Marketing Engineering

Second Edition

Marketing Engineering

Computer-Assisted Marketing Analysis and Planning

Gary L. Lilien
The Pennsylvania State University

Arvind Rangaswamy
The Pennsylvania State University

Second Edition

Co-sponsored by

**Institute for
the Study of
Business Markets**

Prentice
Hall

Upper Saddle River, New Jersey 07458

Library of Congress Cataloging-in-Publication Data
Lilien, Gary L.,
    Marketing engineering: computer-assisted marketing analysis and planning/ Gary L. Lilien,
Arvind Rangaswamy.—2nd ed.
      p. cm.
    Text supplemented by software available free for a year on the Internet or by software which can be
purchased, downloaded, and run by users with Windows 95 and Excel 97 and later versions.
    Includes bibliographical references and index.
    ISBN 0-13-035549-6
    1. Marketing—Data processing. 2. Marketing—Decision making—Mathematical models.
3. Marketing—Decision making—Data processing. I. Rangaswamy, Arvind. II. Title.
      HF5415.125.L54 2001   2001052095
      658.8'02'0285—dc21

Acquisitions Editor: Bruce Kaplan
Editor-in-Chief: Jeff Shelstad
Assistant Editor: Melissa Pellerano
Media Project Manager: Anthony Palmiotto
Marketing Manager: Michelle O'Brien
Marketing Assistant: Christine Genneken
Managing Editor (Production): Judy Leale
Production Editor: Virginia Sheridan
Permissions Coordinator: Suzanne Grappi
Associate Director, Manufacturing: Vincent Scelta
Production Manager: Arnold Vila
Design Manager: Patricia Smythe
Cover Design: John Romer
Cover Illustration: Andrew Stollak
Associate Director, Print/Media Production: Karen Goldsmith
Composition: Open Door Visions
Printer/Binder: Courier Westford

Credits and acknowledgments borrowed from other sources and reproduced, with permission, in this textbook appear on
appropriate page within text.

10 9 8 7 6 5 4 3 2 1
ISBN 0-13-035549-6

Pearson Education LTD.
Pearson Education Australia PTY, Limited
Pearson Education Singapore, Pte. Ltd
Pearson Education North Asia Ltd
Pearson Education, Canada, Ltd
Pearson Educación de Mexico, S.A. de C.V.
Pearson Education–Japan
Pearson Education Malaysia, Pte. Ltd

To my love and best friend,
Dorothy, for sharing her time
with one more book.

—Gary

To Ann for her love and support,
and Cara for providing the
needed distraction.

—Arvind

Contents

Preface   xvii
About the Authors   xxiii

PART I The Basics   1

Chapter 1 Introduction   1

Marketing Engineering: From Mental Models to Decision Models   1
  Marketing and marketing management   1
  Marketing engineering   2
  Why marketing engineering?   5

Marketing Decision Models   6
  Definition   6
  Characteristics of decision models   7
  Verbal, graphical, and mathematical models   8
  Descriptive and normative decision models   11

Benefits of Using Decision Models   13

Philosophy and Structure of the Book   19
  Philosophy   19
  Objectives and structure of the book   21
  Design criteria for the software   22

Overview of the Software   23
  Software access options   23
  Running marketing engineering   24

Summary   25

How Many Draft Commercials Exercise   28

Chapter 2 Tools for Marketing Engineering: Market Response Models   29

Why Response Models?   29

Types of Response Models   31

Some Simple Market Response Models   33

Calibration   37

Objectives   39

Multiple Marketing-Mix Elements: Interactions   42

Dynamic Effects   42

Market-Share Models and Competitive Effects   44

Response at the Individual Customer Level   46

Shared Experience and Qualitative Models   50

Choosing, Evaluating, and Benefiting From a Marketing Response Model   52

Summary   53

Appendix: About Excel's Solver   54

How Solver Works   56

Conglomerate, Inc. Promotional Analysis   58

Conglomerate, Inc. Response Model Exercise   60

PART II Developing Market Strategies   61

Chapter 3 Segmentation and Targeting   61

The Segmentation Process   61

Defining segmentation   61

Segmentation theory and practice   62

The STP approach   64

Segmenting markets (Phase 1)   66

Describing market segments (Phase 2)   68

Evaluating segment attractiveness (Phase 3)   69

Selecting target segments and allocating resources to segments (Phase 4)   70

Finding targeted customers (Phase 5)   73

Defining a Market   75

Segmentation Research: Designing and Collecting Data   78

Developing the measurment instrument   78

Selecting the sample   79

Selecting and aggregating respondents   79

Segmentation Methods   83

Using factor analysis to reduce the data   84

Forming segments by cluster analysis: Measures of association   84

Clustering methods   88

Interpreting segmentation study results   92

Behavior-Based Segmentation: Cross-Classification, Regression, and Choice Models   96

Cross-classification analysis   96

Regression analysis   96

Choice-based segmentation   97

Customer Heterogeneity in Choice Models   101

Implementing the STP Process   102

Summary   103

Conglomerate Inc.'s New PDA (2001)   104

Introducing the Connector   104

The History of the PDA   105

PDA Types   105

The PDA Customer   106

PDA Features   106

Facts About the PDA Market   106

The HVC Survey   107

The Questionnaire   107

Questions for determining segmentation-basis or needs variables   107

Questions for determining variables for discriminant analysis   108

Appendix: PDA Features Guide   110

Operating system   110

Screen   110

Memory   110

Ergonomics   111

Synchronization   111

Batteries   111

Modem & online services   111

Web   111

Email, etc.   111

Handwriting recognition   111

Other software   112

Accessories   112

Audio 112

ABB Electric Segmentation Case   113

History   113

Situation in 1974   113

New Strategy at ABB Electric   113

Establishing the MKIS Program   114

Choice Modeling   115

Postscript: Situation in 1988   116

Chapter 4 Positioning   117

Differentiation and Positioning   117

Definition   117

Positioning Strategy   118

Positioning Using Perceptual Maps   119

Applications of Perceptual Maps   122

Perceptual Mapping Techniques   128

Attribute-based methods   128

Similarity-based methods for perceptual mapping   136

Joint-Space Maps   139

Overview   139

Simple joint-space maps   139

External analysis using PREFMAP3   *141*

Incorporating Price in Perceptual Maps   145

Summary   146

Appendix: Factor Analysis for Preprocessing Segmentation Data   147

Positioning the Infiniti G20 Case   148

Introducing the G20   148

Background   148

Research Data   148

Chapter 5 Strategic Market Analysis: Conceptual Framework and Tools   155

Strategic Marketing Decision Making   155

Market Demand and Trend Analysis   159

Judgmental methods   160

Market and product analysis   161

Time-series methods   162

Causal methods   167

What method to choose?   174

The Product Life Cycle   175

Cost Dynamics: Scale and Experience Effects   180

Summary   183

Bookbinders Book Club Case   185

The Bookbinders Book Club   185

Chapter 6 Models for Strategic Marketing Decision Making   188

Market Entry and Exit Decisions   188

Shared Experience Models: The PIMS Approach   198

Product Portfolio Models   201

The Boston Consulting Group (BCG) approach   201

The GE/McKinsey approach   203

Financial models   204

Analytic Hierarchy Process   205

Competition   208

Summary   212

ICI Americas R&D Project Selection Case   213

Product Planning Using the GE/McKinsey Approach at Addison
Wesley Longman Case   216

Background   216

The new marketing texts   217

The new marketing book promotional challenge   217

Applying the GE approach   217

Appendix: Details of the Three Books from AWL
Promotional Material   220

Portfolio Analysis Exercise   223

Jenny's Gelato Case   226

ACME Liquid Cleanser Exercise   231

Background   231

The Compete Model   231

PART III   Developing Marketing Programs   233

Chapter 7   New Product Decisions   233

Introduction   233

New Product Decision Models   236
  Models for identifying opportunities   236
  Models for product design   238
  Models for new product forecasting and testing   239

Conjoint Analysis for Product Design   239
  Introduction   239
  Conjoint analysis procedure   242
  Other enhancements to the basic conjoint model   250
  Contexts best suited for conjoint analysis   251

Forecasting the Sales of New Products   253
  Overview of the Bass model   253
  Technical description of the Bass model   255
  Extensions of the basic Bass model   261

Pretest Market Forecasting   263
  Overview of the ASSESSOR model   264
  The preference model   266
  Trial-repeat model   268
  The validity and value of the ASSESSOR model   271

Summary   271

Forte Hotel Design Exercise   272

Forte Executive Innes   272

Company Background   272

Preliminary Evaluation   272
  Conjoint Analysis (Matching hotel attributes to customer preferences)   274

Zenith High Definition Television (HDTV) Case   277

HDTV Background   277

Zenith HDTV Efforts to Date   279

The TV Market   279

Forecasts of HDTV Sales   281

Johnson Wax: Enhance Case (A)   283

Instant Hair Conditioner   283

S.C. Johnson & Company   283

New-Product Development at Johnson Wax   284

The Hair Conditioning Market   284

Agree   285

Enhance Product Development   286

The ASSESSOR Pretest Market   286

ASSESSOR Results   288

    Trial and repeat model   290

    Preference model estimates of share   291

Recommendations   292

Chapter 8 Advertising and Communications Decisions   302

The Bewildering Nature of Advertising   303

Advertising Effects: Response, Media, and Copy 304

    Advertising response phenomena   304

    Frequency phenomena   308

    Copy effects   309

Advertising Budget Decisions   310

Media Decisions   319

Advertising Copy Development and Decisions   324

    Copy effectiveness   324

    Estimating the creative quality of ads   327

    Advertising design   328

Summary   335

Blue Mountain Coffee Company Case   336

Blue Mountain's Market Position   336

Operation Breakout   337

Planning for Fiscal Year 1995   340

    The market planning model   340

    Recent developments: The U.S. coffee market in transition   341

Convection Corporation Case   343

Using a Communication Planning Model to Aid
   Industrial Marketing Budget Decisions   343

Background   343

   Heatcrete 4000   344

   Ceratam   344

   Flowclean Sootblowers   345

   Corlin Valve   346

ADVISOR: An Approach to Marketing Budget Planning   347

   Budget task force meeting   348

Johnson Wax Ad Copy Design Exercise   353

Chapter 9 Salesforce and Channel Decisions   354

Introduction to Salesforce Models   354

   Sales-response models for representing the effects of sales activities   354

   Salesforce management decisions   356

Salesforce Sizing and Allocation   357

   Intuitive methods   357

   Market-response methods (the Syntex model)   359

Extending the Syntex Model: Reallocator   365

Sales Territory Design   366

   The GEOLINE model for territory design   367

Salesforce Compensation   369

   Using conjoint analysis to design a bonus plan (the MSZ model)   370

Improving the Efficiency and Effectiveness of Sales Calls   373

   The CALLPLAN model   373

Marketing Channel Decisions   379

   The gravity model   379

Summary   384

Syntex Laboratories (A) Case   386

Company Background   386

Syntex Laboratories   386

Syntex Labs' Product Line   387

   Naprosyn   387

   Anaprox   387

   Topical Steriods   387

   Norinyl   388

   Nasalide   388

The Sales Representative   388

Sales Management at Syntex Labs   389

Sales Force Size   389

Call Frequency   390

Allocation of Sales Efforts Across Products and Physician Specialties   390

Geographic Allocation of Sales Force   390

Sales Force Strategy Model   391

Model Development Process   392

Defining the model inputs   392

Model Structure   393

Results of the SSM Analysis   395

Management implications   395

The John French Exercise: Sales Call Planning for UBC (CALLPLAN)   409

J&J Family Video Case   411

Chapter 10   Price and Sales Promotion Decisions   414

Pricing Decisions: The Classical Economics Approach   414

Pricing in Practice: Orientation to Cost, Demand, or Competition   418

Cost-oriented pricing   418

Demand-oriented pricing   419

Competition-oriented pricing   422

Interactive Pricing: Reference Prices and Price Negotiations   424

Price Discrimination   426

Understanding price discrimination   426

Geographic price discrimination   428

Temporal price discrimination   429

Nonlinear pricing or quantity discounts   433

Other forms of price discrimination   434

Pricing Product Lines   434

Sales Promotions: Types and Effects   435

Objectives of promotions   436

Characteristics of promotions   436

Aggregate Models to Analyze Promotional Effects   440

Analyzing Individuals' Responses to Promotions   444

Summary   448

Account Pricing for the ABCOR2000 Exercise   449

Background   449

    The value spreadsheet   450

Price Planning for the ABCOR2000 Exercise   451

The Problem   452

Paving I-99 Exercise   453

    Part 1: Training Exercise   453

    Part 2: The bid-competition simulation   454

Forte Hotel Revenue Management Exercise   455

How the Generalized Revenue Model Works   456

Massmart Inc. Case   458

Background   458

Scanner-Panel Data   459

The Promotion Model   460

PART IV   Conclusions   462

Chapter 11   Marketing Engineering: A Look Back and a Look Ahead   462

Marketing Engineering: A Look Back   462

Using Marketing Engineering Within Firms   465

Marketing Engineering: A Look Ahead   467

Postscript   480

References   481
Subject Index   499
Company Index   511
Name Index   515

Preface

Several forces are transforming the structure and content of the marketing manager's job. As a profession, marketing is evolving. It is no longer based primarily on conceptual content. Marketing resembles design engineering—it consists of putting together data, models, analyses, and computer simulations to learn about the marketplace and to design effective marketing plans. While many view traditional marketing as art and some view it as science, the new marketing increasingly looks like engineering (that is, combining art and science to solve specific problems). Our purpose in writing this book is to help educate and train a new generation of marketing managers.

Several key forces are changing the marketer's job:

Pervasive high-powered personal computers on networks: During the 1980s marketing managers used personal computers mainly for such tasks as composing letters and presentations and doing simple spreadsheet analyses. Today many marketing managers have the equivalent of an early supercomputer on their desks. And that computer is networked to other PCs and to the company's mainframe on a local area network (LAN), and to external computers and databases all over the world through the Internet. This means that a marketing manager can access current data, reports, and expert opinions, and he or she can also combine and process that information in new ways to enhance decision making. Today basing decisions on such information is a minimum requirement to be a player in many industries.

Exploding volumes of data: A brand manager in the packaged goods industry now sees perhaps a thousand times the volume of data (more frequently collected in finer detail) he or she saw five years ago. The growth of e-commerce, database marketing and direct marketing parallels data explosions in other industries as well. The human brain, however, has not become comparably more powerful in the same period. More data cannot lead to better decision making unless managers learn how to use that data in meaningful ways. If data are a burden, then insights provide relief.

Reengineering marketing activities: All over the world organizations face increasingly well-informed customers who seek value. As a result they are carefully scrutinizing the productivity of all management processes. To reduce their costs and to improve productivity, they are reengineering many marketing functions, processes, and activities. They are reengineering such activities as segmentation and targeting, new product development, market measurement and analysis, and customer satisfaction management for the information age.

Flatter, right-sized organizations: Organizations could respond effectively to the afore-mentioned trends using traditional organizational mechanisms if they trained an army of specialists to harness computer hardware, software, networks, and data. They do not have that luxury. Global competition is driving organizations everywhere to do more with fewer employees. Managers are finding themselves empowered (i.e., without support staff): they have the hardware, software, and data at their desks and are expected to use them, operating independently.

Marketing managers must learn to function in the rapidly changing environment and to exploit evolving trends. Firms and business schools can help marketing managers to cope in two ways. They can offer traditional, concept-based education and training, with the hope that good people will figure out on their own how to cope with the changing environment. The education-as-usual approach will always have some success—well-motivated and intelligent marketers will figure out how to get reasonable value from the new resources. This approach is analogous to lecturing golf novices on the rules and giving them golf clubs and self-training books. Through study, networking, and observing successful golfers, some novices will become pretty good golfers. Others will become duffers. Still others will quit the game because it seems too hard. The lack of formal training limits development.

Those who want to excel need lessons, especially early on. Hence another way to help marketing managers respond to the changes is to provide information-age-specific education and training. There will always be an important role for marketing concepts, and using the powerful information tools now available requires sound conceptual grounding. But marketers need much more than concepts to fully exploit the resources available to them. They need to move from conceptual marketing to marketing engineering: *using computer decision models in making marketing decisions.* In this book we integrate concepts, analytic marketing techniques, and operational software to train the new generation of marketers, helping them to become marketing engineers.

OBJECTIVES FOR THE STUDENT

We designed this book for you, the business school student or marketing manager, who seeks the education you need to perform effectively in information-technology-intensive environments. Most traditional books focus on marketing from conceptual, empirical, or qualitative perspectives. With this book we aim to train marketing engineers to translate concepts into context-specific operational decisions and actions using analytical, quantitative, and computer modeling techniques. We link theory to practice and practice to theory.

Our specific objectives for the book are

- ■ To help you gain an understanding of the role of analytical techniques and computer models for enhancing marketing decision making in modern enterprises
- ■ To improve your skills in viewing marketing processes and relationships systematically and analytically
- ■ To expose you to a number of examples demonstrating the value of marketing engineering in real managerial contexts
- ■ To provide you with a software toolkit, a companion product of this book, that will enable you to apply marketing engineering to real marketing decision problems

Our pedagogical philosophy embraces two main principles: *learning by doing* and *end-user modeling.* Most of the concepts we describe have software implementation and at least one problem or case you can resolve by using the software. You may make errors and struggle at times, attempting to apply the tools. That is part of the learning-by-doing process; you will learn what the tools and software can do as well as what they cannot do. Traditional methods of teaching in business schools (i.e., lectures and case analyses) do not go far enough in helping students to make decisions, assess risks, and solve problems. The learning-by-doing approach extends traditional marketing education. With model-based tools for decision making, you can learn to anticipate and deal with the potential consequences of your decisions—this will help you improve your strategic thinking, sensitize you to customer needs, force you to anticipate competitive moves, and develop implementation plans. In short, you should not only learn to improve how you make marketing decisions, but also how to derive the maximum benefits from your decisions.

Decision models range from large-scale, enterprise-wide applications to those that can be quickly put together by an individual with an understanding of basic marketing and marketing engineering. We emphasize end-user modeling here. End-user modeling has the characteristics of good engineering: do as good a job as you can with the time and resources you have available.

Good end-user modeling provides direct benefits, permits rapid prototyping for more elaborate approaches, and makes the user a better customer (and critic) of larger, enterprise-wide applications. We are not trying to train you to be a technical specialist. Rather we hope to prepare you to put together technically simple but operationally useful decision models and to become astute users of those models and of the results of models that others have developed.

NEW FOR THE SECOND EDITION

The first edition of Marketing Engineering, published four years ago, had as its objective to provide the background and tools needed to train information-age marketers. Our aim was to help marketing students move from conceptual marketing to marketing engineering—to access and use computer decision models when making marketing decisions. As such, that edition combined 26 different software tools with a two-volume book and tutorial package that implemented our pedagogical philosophy: learning by doing and end-user modeling.

The positive (and negative feedback) associated with the first edition has lead to this second edition. Reviews of the concepts and the tools that we included were very positive. Hence, while we have updated the material and the references, we have changed very little of the core of the book, either in terms of the basic textual material or in terms of specific implementations of our software.

Criticisms of the book were mainly associated with

- Its high price, necessitated by the breadth of the ME package—two volumes, CD-ROM, 26 software packages, instructor's manual, videotapes, and web site;
- The difficulty and complexity of getting the latest software distributed and working on different systems; and
- The limited set of data sets/cases for classroom use.

This second edition addresses these concerns by a redesign of the ME package to be accessible through the Internet. While a single softcover textbook remains, there is no longer a CD-ROM or a tutorial volume included with the text. Cases and exercises have been integrated into the single volume; tutorials (and other electronic components of the text) are now available on the Internet at *www.mktgeng.com*.

Adopters have three options for accessing the software:

1. The latest version of the software will be available to book adopters for free for a year on the Internet (but will require the current versions of Windows and Excel to run).
2. Academic adopters can have a version installed and made available on a local area network to speed up response time.
3. For most rapid response, individuals can purchase, download and run the software locally, without the need for an Internet connection. (This version will support versions of Excel 7 and later under Windows 95 and later.)

Thus, in this second edition, we have:

- Revised the text, with corrections, and enhancements and combined the text with the cases into a single volume.
- Made the software available separately from the book with access options as noted above.
- Made enhancements to several of the most frequently used software modules.

ORGANIZATION

The text for the second edition is organized as follows:

In Part 1 (Chapters 1 and 2) we introduce and define marketing engineering and develop key marketing engineering building blocks—market response models.

In Part 2 (Chapters 3 through 6) we focus on strategic marketing issues such as segmentation, targeting, positioning, market selection, portfolio analysis, market measurement, and strategic planning.

In Part 3 (Chapters 7 through 10) we address tactical marketing issues such as product design, advertising and communications, salesforce deployment, outlet location, and price and promotion decisions.

In Part 4 (Chapter 11) we conclude, summarizing some key points and highlighting new developments that are driving the future of marketing engineering.

Each chapter also contains cases and problem sets that are keyed to the major concepts. We have also created a Web site, *www.mktgeng.com*, to provide the software for running the models described in the book. The Web site contains tutorials, help files, tips and other resources for using our software and for deriving the maximum benefits from marketing engineering. We update this site frequently to ensure that you will always have access to the latest software and accompanying resources.

In addition, instructors who adopt the book receive videotapes that highlight award-winning marketing engineering applications and the impact that those applications have had at the following firms:

- ABB Electric (the profitable use of choice-based segmentation)
- Marriott Hotels (the use of conjoint analysis to design the Courtyard by Marriott hotel)
- ASSESSOR (the use of the ASSESSOR pretest market model and procedure at hundreds of firms)

- AT&T (the use of systematic copy testing to develop AT&T's cost-of-visit advertising campaign)
- Syntex Labs (the use of judgmental response functions to size and allocate a salesforce)
- American Airlines (the use of a yield management system to increase profits)

USES OF THE BOOK FOR INSTRUCTORS

We designed this book primarily as a text for a one-semester, capstone MBA course. Students need not have strong backgrounds in quantitative methods; however, it will be helpful if they have some quantitative and marketing background and some facility with microcomputers and related (Windows-based) software. We have used the material successfully in executive programs and in undergraduate classes as well.

As there are 26 software modules (each with a different focus), the book includes twice as much material as can be covered in a normal one-semester course. The software and related problems should be viewed as a menu; students need not use all the software to gain benefits from the material. Indeed we find that students can readily absorb only 6 to 10 modules in a semester. For shorter courses and executive programs, you should make a much more limited selection.

Many of the software modules are intended for general use (i.e., not just for the problem set provided); they can be used for term projects that can provide a very valuable learning experience.

Many of us recognize that reading textbooks or listening to lectures is not the best way to learn marketing decision making. Instead, students should experience marketing in a way that leaves behind enduring lessons. Therefore, the best way for students to learn marketing engineering is to encourage them to use the software, to do the problems, and cases.

The software empowers students to solve marketing problems. We find that classes work best when we keep lectures to a minimum and have one or two student groups present their problem analyses to the rest of the class, which acts as (skeptical) management. This follows the learning-by-doing philosophy and makes students responsible for their own learning. It also simulates how marketing engineering works in the real world.

ACKNOWLEDGMENTS (2nd Edition)

As with the first edition, this book includes a text, software modules, tutorials, help files, problem sets, cases, a Web site and supplementary material. The creation of this portfolio was a major undertaking that could not have been accomplished without the support of many people and institutions.

We gratefully acknowledge the support of the companies that sponsor Penn State's Institute for the Study of Business Markets (ISBM—the book's co-publisher), and the ISBM's Executive Director and Marketing Engineering's chief cheerleader, Ralph Oliva, for the financial and institutional support needed to make this project a continuing reality.

The preface to the first edition of the book paid tribute to the many people whose intellectual contributions and hard work made that edition possible. We redouble our thanks to all who helped make the first edition possible and we single out below those who contributed specifically to this second edition.

An inspiring experience for us is the steadfast support of the many colleagues who have adopted the book and are our ambassadors. We know there would be no second edition of the book without them. Several of these ambassadors, including Chris Dubelaar, Josh Eliashberg, Ujwal Kayande, Vijay Mahajan, Carl Mela and Liz Wilson, have continued to provide helpful comments and suggestions (many of which we have implemented). We thank the students in our classes at Penn State and those in courses elsewhere who have been persistent in their demands that we keep improving the software.

While we continue to write portions of the software, we are involved more in design and testing than in actual coding. Our chief software engineer, Andrew "Nuke" Stollak, together with Laurent Müllender and Daniel Soto-Zeevaert wrote most of the new code (and developed the Web site) for the second edition. We also acknowledge the continuing contributions of Animesh ("Conjoint man") Karna. Two new additions to our team, Srikant Vadali and Vishwanath Ramrao, are enhancing our algorithms and making them more scalable and robust. We offer special thanks to Jean-Marie Choffray, who takes great pleasure in reminding us that software is never done, only abandoned. He has provided a flow of high-quality programming talent from the University of Liège, Belgium, to make sure that our software is not abandoned.

Bruce Kaplan and the staff at Prentice Hall continue to nurture this rather unusual project, helping us transform our concepts into physical reality. Grace Sikorski, Ray Liddick and Michelle Richardson provided very able copyediting and production support.

Finally, we offer special thanks to Mary Wyckoff who, once again, supported and managed the whole process. She continues to put up with our unreasonable demands and unrealistic deadlines and does so with unfailing good humor.

Behind every book is a generous group of family and friends. So it is in our case. In particular, our wives and daughters just let us be who we are, and for that, we are eternally grateful.

This book and related material represent a highly collaborative effort and our contributions are intimately intertwined. We continue to enjoy that collaboration, learn from each other, and marvel at the value of positive synergies.

Gary L. Lilien
Arvind Rangaswamy

About the Authors

GARY L. LILIEN

Gary L. Lilien, who coined the term *marketing engineering*, is Distinguished Research Professor of Management Science at the Smeal College of Business at Penn State. He is also co-founder and Research Director of the Institute for the Study of Business Markets at Penn State, an organization aimed at fostering research and interchange in nonconsumer markets. He holds three degrees in operations research, from the School of Engineering at Columbia University. Previously, Prof. Lilien was a member of the faculty at the Sloan School at MIT. His research interests are in marketing engineering, market segmentation, new product modeling, marketing-mix issues for business products, bargaining and negotiations, modeling the industrial-buying process and innovation-diffusion modeling.

Prof. Lilien is the author or co-author of 12 books (including *Marketing Models* with Philip Kotler) and over 80 professional articles. He was Departmental Editor for Marketing for Management Science; is on the editorial board of the *International Journal for Research in Marketing* and the *Journal of Business to Business Marketing*; is Functional Editor for *Marketing for Interfaces*, and is Area Editor for *Marketing Science*. He is former Editor in Chief of Interfaces. He served as President as well as Vice President/Publications for the Institute of Management Sciences. He is U.S. Coordinator for the European Marketing Academy.

Prof. Lilien is a winner of the Alpha Kappa Psi award for the outstanding article in the Journal of Marketing and is the Philip M. Morse Distinguished Lecturer of the Institute for Operations Research and the Management Sciences (INFORMS), 2001–2003. He received honorary doctorates from the University of Liège, the University of Ghent, and Aston University.

Prof. Lilien's consulting clients include AT&T, DuPont, Exelon, the Federal Reserve Bank, Hewlett-Packard, IBM, Kodak, Pillsbury, PP&L, Sprint, 3M, and Xerox.

Prof. Lilien is three-time winner and seven-time finalist in the Penn State Squash Club Championship and has substantial collections of fine wines and unusual porcine objects.

ARVIND RANGASWAMY

Arvind Rangaswamy is the Jonas H. Anchel Professor of Marketing at Penn State, where he is also co-founder and Research Director of the eBusiness Research Center. He received a PhD in marketing from Northwestern University, an MBA from the Indian Institute of Management, Calcutta, and a B.Tech from the Indian Institute of Technology, Madras. Before joining Penn State, he was a faculty member at the J. L. Kellogg Graduate School of Management, Northwestern University, and at the Wharton School, University of Pennsylvania. He is actively engaged in research to develop concepts, methods, and models to improve the efficiency and effectiveness of marketing using information technologies, including such topics as marketing modeling, online customer behavior, and online negotiations.

Prof. Rangaswamy has published numerous articles in such leading journals as *Marketing Science*, the *Journal of Marketing Research*, *Management Science*, the *Journal of Marketing*, the *International Journal of Research in Marketing*, *Marketing Letters*, *Psychometrika*, *Multivariate Behavioral Research*, and the *Journal of Economics and Statistics*. He is Area Editor for *Marketing Science* and serves on the editorial boards of the *Journal of Interactive Marketing*, the *International Journal of Intelligent Systems in Accounting, Finance and Management*, the *Journal of Service Research*, and the *Journal of Business-to-Business Marketing*.

Prof. Rangaswamy is a Fellow of the IC² Institute, an IBM Faculty Partner, and the Chair of the e-Business Section of the Institute for Operations Research and the Management Sciences (INFORMS). He is the Program Director for Electronic Markets and Marketing Information Systems and a member of the Advisory Board at Penn State's Institute for the Study of Business Markets.

Prof. Rangaswamy has consulted for a number of companies including Marriott, Xerox, IBM, Kodak, Nokia, PPG Industries, AT&T, TVS (India), Bristol-Myers Squibb, Walker Digital, and Peapod.

Prof. Rangaswamy is an avid and successful trader on eBay and other auctions, where he blends his research with his personal interest in rare Indian stamps and postal history.

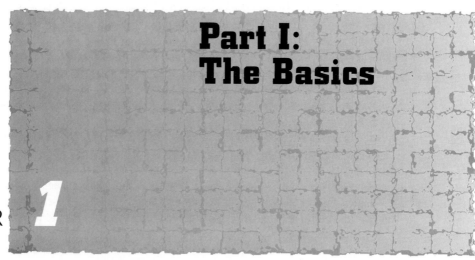

CHAPTER **1**

Introduction

In this chapter, we

- Define marketing engineering
- Identify the trends that make it important to learn about the emerging field of marketing engineering
- Indicate how marketing engineering facilitates decision making
- Highlight the benefits and challenges associated with the marketing engineering approach to decision making
- Summarize the philosophy and structure of the book
- Introduce the software provided with this book to support the marketing engineering concept

MARKETING ENGINEERING: FROM MENTAL MODELS TO DECISION MODELS

Marketing and marketing management

Marketing is pervasive in market economies around the world. Many people associate marketing with its most manifest characteristics, namely, advertising and retailing, which represent only a small part of the functions and processes that make up marketing. Formally marketing is a *societal* and *managerial process* by which *exchanges* are brought about in an economy to satisfy the *needs and wants* of *individuals* and *organizations*. At the core of a market economy are the millions of voluntary exchanges that take place daily between consenting parties. An exchange occurs if two or more parties come together, each having something of value to offer to the other(s). We all engage in a number of exchanges every day. Whenever you go to a grocery store, make an airline reservation, order a book from Amazon.com, visit a hairdresser, bid in an eBay auction, or send out a résumé, you are participating in this exchange process.

In modern economies, both buyers and sellers take steps to initiate desirable exchanges and exchange relationships in the marketplace. Marketing management facilitates this exchange process and can be viewed as a management philosophy with associated processes and activities that enable individuals and firms to proactively bring about desirable exchanges. As an example, let us consider how marketing management facilitates exchanges between a firm, Conglomerate, Inc., and its customers: Conglomerate uses marketing insights and techniques to choose who to sell to (to target a segment of the market), to design its physical product offerings, to set prices, to position its products relative to those of competitors, and to develop support services and the distribution mechanisms it needs to deliver its products to customers. The firm's goal is to maximize its returns, while at the same time providing value to customers through the exchange process. To effect the matching and exchange process, Conglomerate has to make targeted customers aware of its products (through advertising, promotion, and personal selling) and to ensure that its offerings provide more value than those of its competitors in the eyes of its current and potential customers. This entire marketing management process is founded on an intimate knowledge of what customers value, what they know about Conglomerate's (and competitive) offerings, and the process those customers go through in gathering information and effecting exchange (e.g., visiting the store, ordering by phone, or through personal negotiation).

At the heart of marketing management is the ability to understand customers and markets and to translate this understanding into decisions and actions that produce desirable exchanges in the marketplace. While marketing management begins and ends with customers, it serves the goals of the marketer.

Marketing engineering

Marketing managers must make ongoing decisions about product features, prices, distribution options, sales compensation plans, and so forth. In making these decisions, managers choose from among alternative courses of action in a complex, uncertain world. Like all decisions involving people, marketing decision making involves judgment calls. A typical approach to systematic decision making is to develop a mental model of the decision situation that combines known facts with intuition, reasoning, and experience. For example, in deciding how much to spend on advertising, managers can use different approaches:

Rely on experience: Marketing managers often say that experience is the best teacher. By trying different advertising programs over the course of their careers, managers develop mental models of the levels of advertising that are appropriate under different conditions. To set the advertising budget, they may rely on this mental model or they may tap into the experience and wisdom (mental models) of colleagues and consultants.

Use practice standards: Companies that are successful often codify their decisions as practice standards, principles, or rules of thumb. These are essentially the collective mental models for the organization. Typically these rules are in the form of ratios (e.g., "advertising expenses to sales ratio should be 5 percent" or "30 percent of our advertising should be used for new products"). Using practice standards, managers might set the advertising budget as a fixed percentage of projected sales for the current year.

In many cases such mental models may be all that managers need to feel psychologically comfortable with their decisions. Yet mental models are prone to systematic errors. No one can deny the value of experience. But experience is unique to every person, and there is no objective way to choose between the best judgment based only on the experience of Mary versus Tom. Experience can also be confounded with a responsibility bias: sales managers might choose lower advertising budgets in favor of higher expenditures on personal selling, whereas advertising managers might prefer larger advertising budgets.

The use of practice standards can also lead to critical errors: they may be good on average, but they ignore idiosyncratic elements of a decision context. Suppose that a new competitor enters the market with an aggressive advertising program, which results in a decrease in the firm's sales. A fixed advertising-to-sales ratio would then prescribe a *decrease* in advertising, while other reasonable mental models would suggest some form of retaliation based on increased advertising. Rarely do practice standards provide the flexibility to act in changing marketing environments, where sound decisions are in fact most needed.

As an alternative approach to deciding advertising expenditures, managers might choose to build a spreadsheet decision model of how the market would respond to various expenditure levels. They could then use this model to explore the sales and profit consequences of alternative expenditure levels before making a decision.

This book is about the use of decision models for making marketing decisions. We use the term *marketing engineering* (ME) to refer to this approach. In contrast, relying solely on mental models may be referred to as *conceptual marketing*. Marketing engineering is not a substitute for conceptual marketing; rather, ME complements it, with the combination being greater than the sum of its parts.

To illustrate the marketing engineering approach and its potential value, we summarize below some real-world examples that we expand on in later chapters. The book includes software implementations of simple versions of these models.

ABB Electric, a manufacturer and distributor of power-generation equipment, wanted to increase its sales and market share in an industry that was facing a projected 50 percent drop in demand. By carefully analyzing and tracking customer preferences and actions, it determined which customers to focus its marketing efforts on and what features of its products were most important to those customers. Its managers used a marketing engineering tool called *choice modeling* to provide ongoing support for their segmentation and targeting decisions. The firm credits its modeling effort as being a major factor in its successful performance in a declining market.

Marriott Corporation was running out of good downtown locations for new full-service hotels. To maintain its growth, Marriott's management planned to locate hotels outside the downtown area that would appeal to both business travelers and weekend leisure travelers. The company designed and developed the highly successful Courtyard by Marriott chain using a marketing engineering tool called *conjoint analysis*.

American Airlines faces the ongoing problem of deciding what prices to charge for its various classes of service on its numerous routes and determining how many seats on each scheduled flight to allocate to each class of service. Too many seats sold at discount prices, overselling seats on a flight, or allowing too many seats to go empty leads to low revenues. Maximizing revenue in a competitive environment is crucial to the successful operation of the firm. It uses a marketing engineering tool called *yield management* to fill its planes with the right mix of passengers paying different fares.

Syntex Laboratories was concerned about the productivity of its salesforce. In particular, managers were unsure whether the size of the salesforce was right for the job it had to do and whether the firm was allocating its salesforce effort to the most profitable products and market segments. The company used a resource sizing and allocation tool that we call *Syngen* to evaluate the current performance of its salesforce and to develop salesforce deployment strategies that were in line with its long-term growth plans.

Johnson's Wax and many other firms in the packaged goods industry try to predict the likely success of their new products in a cost-effective manner and to use this information to decide how best to proceed in developing a new product. Traditionally these firms relied on test marketing to get a reading on the likely success of the new product. However, test marketing is expensive, and it is also transparent to competitors.

The company realized dramatic cost reductions in its new product testing program without harming decision effectiveness by implementing a marketing engineering tool called ASSESSOR, a pretest market measurement and modeling system.

Exhibit 1.1 is an overview of the marketing engineering approach to decision making—using computer models to help transform objective and subjective data about the marketing environment into insights, decisions, and implementation of decisions.

Data are facts, beliefs, or observations used in making decisions. Thus numbers representing dollar sales in the previous month in various sales territories are data. So is the belief that the brand name *Coke* evokes a positive emotion, or the observation that a competitor has introduced a new product. A common misconception is that decision models require objective data. This is not the case. As we will show with several models in this book, the marketing engineering approach is useful even when one uses only beliefs (subjective data) as inputs to models.

Information refers to summarized or categorized data. For example, the average or the standard deviation of sales across all territories or the classification of sales as low or high constitutes information.

Insights provide meaning to the data or information, and they help the manager gain a better understanding of the decision situation. For example, insights offer us plausible explanations for why sales vary a lot between territories, or why some territories have consistently low sales performance. Information is a derived property of the data. On the other hand, managers gain insight as they mull over and process data and information (using either mental models or decision models) and as they incorporate information with their own internal knowledge.

A *decision* is a judgment favoring a particular insight as offering the most plausible explanation or favoring a particular course of action. For example, choosing to devote more effort in subsequent periods to territories with low sales constitutes a decision. Thus decisions provide purpose to information and insights.

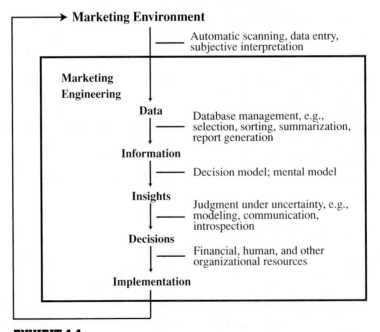

EXHIBIT 1.1
The marketing engineering approach to decision making helps transform objective and subjective data about the marketing environment into decisions and decision implementations.

Finally, *implementation* is the set of actions the manager or the organization takes to commit resources toward physically realizing a decision. For example, a decision may require hiring and training more salespeople to work in poorly performing territories.

Although marketing engineering encompasses all the elements shown in Exhibit 1.1, we will focus mostly on ways to transform information and insights into decisions. Several cases in the book highlight key issues that arise in implementing model-based decisions within organizations.

In many ways computer models are simply tools that managers can use to explore the potential consequences of their decisions. The idea of using computer models to enhance decisions is not new. Researchers and practitioners have long developed and implemented powerful models that facilitate decision making in real-world marketing settings. (For case studies and examples, see Lilien, Kotler, and Moorthy (1992), Lilien and Rangaswamy (2001a,b), Little (1970), Rangaswamy (1993), and Wierenga and van Bruggen (2000).) Yet until recently much of the knowledge about marketing decision models resided in specialized academic journals or required considerable technical expertise to use. As a result, despite their potential value, these models have not seen the extent of managerial use indicated by their potential.

Recent advances in computer hardware and software now make it possible to put these models in the hands of every marketing manager. Several hundred commercially available canned software decision aids are of potential interest to marketers. At the same time, almost no associated teaching material is available to help marketing managers learn to be intelligent users and consumers of the available marketing models. We designed this book to serve this purpose.

Why marketing engineering?

Many marketing managers succeed without relying on computer models. Conceptual marketing based on deep insights and years of experience may often be sufficient for making good decisions. Such tasks as identifying the market segments that are likely to be most attractive to a firm, positioning a product in a competitive setting, or anticipating customer response to a proposed marketing program can all be based on conceptual marketing. However, is conceptual marketing sufficient for the marketing managers of the future? Should you bet your future on relying only on intuitive methods when the marketing environment is undergoing major changes? The following trends are fundamentally changing the marketing manager's job.

High-powered personal computers connected to networks are becoming ubiquitous: Like other professionals, marketing managers are increasingly depending on computers to perform their jobs. Even managers in small firms use PCs. According to Dataquest (*www.dataquest.com*), worldwide shipments of PCs are expected to exceed 130 million units in 2001; there were already over 500 million PC's in use worldwide at the end of the year 2000. Many marketing departments have more computing power today than entire firms did five years ago. A senior marketing executive told us recently, "Ten years ago in my department, we had lots of people and very little software. Today we have lots of software and very few people." These computers are being networked with other computers through local area networks (LANs) and, in some cases, connected to external computers and databases all over the world through wide area networks (WANs), such as the Internet. According to Nielsen-Netratings (*www.netratings.com*) about 430 million people globally had access to the Internet at the end of March 2001.

Although many managers currently use their PCs mainly for word processing and e-mail, sophisticated managers have begun to use their computers to access, combine, and process different types of information to improve their decisions. The most common analysis tools available to managers are spreadsheet programs, like Excel from Microsoft. According to a Microsoft official, about 245 million people worldwide use Microsoft Office products, of which Excel is a component. (Computerworld, June 4, 2001, p. 10). With the wider availability and use of these tools, computer-assisted decision making is becoming important in many firms.

The volume of data is exploding: The automatic electronic capture of data related to transactions with consumers is generating massive amounts of potentially useful information about the preferences and behavior of customers. For example, the typical brand manager in the packaged goods industry is inundated with 1000 times the volume of data (more frequently collected in finer detail) than was available five years ago. The growth of direct marketing and Internet shopping has led to similar data explosions in other industries as well. For example, an online company such as amazon.com collects over 30 gigabytes (30,000 megabytes) of data every day in its server logs. While available data has grown exponentially, the human brain has not advanced in a comparable manner to process and interpret these data. Managers need new concepts, methods, and technologies, such as marketing engineering, to make decisions in data-intensive environments.

Firms are reengineering marketing: The new corporate mantra seems to be "flatter organizations, ad hoc teams, outsourcing, and reduced cycle times." In this environment, firms are reengineering marketing functions, processes, and activities for the information age. In the reengineered firm, centralized decision making, characteristic of traditional hierarchical organizations, is giving way to decentralized decision making that is characteristic of entrepreneurial organizations. As a consequence marketing managers are increasingly dealing directly with market information and using computers to do tasks that were once done by staff support people.

These changes are forcing an evolution in the marketing manager's job from one based primarily on conceptual skills to one that is more akin to the way an engineer works—putting together data, models, analyses, and computer simulations to design an effective marketing program. As Peter Francese, president and founder of Marketing Tools puts it, "emerging corporations don't have any need for classical marketing education. What they have a need for is understanding customers. What they want to know is how to analyze databases—supplier databases, demographic and geographic databases. . . . If you presented one of your students to me and asked me to hire him or her, I'd give that student a diskette and say, 'Here are some of my customers. Tell me what I should do.' There are no right answers. You either fail to create greater value and you're out of a job, or you create more income for the company and you continue to be employed. It's that simple. That's the test, and it's being applied to middle managers all over the country" (quoted in *Selections*, Spring 1996, published by the American Management Admission Council).

Marketing engineering is a way to capitalize on these trends. It is not, however, a panacea for coping with complex and uncertain decision environments. Markets are not controlled settings where careful observation or analysis will permit clear and unambiguous understanding. But neither are they so complex as to defy understanding. They fall somewhere between these two extremes. Marketing engineering enables us to capture the essence of marketing phenomena in well-specified models, and it improves our ability to make decisions that influence market outcomes.

MARKETING DECISION MODELS

Definition

Decision models are a special category of models that provide the foundation for marketing engineering, in much the same way that a skeleton provides the structure for the human body. We first define a generic model and then articulate what we mean by a decision model.

A model is a *stylized representation* of reality that is easier to deal with and explore for a *specific purpose* than reality itself. Let us explore key terms in this definition:

Stylized: Models do not capture reality fully but focus only on some aspects. They are simplified depictions, or analogies, of real-world phenomena and systems. For example, as a model a road map contains only some geographical aspects of the landscape such as main roads, rivers, and towns and ignores many other aspects, such as hills and valleys, vegetation, and buildings in an area. A map that is as large as the geography it represents adds little value.

Representation: A model is only a convenient analogy that may bear little resemblance to the physical characteristics of the reality it is trying to capture. For example, a map printed on paper has little physically in common with the terrain it represents. Most marketing models use verbal, graphical, or mathematical representations. The marketing decision models we describe in this book are often presented as mathematical equations embedded within a set of logical relationships, bearing no obvious physical resemblance to a marketplace of customers. In our view, the ability of a model to fully represent reality is less important than its ability to change people's minds. (Note that models can also represent artificial worlds, as in virtual reality simulations.)

Specific purpose: People develop models with a specific purpose in mind. Cartographers design road maps so that you can find a route from one location to another, estimate the time or distance between locations, or plan a long trip. They do not design them for settling property disputes or planning crop planting. Likewise, modelers design marketing decision models to highlight some aspects and ignore others. The purpose of a marketing model could be to understand or influence certain types of behavior in the marketplace (e.g., repeat purchase of the firm's products), to improve planning and prediction associated with a specific marketing issue (e.g., customer response to a new ad campaign), or to facilitate communication within the firm about a particular marketing problem.

This book is about a special category of models called *interactive decision models*. These are computer models (i.e., simplified representations of reality encoded as packaged software) that can be customized to a specific decision situation faced by a manager. They provide simulated learning environments where a manager can interactively explore the consequences of alternative actions while avoiding the expense, dangers, and irreversibility of the real world. Such models are tools for the mind, to help managers use objective and subjective data to support their decisions. The models serve the same purpose as flight simulators for training pilots or practice sessions for football players to prepare for a game. In some situations, decision models do not lead directly to decisions but enable managers to test and update their mental models of market behavior, perhaps leading to changes in future decisions.

Characteristics of decision models

The decision models we describe in the book incorporate explicit statements of *purpose*, *assumptions*, *variables*, and *relationships* of interest.

A decision model has a well-defined *purpose*, which represents the reason for its construction and circumscribes its domain of applicability. For example, the ADBUDG model (Chapter 8) is designed primarily to help managers arrive at good advertising budgets. The clustering model (Chapter 3) is useful for identifying attractive market segments. A model could have several secondary purposes as well. For example, the ADBUDG model could be used to simulate the sales effect of different advertising spending levels; that is, as a forecasting tool.

Assumptions provide the context or framework for a model. For example, a model to evaluate the advertising budget for a product could include the following assumptions:

- Product sales are related to its advertising.
- Sales will go up if advertising is increased.
- There is a maximum level of sales for this product. No amount of advertising will make it possible for sales to exceed this maximum level.
- Increased advertising will decrease customers' sensitivity to the price of the product.

All models contain assumptions, either explicit or implicit, and unlike mental models, decision models require that these assumptions be made explicit. This explicitness also allows managers to more clearly evaluate the consequences of modifying their assumptions and provides them a means of communicating and sharing their assumptions with others in the organization.

Variables are those aspects of a marketing phenomenon that are not fixed. In a marketing system, many things can vary: the firm's sales, the likelihood that customers will purchase a new product, the calling patterns salespeople use, and the intensity of competition. We distinguish between three types of variables. *Controllable* variables are those that the firm controls, such as the level of advertising and the product features to be designed into a new product. *Noncontrollable* variables are those that are under the control of other players in the market, such as suppliers and competitors. Although a firm may try to influence a noncontrollable variable, it cannot manipulate it directly. *Environmental* variables are noncontrollable variables that are not under the control of any one player in the marketing system. These variables include general trends, such as the aging of the population, and variables whose values are determined by the actions of a number of different actors, such as new regulations or industry capacity. Together, controllable, noncontrollable, and environmental variables are referred to as *independent* or *input* variables. In contrast, *dependent* or *output* variables are those whose values are determined by a set of independent variables. For example, in many marketing models, product sales are driven by the level of advertising spending and the quality of the product. Although the distinction between independent and dependent variables may not always be precise, it is still a useful one.

Relationships between the variables, based on marketing theories and managerial insights, specify how changes in one variable affect another variable. For example, a change in *package design* can be hypothesized to increase *customer attention* at the point-of-purchase. Most marketing decision models use mathematical functions to represent how independent variables (e.g., advertising expenditures) affect dependent variables (e.g., sales). In Chapter 2 we provide details of the concepts, specification, calibration, and interpretation of the various types of relationships among marketing variables.

Verbal, graphical, and mathematical models

One way to distinguish between decision models is on the basis of their structural characteristics: verbal, graphical, or mathematical.

Verbal models are described in words. For example, Lavidge and Steiner (1961) state that advertising moves consumers' mental states along the following chain:

awareness *to* knowledge *to* liking *to* preference *to* conviction *to* purchase.

This model specifies the variables influenced by advertising and the sequence in which this influence will take place. The model also suggests that an increase in advertising will lead to an increase in awareness, which will lead to an increase in knowledge, eventually leading to an increase in purchase. However, it does not specify the magnitude of increase in these variables for a given increase in advertising. This lack of quantification is a fundamental limitation of verbal models, especially when they are used for decision making. On the other hand, verbal models are easy to explain, are intuitively understandable, and in many cases are sufficient for the purpose at hand.

Almost all models start out as verbal models and are then refined into the other types. Some of the most important models of individual, social, and societal behavior, such as those of Freud, Marx, and Darwin, are verbal models. We all use verbal models all the time, even without being aware of it.

EXAMPLE

Try this exercise. The next time you are feeling guilty about something (you were out later than you said you would be, and your partner or parent seems upset and asks for an explanation), check to see if you use a verbal model to "pretest" possible explanations before offering one. You consider saying, "I got a flat tire on the way home," and you expect a sympathetic reaction, or alternatively, "I was out drinking with friends and lost track of time," and you expect an angry reaction. If you go through this process, you are conducting a thought experiment, using a verbal model to forecast the reaction of your partner or parent. You then choose an explanation (suppose you really *were* out drinking), balancing the goal of getting sympathy instead of a reprimand against the moral cost of stretching the truth. If the reaction you get is the one you had expected, your model is confirmed, and you become more confident of your mental model; if you get an unexpected reaction, you will modify or abandon your verbal model.

Graphical models are represented in the form of pictures or charts. Examples include road maps, organizational charts, and flow diagrams. These models describe the overall nature of a phenomenon, stripped of nonessentials, so that the viewer can grasp the whole and select specific relationships for closer examination. We are all familiar with the notion that a picture is worth a thousand words. Graphical models are parsimonious compared with

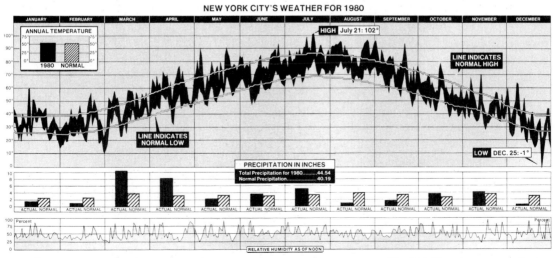

New York Times, January 11, 1981, p. 32

EXHIBIT 1.2
The graphical model of New York City weather for 1980 displays an amazing amount of information with great parsimony. *Source: New York Times,* January 11, 1981, p. 32.

verbal models, and at the same time they are more explicit in representing relationships. To understand the power and parsimony of a graphical representation, look at Exhibit 1.2, which summarizes the weather records of New York City for an entire year.

Graphical models help illuminate and identify key issues relevant to a phenomenon, aid communication about the phenomenon, and guide analysis. In addition graphical models provide a bridge between verbal models and the more formal mathematical models.

Mathematical models specify the relationships embodied in a model in the form of equations. For example, the relationship between advertising expenditure and sales often incorporates two important properties: saturation and diminishing returns (see Chapter 2). Saturation suggests that after some point, no amount of additional advertising will increase sales. Diminishing returns suggest that each incremental unit of advertising will lead to progressively decreasing increases in sales. These properties can be represented in the form of an equation:

$$\text{Sales} = a\left(1 - e^{-bx}\right) \tag{1.1}$$

where a is the market potential for the product (i.e., the maximum sales that would be achieved at infinite levels of advertising), e is the exponent, x is the proposed advertising expenditure, and b is a parameter that indicates that rate at which sales will approach the market potential as the level of advertising expenditure is increased. This equation can also be represented graphically as in Exhibit 1.3.

In a mathematical representation, both the nature and the magnitude of the relationships between variables must be specified. This quantification allows the manager to explore how variations in the level of an independent variable (e.g., advertising) influence both the direction and the level of the dependent variable of the model (e.g., sales). A disadvantage of mathematical models is that many managers are not comfortable dealing with mathematical representations. They think of them as mysterious "black boxes," because they do not see intuitively how the models work. However, advances in software and hardware are making it

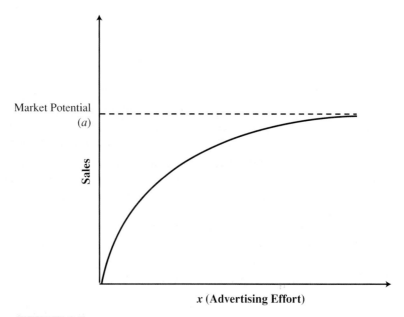

EXHIBIT 1.3
This is a graphical representation of a mathematical model—sales = $a(1-e^{-bx})$—showing the relationship between advertising effort and sales. This function incorporates the properties of saturation and diminishing returns.

easier to provide graphical representations of equations and model outputs, as is the case with many of the software implementations of decision models in this book.

Widely available spreadsheet software, such as Excel, has also made it easier to work with mathematical representations such as Eq. (1.1). For example, marketing spreadsheets typically include planned marketing expenditures and the associated gross and net revenues. However, in most cases the model developer does not establish a relationship, within the spreadsheet, between marketing inputs (e.g., advertising) and sales revenues. Thus marketing inputs only affect net revenue as a cost item. We refer to such spreadsheets as "dumb" models. They make little sense because they are silent about the nature of the relationship between marketing inputs and outputs. For the spreadsheet to make sense, the model developer must define objectives and variables explicitly and specify the relationships among variables. In a "smart" model, an equation such as Eq. (1.1) will be embedded in the spreadsheet. The manager can then look at the effect of advertising on both sales and revenues to see if increases or decreases in advertising can be justified. This is precisely how we will approach the advertising expenditure decision in Chapter 8.

Each of the three types of models has its particular strengths and weaknesses. The same marketing phenomenon can be represented in verbal, graphical, or mathematical forms, depending on the purpose of the model and the level of knowledge about that phenomenon. Exhibit 1.4 contains verbal, graphical, and mathematical models that describe the trajectory of sales of a new product. The verbal model provides a starting point for developing the more refined graphical and mathematical models. The graphical representation adds finer details about the model, and finally the formal mathematical representation adds precision. The sequence from verbal to graphical to mathematical representations is the path by which many models are actually developed. For this phenomenon the mathematical model can make more specific numerical predictions (though not necessarily more accurate ones) of future sales of the new product than both the graphical and verbal models. In turn, the graphical model will have higher specificity of predictions than will the verbal model.

Today's computer technologies enable us to develop models that combine verbal, graphical, and mathematical representations. For example, the user interface may be based on a verbal model, computations may be based on a mathematical model, and the results may be displayed graphically.

Descriptive and normative decision models

Decision models can also be categorized according to the kinds of managerial question they address. We distinguish between two main types: those that are descriptive or predictive, and those that are normative. This book includes decision models of both types.

Descriptive (predictive) decision models: Descriptive models address the question, "What will happen if we do X?" For example, a manager's decision about whether or not to introduce a new product might depend on the likely total sales for the product line if the new product is introduced; a decision to go ahead with a two-for-one promotional offer might depend on the incremental profit that might be generated by that promotion. Using descriptive models the manager conducts "simulations" to evaluate the consequences of marketing actions. Once we develop a descriptive model, we can use it equally well with numbers from the marketplace, or numbers we make up to explore alternative scenarios. For example, the manager might use a descriptive model to compute the likely sales of the product line under various scenarios, taking into account both the sales of the new product and the cannibalization of other products in the product line.

Descriptive models are useful for (1) exploring the impact of a set of alternative assumptions (scenarios), (2) finding explanations (diagnostics) for a phenomenon by identifying the specific variables and relationships that form causal links (e.g., poor new product

Verbal Model

Sales of a new product often start slowly as "innovators" in the population adopt the product. The innovators influence "imitators," leading to accelerated sales growth. As more people in the population purchase the product, total sales continue to increase but sales growth slows down.

Graphical model (a)

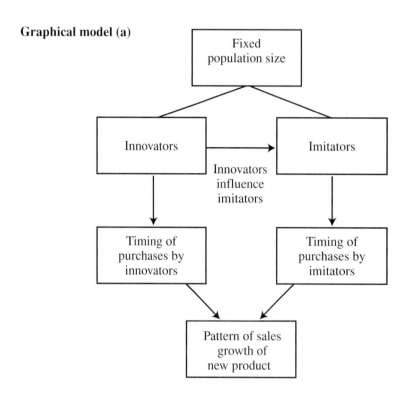

Graphical model (b)

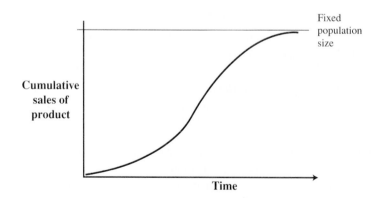

Mathematical model

$$\frac{dx_t}{dt} = (a + bx_t)(N - x_t)$$

x_t = Total number of people who have adopted product by time t
N = Population size
a, b = Constants to be determined. The actual path of the curve in graphical
model (b) will depend on these constants.

EXHIBIT 1.4
Sales of a new product can be represented in several ways: as a verbal model or description; as a graphical model (a) showing what factors influence the pattern of sales growth and (b) showing the pattern of cumulative sales; and as a mathematical model using a differential equation.

sales are due to low repeat purchase rates caused by poor product design) and (3) predicting possible outcome(s) when model inputs are extended to parameter regions other than those used for developing the model (e.g., what will sales be next month?). The ASSESSOR model (Chapter 7) is a successful descriptive and predictive model in marketing that helps managers decide whether to introduce a new product into the market.

Normative decision models: Normative decision models address the question, "What is our best course of action in a given situation?" For example, a manager might want to determine the best location for a new store or the best level of advertising for a particular product. Normative models are designed to help managers to answer such questions by enabling them to explore the value of a decision option under different scenarios: The managerial question can be modeled as a *constrained optimization* problem where the *objective function* measures the value to the firm of a particular decision option and the constraints limit the range of allowed variation in the decision options. When the manager has only a few options, case studies or simulations using descriptive models may be adequate. When he or she is faced with many options to choose from, formal mathematical procedures are needed to identify good options (see the Appendix to Chapter 2).

Firms have used normative decision models in marketing to resolve such problems as allocating salesforce resources to products and markets (see Chapter 9), media planning, designing retail shelf space, and locating stores. Normative models are often referred to as *prescriptive models* because such models can prescribe effective courses of action from among numerous options available without being driven by an explicit optimization of an objective function (see, for example, the ADCAD model in Chapter 8).

Hybrid models combine descriptive and normative elements. For example, conjoint analysis models (Chapter 7) contain descriptive models to represent the utility functions of a sample of customers and normative models to identify the best new product to satisfy a target segment of customers.

BENEFITS OF USING DECISION MODELS

The basic premise of marketing engineering is that the model-building process improves decisions. Let us look at some of the ways in which this comes about (Exhibit 1.5):

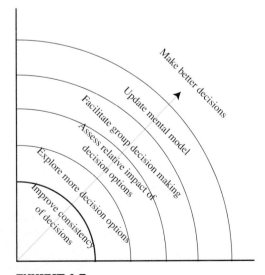

EXHIBIT 1.5
Managers derive a spectrum of benefits from using decision models, leading ultimately to better decisions.

Types of judgments experts had to make	Mental Model*	Subjective Decision Model**	Objective Decision Model***
Academic performance of graduate students	.19	.25	.54
Life expectancy of cancer patients	−.01	.13	.35
Changes in stock prices	.23	.29	.80
Mental illness using personality tests	.28	.31	.46
Grades and attitudes in psychology course	.48	.56	.62
Business failures using financial ratios	.50	.53	.67
Students' ratings of teaching effectiveness	.35	.56	.91
Performance of life insurance salesman	.13	.14	.43
IQ scores using Rorschach tests	.47	.51	.54
Mean (across many studies)	.33	.39	.64

* Outcomes directly predicted by experts.
** Subjective Decision Model: Outcomes predicted by subjective linear regression model, formalizing past predictions made by experts.
*** Objective Decision Model: Linear model developed directly from data.

EXHIBIT 1.6
Degree of correlation with the true outcomes of three types of models, showing that even subjective decision models are superior to mental models, but that formal, objective models do far better. *Source*: Russo and Schoemaker 1989, p. 137.

Applicant	Personal Essay	Selectivity of Undergraduate Institution	Undergraduate Major	College Grade Average	Work Experience	GMAT Verbal	GMAT Quantitative
1	Poor	Highest	Science	2.50	10	98%	60%
2	Excellent	Above avg	Business	3.82	0	70%	80%
3	Average	Below avg	Other	2.96	15	90%	80%
⋮	⋮	⋮	⋮	⋮	⋮	⋮	⋮
117	Weak	Least	Business	3.10	100	98%	99%
118	Strong	Above avg	Other	3.44	60	68%	67%
119	Excellent	Highest	Science	2.16	5	85%	25%
120	Strong	Not very	Business	3.98	12	30%	58%

EXHIBIT 1.7
Input data for all three models—namely, mental model, subjective decision model, and objective decision model—used for predicting the performance of graduate students. See first row of Exhibit 1.6. *Source*: Russo and Schoemaker 1989, p. 132.

Improve consistency of decisions: One benefit of models is that they help managers to make more consistent decisions. Consistency is especially desirable in decisions that they make often. Several studies have shown the value of consistency in improving predictions (Exhibit 1.6).

Exhibit 1.7 lists variables experts often use to predict the academic performance of graduate business students (the first row of Exhibit 1.6). The formalized intuition of experts captured in a simple linear model outperforms the experts themselves! Accuracy here improved from 19 percent correlation with the actual student performance to 25 percent correlation. An explanation for this improvement is that the decision model more consistently applies the expertise of the experts to new cases.

The third column in Exhibit 1.6 lists the accuracy of an "objective" linear regression model. For the academic performance study the independent variables for the regression model were the same factors used by the experts, but the dependent variable was a known measure of the academic performance of the graduate students. The predictions in this case were based on a hold-out sample of data to which the objective model was applied. For this model the correlation of the predictions with the true outcomes was 54 percent. Exhibit 1.6 also shows the average correlations between predictions and true outcomes across several studies. We see that subjective decision models had an average correlation of 39 percent with true outcomes as compared with 33 percent for the intuitive mental models. For more details about these studies, see Camerer (1981), Goldberg (1970), and Russo and Schoemaker (1989).

In sum these results point to a few interesting conclusions: (1) When you can build an objective model based on actual data, you will generally make the best predictions. However, in many decision situations we do not have data that show the accuracy or the consequences of past decisions made in the same context. In such cases the next best option is to codify the mental model decision makers use into a formal decision model. The calibrating of response models using the decision calculus method (Chapter 2) is a way to formalize the mental models of decision makers. (2) Among these three types of models, the least accurate is the mental model. However, on average all three types of models had a positive correlation with the truth, whereas a model with random predictions would have zero correlation with the truth. (3) Managers should focus their attention on finding variables useful for prediction but should use decision models to combine the variables in a consistent fashion.

Explore more decision options: In some situations the number of options available to the decision makers is so large that it would be physically impossible for them to apply mental models to evaluate each option. For example, in allocating a firm's sales effort across products and market segments, in deciding which media vehicles to use for an advertising campaign, or in pricing the various travel classes and routes of an airline, thousands of possible options are available to managers. The manager may develop decision heuristics that help cut down the number of options to be evaluated. The use of heuristics helps refine the mental model to incorporate additional considerations that narrow the number of decision options. But such pruning of decision options may lead to worse decisions than considering each of the available options more carefully. An alternative approach is to develop a computer decision model that facilitates the exploration of more options. By exploring more options, managers are more likely to move away from their prior dispositions (anchor points). A number of decision models of this type are available to marketing managers, and these have been shown to improve decisions. For example, several salesforce-allocation models have resulted in a 5 to 10 percent improvement in profitability with no additional investments (Fudge and Lodish 1977; Rangaswamy, Sinha, and Zoltners 1990; Sinha and Zoltners 2001).

Assess the relative impact of variables: In some situations, the decision options may be few, but the variables that might affect the decision may be numerous. For example, in test marketing a new product a manager may be considering only two decision options—withdraw the product or introduce it in selected markets—but many variables may influence this decision. Such variables as competitor and dealer reactions, consumer trial rates, competitive promotions, the brand equity associated with the brand name, and the availability of the product on the shelf all influence product sales. Here a decision model would provide the manager with a framework to more fully explore each decision option and to understand the impact of each of the variables on product sales. The model would also serve as a diagnostic tool in helping the manager assess the relative importance of the variables in influencing test market sales of the product. Models such as ASSESSOR (discussed in Chapter 7) have been successfully used in test marketing. Urban and Katz (1983) report that, on average, the use of the ASSESSOR model offers a 6:1 benefit:cost ratio.

Facilitate group decision making: Modeling provides focus and objectivity to group decision making by externalizing ideas and relationships that reside inside the minds of decision makers. In the same way that an explicit agenda helps direct meetings, the model or the results from a modeling effort can help a group deliberate and converge on a decision. For example, discussions on allocating resources tend to degenerate into turf battles, like congressional budget debates. However, if the entire group participates in a decision modeling exercise, then group discussions can be directed toward *why* someone prefers a particular allocation, rather than focusing simply on *what* allocation that person prefers. Likewise, if the members of a group agree on a modeling approach, then they may view the model results as unbiased and coming from an external source and therefore favor more rational (less emotional) decision options.

Update mental models: Marketing managers have mental models of how their markets operate. They develop these models through trial and error over years of experience, and these mental models serve as valuable guides in decision making. Yet in forming these mental models they may not take advantage of how managers in other industries have approached similar problems, or they may not incorporate academic research that addresses such problems. When managers are exposed to decision models, they update their own internal mental models in subtle but significant ways. Formal models require that key assumptions be made explicit, or their structure may require new ways of thinking about a familiar problem, resulting in learning that may affect future decisions. Although new learning is an indirect benefit of using models, in many cases it is the most important benefit. As a rough analogy, recall your first view of the sky through a telescope. It not only provided a clearer picture of familiar celestial objects but perhaps also altered your conception of the universe by revealing many new objects and providing more detail about the familiar objects.

Using decision models can produce all of these benefits. While managers can potentially realize one or more of these benefits in any decision situation, we must remember that the mere availability or use of a decision model does not guarantee better decisions or the realization of increased value for the firm.

Although models can produce significant benefits, many managers are reluctant to use models. This reluctance arises partly from the lack of simple-to-use computer software implementations of many marketing models. However, some managers may choose not to use a model even if they are familiar with it and the model is inexpensive, readily available, and provides quick results. Here are some of the reasons why:

> *Mental models are often good enough:* Evolution has provided us with a brain that is an efficient processor of all kinds of information, particularly information that is visual in nature. However, managers mistakenly believe that because mental models do well most of the time, they will also suffice when decisions concern complex and dynamic market behavior. To understand this, look at the sketchy visual information in Exhibit 1.8 and the table of data from a marketing report in Exhibit 1.9. In the case of the picture the brain sorts out the pattern quickly even though the picture is fuzzy, whereas in the other case the pattern represented by the numbers is unclear, even though the numbers themselves are very precise. If you look at the picture in Exhibit 1.8 carefully, you may even be able to tell what kind of dog is shown in the picture. On the other hand, you will find it difficult to immediately see any "big picture" in the data of Exhibit 1.9.
>
> Mental models, however, are not always effective, especially when the information does not form a familiar pattern. The pattern-matching ability of the human brain is helpful for making decisions when a new situation has a pattern similar to past situations, but not otherwise. Indeed, in an experimental study involving forecasting, Hoch and Schkade (1996) find that mental models perform much better in predictable decision environments than in unpredictable environments, where an overreliance on familiar patterns can lead to misleading insights.

EXHIBIT 1.8
Visual pattern of information, showing how you can "get the picture" even with sketchy visual information. *Source*: Morton Hunt 1982, p. 72.

Models don't solve managerial problems, people do: It is unrealistic to expect models to directly solve managerial problems, because by design, they are incomplete. Yet, this is precisely what many managers would like. Realistically, the relevant question is how should we use models to solve problems, not how models will solve problems. The former requires combining model-based analyses with managerial judgments, which often demands more effort, trained managers, motivation to use models, etc. If models are to be used in conjunction with a manager's judgments, some managers may legitimately argue, why not rely just on sound judgments? However, this is not a good argument. As Hogarth (1987, p. 199) notes, "When driving at night with your headlights on, you do not necessarily see too well. However, turning your headlights off will not improve the situation." Indeed, as we have often heard said, "All models are wrong; some are useful."

Decision models and mental models should be used in conjunction, so that each works to strengthen the areas where the other is weak. Mental models can incorporate idiosyncratic aspects of a decision situation, but they also overfit new cases to old patterns. On the other hand, well-designed decision models are consistent and unbiased, but they underweight idiosyncratic aspects. Managers also tend to evaluate decisions with successful outcomes more positively than the same decisions with unsuccessful outcome's. This is termed *outcome bias* and limits a manager's ability to objectively learn from the past decisions to further improve future outcomes (Baron and Hershey 1988). In a forecasting task, Blattberg and Hoch (1990) find that predictive accuracy can be improved by combining the forecasts generated by decision models with forecasts from mental models. Furthermore, they report that a 50-50 (equal weighting) combination of these two forecasts provides high predictive accuracy.

Managers do not observe the opportunity costs of their decisions: Managers observe only the consequences of decisions they have actually made and not the consequences of those they didn't. Therefore they are often unable to judge for themselves whether they could have made better decisions by using decision models. Without this ability to observe the value of systematic decision making, many managers continue to do

Category: Frozen Dinner
Volume is expressed in pounds
Quarter ending Sept 1987
Including only brands purchased by 0.5% or more of all households

Category: Frozen Dinner	Data Reflect Grocery Store Purchases Only							Percent Volume with the Specified Deal						
	Category volume share	Type volume share %	% of hshlds buying %	Volume per purch	Purch. per buyer	Share category reqmts %	Price per volume	Any trade deal %	Print ad feature %	In store display %	Shelf price reduc %	Store coupon %	Mfr coupon %	Avg. % off on price deals
Category: Frozen Dinners	927.5+	100.0	26.7	1.5	2.3	100	2.80	26	12	5	23	0	8	21
Type: Frozen Dinner	100.0	100.0	26.7	1.5	2.3	100	2.80	26	12	5	23	0	8	21
All American Gourmet	10.1	10.1	5.3	1.1	1.6	45	2.71	34	15	8	30	0	3	18
The Budget Gourmet	10.1	10.1	5.3	1.1	1.6	45	2.71	34	15	8	30	0	3	18
Campbell Soup Co.	34.9	34.9	11.4	1.4	2.0	61	3.22	8	3	1	7	0	6	18
Le Menu Light Style	2.4	2.4	1.7	0.9	1.5	24	4.44	18	8	3	15	0	27	20
Swanson	17.4	17.4	6.3	1.3	2.0	48	2.58	9	4	1	9	0	3	18
Swanson Hungryman	8.0	8.0	2.8	1.7	1.6	43	2.68	3	0	0	3	0	3	13
Swanson Le Menu	6.5	6.5	3.1	1.1	1.8	36	5.05	6	1	0	6	0	10	15
Conagra	38.7	38.7	13.6	1.5	1.8	59	2.32	39	19	7	36	0	7	22
Banquet	18.4	18.4	6.2	1.7	1.7	56	1.73	47	25	10	43	0	1	20
Banquet Manpleaser	2.2	2.2	0.9	1.8	1.3	38	1.75	29	12	9	24	0	1	13
Classic Lite	2.6	2.6	1.9	0.9	1.4	24	4.65	24	7	1	21	0	21	25
Dinner Classics	7.4	7.4	4.0	1.1	1.6	32	3.99	27	15	6	24	0	25	27
Morton	6.4	6.4	2.5	1.5	1.6	50	1.44	31	15	3	41	0	1	16
Patio	1.0	1.0	0.6	1.1	1.5	29	1.88	51	15	0	48	0	8	22
General Foods	2.2	2.2	1.1	1.2	1.6	42	3.68	24	8	2	24	0	54	38
Birds Eye Fresh Creat.	2.2	2.2	1.1	1.2	1.6	42	3.68	24	8	2	24	0	54	38
Nestlé Company	1.9	1.9	1.3	1.1	1.3	26	4.68	26	10	5	16	0	35	23
Stouffer Dinner Supreme	1.8	1.8	1.2	1.1	1.3	26	4.69	27	10	6	16	0	36	23
O'Donnel-USEN	0.7	0.7	0.6	0.8	1.3	26	2.87	31	17	7	18	1	5	28
Taste O Sea	0.7	0.7	0.6	0.8	1.3	26	2.87	31	17	7	18	1	5	28
Aggregated Vendors	8.2	8.2	4.3	1.1	1.6	37	3.01	24	11	4	20	0	15	24
Private Label	1.8	1.8	0.5	1.9	1.7	47	1.62	39	16	13	39	0	0	14

EXHIBIT 1.9

In this table from a marketing report, we are given a great deal of numerical information but may have difficulty seeing a pattern (do you see one?). In general we have far less ability to see a pattern in numerical information than we do in visual information (see Exhibit 1.8).
Adapted from: The Marketing Fact Book, Information Resources, Inc., Chicago.

what is intuitively comfortable for them. In some industries, such as mutual funds, managers are rewarded based on their performance compared with that of managers of funds with similar risk portfolios. Here managers can observe indirectly the consequences of decisions they did not make. It is not surprising then that the financial services industry is one of the heaviest users of computer modeling to support decisions.

With the automatic capture of customer transaction data, marketing managers can now establish stronger links between their decisions and market outcomes. For example, in the packaged goods industry weekly data are available that include measures of in-store environment (e.g., special displays, price discounts) and consumer purchases for all brands in a product category. With these data we can track the performance of competing brands and the promotional strategies used by each of them. This ability to link managerial decisions with market performance has led to increased use of decision models in this industry.

Models require precision: Models require that assumptions be made explicit, that data sources be clearly specified, and so forth. Some managers perceive all this concreteness as a threat to their power base and a devaluation of their positions, particularly middle managers in hierarchical organizations. Using models is analogous to thinking aloud. Many people in traditional organizations may be uncomfortable revealing their thoughts. A typical role of middle managers in traditional organizations has been to gather information from the front lines and structure that information to facilitate top management decision making. However, as information management becomes more computerized and decentralized, middle managers need to focus more on the decision consequences of information. Rarely does information by itself lead to better decisions. Only when decision makers draw insights from information and use those insights as a basis for action does information translate into value for an organization.

Models emphasize analysis: Managers prefer action. Little (1970) noted this many years ago. In the past, managers could call on corporate support staff whenever they needed help with analysis, so that they could concentrate on what they liked to do best. In today's flatter organizations, support staff is increasingly a luxury that few firms can afford.

In sum, while there are many potential benefits of using decision models, there are also numerous barriers to actually realizing those benefits. Indeed, many empirical studies of decision support system (DSS) effectiveness report mixed findings (see reviews in Sharda, Barr, and McDonnel 1988; Lilien, Rangaswamy, Starke, and van Bruggen 2001). In a given context, the value of a model could come from a number of sources, including improved decision consistency, more decision options, reduced uncertainty associated with decisions, higher precision of forecasts, faster decision making, greater organizational involvement, and so forth. Some of these benefits are hard to quantify. We leave you with the following thought: the best decision models are those that help produce important and valuable decisions, especially decisions that could not be guessed a priori. See Sinha and Zoltners (2001) for compelling arguments and examples supporting this view.

PHILOSOPHY AND STRUCTURE OF THE BOOK

Philosophy

We designed this book for business school students and managers who wish to train themselves to function in marketing organizations in the information age. We hope to impart knowledge of the concepts and tools underlying decision models and of the skills needed to apply the models we describe for real-world marketing decision making. This is an advanced book that requires you to be familiar with the basic concepts of marketing, as covered in an introductory course. You should also be familiar (though not necessarily proficient!) with basic business mathematics (algebra, statistics, and elementary calculus). The most important requirement is a *willingness* to approach problems in a systematic and logical manner.

The book straddles theory and practice, and we try to demonstrate how they reinforce each other. It will not take you long to learn how to run the software implementations of the various decision models we describe. However, you will need patience and diligence to learn and internalize the underlying principles of the modeling approaches in a way that will allow you to use them effectively in decision situations you will encounter in the future.

We based this book on two fundamental principles: *learning by doing* and *end-user modeling*.

Learning by doing: We believe that the best way to learn about marketing engineering is to put yourself in situations that require you to make decisions. Instead of focusing on modeling theory, we challenge you with practical exercises in marketing decision making. We hope that in making these decisions you will develop the ability to recognize a broad range of marketing decision problems, to structure problems to facilitate decision making, to carry out logical analyses, and to present the results of the modeling effort in a nontechnical manner to interested audiences.

As you use the models described in this book, you will have questions about their adequacy, their advantages, and their limitations, and you may want to know how to adapt the models to related problem areas. It is when you try to answer these questions in actual decision contexts that real learning takes place. To learn to ride a bike, you need to get on and try it. Merely learning about the laws of mechanics or watching other people ride bikes will not make you a bike rider. Learning by doing in the real world is expensive and error prone. This book and software simulate a safe and structured environment in which to explore and experiment with alternative courses of action.

End-user modeling: Decision models in marketing range from very sophisticated models that are developed by a team of experts (e.g., the Marriott conjoint study and the American Airlines yield management system mentioned earlier) to those that can be quickly put together by an individual (end user) with a basic knowledge of marketing and marketing engineering. In this book, we emphasize end-user models, which have the following key characteristics (Powell 1996):

- The modeling process is initiated and completed by an individual who has to deal with a business problem. The user is rarely a technical analyst or a modeling specialist. The objective of the modeling effort is to gain a better understanding of the specific decision problem and the alternative courses of action available to the user, i.e., the most important outcome of the modeling activity may be a better understanding of the user's goals and priorities.
- The modeling effort is nonmathematical in nature, although the underlying models themselves may be mathematical. The user relies on graphics, spreadsheets, and canned software to put together a model to reflect his or her understanding of the business problem.
- The user develops the model under budget and time constraints, and it has the characteristics of a good engineering solution—do as good a job as you can, cheaply, and with what you can obtain easily. The modeler uses whatever information is readily available along with a healthy dose of creativity. The model itself may be less thorough and scientific than models developed by academic researchers or by professional management scientists. Judgment plays a big role in generating inputs to the model and in interpreting the results.

	End-user models	**High-end models**
Scale of problem	Small to medium	Small to large
Time availability (for setting up model)	Short	Long
Costs/benefits	Low to medium	High
User training	Moderate to high	Low to moderate
Technical skills for setting up model	Low to moderate	High
Recurrence of problem	Low	Low or high*

*Low for one-time studies (e.g., Marriott conjoint study) and high for models in continuous use (e.g., American Airlines yield management system).

EXHIBIT 1.10
Two extremes of marketing decision models: end-user versus high-end models. Although the marketing engineering approach applies to both types of models, we focus on end-user models in this book. Source: Stephen G. Powell 1996.

- The models are often used for generating directional insights rather than for providing specific numerical guidelines. In contrast to full-blown decision support systems (e.g., a yield management system), end-user models produce outputs that are useful for the general patterns they reveal (e.g., the feasible range of prices) and not for their own sake.

Exhibit 1.10 summarizes these and other differences between end-user models and high-end models. Success with end-user models may provide the impetus for managers to develop organization-wide implementations of the models in the form of decision support systems that are linked to corporate databases.

Objectives and structure of the book

Our primary objective is to get you to personally experience the value of the marketing engineering approach. We have been involved in conceptualizing and implementing many decision models, and we have experienced the opportunities, the challenges and frustrations, the excitement, and the "Aha!" moments associated with making models work in organizational settings. In many instances we have also seen that models offer considerable value to modern enterprises. We want to share with you our insights and experiences and those of others in academia and industry with similar experiences.

Although you will work hands-on with models, our objective here is *not* to train you to be an analyst or a modeler. Rather, our main goal is to help you to become an astute user of models and a knowledgeable consumer of modeling results generated by others. In particular, we hope that this book will enable you to recognize decision situations that could benefit from the marketing engineering approach and that it will help you focus the modeling effort and interpretation of results to facilitate the decision making process. Specifically we hope to accomplish the following objectives:

- Show how and why the marketing engineering approach *can* enhance marketing decisions
- Provide a basic understanding of the most successful marketing decision models, and offer examples showing why they are successful

- Help you improve your skills in understanding and formulating marketing processes and relationships analytically
- Give you hands-on experience applying decision models

We chose the models in the book to be both theoretically sound and practically useful. The models are either based on academic research that provides some justification for them, or they have been widely used in industry. Thus the models are robust and have been tested in field settings.

In Chapter 2 we focus on how to build models. In Chapters 3 through 6 we focus on strategic marketing issues, such as segmentation, positioning, portfolio analysis, and market measurement and strategic planning. In Chapters 7 through 10 we explore many tactical issues, such as product design, setting advertising budgets, salesforce deployment, store location, and yield management. Finally, in Chapter 11 we summarize the key points for you to take from the book and speculate on the future of marketing engineering. For each chapter we include examples, cases, and exercises to illustrate the concepts covered in the chapter and to gradually ease you into the underlying structure of the models.

There are mathematical descriptions of many models here. We recommend that if you have difficulty with mathematics, skip over the math as you read, do the case problems with the software, and use the mathematics to help deepen your understanding.

Design criteria for the software

This book is best used in conjunction with the companion software tools. The book contains the conceptual material that you will need to understand the decision models embedded in the software. The software helps you learn to apply these concepts and models for making decisions in managerial settings. We used several criteria in designing the software to ensure that it is compatible with our objectives for the book:

It runs under the Windows Operating System: The software will run on IBM-compatible machines running Windows 95, 98, ME, NT, 2000 and XP operating systems. This means you cannot run this software as a native application on Apple/Macintosh computers. We recommend that the software be installed only on PCs with the Intel Pentium chip or higher, with a minimum of 32 MB of RAM.

It links to Microsoft Excel: In addition to the Windows operating system, you should have the Microsoft Excel spreadsheet program, versions 7 or higher, to take full advantage of the software. Excel is required for running all the spreadsheet models in marketing engineering. In addition Excel may be used to set up the data for other models, such as cluster analysis (Chapter 3) and promotional analysis using the multinomial logit model (Chapter 10).

It provides access to all software from a single menu: A major benefit of this software package is that it allows you to access all the programs from a common window. However, all the programs may not work in the same way or have the same menu options. This is because each program is designed to address a specific problem area and, therefore, may contain idiosyncratic menu options. At the same time, we have tried to make similar programs have similar menu structures and look and feel the same. Thus, for example, all the spreadsheets are similar in many ways, although submenu options may be different.

It covers the major areas of marketing decision making: We have tried to include representative decision models from all major areas of marketing decision making. Naturally some areas are stronger than others, given our own interests and the availability of software that is compatible with the goals of this book.

It runs on local area networks (LANs): The software will also run on file-sharing networks that support the TCP/IP Protocol.

It restricts commercial use: All the software tools we provide are educational versions that have some built-in restrictions that limit their value in commercial applications. All the basic features however, remain intact. We have imposed such restrictions as limits on data size or the inability to save large-scale problems for later use, to ensure that most commercial-size applications cannot be executed with the educational version. You *will* be able to use a part of your data to evaluate whether it would be beneficial to attempt a full-scale application of the decision model to a particular problem.

You can access the software implementations of the models described in this book in one of three ways, described in the next section. For all three options, you will need access to Microsoft Excel 7 or higher to run models that are implemented as spreadsheets. Also the tutorials describing how to use each marketing engineering module are available both at *www.mktgeng.com/tutorials* and on the CD-ROM.

Like other newly developed products, this software is subject to continuous improvement. Writing a book is quite different from putting together a complex piece of software, where even small errors can turn out to be critical. Please visit our Web site, *www.mktgeng.com* to obtain the latest updates and tips for using this software or to give us suggestions for improving the software.

OVERVIEW OF THE SOFTWARE

In this section, we assume that you have some working knowledge of the Microsoft Windows operating system and the Microsoft Excel spreadsheet program.

Software access options

Option 1: Accessing Marketing Engineering online from our servers: If you have Windows 2000 or XP, and a high bandwidth connection you can run the Marketing Engineering software directly from our servers. This book comes with a license to use our software for one year after registration. If you choose this option you must be connected to the Internet while installing or running the Marketing Engineering software.

To install the software, first register by visiting our Web site: *www.mktgeng.com/register*. The instructions at this site will grant you access to the software and guide you through the installation. During the registration process, you will need the unique authentication code that is included in this book. The license is for educational use of our software, and includes access to the online software, FAQ, online tutorials, online help files, and technical support. When you have successfully registered, you will have to download the installation setup file (*setup.exe*; approx. 15 Mb). On completion of the download, run *setup.exe* and follow the on-screen instructions to complete the installation procedure (**Remember that you must be online both during the installation procedure and subsequently to run the software**). The installation procedure will automatically configure your computer to connect to our servers.

Option 2: Accessing Marketing Engineering locally from your PC: If you do not have Windows 2000 or XP, you will not be able to run Marketing Engineering from our server and you should purchase a CD. Even if you have Windows 2000, or XP, you may want the convenience and reliability of having a local version of the Marketing Engineering program on your PC. In addition, if you want to run the Geodemographic Site Planning model, you will need the CD—this application does not currently run in a server environment. You can purchase a CD through our Web site: *www.mktgeng.com/register*.

You will be given an option to download the CD directly (although the file is quite large and will require a high-speed connection to complete the download successfully) or to order a physical CD, with several delivery options. To install the software from a CD, insert the CD in your CD Drive and follow the online instructions. If you encounter any problems during installation, visit the FAQ section at our Web site.

Option 3: Accessing Marketing Engineering from a local area network: If you purchased this book as a requirement for a course, check with your instructor to see if your school has a network version of the Marketing Engineering software installed on your school's computer network. Alternatively, if you are with a firm, your firm may have a site license for the software, in which case it would be available on your company's server. In these cases, you will not have to buy a CD.

Running Marketing Engineering

After you install Marketing Engineering on your computer (either the online version or CD version), you will see a marketing engineering shortcut on your Desktop. Click on the icon to start the program. This shortcut will run the shell, i.e., the main application controlling the full package of Marketing Engineering software (see screen below).

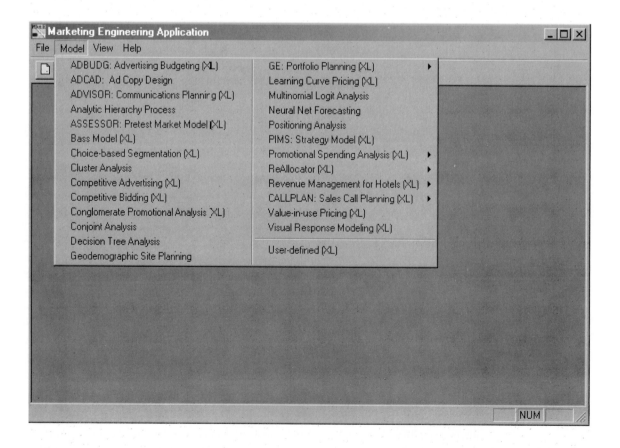

To run an application, click on that application in the **Model** menu. The models vary in terms of their underlying structures. Many of the models are in the form of Excel spreadsheets. Some of the spreadsheet models (e.g., GE planning matrix, CALLPLAN: Sales Call Planning model) accept data sets provided by the user. Other spreadsheet models (e.g., ADBUDG advertising budgeting, ASSESSOR pre-test market model) come with built-in data specific to a case and cannot easily be modified to accept new data sets. The shell will automatically open Excel if the application you are running is a spreadsheet model. The program also contains several non-Excel models, all of which accept new data provided by the user. Most of these models (except ADCAD and AHP) offer links to Excel, and also contain a built-in Excel-compatible spreadsheet facility. Exhibit 1.11 lists the modules available in the companion software and the cases or exercises that accompany a software module.

Installing Solver module in Excel: Several marketing engineering applications (e.g., CALLPLAN: Sales Call Planning model and the ADBUDG model) require the Solver optimization module. If you have not installed the Solver tool within Excel on your system, run the Excel or MSOffice setup program and add the Solver tool.

Changing the default directories used by the Marketing Engineering program: You can customize the directories where Marketing Engineering looks for data files and where it writes out temporary files. Select the **Help** menu and click on the **Preferences** option. Indicate your preferred locations for files. Note that the directory containing Excel spreadsheets must be one level below the directory where the Marketing Engineering program (mktgeng.exe) is installed.

Learning to use the software: To obtain details about the operation of any of the software modules, you should access the associated tutorial through our Web site or from the CD you have obtained. We strongly urge all users to follow the step-by-step illustration of software use included with each of the tutorials.

SUMMARY

In this chapter our primary objective was to introduce the emerging field of marketing engineering—the use of interactive computer decision models to facilitate marketing decisions. More and more marketing managers are functioning in decision environments characterized by increasing amounts of data, information (summarized data), and computing resources. Yet few business schools currently offer courses to train marketing managers in the tools and concepts of marketing decision models, which we believe will help you succeed in such environments. We developed this book to provide in one package both the concepts and software tools that we hope will become a part of the marketing curriculum at business schools.

The marketing engineering approach is centered around interactive decision models, which are customizable computerized representations of marketing phenomena that enhance managerial decision making. We described the many potential benefits of using decision models, including improving the consistency of decisions, gaining the ability to evaluate more decision options, assessing the relative impact of different factors in influencing a decision, and updating one's own mental model of market behavior. We also summarized several reasons that many managers do not currently use decision models in spite of their potential benefits.

Marketing Engineering Software

Excel Spreadsheets

ADBUDG: Advertising budgeting (Ch. 8)
  Blue Mountain Coffee case
ADVISOR: Communications planning (Ch. 8)
  Convection Corporation case
ASSESSOR: Pretest market model (Ch. 7)
  Johnson's Wax: Enhance a case
Choice-based segmentation (Ch. 3)
  ABB Electric segmentation case
Competitive advertising (Ch. 6)
  Acme liquid cleanser exercise
Competitive bidding (Ch. 10)
  Paving I-99 exercise
Conglomerate Inc. promotional analysis (Ch. 2)
GE: Portfolio planning (Ch. 6)
  Portfolio analysis exercise
Generalized Bass model (Ch. 7)
  Zenith high definition TV case
Learning curve pricing (Ch. 10)
  Price planning for the ABCOR2000 exercise
PIMS: Strategy model (Ch. 6)
  Portfolio analysis exercise
Promotional spending analysis (Ch. 10)
  MassMart Inc. case
Reallocator Resource allocation model (Ch. 9)
  Syntex Laboratories A case
CALLPLAN: Sales call planning (Ch. 9)
  The John French exercise
Revenue management for hotels (Ch. 10)
  Forte hotel revenue management exercise
Value-in-use pricing (Ch. 10)
  Account pricing for the ABCOR2000 exercise
Visual response modeling (Ch. 2)
  Conglomerate Inc. response model exercise

Non-Excel Models

ADCAD: Ad copy design (Ch. 8)
  Johnson's Wax: Enhance A case
Cluster analysis (Ch. 3)
  Conglomerate Inc.'s new PDA case
Conjoint analysis (Ch. 7)
  Forte hotel design exercise
Multinomial logit analysis (Ch. 5)
  Bookbinders Book Club case
Positioning analysis (Ch. 4)
  Positioning the Infiniti G20 case

Non-Excel Models Provided by Commercial Vendors

Analytic Hierarchy Process (Ch. 6)
  Jenny's Gelato case
Decision tree analysis (Ch. 6)
  ICI America's Project Selection case
Geodemographic site planning (Ch. 9)
  J & J Video Store case
Neural net forecasting (Ch. 5)
  Bookbinders Book Club case

EXHIBIT 1.11
Marketing engineering software and associated cases and exercises

We emphasize learning by doing. The more you apply the concepts and tools to real decision problems, the more you will learn about marketing engineering and its value. We also emphasize end-user models, that is, models that you can either develop or use directly without having to bring in technical experts. As a result we hope that you will use the software provided in the book to deal with problems you encounter in your jobs, at least as a starting point, before undertaking or authorizing more extensive modeling efforts.

Finally, we also provided an overview of the software that accompanies the book, focusing on the software design criteria and tips for installation and use. *So get ready for marketing engineering!*

HOW MANY DRAFT COMMERCIALS EXERCISE[1]

Your boss directs TV advertising for a large corporation. Currently, the corporation's outside advertising agency creates a draft commercial and, after getting your boss' approval, completes production and arranges for it to be aired.

Your company's advertising budget is divided between creating and airing commercials. Your boss is considering increasing the proportion of the budget devoted to the first "creative" part of the process. He would do this by commissioning multiple ad agencies to each independently develop a draft commercial. He would then select the one for completion and airing that he determines would be most effective for promoting sales.

The standard technique for evaluating a draft commercial involves showing it to a trial audience and asking what they remembered about it later ("day after recall"). Both the effectiveness of a commercial and the exposure it receives will influence sales.

Your boss wants you to develop a marketing engineering approach for determining the "optimum" number of draft commercials to commission.

EXERCISE

Assemble your marketing engineering team in a room. Identify one member of the group to serve as an observer/reporter. The selected observer is not permitted to say anything during the modeling session.

Your team must deliver a model capable of answering your boss' question. You do not have to answer the question; just develop a model that can be used to do so.

Use a combination of equations, words, diagrams, flowcharts, or graphs to express your model. Remember that someone else has to make sense of the model you develop.

In the class, each team will present its model and the observer for the team will then report on one admirable aspect of the team's process.

---

1. This exercise is adapted from an exercise developed by Professor Thomas R. Willemain of Rensselaer Polytechnic Institute for classroom use, and is used here with his permission. See O'Connor et al. (1996) and Gross (1972) for reference.

CHAPTER **2**

Tools for Marketing Engineering: Market Response Models

As we discussed in Chapter 1, decision models form the core of the marketing engineering approach to addressing marketing problems. The building blocks for decision models are market response models.

Our goals for this chapter are to

- Define and classify market response models, the key components of the marketing engineering approach to decision making
- Provide details of some of the types of market response models that will concern us here:
  - Aggregate market response models, to represent response behavior in the market as a whole
  - Individual response models (which can be "added up") to represent the market
  - Other market response models (shared experience models, qualitative response models)
- Develop criteria for calibrating and selecting response models
- Describe some alternative ways to specify decision model objectives
- Outline criteria for selecting response models

Software linked to this chapter includes a tool called visual response modeling, which gives you hands-on experience with building simple response models. In the appendix to this chapter we discuss Excel's Solver tool and how it can help you to find good values of parameters for response functions and to determine cost-effective marketing strategies.

WHY RESPONSE MODELS?

Marketing systems present a number of challenges—the market is not a simple laboratory where you can carefully observe processes to understand them clearly and unambiguously. The following example of possible response effects of a marketing effort illustrates some of these challenges.

Suppose a soft drink manufacturer has developed an ad campaign and wants to determine how effective it is so that it can determine how to introduce the campaign into the market. The campaign could have an immediate effect on customer awareness, attitudes, or preference for the brand, on sales of the brand this week, or on these variables sometime in the future. Let us focus only on the current sales effects for the moment; those effects may be influenced by the current advertising campaigns of other soft drink manufacturers, by the prices of that brand and of competitive brands, and by the promotions the firm is currently running in the marketplace. Some of these effects are controllable (such as trade promotions to retailers), while others are not, such as the price the consumer sees. (The price to the consumer is set by retailers, some of whom may decide to run their own promotions or to not pass on the trade discounts to consumers.) The firm's advertising campaign may have a message that differentially appeals to certain demographic or age groups, and different markets around the country have different proportions of these groups. The advertised soft drink can be purchased through supermarkets, through giant retailers (like Wal-Mart), through convenience stores (like 7 Eleven), through vending machines, through fast food outlets, and the like. Each of these channels is likely to produce a different level or type of sales response. The response may differ by package size (12 pack vs. individual 12 oz. vs. 64 oz.), package type (aluminum can vs. plastic), and the like. And what if there are diet and nondiet versions of the product? Caffeinated and decaffeinated versions? And what if the manufacturer has an entire line of soft drinks and is interested in determining possible synergies (helping other company brands) and cannibalization (stealing sales from some of its other products)?

We could complicate this example even more (we did not really indicate what the firm's goals were or whether nonsales objectives, such as building awareness or brand preference, were to be considered), but we hope the point is clear—marketing decisions take place in an environment that is difficult to analyze or control.

Because of the complexities of marketing problems and the limitations of mental models for decision making, the marketing engineering (ME) approach is of increasing interest to managers. This approach requires that the following be made explicit:

Inputs: The marketing actions that the marketer can control, such as price, advertising, selling effort, and the like—the so-called marketing mix—as well as noncontrollable variables, such as the market size, competitive environment, and the like

Response model: The linkage from those inputs to the measurable outputs of concern to the firm (customer awareness levels, product perceptions, sales levels, and profits)

Objectives: The measure that the firm uses for monitoring and evaluating those actions (e.g., the level of sales in response to a promotion, the percentage of a target audience that recalls an ad)

Response models function within the framework of marketing decision models (Exhibit 2.1). A firm's marketing actions (arrow 1) along with the actions of competitors (arrow 2) and environmental conditions (arrow 3) combine to drive the market response, leading to key outputs (arrow 4). Those outputs are evaluated relative to the objectives of the firm (arrow 5),

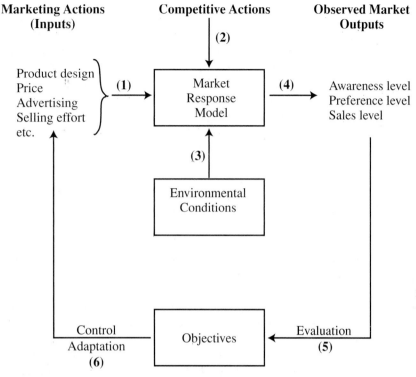

EXHIBIT 2.1
Market response models translate marketing inputs, competitive actions, and environmental variables into observed market outputs within the framework of a marketing decision model—arrow 6, the decision-modeling link.

and the firm then adapts or changes its marketing actions depending on how well it is doing (arrow 6)—the decision-modeling link.

The ME approach enables managers to be more systematic about how they make decisions in partially structured decision situations. Without ME, we see such statements as: ". . . sales in Minneapolis are down 2.3 percent relative to forecast [Goal: meet or exceed forecast?]; I suggest that we increase our promotional spending there by 10 percent over the previous plan [Assumption: an increase in current promotional spending (input) will lead to a (short-term?) sales response of at least +2.3 percent, and this will be cost-effective]."

With ME we might get: "Sales are down 2.3 percent in Minneapolis. After including that information in our database and recalibrating our Minneapolis response model, it looks as if a promotional spending increase of 12.2 percent will maximize our profit in that market this quarter."

The response models that are used in the ME approach are usually mathematical models, although some formalized verbal models are used as well.

TYPES OF RESPONSE MODELS

To the craftsman with a hammer, the entire world looks like a nail, but the availability of a screwdriver introduces a host of opportunities! So it is with marketing models. One of our goals is to expose you to a range of models, both conceptually (through this book) and operationally (through the associated software).

Response models can be characterized in a number of ways:

1. By the number of marketing variables; do we consider the relationship between advertising and sales alone (a one-variable model) or do we include price as well (a two-variable model)?
2. By whether they include competition or not; does our model explicitly incorporate the actions and reactions of competitors or is competition considered simply part of the environment?
3. By the nature of the relationship between input variables—such as advertising—and output (dependent) variables—such as sales; does every dollar of advertising provide the same effect on sales (a linear response) or are there ranges of spending where that additional dollar gives larger or smaller returns (an S-shaped response)?
4. By whether the situation is static or dynamic; do we want to analyze the flow of actions and market response over time or simply consider a snapshot at one point in time?
5. By whether the models reflect individual or aggregate response; do we want to model the responses of individuals (for direct marketing or targeting specific sales efforts) or overall response (the sum of the responses of individuals)?
6. By the level of demand analyzed (sales versus market share); to determine the sales of a brand one can try to analyze brand sales directly (the most common approach) or one can analyze market share and total market demand separately (the product of the two is sales).

In this chapter we will focus first on the simplest of the model types: aggregate response to a single marketing instrument in a static, noncompetitive environment. Then we will introduce additional marketing instruments, dynamics, and competition.

Before we proceed, we need vocabulary:

We use several terms to denote the equation or sets of equations that relate *dependent variables* to *independent variables* in a model (described in Chapter 1), such as *relationship*, *specification*, and *mathematical form*.

Parameters are the constants (usually the *a*'s and *b*'s) in the mathematical representation of models. To make a model form apply to a specific situation, we must estimate or guess what these values are; in this way we infuse life into the abstract model. Parameters often have direct marketing interpretations (e.g., market potential or price elasticity).

Calibration is the process of determining appropriate values of the parameters. You might use statistical methods (i.e., estimation), some sort of judgmental process, or a combination of approaches.

For example, a simple model is

$$Y = a + bX. \tag{2.1}$$

In Eq. (2.1), X is an *independent variable* (advertising, say), Y is a *dependent variable* (sales), the model form is linear, and a and b are *parameters*. Note that a in Eq. (2.1) is the level of sales (Y) when X equals 0 (*zero advertising*), or the *base* sales level. For every dollar increase in advertising, Eq. (2.1) says that we should expect to see a change in sales of b units. Here b is the slope of the sales/advertising response model. When we (somehow) determine that the right value of a and b are 23,000 and 4, respectively, and place those values in Eq. (2.1) to get

$$Y = 23{,}000 + 4X, \tag{2.2}$$

then we say we have *calibrated* the model (given values to its parameters) (Exhibit 2.2).

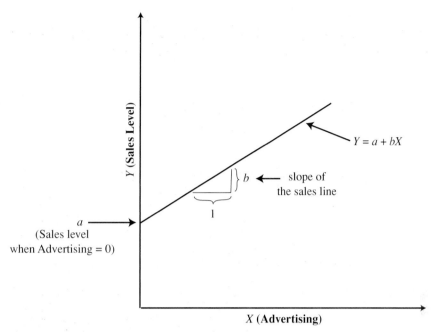

EXHIBIT 2.2
Interpreting the coefficients of a linear response model.

SOME SIMPLE MARKET RESPONSE MODELS

This book is *not* about building complex and complete market response models. Applying even simple, disciplined analysis to marketing problems can yield great benefits as compared with relying on mental models. And using complex models is not necessarily better; indeed their very complexity may hinder people's understanding and use of them. It is best to start with simple tools and gradually add complexity if it is useful.

In this section, we will provide a foundation of simple but widely used models of market response that relate one dependent variable to one independent variable in the absence of competition. The linear model shown in Exhibit 2.2 is used frequently, but it is far from consistent with the ways markets appear to behave.

Saunders (1987) summarizes the simple phenomena that have been reported in marketing studies and that we should be able to handle using our toolkit of models (Exhibit 2.3). In describing these eight phenomena here, we use the term *input* to refer to the level of marketing effort (the X or independent variable) and *output* to refer to the result (the Y or dependent variable):

P1. Output is zero when input is zero.

P2. The relationship between input and output is linear.

P3. Returns decrease as the scale of input increases (every additional unit of input gives *less* output than the previous unit gave).

P4. Output cannot exceed some level (saturation).

P5. Returns increase as scale of input increases (every additional unit of input gives *more* output than the previous unit).

P6. Returns first increase and then decrease as input increases (S-shaped return).

P7. Input must exceed some level before it produces any output (threshold).

P8. Beyond some level of input, output declines (supersaturation point).

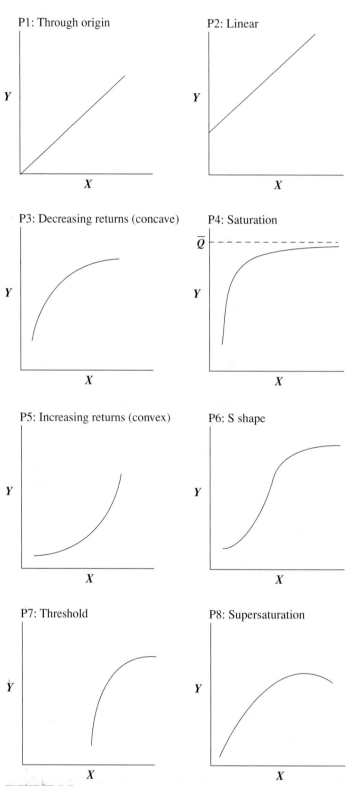

EXHIBIT 2.3
Pictorial representation of Saunders' response model phenomena.

The phenomena we wish to incorporate in our model of the marketplace depend on many things, including what we have observed about the market (data), what we know about the market (judgment or experience), and existing theory about how markets react. We now outline some of the common model forms that incorporate these phenomena.

The linear model: The simplest and most widely used model is the linear model:

$$Y = a + bX. \tag{2.3}$$

The linear model has several appealing characteristics:

- Given market data, one can use standard regression methods to estimate the parameters.
- The model is easy to visualize and understand.
- Within specific ranges of inputs, the model can approximate many more complicated functions quite well—a straight line can come fairly close to approximating most curves in a limited region.

It has the following problems:

- It assumes constant returns to scale everywhere, i.e., it cannot accommodate P3, P5, or P6.
- It has no upper bound on Y.
- It often gives managers unreasonable guidance on decisions.

On this last point, note that the sales slope ($\Delta Y / \Delta X$) is constant everywhere and equal to b. Thus if the contribution margin (assumed to be constant, for the moment) is m for the product, then the marginal profit from an additional unit of spending is bm. If $bm > 1$, more should be spent on that marketing activity, without limit—that is, every dollar spent immediately generates more than a dollar in profit! If $bm < 1$, nothing should be spent. Clearly this model is of limited use for global decision making (It says: spend limitless amounts or nothing at all!), but locally the model suggests whether a spending increase or decrease is appropriate.

Linear models have seen wide use in marketing, and they readily handle phenomena P1 and P2. If X is constrained to lie within a range ($\underline{B} \leq X \leq \bar{B}$), the model can accommodate P4 and P7 as well.

The power series model: If we are uncertain what the relationship is between X and Y, we can use a power series model. Here the response model is

$$Y = a + bX + cX^2 + dX^3 + \cdots \tag{2.4}$$

which can take many shapes.

The power series model may fit well within the range of the data but will normally behave badly (becoming unbounded) outside the data range. By selecting parameter values appropriately the model may be designed to handle phenomena P1, P2, P3, P5, P6, and P8.

The fractional root model: The fractional root model,

$$Y = a + bX^c \text{(with } c \text{ prespecified),} \tag{2.5}$$

has a simple but flexible form. There are combinations of parameters that give increasing, decreasing, and (with $c = 1$) constant returns to scale. When $c = 1/2$ the model is called the *square root model*. When $c = -1$ it is called the *reciprocal model*; here Y approaches the value a when X gets large. If $a = 0$, the parameter c has the economic interpretation of elasticity (the percent change in sales, Y, when there is a 1 percent change in marketing effort X). When X is price, c is normally negative, whereas it is positive for most other marketing variables. This model handles P1, P2, P3, P4, and P5, depending on what parameter values you select.

The semilog model: With the functional form

$$Y = a + b \ln X, \tag{2.6}$$

the semilog model handles situations in which constant percentage increases in marketing effort result in constant absolute increases in sales. It handles P3 and P7 and can be used to represent a response to advertising spending where after some threshold of awareness, additional spending may have diminishing returns.

The exponential model: The exponential model,

$$Y = ae^{bX} \text{ where } X > 0, \tag{2.7}$$

characterizes situations where there are increasing returns to scale (for $b > 0$); however, it is most widely used as a price-response function for $b < 0$ (i.e., increasing returns to decreases in price) when Y approaches 0 as X becomes large. It handles phenomena P5 and, if b is negative, P4 (Y approaches 0, a lower bound here).

The modified exponential model: The modified exponential model has the following form:

$$Y = a(1 - e^{-bx}) + c. \tag{2.8}$$

It has an upper bound or saturation level at $a + c$ and a lower bound of c, and it shows decreasing returns to scale. The model handles phenomena P3 and P4 and is used as a response function to selling effort; it can accommodate P1 when $c = 0$.

The logistic model: Of the S-shaped models used in marketing, the logistic model is perhaps the most common. It has the form

$$Y = \frac{a}{1 + e^{-(b+cX)}} + d. \tag{2.9}$$

This model has a saturation level at $a + d$ and has a region of increasing returns followed by decreasing return to scale; it is symmetrical around $d + a/2$. It handles phenomena P4 and P6, is easy to estimate, and is widely used.

The Gompertz model: A less widely used S-shaped function is the following Gompertz model:

$$Y = ab^{cX} + d, \ a > 0, \ 1 > b > 0, \ c < 1. \tag{2.10}$$

Both the Gompertz and logistic curves lie between a lower bound and an upper bound; the Gompertz curve involves a constant ratio of successive first differences of log Y, whereas the logistic curve involves a constant ratio of successive first differences of $1/Y$. This model handles phenomena P1, P4, and P6. (The better known logistic function is used more often than the Gompertz because it is easy to estimate.)

The ADBUDG Model: The ADBUDG model, popularized by Little (1970), has the form

$$Y = b + (a - b) \frac{X^c}{d + X^c}. \tag{2.11}$$

The model is S-shaped for $c > 1$ and concave for $0 < c < 1$. It is bounded between b (lower bound) and a (upper bound). The model handles phenomena P1, P3, P4, and P6, and it is used widely to model response to advertising and selling effort.

Even readers with good mathematical backgrounds may not be able to appreciate the uses, limitations, and flexibility of these model forms. A software tool called visual response modeling, included with the book, allows you to "see" these models. The software also enables you to develop your own models. More importantly, the tool allows you to calibrate the models (either statistically or judgmentally) and see how they change in shape and behavior when the parameters change. Some experience with the visual response modeler software should help make the abstract mathematical equations more transparent.

CALIBRATION

Calibration means assigning good values to the parameters of the model. Consider the simple linear model (Eq. 2.3). If we want to use that model, we have to assign values to a and b. We would want those values to be good ones. But what do we mean by *good*? A vast statistical and econometric literature addresses this question, but we will try to address it simply and intuitively:

Calibration goal: We want estimates of a and b that make the relationship $Y = a + bX$ a good approximation of how Y varies with values of X, which we know something about from data or intuition.

People often use least squares regression to calibrate a model. In effect, if we have a number of observations of X (call them x_1, x_2, etc.) and associated observations of Y (called y_1, y_2, etc.), regression estimates of a and b are those values that minimize the sum of the squared differences between each of the observed Y values and the associated "estimate" provided by the model. For example, $a + bx_7$ would be our estimate of y_7, and we would want y_7 and $a + bx_7$ to be close to each another. We may have actual data about these pairs of X's and Y's or we may use our best judgment to generate them ("What level of sales would we get if our advertising were 10 times what it is now? What if it were half of what it is now?").

When the data that we use for calibration are actual experimental or market data, we call the calibration task "objective calibration" (or objective parameter estimation). When the data are subjective judgments, we call the task "subjective calibration."

In either case we need an idea of how well the model represents the data. One frequently used index is R^2, or R-square. If each of the estimated values of Y equals the actual value of Y, then R-square has a maximum value of 1; if the estimates of Y do only as well as the average of the Y values, then R-square has a value of 0. If R-square is less than 0, then we are doing worse than we would by simply assigning the average value of Y to every value of X. In that case we have a very poor model indeed!

Formally R-square is defined as

$$R^2 = 1 - \frac{\text{(Sum of squared differences between actual } Y\text{'s and estimated } Y\text{'s)}}{\text{(Sum of squared differences between } Y\text{'s and the average value of } Y)}$$

EXAMPLE

Suppose we have run an advertising experiment across a number of regions with the following results:

Region	Annual Advertising (per capita)	Annual Sales Units (per capita)
A	$ 0	5
B	2	7
C	4	13
D	6	22
E	8	25
F	10	27
G	12	31
H	14	33

Let us take the ADBUDG function (Eq. 2.11). If we try to estimate the parameters of the ADBUDG function (a, b, c, d) for these data, to maximize the R-square criterion, we get

$$\hat{a} = 39.7, \ \hat{b} = 4.6, \ \hat{c} = 2.0, \ \hat{d} = 43.4, \ \text{with } R^2 = 0.99.$$

Exhibit 2.4 plots the results, showing how well we fit these data. (Try using the visual response modeling software to duplicate this analysis.)

In many cases managers do not have historical data that are relevant for calibrating the model for one of several reasons. If the firm always spends about the same amount for advertising (say 4 percent of sales in all market areas), then it has no objective information about what would happen if it changed the advertising-to-sales ratio to 8 percent. Alternatively, the firm may have some historical data, but that data may not be relevant because of changes in the marketplace such as new competitive entries, changes in brand-price structures, changes in customer preferences, and the like. (Consider the problem of using year-old data in the personal computer market to predict future market behavior.)

As we pointed out in Chapter 1, formal models based on subjective data outperform intuition. To formally incorporate managerial judgment in a response function format, Little (1970) developed a procedure called "decision calculus." In essence, decision calculus asks the manager to run a mental version of the previous market experiment.

Q1: What is our current level of advertising and sales?
　　Ans.: Advertising = $8/capita; sales = 25 units/capita.
Q2: What would sales be if we spent $0 in advertising? ($A$ = $0/capita)
Q3: What would sales be if we cut 50 percent from our current advertising budget (A = $4/capita)?
Q4: What would sales be if we increased our advertising budget by 50 percent (A = $12/capita)?
Q5: What would sales be if advertising were made arbitrarily large? (A = $∞/capita)

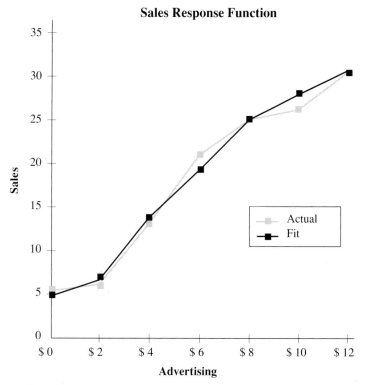

EXHIBIT 2.4
Calibration example using ADBUDG function, with R^2 = 0.99.

Suppose that the manager answered Questions 2 through 5 by 5, 13, 31, and 40, respectively; we would get essentially the same sales response function as in the previous example.

The Conglomerate Inc. promotional analysis case at the end of this chapter and the John French exercise and the Syntex Labs case (Chapter 9) employ this judgmental response modeling approach.

OBJECTIVES

Consider the role of the objectives in Exhibit 2.1. To evaluate marketing actions and to improve the performance of the firm in the marketplace, the manager must specify objectives. Those objectives may have different components (profit, market share, sales goals, etc.), and they must specify the time horizon, deal with future uncertainty, and address the issue of "whose objectives to pursue."

EXAMPLE

You have just constructed an advertising response model for Blue Mountain Coffee (see Blue Mountain Coffee case). It gives three outputs: short-term profit (after one year), long-term profit (after three years), and long-term market share (after three years). Suppose that the advertising level that maximizes short-term (annual) profit is $1 million per quarter, the advertising level that maximizes long-term (three year) profit is $2 million per quarter, and that our market share will be maximized at the end of three years if we spend $3 million per quarter. What should we do?

As this example suggests, there is no single (or natural) objective. We will introduce here some of the key issues to consider in setting objectives and develop them through the exercises in the rest of the book.

Short-run profit: The simplest and most common objective (in line with our focus on a single marketing element in a static environment) is to maximize short-run profit. The equation focusing on that single marketing element in a static environment is

$$\text{Profit} = (\text{Unit price} - \text{Unit variable cost}) \times \text{Sales volume} - \text{Relevant costs}$$

(2.12a)

$$= \text{Unit margin} \times \text{Quantity} - \text{Relevant costs.}$$

(2.12b)

We can use response models to see how the sales volume in Eq. (2.12a) is affected by our marketing actions. If our focus is on price, then (assuming costs are fixed) as price increases, unit margin goes up and quantity sold generally goes down. If we focus on another marketing instrument, such as advertising, then margin is fixed, quantity goes up, but costs go up as well.

Relevant costs generally consist of two components: fixed and discretionary. Discretionary costs are those associated with the marketing activity under study and should always be considered. Fixed costs include those plant and overhead expenditures that should be appropriately allocated to the marketing activity. Allocating fixed costs is thorny and difficult; it keeps accountants employed and frequently frustrates managers of profit centers. For our purposes only two questions are relevant concerning fixed costs:

Are the fixed costs really fixed? Suppose that tripling advertising spending leads to a 50 percent sales increase, leading in turn to the need to increase plant size. These costs of capacity expansion must be taken into account. Normally fixed costs are locally fixed; that is, they are fixed within the limits of certain levels of demand and shift to different levels outside those regions. As with our response models, as long as we focus locally most fixed costs are indeed fixed.

Are profits greater than fixed costs? If the allocated fixed costs are high enough, absolute profitability may be negative. In this case the decision maker may want to consider dropping the product, not entering the market, or some other action.

Long-run profit: If a marketing action or set of actions causes sales that are realized over time, we may want to consider profit over a longer time horizon. If we look at the profit stream over time, then an appropriate way to deal with long-run profits is to take the present value of that profit stream:

$$PV = Z_0 + Z_1 r + Z_2 r^2 + Z_3 r^3 + \cdots$$

(2.13)

where Z_1 is the profit for period i, and $r = 1/(1 + d)$, with d being the discount rate. The discount rate d is often a critical variable; the closer d is to 0, the more oriented to the long term the firm is, whereas a high value of d (over .25 or so) reflects a focus on more immediate returns. In practice the more certain the earnings flow, the lower the discount rate that firms use.

Dealing with uncertainty: Managers know few outcomes of marketing actions with certainty. Consider the following:

EXAMPLE

Conglomerate, Inc., is considering two possible courses of action: continuing with its current laser pointer, whose profit of $100,000 for the next year is known (almost for sure); or bringing out a replacement that would yield a profit of $400,000 if it is successful (likelihood = 50 percent) or a loss of $100,000 if it is unsuccessful (likelihood = 50 percent). What should it do?

If the firm had lots of money and the ability to make many decisions of this type, on average it would make 50% × $400,000 + 50% × $100,000 or $150,000 with the new product, and so it seems clear that this is the better decision. But if the firm (like capital markets) values more certain returns over less certain ones, then the decision is not that clear. What about a $310,000 gain verses the $100,000 loss for an average gain of $105,000, but a 50 percent chance of losing $100,000? Is it worth the risk?

In Chapter 6 we discuss decision-tree analysis, which formalizes a preference for more rather than less certainty—a concept known as *risk aversion*. For the moment we introduce two useful, closely related concepts: certainty monetary equivalent and risk premium.

Consider Conglomerate, Inc.'s, risky investment. And suppose that Conglomerate's managers would be just indifferent between the 50-50 chance of a $400,000 profit or a $100,000 loss and a $125,000 gain for sure. We call the $125,000 in this case the *certainty monetary equivalent* for the risky investment. The difference between the average gain ($150,000) and the certainty monetary equivalent ($125,000) is called the *risk premium*.

Either formally through utility theory (Lilien, Kotler, and Moorthy 1992) or informally by applying some combination of high discount rates or risk premiums, Conglomerate's managers should incorporate their attitude toward risk in evaluating potential actions when the outcomes are uncertain.

Multiple goals: Although profit of some sort is an overriding goal of many organizations, it is not the only factor managers consider in trying to decide among possible courses of action. Managers may say, "We want to maximize our market share and our profitability in this market!" or "We want to bring out the best product in the shortest possible time." Such statements are attractive rhetoric but faulty logic. For example, one can almost always increase market share by lowering price; after some point, however, profit will be decreasing while market share continues to increase. And when price becomes lower than cost, profit becomes negative even though market share is still increasing!

If a firm has two or more objectives that possibly conflict, how can the decision maker weight those goals to rank them unambiguously? A sophisticated branch of analysis called multicriteria decision making deals with this problem. The simplest and most common approach is to choose one (the most important) objective and to make all the others constraints; then management optimizes one (e.g., a profit criterion) while considering others to be constraints (e.g., market share must be at least 14 percent).

A second approach is *goal programming*, in which managers set targets for each objective, specify a loss associated with the difference between the target and actual performance, and try to minimize that loss. *Trade-off analysis* (Keeney and Raiffa 1976) and the analytic hierarchy process (Chapter 6) are further procedures for handling multiple objectives and trade-offs among objectives. Ragsdale (2000) provides a nice discussion of how to implement multiobjective optimization in a spreadsheet framework. The software associated with the Blue Mountain Coffee case implements a multicriteria approach.

Whether you use a simple formal method, such as the approach employing a single goal plus constraints, or a more sophisticated method of dealing with trade-offs among goals, it is critical that you neither ignore nor poorly assess important goals.

After you have specified goals or objectives, the ME approach facilitates the process of decision making—suggesting those values of the independent variables (such as level of advertising, selling effort, or promotional spending) that will best achieve these goals(s) (such as maximize profit, meet target levels of sales, or maximize market share). Throughout this book we will be exploring ways of finding those values.

We will use optimization procedures often in our search for good marketing policies (good values for our independent variables). The Excel-based software in the book relies on an add-in module called Solver for optimization problems that require model calibration (searching for the best values for the parameters of response models) or model optimization (looking for the best values for independent variables). In the appendix to this chapter, we describe how Solver works.

MULTIPLE MARKETING-MIX ELEMENTS: INTERACTIONS

In the section on calibration we dealt with market response models of one variable. When we consider multiple marketing-mix variables, we should account for their interactions. As Saunders (1987) points out, interactions are usually treated in one of three ways: (1) by assuming they do not exist, (2) by assuming that they are multiplicative, or (3) by assuming they are multiplicative and additive. For example, if we have two marketing-mix variables X_1 and X_2 with individual response functions $f(X_1)$ and $g(X_2)$, then assumption (1) gives us

$$Y = af(X_1) + bg(X_2);$$
(2.14)

assumption (2) gives us

$$Y = af(X_1)g(X_2);$$
(2.15)

and assumption (3) gives us

$$Y = af(X_1) + bg(X_2) + cf(X_1)g(X_2).$$
(2.16)

In practice when multiple marketing-mix elements are involved, we can resort to one of two forms: the (full) linear interactive form or the multiplicative form. The full linear interactive model (for two variables) takes the following form:

$$Y = a + bX_1 + cX_2 + dX_1X_2.$$
(2.17)

Note here that $\Delta Y/\Delta X_1 = b + dX_2$, so that sales response to changes in marketing-mix element X_1 is affected by the level of the second variable, X_2.

The multiplicative form is as follows:

$$Y = aX_1^b X_2^c.$$
(2.18)

Here $\Delta Y/\Delta X_1 = abX_1^{b-1}X_2^c$, so that the change in the response at any point is a function of the levels of both independent variables. Note here that b and c are the *constant* elasticities of the first and second marketing-mix variables, respectively, at all effort levels X_1 and X_2.

DYNAMIC EFFECTS

Response to marketing actions does not often take place instantly. The effect of an ad campaign does not end when that campaign is over; the effect, or part of it, will continue in a diminished way for some time. Many customers purchase more than they can consume of a product during a short-term price promotion. This action leads to inventory buildup in customers' homes and lower sales in subsequent periods. Furthermore, the effect of that sales promotion will depend on how much inventory buildup occurred in past periods (i.e., how much potential buildup is left). If customers stocked up on brand A cola last week, a new promotion this week is likely to be less effective than one a long period after the last such promotion.

Carryover effects is the general term used to describe the influence of a current marketing expenditure on sales in future periods (Exhibit 2.5). We can distinguish several types of carryover effects. One type, the *delayed-response effect*, arises from delays between when marketing dollars are spent and their impact. Delayed response is especially evident in industrial markets, where the delay, especially for capital equipment, can be a year or more. Another type of effect, the *customer-holdover effect*, arises when new customers created by the marketing expenditures remain customers for many subsequent periods. Their later purchases should be credited to some extent to the earlier marketing expenditures. Some percentage of such new customers will be retained in each subsequent period; this phenomenon gives rise to the notion of the *customer retention rate* and its converse, the *customer decay rate* (also called the attrition or erosion rate).

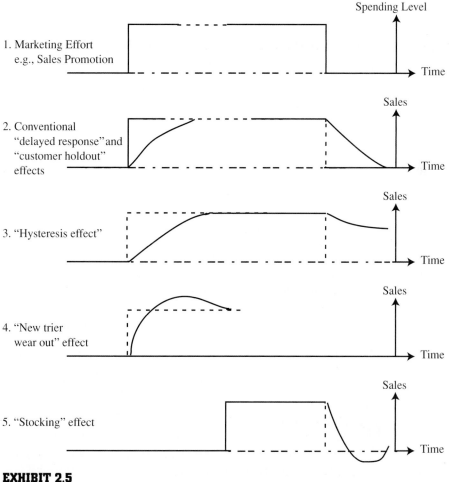

EXHIBIT 2.5
Some types of dynamic marketing responses. *Source*: Saunders 1987, p. 33.

A third form of delayed response is *hysteresis*, the asymmetry in sales buildup compared with sales decline. For example, sales may rise quickly when an advertising program begins and then remain the same or decline slowly after the program ends.

New trier effects, in which sales reach a peak before settling down to steady state, are common for frequently purchased products, for which many customers try a new brand but only a few become regular users.

Stocking effects occur when a sales promotion not only attracts new customers but encourages existing customers to stock up or buy ahead. The stocking effect often leads to a sales trough in the period following the promotion (Exhibit 2.5).

The most common dynamic or carryover effect model used in marketing is

$$Y_t = a_0 + a_1 X_t + \lambda Y_{t-1}. \tag{2.19}$$

Equation (2.19) says that sales at time t (Y_t) are made up of a constant minimum base (a_0), an effect of current activity $a_1 X_t$, and a proportion of last period's sales (λ) that carries over to this period. Note that Y_t is influenced to some extent by all previous effort levels $X_{t-1}, X_{t-2}, \ldots, X_0$, because Y_{t-1} depends on X_{t-1} and Y_{t-2}, and in turn Y_{t-2} depends on X_{t-2} and Y_{t-3}, and so on. The simple form of Eq. (2.19) makes calibration easy—managers can either guess λ directly as the proportion of sales that carries over from one period to the next or estimate it by using linear regression.

MARKET-SHARE MODELS AND COMPETITIVE EFFECTS

Thus far we have ignored the effect of competition in our models, assuming that product sales result directly from marketing activities. Yet, if the set of product choices characterizing a market are well defined, we can specify three types of models that might be appropriate:

- Brand sales models (Y)
- Product class sales models (V)
- Market-share models (M)

Note that by definition

$$Y = M \times V. \tag{2.20}$$

Equation (2.20) is a powerful reminder that we obtain our sales (Y) by extracting our share (M) from the market in which we are operating (V). Thus an action we take may influence our sales by affecting the size of the market (V), our share of the market (M), or both. It is possible that an action of ours may result in zero incremental sales in at least two ways. First, it might have no effect at all. But second, it might entice a competitive response, leading to a gain in total product class sales (V goes up) while we lose our share of that market (M goes down). Equation (2.20) allows us to disentangle such effects.

Models of product class sales (V) have generally used many of the analytic forms we have introduced earlier, using time-series or judgmental data and explaining demand through environmental variables (population sizes, growth, past sales levels, etc.) and by aggregate values of marketing variables (total advertising spending, average price, etc.). Market-share models are a different story. To be logically consistent, regardless of what any competitor does in the marketplace, each firm's market share must be between 0 and 100 percent (range restriction) and market shares, summed over brands, must equal 100 percent (sum restriction).

A class of models that satisfy both the range and the sum restrictions are attraction models, where the attraction of a brand depends on its marketing mix. Essentially these models say our share = us/(us + them), where "us" refers to the attractiveness of our brand and (us + them) refers to the attractiveness of all brands in the market, including our brand.

Thus the general attraction model can be written as

$$M_i = \frac{A_i}{A_1 + A_2 + \cdots + A_n} \tag{2.21}$$

where

A_i = attractiveness of brand i, and $A_i \geq 0$, and

M_i = firm i's market share.

Attraction models suggest that the market share of a brand is equal to the brand's share of the total marketing effort (attractiveness).

While many model forms of A's are used in practice, two of the most common are the linear interactive form and the multiplicative form outlined in the section on interactions of marketing-mix elements. Both of these models suffer from what is called the "proportional draw" property. We can see this best via an example:

EXAMPLE

Suppose $A_1 = 10$, $A_2 = 5$, and $A_3 = 5$.
In a market with A_1 and A_2 only,

$$m_1 = \frac{10}{10 + 5} = 66\,\tfrac{2}{3}\,\% \text{ and } m_2 = \frac{5}{10 + 5} = 33\,\tfrac{1}{3}\,\%.$$

Suppose A_3 enters. Then after entry,

$$\overline{m}_1 = \frac{10}{10 + 5 + 5} = 50\%,\ \overline{m}_2 = 25\%,\ \text{and } \overline{m}_3 = 25\%.$$

Note that brand 3 draws its 25 percent market share from the other two brands, $16\,\tfrac{2}{3}$ percent from brand 1 and $8\,\tfrac{1}{3}$ percent from brand 2—that is, proportional to those brands' market shares. But suppose that brand 3 is a product aimed at attacking brand 1; one would expect it to compete more than proportionally with brand 1 and less than proportionally with brand 2.

Thus when using simple market-share models, be sure that all the brands you are considering are competing for essentially the same market. Otherwise you will need to use extensions of these basic models that admit different levels of competition between brands (L. Cooper 1993).

RESPONSE AT THE INDIVIDUAL CUSTOMER LEVEL[1]

Thus far we have looked at market response at the level of the entire marketplace. However, markets are composed of individuals, and we can analyze the response behaviors of those individuals and either use them directly (at the segment or segment-of-one level) or aggregate them to form total market response.

Because information at the individual level is now widely available, researchers are increasingly interested in response models specified at the individual level. The information comes from scanner panels, where a panel of consumers uses specially issued cards for their supermarket shopping, allowing all purchase information—captured by bar-code scanners—by that consumer to be stored and tracked; database marketing activities, which capture purchase information at the individual level; and other sources.

Whereas aggregate market response models focus, appropriately, either on brand sales or market share, models at the individual level focus on purchase probability. Purchase probability at the individual level is equivalent to market share at the market level; indeed, by summing purchase probabilities across individuals (suitably weighted for individual differences in purchase quantities, purchase timing, and the like), one gets an estimate of market share. Hence it should not be surprising that the most commonly used individual response models have forms that are like Eq. (2.21), our general market-share response model. At the individual level, the denominator represents all those brands that an individual is willing to consider before making a purchase.

The specific functional form most commonly used to characterize individual choice behavior is the multinomial logit model. A simple form of the multinomial logit model is

$$P_{i1} = \frac{e^{A_{i1}}}{\sum_j e^{A_{ij}}} \tag{2.22}$$

where

A_{ij} = attractiveness of product j for individual i

$$= \sum_k w_k b_{ijk} \tag{2.23}$$

b_{ijk} = individual i's evaluation of product j on product attribute k (product quality, for example), where the summation is over all products that individual i is considering purchasing; and

w_k = importance weight associated with attribute k in forming product preferences.

Equation (2.22) gives the probability of individual i choosing brand 1. Analogous equations may be specified for the probabilities of individual i choosing the other brands. We can estimate the importance weights w_k in a number of different ways, depending on whether we have information on *likelihood-of-purchase* measures or whether we have observations of actual recent purchase events. In either case the weights are often called "revealed importance weights," because they are revealed by an analysis of the past behavior (e.g., choice) of consumers rather than by directly asking consumers. They are interpreted in much the same way as regression coefficients.

What is the value of using the logit form (Eq. 2.22)? The answer, briefly, is that the structure of logit mirrors the differential sensitivities we expect in actual choice behavior.

---

1. This section draws on material from Huber (1993).

To see how this works, consider the properties of logit. It assumes that each choice alternative has an intervally scaled measure of attractiveness. The predicted probability that an individual chooses an alternative is simply the exponent of its utility over the sum of the exponents of all alternatives in the set.

The exponentiation in (2.22) ensures that the probabilities are always positive, since the exponentiation of any real number is always positive. Exponentiation also ensures that the probabilities do not change if all the measures of attractiveness are increased by a constant. Thus the measures of attractiveness need only form interval scales, something quite useful since most customer-based measures only achieve interval quality.

A major value of logit is that it produces an S-shaped curve, tracking the expected relationship between attractiveness and choice. Graphing Eq. (2.22) as a function of A_{ij} produces an S-shaped curve that asymptotes to zero for very unattractive brands and to one for very attractive ones.

In most applications of the logit model, the attractiveness of a product (or, more generally, a choice alternative) is assumed to be a function of its characteristics. This function is typically linear as in Eq. (2.23).

With this specification the marginal impact of a change in an attribute of an alternative b_{ilk} takes a particularly simple form. The derivative of P_{il} as a function of b_{ilk} is

$$\frac{dP_{il}}{db_{ilk}} = w_k P_{il}^*(1 - P_{il}^*)$$

(2.24)

where P_{il}^* is the predicted probability of choosing product 1 in the current choice set based on the model. Thus the marginal value of a change in one variable is a function of the predicted probability of choosing the alternative. A graph of Eq. (2.24) is given in Exhibit 2.6. The marginal impact of a given marketing effort is maximized when the probability of choosing the brand is .5, but the marginal impact approaches zero when the probability of choosing that brand is near zero or close to one. Thus the logit model has a nice behavioral property: it ensures that the incremental impact of marketing effort is at its peak when the consumer is "on the fence" about choosing it.

Thus a good reason to use logit is that it mimics the way we expect choice behavior to occur. Another choice model, probit (Daganzo 1979), also has this property, and indeed it is empirically indistinguishable from logit, except for very extreme probabilities. Probit, however, is far more difficult to estimate. Thus logit is generally preferred over probit simply because the available computer programs are easier to run.

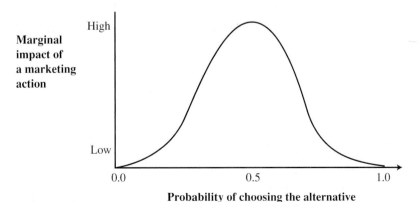

EXHIBIT 2.6
The marginal impact of marketing effort depends on the probability of choice.

The important point is that both logit and probit are better than a linear probability model, which simply predicts P_{il} as a function of a linear combination of the b_{ilk}'s. The linear probability model assumes a constant probabilistic impact of any change in the b_{ilk}'s. That is counter to our ideas of what the impact of external factors on choice ought to be and can result in predicted probabilities that are less than zero or greater than one! We illustrate some properties of the logit model in the following example:

EXAMPLE

Suppose that someone performed a survey of shoppers in an area to understand their shopping habits and to determine the share of shoppers that a new store might attract. The respondents rated three existing stores and one proposed store (described by a written concept statement) on a number of dimensions: (1) variety, (2) quality, (3) parking, and (4) value for the money (Exhibit 2.7). By fitting shoppers' choices of existing stores to their ratings through the logit model, we can estimate the coefficients [w_k]:

$$A_j = w_1 b_{j1} + \cdots + w_k b_{jk} + \cdots + w_K b_{jK}, \tag{2.25}$$

where

A_j = attractiveness of store j;

b_{jk} = rating for store j on dimension k, $k = 1, \ldots, K$; and

w_k = importance weight for dimension k.

The data in Exhibit 2.7 come from a group of similar customers. Exhibit 2.8 gives the share of the old stores with and without the new store, the potential share of the new store, and the draw estimated from this group.

The multinomial logit model has seen wide application, but it includes several assumptions that may limit its applicability. The assumption that invites the most criticism is the "proportional draw" assumption that we discussed in the section on market-share models. In column e of Exhibit 2.8, the draw is proportional to market share. In other words, this model assumes that all individuals consider all brands in their choice process, that they do not go through any prescreening or eliminate some brands. (This prescreening is often referred to as a consideration process.)

Attribute ratings by store

Store	Variety	Quality	Parking	Value for Money
1	0.7	0.5	0.7	0.7
2	0.3	0.4	0.2	0.8
3	0.6	0.8	0.7	0.4
4 (new)	0.6	0.4	0.8	0.5
Importance weight	2.0	1.7	1.3	2.2

EXHIBIT 2.7
Ratings and importance data for the store-selection example.

Store	(a) $A_i = w_k b_{jk}$	(b) e^{A_i}	(c) Share estimate without new store	(d) Share estimate with new store	(e) Draw [(c) – (d)]
1	4.70	109.9	0.512	0.407	0.105
2	3.30	27.1	0.126	0.100	0.026
3	4.35	77.5	0.362	0.287	0.075
4	4.02	55.7		0.206	

EXHIBIT 2.8
Logit model analysis of new store share example.

Researchers have developed several ways to deal with the proportional draw problem. One way is a priori segmentation; the researcher segments the market into groups that *do* consider (different) sets of brands differently. Another alternative is to group products (rather than customers) into groups that more directly compete with one another. If we view the choice process as a hierarchy, we can then assume that consumers select among branches of a tree at each level of the hierarchy (Exhibit 2.9). The consumer might first choose the form of the deodorant and then, conditional on that choice, choose the brand. The form of the logit model that applies here is called the nested logit, and it incorporates an equation like (2.22) for the selection of product form (the upper level of the hierarchy) and a separate logit model for brand (conditional on the selection of form) at the lowest level of the hierarchy.

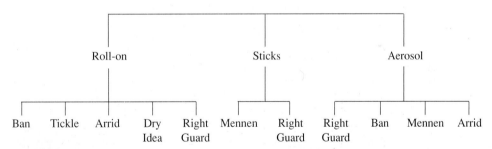

EXHIBIT 2.9
Consumer decision hierarchy for deodorant purchase. *Source*: Urban and Hauser 1980, p. 92.

The nested logit model can be represented as

$$P^i_{jk} = P^i_{k|j} P^i_j$$

where

P^i_{jk} = probability that individual i chooses brand k and product form j

P^i_j = probability that individual i chooses product form j

$P^i_{k|j}$ = probability that individual i chooses brand k *given* he or she has chosen product form j

(We drop the superscript i in the discussion below for simplicity.)

If we assume attractiveness is separable, we get

$$A_{jk} = A_j + A_{k/j} \tag{2.26}$$

where

A_{jk} = attractiveness of product j and brand k

A_j = attractiveness of product form j

$A_{k/j}$ = attractiveness of brand k (when in product form j)

The brand choice (bottom level of the hierarchy in Exhibit 2.8) can be represented as a multinomial logit model as before:

$$P_{k/j} = \frac{e^{A_{k/j}}}{\sum_{\ell} e^{A_{\ell/j}}} \tag{2.27}$$

Under suitable assumptions, the product form probability has a similar structure:

$$P_j = \frac{e^{\mu[A_j + \ell n(\sum \exp A_{\ell/j})]}}{\sum_{\ell'} e^{\mu[A_{\ell'} + \ell n(\sum \exp A_{\ell/\ell'})]}} \tag{2.28}$$

where μ above is a normalizing constant.

Substituting Eq. (2.28) and Eq. (2.27) in Eq. (2.25) gives the full equation for the nested logit model. (See Roberts and Lilien, 1993, for a more complete discussion).

Individual choice models of all sorts are difficult to estimate. If we measure only choices (yes–no or 0–1 responses) and not market shares, then we generally cannot use regression-based methods These other procedures (maximum likelihood estimation is the most common) give outputs that can generally be interpreted like regression coefficients (see Chapter 3).

We illustrate the use of logit response models with the ABB Electric Case (Chapter 3), the ASSESSOR model (Chapter 7), the gravity model (Chapter 9), and the promotion spending analysis model (Chapter 10).

SHARED EXPERIENCE AND QUALITATIVE MODELS

So far in this chapter we have focused on quantitative response models—equations that develop a formal analytic structure of the marketplace. We will now introduce two other forms of modeling that have proved valuable: shared experience and qualitative models. We will discuss both in more depth in later chapters.

Shared experience models: If we do not have data about the way a market responds (or even if we do), it may be valuable to pool the experience of a wide range of businesses and develop norms or guidelines for response behavior from the pooled data. There are many ways that such pooling takes place. One example is benchmarking (comparing one's operations against acknowledged good alternatives).

In marketing there are a number of shared experience models. Two that we will explore are PIMS and ADVISOR. The PIMS model is based on the idea that by pooling the information on experiences of a sample of successful and unsuccessful businesses, one can gain useful insights and guidance for developing successful business strategies. ADVISOR relates the determinants of spending levels for business product advertising and selling to product, market, and environmental characteristics, providing norms for those spending levels. Neither model has a causal basis, although both provide clues about what might lead markets to respond in certain ways. Both are based on regression models, where the regressive weight inferred from a sample of practice might be applied to new situations to develop guidelines for action. We cover PIMS in Chapter 6 and ADVISOR in Chapter 8.

New types of benchmarking procedures provide real time feedback to participants—a form of data currency—so that participants have stronger incentives to provide timely and accurate data (visit *www.ebrc.psu.edu/benchmark* for an example).

Qualitative response models: Some decision situations call for qualitative insights (the development of new copy for an advertising campaign, the structure of a negotiation between a buyer and a seller from different cultures, etc.). The experience of knowledgeable practitioners and guidelines generated by academic research can be useful in these situations. Qualitative response models help us to represent qualitative knowledge and insights.

In the physical sciences, mathematical models can often provide parsimonious and fairly accurate descriptions of phenomena. A well-known example is the equation $E = mc^2$, where an extraordinary range of physical phenomena are reduced to four symbols. In marketing, however, analytic functions are mostly a convenience, not necessarily accurate representations of phenomena. If a particular phenomenon can at best be described in a qualitative fashion, then a precise numerical model may be inappropriate for representing what is known. For example, if we can characterize consumer response to an ad only as positive, neutral, or negative, then a precise numerical model is inappropriate. Such a model would require managers to come up with an exact numerical value rather than allowing them to express exactly what they know. Here are two examples of qualitative response functions:

> *Example 1:* The likely response to a price reduction by a competitor might be (1) match the new price, (2) maintain the current price, (3) change TV advertising, (4) increase trade promotion, or (5) fire the brand manager. These options do not fall along a continuum that can be succinctly represented by smooth analytic functions.

> *Example 2:* The following response function might specify how a retailer might react to a trade promotion (McCann and Gallagher 1990): "This retailer always accepts a deal, but what he does with it is based on coop (shared) advertising dollars. If the deal includes coop money, the retailer will accept the deal and pass on all of the discount to the consumer. If the discount is greater than 30 percent, he will put up a big display. Otherwise, the retailer leaves the item at regular price and does not use an ad feature or a display."

We can use qualitative response functions in decision models by adopting nonmathematical representation schemes. Perhaps the most widely used approach is a rule-based representation. The response model is stated in the form of rules, which are statements joined by the connectives AND, OR, and NOT and properly specified by qualifiers FOR ALL and THERE EXISTS. Using this representation, we can state Example 2 as a set of rules in computer representation form:

If the deal includes coop money,
Then the retailer will accept the deal.

If the deal includes coop money,
Then the retailer will pass on all the discount to the consumer.

If the deal discount is greater than 30 percent,
Then the retailer will put up a big display.

If NOT (the deal includes coop money) AND
NOT (discount is greater than 30 percent),
Then the retailer will sell the item at regular price.

If NOT (the deal includes coop money) AND
NOT (discount is greater than 30 percent),
Then retailer will use ad feature = No.

If NOT (the deal includes coop money) AND
NOT (discount is greater than 30 percent),
Then retailer will use display = No.

When a response model consists of a set of rules, we can use artificial intelligence techniques, particularly logical inference, to derive recommendations in specific decision situations. Such rule sets are used for developing expert systems. In Chapter 8 we describe such an expert system called ADCAD for designing TV commercials.

CHOOSING, EVALUATING, AND BENEFITING FROM A MARKETING RESPONSE MODEL

The model forms we have described in this chapter present a number of trade-offs. One model form is not better than another. Each is good in some situations and for some purposes. We need to consider the model's use. Although a number of criteria are useful in selecting a model, here are four we suggest that apply specifically to response models:

Model specification
- Does the model include the right variables to represent the decision situation?
- Are the variables, as represented, managerially actionable?
- Does the model incorporate the expected behavior of individual variables (e.g., diminishing returns, carryover effects, or threshold effects)?
- Does the model incorporate the expected relationships between variables (e.g., patterns of substitutability and complementarity)?

Model calibration
- Can the model be calibrated by using data from managerial judgment or historical data, or through experimentation?

Model validity and value
- Does the level of detail in the model match that in the available data?
- Does the model reproduce the current market environment reasonably accurately?
- Does the model provide value-in-use to the user?
- Does the model represent the phenomenon of interest accurately and completely?

Model usability

- Is the model easy to use? (Is it simple, does it convey results in an understandable manner, and does it permit users to control its operation?)
- Is the model as implemented easy to understand?
- Does the model give managers guidance that makes sense?

When we select a model, we can summarize these criteria in one question: "Does this model make sense for this situation?" That is, does the model have the right form, can it be calibrated, is it valid, and is it useful? If the answers are all *yes*, then the model is appropriate.

Note that a great deal of the benefit or usefulness associated with modeling involves related activities. Sinha and Zoltners (2001), in reflecting on over 2000 projects with several hundred firms over 25 years, report that, often, over 95% of the total effort is spent on issues such as problem finding, database management, change management, and implementation. Often the benefits of modeling are subtle—for example, as we will see in Chapter 9, a problem framed as salesforce sizing can be profitably viewed largely as a reallocation problem.

Sinha and Zoltners (2001) also point out the value of some simple model-based insights; for example, despite the fact that when a marketing activity becomes more effective (its sales elasticity increases) it is optimal to spend more on that activity, most managers believe that such an increase in effectiveness should permit decreases in spending in the activity. Models help uncover such flaws in intuition.

Most marketing managers make decisions based largely on mental models. The more formal model building process we have outlined here permits them to refine and update those mental models and combine them with their judgment to realize the large benefit enabled by that combination (Hoch 2001).

SUMMARY

In this chapter we have given a very brief overview of market response models—the toolkit for marketing engineering. We have also introduced many concepts and the related vocabulary.

We have defined, classified, and provided details of some simple, commonly used response models. We also have outlined how you can calibrate them, what criteria are most appropriate to use as model objectives, and how you can best select a model.

But you cannot learn to ride a bicycle by reading a book about it—you have to get on and try it out. That is what we want you to do now. We strongly recommend that you try the Conglomerate, Inc. promotional exercise and visual response modeling exercises now. The former will give you some experience with judgmental calibration, with building models in Excel, and with using Excel's Solver tool to develop guidelines for marketing action. The visual response modeling exercise is linked to the Conglomerate, Inc. promotional analysis exercise and shows you how to build a response model.

There is enormous potential value in learning to ride the ME bicycle—jump on and try it out!

Chapter 2 Appendix
ABOUT EXCEL'S SOLVER

We have used the Excel spreadsheet program as a platform to implement many of the marketing models in this book, because spreadsheets are excellent tools for viewing data and for building models. Moreover, spreadsheets provide utilities—such as graphing capabilities—that facilitate analysis. And finally, and important to us, they offer links to other utilities that greatly expand the domain of an application. Excel's Solver add-in function (be sure your installation of Excel has this add-in feature before working with the Marketing Engineering software) is such a utility, and it is used in many of the Excel software tools.

Solver is a program that solves linear and nonlinear optimization problems, with or without constraints. In English this means that

- If you can specify sales as a function of advertising spending, then Solver will tell you what level of advertising will maximize your profits. It will optimize the marketing mix.
- If you are looking for some model parameters that will make a function represent data best, Solver will determine which parameters minimize squared differences between actual values and predicted values (model calibration—via least squares regression).
- If you want to determine what level of marketing effort will help you meet a sales target, Solver will help you determine the value that will do it (market-mix target setting).

All of these problems (and optimization problems in general) have three basic components: decision variables, constraints, and an objective function.

Decision variables are mathematical representations of the marketing-mix variables that we wish to set. An example variable is "Promotional spending (X) in Albuquerque (i) in July (t)," which we will represent below by X_{it}.

Constraints: All marketing problems have constraints. Promotional spending cannot be less than 0 (nonnegativity constraint). The number of sales calls in a period must be both nonnegative and an integer (integer constraint). The total promotional budget may be set at a fixed amount (equality constraint) or as a ceiling (inequality constraint).

Objectives: In the text of Chapter 2, we discussed objectives. We must specify the objective as the (single) criterion that we wish to maximize (profit), minimize (sum of squared deviations), or set equal to a target (a specific target ROI, for example).

We can characterize an optimization problem mathematically as follows:

(Decision Variables)

Find

$\{X_{it}\}$; $X_{it} \geq 0$ for $i = 1, \ldots,$ number of markets and $t = 1, \ldots$ end of
planning period.

(Objective)

To

$$\text{Max (or Min) } Z\left(\left\{X_{it}\right\}\right)$$

(Constraints)

Subject to

$$f_j\left\{X_{it}\right\} \geq b_j \text{ (or } \leq b_j, \text{ or } = b_j) \text{ for } j = 1, \cdots \text{ number of constraints.}$$

EXAMPLE

Find

$\quad X$ (the level of advertising spending—the decision variable)   (2A.1a)

To

$$\text{Max } \$0.70 \times \left(5 + 30 \times \left(\frac{X^2}{15 + X^2}\right) - X\right) \text{—the objective} \qquad (2A.1b)$$

(i.e., margin TIMES sales response to advertising LESS advertising expenditures)

Subject to

$\quad X \geq 0$ (advertising must be nonnegative—constraint).   (2A.1c)

This problem can be set up in a spreadsheet using Solver quite simply; the following spreadsheet implements the model:

D6			=0.7*(5+30*(D4^2/(D4^2+15)))-D4			
	A	B	C	D	E	F	G
1							
2							
3							
4		Advertising Level (X) =		$7.25			
5							
6		Profit =		$12.59			
7							
8							
9							
10				Advertising	Profit		
11				$0.00	$3.50		
12				$0.25	$3.34		
13				$0.50	$3.34		
14				$0.75	$3.51		

By selecting solver from the **Tools** menu, we set up the optimization as

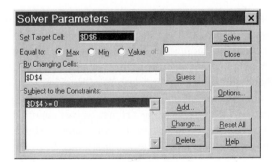

Note that in this structure we

Set Cell: D6 (our profit objective)

Equal to Max

By Changing Cells: D4 (advertising spending)

Subject to the Constraints:

D4 ≥ 0.

Solver then finds the optimal value of advertising ($7.25 in this case). See your Excel User's Guide or select Excel **Help** to obtain more details on setting up optimization problems using Solver.

HOW SOLVER WORKS

The Solver implemented in Excel (produced by a software firm called Frontline Systems) uses numerical methods to solve equations and to optimize linear and nonlinear functions with either continuous variables (as in advertising spending) or integer variables (number of account-visits in a quarter). The methods used are iterative; generally Solver calculates how small changes in the decision variables affect the value of the objective function. If the objective function improves (profit increases in our case), Solver moves the decision variables in that direction. If the objective function gets worse, Solver moves in the opposite direction. If the objective function cannot be improved by either an increase or a decrease in any of the decision variables, Solver stops, reporting at least a local solution.

The field of nonlinear, constrained optimization (especially with integer variables) is quite complex and beyond the scope of this book. (See Lilien, Kotler, and Moorthy 1992, Appendix A) for more discussion. Ragsdale (2000), and Winston, Albright, and Albright (2000) provide practical introductions to analyses and optimization with spreadsheets and www.optimization-online.org provides a wide variety of resources. However, you should be aware of some situations that can occur with nonlinear optimizers.

1. *Local optima*: While Solver may have found the top of a hill (the highest point in the region), there may be a higher peak elsewhere. Solver would have to go DOWN from the local peak and begin searching elsewhere to find it. In other words, Solver would need a new starting value (values in the "By Changing Variable" cells in the "Solver Parameter" box) to find the optimum.

EXAMPLE

Note the graph that follows of the advertising spending function that we optimized. Suppose that we started Solver with the level of advertising = 0. Note that advertising spending cannot be negative and that profit initially decreases with increases in advertising spending because we have an advertising response model with a threshold. (The form of Eq. [2A.1b] has us subtracting advertising spending from the sales/profit response function. If the latter is flat, the profit function will be decreasing.) Hence Solver cannot decrease advertising spending to less than zero (because of the constraint) and it does not want to go up (as, locally, at least, that would decrease profitability), and so we are at a local maxi-

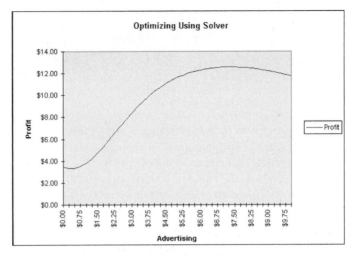

Note: Profit goes down initially when Advertising is near 0.

mum. However, if we start the problem with advertising at 1.0 or greater, Solver will correctly find the optimum value at $7.25.

What this example illustrates is that when you are using market response functions that have threshold effects, you may need to try different starting values to be sure that you have reached a global optimal solution. Several of the software programs, like Syngen, have built-in options that permit you to, in effect, try a different starting value if Solver fails to converge or gives you a local solution.

2. *No feasible solution*: Suppose that we set two constraints: $X > 6$ and $X < 3$. Clearly both of these constraints cannot be satisfied at the same time, and Solver will fail to provide any solution. While the example here makes the lack of any feasible solution obvious, in larger problems this is often quite subtle.

3. *Other problems*: General nonlinear optimizers like Excel's Solver are remarkable technical additions to the analyst's toolkit. With their power and flexibility come a variety of other problems, however. The user who wants to use Solver directly in market analyses or who wants to adapt or adjust the operation of some of the software that uses Solver may run into a number of other questions or problems, many of which are addressed in Excel's Help and at *www.frontsys.com*.

Some of those problems are caused by the way the user formulates the specific problem and employs Solver's options. Other problems may be caused by bugs in your version of Excel and in Excel's link to your operating system (your version of Windows). If the results you are getting do not make sense, it may help to quit Windows or even to reboot your computer before trying to solve the problem again.

CONGLOMERATE, INC. PROMOTIONAL ANALYSIS

UBC (Unsweetened Breakfast Cereals) is one of Conglomerate, Inc.'s oldest divisions, competing heavily with Kellogg Co. and General Mills. Historically the division has been setting its own annual promotional budgets (across all six brands in the market) based on managerial judgment and rules of thumb.

UBC recently began to develop promotional response model tools to help it decide the level and allocation of promotional spending. It started with a prototype spreadsheet. The spreadsheet is intended to encourage discussion about the appropriate level of consumer promotions for four of its markets and to familiarize brand managers with marketing engineering and the related software tools and ideas. In this case, they were to learn about response modeling and optimization with Excel's Solver tool.

To get feedback on the value of the prototype, UBC purposely left the software incomplete. It is asking you (as a brand manager) to complete the missing cells in the spreadsheet (gross and net profit) using Excel formulas.

In addition, the brand group has been through a judgmental calibration exercise as background for promotional-response modeling. In essence, UBC asked the group the following questions: What would happen to sales response for UBC brands as a whole if UBC spent $0? Fifty percent of the base level of promotional spending? One hundred and fifty percent of the base? An unlimited amount?

Using the brand managers' answers to these four questions, the software constructs a response model, which relates the amount of promotional spending to the sales that result from that spending.

The training session is designed to accomplish several goals:

- Familiarize you with building formulas in Excel
- Introduce you to the functionality of Excel's Solver tool
- Introduce the concepts of response functions and judgmental calibration
- Produce a preliminary promotional budget (and some sensitivity analysis) for these four Northeast regional markets
- Provide design feedback for a more complete, operational decision support tool

NOTE: The only cells you should change when running Solver are Cells D4 to G4—the percent of base promotional spending. The program updates the actual spending in cells D17 through G17 automatically.

In your analysis, consider several scenarios:

Scenario 1: Optimal budget and allocation with no constraints.

Scenario 2: Optimal allocation with the same, planned (base) level of promotional spending.

Scenario 3: Optimal budget and allocation if promotional spending must be increased or decreased proportionally in all markets. (Hint: Set cells E4, F4, and G4 equal to cell D4 and change only D4 in the optimization.)

Scenario 4: Optimal budget and allocation as in scenario 1 but with the saturation spending response for Philadelphia set lower than that in the base calibration (say 2.0 versus the current level of 2.9). (An outside consultant says that Philadelphia is not nearly as sensitive to promotions as the brand group had originally guessed.)

After running through these scenarios, make suggestions to the marketing-engineering software designers about the uses and limitations of the tool (including enhanced versions) for the UBC division. The following issues have come up in earlier discussions: use at the brand level versus the SBU level, dynamics of market response, competition, other (missing) marketing-mix elements, model validation, and the like. What are the most critical characteristics to include in such a tool to ensure its broad use?

CONGLOMERATE, INC. RESPONSE MODEL EXERCISE

As part of the promotional resource allocation exercise that UBC's managers performed (see Conglomerate Inc. Promotional Analysis), they had to construct a response model. A response model relates a variable under the control of management (promotional spending in this case) with an important output (such as sales, the variable we focus on here). The result is a relationship between promotional spending and sales that can be linked to profit through a formula such as, for example,

Profit = Sales(Promotional $) × (Unit price –Unit cost) –Promotional $

Marketing Engineering provides a tool called Visual Response Modeler to develop and explore both response models and related profit functions.

In conjunction with the Conglomerate, Inc. Promotional Analysis exercise, we will explore the promotional spending response analysis for New York.

Input information (drawn from the Conglomerate, Inc. Promotional Analysis spreadsheet):

Promotional Spending ($MM)	Sales (MM units)
$0.00	6.3
$0.44	6.7
$0.87	8.0
$1.31	9.3
$5.00 (very large amount)	11.8

Price (to the trade) = $2.25
Cost to deliver to the trade = $1.69
(including manufacturing, shipping, and allocated overhead)

EXERCISES

1. Use Modeler to estimate the parameters of the response function and set up the associated profit function. Use ADBUDG for this purpose, as well as the associated profit function that has the form above. (You will have to go through the **Data Maintenance** step—inputting and calibrating the model.)
   a) Analyze the associated function (look at small variations around the parameter estimates) and variations in the parameters for the profit function.
   b) What does the model suggest as the best level of promotional spending? (Does this correspond with what you saw in the Conglomerate, Inc. Promotional Analysis exercise?)
   c) What happens to that optimal spending level if
      ■ The market saturates at 13.8MM units rather than the 11.8MM above?
      ■ Improvements in logistics allow us to reduce the cost of delivered goods to New York to $1.39/unit from $1.69/unit?
2. Comment on the strengths and weaknesses of Visual Response Modeling software as an aid to exploring and building models of market response to marketing effort.

**Part II:
Developing
Marketing
Strategies**

CHAPTER *3*

Segmentation and Targeting

Segmentation, the process of dividing the market into consumer groups with similar needs and developing marketing programs that meet those needs, is essential for marketing success: the most successful firms drive their businesses based on segmentation. Targeting is the process of selecting that segment or those segments in a market to serve. In this chapter we discuss

■ Segmentation, the process of dividing customers into groups whose valuations of products are similar within groups and who differ across those groups
■ Defining a market: the set of products that are substitutes for one another within a usage segment
■ Segmentation research, the design of segmentation studies and associated data collection procedures to support a segmentation strategy
■ Segmentation methods, the models and procedures available to segment the market and to profile the segments, based on the data collected from segmentation research
■ Behavior-based segmentation, an approach to segmentation grounded not on direct measurement of customer values but on inference of those values based on customer purchase behavior
■ Targeting—how to evaluate the attractiveness of segments, select segments to serve, and identify customers in target segments.

Associated with this chapter are four key pieces of software: one that performs clustering and discriminant analysis, one that implements choice-based segmentation, and two that prioritize segments.

THE SEGMENTATION PROCESS

Defining segmentation
Markets are heterogeneous. Customers differ in their values, needs, wants, constraints, beliefs, and incentives to act in a particular way. Products compete with one another in at-

Professor Grahame R. Dowling is co-author of this chapter.

tempting to satisfy the needs and wants of those customers. By segmenting the market, firms can better understand their customers and target their marketing efforts efficiently and effectively. Through segmentation an organization strives to attain a happy middle ground where it does not rely on a common marketing program for all customers, nor does it incur the high costs of developing a unique program for each customer.

Three definitions are critical to the concept of segmentation:

A *market segment* is a group of actual or potential customers who can be expected to respond in a similar way to a product or service offer. That is, they want the same types of benefits or solutions to problems from the product or service, or they respond in a similar way to a company's marketing communications.

Market segmentation is the process of dividing customers whose valuations of a product or service vary greatly into groups or segments containing customers whose valuations vary very little within the group but vary greatly among groups.

A *target market* is a market that a company chooses to serve effectively and profitably.

Three fundamental factors provide the conditions that create an opportunity for a firm to successfully segment a market. First and most necessary is heterogeneity of customer needs and wants. In these circumstances customers actively seek and pay a premium for products and services that better meet their needs and wants. Second, although customers may be heterogeneous, they do cluster into specific groups whose members' needs are more similar to those of other customers in that group than they are to the needs of customers in other groups. Finally, the costs of serving customers in a segment must be no more than they are willing to pay, although they may be higher than the costs of serving an average customer. When customer needs differ or when the costs of serving different types of customers vary substantially, a firm that does not segment a market presents its competitors with an opportunity to enter the market.

At one extreme, a firm could think of each customer as a unique market segment: a segment of one. The business and production processes of most companies make it too costly to serve such small segments, and so they must strike a balance between the cost of serving a segment and the value customers get from their products—products designed to fit the needs of particular customers provide more customer utility than products that fit the average need. Because it provides this extra customer utility, the manufacturer may be able to charge a higher price for the more customized products, and it may reduce competitive pressure by making it more difficult for other manufacturers to tailor better products to meet the segment's needs.

Segmentation theory and practice

Firms use segmentation research to answer a wide variety of questions about the varying responses of market segments to marketing strategies (price changes, new product offerings, promotional plans, etc.), and about selecting and defining target segments for planned offerings. Some typical management problems addressed by segmentation studies are the following:

Which new-product concepts evoke the highest respondent interest, and how do the evaluations of these concepts differ by respondent group—heavy versus light users of the product and users versus nonusers of the company's brand?

In terms of target markets for a new-product concept, how do potential heavy and light users differ by demographic and socioeconomic characteristics, attitudes, and product-use characteristics?

Can the market for potential new products be segmented in terms of customers' price sensitivity (or other benefits sought)? What are the concept evaluations, attitudes, product use, demographic, and other background characteristics of the various price-sensitive segments (Wind 1978, p. 318)?

However, such questions have little to do with the basic theory of segmentation, which focuses on the relationship between customer characteristics, varying responses to potential products, and the optimal development of a marketing strategy. We try to bridge the gap between theory and real-world problems here.

To answer the management questions we have raised, we develop a segmentation model. The market segments identified in the model should satisfy three conditions: homogeneity/heterogeneity, parsimony, and accessibility. *Homogeneity* is the measure of the degree to which the potential customers in a segment (a) have similar responses to some marketing variable of interest, and (b) are different from other groups of customers. Unfortunately, no segmentation is perfect; members of different segments frequently show considerable overlap in their responses to marketing variables. *Parsimony* is a measure of the degree to which the segmentation would make every potential customer a unique target. If a study is to be useful to managers, it should identify a small set (often between three and eight) of groupings of substantial size. Finally, *accessibility* is the degree to which marketers can reach segments separately using observable characteristics of the segments (descriptor variables).

A segmentation model requires a dependent variable, usually called a segmentation *basis*, and independent variables, or segment *descriptors*. The segmentation basis should describe why customers will respond differently (why they value offerings differently, i.e., their needs and wants) while segment *descriptors* (like age, income, use of media) help marketers deliver different product or service offerings to various customer segments. In practice the distinction between bases and descriptors is contingent on the reasons for conducting the segmentation study. Analytical methods such as regression or discriminant analysis can be used to relate segment membership to descriptors. Analysts use the resulting equation (e.g., discriminant function) to predict whether a potential customer belongs to a specific segment.

Given a measure of managerial interest, such as purchase likelihood, we can use relevant segment variables (descriptors) to discriminate among segments of the population along the criterion (basis) of interest. A relevant segmentation descriptor for responsiveness to solar water-heating systems might be different climates—solar regions—in which individuals live (Exhibit 3.1a). An irrelevant segmentation descriptor for the same product would be the educational level of the potential buyer (Exhibit 3.1b).

In practice segmentation approaches focus either on descriptions of customers or on their observed or likely values or actions, although some approaches blend the two. Many articles tout one approach over another. Most of these arguments are moot, partly because no method exists for determining how similar two customers are who differ on a number of needs and behavioral dimensions. The management problem at hand, combined with cost and information on availability, should point to the best approach to use. Also, the best approach depends on the reason for undertaking the segmentation study. Wind's (1978) recommendations about appropriate bases for different types of marketing problems (Exhibit 3.2) underscore this point.

There is no single segmentation approach. The marketing problem, the timing, the availability of relevant data, and similar considerations should dictate the appropriate approach.

Segmentation is best viewed as the first step in a three-step process of segmentation, targeting, and positioning (STP). Segmentation groups customers with similar wants, needs, and responses. Targeting determines which groups a firm should try to serve (and how). Positioning addresses how the firm's product will compete with others in the targeted segment. We address the first two steps in this chapter and describe positioning in the next.

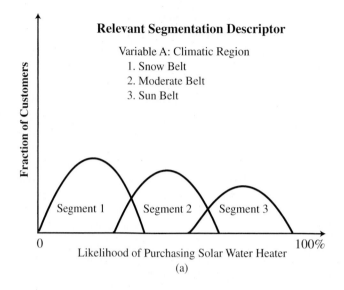

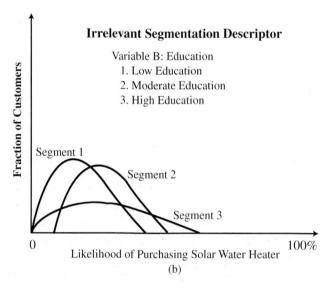

EXHIBIT 3.1

Relevant and irrelevant segment descriptors: relevant descriptors separate segments (a) while irrelevant ones do not (b).

The STP approach

Segmentation has two phases:

Phase 1   Segment the market using demand variables (e.g., customer needs, wants, benefits sought, problem solutions desired, and usage situations).

Phase 2   Describe the market segments identified using variables that help the firm understand how to serve these customers (e.g., shopping patterns, geographic location, clothing size, spending power, and price sensitivity), how to talk to these customers (e.g., media preference and use, attitudes, activities, interests, and

For General Understanding of a Market
Benefits sought (in industrial markets the criterion used is purchase decision)
Product-purchase and product-use patterns
Needs
Brand-loyalty and brand-switching patterns
A hybrid of the variables above

For Positioning Studies
Product use
Product preference
Benefits sought
A hybrid of the variables above

For New-Product Concepts (and New-Product Introduction)
Reaction to new concepts (intention to buy, preference over current brand, etc.)
Benefits sought

For Pricing Decisions
Price sensitivity
Deal proneness
Price sensitivity by purchase/use patterns

For Advertising Decisions
Benefits sought
Media use
Psychographic/lifestyle
A hybrid (of the variables above and/or purchase/use patterns)

For Distribution Decisions
Store loyalty and patronage
Benefits sought in store selection

EXHIBIT 3.2
The most appropriate segmentation bases depend on the managerial use of the segmentation. There is no single, best segmentation. *Source*: Wind 1978, p. 320.

opinions), and buyer switching costs (the costs associated with changing products or suppliers).

Targeting has three phases:

Phase 3 Evaluating the attractiveness of each segment using variables that quantify the demand possibilities of each segment (e.g., its growth rate), the costs of serving each segment (e.g., distribution costs), the costs to the firm of producing the products and services the customers want (e.g., production and product differentiation costs), and the fit between the firm's core competencies and the target market opportunity.

Phase 4 Selecting one or more target segments to serve based on the profit potential of the segments and their fit with the firm's corporate strategy, and determine the level of resources to allocate to those segments.

Phase 5 Finding customers and prospects in targeted segments.

Positioning is the final phase (Chapter 4):

Phase 6 Identify a positioning concept for the firm's products and services that attracts target customers and that enhances the firm's desired corporate image.

We elaborate on the first four phases next (segmentation and targeting) and address Phase 5 (positioning) in Chapter 4.

Segmenting markets (Phase 1)

Of the many possible ways to segment markets, we recommend segmenting based on customers' needs and the situations in which they use the product. Given this perspective, we can segment markets in two ways. We can start with characteristics of customers that are easy to identify and see if the resulting customer groups have different needs. For example, do people in New York have different entertainment needs than those in Fort Lauderdale? Alternatively, we can group customers based on their needs and then search for discriminating characteristics that enable us to identify groups that differ in their need. For example, are customers who frequent live entertainment venues price sensitive, heavy users, and so forth? The first approach is often called *convenience-group* or *a priori* segmentation. That is, we form market segments based on how convenient they are to serve. Companies serving industrial markets often use convenience-group or a priori segmentation; it is a reactive form of market segmentation.

Whenever possible, firms should be proactive in segmenting the market. They should identify differences in customers' needs, wants, and preferences and then see if they can design products and strategies to profitably serve these different needs. We suggest a five-step approach.

Step 1 is to explicitly outline the role of market segmentation in the company's strategy. How will it help the firm to establish a competitive advantage, and what other actions might the firm take to achieve its objectives? For example, the firm's abilities to develop truly new products or business processes are two strategic factors that may influence the way it segments its markets. The underlying cost (dis)advantage arising from the firm's position on its experience curve is another factor to consider. A firm should not segment the market without first considering its overall strategic intent and its core competencies.

Step 2 is to select a set of segmentation variables. These variables should be based on some aspect of a potential customer's needs or wants and should reflect differences between customers. To do this the firm needs intimate knowledge of the factors that drive demand for its products and services. Geodemographic segmentation (often used in direct marketing) focuses on the location, income, sex, marital status, and other such characteristics of target customers. In many consumer markets, the segmentation variables reflect customer differences on perceptual dimensions (see Chapter 4) and often concern geodemographic and socioeconomic characteristics. In industrial markets, the benefits the customers seek depend less on the psychological and socioeconomic characteristics of the individual making the purchase decision and more on the end use of the product and the profitability it generates (see Chapter 10 and the value-in-use concept). In the end, the segmentation variables one chooses should isolate groups of customers whose needs are similar within a group, but are different from the needs of other groups.

Step 3 is to choose the mathematical and statistical procedures one can use to aggregate individual customers into homogeneous groups or segments; this entails an implicit strategic decision: Are customer segments to be discrete (each customer in only one segment), overlapping (a customer can be in two or more groups), or fuzzy (each customer is assigned a proportional membership in each segment). Assigning each customer to a single segment is easier to understand and to apply, but we may be sacrificing information. Overlapping or fuzzy segments are intuitively more appealing, more realistic, and theoretically more accurate. However, under these fuzzy circumstances developing a segmentation strategy is much more complex, since the firm needs to position identical products differently to the different overlapping segments.

In steps 4 and 5, the firm must make two crucial decisions: *step 4* is to specify the maximum number of segments to construct based on the segmentation variables; *step 5* is to search across those segments to determine how many of those segments to target. We have no theory to guide us in deciding on the correct number of segments; this is more art than science.

Firms decide on the number of segments to target using both statistical criteria and managerial judgment. What usually happens is that firms split the (potential) market into two groups, then three groups, four groups, and so on, up to the maximum number of segments they have decided to consider. They examine each of these segment structures using various managerial and statistical criteria to eliminate any groups that are statistically or managerially unsuitable. This process invariably leads to conflict. Middle managers and salespeople naturally focus on a large number of narrowly defined market segments, while upper managers tend to view the market as comprising a small number of broadly defined segments (Exhibit 3.3).

EXAMPLE

Dowling and Midgley (1988) found that they could use two market structures to reflect needs in the Australian women's clothing market. Splitting the market into three segments was appropriate for making broad strategic decisions, while six segments were more appropriate for tactical marketing decisions. The narrow tactical segments are related to the broad strategic segments (Exhibit 3.3). The six tactical segments rank weakly from low fashion to high fashion. These tactical segments aggregate up into three broader strategic segments, again ranging roughly from low to high fashion. With both coarse and fine structures of segments, top managers can develop strategy at the broad level, while middle managers and salespeople can—and really must—implement it at the narrow level. The only complication is that the small segments have no one-to-one relationship with the large segments. For example, in Exhibit 3.3 the innovative communicators include higher-status leaders but overlap with two other segments at the tactical level (low-status leaders and professional singles). The segmentation strategy must account for this so that managers can determine how to implement the strategy (e.g., which distribution channels to use and which advertising message to use).

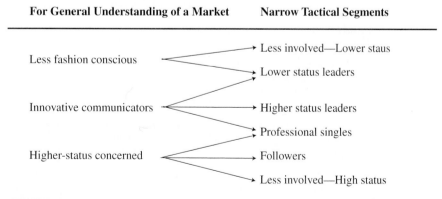

For General Understanding of a Market	Narrow Tactical Segments
	Less involved—Lower staus
Less fashion conscious	Lower status leaders
	Higher status leaders
Innovative communicators	Professional singles
	Followers
Higher-status concerned	Less involved—High status

EXHIBIT 3.3
Resolving the conflict between needs for segmentation at different levels in the Australian women's clothing market. Top management usually focuses on the broad strategic segments while middle management is concerned with narrower segments.

In the case of industrial markets, Robertson and Barich (1992) found that, at the broad strategic level, they could break customers down into three groups: first-time prospects, novices, and sophisticates. First-time prospects are new to the market and have just begun to evaluate vendors. Novices have purchased the product but are still uncertain about its usefulness and appropriateness. Sophisticates have purchased and used the product and are knowledgeable about it (Exhibit 3.4). Although Robertson and Barich's approach is limited, it illustrates a basic form of segmentation, one that is based on knowledge-based needs that are independent of the idiosyncratic nature of the individual market. According to them, industrial markets generally exhibit these knowledge-based segments.

Describing market segments (Phase 2)

After isolating a number of segments in a market, one must describe these segments. The variables you choose to describe the various market segments should highlight the profit potential (price sensitivity and size) of each segment and how the company might serve these segments. You can use two general types of variables for this purpose: those that outline broad market characteristics and those that provide insight into serving one or more of the market segments.

For consumer and industrial markets, you can use broadly similar variables to describe the various segments (Exhibit 3.5). Using these variables you can profile the segments in the market to find actual and potential customers, to understand their purchase motivations, and to understand how to communicate with them.

Many combinations of variables can be used to describe a market (Exhibit 3.5). In determining strategy, you should select variables that help you to

- Measure the size and purchasing power of the segments
- Determine the degree to which you can effectively reach and serve the segments
- Develop effective programs to attract customers

Properly implemented, this approach normally leads to readily distinguishable segments.

First-Time Prospects	Novices	Sophisticates
Dominant Theme: "Take care of me"	**Dominant Theme:** "Help me make it work"	**Dominant Theme:** "Talk technology to me"
Benefits Sought: Knowledge of my business Honest sales representative Vendor who has experience Sales representative who can communicate in an understandable manner	**Benefits Sought:** Easy-to-read manuals Technical support hotlines A high level of training Sales representative knowledgeable about products and services	**Benefits Sought:** Compatibility with systems Customization Track record of vendor Sales support and technical assistance
What's Less Important: Sales representative's knowledge about products and services	**What's Less Important:** Honest sales representative Knowledge of my business	**What's Less Important:** Sales representative who can communicate in an understandable manner Training Trial Easy-to-read manuals

EXHIBIT 3.4
Robertson and Barich's classification of three generic segments in industrial markets and what they value. *Source*: Robertson and Barich 1992.

	Consumer	**Industrial**
Segmentation Bases	Needs, wants, benefits, solutions to problems, usage situation, usage rate	Needs, wants, benefits, solutions to problems, usage situation, usage rate, size*, industry*
Descriptors		
• Demographics/ Firmographics	Age, income, marital status, family type and size, gender, social class, etc.	Industry, size, location, current supplier(s), technology utilization, etc.
• Psychographics	Lifestyle, values, and personality characteristics	Personality characteristics of decision makers
• Behavior	Use occasions, usage level, complementary and substitute products used, brand loyalty, etc.	Use occasions, usage level, complementary and substitute products used, brand loyalty, order size, applications, etc.
• Decision making	Individual or group (family) choice, low- or high-involvement purchase, attitudes and knowledge about product class, price sensitivity, etc.	Formalization of purchasing procedures, size and characteristics of decision making group, use of outside consultants, purchasing criteria, (de)centralized buying, price sensitivity, switching costs, budget cycle, etc.
• Media patterns	Level of use, types of media used, times of use, etc.	Level of use, types of media used, times of use, patronage at trade shows, salespeople, etc.

*These are "macro-segmentation"— or first stage—bases.

EXHIBIT 3.5

A list of common bases and descriptors that can be used to segment and describe markets, noting the differences between consumer and industrial variables.

Evaluating segment attractiveness (Phase 3)

In the next phase you choose one or more markets to serve. We suggest that you use nine measures, grouped into three broad factors, to evaluate the attractiveness of a segment of customers (Exhibit 3.6). One factor (criteria 1 and 2) concerns the size of the group and its growth potential. Although bigger, faster-growing segments seem intuitively appealing, what constitutes the right size and growth potential for a company will depend on its resources and capabilities.

The second factor concerns the structural characteristics of the segment and includes four criteria (criteria 3, 4, 5, and 6): competition, segment saturation, protectability, and environmental risk. Porter (1980) identified a set of competitive factors (criterion 3) that is widely used to assess competitive rivalry in a market segment. That set includes such items as barriers to entry, barriers to exit, the threat of new entrants, pressure from substitute products, customer bargaining power, and supplier bargaining power. A company should also assess whether the existing competitors in the market are serving all the obvious segments or if they have left gaps in the market.

The third factor, product-market fit, includes criteria 7, 8, and 9. A company should ask at least three types of screening questions. First, does serving a segment fit the company's strengths and its desired corporate image? Second, can the company gain any synergy from serving this segment? Third, can the company sustain the costs of entering this segment, and can it price its products and services to achieve the desired margins and re-

Criterion	Examples of Considerations
I. Size and Growth	
1. Size	• Market potential, current market penetration
2. Growth	• Past growth forecasts of technology change
II. Structural Characteristics	
3. Competition	• Barriers to entry, barriers to exit, position of competitors, ability to retaliate
4. Segment saturation	• Gaps in the market
5. Protectability	• Patentability of products, barriers to entry
6. Environmental risk	• Economic, political, and technological change
III. Product-Market Fit	
7. Fit	• Coherence with company's strengths and image
8. Relationships with other segments	• Synergy, cost interactions, image transfers, cannibalization
9. Profitability	• Entry costs, margin levels, return on investment

EXHIBIT 3.6
Some suggested criteria to use when evaluating segment attractiveness: use the ones that are most appropriate in your industry and for your business problem.

turns on investment? Many companies have tried to grow and failed by pursuing a market segment that offers a high return on investment but a poor fit with the firm's current capabilities. This strategy is sometimes referred to as the "unrelated diversification trap."

Selecting target segments and allocating resources to segments (Phase 4)

After developing the criteria to evaluate the attractiveness of various market segments, the firm must select which segments to serve. It has five basic options (Kotler 1997, p. 284):

- ■ To concentrate on a single segment
- ■ To select segments in which to specialize
- ■ To provide a range of products to a specific segment
- ■ To provide a single product to many segments
- ■ To cover the full market (all products to all segments)

Which option should the firm choose? A small company with limited resources probably cannot serve the full market. Despite their being able to serve the entire market, big companies should make a strategic choice. Most often firms use a simple heuristic; for example, they select those segments that rate highest on the attractiveness criteria described in the previous section. Sometimes managers use a matrix (Exhibit 3.7) to help them evaluate the opportunities facing the firm. For segments (such as E and A) that are very attractive and match the firm's competencies very well or the opposite, they can make clear decisions; serve segment E and keep out of segment A. They must make true strategic decisions for segments whose attractiveness, or in which the firm's competencies, are not so extreme (B, C, and D), trading off segment attractiveness against the core strengths and competencies of the company.

This type of analysis was originally developed by General Electric, and it relies on a fairly common form of portfolio matrix.

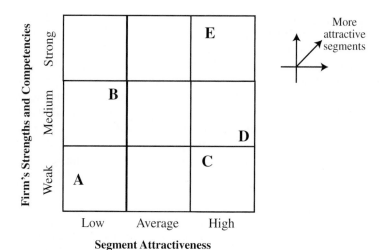

EXHIBIT 3.7
Selecting segments to serve: We plot five segments—A through E—along segment attractiveness and firm competence dimensions and note that segments are more attractive as we move in a northeasterly direction.

A six-step procedure to implement this process is as follows:

1. *Specify drivers of each dimension.* The firm may start with the dimensions suggested in Exhibit 3.6, but should carefully determine those factors that are important to its specific, overall strategy.

2. *Weight drivers.* Here, the firm must assign relative importance weights to the drivers, again a critical strategic decision. Some form of consensus-building process is usually required to come to agreement on a set of weights.

3. *Rate segments on each driver.* This scoring process is normally a consensus-building process like the one that develops the weights.

4. *Multiply weights times rates for each segment.* This is simply an arithmetic operation.

5. *View resulting group.* The graph helps interpret the results of the analysis (Exhibit 3.7).

6. *Review/sensitivity analysis.* The process should be repeated with other weights (there may be no consensus) and other ratings.

Chapter 5 provides an illustration of the use of this procedure with our GE.xls software.

When a company targets only its most attractive segment, it concentrates all its resources on serving a single group of customers. This focus should enable the firm to understand and serve the needs of this segment. Such concentration in a single segment, however, comes at a price; the company has exposed itself to high risk: it has put all its eggs in one basket.

EXAMPLE

McDonald's originally focused on lunchtime and dinnertime hamburger customers. But how could it make its existing business grow? It targeted the fast food breakfast-eater, opening earlier and adding such items as Egg McMuffins to the menu. It also targeted other tastes (beyond hamburgers), adding chicken products (McNuggets) to the menu. It tested pizza varieties in a number of locations with mixed results. The firm continues to balance the benefits of targeting multiple segments against the costs of serving those new segments and of possibly becoming less attractive to its traditional loyal (hamburger) customers.

EXAMPLE

Lotus Corporation's product, Lotus 1-2-3, targeted spreadsheet users. It lost market share to Microsoft's Excel product, especially after Microsoft included Excel as part of the Microsoft Office suite of software, running under a Microsoft operating system. It appeared that the spreadsheet segment was so narrow that Lotus could not defend its spreadsheet from competition from office suites. Lotus developed Lotus Notes (among other products) to address different but related needs and is busily defending that broader segment from competition.

To reduce the risk associated with choosing a single segment, a company may instead decide to serve two or more segments. The selection of these segments can be analyzed in two steps. First, which segments pass the attractiveness criteria we have outlined? Second, which of these acceptable segments offers the best combination of risk and return to the company, given its risk tolerance?

A variant of the single-segment strategy is market specialization. Here the company identifies a particular segment and offers a broad range of products and services to meet its needs. For example, the explosives divisions of both DuPont and ICI target open-cut and underground mines with a range of different explosives (for example, wet hole and dry hole), and blasting control systems.

A variant of this market specialization strategy is product-line specialization. Here the company makes one product or a limited range of products for sale to any customer who can pay. For example, Boeing makes aircraft, Kodak makes film, Intel makes computer chips, and MGM makes movies. When you think of a particular product category, such as cola or rental cars, it is often a product specialist (Coke or Pepsi, or Hertz or Avis) that comes to mind.

Finally, a firm such as IBM may choose to provide something for everyone. But trying to serve multiple types of customers simultaneously can be costly, since most companies alter their product offerings for different market segments. They do this by varying the physical product or by varying such nonproduct attributes as price, packaging, warranty, distribution, and image-based advertising. Most changes combine product and nonproduct attributes. However, if they can achieve substantial economies of scale, they may change only the brand name, packaging, advertising, and price.

Differentiated products targeted to different market segments typically create higher sales than a single product targeted to the average customer. However, differentiated marketing almost always increases the costs of doing business (e.g., product modification costs, production costs, administrative costs, inventory costs, and promotion costs). Exhibit 3.8 illustrates these market-coverage options.

OPTIONS

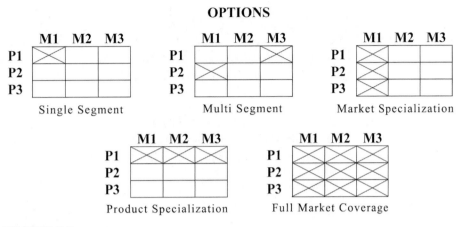

EXHIBIT 3.8
Selecting the level of marketing coverage via a product (P) market (M) matrix.

Finding targeted customers (Phase 5)

We may seek customers who are price sensitive or quality conscious, but customers don't walk around with tags providing that information. The only tags they display are those associated with their demographic profile or firmographic (industry, size, location) profile. But demographics and firmographics are notoriously poor identifiers of customer value segments. So, here is our problem—what is easy to observe is often a poor predictor of what motivates behavior.

Forsythe et al., (1999) suggest three strategies that have proven successful for identifying specific customers whose values and needs do not correlate well with easy-to-gather identifiers:

Customer self-selection: The basic idea here is for the customer and the company to reverse roles. The company might offer a range of products that fit the needs of different target segments and the customers' task is to sort through this assortment and pick the product that best fits their needs. We see this approach applied in retail settings like supermarkets—there is a wide variety of breakfast cereals on the shelf from the same manufacturer and customers choose the best one for them. If customers are price sensitive, then they may choose a brand with a coupon and take the trouble to redeem it. The not-so-price-sensitive customers forget about the coupon and pay full price.

Branding and packaging the same product in different ways can achieve the same result. Using different distribution channels to deliver the same product can also be a way to reach different segments. These approaches are most suitable when the number of customers is large and the dollar volume for each of them is small.

Another way to help customers self-select into the correct customer-value segment is to advertise in such a way that customers can see the range of segments and choose the one that best represents their needs. Companies selling investment products often use this approach. In the brochure or Web site introducing the investments, there is a section that asks prospective customers to determine their income and expense flows, risk profile, wealth situation, income needs, and so forth. On the basis of this self-analysis, they are then directed to the products that best suit their needs.

Scoring methods: In this approach, we employ the results of the discriminant analysis used to profile the target segment(s), described later in this chapter, to create a small set of questions for customers to answer. Typically, in the segmentation study, there are many more descriptive questions asked than are needed to reliably profile each segment. The role of discriminant analysis is to find a small subset of variables that can be turned into questions for consumers to answer so that they can be assigned to their correct segment.

Typically, five to ten questions from the discriminant analysis are required to assign a customer to a segment reliably. Salespeople can ask these when prospecting for new customers or when visiting existing customers. They can be included as part of the customer profiling process via a call center or executed on the Web. These can also be used to segment the current customer database—for example, a questionnaire can be mailed or e-mailed to customers or they can be contacted by customer service representatives. Hence, over a short period of time it is possible to overlay a new segmentation scheme onto the existing customer database.

Dual objective segmentation: This approach merges some of the easier-to-collect needs data with the demographic data to develop a mix of basis and descriptor variables. The approach trades off some precision in understanding customer needs and values against the ease of identifying people or firms based on the demographics. The idea is to produce a set of actionable segments.

EXAMPLE

Berrigan (1999) describes a disguised example from East Coast Telecom (Telecom with Heart) whose Web site directs the customer to a series of questions that "help identify your needs and suggest the products and services that are the best fit for you." A series of questions follow (see flowchart of questions starting at one place in the Web site in Exhibit 3.9. On the basis of those questions, the system places the customer in a segment and suggests the best product for that segment.

Integration of Targeting and Relationship Management

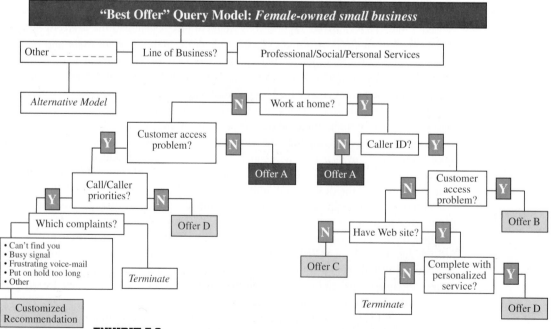

EXHIBIT 3.9
The sequence of questions asked over the Web to classify customers into segments.

DEFINING A MARKET

We have been using the word *market* but have not defined it yet. To segment a market, one must first define that market. While the term *market* is often used loosely, the traditional approach to describing markets has been to use both a generic title and physical properties. For example, we use "auto market" (a generic title) and the size of the car—subcompact, compact, midsize, or full size (a physical property). The idea behind this traditional approach is that more (actual or perceived) competition exists within markets than across markets. It is most useful to define markets to reflect the way consumers view them.

Kotler (1997, p. 13) defines a product market as follows:

> A market consists of all the potential customers sharing a particular need or want who might be willing and able to engage in exchange to satisfy that need or want.

By this definition the physical product alone does not define a market; the same physical product may compete in different markets, and different physical products may compete in the same market. For example, the same (physical) automobile may be sold to a consumer or to a taxi company (fleet sales); the needs and buying behaviors of the manager of fleet operations and the individual customer are quite different. And both a PC and a mechanical typewriter, very dissimilar physical products, can provide "word processing solutions" (see the following example).

EXAMPLE

A classical example from the 1980s demonstrates two ways to define the word processor market. In Exhibit 3.10 we define the market as electric typewriters or electromechanical equipment to solve word processing needs. Firm A sees its market share increase but both its sales and total market sales decline in this market.

Shipments

	1980	1981	1982	1983	1984	1985
A (Us)	403,027	495,192	548,905	550,351	541,388	515,000
B	369,916	388,520	349,396	323,005	342,197	297,000
Other	367,057	324,010	343,885	370,374	202, 495	129,070
Total	1,140,000	1,207,722	1,242,186	1,243,730	1,086,080	941,070

Market Shares (%)

	1980	1981	1982	1983	1984	1985
A (Us)	35.4	41.0	44.2	44.2	49.8	54.7
B	32.4	32.2	28.1	26.0	31.5	31.6
Other	32.2	26.8	27.7	29.8	18.6	13.7

EXHIBIT 3.10
(Fictitious) Electric typewriter shipment data. If firm A defines itself as a typewriter manufacturer, it sees declining sales but increasing market share in a declining market.

If we broaden the market definition to include electronic solutions (Exhibit 3.11), we get a different picture: Firm A's share of a growing market is declining along with its sales.

How do we know which definition of a market is right? It depends on the strategic orientation of the firm, and what marketing actions (milk the business, invest in new technology, or divest, for example) are appropriate depending on what definition the firm chooses.

Shipments

	1980	1981	1982	1983	1984	1985
A (Us)	403,027	495,192	548,905	550,351	541,387	515,000
B	369,916	388,520	349,396	323,005	342,197	297,000
Other electric	367,057	324,010	343,885	370,374	202,495	129,070
Electronic word processors	60,040	112,220	209,800	392,352	733,699	1,372,016
Total	1,200,040	1,319,942	1,451,986	1,636,082	1,819,778	2,313,086

Market Shares (%)

	1980	1981	1982	1983	1984	1985
A (Us)	33.6	37.5	38.7	33.6	29.8	22.3
B	30.8	29.4	24.1	19.7	18.8	12.8
Other electric	30.6	24.5	23.7	22.6	11.1	5.6
Electronic word processors	5.0	8.5	14.4	24.0	40.3	59.3

EXHIBIT 3.11
Word processor shipments data. If firm A is in the word processing market, its market share is eroding in a rapidly growing market.

Day, Shocker, and Srivastava (1979) classify methods for identifying product markets by whether they rely on behavioral or judgmental data. Exhibit 3.12 presents their basic classification.

Economists consider *cross-elasticity of demand* to be the standard criterion against which other criteria should be judged. Essentially, if the price of product *i* goes up and that

Purchase or Use-Behavior Approaches	**Customer-Perception or Judgmental Approaches**
Cross-elasticity of demand Similarities in behavior Brand switching	Decision-sequence analysis Perceptual mapping Technology-substitution analysis Customer judgments of substitutability

EXHIBIT 3.12
Analytic methods for defining product markets are based either on what customers do or what customers say. *Source:* Day, Shocker, and Srivastava 1979, p. 11.

causes demand for product *j* to go up, *i* and *j* are said to be in the same market. This approach, despite its logic, may be limited because (1) it assumes a firm has no response to another's price changes, (2) it is static and cannot accommodate changes in the composition of the market for the product, and (3) it is difficult to estimate cross-elasticity in relatively stable markets, where data vary very little. (Most cross-elasticity studies rely on some form of regression analysis, using methods like Excel's regression tool.)

We can also define a market by looking at *similarities in use behavior*, that is, what customers buy. Cocks and Virts (1975) addressed the question of the substitutability of drugs with different chemical makeups but of similar therapeutic value. A panel of 3,000 physicians provided data on the need for the drug (the diagnosis) as well as the drugs they prescribed to treat the problem. As more detailed data on consumption behavior become available, we expect that use of this approach will increase. (Tools like our cluster analysis program can segment based on use behavior.)

We can look at *brand switching* to discover markets. A matrix of brand-switching proportions breaks down into competitive markets, with high switching rates between brands in the same market, but with low switching rates across markets. The approach is applicable in relatively stable markets with high repeat-purchase rates, such as the soft drink market (Exhibit 3.13).

Current Purchase Occasion

		Coke	Diet Coke	Pepsi	Diet Pepsi	Sprite	Diet Sprite	Total
	Coke	53%	9%	27%	4%	5%	2%	100%
Last	Diet Coke	12%	61%	4%	15%	2%	5%	100%
Purchase	Pepsi	24%	3%	58%	9%	5%	1%	100%
Occasion	Diet Pepsi	4%	14%	11%	63%	2%	6%	100%
	Sprite	21%	2%	17%	3%	52%	6%	100%
	Diet Sprite	2%	15%	2%	12%	7%	61%	100%

EXHIBIT 3.13
Segmentation by brand switching: a brand-switching matrix suggesting a cola/noncola segment and a diet/nondiet segment: i.e., highest switching levels are Coke → Pepsi; Pepsi → Coke; Diet Coke → Diet Pepsi and Coke; Diet Pepsi → Diet Coke and Pepsi; Sprite → Coke/Pepsi; and Diet Sprite → Diet Coke/Diet Pepsi.

All the methods that rely on behavioral data to define a market suffer from analyzing *what was* rather than focusing on *what might be*. For instance, problems such as lack of availability may prevent substitution of one brand for another when they might otherwise be substitutes. Unless researchers gather data in a laboratory-based setting, using behavioral methods may bias the definition of a market. To complement behavioral data, consumer perceptions and judgments are useful.

In analyzing consumers' *decision sequence*, researchers consider protocols or descriptions of the consumer decision-making process that indicate the sequence in which people use decision criteria to choose products (Bettman 1971). For example, they might ask a potential customer "When choosing a margarine, do you chose a form first (stick versus tub), a raw material first (corn oil, safflower oil, etc.), or a brand first?" Because respondents are not used to this type of introspection, there is a danger that the stated responses may not truly reflect reality.

Perceptual mapping represents in a geometric space the way customers think about products (Chapter 4). Those brands that are close together on the map form a market and are substitutes. The approach is flexible and has seen wide use in market-definition studies.

Another way of determining how products (industrial products, generally) are likely to compete is to look at *technology substitution*. The rate at which one material is substituted for another (e.g., polyvinyl for glass in bottles) indicates its relative utility in each use situation. One can calculate an economic measure of relative utility that can be used to estimate substitutability among competing products or technologies in certain situations.

Consumer judgments of substitutability can be gathered in various ways, ranging from simply asking customers to methods with more diagnostic power. (Day, Shocker, and Srivastava [1979] give a critical review of these methods.)

While we have a wide range of methods for defining markets, in choosing a method we must take into account both management's needs and the cost and availability of data. We have yet to resolve Day, Shocker, and Srivastava's (1979) concern: "The most persistent problem is the lack of defensible criteria for recognizing [market] boundaries" (p. 18), and we must blend judgment with one or more of the methods outlined in this section.

SEGMENTATION RESEARCH: DESIGNING AND COLLECTING DATA

While there are many ways to segment markets and many data sources, both internal and external to the firm, we will focus here on a typical formal segmentation research study, based on the collection of primary source data.

Such a study consists of four key steps:

1. Developing the measurement instrument (survey form, for example): what information do we want to collect and how should we collect it?
2. Selecting a sample: who (what respondents? where? in what households or organizations?) are we studying?
3. Selecting and aggregating respondents: how can we take different responses from several individuals in a household or an organization and use them to predict how the household or organization will behave?
4. Analyzing the data and segmenting the market: what statistical procedures can we use to segment (potential) customers and to describe aspects of their behavior that are crucial to serving their needs?

These topics are covered in much more detail in market research texts; what we try to do here is to outline the key issues and illustrate the important points. (Note that when you are dealing with data from a secondary source—data already collected—steps 1 and 2 have been bypassed, but you still must follow steps 3 and 4.)

Developing the measurement instrument

Measurement instruments for segmentation studies are usually designed to collect several types of data:

- Demographic descriptors, such as age, income, marital status, and education, on the consumer side, and industry classification, size (number of employees or sales), and job responsibilities on the industrial side
- Psychological descriptors, such as activities, interests, and lifestyle, for consumer and service markets
- Demand, including historical purchases or consumption and anticipated future purchases
- Needs, which could be stated needs or needs inferred through such methods as conjoint analysis (Chapter 7) or value-in-use analysis (Chapter 10)
- Attitudes, which could be about products, suppliers, risk of purchase, or the adoption process in general
- Media and distribution channel use, such as the types and amount of media used and where products and services are typically bought

Usually the data collected in a segmentation study are structured into a *data matrix*; the columns in the matrix correspond to the variables measured and each row contains the responses of one respondent. Exhibit 3.14 shows part of a data matrix from a study of needs for organizational use of PCs. Even when a particular study does not organize data in this way, it is a useful way to think about segmentation data.

In collecting data, and constructing a data matrix, you should address a number of issues:

Q1: Who is the respondent? Different respondents in the same household or, more critically, in the same organization may give quite different responses. (A husband, a wife, and their children may have quite diverse opinions about what constitutes an ideal vacation; design engineers and purchasing agents have different views about key purchasing criteria.)

Q2: What kind of data are you gathering? Nominal data, such as yes–no, or industry classification data, are not easy to compare with data obtained from rating scales.

Q3: Are the measurement scales the same? If the scales are different (agree–disagree on a 1 to 7 scale vs. estimated demand on a 1- to 10,000-unit scale), you need some form of data standardization.

Q4: Are the variables correlated? Often several variables measure different aspects of the same thing: For example, if "quality of service" and "on-time arrival" mean the same thing to airline customers, perceptions and importance ratings for those items should be combined in some way to avoid double counting.

Q5: How should you handle outliers, that is, unusual respondents? Some outliers represent incorrect data, while others may represent unique situations that are better discarded. But some outliers represent new, emerging segments!

Selecting the sample

For any market research study, the analyst must define the population to be studied (the *universe*) and the means for gaining access to a representative sample of that universe (the *sampling frame*). The sample universe might be all U.S. firms, the sample frame might be the list of those firms that are furnished by Dun and Bradstreet, and the sample might be the actual firms selected for study from the Dun and Bradstreet list. For exploratory research or for small-sample studies, using a convenience sample or judgmental approach is appropriate.

For quantitative research, analysts usually use some form of probability sample, such as

- Simple, random sampling, where every member of the sample frame has an equal chance of being chosen to be a member of the sample
- Cluster sampling, where the unit of selection is a group (say, all households on a street) and each group has an equal chance of being selected as a member of the sample
- Stratified sampling, where the sampling frame is broken into strata that the user believes are different from one another but whose members are relatively homogeneous, and where simple random sampling within each strata is used to generate the sample

Where possible, we recommend some form of stratified sampling, with larger samples taken from more "important" strata (e.g., heavy users, likely brand switchers, larger organizations, or target demographic segments).

Selecting and aggregating respondents

Even in households, people make many purchases for the household as a whole (vacation spot, entertainment event, etc.), basing the purchase on the preferences of several parties.

Company	Job title	SIC code	# PCs	# employees	Office use	LAN	Color	Mem. needs	Speed needs	Storage needs	Wide connect	Periph.	Budget
#1	design eng.	361	6	8	3	4	5	6	6	6	1	3	$5,000
	purch. agent	361	6	8	3	4	4	4	4	5	1	2	$2,500
#2	design eng.	363	4	5	3	4	6	5	5	5	2	4	$5,500
	purch. agent	363	4	5	3	4	4	3	3	4	1	1	$3,000
#3	design eng.	871	75	82	2	5	5	6	6	5	2	3	$6,500
	purch. agent	871	75	82	2	4	4	5	5	3	1	2	$4,000
#4	design eng.	871	52	57	2	5	5	6	6	5	1	3	$4,500
	purch. agent	871	52	57	2	5	3	4	4	4	1	2	$2,500
#5		602	90	100	6	4	2	3	3	5	7	2	$2,500
#6		621	8	9	7	5	1	4	4	4	7	2	$3,200
#7		731	61	68	4	3	7	5	5	7	2	5	$5,500
#8		733	4	5	3	4	7	7	7	6	1	6	$3,250
#9		731	3	3	4	5	7	7	7	7	2	6	$5,700
#10		653	7	8	7	7	3	1	1	4	3	1	$2,500
#11		654	54	60	6	6	2	2	2	5	2	2	$2,000
#12		672	18	20	5	5	1	2	2	4	3	2	$2,750
#13		811	225	250	7	6	2	2	2	4	4	1	$2,200
#14		451	32	36	6	7	1	1	1	5	2	1	$2,400
#15		801	3	3	6	6	1	1	1	4	2	2	$1,999
Means		661.73	42.80	47.60	4.73	5.07	3.67	3.87	3.87	5.07	2.73	2.87	$3,700
std. dev.		163.33	58.41	64.74	1.83	1.16	2.41	2.26	2.26	1.03	1.91	1.68	$1,572

Demographic Variables

Needs

EXHIBIT 3.14

This abbreviated data matrix for industrial PC purchases shows demographic data, stated needs, respondent attitudes, and conjoint part worths (inferred needs).

In organizations, a number of individuals representing different points of view may be involved in purchase decisions, including a purchasing agent (frequently most interested in price, service, and on-time delivery), a user (interested in certain specific features), a gatekeeper (involved heavily in managing and maintaining supplier relationships), the financial analysts (interested in the impact on finances—perhaps willing to trade off higher initial costs for savings elsewhere). Exhibit 3.15 illustrates that the purchasing agents from the data set shown in Exhibit 3.14 have less need for features than the design engineers (who would be the users).

In choosing a sample you must consider two key issues:

- How many respondents per unit should you survey?
- If there is more than one respondent per unit, how should you aggregate their responses?

Common sense tells us that if everyone in a household or an organization agrees about their needs, then we need only a single respondent. However, Wilson, Lilien, and Wilson (1991) found that when a firm has little prior experience with the purchase and when the purchase is critically important to the firm, the responses of a single respondent can be misleading.

When the needs of those within the group differ, Wilson, Lilien, and Wilson (1991) show that it is important to study the two or three people who have the most influence in the decision and to aggregate their responses in such a way that the aggregated preference scores are higher for those alternatives that require the least compromise for the individuals involved in the decision process.

(EXHIBIT 3.14 cont.)

Leading edge	Cen-tralized	Slack	Price			Memory		Tasks			
			1000	1500	2000	32MB	128MB	4	8	12	16
4	4	6	0.6	0.4	0.2	0.1	0.9	0.2	0.3	0.4	0.6
3	5	4	0.9	0.8	0.6	0.2	0.9	0.4	0.5	0.5	0.6
7	6	5	0.3	0.3	0.3	0.1	0.8	0.3	0.5	0.8	0.9
5	5	6	0.8	0.7	0.5	0.3	0.7	0.2	0.4	0.7	0.8
6	6	5	0.6	0.6	0.4	0.2	0.8	0.3	0.4	0.7	0.8
4	7	6	0.8	0.7	0.5	0.3	0.6	0.4	0.5	0.5	0.7
6	5	5	0.4	0.3	0.2	0.3	0.7	0.1	0.6	0.8	0.9
4	5	5	0.9	0.7	0.5	0.3	0.7	0.4	0.7	0.8	0.7
6	6	6	0.5	0.3	0.3	0.4	0.6	0.4	0.5	0.6	0.7
6	6	7	0.6	0.6	0.4	0.3	0.7	0.1	0.5	0.6	0.7
7	7	6	0.7	0.5	0.4	0.1	0.8	0.3	0.5	0.6	0.8
7	7	2	0.4	0.8	0.6	0.2	0.9	0.2	0.7	0.8	0.9
6	6	2	0.5	0.4	0.1	0.1	0.9	0.1	0.5	0.7	0.9
3	3	3	0.8	0.5	0.5	0.3	0.7	0.5	0.4	0.4	0.4
2	2	7	0.8	0.7	0.5	0.5	0.5	0.4	0.6	0.7	0.8
1	3	3	0.9	0.7	0.4	0.4	0.7	0.5	0.5	0.5	0.5
3	1	4	0.7	0.6	0.5	0.3	0.8	0.6	0.5	0.4	0.3
2	2	5	0.8	0.4	0.3	0.4	0.7	0.4	0.5	0.5	0.4
1	2	2	0.7	0.4	0.4	0.5	0.6	0.2	0.4	0.5	0.5
4.47	4.40	4.53	0.62	0.50	0.37	0.38	0.74	0.31	0.49	0.60	0.67
2.26	2.06	1.77	0.17	0.16	0.13	0.14	0.12	0.16	0.10	0.15	0.21

Attitude Measures

Conjoint Part Worths

EXAMPLE

In a study of the market for industrial cooling equipment, Choffray and Lilien (1978) found that a number of types of people often participated in making the decision. They developed an instrument called a decision matrix to assess the likelihood of a person participating in the decision (Exhibit 3.16).

Three types of individuals who *were not firm employees* influenced the decision—HVAC (heating, ventilation, and air conditioning) consultants, architects and contractors, and air conditioning (A/C) manufacturers. (Note how this observation expands the definition of the sample universe and the sampling frame.)

After a macrosegmentation phase, in which they segmented the market by industry type and location, Choffray and Lilien (1978) further (micro)segmented the market according to the decision structure in the organization (as reflected in the decision matrix)—that is, they grouped firms together who reported similar decision matrices. Interestingly, another part of their research showed more differences in attitudes and preferences by job category than by firm. The responses of purchasing agents in one firm (A) were more like those of purchasing agents in another firm (B) than responses of design engineers in firm A.

They found four major microsegments (Exhibit 3.17). We will focus on segment 4 here, primarily consisting of top managers and HVAC consultants.

Top managers and HVAC consultants are almost exactly opposite in what they consider important (Exhibit 3.18). Top managers value modernity, energy savings, and low operating costs most highly, while HVAC consultants think these

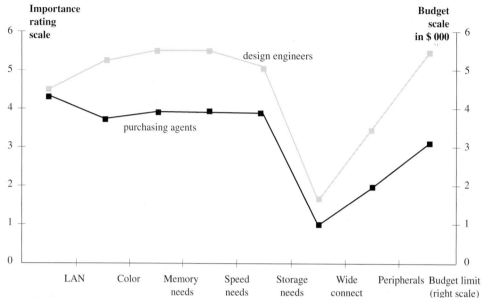

EXHIBIT 3.15
Needs assessment for PCs of engineers vs. purchasing agents from data in Exhibit 3.13, showing that design engineers are generally more concerned about product features than are purchasing agents, who try to adhere to a tighter budget.

	Decision Phases				
Decision Participants	**1** Evaluation of A/C needs, specifications of system requirements	**2** Preliminary A/C budget approval	**3** Search for alternatives, preparations of a bid list	**4** Equipment and manufacturer evaluation*	**5** Equipment and manufacturer selection
Company personnel					
• Production and maintenance engineers	5%	0%	10%	25%	10%
• Plant or factory managers	20%	20%	10%	15%	20%
• Financial controller or accountant	0%	30%	5%	10%	5%
• Procurement or purchasing department personnel	0%	0%	40%	10%	5%
• Top management	10%	50%	0%	0%	40%
External personnel					
• HVAC/engineering firm	20%	0%	20%	25%	10%
• Architects and building contractors	25%	0%	15%	15%	10%
• A/C equipment manufacturers	20%	0%	0%	0%	0%
Column total	100%	100%	100%	100%	100%

*Decision phase 4 generally involves evaluation of all alternative A/C systems that meet company needs, whereas decision phase 5 involves only the alternatives (generally 2–3) retained for final selection.

EXHIBIT 3.16
Decision matrix for the industrial air conditioning study, showing that the purchase process has several phases and that individuals both inside and outside the firm (such as heating, ventilation, and air conditioning—HVAC—engineers) influence the purchase decision.

	Segment 1	Segment 2	Segment 3	Segment 4
Microsegment size in potential market	12%	31%	32%	25%
Major decision participant categories in equipment selection decision (frequencies of involvement)	Plant Managers (1.00)	Production Engineers (.94)	Production Engineers (.97)	Top Managers (.85)
	HVAC Consultants (.38)	Plant Managers (.70)	HVAC Consultants (.60)	HVAC Consultants (.67)

EXHIBIT 3.17
Major microsegments of organizations in the industrial air conditioning study, showing those categories of decision makers who are most influential in equipment selection (1.00 = maximum influence).

	More Important	Less Important
Production Engineers	Operating cost Energy savings Reliability Complexity	First cost Field proven Substitutability of components
Plant Managers	Operating cost Use of unproductive areas Modernness Power failure protection	First cost Complexity Substitutability of components
Top Managers	Modernness Energy savings Operating cost Fuel rationing protection	Noise level in plant Reliability
HVAC Consultants	Previous system experience Ease of installation Modularity/accessibility Reliability	Modernness Energy savings Operating cost

EXHIBIT 3.18
Issues of importance for each category of decision participant, showing clear conflict between HVAC consultants and top managers.

issues are of little importance. These and other results of this study showed that to target a marketing strategy to this segment, a firm should focus on the value compromises participants in a purchase decision would need to make.

SEGMENTATION METHODS

After you have administered the measurement instrument to the people in your sample, you should be able to assemble the resulting data into a usable data matrix. You are now ready to do the segmentation analysis, which consists of data reduction, segment formation, and interpretation of results.

Wedel and Kamakura (2000) classify segmentation methods according to whether they are a priori methods (where the segments are determined by the researcher in advance) and post-hoc methods (where data analysis determines the number and type of segments). The clustering methods that we describe here (as well as the latent class approach we describe later) fall into the post-hoc category. The following section addresses a priori methods.

Using factor analysis to reduce the data

In many segmentation studies, researchers collect data on a wide battery of attitude- and needs-based items. If many of those items measure similar or interrelated constructs, then subsequent analyses may lead to misleading conclusions because some data are over-weighted and other data underweighted. Analysts also should drop irrelevant variables (i.e., those on which customers do not differ) from the study. Research has shown that including even a couple of irrelevant variables can damage the detection of the segment structure in the data (Milligan and Cooper 1987).

In factor analysis, we use several methods to reduce a large set of data to a smaller set. Specifically, we analyze the interrelationships among a large number of variables (attitudes, questionnaire responses) and then represent them in terms of common, underlying dimensions (factors). As these methods are central to constructing perceptual maps and conducting positioning studies, we will elaborate on them in more detail in Chapter 4 and in the appendix to that chapter.

Forming segments by cluster analysis: Measures of association

To form segments or clusters, you must

- Define a measure of similarity (or dissimilarity—distance) between all pairs of elements (individuals, families, Decision Making Units, etc.)
- Develop a method for assigning elements to clusters or groups

Exhibit 3.19 illustrates the issue: to form the (three) clusters there, we need to know the distances between all pairs of respondents or clusters of respondents. While this exhibit covers only two dimensions, it actually exists in multidimensional space: the number of dimensions equals the number of factors you retained in the previous, data-reduction step.

The most common method of grouping elements is the cluster analysis method. Cluster analysis is a set of techniques for discovering structure (groupings) within a complex body of data, such as the data matrix used in segmentation analysis. We can explain the concept by considering a deck of cards. Each card varies from the other cards along three dimensions (variables): suit, color, and number. If you are asked to partition a pack of cards into two distinct groups, you might sort them into red and black, or into numbered cards and picture cards. While you can partition a pack of cards intuitively, partitioning a large number of items into groups can be very complex, especially if those items vary along a number of different dimensions.

To understand the complexity, consider partitioning 25 items (or respondents in our case) into two groups, with at least one item in a group. There are $2^{24}-1$ (16,777,215) possible partitions. In partitioning 25 items into five groups, the number of possibilities is an astounding 2,436,684,974,110,751 (2.44×10^{15}). Clearly we need a systematic and feasible method of finding a good partition. We can use cluster analysis to address this problem. (It is also called *numerical taxonomy* by biologists, *unsupervised pattern recognition* by computer scientists, *regionalization* or *clumping* by geographers, *partitioning* by graph theorists, *seriation* by anthropologists, and *segmentation* by marketers.) To perform a cluster analysis, you must select variables and construct a measure of association between all pairs of items.

Choosing variables: Variables that have similar values for all your respondents do not provide a good basis for distinguishing between respondents. On the other hand, in-

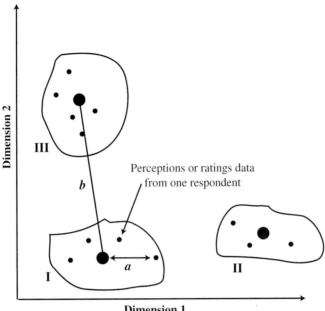

EXHIBIT 3.19
This exhibit illustrates how distance is measured in cluster analysis. Here there are three clusters (I, II, and III); distance *b* is the distance from the center of cluster I to the center of cluster III, and *a* is the distance from the center of cluster I to one of its member respondents.

cluding variables that strongly differentiate between respondents but that are not relevant for the purposes at hand will yield misleading results. We suggest including a number of variables, so that adding or deleting any one variable will not appreciably affect the results.

Defining measures of similarity between individuals: Most cluster analyses require you to define a measure of similarity for every pair of respondents. Similarity measures fall into two categories, depending on the type of data that are available. For scaled data you use distance-type measures. For nominal data (male/female, for example) you use matching-type measures. When the data type is mixed, other segmentation methods, for example, automatic interaction detection (AID)—described in the next subsection—may be most appropriate.

The following example illustrates the use of *matching coefficients*.

EXAMPLE

We ask respondents from four organizations that will purchase a copier to state which of its eight features (F) are essential, (F1=sorting, F2=color, etc.) with the following result:

	F1	*F2*	*F3*	*F4*	*F5*	*F6*	*F7*	*F8*
	Essential Features? (Yes or No)							
Organization A	Y	Y	N	N	Y	Y	Y	Y
Organization B	N	Y	N	N	N	Y	Y	Y
Organization C	Y	N	Y	Y	Y	N	N	N
Organization D	Y	N	N	N	Y	Y	Y	Y

We can define one similarity measure (among the organizations across these eight features)—a similarity coefficient—as

Similarity coefficient=number of matches/total possible matches (08).

The resulting associations are shown in Exhibit 3.20.

Researchers develop other types of matching coefficients in a similar fashion, often weighting differences between positive and negative matches differently. For example, suppose we counted only the number of positive (Yes-Yes) matches; in that case there would still be a possibility of eight matches, but organizations A and B would have only four of those possible eight matches (4/8) instead of the six (6/8) shown in Exhibit 3.20.

Organization

	A	B	C	D
D	1			
C	6/8	1		
B	2/8	0/8	1	
A	7/8	5/8	3/8	1

Organization

EXHIBIT 3.20
Similarity data for "essential features" data: firms A and B match on 6 of their essential features needs (Y-Y or N-N) out of 8 possible matches.

Distance-type measures fall into two categories: measures of similarity or measures of dissimilarity, where the most common measure of similarity is the correlation coefficient and the most common measure of dissimilarity is the (Euclidean) distance.

Two common distance measures are defined as follows:

- Euclidean distance $= \sqrt{\left(x_{1i} - x_{1j}\right)^2 + \cdots + \left(x_{ni} - x_{nj}\right)^2}$,   (3.1)

where i and j represent a pair of observations, x_{ki} = value of observation i on the kth variable, and 1 to n are the variables.

- Absolute distance (city-block metric) $= \left|x_{1i} - x_{1j}\right| + \cdots + \left|x_{ni} - x_{nj}\right|$,   (3.2)

where I I means absolute distance.

All distance measures are problematic if the scales are not comparable, as the following example shows.

EXAMPLE

Consider three individuals with the following characteristics:

	Income ($ thousands)	Age (years)
Individual A	34	27
Individual B	23	34
Individual C	55	38

Straightforward calculation of Euclidean distances across these two characteristics gives

$$d_{AB} = 13.0, \ d_{AC} = 23.7, \ \text{and} \ d_{BC} = 32.$$

However, if age is measured in months, rather than years, we get

$$d_{AB} = 84.7, \ d_{AC} = 133.6, \ \text{and} \ d_{BC} = 57.$$

In other words, when we use months individuals B and C are closest together; when we use years they are farthest apart!

To avoid this scaling problem, many users standardize their data (subtract mean and divide by the standard deviation) before doing the distance calculation. This allows them to weight all variables equally in computing the distance in Eq. (3.1). In some cases, however, it is important not to standardize the data; for example, if the segmentation is being done on needs data obtained by such procedures as conjoint analysis (Chapter 7), the values of all the variables are already being measured on a common metric.

A frequently used measure of association is the correlation coefficient, calculated as follows:

$$X_1, \cdots, X_n = \text{Data from organization } x,$$
$$Y_1, \cdots, Y_n = \text{Data from organization } y;$$

$$x_i = X_i - \overline{X}, \ y_i = Y_i - \overline{Y} \ (\text{difference from mean values } \overline{X} \text{ and } \overline{Y}); \qquad (3.3)$$

$$\text{then } r_{xy} = \frac{x_1 y_1 + \cdots + x_n y_n}{\sqrt{\left(x_1^2 + x_2^2 + \cdots + x_n^2\right)\left(y_1^2 + y_2^2 + \cdots + y_n^2\right)}}$$

Warning: The correlation coefficient incorporates normalization in its formula. However, it also removes the scale effect. So an individual who gives uniformly high ratings (7's on a 1 to 7 scale) on all items would be perfectly correlated (r=1) with two other individuals, one who also gave all high ratings and another who gave all low ratings (all 1's on a 1 to 7 scale)! For this reason, we feel that, while correlation coefficients are commonly used in segmentation studies, the results of such studies should be carefully scrutinized.

We recommend that if you have scaled data, you standardize that data first (subtract its mean and divide by its standard deviation) and use a Euclidean distance measure.

Clustering methods

After developing a matrix of associations between the individuals in every pair, you are ready to cluster. There are two basic classes of methods:

- Hierarchical methods, in which you build up or break down the data row by row
- Partitioning methods, in which you break the data into a prespecified number of groups and then reallocate or swap data to improve some measure of effectiveness

Our software includes one method of each type—Ward's (1963) (hierarchial) and *K*-means (partitioning).

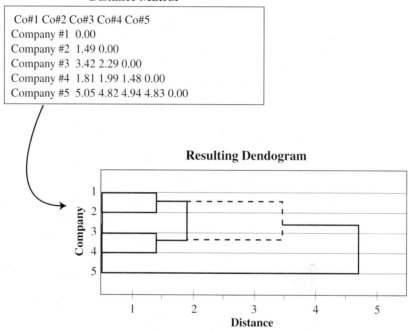

Distance Matrix

Co#1 Co#2 Co#3 Co#4 Co#5
Company #1 0.00
Company #2 1.49 0.00
Company #3 3.42 2.29 0.00
Company #4 1.81 1.99 1.48 0.00
Company #5 5.05 4.82 4.94 4.83 0.00

Resulting Dendogram

EXHIBIT 3.21
This distance matrix yields one dendogram for single linkage clustering (solid line) and another for complete linkage clustering (dotted line). The cluster or segments formed by companies 1 and 2 join with the segment formed by companies 3 and 4 at a much higher level in complete linkage (3.42) than in single linkage (1.81). In both cases company 5 appears to be different from the other companies—an outlier. A two-cluster solution will have A=5, B={1, 2, 3, 4}, while a three-cluster solution will have A=5, B=(1, 2), and C=(3, 4).

Hierarchical methods produce "trees," formally called dendograms. Hierarchical methods themselves fall into two categories: build-up (agglomerative) methods and split-down (divisive) methods.

Agglomerative methods generally follow this procedure:

1. At the beginning you consider each item to be its own cluster.
2. You join the two items that are closest on some chosen measure of distance.
3. You then join the next two closest objects (individual items or clusters), either joining two items to form a group or attaching an item to the existing cluster.
4. Return to step 3 until all items are clustered.

Agglomerative methods differ in how they join clusters to one another:

In *single linkage clustering* (also called the nearest neighbor method), you consider the distance between clusters to be the distance between the two closest items in those clusters.

In *complete linkage clustering* (also called the farthest neighbor method), you consider the distance between two clusters to be the distance between the pair of items in those clusters that are farthest apart; thus all items in the new cluster formed by joining these two clusters are no farther than some maximal distance apart (Exhibit 3.21).

In *average linkage clustering*, you consider the distance between two clusters A and B to be the average distance between all pairs of items in the clusters, where one of the items in the pair is from cluster A and the other is from cluster B.

In *Ward's method*, one of the two methods included in the software, you form clusters based on the change in the error sum of squares associated with joining any pair of clusters (see the following example).

EXAMPLE

This example is drawn from Dillon and Goldstein (1984). Suppose that we have five customers and we have measurements on only one characteristic, intention to purchase on a 1 to 15 scale:

Customer	Intention to purchase
A	2
B	5
C	9
D	10
E	15

Using Ward's (1963) procedure, you form clusters based on minimizing the loss of information associated with grouping individuals into clusters. You measure loss of information by summing the squared deviations of every observation from the mean of the cluster to which it is assigned. Using Ward's method you assign clusters in an order that minimizes the error sum of squares (ESS) from among all possible assignments, where ESS is defined as

$$ESS = \sum_{j=1}^{k} \left(\sum_{i=1}^{n_j} X_{ij}^2 - \frac{1}{n_j} \left(\sum_{i=1}^{n_j} X_{ij} \right)^2 \right), \tag{3.4}$$

where X_{ij} is the intent to purchase score for the ith individual in the jth cluster; k is the number of clusters at each stage; and n_j is the number of individuals in the jth cluster. Exhibit 3.22(a) shows the calculations, and Exhibit 3.22(b) is the related dendogram. The ESS is zero at the first stage. At stage 2, the procedure considers all possible clusters of two items; C and D are fused. At the next stage, you consider both adding each of the three remaining individuals to the CD cluster and forming each possible pair of the three remaining unclustered individuals; A and B are clustered. At the fourth stage, CDE form a cluster. At the final (fifth) stage, all individuals are ultimately clustered.

In using divisive methods, you successively divide a sample of respondents. One popular method is automatic interaction detection (AID). It can be used with both categorical and scaled data. It works as follows: you determine group means on the dependent variable—brand usage, for example—for each classification of the independent variables and examine all dichotomous groupings of each independent variable. Suppose that there are four categories of job classification: professional, clerical, blue-collar, and other. You examine the group means on the dependent variable for all *dichotomous* groupings: blue-collar versus the other three categories, blue-collar plus professional versus the other two categories, and so on.

First Stage:	$A = 2$	$B = 5$	$C = 9$	$D = 10$	$E = 15$
Second Stage:		$AB =$ 4.5	$BD = 12.5$		
		$AC = 24.5$	$BE = 50.0$		
		$AD = 32.0$	$CD = 0.5$		
		$AE = 84.5$	$CE = 18.0$		
		$BC =$ 8.0	$DE = 12.5$		
Third Stage:	$CDA = 38.0$	$CDB = 14$	$CDE = 20.66$	$AB = 5.0$	
	$AE = 85.0$	$BE = 50.5$			
Fourth Stage:		$ABCD = 41.0$	$ABE = 93.17$	$CDE = 25.18$	
Fifth Stage:			$ABCDE = 98.8$		

EXHIBIT 3.22(a)
Summary calculations for Ward's ESS (Error Sum of Square) method. *Source:* Dillon and Goldstein 1984, p. 174.

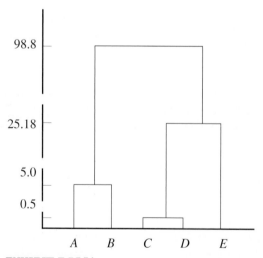

EXHIBIT 3.22(b)
Dendrogram for Ward's ESS method. *Source:* Dillon and Goldstein 1984, p. 174.

Then you split each independent variable into two nonoverlapping subgroups providing the largest reduction in unexplained variance. You choose the split to maximize the between sum of squares (BSS) for the ith group (the group to be split).

You then split the sample on the variable yielding the largest BSS, and the new groups formed become candidates for further splitting. The output can take the shape of a tree diagram, each branch splitting until terminated by one of three stopping rules: (1) a group becomes too small to be of further interest, (2) a group becomes so homogeneous that further division is unnecessary, or (3) no further possible division would significantly reduce BSS.

EXAMPLE

Assael and Roscoe (1976) reported on a market-segmentation study for AT&T to identify heavy and light long-distance callers. They studied a sample of 1,750 individuals, all from the southern region. Exhibit 3.23 shows the output of the AID analysis, and Exhibit 3.24 shows the tree and intermediate splits.

This analysis shows that one can segment the long-distance market based on demographic and telephone-equipment characteristics. Exhibit 3.22 shows that the segment with the most concentrated use, those with incomes over $15,000, represents 29 percent of long-distance billing but accounts for only 15.4 percent of the sample. In addition, the most- and the least-concentrated-use segments differ in expenditures three to one.

In terms of marketing strategy, this study suggests that income alone is one criterion for reaching the heavy-use segment. It also identifies a relatively heavy-use segment (Exhibit 3.24) among those who have low incomes but have high socioeconomic status and have one or more extension phones.

Partitioning methods, unlike hierarchical methods, do not require you to allocate an item to a cluster irrevocably—that is, you can reallocate it if you can improve some criterion by doing so. These methods do not develop a treelike structure; rather they start with cluster centers and assign those individuals closest to each cluster center to that cluster.

The most commonly used partitioning method is *K-means clustering*. The procedure works as follows:

Segment Profile	Average Long-Distance Bill	Percent of Sample	Percent of Total Long-Distance Billing Accounted for by Segment
1. Income $15,000 and over	$11.10	15.4	29.0
2. Income less than $15,000, one or more phones, higher socioeconomic status based on education and occupation	7.56	15.6	20.1
3. Same as 2 but medium to low socioeconomic status	5.16	18.6	16.2
4. Income under $15,000, one phone, and family has teenage children	7.38	5.1	6.4
5. Same as 4 but no teenage children	3.69	45.3	28.3

EXHIBIT 3.23
Final output of AID analysis of the long-distance-telephone market. *Source*: Assael and Roscoe 1976, p. 70.

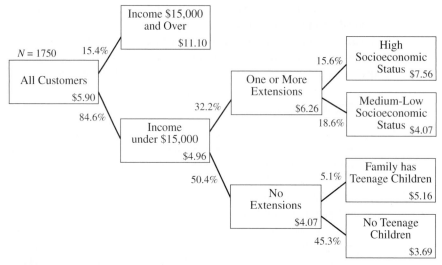

EXHIBIT 3.24
AID tree from segmentation of the long-distance market by average monthly long-distance expenditures in 1972, showing the optimal breakdowns for each customer variable.
Source: Assael and Roscoe 1976, p. 70.

1. You begin with two starting points and allocate every item to its nearest cluster center.
2. Reallocate items one at a time to reduce the sum of internal cluster variability until you have minimized the criterion (the sum of the within-cluster-sums of squares) for two clusters.
3. Repeat steps 1 and 2 for three, four, or more clusters.
4. After completing step 3, return to step 1 and repeat the procedure with different starting points until the process converges—you no longer see decreases in the within-cluster sum of squares.

While there are many ways to determine starting points, we recommend using the output of Ward's procedure to give good starting points (this is the procedure we use in our software).

The number of clusters (K) to use is usually based on managerial judgment, but certain indices can also help you to determine an appropriate number of clusters. In hierarchical clustering, you can use the distances at which clusters are combined as a criterion—for example, in the dendogram output from our software (Exhibit 3.21). In using partitioning methods, you can study the ratio of total within-group variance to between-group variance and use the number of clusters at which this ratio stabilizes. In either case you are looking for a big improvement in your criterion followed by a smaller improvement as an indication that there is little benefit in producing finer clusters.

Interpreting segmentation study results

After forming your segments by following one of the foregoing methods, you need to interpret the results and link them to managerial actions. You can base targeting and positioning decisions on the results of a segmentation analysis. Technically, you need to address such issues as how many clusters you should retain, how good your clusters are, the possibility that there are really no clusters, and how you should profile the clusters.

How many clusters should you retain? There is no unambiguous statistical answer to this question. You should determine the number of clusters by viewing the results of your cluster analysis in light of the managerial purpose of the analysis.

How good are your clusters? How well would the clusters obtained from this particular sample of individuals generalize to the sampling frame? No one statistical or numerical scheme helps you to judge the validity of clusters. You need knowledge of the context to make sense of the results. You should also ask: Do the means of basis variables in each cluster make intuitive sense (have face validity)? Can I think of an intuitively appealing name, for example, techno-savvy or mobile bloomers, for each of the resulting clusters?

Are there really no clusters? Do not overlook this possibility. If only a few basis variables show meaningful differences between individuals, it is possible that no really distinct segments exist in the market.

You can describe clusters informally by profiling them or more formally by using a method such as discriminant analysis. In *cluster profiling*, you prepare a picture of the clusters you found based on the variables of interest—both those variables you used for the clustering (the bases) and those variables withheld from the clustering but that you will use to identify and target the segments (the descriptors). Typically you report the average value of both the basis and the descriptor variables in each cluster in the profile.

Exhibit 3.25 is a snake chart, based on the data in Exhibit 3.15 where we only look at responses from design engineers. One segment concerned with buying PCs has a high relative need for power, color, storage, and peripherals and is not price sensitive (basis). We have labeled this the design segment. The other (business) segment is more interested in office use, local area networks (LAN's), and wide area connectivity and is quite price sensitive.

Profiling of the other (descriptor) variables in Exhibit 3.15 will show that the "design" segment is made up primarily of design engineers from smaller firms.

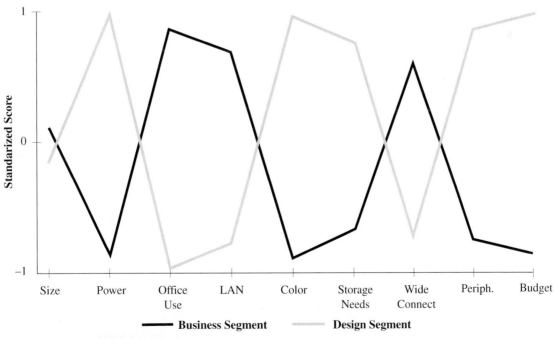

EXHIBIT 3.25
Segment profiles (snake chart) for two segments based on the data from Exhibit 3.15.

Using *discriminant analysis*, you look for linear combinations of variables that best separate the clusters or segments; in cluster profiling, you separate a group one item at a time. Specifically, in using discriminant analysis you look for linear combinations of *descriptors* that maximize between-group variance relative to within-group variance.

EXAMPLE

Exhibit 3.26 shows the results of a segmentation study on the need for wireless internet access, where one segment (X) is the high-need segment and other segment (O) is the low-need segment.

In the exhibit two segments or clusters determined from cluster analysis are plotted on two descriptor variable axes: number of employees and firm profitability. Segment X apparently comprises firms with fewer employees and higher profitability than segment O. Firm size appears to discriminate better than firm profitability. (While the output of discriminant analysis provides formal ways to see this, our picture shows that there is more of a split between X's and O's from east to west—number of employees—than from north to south—profitability).

Discriminant analysis ties us intimately to the targeting decision. As the discriminant function in Exhibit 3.26 moves toward the northwest, the likelihood of segment X membership increases. Indeed, if such descriptor variables as number of employees and firm profitability are readily available, you can assign a likelihood of segment membership to any organization in the target market, even if that organization was not in the original segmentation study sample, addressing the customer-identification challenge in Phase 5 of the STP approach to segmentation discussed earlier.

How can you determine how good the results of a discriminant analysis are? We suggest the following:

To determine the *predictive validity of discriminant analysis* (how well the discriminant functions, taken as a whole, predict the group membership of each individual included in the analysis) you do this: Form a *classification matrix* that shows the actual cluster to which an individual in the sample belongs and the group to which that individual is predicted to belong. (You determine predicted group membership by computing the distance between an individual and each group centroid along the discriminant function[s]. You assign each individual to the group with the closest centroid.) The *hit rate* gives the proportion of all the individuals that are correctly assigned. The higher the hit rate, the higher the validity of the discriminant functions in finding meaningful differences among the descriptor variables between the clusters. (In our software, we compute the hit rate on the same sample on which we develop the discriminant functions. This is a weaker method for predictive validation than using a *hold-out sample* for validation.)

The statistical significance of each discriminant function indicates whether that discriminant function provides a statistically significant separation between the individuals in different clusters. (Note: If there are n clusters and m descriptor variables, then the maximum number of discriminant functions is equal to the smaller of n-1 and m.)

The variance explained by each discriminant function is a measure of the operational significance of a discriminant function. Sometimes, especially if you have a large sample, a discriminant function that is statistically significant may actually explain only a small percentage of the variation among the individuals. Discriminant functions that explain less

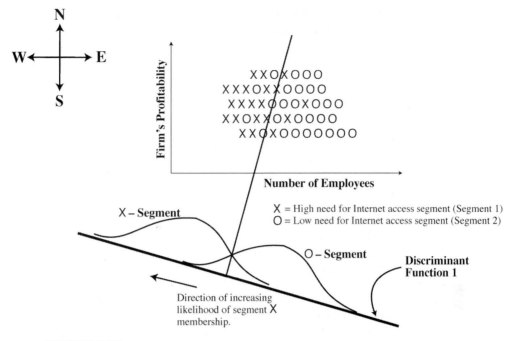

EXHIBIT 3.26
Two-group discriminant analysis example, showing that the number of employees discriminates well between the clusters while the firm's profitability does not.

than about 10 percent of the variance may not provide sufficient separation to warrant consideration.

The correlations between your variables and the discriminant functions are also called *structure correlations* and *discriminant loadings*. If a variable has high correlation with a statistically and operationally significant discriminant function, then that variable is an important descriptor variable that discriminates among the clusters. The square of the correlation coefficient is a measure of the relative contribution of a variable to a discriminant function. To facilitate interpretation in the output of our software, we report the correlations between variables and discriminant functions in the order of absolute size of correlation within each discriminant function, putting the most important variable first. If correlations are small for a variable, it means either that the variable does not offer much discrimination between clusters, or that it is correlated with other variables that overshadow its effects.

You can *use relevant descriptors to profile a cluster.* Discriminant analysis provides information that is useful in profiling clusters. You should first examine the mean values of descriptor variables that are highly correlated (say, absolute correlations greater than 0.6) with the most important discriminant function. If these means are sufficiently different and managerially meaningful, you can use these variables as the basis on which to develop marketing programs for the selected segments. You should then look at the mean values of the descriptor variables that are associated with the next most important discriminant function, and so on, repeating the procedure for each discriminant function.

BEHAVIOR-BASED SEGMENTATION: CROSS-CLASSIFICATION, REGRESSION, AND CHOICE MODELS

The approach we described in the previous section assumes that there is a set of variables (bases) that we want to use to develop market segments.

If the goal of the segmentation study is simply to identify individuals or groups with a high propensity to buy, researchers often use other methods: (1) cross-tabulation, (2) regression analysis, and (3) choice models. In each case, the goal is to relate some descriptor variables to a measure of propensity to buy (susceptibility to our marketing effort). According to Peppers and Rogers (1993), an industry's best customers outspend its average customers by a factor of 16:1 in the retail industry, 12:1 for airlines, and 5:1 in hotels.

Cross-classification analysis

Cross-classification, or contingency table analysis, classifies data into two or more categories or dimensions. In spite of the proliferation of more sophisticated techniques, cross-classification is still a widely used segmentation technique. However, cross-classification becomes unwieldy if you have more than two or three classification variables. In addition, if segmentation bases are continuous, the breakpoints you select for cross-classification may obscure some important relationships. Cross-tabulation is also not appropriate if significant interactions exist among the variables. (Note: Excel offers an add-in called Cross-tab Sheet Function that can be used to execute cross-classification analysis.)

EXAMPLE

A cross-classification of product usage against a preference scale, split at the 50 percent point, shows little predictive ability (Exhibit 3.27a). Splitting the same sample at both the 50 percent and the 90 percent points, however, reveals an important relationship (Exhibit 3.27b).

Regression analysis

Multiple-regression-based procedures overcome many of the problems found in cross-classification. In a typical multiple-regression study, the dependent variable is usually some

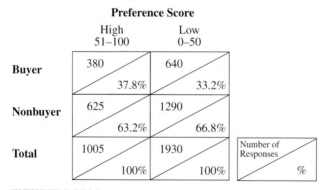

EXHIBIT 3.27(a)
With a 50-50 split on preference score in this cross-classification, high preference score shows a weak (37.8 vs. 33.2 percent) relationship to purchasing behavior.

Preference Score

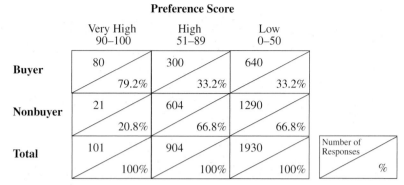

EXHIBIT 3.27(b)
Splitting the "High" category from (a) into "Very High" and "Medium" reveals a strong relationship between "Very High" preference and purchase.

measure of consumption, and the independent variables are socioeconomic and demographic variables postulated to vary with consumption. (Excel's add-in Analysis Tools include an easy-to-use regression package.)

EXAMPLE

McCann (1974) used regression analysis to determine differences in response rates (advertising, price, and promotion sensitivity) for different market segments. He studied the purchasing behavior for 29 brands of a frequently purchased consumer product by a panel of 7,500 consumers over a period of over four years.

He found that such descriptors as usage rate, household income, homemaker's age, area population, household size, and employment status were significant in explaining differences in market response. He used that information to develop "segmentation coefficients" (the products of the relative size, level of demand, and response rate of the segments) and used them to rank segments for attractiveness and to decide which to target.

Choice-based segmentation

An increasingly common approach to segmentation, especially in direct marketing (also called database marketing), is choice-based segmentation. In choice-based segmentation we perform the analysis at the level of the individual, relating that individual's likelihood of purchase (or response to a proposed marketing program) to variables that the firm has in its database, such as geodemographics, past purchase behavior for similar products, and attitudes or psychographics. Individual choice models—such as the logit model described in Chapter 2—relate these variables to likelihood of choice.

With a new product offering, a direct marketer chooses a sample from a large database and sends out the offer. It then observes who purchases (and how much) and uses that information to estimate the parameters of the response function:

Probability of purchase $= f$(geodemographics,

past purchase, psychographics, etc.) (3.5a)

or

$$\text{Probability of Purchase} \ = \ \frac{1}{1 \ + \ \exp\left(b_0 \ + \ \sum b_i x_i\right)}, \tag{3.5b}$$

where

b_i = importance of the ith basis variable, geodemographics, past purchase, etc.; and

x_i = value of the ith variable.

The firm then applies Eq. (3.5) to its database, plugging in values for the variables on the right-hand side of the equation to get *a predicted probability of purchase*. Equation (3.5b) is called a binary logit model and is closely related to Eq. (2.22).

The firm then uses that probability of purchase information to calculate an expected customer profitability. The firm directs the marketing campaign to those customer segments whose expected profitability in Eq. (3.6) exceeds the cost of reaching the segment:

Expected (gross) customer profitability = Probability of purchase

$\times$ Likely purchase volume if a purchase is made

$\times$ Profit margin (for this customer). (3.6)

EXAMPLE

Exhibit 3.28 shows part of a direct marketing database after the firm has completed the choice modeling step just discussed. Choice modeling provided the data in column *A*—purchase probability. The question, then, is which customers should the firm target?

Suppose that the total cost of reaching one of these customers is $3.50. What should the firm do? Firms commonly use several approaches to answer this question. First, if the firm looks at the average expected profit, it may decide to target all 10 groups and make a small profit $(10\times(\$3.72–\$3.50) = \$2.20)$.

Or it may target customers 1, 3, 5, and 6 and make

$$\$6.51 \ + \ \$3.62 \ + \ \$6.96 \ + \ \$6.20 \ - \ (4 \times \$3.50) = \$9.29.$$

Notice that by using choice-based modeling the firm can target customers to improve profitability by over 400 percent.

Finally, using a more traditional segmentation by average purchase volume, the firm would target, say 30 percent, or the three largest customers in this case—2, 4, and 9—and lose $5.02!

In practice firms may do analysis at the level of a group or an a priori segment and then determine which of those segments to target. However, it is increasingly common for firms to do the analysis at the individual level and then sort the customer database in decreasing order of expected customer profitability (Exhibit 3.28, column *D*). The firm then targets customers who exceed some threshold (a profitability measure) or fall into the most profitable percentage of the database.

Customer	A Purchase Probability	B Average Purchase Volume	C Margin	D Customer Profitability = A×B×C
1	30%	$ 31.00	0.70	$6.51
2	2%	$143.00	0.60	$1.72
3	10%	$ 54.00	0.67	$3.62
4	5%	$ 88.00	0.62	$2.73
5	60%	$ 20.00	0.58	$6.96
6	22%	$ 60.00	0.47	$6.20
7	11%	$ 77.00	0.38	$3.22
8	13%	$ 39.00	0.66	$3.35
9	1%	$184.00	0.56	$1.03
10	4%	$ 72.00	0.65	$1.87

Average Expected Profit = $3.72

EXHIBIT 3.28
Choice-based segmentation example for database marketing: target those customers whose (expected) profitability exceeds the cost of reaching them by comparing column D with the cost to reach that customer.

Choice-based segmentation can be used in a number of ways. We describe one creative and profitable use of choice models in the next example.

EXAMPLE

ABB Electric—achieving the fruits of segmentation: In its third year of existence, ABB Electric of Wisconsin faced a 50 percent drop in total industry sales. The company sold medium-sized power transformers, breakers, switchgear, relays, and the like, to electric utilities in the North American market. As a new firm in an industry dominated by General Electric, Westinghouse, and McGraw-Edison, ABB had to find a way to win customers from these major competitors or it would go out of business.

In 1974 ABB engaged a consultant, Dennis Gensch, to upgrade its information and to help it to gain insight into its customers. Gensch used customer research and consumer-choice models to better understand the preferences and the decision-making process of ABB's customers. He then helped ABB to use choice-based segmentation to segment its market and to design new products and a service program to better fit the needs of the customers it targeted.

At the heart of ABB's success was the insight it gained into its customers and how to segment the market to target its products and services. First, Gensch and ABB isolated the 8 to 10 attributes that customers used to select among alternative suppliers. They then used these characteristics to predict choice behavior and to form segments of customers who valued different combinations of these attributes differently.

Specifically, what Gensch did was to estimate the choice probability for every customer for every major brand in the market (using a logit model like Eq. [2.22]). He then tested for significant differences in those choice probabilities and used those differences to assign customers to one of four segments:

1. *ABB loyal:* Customers for whom the probability of choosing ABB was significantly higher than it was for choosing any other competitor
2. *Competitive:* Customers whose probability of choosing ABB was the highest, but *not* highest by a statistically significant amount relative to the next best alternative
3. *Switchable:* Customers who preferred a competitor to ABB, but for whom ABB was a close (not statistically significantly different) second
4. *Competitor loyal:* Customers who preferred a competitor to ABB by a statistically significant amount

ABB used this segmentation scheme to focus its marketing efforts. The result was a substantial gain over "business as usual" with no incremental marketing spending. (Gensch, Aversa, and Moore 1990). Exhibits 3.29(a) and (b) show the type of input data and some of the resulting output one gets from this type of choice modeling. Our ABB Electric segmentation case uses these data.

Customer Attitude and Choice Data (Basis)

Brand	Cust. ID	Purch. Vol.	District	Choice	Price	Energy Loss	Maint.	Warranty	Spare Parts	Ease Install	Prob. Solv.	Quality
A	1	$761	1	0	6	6	7	6	6	5	7	5
B				1	6	6	6	7	9	9	7	5
C				0	6	5	7	5	3	4	7	6
D				0	5	5	6	7	8	2	6	5
A	2	$627	1	0	3	4	5	4	4	5	6	4
B				0	3	4	5	4	7	3	5	5
C				0	4	5	5	5	5	7	6	4
D				1	4	5	6	5	4	5	5	6
A	3	$643	2	1	6	6	7	7	6	7	7	6
B				0	5	6	7	7	5	6	8	6
C				0	5	6	7	5	5	8	6	5
D				0	6	5	5	4	2	8	6	5
A	4	$562	3	0	6	6	5	5	4	5	5	5
B				0	5	5	6	5	4	6	7	5
C				0	4	4	5	4	6	7	5	3
D				1	4	4	6	7	7	8	7	5

EXHIBIT 3.29(a)
Choice-based segmentation data for ABB-type analysis. Read as follows: customer 1 has annual purchase volume of $761,000, is in district 1, bought brand B last, rates price level as 6, 6, 6, 5 (on a seven-point scale) for brands A, B, C, D, respectively, and so forth.

Customer	Annual Purchase Volume ($K)	District	Firm Chosen	Estimated Purchase Probabilities				
				A(BB)	Firm B	Firm C	Firm D	Type
1	$761	1	B	13.9%	83.8%	2.3%	0.0%	4 lost
2	$625	1	D	0.0%	0.0%	2.2%	97.8%	4 lost
3	$643	2	A	54.3%	45.7%	0.0%	0.0%	2 competitive
4	$562	3	D	39.4%	49.2%	0.0%	11.4%	1 switchable

EXHIBIT 3.29(b)
Output of choice model—giving both probability of purchase and "switchability" indicators for each customer.

CUSTOMER HETEROGENEITY IN CHOICE MODELS

Individual customers differ in their attitudes, tastes and in the rules that they use for making judgments and decisions. The choice models above assumed that all customers share the same purchase probability rule. While we rarely have sufficient data about each individual to build separate individual response or choice models, we may still want to account for the customer heterogeneity that exists in the population. Customer heterogeneity can be classified into two categories: (1) observed heterogeneity (e.g., customers differ on observable characteristics such as gender), and (2) unobserved hetergeneity (e.g., customers differ in terms of their price sensitivity). Observed heterogeneity can be modeled directly by including associated independent variables (e.g., gender) in the choice model. However, the same idea does not work for modeling unobserved heterogeneity (e.g., we cannot construct a variable for price sensitivity because we do not observe it). A common approach for accommodating unobserved heterogeneity is to use finite mixture modeling, in which each segment follows its own choice rule. In the framework of logit models, unconditional purchase probability is then assumed to be a mixture of several conditional purchase probabilities, where each conditional probability corresponds to a segment. Then, given the actual choices people make, we can infer the most likely values of these segment-level parameters (e.g., price sensitivities for different segments) from the data, i.e., we simultaneously form segments as well as estimate the unknown choice process within each segment through an approach called maximum likelihood estimation.

EXAMPLE

Assume we have a two-brand market, with brands A and B, whose major difference is in price and that each customer i's "attractiveness" for these can be assessed as

$$\text{Attractiveness of brand A for customer i is } \left[\frac{P_B}{P_A}\right]^{k_i}, \tag{3.7}$$

where P_A , P_B =   prices of the brands

k_i = price sensitivity parameter for customer i, where the higher the value of k, the more price sensitive the customer i.

Now, according to this model, the probability that customer i buys brand A can be assessed as

$$P_i(A|k_i) = \frac{(p_B/p_A)^{k_i}}{(p_B/p_A)^{k_i} + (p_A/p_B)^{k_i}} \tag{3.8}$$

$$P_i(B|k_i) = 1 - P_i(A|k_i)$$

and

Assume that customers are of one of two types, low price sensitivity *(k_l)* or high price sensitivity *(k_h)*, where we know neither the level of price sensitivity *(k)* nor the proportion of the population with that level of sensitivity *(b_l , b_h)*, i.e., the mixing distribution. What can we say about the (unconditional) probability of a customer buying brand A?

Using the formula for total probability we get

(3.9)

$$P(A) = P(A|k_l)\, b_l + P(A|k_h)\, b_h$$

where $P(A|k_l)$ and $P(A|k_h)$ are determined from Eq. 3.8.

The challenge here is to estimate the four parameters in Eq. (3.9): k_l, k_h (the levels of price sensitivity) and b_l, b_h (the proportions of the population with those levels of price sensitivity—the weights in the mixing distribution), given observed choices that customers make in different price situations.

In the example above, we assumed two segments (high and low price sensitivity) and that individual purchase probabilities varied only by price sensitivity. In general, response models will have a number of parameters (like price sensitivity here) and the number of segments will not be known in advance. A number of methods have been developed to (a) estimate the number of segments that best fit the data, (b) estimate the parameters of the response model and the proportions of the population that belong to each segment, and (c) assign individuals to the segment they most likely belong to whether or not their purchase behavior was used to estimate the parameters of the model (Wedel and Kamakura, 2000).

In the software associated with this book, we use the EM (Expectation Maximization) algorithm to simultaneously estimate the number and size of segments and the parameter values for each segment.

There are several indices to assess the goodness of fit of the estimates that function similarly to the R^2 index associated with regression models: (1) Hit ratio–the proportion of out-of-sample observations correctly classified by the estimated model; the higher this ratio, the higher the predictive validity of the model, with a maximum possible value of 1; and (2) AIC (Akaike Information Criterion), BIC (Bayesian Information Criterion), and CAIC (Consistent AIC), all of which indicate superior model performance the closer they are to 0. For details on these indices as well as about the EM algorithm, see Jagpal (1999) and Wedel and Kamakura (2000), both of whom also describe other methods (e.g., random coefficient logit or probit models) for representing and estimating heterogeneity.

IMPLEMENTING THE STP PROCESS

In practice, the best segmentation scheme means little until it is implemented. There are numerous challenges to implementation, including the firm's strategic situation, its corporate capabilities, as well as organizational issues (such as top management support), operational issues, information technology limitations, competitors' actions and financial consequences. Dowling, et al (2001) discuss these challenges in detail.

In many organizations, a key impediment to implementation is the structure of the marketing organization. It is hard to focus on the customer when one has the title of brand manager, marketing manager, advertising manager, pricing specialist, trade marketing manager, and the like. To focus on customers, companies need "customer segment managers," job titles that are rare but increasing in visibility these days.

We urge firms to run pilot tests to validate their segmentation strategy. This means testing whether or not the anticipated benefits from segmentation will be realized, as well as determining if the buyers hypothesized to respond favorably actually do so.

However, after launch, the effectiveness of the program must be carefully monitored. In particular, the response of aggressive competitors may dampen the effectiveness of the new program. The initial enthusiasm of the salesforce or distributors may also wane over time if not monitored and stimulated to maintain the level of focus required.

The reactions of competitors, the dynamics of changing customer tastes, and other factors require managers to continually review their segmentation scheme and determine its validity. Otherwise, what might have started as a vital segmentation that creatively guided marketing decisions can become out of date and lead to poor results. That is why segmentation must be viewed as an ongoing strategic decision process.

SUMMARY

In segmenting a market we divide it into distinct subsets of customers, where each subset (which could be as small as an individual customer) reacts to messages and product offerings differently—that is, has different needs. Marketing opportunities increase when a firm recognizes these differences and measures them. Market segmentation as a theory helps you to understand and explain these differences; as a strategy, our focus here, it helps you to exploit the differences. You can exploit the differences by using the STP approach.

Segmentation requires us to define a market, which we believe should be defined on the basis of shared customer needs, not on the basis of product similarities. To do a sound segmentation, you must specify the objectives for the study, define a sample, collect relevant data, analyze them, and interpret the results. People use a number of techniques to address segmentation problems, including cluster analysis, discriminant analysis, cross-classification analysis, AID, regression, and choice models.

Once a firm completes a segmentation analysis and targets one or more segments, it has to implement a segmentation scheme. Implementing segmentation consists of two related tasks:

1. You must allocate resources and develop a specific marketing program for each target segment: developing product features, price, distribution channels, and ad messages that are appropriate to that segment.
2. You must also identify current or potential customers and determine their segment membership. If you describe potential customers along the same descriptor variables that you used in developing the targeting scheme, then you can use the discriminant function(s) to predict the segment membership of any potential new customer.

By following these two steps, the firm can identify the target segment to which any current or potential customer belongs and direct the appropriate marketing program to that customer.

CONGLOMERATE INC.'S NEW PDA (2001)[1]

INTRODUCING THE CONNECTOR

Conglomerate Inc; a major US wireless carrier, has teamed up with a PC manufacturer to form a joint venture, Netlink, to develop, produce and market a hybrid product integrating a Personal Digital Assistant (PDA) with a "smart" cellular phone. Its first product is tentatively called ConneCtor. ConneCtor directly transmits and receives both data and voice. It is lightweight but heavier than a cell phone whose shape it emulates. It comes with a backlit grayscale LCD screen of moderate resolution. Its operating system is the PalmOS, which is common in PDAs. Thus, ConneCtor allows the user, among other things, to access the standard tools of Personal Information Management (PIM) and also performs standard cell phone functions.

ConneCtor can send and receive faxes and e-mail, access the Internet, and record voice messages. Users can input data to the PDA in the following ways:

- By typing on the on-screen keyboard
- By using the numerical keyboard
- By writing on the screen (using handwriting recognition software)
- By speaking into the phone, using a voice recorder.

---

1. This case was developed by Katrin Starke and Gary L Lilien. It describes a hypothetical situation.

An additional feature of ConneCtor is its ability to establish wireless links to other ConneCtors for voice and data transfer or to cell phones for voice transfer. For direct data transfer, the product includes an infrared port and also ships with a USB synchronization cradle. In summary, the key features of ConneCtor are:

- Instant communication for voice and data
- Cell phone, pager, fax and e-mail, and instant messaging
- PIM functions
- Digital voice recorder
- Enabled voice commands
- PalmOS application base.

THE HISTORY OF THE PDA

The Personal Digital Assistant (PDA) is basically a hand-held computer. In 1984 the first PDA, the Psion1, was introduced. It could store addresses and phone numbers, keep a calendar, and included a clock and calculator. In 1993, Apple introduced the Newton PDA, which was too bulky, too expensive, and had handwriting recognition too inaccurate to be successful. However, the excitement surrounding the Newton hinted that there could be a market for such devices. The broad acceptance of PDA technology then materialized in 1996, when Palm Inc. came out with the Palm Pilot that featured an elegant user interface and a reliable character-recognition system.

By 2001, PDAs had evolved to offer many applications including wireless Internet capabilities, games, and music playback. PDAs are designed for very specific tasks and environments: there are custom-built PDAs for amateur astronomers, truck drivers, and teachers. In addition, there is specialized software available to fit specific needs; for example, people in the medical fields can obtain software that lists thousands of drugs with their dosages and interactions.

PDA TYPES

The 2001 palm-sized PDA market was mainly composed of two types, each with its own philosophy: (1) the PDA/Palm devices run PalmOS, whose developers sought to make PDAs simple but functional products focusing on Personal Information Management (PIM) tasks; (2) the PDA/Pocket PCs run the more complex operating system, Microsoft Windows CE, which allows these PDAs to offer extensive features. In addition, "smart" phones are breaking into the PDA world. These wireless application protocol phones extend traditional cell phones with PDA functions such as email and Web access.

The original Palm Pilot embodied the PDA/Palm design mission. It provided a simple organizational device, composed of a calendar, an address book, and a to-do list with e-mail and Internet access. It also had a character-recognition system that worked for most people. Handspring, Palm's biggest competitor, introduced snap-on modules to expand the Handspring Visor and allow many applications, including an MP3 player, a web cam, and digital camera. These features appealed to the youth market and enabled Handspring to gain considerable market share. In 2001, Palm also offered this same degree of expandability and was able to maintain a market share of more than two-thirds; in addition, all of Palm's close competitors licensed its operating system, PalmOS. Several electronic manufacturers have developed similar devices; for example, Sony introduced Clie as a direct competitor to Palm and Handspring.

PocketPCs make up the other group of PDAs, whose manufacturers include Compaq, Hewlett-Packard, Psion, and Casio. These hand-held computers come with a large application suite of pocket Windows applications, e.g., a scaled-down version of MS Office. They usually come with more memory than PDA/Palms and with a range of accessories to be added to the devices (e.g., digital cameras, web cams). However, they are bulkier, heavier, and more expensive. In contrast, PDA/Palms perform basic tasks very well and, unlike the PocketPCs, synchronize with non-Windows systems.

A new technological thrust in 2001 involved the adoption of wireless technology for the PDA with manufacturers trying to assess if and how to add wireless capabilities. Wireless technology would make synchronization possible without docking, making PDAs true communication tools. AT&T, Nokia, and other cellular phone companies have started developing wireless phones with some PDA functions.

THE PDA CUSTOMER

As PDA designs have evolved, manufacturers have targeted different segments based on differing lifestyle and business needs. Palm initially captured innovators, people eager to adopt a new gadget. A typical early PDA user was a professional, high-income male. He was over 30 and probably worked in a technology field. Even as of September 2000, 93 percent of PDA users were male, according to IDC, a Massachusetts technology consulting firm.

Another major group of users is the mobile professional. Since this group frequently needs access to e-mail and the Internet while away from the office, it is also driving progress on the wireless front. A recent study by the University of California at Berkeley indicated that nearly half of the users had a technical job dealing with computers, and the overwhelming majority of the respondents rated themselves as technically sophisticated.

To attract more mainstream buyers in 2001, companies were working on increasing the usability of the PDA and its general appeal to nonbusiness users. For example, the new Claudia Schiffer Palm (sold via her Web site) is supposed to give Palm a sexier image, and Handspring's Visor line comes in many colors. Palm's affordable M series ($150) targets college students and other nonprofessional consumers. It is expected that such efforts will eventually open up the largely untapped young consumer and female market.

However in 2001, it appeared unlikely that the bulk of the mainstream population would enthusiastically embrace the PDA. A PDA was still relatively pricey and fairly limited. Handwriting recognition was slow and lacked quality, and keyboard facilities were either non-existent, too big to carry, or too small to use. The display screen was too small for most applications other than text display. Internet connections were generally both slow and expensive. In addition, the mainstream market appeared to have little need for many of the more sophisticated features the PDAs were able to offer.

PDA FEATURES

Given all the available design options, new product entries must make trade-offs between features. Customers want easy portability, but with more functions the PDA becomes heavier and bulkier. PDA users' needs are heterogeneous. Those who are looking for a high-tech way to store contact and appointment data may be satisfied with the basic models that cost $200 or less. They also are likely to prefer to keep a PC and cell phone separately rather than having an integrated PDA system that could do both. Users who plan to use the PDA as an extension of a PC by creating and accessing documents, sending e-mail, and doing basic Web surfing, might consider a Pocket-PC in the range of $350–$600. The appendix provides more details on PDA features.

FACTS ABOUT THE PDA MARKET

In 2001, many companies participated in the PDA market, bringing in a variety of new products designed to appeal to new audiences. The market was changing and growing rapidly. PDA unit sales totaled 1.3 million in 1999 and more than doubled, totaling 3.5 million in 2000 (Source: NPD INTELECT in Business 2.0). IDC, a research and analysis company, predicts worldwide sales of hand-held computing devices will reach 60 million by 2004.

In December 2000, the top five PDA brands in the United States (Source: NPD INTELECT) were:

Rank	Brand	Unit Share
1	Palm	72.1%
2	Handspring	13.9%
3	Casio	6.0%
4	Hewlett Packard	2.3%
5	Compaq	2.0%

The prices for PDAs have been relatively stable. According to NPD INTELECT, the average price of a PDA was $324 in 2000, down from $350 the year before.

THE HVC SURVEY

Netlink's management hired a market research firm, Happy Valley Consultants (HVC), to collect information about the needs of ConneCtor's potential customers. Netlink wants to use the data that HVC collected to identify segments within the market for PDAs, target appropriate segment(s) for ConneCtor, and position ConneCtor in the chosen segments.

For the targeting task, Netlink recognized that it had to develop criteria for segment selection. Using the items in Exhibit 3.6 as a starting point, Netlink identified two sets of key targeting criteria:

- Product-target market fit, in terms of Conglomerate's technical strengths, market needs and the ability of the current (or future) ConneCtors to meet those needs.
- Segment size and growth expectations, including both first purchases and upgrade/replacement buys.

THE QUESTIONNAIRE

HVC surveyed the market, looking at a range of occupation types. The survey included screening items that asked respondents if they had or would consider a PDA and if their job included time away from the office. Only those respondents who answered affirmatively to these questions were retained for further analysis.

The questionnaire asked the respondents to provide data on two kinds of variables: segmentation-basis or needs variables and variables that could be used in discriminating between or targeting the segments.

Questions for determining segmentation-basis or needs variables

X1   Whenever new technologies emerge in my field, I am among the first to adopt them.
            (1 = Strongly disagree ... 7 = Strongly agree)

X2   How often do you use a pager or an Instant Messaging service?
            (1 = Never ... 7 = Very often)

X3   How often do you use a cell phone?
            (1 = Never ... 7 = Very often)

X4   How often do you use personal information management tools; e.g., scheduler, contact-management tools, to-do list?
(1 = Never ... 7 = Very often)

While away from your office (including remote locations)...
X5   how often do others send you time-sensitive information?
(1 = Never ... 7 = Very often)
X6   how often do you have to send time-sensitive information?
(1 = Never ... 7 = Very often)
X7   how often do you need remote access to information?
(1 = Never ... 7 = Very often)
X8   how important is it for you to share information rapidly (e.g., synchronize information) with other people, e.g., colleagues?
(1 = Not at all important ... 7 = Very important)
X9   how important is it for you to view information on a large-sized, high-resolution display?
(1 = Not at all important ... 7 = Very important)
X10   how important is it for you to have constant access to e-mail?
(1 = Not at all important ... 7 = Very important)
X11   how important is it for you to have permanent Web access; e.g., real-time stock prices, news?
(1 = Not at all important ... 7 = Very important)
X12   how important is it for you to use multimedia features; e.g., playing of music, video, and games?
(1 = Not at all important ... 7 = Very important)
X13   How important is it for you to have a communication device that is not bulky?
(1 = Not at all important ... 7 = Very important)

How much would you be willing to pay for a palm-sized PDA with the following features: instant communication from PDA to PDA, cellular phone, instant messaging, instant file sharing, e-mail, Web access, fax, personal information management features (e.g., scheduler, calculator, address book)?
X14   a) Monthly (for all services that you use)?
(1 = Not at all important ... 7 = Very important)
X15   b) Invoice price for the PDA device with all the features?
(1 = Not at all important ... 7 = Very important)

Questions for determining variables for discriminant analysis
Z1   Age
Z2   Education (1 = High school, 2 = Some college, 3 = College graduate, 4 = Graduate degree)
Z3   Income

Type of industry or occupation: (0 = No, 1 = Yes)
Z4   Construction
Z5   Emergency (fire, police, ambulance, etc.)
Z6   Sales (insurance, pharmacy, etc.)
Z7   Maintenance and service
Z8   Professional (e.g., executive, lawyers, consultants)
Z9   Computer (e.g., computer programmer, software engineer)

Z10   Do you own a PDA? (0 = No, 1 = Yes)

Z11   Do you own a cell phone? (0 = No, 1 = Yes)

Z12   Do you own or have personal access to a desktop/notebook computer? (0 = No, 1 = Yes)

Z13   How often do you spend time away from the office? (1 = Rarely ... 7 = Almost every day)

Media consumption (Readership of magazines) (0 = No, 1 = Yes)

Z14   Business week

Z15   PC Magazine

Z16   Field & Stream

Z17   Modern Gourmet

EXERCISES

1. Run cluster analysis (without Discrimination) on the data to try to identify the number of distinct segments present in this market. Consider both the distances separating the segments and the characteristics of the resulting segments.

2. Identify and profile (name) the clusters that you select. Given the attributes of ConneCtor, which cluster would you target for your marketing campaign? (Consider using a form of the GE matrix approach for this task.)

3. Rerun the analysis in Exercise 1 with Discrimination. How would you go about targeting the segments you picked in question 2?

4. How has this analysis helped you to segment the market for ConneCtor?

5. What concerns do you have with the approach (data collection, analysis, etc.) so far?

6. What are the next steps you would recommend for Netlink and the development of ConneCtor?

APPENDIX: PDA FEATURES GUIDE[2]

Operating system

There are a number of different operating systems (OS's) used for PDAs. The two main OS are PalmOS and Windows CE from Microsoft. Both license their systems to other manufacturers. Another system, EPOC from Symbian, is especially prevalent in Europe. Some manufacturers, such as Apple (Newton), use proprietary operating systems. A PDA should be compatible with the user's desktop computer. When using a PDA in a corporate environment, it is important to have compatibility with other PDAs; that way, co-workers using the same OS can swap data more easily.

Windows CE is basically a mini version of Windows, similar in look and feel to Windows 95/98. PocketPCs typically run Windows CE that Microsoft released for small devices like PDAs and set-top TV controllers. PocketPCs can only directly synch with other MS operating systems; i.e., this poses a problem for Mac users.

Palm OS is most common with palm-sized PDAs none of which come with a built-in keyboard. Developed by 3Com/Palm Computing, this is the OS for all Palm models, certain IBM Workpad models, and the Handspring Visor. The Palm OS is simple, speedy, and easily customizable via third party software and shareware programs. Its Palm OS is compatible with Windows, Mac, OS/2, Unix and Linux given the right software.

EPOC is an OS developed by Symbian, a joint venture of Psion, Ericsson, Motorola, Nokia and Matsushita. This OS is used for mobile wireless devices like smart phones as well as PDAs. In many ways, this OS resembles Windows and is fully Windows compatible. However, EPOC tends to run faster and use less power than Windows CE. With the proper software, EPOC also supports Mac, Psion, Ericsson and some others.

Screen

Most PDAs are monochrome models, but color is becoming popular. Color is more expensive, it drains batteries faster, and a color screen might wash out in direct sunlight. It is also advisable to get a screen with a backlight, which makes it easier to read under a variety of lighting conditions including the dark.

The greater a screen's resolution is, the sharper the image will be. Resolution on PDAs is limited by the compactness of the screens. On Palm units, screens are roughly 4 inches across the diagonal with resolutions up to 240 x 320.

Memory

PDAs need memory to store the operating system, standard applications, additional software, data, etc. Although more memory is usually better, storage capacity between models with different operating systems should not be directly compared, e.g., a PalmOS running model with 4 MB of RAM will store more data than a 4 MB model running Windows CE. To allow more applications to run, the memory of many PDAs can be upgraded. Other PDAs support removable storage like CompactFlash. However, greater memory leads to shorter battery life.

2. Source *www.viewz.com*

Ergonomics

PDAs come in a wide range of sizes: from credit card to book size. Size, weight, and hands-on feel directly influence the PDA's portability.

Synchronization

Synchronization refers to the two-way process that exchanges and updates information between the PDA and the user's computer. The connection can be via cable or, significantly slower, via the Infrared port. Most devices come with a special stand or cradle that facilitates synchronization and often recharges the PDA's batteries.

With the right software and appropriate connection, a PDA can sync with a PC remotely; for example, PDAs can access and synchronize with data stored on a corporate network. Other programs allow syncing over the Internet by keeping the information on a web server. When using the same OS, users swap information by syncing their PDAs with another user's devices, e.g., using Infrared transfer.

Batteries

Most PDAs come with rechargeable batteries, and many also work with regular alkaline batteries. Among the rechargeable batteries, Lithium-ion–based ones are the most expensive, but they hold onto their charge longer when not in use. Battery life also depends on how extensively the PDA is used. Monitoring the life of the battery is useful to avoid losing all data in case of power failure.

Modem and online services

Mobile access to the office/home PC is possible with a PDA modem or cable adaptor. Most PDAs support at least optional modems. For complete mobility, a wireless modem and wireless network access are needed.

Web

Monitor size and quality constraints strain the Web-surfing experience. However, there are several special Web browsers for PDAs that reformat regular Web content so it can be viewed on a PDA. "Web clipping" services exist that answer requests by sending back stripped down "clips" of information from participating sites. Other applications, like ProxiWeb, use proxy servers to reformat Web content before it gets sent. Lastly, PDAs can be used to download web content for offline viewing—even if the PDA does not have a modem; every time the user synchronizes the PDA, the Web content is updated through the user's PC Internet connection.

E-mail, etc.

A PDA can be used to read, write, send, and receive e-mail either by synchronizing e-mail with a desktop or directly online by using a modem. The writing of e-mails, however, is cumbersome on most PDAs, especially if there is no keyboard. Applications also exist for Usenet, and instant messaging.

Handwriting recognition

PalmOS-based devices and PocketPCs come with a touch-screen and handwriting recognition software for writing text. PDA/Palm handwriting recognition programs require that the user learn a predefined set of pen strokes to form characters. Some handwriting programs let the user customize standard pen strokes to suit the user's writing style. For Windows CE, there is a full recognition application (no pen strokes to learn) available that allows writing anywhere on the screen, but recognition is slower and uses more memory.

Other software

A PDA comes bundled with a variety of software: e.g., synchronization software, PIM applications (calendar, addresses, to-do-list, etc.), and handwriting recognition software. In addition, there is plenty of third-party commercial software, shareware, and freeware available —at least for PalmOS, Windows CE, and EPOC, but not for PDAs with a proprietary OS.

Accessories

Sync cradles or cables are usually included in the price of the PDA. Internal modems are sometimes included in the upfront price, but add-on or wireless modems are extra. Other accessories include small keyboards for palm units, AC adapters, and styluses that double as pens and bar scanners. Protective screen overlays or carrying cases are also available to increase durability and style.

Audio

PDAs have differing audio capabilities. Virtually all have built-in speakers for alert noises. Others have internal microphones for recording notes or limited voice recognition uses. Depending on the device, there may be jacks for headphones or external microphones. Audio features will be especially important for users who want to use a PDA for multimedia purposes, e.g., watching video clips or listening to MP3s. In general, PocketPC units offer more audio features, although there are add-on audio accessories for Palm OS devices as well.

ABB ELECTRIC SEGMENTATION CASE[1]

HISTORY

In March 1970, ABB Electric was incorporated as a Wisconsin-chartered corporation with initial capital provided by ASEA-ABB Sweden and RTE Corporation. The new firm's management was to operate independently of the parent company. The company mission was to design and manufacture a line of medium-sized power transformers to market in North America. The firm produced such electrical equipment as transformers, breakers, switchgears, and relays used in distributing and transmitting electrical energy. Four main types of customers buy this electrical equipment: (1) investor-owner electrical utilities (IOUs), the largest segment; (2) rural electrification cooperatives (RECs); (3) municipalities; and (4) industrial firms. Most of ABB Electric's customers were electrical utilities.

SITUATION IN 1974

After three years of operation, ABB Electric was approaching the breakeven point when it encountered a serious problem. Its market share in 1974 was around 6 percent. In 1974, total industry sales of electrical equipment dropped 50 percent compared to 1973. Further ABB Electric was a small player in an industry dominated by large competitors such as General Electric, Westinghouse, and McGraw-Edison.

ABB Electric faced several other issues at this time. The salesforce relied on traditional methods of selling and was not well focused. The salespeople acted independently and did whatever they thought they needed to do to close sales quickly. At the same time, the board of directors was pushing for standardization of products and cost reduction. The board felt that to compete effectively against the larger companies and to improve its current position of marginal profitability, ABB Electric would need a cost advantage. The directors thought this particularly important because all the major competitors made good-quality products that were similar to ABB Electric's. ABB Electric would have to find some way to differentiate itself in the marketplace.

Virtually all of ABB Electric's sales were to one type of customer, the investor-owned electrical utilities. Because these utilities already had substantial inventories, sales to this group were projected to fall as much as 80 percent per year for the next two or three years. ABB's salesforce focused most of its effort on this market segment. As a result the company had little penetration among the over 3,000 RECs and over 100,000 small municipalities and industrial companies who tended to purchase occasionally or only once. Westinghouse, General Electric, and McGraw-Edison were well-established, long-time suppliers to RECs, municipalities, and industrial customers.

NEW STRATEGY AT ABB ELECTRIC

ABB Electric's research indicated that the market for electrical equipment would remain flat well into the 1980s. This would cause downward pressure on the prices of all products sold to customers in this market. Daniel Elwing, president and CEO of ABB Electric, concluded that the only way ABB Electric could grow in this environment would be to in-

---

1. Case developed by Katrin Starke and Arvind Rangaswamy. It describes a real situation using hypothetical data.

crease its market share. This meant that ABB Electric had to steal customers away from its competitors.

To support its new marketing strategy, ABB Electric decided to develop a marketing information system (MKIS) to support decision making. To seed the MKIS database, ABB Electric hired a marketing research firm to conduct a survey to provide information about customer needs. This firm thought that it was critical that ABB Electric understand the diverse problems and needs of its potential customers better than its competitors. It also felt that such information would be useful for segmenting the electrical equipment market and would contribute toward making ABB Electric a customer-driven company. ABB Electric hired Professor Dennis H. Gensch to develop segmentation models and to show its employees the value of using formal models to implement its segmentation strategies.

ESTABLISHING THE MKIS PROGRAM

ABB Electric hired a marketing research company to design a survey to determine the product attributes most important to current and potential customers. A pretest questionnaire asked electrical equipment purchasers to rate the importance of 21 product and service attributes (e.g., maintenance requirements, invoice price, and warranty) and then to rate the major suppliers in the industry on a poor to good scale on each attribute.

The firm used factor analysis techniques (see Chapter 3 of the text) to analyze the responses to determine nine important and fairly independent attributes that influence the purchase of electrical equipment. It mailed its final questionnaire to 7,000 key decision makers at utilities, RECs, municipalities, and industrial firms who purchase electrical equipment. Respondents evaluated each supplier known to them on the nine selected attributes. They also gave an overall rating to each supplier and indicated the supplier from whom they had purchased a particular type of equipment the last time they purchased it.

Sample Survey Question

Supplier Performance Rating
List the suppliers you are considering or would consider when purchasing your next substation:

_____   _____
_____   _____
_____   _____

For each supplier on your list, indicate your perception of this supplier on the following attributes:

Invoice Price	Poor	Good

Supplier A |————————————————————|
Supplier B |————————————————————|
Supplier C |————————————————————|
Supplier D |————————————————————|

The firm received completed questionnaires from 40 percent of the sample. In a follow-up phone check of nonrespondents, it detected no significant nonresponse bias. This data formed the nucleus of the MKIS database.

Data analyses indicated that the following attributes were the most important to customers when deciding to purchase electrical equipment (not in order of importance):

- Invoice price
- Energy losses
- Overall product quality
- Availability of spare parts
- Problem-solving skills of salespeople
- Maintenance requirements
- Ease of installation
- Warranty

Professor Gensch held the view that different segments of customers would weight these attributes very differently in selecting suppliers, partly because they differed in technical sophistication and partly because they were subject to different sales-force call patterns and different promotional efforts. After reviewing the data, the marketing staff decided on three ways to distinguish between companies: by type, size, and geographic location.

CHOICE MODELING

In addition to determining the important attributes as stated by customers, Professor Gensch suggested that ABB Electric determine the most important factors based on the supplier choices customers actually made. He thought that what customers say is important may not match what actually is important when they decide on suppliers. To get at this, he developed a choice model based on multinomial logit analysis. He then developed a segmentation scheme based on the probability that a customer would choose a particular supplier (the probabilities sum to 1 for each customer):

ABB Electric Loyal Segment (Loyal): Customers in this segment have a probability of purchasing from ABB Electric that is *significantly higher* than the probability that they would buy from the next closest competitor.

Competitive Segment (Competitive): Customers in this segment have a *slightly higher* probability of purchasing from ABB Electric than from the next most preferred supplier. Thus the probability of purchasing from ABB Electric is highest, but not significantly above the probabilities of purchasing from one or more competitors.

Switchable Segment (Switchable): Customers in this segment have a *slightly lower* probability of purchasing from ABB Electric than their most preferred supplier. Thus the probability of purchasing from a competitor is highest, but not significantly higher than the probability of purchasing from ABB Electric.

Competitor Loyal Segment (Lost): Customers in this segment have a *significantly lower* probability of purchasing from ABB Electric than from their most preferred supplier. Thus these customers are highly likely to buy only from a competitor and can be classified as lost customers.

ABB Electric used this segmentation scheme to focus its sales effort primarily at the Competitive and Switchable segments. It redesigned its entire marketing program with this in mind. The salesforce spent more time calling on prospects in these segments. ABB customized its brochures to focus on the "hot buttons" specific to each segment. Most important it continuously updated the MKIS database with new data and it institutionalized this approach to targeting across the organization.

POSTSCRIPT: SITUATION IN 1988

ABB Electric has strengthened its position well beyond expectations. Its market share reached 40 percent in 1988. Along with a larger market share came improvements to its profitability. The overall market remains flat and forecasters predict that it will remain flat into the near future. However, ABB Electric was able to establish a competitive edge against much larger competitors.

EXERCISES

Suppose you are the regional sales manager for ABB Electric, and you have been given a budget for a supplementary direct marketing campaign aimed at 20 percent of the companies in your region.

1. At present you have information about the location of customers (districts 1, 2, and 3) and the sales potential of each account or prospect. Based on this information alone, to what companies would you direct the new direct marketing program? Specify the accounts and customer or prospect types.
2. Use the choice modeling approach based on the responses provided by 88 firms from your region. The data consists of the evaluation of ABB Electric and the three main competitors on eight variables: (1) Price, (2) Energy losses, (3) Maintenance requirements, (4) Warranty, (5) Availability of spare parts, (6) Ease of installation, (7) Salesperson problem solving support, and (8) Perceived product quality. Perform a customer-loyalty–based segmentation for your customers and prospects.

   ■ Which variables are the key drivers of choice in this market?
   ■ Based on your analyses, on which firms would you focus your efforts?

3. Assume that marketing efforts targeted at companies in the Loyal and Lost categories result in no incremental gain. On the other hand, suppose that you could retain or win half the companies in the Switchable and Competitive segments with this program. How much improvement in sales productivity can you realize by applying this choice model to the allocation of your efforts?
4. What other recommendations would you offer to ABB Electric to improve its segmentation marketing program?
5. Comment on the uses and limitations of this modeling approach.

CHAPTER **4**

Positioning

In this chapter, we

- Highlight the importance of positioning strategy
- Describe how positioning analyses can be used in developing new products, in positioning existing products, and in analyzing market structures
- Discuss several techniques for positioning a firm and its products

DIFFERENTIATION AND POSITIONING

Definition

When you think of safe cars, the one that likely comes to mind is the Volvo. When you want a cold medicine at night, you probably think of Nyquil. If you are looking for healthy frozen food, you probably reach for Healthy Choice. These are products (more generally, offerings) that have a well-defined position in the minds of customers. They are differentiated from the other offerings in the market on one or more dimensions of importance to customers. "Positioning" in the minds of customers typically results from firms following deliberate strategies to design products with particular characteristics and to communicate with the targeted customers about those products. A common way to convey a product's positioning is through its advertising. One of the best-known positioning statements is Avis': "We're number two. We try harder." Reis and Trout (2001) document many other examples in which a firm's positioning strategies were instrumental to its long-term success.

Differentiation is the creation of tangible or intangible differences on one or two key dimensions between a focal product and its main competitors. *Positioning* refers to the set of strategies that firms develop and implement to ensure that these differences occupy a distinct and important position in the minds of customers. Thus Kentucky Fried Chicken differentiates its chicken meal by using its unique blend of spices, cooking vessels, and cooking processes. It conveys these differences to the market through its communications programs, which emphasize that its chicken is "finger-lickin' good." In short, differentiation is what you do to a product to make it different from competing products. Positioning is what you try to do to the minds of customers to help them perceive the product differences clearly. If a mouthwash provides a fresher breath, then this attribute could be positioned in the minds of customers by showing a kissing couple (who use the product). If a detergent has stronger cleaning power, that characteristic could be positioned in customers' minds by showing more bubbles. Reis and Trout (2001) state this succinctly: you don't find uncola in a 7-Up. You find it in the consumer's head.

Positioning Strategy

There are many dimensions that can be leveraged for positioning a product, or more generally, a brand or offering. These include *lifestyle or self-concept* (e.g., MTV is for the anti-establishment, hip, and under-30 audience), *product attribute* (e.g., amazon.com is the world's largest bookstore), *product benefit* (e.g., Discount Air Express: Overnight, not overpriced), *competition* (e.g., Listerine kills more germs than competing products; Meisterbrau tastes like Budweiser at a fraction of its price), and *time* (e.g., Nyquil is the night-time cold medicine).

Today's markets are crowded with offerings. In the U.S., there are over 25,000 products in a typical grocery store, and over 150 models of cars in auto dealerships. There are thousands of mutual funds and financial instruments for customers to choose from. Physicians can prescribe from over 100,000 drugs. Purchase managers can choose from millions of products and supplies with varying levels of service. What can a firm do to create memorable and unique representations of its offerings in the minds of its target customers to help it get beyond the clutter?

Today's markets are also fragmented. When a firm offers a single product to a single market and competes against a single competitor, finding a distinctive product position and communicating it consistently is perhaps not that difficult. However, if a firm serves ten market segments with four offerings (e.g., local telephone service, long-distance service, wireless voice, and wireless messaging) against ten competitors, it may require as many as four hundred distinct communication messages. The complexity created by the growth of the Internet adds to this challenge. Many online customers now use search engines to locate products and sites of relevance to them. There is an ongoing struggle for keyword positioning so that the firm's products and brands are listed higher in the search engine results. For example, a Google search (*www.google.com*) in June 2001 on the keywords safe car, car+safe, and car+safety did not bring up Volvo in the first 10 listings. Thus, a key question for firms is, what overall brand position should it convey in fragmented markets, while still tailoring communications to individual segments?

To position products in crowded and fragmented markets, firms need systematic approaches to design and develop their offerings in such a way that members of their target segments both perceive the offerings to be distinct and value them more than they do the competitive offerings. As a first step, managers must understand the dimensions along which target customers perceive the offerings in a category and how those customers view the firm's offer relative to the competitive offers. In other words, the managers have to understand the competitive structure of their markets as perceived by their customers: How do our customers (current or potential) view our brand? Which brands do those customers perceive to be our closest competitors? What product and company attributes seem to be most responsible for these perceived differences?

Once managers have answers to these questions, they can assess how well or how poorly their offerings are positioned in the market. They can then identify the critical elements of a marketing plan that differentiate their offerings from those of competitive offerings: What should we do to get our target customer segments to perceive our offering as different?

Based on customer perceptions, which target segments are most attractive? How should we position our new product with respect to our existing products? What product name is most closely associated with attributes our target segment perceives to be desirable?

If a firm develops a clear positioning strategy, it should be able to complete the following sentence in a succinct manner: For [*target segment*], the [*offering*] is [*positioning claim*] because [*single most important support*]. For example, Iomega, the maker of Zip disks and drives could complete the sentence as follows: For *PC Users*, the *IOMEGA Zip drive* is *the best available portable storage device* because it *is the most cost-effective system*. J. C. Penney's positioning statement is less precise: For *"Modern Spenders" and "Starting Outs," in mid-income levels who shop for apparel, accessories, and home furnishings* we offer *private-label, supplier exclusive, and national brands* that *deliver greater value than that of our competition* because of *our unique combination of quality, selection, fashion, service, price, and shopping experience. (www.jcpenney.com, June 2001)*

POSITIONING USING PERCEPTUAL MAPS

There are many intuitive approaches that managers use to develop an understanding of the competitive structure of their markets. The perceptual mapping methods described in this chapter provide formal mechanisms to depict the competitive structure of markets in a manner that facilitates differentiation and positioning decisions. Before considering such mapping models, let us look at an example of a perceptual map and see how it facilitates managerial decisions.

A *perceptual map* is a graphical representation in which competing alternatives are plotted in a Euclidean space (Exhibit 4.1). The map has the following characteristics: (1) The pairwise distances between product alternatives directly indicate the "perceived similarities" between any pair of products, that is, how close or far apart the products are in the minds of customers. (2) A vector (i.e., line) on the map (shown by a line segment with an arrow) indicates both magnitude and direction in the Euclidean space. Vectors are usually used to geometrically denote attributes of the perceptual maps. (3) The axes of the map are a special set of vectors suggesting the underlying dimensions that best characterize how customers differentiate between alternatives. Most frequently, orthogonal axes (straight lines at right angles) are used to represent the dimensions of the map, although nonorthogonal axes can also be used. In either case the axes can be rigidly rotated to aid interpretation. For example, in a two-dimensional map the horizontal and vertical axes are often used to characterize the two dimensions of the map. However, the axes can be rotated so that the southwest to northeast becomes one axis, and southeast to northwest becomes the other axis.

EXAMPLE

To understand the above points, consider the perceptual map in Exhibit 4.1, which summarizes how a group of customers views the beer market and contains a number of useful insights about the nature and structure of this market (Moore and Pessemier 1993).

First, the map shows the intensity of competition between the brands—the closer two brands are together in the map, the more similar they are perceived to be by customers, and therefore, are more direct competitors. Beck's and Heinekin are close competitors, whereas Old Milwaukee and Coors Light are far apart from each other and are not direct competitors. We can also see, for example, that the distance (dissimilarity) between Budweiser and Miller is about the same as the distance between Coors and Michelob, suggesting that the intensity of competition between these pairs of brands is roughly of the same order.

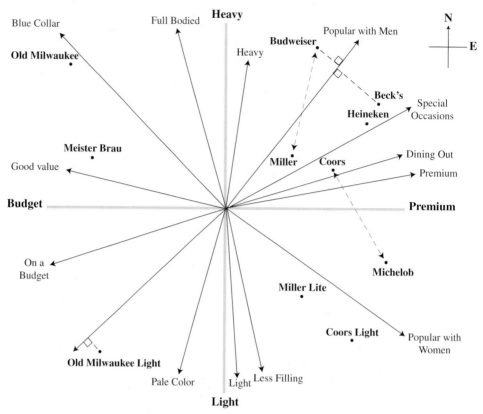

EXHIBIT 4.1

A perceptual map of the beer market, showing (among other things) that Budweiser is the most popular beer with men while Old Milwaukee Light is the least popular with men. The map summarizes customer evaluations of beer on 13 attributes into two dimensions: (1) budget–premium and (2) light–heavy. *Source*: Moore and Pessemier 1993, p. 145.

Second, the map summarizes how customers perceive each brand on each attribute. For example, Budweiser is the most popular beer with men (Beck's is nearly as popular with men). To see this, move your eye in a northeast direction along the line "Popular with Men." The farther away from origin a beer is located along this direction, the more popular it is with men. This also means that, as you move in the opposite direction (i.e., southwest) away from the origin, the beers become less popular with men. Thus, Old Milwaukee Light is least popular with men. Customer perceptions of these beers along each of the 13 attributes can be interpreted in the same manner.

Third, the map shows the relationships between the attributes. The smaller the angle between any two vectors, the more correlated they are with each other. For example, beers that are "popular with men" are also likely to be "heavy." Of particular interest is the relationship between the vertical and horizontal axes and the attributes. The horizontal axis (in the east direction) is more closely aligned with the attributes "premium," "dining out," and "special occasions" (i.e., they are pointing in nearly the same direction as the horizontal axis). Likewise, in the westerly direction, the horizontal axis is most closely aligned with the attributes "on a budget" and "good value." Thus, the horizontal axis (the west-east dimension) indicates an underlying dimension of "budget-premium," along which customers seem to characterize their perceptions of the differences between these beers. Note that the axes can be rotated (rigidly) to improve interpretation.

Fourth, the length of each attribute line indicates how well that attribute differentiates between the beers. The longer the line the stronger is the differentiation. Thus, customers are better able to differentiate between the brands on the attribute, "popular with men" than on the attribute, "good value."

Thus, the map captures many of the significant factors defining the competitive structure of the beer market as perceived by the customers in this market. We can draw several other conclusions from this map:

- Michelob is located between the "heavy" beers and the "light" beers, thus being a weak competitor in both markets.
- Old Milwaukee Light has very little direct competition (i.e., there is a gap in the market with no other brand located close to it), indicating potential opportunity for a new beer positioned in this quadrant. To be in this quadrant, a beer needs to be pale in color, be viewed as appropriate for someone on a budget, not be a beer for special occasions, not be perceived as a premium beer, etc. Of course, before positioning a brand in this quadrant, we need to first assess whether there would be a sufficient number of customers who would prefer/buy such a beer.
- Whether or not a beer is popular with women does not indicate anything about whether it will be popular with men (these two attributes are perpendicular to each other). Thus, although Beck's and Budweiser are equally popular with men, among women, Beck's is more popular than Budweiser.

In spite of its potential value in offering these insights, the map in Exhibit 4.1 does not say much about the brand locations that are most attractive to customers, except in broad terms such as "popular with men." For example, the map does not indicate whether more customers prefer heavy premium beers or light budget beers. Without such insights, firms risk investing in differentiating products along dimensions that are not aligned with increased customer preference. An example of such ineffective differentiation is the Westin Stamford Hotel in Singapore, which advertises that it is the world's tallest hotel, an attribute that is not important to any customer segment (Kotler 1991). To identify meaningful dimensions for differentiation, a perceptual map should incorporate the preferences of customers. Later in this chapter we describe "joint-space" techniques to incorporate both perceptions and preferences within the same map.

Perceptual maps facilitate decision making by enabling managers to *summarize* and *visualize* key elements of the market structure for their products. By summarizing a large amount of information, such maps help managers to think strategically about product positioning. For example, the underlying dimensions of *budget–premium* and *light–heavy* capture the combined essence of several attributes on which beers differ. By thinking about competitors in the beer market along these underlying dimensions, instead of along individual product attributes, managers gain a strategic focus to use in product positioning decisions. The use of underlying dimensions to summarize information parallels the process that people use to simplify cognitive tasks. The brain organizes information into categories and relationships, rather than keeping information in random lists. We use such terms as *brilliant* or *arrogant* as summary descriptors of people, basing these descriptions on many different things they do, and we place political candidates on a liberal–conservative dimension to characterize their combined stands on a number of issues such as abortion, economic policies, aid to foreign countries, and military affairs. We *observe* other people's actions, but we *infer* the underlying characteristics of brilliance, arrogance, or liberalism. Likewise, we measure how people perceive products in the market, but we infer the underlying dimensions that determine these perceptions.

EXAMPLE

This example is adapted from Grapentine (1995). Two automobile manufacturers want to identify the physical features of a car that customers find attractive. Both manufacturers have a sample of target customers evaluate their vehicles on a series of attributes that describe the perceived attractiveness of these cars' physical features.

Manufacturer A conducts its study without developing a perceptual map showing how the various physical features of a vehicle are interrelated to influence perceived attractiveness. That is, it examines only the direct impact of each attribute on physical attractiveness. It finds that (1) its vehicle receives a relatively low rating on the grill design attribute, and (2) this attribute is highly correlated with the vehicle's overall attractiveness rating. Manufacturer A tells its engineers to redesign the grill to make the car more attractive.

Manufacturer B develops a perceptual map that helps it to determine the underlying dimensions that summarize the attributes used in the study, and it develops a framework to articulate how these dimensions influence perceived vehicle attractiveness. Manufacturer B finds that ratings of the grill are highly correlated with ratings of other attributes, such as those for the design of the outdoor mirrors, the slope of the hood, the design of the windshield, and the impact rating of front bumpers. Guided by this analysis manufacturer B recognizes that the attributes, as a group, reflect consumers' perceptions of the vehicle's aerodynamics. Instead of telling its engineers to change the design of the grill, it instructs them to change the car's aerodynamic styling.

In addition to summarization, maps offer managers a pictorial view of the competitive structure of their markets, helping them to sharpen their thinking about how their market works. People are better at processing visual than numerical information. Although managers may be able to describe verbally how their customers perceive the structure of a market, a data-derived map provides finer details. The details in a perceptual map are especially helpful to those making decisions in new contexts, such as when the firm is developing a positioning strategy for a new product. Other options, such as bar charts and snake plots (Exhibit 4.2), are also available to pictorially summarize customer perceptions. However, plots of this type are difficult to interpret if they include more than three or four alternatives. In addition, snake plots suggest that managers pay equal attention to all attributes, thereby implicitly assigning the same weight to each attribute.

APPLICATIONS OF PERCEPTUAL MAPS

The value of a perceptual map stems from the notion that perception is reality; that is, customer perceptions, in part, determine customer behavior. A primary use of perceptual mapping is to provide insights into the market structure for a defined set of competing alternatives. Because any location on a map results from the combined effects of a number of beliefs and perceptions, the map suggests which attributes of a product the firm should modify to effect a desired change in the position of the product. For example, the map in Exhibit 4.1 could help identify what attributes management must change to position

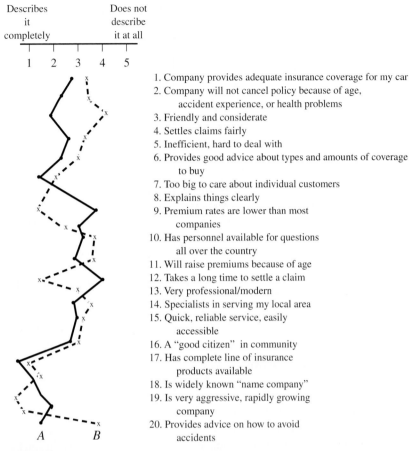

Describes
it
completely

Does not
describe
it at all

1   2   3   4   5

1. Company provides adequate insurance coverage for my car
2. Company will not cancel policy because of age,
   accident experience, or health problems
3. Friendly and considerate
4. Settles claims fairly
5. Inefficient, hard to deal with
6. Provides good advice about types and amounts of coverage
   to buy
7. Too big to care about individual customers
8. Explains things clearly
9. Premium rates are lower than most
   companies
10. Has personnel available for questions
    all over the country
11. Will raise premiums because of age
12. Takes a long time to settle a claim
13. Very professional/modern
14. Specialists in serving my local area
15. Quick, reliable service, easily
    accessible
16. A "good citizen" in community
17. Has complete line of insurance
    products available
18. Is widely known "name company"
19. Is very aggressive, rapidly growing
    company
20. Provides advice on how to avoid
    accidents

A   *B*

EXHIBIT 4.2
In this example of positioning by profile chart analysis, insurance company A is compared with its leading competitor B using customer evaluation on 20 attributes. *Source:* Wind 1982, p. 82.

Michelob clearly either as a light premium beer or as a heavy premium beer, instead of occupying an intermediate position. By making assumptions about how changes in the physical characteristics of a product influence customer perceptions, managers can tentatively predict the sales or market shares that would be associated with alternative positions on a map. Green (1975) urges caution here, pointing out that the primary use of perceptual maps should be providing diagnostic insights, rather than making specific predictions about sales.

In addition to their use in general positioning decisions, perceptual maps are particularly useful in several specific areas of marketing. We list four such areas:

1. *New product decisions*: Perceptual mapping is used to support new product decisions (Dolan 1993). It is useful in the opportunity-identification stage of new product development to locate gaps in the market, as a way to provide focus for new product development efforts. It is also useful in the concept-testing stage to evaluate the potential for the new concept in the context of other existing products and to identify segments who would find the product most appealing. GM used such a map (Exhibit 4.3) to evaluate the Buick Reatta, both as a concept and after a test drive (Urban and Star 1991, p. 280). This map helped reassure GM management that the Reatta had a distinct new upscale image compared with the other models of Buick. A gap in the market does not necessarily indicate that there is a market in the gap, which was the

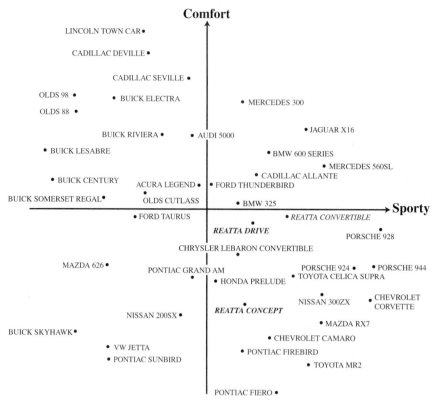

EXHIBIT 4.3

A perceptual map showing that the Reatta is perceived differently from other Buick cars, and after driving it (Reatta Drive), the Reatta is perceived better in comfort than before driving (Reatta Concept). *Source*: Urban and Star 1991, p. 280.

case with Buick Reatta. General Motors sold only a few thousand cars before it started discounting the price of the car to reduce the inventory. Later in this chapter, we describe joint-space maps that incorporate both perceptions and preferences of customers. Such maps can be used to detect not only the gaps in the markets, but also whether there are viable market segments in the gap.

We can also use perceptual maps to evaluate candidate names for a new product on a defined set of criteria. For example, when this book was at the concept stage, we evaluated potential titles using the following adjectives: boring, complicated, leading-edge, pretentious, relevant, and unique. Several faculty members in business schools in the United States responded to a structured questionnaire after going through a packet of information that contained the book outline and a demonstration version of the software. Another way to obtain data for naming a product is to ask potential customers to state all the things that come to mind when they hear a particular title. Then you can use the number of mentions of each attribute as data for developing a perceptual map.

2. *As a check on managers' views of competitive structure and positioning*: Marketing managers have their own perceptions of how their customers and noncustomers perceive the different brands. These perceptions may or may not be consistent with how various customer segments actually view the different brands. Perceptual maps can provide managers with important insights on whether, how, and why their perceptions coincide with customer perceptions. For example, a manager noting the contributions of a perceptual mapping study said:

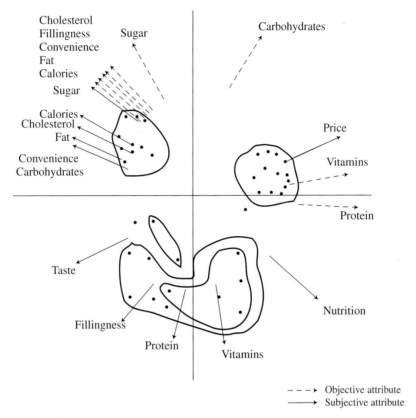

EXHIBIT 4.4
Two-dimensional perceptual configuration of 40 food products and their "perceived" and objective attributes, showing that characteristics like taste, fillingness, and perceived nutrition are not closely related to objective measures. Each dot represents a product. *Source:* Wind 1982, p. 90.

> Some of the facts we learned from this study shocked us. We had focused on physical product benefits as a basis for competitive advantage. Instead we found a market more interested in service issues. (Siemer 1989)

Wind (1982, p. 90) compared customer perceptions of food products to the "objective" perceptions of food technicians (Exhibit 4.4). That study included 40 different products and new-product concepts evaluated along 12 attributes. The study showed little relationship between objective characteristics and subjective perceptions concerning attributes such as fillingness, carbohydrates, proteins, and vitamins. On the other hand, there was a stronger relationship between subjective perceptions and such objective attributes as caloric content, sugar, fat, cholesterol, and convenience of preparation. These insights helped the firm to position the new products in a way that would not lead customers to overestimate undesirable attributes such as fattening. In many product categories, objective data are available through such sources as *Consumer Reports* and *PC Magazine*. In some cases these sources also publish maps of these objective data; Exhibit 4.5, for example, summarizes the price-performance characteristics of several brands of modems.

3. *Identifying who to compete against*: Many marketers try to differentiate their products from those of their competitors. However, in some highly competitive markets,

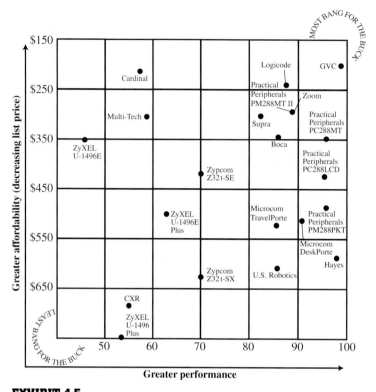

EXHIBIT 4.5
A map positioning high-speed modems in a "price-performance" space. *Source: PC Magazine,* September 13, 1994, p. 282.

there are few gaps or opportunities to find distinct positions. In such cases it may be useful to select specific competitors to target, based on an understanding of their weakest points. Perceptual maps can highlight what attributes are associated with close substitutes and what points of difference among the substitutes are least relevant in influencing customer preferences (Wyner and Owen 1994). Thus perceptual maps can provide insights about differences between competitive products that customers do not notice (i.e., the company or its competitor has not successfully communicated these differences to customers) and insights about differences that customers notice but do not care about (i.e., products are differentiated, but the differences do not significantly influence customer preferences, such as Jolt Cola, which has twice the caffeine of other colas).

4. *Image or reputation studies*: Image is a multidimensional concept that serves as a summary of what a firm stands for, as perceived by its various stakeholders. The objective of image or reputation studies is both to understand how stakeholders perceive a firm and to design an image that is consistent with the firm's strategic objectives. Perceptual maps offer a good way to summarize the key results of such studies.

Exhibit 4.6 shows a perceptual map comparing various retailers (e.g., regional chains, discount chains, and independent hardware stores) who compete for the do-it-yourself segment of the home improvement market in Chicago (Johnson 1994). This study was undertaken by independent retailers who were losing market share all across the United States to discount chains such as Wal-Mart and mega home centers such as Lowe's and Home Depot. The perceptual map is based on customer

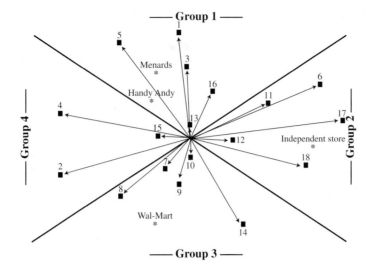

Attributes included in this study

1. Has hard-to-find items
2. Has good prices
3. Stocks preferred brands
4. Offers many price levels
5. Stocks unique products
6. Offers assistance and information
7. Place doesn't feel intimidating
8. Has convenient hours
9. Provides quick checkouts
10. Has easy-to-find departments
11. Will special order
12. Has convenient location
13. Keeps products in stock
14. Has good customer service
15. Has displays which highlight specials
16. Provides installation
17. Offers special services
18. Has sufficient number of employees

EXHIBIT 4.6
Image study of retailers in the do-it-yourself segment in Chicago, using a perceptual map. The map shows that customers perceive Wal-Mart to be convenient, the independent store to provide good customer service, and the regional chain to offer a good assortment of products. *Source:* Johnson 1994, p. 57.

ratings of various retailers on 18 attributes. The map indicates that customers perceive Wal-Mart to be the most convenient, the two regional chains (Menards and Handy Andy) to stock hard-to-find items and preferred brands, and the independent store to offer the best customer service. The three types of retailers have occupied distinct positions on the map, and the regional chains are viewed as similar stores (they are located near each other on the map). One way for the independent store to remain viable in this market is by maintaining and strengthening its superior customer service. About 40 percent of the customers had shopped there in the previous 12 months. The map also suggests that there is a potential opportunity for a new retailer to differentiate itself by offering lower prices (with possibly lower levels of service), an area of the map with no existing retailers.

PERCEPTUAL MAPPING TECHNIQUES

Psychometricians first developed perceptual mapping techniques to map psychological measurements of how people perceive things that vary on multiple dimensions. Marketers have adapted these multidimensional scaling (MDS) methods to represent customer perceptions and preferences for a set of entities (brands, geometric shapes, department stores, presidential candidates, etc.) on a map in Euclidean space.

Customer behavior is influenced by both perceptions and preferences. Two products may be perceived to be different, although physically they may essentially be the same. For example, Toyota Corolla and Chevy Prizm are physically nearly identical cars with different names. However, customers perceive the Corolla to be superior to the Prizm. In other cases customers may not be able to perceive any differences even when the products are different. For example, in blind taste tests most customers cannot identify different brands of beer or cola. Customers are also unable to identify different brands of wine even when their prices differ by several hundred percent (experts, however, can distinguish different wines).

MDS methods vary depending on the nature of input data (e.g., similarities data, perceptions data, or preference data) and how these data are manipulated to derive the map (Exhibits 4.7 and 4.8). We will describe three major approaches in greater detail: (1) perceptual maps from attribute-based data, (2) perceptual maps from similarity-based data, and (3) joint-space maps that include both customer perceptions and their preferences. (Cooper [1983] and Green, Carmone, and Smith [1989] describe these methods in detail.)

Attribute-based methods

Managers can use attribute-based methods to derive perceptual maps from data consisting of customer evaluations of products (more generally, competing alternatives) along pre-specified dimensions. There are four major steps to this method.

Step 1: Identify the set of products and the attributes on which those products will be evaluated. The attributes you choose to include in the analysis depend on the objectives of the study. For strategic positioning studies you should select a broad set of competing alternatives and attributes. For example, the alternatives can be product class (e.g., mutual funds, bonds, and stocks in the financial services industry) or product forms (e.g., subcompact, compact, and intermediate in the automobile industry). For tactical positioning studies, the al-

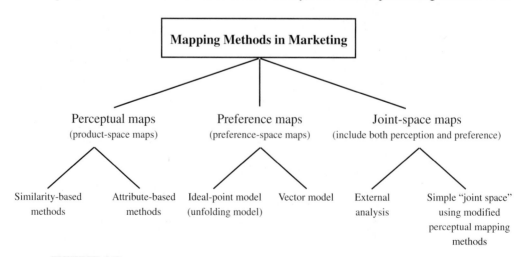

EXHIBIT 4.7
Mapping methods used in marketing fall into three categories: (1) perceptual maps,
(2) preference maps, and (3) joint-space maps.

Model	Input	Output	Computer programs	Comments
Perceptual map from similarity-based methods	Data matrix (or submatrix) consists of perceived pairwise similarities or other distance measures (e.g., correlations) between alternatives. The data may come from a single individual or be averaged across members of a target segment.	Spatial map showing the locations of the product alternatives.	KYST MDSCAL INDSCAL	Particularly useful when market structure is primarily based on intangible attributes such as image, aesthetics, smell, or taste.
Perceptual map from attribute-based methods	Data matrix consists of ratings of alternatives on a prespecified set of attributes. The data may either be from a single individual, or be averaged across members of a target segment.	Spatial map showing both the location of alternatives and the directional vectors associated with the attributes.	Factor Analysis (MDPREF) Discriminant Analysis	Particularly useful when market structure is driven primarily by tangible attributes, such as physical features of the product, its performance, and its service characteristics.
Preference map from ideal-point methods (Unfolding model)	Data matrix consists of the stated or derived preferences of individuals over a set of alternatives. Preferences may be rank-orders (nonmetric unfolding model) or ratings (metric unfolding model).	Spatial map showing the locations of the alternatives and the ideal points of the individuals. An ideal point refers to an individual's most preferred combination of the underlying dimensions defining the product space and will vary from individual to individual.	KYST GENFOLD ALSCAL	Particularly useful in categories where segment preferences are not uni-directional but exhibit an inverted U-shape. For example, preference for coffee brands may decline as the available options become either "stronger" or "weaker" in flavor as compared with an individual's ideal brand.
Preference map from vector method	Data matrix consists of the stated or derived preferences of individuals over a set of alternatives, where preferences are measured on a rating scale.	Spatial map showing the locations of the alternatives and the directional vectors associated with the preferences of each individual.	MDPREF	Useful in categories where segment preferences are unidirectional along the underlying attributes. For example, if competition is driven by factors such as quality, value, or speed of response, preferences are likely to be increasing in a unidirectional manner.
Joint-space map from external analysis	Data matrix consists of the stated or derived preferences of individuals over a set of alternatives, supplemented with data giving locations of the alternatives from a perceptual map.	Spatial map showing the locations of the alternatives, the directions of the attributes, and the ideal points or the preference vectors of individuals.	PREFMAP-3 GENFOLD	These are full-fledged systems with a number of processing options.
Simple joint-space map obtained from modified perceptual mapping methods	Data matrix may consist of (1) data like that in the similarity-based method where one of the alternatives is a hypothetical ideal-point of the individuals, or (2) data like that in the attribute-based method where one of the alternatives is the hypothetical ideal-point of the individuals, or all alternatives are rated on a "preference" attribute.	For data in (1), the spatial map provides the location of the alternatives, including the ideal alternative, and for data in (2), the spatial map provides the locations of all the alternatives, including the ideal alternative, and a directional vector for each attribute.	MDSCAL KYST INDSCAL MDPREF	These methods are fairly simple to implement, and they are often insightful.

EXHIBIT 4.8

A summary of the major perceptual and preference modeling methods, their required inputs and outputs, and computer programs that implement each method.

ternatives can be close competitive offerings (e.g., different brands of shampoo or different fragrances in shampoo, such as floral and herbal), and the attributes can be more operational in nature (e.g., color and miles per gallon.) The alternatives you choose should vary along all the chosen attributes. Kotler (1991) has summarized a number of generic attributes that can provide a useful starting point in selecting attributes for the study (Exhibit 4.9).

Step 2: Obtain perceptions data. The data for perceptual mapping typically come from questionnaires administered to a sample of customers in defined target segments. You should first organize the data into a matrix representing customer perceptions of each alternative on each of the prespecified attributes. Customers can either rank or rate all alternatives on one at-

	American	United	USAirways	Continental	Southwest
Convenience	5	8	3	3	8
Punctuality	6	5	5	4	8
Overall Service	8	7	5	4	6
Comfort	6	6	4	4	3

Attribute data for airlines: 1 = worst to 9 = best

FEATURES are characteristics that supplement a product's basic function (e.g., stereo system in a car).

PERFORMANCE refers to levels at which the product's primary characteristics operate.

DURABILITY is a measure of the product's expected operating life.

RELIABILITY is a measure of the probability that a product will malfunction or fail within a specified time period.

SERVICEABILITY is a measure of the ease of fixing a product that malfunctions or fails.

STYLE describes how well the product looks and feels to the customer.

PRODUCT IMAGE refers to attributes that convey the emotional aspects of the product—attributes that stir the heart as well as the mind of the customer. These include attributes such as the prestige or reputation associated with a product/company, the perceived lifestyle of the people who use the product, etc.

DELIVERY refers to all aspects of how the product or service is delivered to the customer. It includes the speed, accuracy, and the care attending the delivery process.

INSTALLATION refers to activities needed to be completed before the product becomes operational in its planned location.

TRAINING AND CONSULTING refer to the support services provided by the company to train the customer and its personnel in the use and maintenance of the product, and to help derive the maximum value from the use of the product.

REPAIR AND MAINTENANCE refers to convenience and quality of services provided by the company to prevent product failures, and to repair the product in the event that it fails to conform to expected performance.

OTHER SERVICES include warranty, availability of "loaners," and services that add value to the customer's purchase or use of the product.

SERVICE IMAGE refers to a number of attributes that contribute to the overall perception of the service. It includes such attributes as competence, friendliness, and courteousness of service employees, the perception of being pampered with personalized attention, etc.

PERCEIVED QUALITY refers to the degree to which the product meets customers' expectations of what the product/service should be. It is closely associated with the other attributes such as features, performance, reliability, durability, etc., that are listed above (Garvin 1987).

EXHIBIT 4.9
Illustrative list of attributes relevant for positioning analysis using attribute-based perceptual mapping methods. *Source*: Adapted from Kotler 1991.

tribute at a time, or customers can rank or rate one alternative at a time along all the attributes. For example, airlines differ along many perceptual attributes, such as convenience, punctuality, overall service, and comfort. The following data matrix *from one customer* illustrates the nature of the data collected, where the customer ratings ranged from 1 to 9 for each attribute.

A key assumption in perceptual mapping is that all customers whose data are used in the study share roughly the same perceptions about the alternatives. Therefore it is important that you obtain data from a homogeneous sample of customers. If you believe that customers are from several different segments, it is better to group them first into separate segments using, for example, cluster analysis (Chapter 3). By averaging responses within each segment, you can generate an "average" data matrix for every segment and then develop a separate perceptual map for each segment.

Step 3: Select a perceptual mapping method. In positioning studies it is not unusual to obtain customer evaluations on 10 or more attributes relevant to the set of alternatives under consideration. However, it is unlikely that all these attributes extract unique information about the perceptions that customers have about these alternatives. It is more likely that subsets of attributes tap the same underlying construct (also referred to as factor, axis, or dimension). Thus perceived overall service and comfort might both be attributes that tap the more fundamental dimension of perceived quality.

Perceptual mapping techniques offer a systematic method for extracting information about the underlying construct(s) from a data matrix consisting of customer perceptions on observable attributes. While there are several methods for doing this with attribute-based data, Hauser and Koppelman (1979) recommend factor analysis. We will describe the factor analysis procedure. The model used in the software accompanying this book is called MDPREF, which contains options for a factor-analytic derivation of perceptual maps (Carroll 1972, and Green and Wind 1973).

Outline of the factor analysis procedure: Factor analysis is a technique for systematically finding underlying patterns and interrelationships among variables (here, attributes), based on a data matrix consisting of the values of the attributes for a number of different alternatives (brands, product classes, or other objects). In particular, it enables us to determine from the data whether the attributes can be grouped or condensed into a smaller set of underlying constructs without sacrificing much of the information contained in the data matrix. Factor analysis is also useful in preprocessing data before undertaking segmentation studies, as described in the appendix to this chapter.

Let X be a matrix with m rows and n columns, in which the column headings are attributes and the rows are alternatives, with the data in the matrix consisting of the average ratings of each alternative on each attribute by a sample of customers. Note that X is the transpose of the example data matrix for perceptual mapping shown in the previous subsection. Let X_s represent a standardized matrix in which each column of X has been standardized. (To standardize a column, for each value we subtract the mean of all values on that attribute and divide by the standard deviation of the values. By standardizing we remove the effect of the measurement scale and ensure that all variables are treated equally in the analysis—i.e., it would not matter whether income is measured in dollars or pesos.) We denote the columns of X_s as $x_1, x_2, \ldots, x_n$.

In the principal-components approach to factor analysis (the most commonly used method in marketing), we express each of the original attributes as a linear combination of a common set of factors, and in turn we express each factor also as a linear combination of attributes, where the jth factor can be represented as

$$F_j = a_{j1}x_1 + a_{j2}x_2 + \cdots + a_{jn}x_n, \tag{4.1}$$

where the a's are weights derived by the procedure in such a way that the resulting factors F_j's are optimal. The optimality criterion is that the first factor should capture as much of the information in X_s as possible, the second factor should be orthogonal to the first factor and contain as much of the remaining information in X_s as possible, the third factor should be orthogonal to both the first and the second factors and contain as much as possible of the information in X_s that is not accounted for by the first two factors, and so forth.

Each value of the original data can also be approximated as a linear combination of the factors:

$$x_{kj} \approx z_{k1}f_{1j} + z_{k2}f_{2j} + \cdots + z_{kr}f_{rj}, \tag{4.2}$$

where the z_{kl}'s and f_{ij}'s are also outputs of the factor analysis procedure.

The relationships characterized by Eqs. (4.1) and (4.2) can be seen more clearly when represented as matrices (Exhibit 4.10). In Exhibit 4.10, the z's are called (standardized) factor scores and the f's are the factor loadings. Then Z_s is the matrix of standardized factor scores, and F is the factor loading matrix, with columns denoted as F_j, and those factor scores represent the correlation matrix of attributes with factors. (Note that the factors-by-attributes matrix in Exhibit 4.10 is actually the transpose of the F matrix.) If $r = n$, that is, if the number of factors is equal to the number of attributes, there is no data reduction. In that case, (4.2) becomes an exact equation (i.e., the approximation symbol in Exhibit 4.10, $\approx$, can be replaced by the equality symbol, $=$) that shows that the standardized data values (x_{kj}'s) can be exactly recovered from the derived factors. All that we would accomplish in that case is to redefine the original n attributes as n different factors, where each factor is a linear function of all the attributes. However, in perceptual mapping we seek r factors (r typically being 2 or 3) that retain as much of the infor-

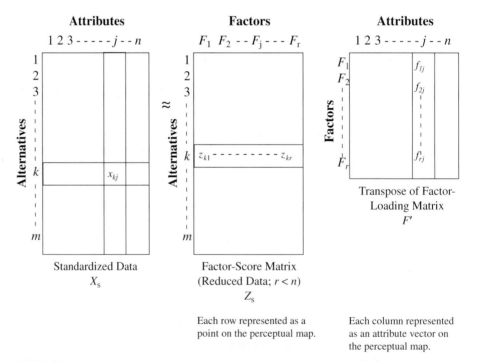

Each row represented as a point on the perceptual map.

Each column represented as an attribute vector on the perceptual map.

EXHIBIT 4.10
A pictorial depiction of attribute-based perceptual mapping. The model decomposes the (standardized) original data matrix (X_s) into two matrices: (1) the standardized factor score (Z_s) matrix and (2) the factor-loading matrix (F); r is the number of factors (dimensions of the perceptual map) and is usually set to be equal to 2 or 3.

mation contained in the original data matrix as is possible. Variance (the dispersion of values around a mean) is a measure of the information content of an attribute. The larger the variance, the higher the information content. Once we standardize the attributes, each attribute contains one unit of variance (except for attributes for which all values are identical, in which case the information content of that attribute is equal to 0). If there are n attributes in the analysis, then the total variance to be explained (information content) is equal to n.

The output of a factor analysis procedure is illustrated graphically in Exhibit 4.11 for the case of two attributes, elegance and distinctiveness, in a study of notebook computers. The procedure first finds a factor along which the points are maximally dispersed (i.e., this factor has the maximal variance when we project the points onto it). In this example the locations of the notebook computers are dispersed much more along factor 1 than factor 2. If factor 1 has a variance equal to 1.7, this factor alone accounts for 85 percent of the information content in the two attributes ($[1.7 / 2.0] \times 100$), suggesting that "elegance" and "distinctiveness" are correlated and possibly refer to a common underlying dimension called "design." The procedure then finds a second factor, orthogonal (perpendicular) to the first, that maximally recovers the remaining variance. In this case the remaining factor will recover 15 percent of the variance; together the two factors explain all the variance in the data. If there are n attributes, the procedure continues in this fashion until it extracts as many factors (up to n), all orthogonal to each other, as are needed to explain the variance in the original data.

Step 4: Interpreting factor analysis output. An important objective of factor analysis is to provide an interpretation of the underlying factors in terms of the original attributes. The key to

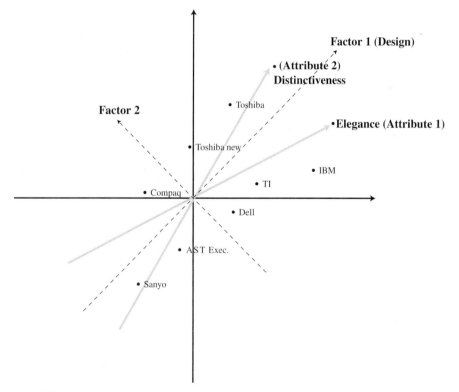

EXHIBIT 4.11
A two-attribute example of factor analysis for notebook computers. "Distinctiveness" and "elegance" are correlated with each other, and they are represented by an underlying factor (dimension) called "design." For this example a one-dimensional map captures most of the variation among the notebook computers.

interpretation is the factor-loading matrix F. By looking at the pattern of the loadings, we should be able to identify and name the factor. Loadings that have high absolute value (high absolute values of correlations) make interpretation easy. In a perceptual map the factor-loading matrix is represented visually as attribute vectors, where correlation between any attribute and a factor is equal to the cosine of the angle between that attribute vector and the corresponding factor.

The factors may be rigidly rotated (i.e., F is transformed by an orthogonal matrix, while at the same time making the corresponding transformation to Z_s) to aid interpretation, forcing attributes to have either big or small cosines with the transformed factors (the transformation is called Varimax rotation). The result is that a set of attributes tends to line up closely with each factor. In this way, attributes tend to be closely aligned with a single factor. We can then better identify the attributes most closely associated with the transformed factors. Although rotation changes the variance explained by each factor, it does not affect the total variance explained by the set of retained factors. *To further aid interpretation, we can draw each attribute vector on the map with a length that is proportional to the variance of that attribute explained by the retained factors.* Exhibit 4.12 is a perceptual map derived from factor analysis, where the length of each attribute vector indicates the proportion of the variance of that attribute recovered by the map.

Variance explained by a factor: Each factor explains a proportion of the total variance in the data as follows:

$$\text{Variance explained by factor } i = f_{i1}^2 + f_{i2}^2 + \cdots + f_{in}^2. \tag{4.3}$$

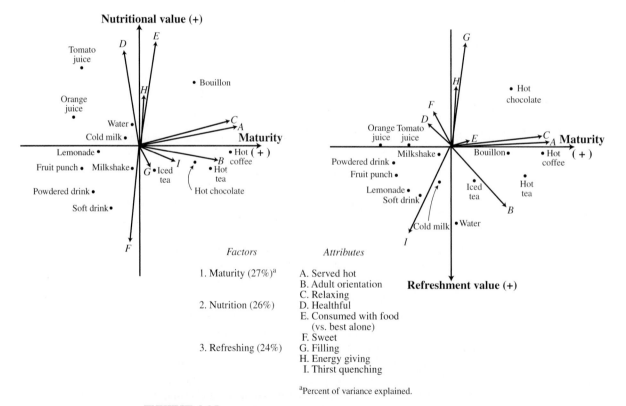

Factors	Attributes
1. Maturity (27%)[a]	A. Served hot
	B. Adult orientation
	C. Relaxing
2. Nutrition (26%)	D. Healthful
	E. Consumed with food (vs. best alone)
	F. Sweet
3. Refreshing (24%)	G. Filling
	H. Energy giving
	I. Thirst quenching

[a]Percent of variance explained.

EXHIBIT 4.12
An example of a three-dimensional attribute-based perceptual map of beverages, where the length of each attribute vector is proportional to the amount of its variance explained by the map. The three dimensions are (1) maturity of target segment, (2) refreshment value, and (3) nutritional value. *Source:* Aaker and Day 1990, p. 574.

The proportion of the variance explained by a single factor equals the variance explained by that factor divided by n, the total variance in the data. In Exhibit 4.12 the proportion of variance explained by the horizontal axis (factor 1) is equal to 0.27, and the variance explained by the vertical axis (factor 2) is equal to 0.26, giving a combined variance explained by the two axes of 0.53. If all n factors are retained, these proportions will sum to one.

Proportion of an attribute's variance explained by the retained factors: A good factor analysis solution explains a significant proportion of the variance associated with each original attribute as follows:

$$\text{Proportion of variance explained for attribute } j = f_{1j}^2 + f_{2j}^2 + \cdots + f_{rj}^2. \quad (4.4)$$

Number of factors retained: If the variance of any attribute is poorly recovered by the retained factors, that attribute is unique and would require additional factor(s) for it to be explained. In that case we might consider going to a higher-dimensional map, say, from a two- to a three-dimensional map. This raises the broader question of how many factors we should retain in a factor-analysis study. Unfortunately, there is no simple answer to this question, although there are several useful guidelines. In the context of perceptual maps, it rarely makes sense to go beyond three dimensions, especially if a three-dimensional map recovers more than 60 to 70 percent of the variance in the original data. Another useful guideline is that every retained factor should individually account for *at least* one unit of variance (equivalent to the variance in a single attribute) and typically should account for substantially more than one unit of variance.

EXAMPLE

In a study of the market for both conventional and solar-powered cooling products for industrial buildings, Choffray and Lilien (1980) found that several different types of individuals participated in the purchase decision process for such equipment. Decision makers included production engineers (those who would be working with and maintaining the equipment), corporate engineers (those designing the systems), plant managers, and senior executives. Using the preceding guidelines (along with additional statistical methods), they determined that even the *number* of dimensions that these groups of individuals used in thinking about cooling systems differed—top managers and production engineers had perceptual spaces that could best be represented in three dimensions, while plant managers and corporate engineers had two-dimensional spaces.

Choffray and Lilien then studied whether it was appropriate to combine the perceptions of these groups. (Roughly this amounts to determining whether the data matrices in Exhibit 4.10 would be the same when they analyzed each group separately and when they combined the perceptions of all groups.) The answer was *no*, even when they used the same number of dimensions for the different groups. Exhibit 4.13 summarizes the qualitative results for plant managers and corporate engineers. Plant managers group operating costs, the system's use of currently unproductive areas, and the protection the system offers against irregularities in the supply of traditional energy sources as their first dimension (factor). Corporate engineers, however, include the system's initial costs, its vulnerability to weather damage, and its complexity.

This example underscores the importance of ensuring that the respondents who provide data for perceptual mapping form a homogeneous group. Alternatively, we could perform some prior segmentation, because the groups may differ both in the number and the makeup of their perceptual dimensions.

	Factor 1	**Factor 2**
Plant Managers	(+) Energy savings (+) *Low cost a/c* (+) Fuel rationing protection (+) *Use unproductive areas* (+) Reduce pollution (+) *State of the art solution* (+) Modern image (+) *Power failure protection*	(−) Field proven (−) Reliability (+) Not fully tested (−) *Substitutability of components* (−) Climate sensitivity
Corporate Engineers	(+) Not fully tested (−) *System's cost* (−) Field proven (−) Reliability (+) *Vulnerability to weather* (+) *Complexity*	(+) Reduce pollution (+) Fuel rationing protection (+) Energy savings (+) Modern image

Notes:
- The factors listed have loadings greater than .50 and are listed in decreasing order of importance.
- Items in italics are important to the corresponding group, but not to the other group.
- The sign to the left of each factor is the sign of the correlation between an attribute and a factor. When the sign is positive (negative), then the factor and the attribute are positively (negatively) related to each other.

EXHIBIT 4.13
Source: Choffray and Lilien 1980, p. 125.

Location of the products (alternatives) in the perceptual map: An important element of the factor analysis output is the factor score matrix, which gives the location of each product on each factor. If we retain only two factors, then the location of the first product in a two-dimensional perceptual map is given by the first two elements in the first row of the factor-score matrix; the location of the second product is given by the first two elements of the second row of the factor score matrix, and so on.

In summary, attribute-based methods provide a powerful set of tools for perceptual mapping. They are particularly useful when the product alternatives are differentiated along tangible attributes that are well understood and evaluated by customers. Compared with similarity-based methods, attribute-based methods identify the underlying dimensions more clearly. A further advantage is that you can develop the maps even when the respondents evaluate only a few alternatives.

Similarity-based methods for perceptual mapping

Similarity-based methods rely on the idea that perceived similarity (or dissimilarity) between alternatives may be conceptualized in terms of psychological distances. With this mapping method we try to produce a spatial map in which the *Euclidean distances* between any two alternatives closely correspond to the degree of similarity that customers perceive between the same pair of alternatives. The techniques for producing such a map differ in their assumptions regarding the nature of the input data and in the algorithms used to translate similarities into distances on the map. In the most common technique any two alternatives, C and D, that respondents perceive to be less similar to each other than another set of alternatives, A and C, are placed on the map at least as far apart as C is from D (to the extent feasible). Similarity-based methods usually require five steps to implement:

Step 1: Identify the alternatives of interest. Usually these alternatives will be competing products or services. The specific set of alternatives we choose depends on the objectives for the study. For strategic positioning studies, it is best to select a broad set of competing alternatives. For tactical positioning studies, we can choose a set of alternatives from among the firm's closest competitors. In either case we should choose alternatives familiar to the customers whose perceptions we are measuring, or we should brief the customers to make them familiar with the alternatives before eliciting their perceptions of these alternatives.

Step 2: Develop a matrix of similarities (also called proximities) between pairs of alternatives. The input data for generating similarity-based perceptual maps is a symmetric matrix consisting of the interproduct similarities (or dissimilarities) perceived by the target segment. The matrix is symmetric because we assume that the similarity (psychological distance) between alternatives A and B is the same as that between alternatives B and A. In the following similarity matrix, we measure similarity on a scale ranging from 1 to 9, with 1 representing "most similar" and 9 representing "most dissimilar."

	Aqua-Fresh	Colgate	Crest	Gleem
Aqua-Fresh	1			
Colgate	2	1		
Crest	4	4	1	
Gleem	7	6	5	1

In this similarity matrix for a few toothpastes, 1 is most similar and 9 is least similar.

Another way to obtain the input data is to ask customers to *rank each pair* directly from the most similar pair to the least similar pair, with the rank 1 being assigned to the most similar pair. Although we can derive a perceptual map separately for each customer from a similarity matrix, typically one first computes average similarities data by averaging the responses of several customers. (Again, it is critical that the group of customers included in the study have reasonably homogeneous perceptions.) Averaging individual responses in this way is an acceptable approximation only if we can reasonably assume that all the customers in the target segment use the same underlying dimensions in comparing the alternatives.

Step 3: Develop the perceptual map. We can generate a perceptual map using one of several computer programs (Exhibit 4.8). The computer mapping program transforms the input data of the similarity between alternatives i and j (δ_{ij}) into distance on a map (d_{ij}). This is the critical step in this analysis, in which we transform "psychological distances" between the alternatives into distances in Euclidean space. The reason for making this transformation is that we can use more powerful analytical methods to interpret a map in Euclidean space. The similarity-based perceptual map in Exhibit 4.14 shows that customers perceive Close-up to be *three times* as far from Dentagard (i.e., three times as dissimilar) as Colgate is from Aqua-Fresh. The ability to quantify judgments is important in the next step: numerically evaluating the *relative* effects of alternative positioning strategies on market shares or on the sales of each alternative.

In general, to satisfy all the constraints (e.g., customers perceive A as most similar to B and least similar to F, which implies that A should be closest to B on the resulting map and farthest away from F) will require a map of $n - 1$ dimensions, where n is the number of product alternatives being evaluated. But maps with more than three dimensions have little managerial value, and so we balance interpretability with the goal of adhering to the constraints. The ideal way to resolve this trade-off is to produce a map in two- or three-dimensional space that summarizes the market structure with visual clarity.

Step 4: Determine the number of dimensions for the map. To make an intelligent decision on the appropriate number of dimensions, we use the notion of (weak) monotonicity, namely, that the rank order of product similarities should be the same (or close to same) as the rank order of distances on the associated perceptual map. Monotonicity requires that if $\delta_{ij} > \delta_{kl}$ then $d_{ij} \geq d_{kl}$, where i, j, k, l are alternatives, the δ's are similarities, and the d's distances on the perceptual map. The monotonicity constraint is always satisfied if the resulting map is in $n - 1$ dimensions. For fewer dimensions, the greater the departure from monotonicity, the less perfect the resulting map. We use the notion of "stress" to measure

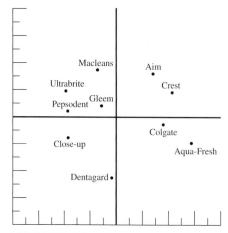

EXHIBIT 4.14
A similarity-based map of toothpastes. The map shows that Ultrabrite and Pepsodent are the closest substitutes in this market; Aqua-Fresh and Close-up, and Aim and Dentagard are least likely to be substituted for each other. *Source:* Malhotra 1993, p. 703.

departures from monotonicity. A stress value of 0 implies a perfect fit, a measure similar to $1 - R^2$ in regression. Stress values less than 0.05 are considered to be good, whereas maps with stress values greater than 0.20 are not generally meaningful. Computer program output typically includes the stress values associated with a map in any given number of dimensions. These programs use one of several formulas for computing stress. A frequently used formula is

$$
\text{Stress} = \sqrt{\frac{\sum_{i<j}\left(d_{ij} - \hat{d}_{ij}\right)^2}{\sum_{i<j}\left(d_{ij} - \bar{d}\right)^2}},
\tag{4.5}
$$

where

d_{ij} = the distance between alternatives i and j in the resulting Euclidean spatial map;

$\bar{d}$ = the average of all d_{ij}'s; and

$\hat{d}_{ij}$ = a set of numerical values that are as close as possible to d_{ij}, but that also represents a monotonic function of δ_{ij}.

To determine the appropriate number of dimensions, we trade off between monotonicity and the number of dimensions. The general idea is to start with one dimension, and increase the number of dimensions until the stress value decreases very little with the addition of each incremental dimension.

The foregoing approach uses "nonmetric analysis" to recover the rank orders in the similarity data. Other approaches based on "metric analysis" attempt to recover either the absolute magnitudes or differences in magnitudes in the similarity data.

Step 5: Interpret the dimensions in the map. As output, the computer program produces points (representing alternatives) in a perceptual map of the dimensionality we choose, along with a set of associated axes. Next we must interpret the axes. One simple way to interpret the map is to look for alternatives in extreme locations on each dimension and then try to determine the differentiating features between these alternatives. We can also shift the origin or rotate the axes to improve interpretation. Usually, however, we will need additional data from the study participants regarding their perceptions of the alternatives to help us interpret the map. (For example, if the study includes measures of product attributes as well, we can correlate the perceptual map positions with the attribute data.)

In summary, similarity-based methods are particularly useful in categories in which it is difficult to articulate the specific attributes on which various alternatives are differentiated (e.g., different fragrances). The maps can help a firm to identify new product opportunities and the competitive structure (e.g., closest competing brands) of the market. However, similarity-based methods do not provide a clear mechanism for interpreting the underlying dimensions of the map, and they generally require at least eight alternatives for the algorithms to produce a reliable map.

JOINT-SPACE MAPS

Overview

A major limitation of perceptual maps is that they do not indicate which areas (positions) of the map are desirable to the target segments of customers and which ones are not. In other words, the maps do not incorporate information about customer preferences or choices. We need to use a *joint-space mapping method* to incorporate both perceptions and preferences in the same map.

Perceptions are fundamentally different from preferences: customers may see Volvo as the safest car, but they may also have a low preference for it. In addition, unlike perceptions preferences do not necessarily increase or decrease monotonically with increases in the magnitude of an attribute. In some cases (e.g., sweetness of soft drink) each customer has an ideal level of the attribute above or below which a product becomes less preferred. In other cases customers always prefer more of the attribute (e.g., quality of a TV set) or always prefer less of an attribute (e.g., waiting time before a car is repaired). Exhibit 4.15 illustrates these different types of preferences. Preference maps that incorporate inverted U-shaped preferences are referred to as ideal-point (or unfolding) models. Maps that incorporate linear preference functions are referred to as vector models. (In a third kind of preference modeling, we can use part-worths to represent arbitrary piecewise linear functions that can approximate both ideal-point and vector preference functions. In Chapter 7, we describe conjoint analysis, which allows for part-worth functions.)

Simple joint-space maps

The simplest way to incorporate preferences in a map is to introduce a hypothetical ideal brand into the set of alternatives that customers evaluate in the attribute-based mapping model. For each respondent, an ideal brand has that individual's most preferred combination of attributes. Assuming that both the perceptions and the preferences of customers in a target segment are fairly homogeneous, we can find the location of the "average" ideal brand using either similarity-based or attribute-based methods. The ideal brand thus becomes simply another alternative that customers evaluate. In the resulting map, locations that are farther away from the ideal point (location of the ideal brand) are less desirable to customers than locations closer to the ideal point. Using this approach in Exhibit 4.16(a), we can view alternative A, which is twice as far from the ideal point as alternative B, as being preferred half as much as B.

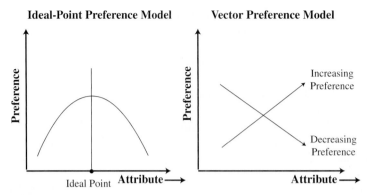

EXHIBIT 4.15
Different types of preference functions. Ideal-point models have an intermediate "best level," e.g., sweetness, whereas for vector models more (or less) is always more (less) preferred, e.g., waiting time, reliability.

Another way to include preferences in attribute-based models is to add an attribute called "preference" on which customers rate all the alternatives to indicate their preferences for these alternatives. When we aggregate and average these preference ratings, we can treat the average ratings as an additional row in the input data matrix to represent an attribute called "preference." The map we generate from this modified data set then includes a preference vector to indicate the direction of increasing preference. An alternative positioned farther along this vector is one for which customers have greater preference. Suppose that alternative A is farthest along the preference vector. Then if B is half as far from A as C is from A along the preference vector, customers prefer B twice as much as C (Exhibit 4.16b).

Exhibit 4.17 shows this approach in evaluating notebook computers. The preference vector shows that customer preference increases with improvements in screen quality and perceived value of the product and decreases with lower levels of battery life. In this example the two-dimensional map recovered over 80 percent of the variance in the preference "attribute." However, if it had recovered a low percentage, say less than 50 percent, then it would be unwise to use the map to interpret preference structure, even though the map

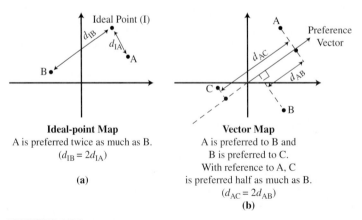

EXHIBIT 4.16
Interpreting simple joint-space maps. In ideal-point maps distances directly indicate preference: the larger the distance from the ideal point, the less preferred the brand. In vector maps the product locations are projected onto a preference vector (dashed lines in b), and distances are measured along the preference vector.

could still be useful for interpreting the perceptual dimensions. When variance recovery for the preference vector is poor, it may be worthwhile to drop some attributes from the analysis to see if we can produce a joint-space map that is easier to interpret.

External analysis using PREFMAP3

Overview: PREFMAP3 is a mapping model based on the assumption that respondents who have common perceptions of a set of alternatives may have widely differing preferences for these alternatives. The model superimposes the preferences of each respondent in a group onto a common perceptual map, developed external to the PREFMAP3 model. The perceptual map can be derived from the same set of respondents using the similarity- or attribute-based approaches described in the previous section.

PREFMAP3 starts with a perceptual map giving the locations of the product alternatives. In the second step it introduces for each respondent either an ideal brand or a preference vector into the map in a manner that ensures maximal correspondence between the input preference ratings (or rankings) for the alternatives and the preference relationships among the alternatives in the resulting joint-space map. Note that each respondent included in the study has a unique ideal point or a preference vector as the case may be.

EXHIBIT 4.17
In this example of a simple attribute-based joint-space map with a preference vector, the direction of increasing preference is indicated by the attribute "preference." Overall preference for notebook computers increases with screen quality, value, and long battery life but is unaffected by expandability, keyboard, and ease of use.

Description of the PREFMAP3 model: The input data for the model is the $N \times m$ preference matrix consisting of the preference ratings of the m alternatives by N respondents as shown in the following table. Here we show preference ratings for five airlines from five customers using a 1 to 9 scale, with 1 indicating most preferred and 9 indicating least preferred.

	Airlines				
	American	United	USAirways	Continental	Southwest
Customer 1	1	7	2	5	8
Customer 2	7	7	4	2	1
Customer 3	4	6	6	6	7
Customer 4	3	1	8	6	2
Customer 5	2	2	3	7	8

Matrix of preference values, s_{ij} where i refers to customer and j refers to product alternatives (airlines).

(If the rating scale is reversed, i.e., if larger numbers indicate increased preference, then multiply every number in the data matrix by –1 to reverse the scale.)

Let s_{ij} denote the value of the preference rating of the jth alternative by the ith customer. The ideal-point version of PREFMAP3 attempts to optimally locate the ideal point of each respondent i on the perceptual map. Define

$$\hat{s}_{ij} = b + ad_{ij}^2, \tag{4.6}$$

where

$\hat{s}_{ij}$ = the estimated rating of alternative j by respondent i, as determined by the procedure for each i and j; $i = 1, 2, \ldots, I$ (# of respondents) and $j = 1, 2, \ldots, J$ (# of alternatives); and

d_{ij} = the squared distance of ideal point i from the fixed location of alternative j on the perceptual map.

The model tries to determine the constants a and b (which may be negative) in Eq. (4.6) such that ($\hat{s}_{ij}$) is as close as possible (i.e., in the sense of minimizing squared distance) to the ratings s_{ij} for all respondents i and all alternatives j given in the preference data matrix. Exhibit 4.18 shows a map produced from a preference mapping model.

In the vector version of PREFMAP3, the model attempts to find a preference vector (i.e., the direction in which preference increases) for each respondent by using the following equation to compute estimated ratings:

$$\hat{s}_{ij} = a_i \sum_{k=1}^{r} x_{ik} y_{jk} + b_i, \tag{4.7}$$

where

a_i = slope of the preference vector;

b_i = intercept term for preference vector;

y_{jk} = coordinate location of alternative j on dimension k, determined from a perceptual map;

x_{ik} = preference vector coordinate on dimension k; and

r = number of dimensions in the perceptual map.

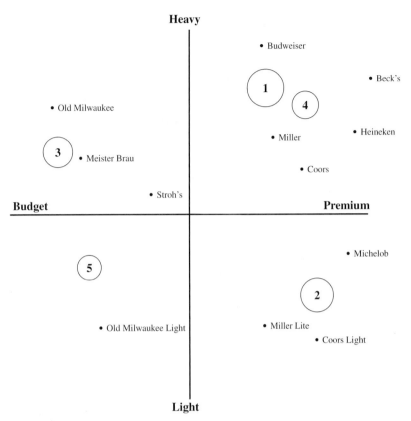

EXHIBIT 4.18
A joint-space map derived from external analysis with groupings of customer ideal points in circles. The size of the circle indicates relative size of the customer segment at that location. *Source*: Moore and Pessemier 1993, p. 146.

Given r and y_{jk} (for all j and k), the model attempts to find a_i, b_i, and x_{ik} such that $\hat{s}_{ij}$ is as close as possible (in the sense of minimizing squared distance) to the ratings s_{ij}. (To draw the map, we can relocate the computed preference vectors by shifting them in a parallel manner so that they pass through the origin.) The product term, $x_{ik} y_{jk}$, in Eq. (4.7) ensures that the preference vector direction on the map will maximally recover the preference ratings s_{ij} for respondent i for all j, for the given positions of the product alternatives ($y_{jk}, j = 1, 2, \ldots, J$ and $k = 1, \ldots, r$).

There are several other options in the PREFMAP3 model, including the use of rank-order preference data and options that allow distances to be differentially weighted so that each dimension is accorded a different level of importance, which can vary by customer. The model can also be structured to use both the ideal-point and vector models on the same map, with the ideal-point mode used for respondents for whom it best recovers the original preference ratings and the vector mode used for the remaining respondents (for whom it best recovers their preferences). A full discussion of these topics will take us well beyond the scope of this book. Further details are available in Carroll (1972), and Green and Wind (1973), and Meulman, Heiser, and Carroll (1986). For this book we implemented the vector model version of PREFMAP3 (Meulman, Heiser, and Carroll 1986).

Interpreting PREFMAP3 results: An advantage of PREFMAP3 is that typically we can visually identify segments of customers on the map. For example, in Exhibit 4.18 the largest group-

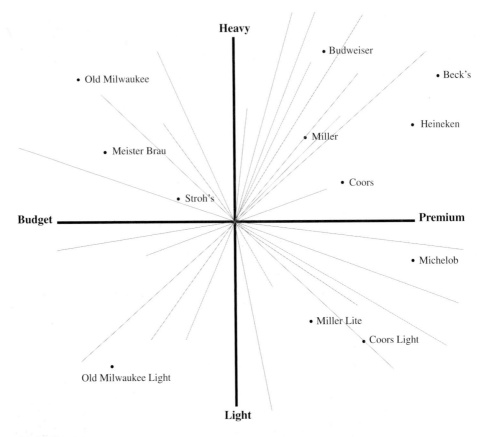

EXHIBIT 4.19

A joint-space map derived from external analysis displaying the preference vectors of 25 respondents. This map is equivalent to the map shown in Exhibit 4.18, which was based on the ideal-point version of external analysis. The lines are denser in the upper right quadrant, suggesting that more respondents prefer the brands in that quadrant. The length of a preference vector indicates the degree to which the map was able to capture the preferences of that respondent.

ing of respondents (ideal points) is in the circle marked 1. These customers prefer Budweiser the most (i.e., their ideal points are located closest to Budweiser), Miller the next most, and so forth. The next largest segment is marked as a circle with the number 2. This segment prefers Coors Light and Michelob most. The model also shows that Stroh's is not the most preferred brand in any segment—it is a "compromise brand" that some respondents may choose (e.g., those in segments 5 and 3) when their most preferred brand is unavailable. Exhibit 4.19 shows a map derived using the vector model version of PREFMAP, which is equivalent to the map shown in Exhibit 4.18 (We have only implemented the vector model version in the Marketing Engineering software suite). To interpret the preference vectors, follow the guidelines we gave for interpreting attributes in Exhibit 4.1, that is, project each product alternative onto the respective vectors.

The preference map allows us to not only visually identify segments, but to also compute an index of predicted market share for any product at any location on the map. The latter requires us to first transform preferences into indices of market shares. We can consider two "choice rules" for doing this (see also Chapter 7): (1) first choice and (2) share of preference. Under the first choice rule, we assume that each customer only purchases the most preferred product (that is, the one closest to the ideal point or the one farthest along a preference vector). Under the share of preference rule, we assume that

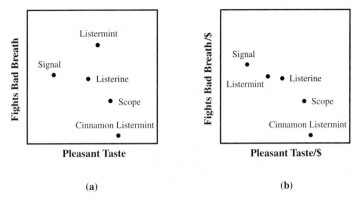

EXHIBIT 4.20
An example of a perceptual map with and without "dollar-metric" modification, showing that Signal is dominated by the other brands on both attributes (a) unless price is considered (b). *Source*: Urban and Star 1991, pp. 138–139.

each customer purchases every product in proportion to its measured preference value (relative to the sum of the preference values for all other products included in the model). The first choice rule is appropriate for infrequently purchased products (e.g., cars), whereas the share of preference rule is appropriate for frequently purchased products (e.g., shampoo or soft drinks). The software automatically does these computations and enables us to explore the potential market performance that can be achieved by repositioning any one product assuming that all other products remain at their original locations on the map.

For some data sets, parameter a in Eq. (4.6) can turn out to be negative for some respondents. These respondents have "anti–ideal-points" such that the closer a product is to such points, the less it is preferred. Anti–ideal-points can cause difficulties in interpretation. This is the primary reason that we have only implemented the vector model in the software. It is also possible that the preference map poorly recovers the preferences of some respondents. This can be detected by checking the proportion of variance (of preferences) that the map explains for each respondent. If there are many such respondents, it may be worthwhile to redo the whole analysis after increasing the number of dimensions of the externally derived perceptual map.

INCORPORATING PRICE IN PERCEPTUAL MAPS

We can represent price in several ways in perceptual maps (Urban and Star 1991). In attribute-based methods we can include price as another attribute along which customers evaluate the products. Or we can include objective prices (the actual prices of the products) as an additional attribute in developing the map.

A completely different way to approach this issue is to divide the coordinates of each alternative by its price along each of the dimensions of the map. We can use this approach with any of the methods described in this chapter. Exhibit 4.20 shows a map of the mouthwash category with and without price included. When the coordinates of each alternative are transformed by its price, the underlying dimension becomes "per-dollar coordinates." Without this transformation it is difficult to see why Signal should survive in the market. Other brands dominate it along both dimensions (Exhibit 4.20a). Listerine is perceived to taste better and to have the same ability to fight bad breath. However, the price-transformed coordinates (Exhibit 4.20b) show that its price-adjusted position makes it an attractive alternative that is not dominated by other alternatives on both dimensions.

SUMMARY

In this chapter we described methods to produce perceptual and preference maps that help us to position products and services in the minds of our customers. Although many of our examples were for consumer products, we can also apply these methods to technical and industrial products and services aimed at business markets.

These mapping techniques enable managers to understand the competitive structure of their markets. Based on this understanding, they can then position their offerings to gain a favorable response from their target segments. Although these techniques are powerful, it is important to understand their limitations so that they we can apply them where they are most useful.

- Perceptual mapping methods provide only a partial explanation of customer perceptions and preferences. They provide insights that are limited by the particular set of alternatives and attributes included in the study—that is, they support positioning efforts within an existing framework. In similarity-based methods the set of alternatives selected for study will limit the set of underlying dimensions that are developed as a basis for positioning. In attribute-based methods the set of attributes chosen limit the dimensions along which new positioning options will be considered. Thus these methods may not encourage managers to think "outside the box" to develop positioning strategies along new attributes.

  We should also remember that the mapping techniques only serve to *represent* perceptions and preferences in a manner that aids decision making. They do not tell us much about *why* customers form certain perceptions or preferences.

- Several technical limitations (e.g., data size restrictions in attribute-based methods, minimum number of alternatives required for similarity-based methods, solutions that yield degenerate maps in joint-space methods, and so forth) make these methods less than perfect in real-world applications.

- There are no "probability models" to provide us statistical guidance in selecting the most appropriate map (for the methods presented here). Thus we cannot statistically estimate whether a map based on data from a particular set of respondents will generalize to the target population of interest. The plausibility of a map is not an indicator of its validity (truth) or even of its reliability (whether we will obtain a similar map when we use data from a new sample of respondents). Some newer mapping techniques, such as PROSCAL (MacKay and Zinnes 1986), incorporate an error model and offer statistical guidance in interpreting maps. However, these models are not yet in wide use.

In spite of these limitations, perceptual and preference maps offer two major benefits: they help managers to (1) view the competitive structure of their markets through the eyes of their customers and (2) communicate with each other about how the market is structured and what they might do to take advantage of that structure. These maps are particularly useful for strategic decision making, especially if the mapping exercise is part of a larger audit of the competitive position of the organization.

Finally, perceptual maps are useful even when there are no data available from customers. Subjective managerial data often provide useful insights. For example, managers developing a new product can each generate individual maps based just on their own perceptions of how the new product stacks up against existing competitors. These maps can stimulate good discussions that will help them develop a positioning strategy for the new product.

Chapter 4 Appendix
FACTOR ANALYSIS FOR PREPROCESSING SEGMENTATION DATA

Segmentation studies often rely on measurements (observations) about individuals on a number of attributes (variables). However, as mentioned in Chapter 3 correlated variables may mask the true segment structure. To address this problem we can use factor analysis to preprocess segmentation data before using cluster analysis. The objective is to reduce the data from a large number of correlated variables to a much smaller set of independent underlying factors, this reduced set retaining most of the information contained in the original data. The derived factors not only represent the original data parsimoniously, they often result in more reliable segments when used in cluster analysis procedures.

The form of factor analysis that is useful for segmentation studies is slightly different from the approach described in this chapter. Let X be a $m \times n$ data matrix consisting of needs (or attitudinal) data from m respondents on n variables. As before, the input data are standardized. Let X_s represent the standardized data matrix. However, here we work with unstandardized factor scores (we denote the factor score matrix as P to distinguish it from the standardized factor score matrix represented as Z_s in Exhibit 4.10). Thus we need a different set of variables to distinguish these factor analysis results from the ones we get in Eqs. (4.1) and (4.2):

$$P_j = u_{j1}x_1 + u_{j2}x_2 + \cdots + u_{jn}x_n, \tag{4A.1}$$

$$x_{kj} \approx p_{k1}u_{1j} + p_{k2}u_{2j} + \cdots + p_{kr}u_{rj}, \tag{4A.2}$$

where

x_i = ith column from the standardized data matrix X_s; x_{ki} is the element in the kth row and ith column of this matrix;

P_j = the jth column of the factor score matrix representing the scores of each respondent on factor j; $P = [P_1, P_2, \ldots, P_r]$ is the factor-score matrix with r retained factors; and

u = "loadings" that characterize how the original variables are related to the factors.

As before, we seek r factors to represent the original data, where r is smaller than n, the number of variables we started with. If we can pick an r that is less than 1/3 of n, but where the retained factors account for more than 2/3 of the variance in the data, we can then consider the preprocessing of the data to be successful. There is, however, always a danger that some important information is lost by preprocessing sample data in a way that masks the true cluster structure. Thus, it is often a good idea to run the model with and without preprocessing of the data through factor analysis, to see which set of results make the most sense. To aid interpretability of the factors, we can orthogonally rotate the initial factor solution (Varimax rotation) so that each original variable is correlated most closely with just a few factors, preferably with just one factor. A full discussion of this topic is beyond the scope of this book.

We can then use the factor-score matrix with r factors as the set of input variables for identifying segments through cluster analysis. By using unstandardized factor scores at this stage, we can determine during cluster analysis whether to standardize the factor scores, an option that we can select within the cluster analysis software provided with this book.

POSITIONING THE INFINITI G20 CASE[1]

INTRODUCING THE G20

In April 1990, Nissan's Infiniti division planned to introduce the G20 in the United States, adding a third model to the existing Infiniti line. The G20 was already available in Europe and Japan under the name Primera. The car, equipped with a four-cylinder engine developing 140 horsepower, would be Infiniti's entry-level luxury car. Initial market response to the G20 in the United States was disappointing, and management wondered how it might retarget or reposition the car to improve its market performance.

BACKGROUND

In 1989, three years after Honda first introduced its Acura line, Toyota and Nissan attacked the U.S. luxury car market, a segment previously dominated by American and German manufacturers.

In November 1989, Nissan launched its new luxury Infiniti division with the $40,000 Q45 as its lead car and the $20,000 M30. However, Nissan was somewhat late: in August 1989, three months before Nissan shipped its first Infiniti, Toyota had introduced Lexus, its luxury brand, with a two-car line comprising the $40,000 LS400 and the entry-level LS250.

As the figures for January to September 1990 showed, Lexus outsold Infiniti by 50,000 to 15,000. The reasons for Infiniti's slow start were threefold:

- First, the Infiniti Q45 came to the market after the Lexus LS400 had established a good market position.
- Second, Lexus had two very good cars, whereas Infiniti's M30 coupe received poor evaluations from the automobile press and from customers.
- Finally, the eccentric Infiniti advertising campaign that showed scenes of nature, but not the car itself, shared some of the blame. ("Infiniti may not be doing so well, but, hey, at least sales of rocks and trees are skyrocketing," commented comedian Jay Leno.)

RESEARCH DATA

Exhibits 1–4 summarize some of the data that Infiniti had in early 1990. Data in Exhibits 1 and 2 are based on a survey of customers from its target segments, described as people between 25 and 35 with annual household incomes between $50,000 and $100,000 (when the survey was administered, the Lexus LS250 was not yet well known to the respondents to be included in the study). The three subsegments in Exhibit 1 (denoted S1, S2, and S3) are based on information provided by Infiniti managers. Exhibit 3 is derived from sales brochures describing the characteristics of each car. Exhibit 4 summarizes demographic and psychographic information about the three subsegments and was compiled from databases supplied by Claritas, Inc.

---

1. This case was developed by Katrin Starke and Arvind Rangaswamy and describes a real situation using hypothetical data.

	G20	Ford T-bird	Audi 90	Toyota Supra	Eagle Talon	Honda Prelude	Saab 900	Pontiac Firebird	BMW 318i	Mercury Capri
Attractive	5.6	4.0	4.6	5.6	4.0	5.2	5.3	3.9	5.7	3.9
Quiet	6.3	3.6	5.2	4.2	3.5	5.4	4.8	2.8	5.0	3.3
Unreliable	2.9	4.2	3.7	2.0	4.3	3.2	3.7	3.9	2.3	4.0
Poorly Built	1.6	4.2	2.6	2.1	4.3	2.8	2.8	4.4	1.8	4.3
Interesting	3.6	5.0	4.0	4.3	3.9	3.4	3.4	5.4	3.3	3.9
Sporty	4.1	4.9	3.8	6.2	4.9	5.1	4.3	5.7	4.1	5.2
Uncomfortable	2.4	4.0	2.4	3.7	4.0	3.3	2.8	4.3	3.5	4.4
Roomy	5.6	3.9	5.3	3.5	3.6	3.9	5.1	3.3	4.3	3.6
Easy to Service	4.6	4.9	3.5	4.9	4.6	5.0	3.8	4.7	4.1	4.6
High Prestige	5.4	3.5	5.6	5.3	2.8	4.7	5.7	3.8	6.4	3.3
Common	3.5	3.6	3.4	2.9	4.3	3.9	1.9	4.3	2.8	3.9
Economical	3.6	3.7	3.6	3.2	4.9	5.0	4.3	3.1	4.3	4.6
Successful	5.3	4.2	5.0	5.5	3.7	5.6	5.3	4.4	5.9	3.9
Avant-garde	4.3	3.6	3.6	4.9	4.4	3.9	4.7	4.1	3.7	4.5
Poor Value	3.4	4.3	4.3	3.5	3.6	2.6	2.9	4.3	3.3	3.8
Preferences										
Overall	6.3	3.9	6.0	5.5	4.0	6.5	6.8	3.0	6.7	4.0
Segment I (S1)	4.3	2.1	6.0	6.1	3.3	6.0	7.5	1.2	8.3	1.7
Segment II (S2)	5.9	6.0	7.7	3.5	3.1	5.5	5.4	2.5	5.4	5.8
Segment III (S3)	8.4	2.1	3.4	8.1	5.8	8.3	8.4	5.3	7.3	3.4

EXHIBIT 1
Survey results with average perception and average preference ratings on a scale from 1 to 9 (G20.DAT).

	G20	Ford T-bird	Audi 90	Toyota Supra	Eagle Talon	Honda Prelude	Saab 900	Pontiac Firebird	BMW 318i	Mercury Capri
1	4.0	7.0	8.0	3.0	4.0	5.0	5.0	1.0	4.0	5.0
2	4.0	8.0	6.0	5.0	8.0	7.0	3.0	1.0	5.0	2.0
3	8.0	5.0	9.0	4.0	1.0	7.0	7.0	2.0	4.0	4.0
4	7.0	1.0	8.0	1.0	4.0	6.0	5.0	5.0	7.0	3.0
5	8.0	8.0	8.0	3.0	5.0	4.0	3.0	2.0	8.0	6.0
6	5.0	6.0	5.0	5.0	2.0	4.0	8.0	4.0	4.0	7.0
7	3.0	9.0	7.0	4.0	4.0	3.0	6.0	4.0	3.0	6.0
8	4.0	7.0	9.0	3.0	1.0	7.0	9.0	3.0	6.0	6.0
9	8.0	6.0	6.0	4.0	5.0	5.0	1.0	2.0	8.0	7.0
10	6.0	4.0	6.0	3.0	2.0	8.0	7.0	3.0	1.0	8.0
11	8.0	6.0	8.0	4.0	6.0	8.0	7.0	1.0	2.0	7.0
12	8.0	5.0	6.0	6.0	2.0	3.0	8.0	1.0	6.0	6.0
13	4.0	2.0	9.0	4.0	1.0	5.0	5.0	4.0	8.0	5.0
14	5.0	5.0	8.0	5.0	6.0	4.0	6.0	1.0	3.0	7.0
15	6.0	5.0	9.0	1.0	3.0	6.0	8.0	3.0	6.0	3.0
16	6.0	3.0	9.0	2.0	7.0	8.0	6.0	3.0	7.0	3.0
17	8.0	5.0	8.0	1.0	1.0	8.0	9.0	2.0	5.0	4.0
18	5.0	9.0	7.0	5.0	2.0	4.0	7.0	5.0	6.0	1.0
19	6.0	7.0	9.0	6.0	2.0	6.0	3.0	5.0	4.0	5.0
20	6.0	9.0	8.0	2.0	3.0	8.0	6.0	1.0	7.0	5.0
21	7.0	7.0	9.0	4.0	1.0	3.0	4.0	1.0	4.0	3.0
22	6.0	9.0	6.0	2.0	3.0	4.0	6.0	1.0	6.0	3.0
23	5.0	4.0	8.0	4.0	1.0	4.0	1.0	1.0	8.0	5.0
24	7.0	4.0	8.0	3.0	2.0	3.0	4.0	6.0	9.0	5.0
25	4.0	9.0	7.0	3.0	1.0	7.0	2.0	1.0	5.0	7.0
26	8.0	2.0	1.0	9.0	4.0	8.0	8.0	5.0	8.0	4.0
27	8.0	6.0	5.0	8.0	4.0	8.0	7.0	7.0	5.0	1.0
28	9.0	1.0	2.0	4.0	9.0	9.0	9.0	4.0	8.0	3.0
29	9.0	2.0	4.0	8.0	7.0	8.0	9.0	8.0	5.0	6.0
30	8.0	3.0	4.0	8.0	7.0	6.0	6.0	4.0	5.0	1.0
31	8.0	3.0	2.0	9.0	5.0	8.0	9.0	5.0	7.0	5.0
32	5.0	1.0	2.0	7.0	5.0	9.0	9.0	7.0	8.0	6.0
33	9.0	1.0	4.0	9.0	6.0	9.0	9.0	5.0	9.0	2.0
34	8.0	2.0	6.0	8.0	7.0	9.0	8.0	5.0	9.0	5.0
35	9.0	1.0	7.0	9.0	5.0	7.0	6.0	6.0	4.0	1.0
36	8.0	1.0	4.0	9.0	6.0	8.0	8.0	3.0	7.0	4.0
37	9.0	2.0	3.0	9.0	5.0	8.0	9.0	7.0	9.0	6.0
38	8.0	2.0	3.0	6.0	5.0	9.0	9.0	3.0	9.0	6.0
39	9.0	2.0	4.0	9.0	7.0	8.0	7.0	7.0	9.0	1.0
40	8.0	3.0	2.0	7.0	5.0	8.0	9.0	5.0	6.0	1.0
41	9.0	3.0	4.0	8.0	8.0	9.0	6.0	2.0	9.0	6.0
42	8.0	3.0	2.0	8.0	6.0	8.0	9.0	4.0	7.0	2.0
43	9.0	2.0	1.0	8.0	6.0	7.0	9.0	5.0	9.0	5.0
44	9.0	2.0	3.0	9.0	7.0	8.0	9.0	7.0	5.0	4.0

EXHIBIT 2

Individual-level preference data, measured on a scale from 1 to 9, with higher numbers representing increased preference (GEOPREF.DAT).

	G20	Ford T-bird	Audi 90	Toyota Supra	Eagle Talon	Honda Prelude	Saab 900	Pontiac Firebird	BMW 318i	Mercury Capri
45	9.0	2.0	3.0	7.0	6.0	9.0	9.0	7.0	5.0	2.0
46	8.0	1.0	2.0	9.0	5.0	8.0	9.0	4.0	9.0	4.0
47	9.0	2.0	3.0	9.0	6.0	9.0	9.0	6.0	8.0	1.0
48	9.0	3.0	6.0	8.0	2.0	8.0	9.0	4.0	8.0	4.0
49	9.0	1.0	2.0	9.0	6.0	8.0	9.0	4.0	7.0	1.0
50	9.0	3.0	6.0	9.0	6.0	9.0	8.0	8.0	7.0	5.0
51	8.0	3.0	5.0	7.0	2.0	8.0	8.0	6.0	8.0	1.0
52	9.0	5.0	4.0	7.0	1.0	2.0	5.0	1.0	9.0	3.0
53	7.0	4.0	4.0	3.0	4.0	9.0	8.0	2.0	5.0	4.0
54	7.0	2.0	6.0	5.0	3.0	7.0	6.0	4.0	8.0	6.0
55	5.0	2.0	3.0	5.0	5.0	8.0	9.0	1.0	9.0	1.0
56	4.0	5.0	6.0	5.0	4.0	9.0	8.0	4.0	6.0	4.0
57	7.0	1.0	7.0	8.0	7.0	7.0	7.0	2.0	6.0	5.0
58	5.0	3.0	3.0	7.0	2.0	8.0	7.0	2.0	9.0	6.0
59	4.0	4.0	5.0	8.0	2.0	6.0	6.0	6.0	6.0	1.0
60	8.0	4.0	9.0	4.0	5.0	5.0	5.0	2.0	7.0	4.0
61	8.0	4.0	5.0	4.0	3.0	6.0	8.0	3.0	7.0	4.0
62	7.0	5.0	7.0	7.0	6.0	6.0	6.0	5.0	7.0	3.0
63	8.0	2.0	2.0	4.0	5.0	8.0	8.0	1.0	9.0	2.0
64	5.0	6.0	4.0	7.0	4.0	4.0	5.0	1.0	8.0	1.0
65	7.0	4.0	4.0	6.0	5.0	3.0	6.0	1.0	6.0	4.0
66	8.0	2.0	9.0	3.0	5.0	7.0	8.0	4.0	6.0	2.0
67	3.0	5.0	8.0	7.0	6.0	3.0	8.0	2.0	9.0	6.0
68	6.0	1.0	3.0	5.0	2.0	9.0	7.0	2.0	6.0	5.0
69	6.0	3.0	8.0	8.0	5.0	8.0	6.0	3.0	3.0	1.0
70	7.0	2.0	8.0	8.0	3.0	9.0	7.0	4.0	4.0	5.0
71	7.0	1.0	7.0	7.0	8.0	8.0	9.0	1.0	9.0	1.0
72	6.0	5.0	5.0	5.0	4.0	6.0	9.0	4.0	8.0	2.0
73	7.0	5.0	4.0	4.0	2.0	6.0	8.0	5.0	9.0	5.0
74	8.0	5.0	6.0	6.0	6.0	7.0	7.0	4.0	8.0	4.0
75	7.0	3.0	6.0	8.0	4.0	7.0	7.0	5.0	5.0	3.0

EXHIBIT 2 cont'd
Individual-level preference data, measured on a scale from 1 to 9, with higher numbers representing increased preference (GEOPREF.DAT).

	G20	Ford T-bird	Audi 90	Toyota Supra	Eagle Talon	Honda Prelude	Saab 900	Pontiac Firebird	BMW 318i	Mercury Capri
Base Price ($)	17,500	15,783	20,200	23,280	16,437	14,945	18,295	12,690	19,900	13,500
Length (Inches)	175	198.7	176	181.9	170.5	175.6	184.5	192.0	170.3	166.1
Width (Inches)	66.7	72.7	67.6	68.7	66.7	67.3	66.5	72.4	64.8	64.6
Height (Inches)	54.9	52.7	54.3	51.2	51.4	29.2	56.1	49.8	53.5	50.2
Curb Weight (lbs.)	2,535	3,600	3,170	3,535	3,100	2,740	2,825	3,485	2,600	2,487
Fuel Economy (Mpg)										
City	24	17	18	17	20	23	20	16	22	23
Highway	32	24	24	22	25	27	26	24	27	28
Horspower, SAE.net (Bhp)	140@ 6,400 rpm	210@ 4,000 rpm	164@ 6,000 rpm	232@ 5,600 rpm	195@ 6,000 rpm	135@ 6,200 rpm	140@ 6,000 rpm	240@ 4,400 rpm	134@ 6,000 rpm	132@ 6,000 rpm
Warranty, Years/Miles,	4/ 60,000	1/ 12,000	3/ 50,000	3/ 36,000	1/ 12,000	3/ 36,000	3/ 36,000	3/ 50,000	3/ 36,000	1/ 12,000

EXHIBIT 3
Some physical characteristics of the cars.

Segment Characteristics	Segment I (Western Yuppie, Single)	Segment II (Upwardly Mobile Families)	Segment III (American Dreamers)
Segment Size	(25%)	(45%)	(30%)
Education	College Grads	College Grads or Some College	College Grads or Some College
Predominant Employment	Professionals	White-Collar	White-Collar
Age Group	25–35	25–35	25–35
Predominant Ethnic Background	White	White	Mix (Asian, White)
Average Household Income	$81,000	$68,000	$59,000
Persons per Household	1.42	3.8	2.4
Percent Married	32%	75%	55%
Watch Late Night TV	27%	9%	17%
Watch Daytime TV	3%	45%	5%
Read Computer Magazines	39%	6%	10%
Read Business Magazines	58%	23%	27%
Read Entertainment Magazines	3%	14%	30%
Read Infant and Parenting Magazines	1%	17%	2%
Rent Movies	43%	85%	38%
Possess an American Express Card	48%	45%	75%
Own Investment Funds	24%	18%	47%
Go Fishing	2%	30%	3%
Sail, Scuba Dive, or Ski	49%	2%	20%

EXHIBIT 4
Data about the segments.

EXERCISES

1. Describe the two (or, if applicable, three) dimensions underlying the perceptual maps that you generated. Based on these maps, how do people in this market perceive the Infiniti G20 compared with its competitors?
2. Infiniti promoted the G20 as a Japanese car (basic version $17,500) with a German feel, basically a car that was like the BMW 318i ($20,000), but lower priced. Is this a credible claim, given the perceptions and preferences of the respondents?
3. Which attributes are most important in influencing preference for these cars in the three segments (S1, S2, and S3) shown on these maps? To which segment(s) would you market the Infiniti G20? How would you reposition the Infiniti G20 to best suit the chosen segment(s)? Briefly describe the marketing program you would use to target the chosen segment(s).
4. What ongoing research program would you recommend to Infiniti to improve its evaluation of its segmentation of the market and positioning of its G20?
5. Summarize the advantages and limitations of the software provided for this application.

CHAPTER **5**

Strategic Market Analysis: Conceptual Framework and Tools

In this chapter (and the next) we develop concepts and tools that we can apply when deploying marketing effort in the long term to different markets and for different products. The topics we cover in this chapter are

■ Strategic marketing decision making, the process and steps that firms use to develop marketing programs
■ Market demand and trend analysis, the methods and tools firms use to assess the current and future size of a market
■ The product life cycle, the long-term evolution of a market
■ Cost dynamics, how costs vary with scale of production and production experience

While we will discuss the use of these concepts and tools in more detail in the next chapter, we discuss the conceptual foundations here.

STRATEGIC MARKETING DECISION MAKING

In a large organization with several business divisions and several product lines within each division, marketing plays a role at each level. At the organizational level, marketing contributes perspectives and demand estimates to help top management decide on the corporation's mission, opportunities, growth strategy, and product portfolio. Corporate strategies provide the context in which division managers formulate strategy in each of the business divisions. Finally, the managers of each product or market within each division develop their marketing strategies within the context of the policies and constraints developed at the divisional and corporate levels.

Most firms have a corporate mission statement, and a related set of objectives, and they define their corporate strategies and related marketing strategies with respect to that mission statement and set of objectives.

The *corporate mission* is the firm's statement of the scope of its activities. For example, Xerox Corporation's mission statement could define whether it is in the business of manufacturing copiers, improving business productivity for its customers, or providing automated office systems or some combination thereof. The actual mission statement for Xerox in 2001 is to be the leader in the global document business, providing document solutions (hardware, software, and services) that enhance business productivity and knowledge sharing.

The firm must translate its mission into a set of directly measurable objectives to make that mission operational. Those objectives normally concern all the firm's divisions. The firm's financial objectives may stress profitability, its accounting objectives may stress cost, its marketing objectives may focus on sales and creativity, and its engineering objectives may stress efficiency. To be useful guidelines for action, these objectives must be stated precisely and they must be easy to understand.

Some examples of objectives are

- To achieve a 15 percent average growth in sales over the next five years (marketing)
- To achieve a growth in after-tax return on investment of 8 percent for the next three years (finance)
- To reduce the costs of manufacturing and allocated overhead per unit of output by 3 percent per year over the next three years (accounting/manufacturing)
- To reduce the rate of product returns by 20 percent within the next three years (engineering/manufacturing)
- To increase customer satisfaction ratings by 30 percent within two years (marketing, service, manufacturing, operations)

As these examples show, achieving objectives requires the close cooperation of several areas of the firm.

In its *corporate strategy*, then, the firm sets forth the actions it intends to undertake to secure a sustainable (long-term) advantage while meeting its corporate objectives. Firms usually state their strategies in terms of what products they plan to offer to what markets or market segments using what technologies. In formulating its strategy, the firm defines the areas it is targeting for growth, the level and focus of its R&D effort, and how it intends to commit its resources over the long term to meet its corporate objectives. The firm's strategy will include the details about product innovation, markets to serve, personnel, R&D, and corporate image. For example, IBM might decide to serve business and home users with its personal computers, and McDonald's might decide to enhance its corporate image as the preeminent family restaurant chain.

Marketing objectives follow from the corporate strategy. Firms usually state their marketing objectives in terms of expectations for market share, sales, or profits over a period of time. Finally, the firm develops marketing strategies to specify how it will achieve its marketing objectives. In this chapter and the next we focus on the key factors that influence firms in formulating these marketing strategies.

Wind and Robertson (1983) have developed a useful framework for structuring the marketing elements that firms consider in developing their strategies (Exhibit 5.1). The framework has three main sections:

Section I: A traditional assessment of market opportunities and business strengths:
          a. An analysis of opportunities and threats in the market and environment
          b. An analysis of business strengths and weaknesses

Section II: The marketing strategy core:
          c. Segmentation and positioning analysis (identifying market segments and the benefits they seek)

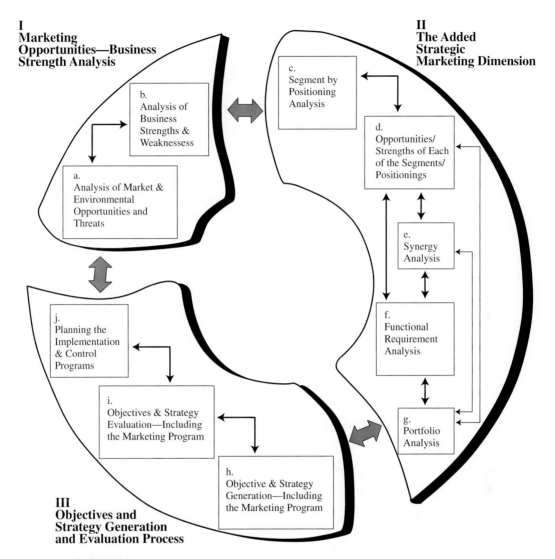

I
Marketing
Opportunities—Business
Strength Analysis

II
The Added
Strategic
Marketing Dimension

c.
Segment by
Positioning
Analysis

b.
Analysis of
Business
Strengths &
Weaknessess

d.
Opportunities/
Strengths of Each
of the Segments/
Positionings

a.
Analysis of Market &
Environmental
Opportunities and
Threats

e.
Synergy
Analysis

j.
Planning the
Implementation
& Control
Programs

f.
Functional
Requirement
Analysis

i.
Objectives & Strategy
Evaluation—Including
the Marketing Program

g.
Portfolio
Analysis

h.
Objective & Strategy
Generation—Including
the Marketing Program

III
Objectives and
Strategy Generation
and Evaluation Process

EXHIBIT 5.1
A marketing-oriented approach to strategy formulation and evaluation. *Source*: Wind and
Robertson 1983, p. 16.

    d. Opportunity analysis (linking the benefits the segments seek with business
       strengths and weaknesses)

    e. Synergy analysis (the positive and negative synergies in advertising, dis-
       tribution, manufacturing, etc., among products, segments, and marketing-
       mix components)

    f. Functional requirement analysis (specification of what products, services,
       and support each segment requires and the company's ability to satisfy
       those requirements)

    g. Portfolio analysis, the analytical core of the process (an integrated view of
       the strategic process, both for existing and new business)

Section III: The objective and strategy generation and evaluation process:

    h. Generation of objectives and strategies

Limitation of Typical Marketing Strategy (Wind & Robertson 1983)	The Marketing Engineering Solution
1. Improper analytic focus	Market definition and understanding of market structure
2. Functional isolation	Integration, especially models of cost dynamics (scale and experience effects), linking production, supply chain values and marketing
3. Ignoring synergy	Marketing-mix/product-line methods
4. Short-run analysis	Dynamic models, especially product life-cycle analysis models
5. Ignoring competition	Competitive-analysis models
6. Ignoring interactions	Proper market-definition models
7. Lack of an integrated view	Integrated models including shared-experience models such as PIMS, product-portfolio models and normative resource-allocation models

EXHIBIT 5.2
Seven limitations of typical marketing strategy and the type of market strategy models that can be used to address these limitations.

    i. Evaluation of objectives and strategies
    j. Implementation, monitoring, and control of the program

Wind and Robertson claim that this framework helps firms to overcome seven important limitations of marketing analysis (Exhibit 5.2); the analytic model-based approaches can be used to address those limitations.

Improper analytic focus: In Chapter 3 we argue that customer needs and values, rather than the physical characteristics of products, define a market. We can use the methods for defining a market described in Chapter 3 in any program to develop a marketing strategy. The size, growth, and development of the market are necessary inputs in developing a strategic process. In addition, we must understand key forecasting issues.

Functional isolation: Analyzing functional requirements is integral to the process of formulating and evaluating a strategy (Exhibit 5.1). Marketing strategy is intimately linked to research and development activities, financial issues, logistics, and manufacturing. In this chapter we will address one aspect of the integration of functions with respect to cost dynamics; in Chapter 7 we describe new product development methods, and in Chapter 9 we deal with several related logistical challenges such as location analysis.

Ignoring synergy: In Chapter 2 we sketched out how response models could accommodate the effect of multiple marketing-mix elements.

Short-run analysis: Most short-run analyses ignore dynamic effects. We will focus on market dynamics at several points in the book, particularly with the ADBUDG model (Chapter 8) and the Bass diffusion model (Chapter 7); in this chapter we explore the factors that underlie the product life cycle.

Ignoring competition: In today's saturated markets, many companies gain sales only at the expense of others; hence a focus on competition is central to the development of sound marketing strategy. In Chapters 2, 6, and 10 we describe models that incorporate the effect of competition.

Ignoring interactions: A major weakness of many market strategy studies is their lack of attention to interactions between products and across market segments. In Chapter 3 we discuss how to define markets properly, which can lessen this problem: In well-defined markets competition occurs within market boundaries but there is little competition across the defined boundaries. In Chapter 9 our resource allocation model permits response-function interactions between products and segments.

Lack of an integrated view: The models we describe in Chapter 6 incorporate an integrated view of strategic marketing.

The marketing strategy component of Exhibit 5.1 has as part of its foundation the size and growth of the market or markets that the firm currently serves or is planning to serve in the future. We discuss the critical issue of analyzing market demand and trends next.

MARKET DEMAND AND TREND ANALYSIS[1]

Defining a market is critical to developing any market-based model. Marketing strategy, with its focus on the long term, depends on defining the market and the market's evolution and dynamics. In this section we deal with assessing market demand and analyzing trends for products that have had some sales history or market experience; we deal with demand estimation for new products in Chapter 7.

In developing market forecasts one needs to carefully define the level of the market under study. We distinguish five levels here (although coarser or finer grain classifications are possible) and illustrate them using Budweiser beer as an example:

The *potential market* is the set of all customers who show interest in a product or service; survey methods can be used to determine its size.

The *available market* is the set of all customers who not only have interest in but sufficient income and access to the product or service. We can determine the available market by linking the potential market to demographic and distribution data.

The *qualified available market* is the set of customers who pass the availability screen and who are qualified to buy. For example, for beer the qualified market might be that part of the available market that is over 21 years old, that is, legal drinkers.

The *served or target market* is the part of the qualified market that the company decides to pursue. Budweiser may decide that (for analysis purposes) the Southeast and Midwest regions constitute its target market.

The *penetrated market* is the set of all customers who have already bought the product or service. For the beer example the penetrated market is all buyers of all brands of beer in the served markets.

---

1. This section draws on a note by Venkatesh Shanker.

Predicting the course of a company's or an industry's market sales is essential if a company is to plan and control its business operations. As markets fluctuate and become more unstable, it becomes an increasingly critical task for marketing management. Without some form of sales projection, firms would have no reasonable starting point for making strategic marketing decisions.

Vital as they are, forecasts are estimates at best. Some firms do better jobs than others, but no one has come up with a perfect method; many companies are beginning to rely on several independent forecasting methods (Exhibit 5.3), hoping to converge on a reliable approach.

Prominent forecasting techniques include judgmental methods, market and survey analyses, time-series analyses, and causal analyses (Exhibit 5.3).

Judgmental methods

There are three main judgmental methods of market forecasting—through salesforce-composite estimates, using a jury of executive opinion, and Delphi and related methods:

Salesforce-composite estimates: Many company managers turn to members of the salesforce for help when assembling clues about future sales. However, few use their estimates without some adjustments. In the first place, sales representatives are biased observers. They may be characteristically pessimistic (if their quotas are related to their forecasts) or optimistic (if they want to expand their set of accounts), or they may go from one extreme to the other because of a recent sales setback or success (recency bias).

If these biasing tendencies can be countered, sales representatives often have more knowledge of or better insight into developing trends than any other single group. They are often especially knowledgeable when the product is fairly technical and subject to a changing technology. And when they participate in the forecasting process, the sales representatives may have greater confidence in the derived sales quotas, and this confidence may increase their incentive to achieve those quotas.

Jury of executive opinion: A common judgmental approach is to combine the views of key stakeholders in hopes of gaining a sounder forecast than might be made by a single estimator. Those stakeholders may be company executives but may also include dealers, distributors, suppliers, marketing consultants, and professional associations.

The main problems with using juries of executives are (1) a tendency to give too much weight to their opinions, (2) the need to infringe on executives' time, and (3) deciding how to weight the individual forecasts to get a consensus (Chase Econometrics, Data Resources, and Wharton Econometrics are secondary sources that provide expert opinion data). Armstrong (1985) provides some useful guidelines on how to address these problems.

Delphi and related methods: In gathering informed opinion, a number of companies are relying on the Delphi method for forecasting, especially for medium- or long-term fore-

Judgmental	Market and Survey Analysis	Time Series	Causal or Correlational Analyses
Salesforce composite	Buyer intentions	Naive methods	Regression analysis
Jury of executive opinion	Product tests	Moving averages	Econometric models
		Exponential smoothing	Input-output analysis
Delphi methods		Box-Jenkins method	MARMA

EXHIBIT 5.3
A classification of market forecasting approaches.

casting. Developed by the RAND corporation in the 1950s, the Delphi method has three key features: (1) anonymous response, in which the study director uses formal methods to obtain anonymous opinions and assessments; (2) interaction and controlled feedback, in which the director organizes interaction through a multiround process with controlled feedback between rounds; and (3) statistical group response, where group opinion is the aggregate of individual opinions in the final round. These features mitigate the effects of dominant individuals, irrelevant comments, and group pressure toward conformity.

Several experiments have shown that the Delphi method does indeed perform rather well (Jolson and Rossow 1971, and Martino 1983). Larréché and Montgomery (1977) use the Delphi method to determine the likelihood that marketing managers will use a number of well-known marketing models. Delphi methods are becoming more popular with the development of "groupware" products like Lotus Notes that can facilitate the process. RAND originally developed the Delphi method to forecast which cities in the United States Russia would attack in a nuclear war—a situation in which there was no objective basis for forecasting.

EXAMPLE

The University of Michigan's Office for the Study of Automotive Transportation conducted a Delphi study with 300 auto industry executives to forecast the sales of electric vehicles 10 years into the future. The surprising result: The consensus favors hybrid (electric-combustion engines), and if the estimates are realized we should see roughly 150,000 hybrid-drive vehicles on the road in 2003 (Thomas and Keebler 1994).

Market and product analysis

Buying intentions: Marketing forecasting is the art and science of anticipating what buyers are likely to do under a given set of conditions. This definition immediately suggests that a most useful source of information would be the buyers themselves. Ideally the firm draws up a probability sample of potential buyers and asks each buyer how much of a product he or she will buy in a given future time period under stated conditions. It also asks buyers to state what proportion of their total projected purchases they will buy from a particular firm or at least what factors would influence their choice of supplier. With this information the firm seems to have an ideal basis for forecasting its sales.

Unfortunately, this method has a number of limitations in practice, the most important of which are (1) the relationship between stated intentions and actual behavior and (2) potential nonresponse bias. (The second problem is particularly critical in industrial markets composed of few buyers.) The value of this method then depends on the extent to which the buyers have clearly formulated intentions and then carry them out. (Haley and Case [1979] and Morrison [1979] discuss the related merits of using stated intentions versus actual behavior.)

Secondary source surveys about buyer intentions are available for both consumer and industrial products. Two indices provide data related to consumer durable purchases and contain information about consumers' present and anticipated future financial positions and their expectations about the economy: the "Consumer Sentiment Measure" from the Survey Research Center at the University of Michigan and the "Consumer Confidence Measure" from Sindlinger and Company. For industrial products the best-known surveys are published by the U.S. Department of Commerce, the Opinion Research Corporation, and McGraw-Hill. Most of their estimates have been within 10 percent of the actual outcomes.

Market tests: The usefulness of opinions, whether those of buyers, sales representatives, or other experts, depends on their cost, availability, and reliability. When buyers typically do not plan their purchases carefully or are very erratic in carrying out their intentions or when experts are not very good guessers, firms need a more direct market test of likely behavior. Unlike forecasts based on buying intentions, which rely on *what people say*, forecasts based on market tests rely on *what people do*. A direct market test is especially desirable for forecasting the sales of a new product or the likely sales of an established product in a new distribution channel or a new territory. When a firm wants a short-run forecast of likely buyer response, a small-scale market test is usually a good solution. (We describe this approach in more detail in Chapter 7.)

Time-series methods

As an alternative (or complement) to surveys, opinion studies, and market tests, many firms prepare forecasts based on statistical analysis of past data (past data arranged in temporal order are referred to as a *time series*). The logic of this approach is that past data incorporate enduring causal relationships that will carry forward into the future and that can be uncovered through quantitative analysis. Thus the forecasting task becomes, in essence, a careful study of the past plus an assumption that the same relationships will hold in the future.

There are a number of time-series analysis and forecasting methods, differing mainly in the way past observations are related to the forecast values.

Naive methods: The simplest time-series forecasting procedure is to use the most recently observed value as a forecast: a naive forecast is equivalent to giving a weight of one to the most recent observation and zero to all other observations. Other naive methods may modify this procedure by adjusting for seasonal fluctuations. These methods are used mainly as a basis for comparing alternative forecasting approaches.

Slightly more sophisticated methods include the following:

- Freehand projection, which is a visual exploration of a plot of time-series observations. This method has the advantage of delivering a forecast quickly and cheaply, and it is easy to understand. However, it is of low accuracy, especially for nonlinear series, and two people may make very different projections.
- Semiaverage projection, in which the analyst divides a time series in half, calculates averages for each half, and draws a line connecting the average points, which the analyst projects to produce a forecast. This method has the same advantages and disadvantages as freehand projection.

Smoothing techniques: The notion underlying smoothing methods is that there is some pattern in the values of the variables to be forecast, which is represented in past observations, along with random fluctuations or noise. Using smoothing methods, the analyst tries to distinguish the underlying pattern from the random fluctuations by eliminating the latter.

One way to lessen the impact of randomness in individual short-range forecasts is to average several of the past values. The *moving-average* approach is one of the simplest procedures for doing so. It weights the past N observations with the value $1/N$, where N is specified by the analyst and remains constant. The larger N is, the greater will be the smoothing effect on the forecast. If a year's worth of monthly data were available, the moving-average method would forecast the next period as 1/12 of the total for the past year. When new data become available, they are used, with the newest observation replacing the oldest. In this sense the average is moving. Typically the method of moving averages is used for forecasting only one period in advance. It does not adapt easily to pattern changes in the data.

Formally, for simple moving averages let

S_t = forecast at time t,

X_t = actual value at time t, and

N = number of values included in average.

Then forecasting with moving averages can be represented as

$$S_{t+1} = \frac{1}{N} \sum_{i=t-N+1}^{t} X_i = \frac{X_t - X_{t-N}}{N} + S_t. \tag{5.1}$$

This equation makes it clear that the new forecast S_{t+1} is a function of the preceding moving-average forecast S_t. Furthermore, if X_t corresponds to a change (e.g., step change) in the basic pattern of variable X, it is difficult for the method to account for that change. Note also that the larger N is, the smaller $(X_t - X_{t-N})/N$ will be and the greater the smoothing effect will be.

Advantages of this technique are that a forecast can be produced in little time, at low cost, and with little technical knowledge. Low accuracy and an arbitrary choice of the number of observations in calculating forecasts are among its disadvantages. Furthermore, simple moving averages are not very effective in the presence of complex data patterns, such as trend, seasonal, and cyclical patterns.

Using another procedure, the *double moving average*, one starts by computing a set of single moving averages and then computes another moving average based on the values of the first.

With a trend, a single or double moving average lags the actual series. Also, the double moving average is always below the simple moving average. Thus it is possible to forecast by taking the difference between the single moving average and the double moving average and adding it back to the single moving average. This forecasting technique is called the *double moving averages with trend adjustments*.

The *exponential-smoothing* approach is very similar to the moving-average method, differing in that the weights given to past observations are not constant—they decline exponentially so that more recent observations get more weight than earlier values. Choice of the smoothing factor is left to the analyst. Most often the analyst selects a value experimentally from a set of two or three different trial values. As with moving-average methods, exponential smoothing has limitations when basic changes are expected in the data pattern. These methods cover a variety of procedures, some of which make adjustments for trends and for seasonality. In essence most adjust the data in some way before applying an exponential-smoothing procedure.

With the foregoing notation, the procedure can be represented by

$$S_{t+1} = \alpha X_t + (1 - \alpha)S_t, \tag{5.2}$$

where $0 \leq \alpha \leq 1$ is selected empirically by the analyst. A high value of α gives past forecasts and past data (included in S_t) little weight, whereas a low value of α weights the most recent period very lightly compared with all other past observations.

The method of *double exponential smoothing* is analogous to that of double moving averages, and easily adapts to changes in patterns, such as step changes.

Smoothing methods are based on the idea that a forecast can be made by using a weighted sum of past observations. In the case of simple moving averages, the individual weights are $1/N$. For exponential smoothing, the analyst has to postulate the declining weighting factor. *Adaptive filtering* is another approach for determining the most appropriate set of weights. It is based on an iterative process that determines weights that minimize forecasting error.

Specifically, all the methods outlined so far are based on the idea that a forecast can be made as a weighted sum of past observations:

$$S_{t+1} = \sum_{i=t-N+1}^{t} W_i X_i, \tag{5.3}$$

where

S_{t+1} = forecast for period $t + 1$;

W_i = weight assigned to observation i;

X_i = observed value at i, as before; and

N = number of observations used in computing S_{t+1} (and so the number of weights required).

Adaptive filtering attempts to determine a best set of weights. The usual criterion is that the weights should minimize the average mean-squared forecasting error.

The *Box-Jenkins (ARMA)* method is a philosophy for approaching forecasting problems. It is the most general of the short-term forecasting techniques and one of the most powerful available today. Using it an analyst can develop an adequate model for almost any pattern of data. However, it is sufficiently complex that its users must have a certain amount of expertise.

Box and Jenkins propose three general classes of models for describing any type of stationary process (processes that remain in equilibrium about a constant mean level): (1) autoregressive (AR), (2) moving average (MA), and (3) mixed autoregressive and moving average (ARMA).

If a series is increasing or decreasing with time, we can remove this (trend) by taking differences,

$$\Delta Y_t = Y_t - Y_{t-1}, \tag{5.4}$$

and then developing an ARMA model for ΔY_t. The original series Y_t can be recovered by successively adding in the ΔY_t, starting at Y_0. If the trend is nonlinear, several successive differences (d) may be required to produce a stationary ARMA series. (Recall that if you differentiate $Y = X^2$ twice—d^2Y/dX^2—you get a constant, 2. The differencing operation here is analogous and produces the same result.) Again, the original series can be recovered by summing d times. Such a series is called an integrated ARMA series, denoted as ARIMA (p, d, q), where p is the order (number of periods used) of the AR part, q is the order of the MA part, and d is the level of difference used to produce stationarity. Multivariate extensions of the ARMA models, known as multivariate ARMA, or MARMA, have been developed. They combine powerful time-series forecasting techniques with explanatory variables and causal models (Hanssens, Parsons, and Schultz 1990). Applying the ARMA and MARMA methods requires more technical expertise and experience than many of the other methods we describe.

EXAMPLE

Exhibit 5.4 shows how some of these forecasting methods perform on data drawn from the National Bureau of Economic Research. Using the mean-

Year	Q1*	Q2	Q3	Q4
1969	11,445	11,573	11,516	11,990
1970	11,704	11,050	11,069	10,705
1971	10,729	10,931	11,832	12,172
1972	12,472	12,840	12,865	13,491
1973	14,324	14,684	14,689	15,473
1974	16,483	16,634	17,245	17,177
1975	16,230	16,562	17,614	18,318
1976	19,148	19,730	19,184	19,424
1977	20,774	21,184	21,052	22,121

* Q1 = quarter 1, and so on.

(a)

1978	(1) Actual	(2) Naive	(3) Averaged on Four Previous Quarters, Moving Average	(4) Moving Average with Trend Adjustment
Q1	22,433	22,121	21,283	22,666
Q2	23,792	22,433	21,698	23,219
Q3	23,980	23,792	22,350	23,772
Q4	25,840	23,980	23,082	24,325
MAPE*	3.78	3.78	7.85	2.53

Exponential Smoothing

1978	(5) $\rho = 0.90$	(6) $\rho = 0.50$	(7) Optimal Box-Jenkins
Q1	22,014	21,397	23,168
Q2	22,391	21,915	23,509
Q3	23,652	22,853	24,133
Q4	23,947	23,416	25,141
MAPE*	4.10	6.65	1.95

*MAPE = mean-absolute-percent error $= \frac{1}{n} \Sigma \, (|\text{actual} - \text{forecast}| \, / \, \text{actual}) \times 100$.

(b)

EXHIBIT 5.4
A comparison of the forecasting accuracy of six forecasting methods; (a) gives actual data for fabricated metal products while (b), columns (2) through (7), gives the forecasting accuracy of six methods. *Source*: National Bureau of Economic Research Series MDCSMS.

absolute-percent error (MAPE) as the measure of forecasting ability, Box-Jenkins does best in this case. However, the naive method is the third best out of the six methods, suggesting that more sophisticated methods do not always perform better than simple ones. (Note that moving-average and exponential-smoothing methods are available through Excel's "analysis tools" add-in.)

Decompositional methods: The forecasting methods described thus far are based on the idea that we can distinguish an underlying pattern in a data series from noise by smoothing (averaging) past values. The smoothing eliminates noise so that we can project the pattern into the future and use it as a forecast. These methods make no attempt to identify individual components of the basic underlying pattern. However, in many cases we can break the pattern down (decompose it) into subpatterns that identify each component of the series separately. With such a breakdown we can frequently improve accuracy in forecasting and better understand the series.

Decompositional methods assume that all series are made up of patterns plus error. The objective is to decompose the pattern of the series into trend, cycle, and seasonality:

$$X_t = f(I_t, T_t, C_t, E_t), \tag{5.5}$$

where

X_t = time series at time t;

I_t = seasonal component (or index) at t;

T_t = trend component at t;

C_t = cyclical component at t; and

E_t = error or random component at t.

The exact functional form of Eq. (5.5) depends on the decompositional method used. The most common form is a multiplicative model:

$$X_t = I_t \times T_t \times C_t \times E_t. \tag{5.6}$$

An additive form is used often, as well.

Although there are a number of decompositional methods, they all seem to follow the same basic process:

1. For the series X_t compute a moving average of length N, where N is the length of the seasonality (e.g., $N = 12$ with monthly data). This averaging will eliminate seasonality by averaging seasonally high periods with seasonally low periods; and because random errors have no systematic pattern, it reduces randomness as well.
2. Separate the outcome of the N-period moving average from the original data period to obtain trend and cyclicality. If the model is multiplicative, you do this by dividing the original series by the smoothed series, leaving seasonality and error:

$$\frac{X_1}{T_t + C_t} (= \text{moving average}) = I_t \times E_t. \tag{5.7}$$

3. Isolate the seasonal factors by averaging them for each data point in a season over the complete length of the series.
4. Specify the appropriate form of the trend (linear, quadratic, exponential) and calculate its value at each period T_t. You can do this by using regression analysis or moving averages with trend adjustments.
5. Use the results to separate out the cycle from the trend + cycle (i.e., the moving average).
6. When you have separated the seasonality, trend, and cyclicality from the original data series, you can identify the remaining randomness, E_t.

Decompositional methods are widely used and have been developed empirically and tested on thousands of series. Although they do not have a sound statistical base, the methods are intuitive and geared to the practitioner and, therefore, the opposite of such procedures as the Box-Jenkins approach, which is derived from theory. Decompositional methods appear to be most appropriate for short- or medium-term forecasting and are mainly suited to macroeconomic series.

Causal methods

The models we have described assume that little is known about the underlying cause of demand and that the future will be pretty much like the past. For these reasons, these time-series methods are most useful for short- or medium-term extrapolations (usually less than a year in the future).

An alternative approach, especially useful when market conditions are not inherently stable, is to express demand as a function of a certain number of factors that determine its outcome. Such forecasts are not necessarily time dependent, which makes them useful for longer-term predictions. In addition, developing an explanatory or causal model facilitates a better understanding of the situation.

Regression and econometric models typically specify the structure of the relationship between demand and its underlying causes.

EXAMPLE

In industrial markets, firms often want to relate product-demand needs to published data for those Standard Industrial Classification (SIC) codes they think have high potential. In these analyses, they often use the number of employees as the most readily available surrogate for customer size.

Customer Number	No. of Employees	Sales in $1000s*
1	110	9.8
2	141	21.2
3	204	14.7
4	377	22.8
5	395	48.1
6	502	42.3
7	612	27.8
8	618	40.7
9	707	59.8
10	721	44.5
11	736	77.1
12	856	59.2
13	902	52.3
14	926	77.1
15	1045	74.6
16	1105	81.8
17	1250	69.7

Total = 823.0

*Regression of sales versus employees gives
sales = $8.52 + 0.61 \times$ no. of employees, $R^2 = 0.77$.

EXHIBIT 5.5
Data on Machinco's customers, their number of employees and current sale level, providing input for a regression model of demand. *Source:* Lilien and Kotler 1983, p. 342.

The Machinco Company makes high-technology components and currently has 17 customers. Exhibit 5.5 shows the number of employees for each customer and the volume of purchases from Machinco.

If we use number of employees as a rough predictor of sales potential, we might relate sales to the number of employees via a linear equation:

$$\text{Sales} = a_0 + a_1(\text{number of employees}). \tag{5.8}$$

Through linear regression, we find that $a_0 = 8.52$ and $a_1 = 0.061$. The U.S. Census of Manufacturers reports that the organizations that are prospective customers for Machinco's product have a total of 126,000 employees. With this information and Eq. (5.8), we find

$$\text{(Potential) sales} = 8.52 + (0.061 \times 126,000) = 7695. \tag{5.9}$$

This value is nearly 10 times the current sales of Machinco (823), which indicates that Machinco could greatly expand its sales to other prospects.

Suppose that the company has two prospects. Company A has 1,600 employees, and company B has 500 employees. A good guess for the sales potential for company A is $8.52 + (0.061 \times 1600)$, or 106 units. Similarly we get 39 units as the potential for company B. (A regression tool is one of Excel's "analysis tool" add-ins.)

Input-output analysis, more widely used in the 1960s and 1970s than today, views the economy as an interrelated system. The input-output principle is the conservation of mass. Everything that is produced has to go somewhere, and when demand for finished products increases, this drives demand for other intermediate (industrial) products.

In a complex and diversified economy, direct consumer sales frequently represent only a portion of the output of a given industry. The rest of its output consists of intermediate products used by its purchasers as input into other production processes. Final demand is that part of the output of an industry that is not sold to another industry but rather is sold to domestic consumers or the government, is exported, or is put into inventory. The sum of final demand in a national input-output table is the gross national product.

Thus we can develop a series of accounting equations:

$$\text{Output of any industry} = \text{Sales to intermediate users} + \text{Final demand}. \tag{5.10}$$

Outputs

	— Processing Sector —		Final Demand	
Inputs	**Agriculture**	**Manufacturing**	**(Consumers)**	**Output Total**
Agriculture	50	40	110	200 stacks of flour
Manufacturing	28	12	60	100 bars of soap
Consumers	160	360	80	600 hours

EXHIBIT 5.6
Example of transactions matrix for input-output analysis.

EXAMPLE

A system of equations like (5.10), one for each industry, is called a transactions matrix. To explain it, we will use an example of a simple economy with three sectors: agriculture, manufacturing, and consumers (Exhibit 5.6).

The agricultural sector produces 200 sacks of flour, the manufacturing sector produces 100 bars of soap, and consumers provide 600 hours of labor. Exhibit 5.6 shows the intersectoral flows. For example, agriculture turned out 200 sacks of flour but used up 50 in the process and sent 40 to the soap manufacturers; the consumers got the rest. Manufacturing sent 28 bars of soap to agriculture, used 12 itself, and sent the remaining 60 bars to consumers.

Each column represents the input structure of the sector. To produce 200 sacks of flour, the farmers needed to consume 50 sacks, to use 28 bars of soap, and to absorb 160 hours of labor. Manufacturing needed 40 sacks of flour, 12 bars of its own soap, and 360 hours of labor to produce 100 bars of soap. And consumers spent the incomes that they received for supplying 600 hours of labor on 110 sacks of flour, 60 bars of soap, and 80 hours of direct services of labor.

To be useful, an input-output table must have many more entries. In practice the intersectoral flows are generally represented in a common unit (dollars) for convenience.

If we now take the output of sector i as absorbed by sector j per unit of total output, we get the input coefficient of a product of sector i into sector j. Mathematically we get

$$a_{ij} = \frac{x_{ij}}{X_j},$$ (5.11)

where

a_{ij} = input coefficient from industry i to industry j;

x_{ij} = sales of industry i to industry j; and

X_j = total sales of industry j.

A complete set of input coefficients for all sectors of a given economy—arranged in the same way as the transactions matrix—is the structural matrix of an economy. Exhibit 5.7 shows the structural matrix of our three-sector economy with a sack of flour = $2, a bar of soap = $5, and an hour of labor = $1.

	To		
From	Agriculture	Manufacturing	Consumers
Agriculture	0.25	0.16	0.37
Manufacturing	0.35	0.12	0.50
Consumers	0.40	0.72	0.13
	1.00	1.00	1.00

EXHIBIT 5.7
Structural matrix for input-output analysis, showing the proportion of each input needed for a unit of output.

To interpret this table, we note that an input coefficient measures the input required from one industry to produce $1 of output in another industry. For example, for every dollar of output in manufacturing, we need $.16 from agriculture, $.12 from manufacturing itself, and $.72 from consumers (labor).

Practically, input-output forecasts provide estimates of industrial growth, of the markets that account for that growth, and of the inputs the industry will require to achieve that growth. However, many firms are not in a single industry, and they must adapt the input-output analysis. One way to do this is to insert the product of an organization as a row in the available tables. Then the company can estimate sales to the various sectors specified in the input-output study and can calculate how much each industry requires from it per dollar of output. It adjusts the row coefficients suitably. The firm can enter itself as a column, and the new structure can be used to produce a forecast for an individual company or a product. Alternatively, the firm can expand the input-output matrix by making a detailed analysis of its target markets and inserting them as sectors in the economy. This may require customized data collection.

Artificial neural networks: In many situations in marketing, a manager might say, "I can tell you what factors I take into account in forecasting sales, but I can't tell you exactly what the relationship is between those factors and sales." Artificial neural networks allow users to develop and use models in such situations.

An artificial neural network is a special kind of model that relates inputs (e.g., advertising) to outputs (e.g., sales) and (arguably) emulates the organization of the human brain. The network consists of an interlinked set of simple processing nodes (neurons), which represent complex relationships among inputs and outputs. The basic ideas behind neural networks come from researchers who are trying to understand how the brain processes information and to develop computer representations of those processing mechanisms.

A commonly used artificial neural network is a multilayered *feedforward* network, as shown in Exhibit 5.8. This network has *three layers*, each layer consisting of a set of neurons. Analysts feed data into the nodes in the input layer, which then process the data and transmit their outputs to each node in the intermediate layer(s), which do further processing before transmitting the transformed data as outputs in the output layer. The output of a neural net is the combined pattern of signals that come from the output nodes. This network is called *feedforward* because the data move along in only one direction, from the input layer to the output layer.

Each node (also called neuron, processing element, or perceptron) in the hidden intermediate layer of the network performs a simple computational task: it combines all the input signals x_i that it receives into a single signal value Z as follows:

$$Z = \sum_i w_i x_i, \tag{5.12}$$

where

w_i = weight associated with the link between a node and its ith input source,

$(-\infty \leq w_i \leq \infty)$; and

x_i = the data value (signal) the node receives from its ith source.

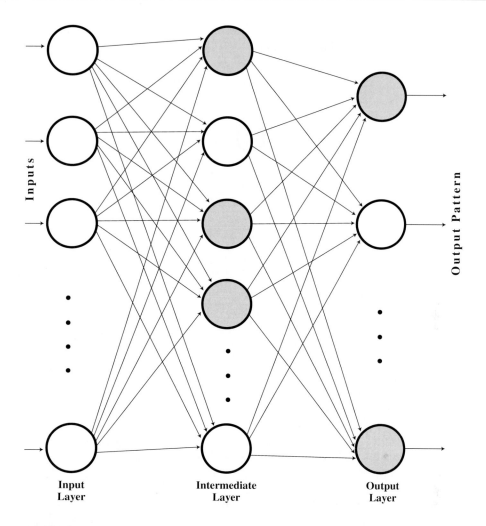

EXHIBIT 5.8
A three-layered feedforward network. The information coming into the input layer is transformed into an internal representation by nodes in the intermediate layer and is then transformed into an output pattern by the nodes in the output layer.

Each node also transforms Z into an output signal (Y) that can take any real value ($-\infty \leq Y \leq \infty$) given real-valued inputs. However, we can use one of several "activation functions" to restrict the range of values output by a node. For example, if we define a threshold value of T for the node, then Y can be transformed into a binary digit (0 or 1) as follows:

$$Y = 1 \text{ if } Z \geq T,$$
$$= 0 \text{ otherwise.} \tag{5.13}$$

Nodes that generate a binary output are called *hard limiters*. Other transformations of Z are also frequently used in neural networks. A common form is the sigmoidal activation function that transforms Y to fall in the range $0 \leq Y \leq 1$:

$$Y = f(Z - T) = \frac{1}{1 + e^{-(Z-T)}}, \tag{5.14}$$

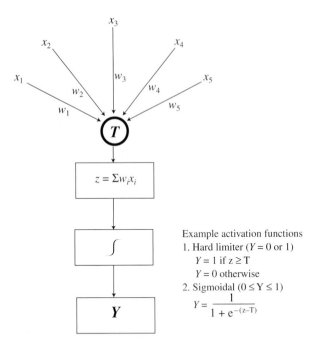

T = Threshold associated with node
$w_1, w_2, ...$ = Network weights associated with incoming signals
$x_1, x_2, ...$ = Input signal values
Y = Output signal from node

EXHIBIT 5.9
Nodes in the intermediate and output layers of a neural network use processing mechanisms like those shown here to transform inputs into outputs.

Hard limiter nodes where the value of Z is higher than the threshold (i.e., $Z > T$) are said to be "active" and have a value equal to 1 (shown shaded in Exhibit 5.8). Corresponding to each pattern of input, the final output of the network is an associated pattern of activation of the output nodes, some active, some not. Thus the neural net transforms an input pattern into an associated output pattern. The computations performed by a node are shown in Exhibit 5.9.

To ensure that a neural net associates the correct outputs with a specific set of inputs, you must "train" the net to strengthen signals (i.e., adjust weights w_i and thresholds T) that most efficiently lead to the correct output, and to weaken incorrect or inefficient signals. Starting with a set of random weights, a computer representation of the network updates the weights and sometimes the thresholds by minimizing an error measure computed from feedback (usually given by the model developer) regarding the correctness of the output in sample cases; thus the network "learns" to associate the correct outputs with specified sets of inputs. The network then retains this learning and uses it when processing new inputs—that is, when it is used for forecasting. One common method for updating weights is called "back propagation," in which error at the output layer is sequentially propagated backward across the network as errors attributable to individual neurons in the intermediate layers.

Theoretically, one can design a multilayered feedforward network with a sigmoidal activation function (given in Eq. [5.14]) to represent any functional relationship at any desired accuracy, if the network contains enough intermediate neurons between the input and output layers. This does not mean, however, that you can train any neural network to correctly represent a sampled relationship. There is no known method for determining just the right number of nodes and levels to represent an unknown response function most appropriately.

Compared with multiple linear regression for representing the relationship between inputs and outputs, neural networks offer two advantages:

1. The user need not specify the structure of the model beforehand. Multilayered networks of the form we have described are general nonlinear estimators that accommodate many kinds of complex nonlinear relationships between inputs and outputs.
2. Neural networks yield more robust fits and predictions than multiple linear regression when data are incomplete or missing. Because neural networks use redundant connections, they are less sensitive than regression to such data problems.

Neural nets have disadvantages as well: even a trained neural net is a black box, and it is difficult to interpret the weights on the network. However, if the primary objective of using the network is to forecast, rather than to provide detailed explanations for a forecast, a neural net may be useful. Neural net forecasting performance depends on several factors including the number of layers in the network, the strength of the learning parameter (slow versus fast learning), and whether the model is overfitted (i.e., whether the model incorporates too many chance variations). Overfitting is similar to the problem of having too many explanatory variables in a regression analysis—you can fit the model perfectly to your data, but the model may be poor at predicting. In the software accompanying the book, part of the data is used for training the neural net, and the rest of the data is used for predictive validation to minimize the chances of overfitting.

Neural nets are so new in the marketing area that no one has developed definitive guidelines on their use, but the method has reported successes, as the following example suggests.

EXAMPLE

First Commerce Corporation, a leading asset banking company, uses a neural network to determine which customers from its database to target for its direct marketing campaigns based on the past behavior of these customers. The company claims that the neural network has helped it increase the response to its direct marketing programs by a factor of four to eight depending on the market segment. The bank conducted an experiment comparing the neural network model with its traditional profiling method (i.e., models that identify customers with desirable profiles). The bank sent out 25,000 letters to customers whose names it had identified as targets using the neural network. These letters did not include prior credit approval. The bank also sent out 100,000 letters to customers whose names were selected in the traditional way and included prior credit approval. The result: while the larger mailing generated 50 more auto loans than the smaller mailing, the smaller mailing generated 100 more loans of all types. (Brokaw, 1997)

In a comprehensive study comparing neural networks to traditional time-series analysis using more than 1,000 data sets, Hill, O'Connor, and Remus (1996) report that neural networks outperform all other methods tested in terms of average forecast accuracy and variance of the forecast errors. They attribute this superior performance to the ability of neural networks to better handle "discontinuities" in most data. In another study, West, Brockett and Golden (1997) conclude that for predicting consumer choices, neural nets outperform discriminant analysis and logistic regression. Lee and Jun (2000) stress caution, showing circumstances in which logistic regression outperforms neural nets (and vice versa).

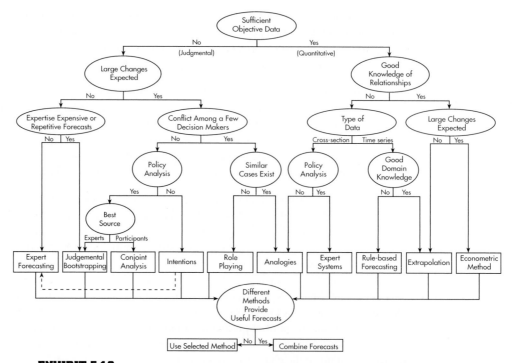

EXHIBIT 5.10
Selection tree for forecasting methods. *Source:* Armstrong, 2001b, p. 376.

What method to choose?

Armstrong (2001b) provides a useful set of research-based guidelines for selecting a fore-casting method. He suggests:

1   *Use structured methods rather than unstructured methods.* While you can't avoid judgment, you should use judgment in a structured way.

2. *Use quantitative methods rather than judgmental methods if enough data exist.* When sufficient data on the dependent variable and independent variables exist, quantitative methods are generally at least as accurate as judgmental methods and often considerably more accurate. The key limitations to this guideline are that the forecaster should be reasonably competent in using the methods and that the methods should be relatively simple (guideline 4).

3. *Use causal methods rather than extrapolation methods, especially if changes are expected to be large.* Extrapolation methods often work quite well and are usu-ally inexpensive. And they give good results for short-term forecasts and when the situation has been and is likely to remain stable over an extended pe-riod. However, when the historical or future environment exhibits large changes, causal methods are best.

4. *Use simple methods unless substantial evidence exists that complexity helps.* Simple methods are generally as accurate as more complex methods. Forecasters often use overly complex methods, which generally fit historical data better but often harm forecast accuracy.

5. *Match the forecasting method to the situation.* The person with many clocks rarely knows the correct time; so it is with forecasting methods. Armstrong (2001b) provides sound evidence to support the flowchart in Exhibit 5.10.

To illustrate the use of the flowchart, if one had sufficient objective historical data, good knowledge of the relationships amongst those data, and large changes were expected, then econometric methods would be most appropriate. In addition, if there are several methods that could provide useful forecasts, one is advised to combine forecasts (Armstrong, 2001c).

Most of the methods we have described so far are based on historical data (the right side of Exhibit 5.10) and, hence are not appropriate for new products. That is because new products, by definition, typically have little sales history, and by their nature, their sales are un-stable. Because the behavioral assumptions and data sources (judgments, pretest market evaluations, first purchase and repeat purchase rates, etc.) differ for new products from those of existing products, special forecasting methods have been developed for new products (Chapter 7).

Armstrong (2001a), along with an associated web site, www.forecastingprinciples.com, provides an up-to-date and comprehensive overview of forecasting findings and references; Yurkiewicz (2000) provides a good review of forecasting software.

THE PRODUCT LIFE CYCLE

An important concept underlying most dynamic business-planning models is the product life cycle. Because a product's sales position and profitability can be expected to change over time, the firm needs to revise its product's strategy periodically. Using the concept of the life cycle, the firm tries to recognize distinct phases in the sales history of the product and its market and to develop strategies appropriate to those stages.

The life-cycle concept comes from many sources. Biological life forms are born, grow, mature, and die. Many human enterprises (like the Roman Empire) have a birth, a heyday, and a decline or death. The length of the product life cycle varies from product to product; it is long for such commodity items as salt, peanut butter, and wine, and short for more differentiated products such as California wine coolers and Darth Vader Halloween masks. Several factors affect the length and form of the product life cycle, including changing needs and wants, changes in technology that lead to close substitutes, and how quickly a new product is adopted in a market.

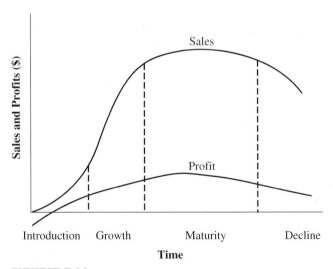

EXHIBIT 5.11
Typical stages in the sales and profit cycles, showing that profit typically lags behind the growth of sales.

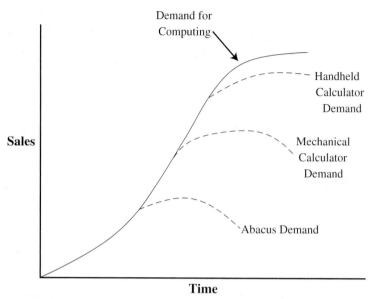

EXHIBIT 5.12(a)
The demand for computing is satisfied over time by different technologies that substitute for one another.

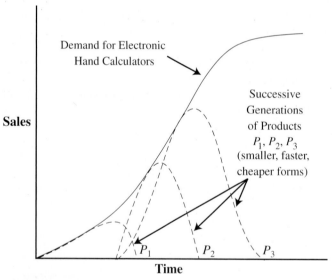

EXHIBIT 5.12(b)
The demand for a product class is driven by the replacement of one generation (product form) by another.

The importance of the life-cycle concept is not that all products have such a product life cycle, or even that a life cycle has specific, distinct stages. Rather, by using the life-cycle concept, firms can anticipate how sales might evolve for a product, and they can develop strategies to influence those sales. For example, in the introductory stage the firm should devote considerable resources to advertising to increase customer awareness of the new product; in the mature stage the firm should devote resources to differentiating and positioning its offering with respect to those of competitors.

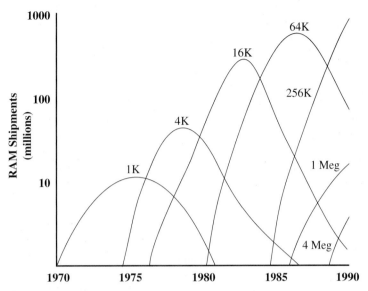

EXHIBIT 5.12(c)
Technological life cycles for random access memories, showing greater peaks and shorter cycle time (a pattern that has continued in the market). *Source*: Urban and Star 1991, p. 96.

In most discussions of the product life cycle (PLC), people portray the sales history of a typical product as following an S-shaped sales curve (Exhibit 5.11). This curve is typically divided into four stages, known as introduction, growth, maturity, and decline. *Introduction* is a period of slow growth as the product is introduced in the market. The profit curve in Exhibit 5.11 shows profits as low or negative in this stage because of the heavy expenses of product introduction. *Growth* is a period of rapid market acceptance and substantial profit improvement. *Maturity* is a period of slowing sales growth, because the product has been accepted by most of its potential buyers. Profits peak in this period and start to decline because of increased marketing outlays needed to sustain the product's position against competition. Finally, *decline* is the period when sales show a strong downward drift and profits erode toward zero.

We can understand this phenomenon as follows. Assume that a human need or want (e.g., calculating power) exists and that a product (e.g., a calculator) satisfies that need. Exhibit 5.12(a) shows how different technologies can successively substitute for one another (leading to a sequence of technology cycles within an overall demand cycle). Exhibit 5.12(b) breaks things down further, showing how successive product forms can replace one another within the context of a single technology cycle. Exhibit 5.12(c) illustrates the effect with actual data from random access memory chips.

The empirical evidence of the existence and applicability of the product life-cycle concept is uneven. In a literature review, Rink and Swan (1979) identified 12 types of product life-cycle patterns. For example, Cox (1967) studied the life cycles of 754 ethical drug products and found that the most typical form was a cycle-recycle pattern (Exhibit 5.13). He explains that the second hump in sales is caused by a promotional push during the decline phase. In another study, Buzzell (1966) reported a scalloped life-cycle pattern (Exhibit 5.13), representing a succession of life cycles based on the discovery of new product characteristics, new uses, or new markets. Exhibit 5.14 shows the cycle-recycle pattern for the Boeing 727 and 747, where redesigns provided several sparks of rejuvenation to the product.

Harrell and Taylor (1981) and Thorelli and Burnett (1981) found that growth rates are only one aspect of the product life cycle; such elements as market innovation, market con-

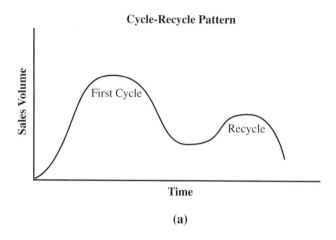

(a)

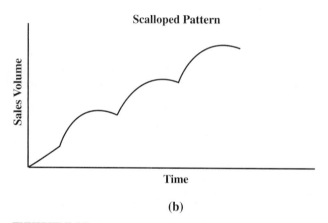

(b)

EXHIBIT 5.13
Two anomalous life-cycle patterns, both featuring forms of rejuvenation after a slowdown or decline in growth.

centration, competitive structure, economic cycles, supply constraints, and replacement sales affect the structure of the life cycle as well.

In fact research results are further confounded by differences in the level of product aggregation and by difficulties with the definition of a new product. Typically there are three possible levels of aggregation: product class (cigarettes), product form (plain filter cigarettes), and brand (Philip Morris, regular or nonfilter). The PLC concept is applied differently in these three cases. Product classes have the longest life histories, longer than particular product forms, and certainly longer than most brands. The sales of many product classes can be expected to continue in the mature stage for an indefinite duration because they are highly related to population (cars, perfume, refrigerators, and steel). Product forms tend to exhibit the standard PLC histories more faithfully. Product forms, such as the dial telephone and cream deodorants, seem to pass through a regular history of introduction, rapid growth, maturity, and decline. On the other hand, a brand's sales history can be erratic because changing competitive strategies and tactics can produce substantial ups and downs in sales and market shares, even to the extent of causing a mature brand to suddenly exhibit another period of rapid growth. Two problems life-cycle researchers tackle frequently are the forecasts of stage transitions and phase duration. Lambkin and Day (1989) explicitly develop such a model to describe and explain the product life cycle.

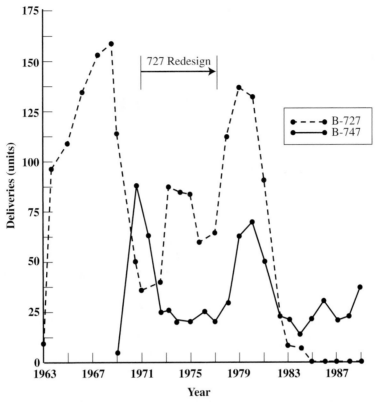

EXHIBIT 5.14
The life cycle of the Boeing 727 and 747, showing the 727's rejuvenation after a redesign in 1971, and a similar pattern for the 747. *Source*: Boeing Commercial Airplane Group 1988, p. 7.

Although some success has been claimed for these methods, they typically rely on data from one phase to forecast the timing and length of the next stage. Accurate long-range forecasting is quite difficult, and therefore little is known about the length and sequence of life-cycle phases (Day 1981). The problems of forecasting phase change and phase length are made more difficult by the widely held belief that life cycles are becoming shorter.

We continue to see applications of life cycle theory used to forecast developments in such diverse areas as tourism (Toh, Kahn, and Koh, 2001), financial services (Javalgi and Dion, 1999), product features (Tholke, Hulfink, and Robken, 2001), and the like.

Two important trends are affecting the use of life-cycle analyses. First, as Kumar (2000) points out, products are likely to be in different stages of their life cycles in differ-ent countries, a point to be taken into account in developing a global marketing strategy. And secondly, as we point out more fully in Chapter 7, improvements in communications technology—the Internet in particular—are leading to more rapid diffusion and are at least partially responsible for shortening product life cycles.

What are we to make of this? Arealistic view is that life-cycle analysis is only one important element in the overall analysis of marketing opportunities. The life cycle acts as a classification device and suggests conditions under which market growth, for example, may occur. During market growth, competitors are better able to enter the market, and new opportunities for product offerings are available in selected market segments. Price and ad-vertising elasticities change over the product life cycle as well, so while there continues to be much discussion concerning definition and measurement, the product life cycle is clearly critical in determining appropriate marketing strategies (Thietart and Vivas 1984). In Chapter 7 we describe several useful tools for developing life-cycle planning models, especially in the introduction and growth stages of the product life cycle.

COST DYNAMICS: SCALE AND EXPERIENCE EFFECTS

Another phenomenon affecting marketing strategy is cost dynamics. One of the most widely discussed findings of the profit impact of marketing strategy (PIMS) program (Chapter 6) is that market share is a primary determinant of business profitability: the PIMS results show that on average a difference of market share between competitors of 10 percent translates into a 5 percent difference in pretax return on investment. One reason for this increase in profitability is that firms with larger market shares have lower costs, partly because of *economies of scale*—very large plants cost less per unit of production to build and run—and partly because of the *experience effect*—the cost of many products declines 10 to 30 percent in real terms each time the company's experience in producing and selling them doubles.

Although researchers have long observed that manufacturing costs seem to fall with cumulative experience and not just with product scale, only recently have they studied this phenomenon carefully and quantified it (Yelle 1979). Initially people believed that only the labor portion of manufacturing costs decreased with cumulative production. The commander of the Wright-Patterson Air Force Base noted in the 1920s that the number of hours required to assemble a plane decreased as the total number of aircraft increased. The relationship between cumulative production and labor costs became known as the *learning curve*.

In the 1960s evidence began mounting that the phenomenon was broader. The Boston Consulting Group (1970), in particular, showed that each time the cumulative volume of production of a product doubled, total value-added costs—sales, administration, and so on—fell by a constant percentage. This relationship between total costs and cumulative production became known as the *experience curve*.

The simplest form of the learning or experience curve is the log-linear model:

$$C_q = C_n \left(\frac{q}{n} \right)^{-b}, \tag{5.15}$$

where

q = cumulative production to date;

n = cumulative production at a particular, earlier time;

C_n = cost of nth unit (in constant dollars);

C_q = cost of qth unit (in constant dollars); and

b = learning constant.

In practice, experience curves are characterized by their *learning rate*. Suppose that each time experience doubles, cost per unit drops to 80 percent of the original level. Then the 80 percent is known as the learning rate. The learning rate is related to the *learning constant* as follows:

$$r = 2^{-b} \times 100, \tag{5.16}$$

or

$$b = \frac{\ln 100 - \ln r}{\ln 2} \tag{5.17}$$

where

r = learning rate (percentage); and

b = learning constant.

Exhibit 5.15 shows how costs fall with experience for various learning rates and levels of experience.

Alberts (1989) contends that most cost declines are caused partly by innovations and partly by economies of scale. Innovation-based causes of cost reductions include

1. Operator innovations—in which workers figure out how to procure, manufacture, and distribute goods more efficiently with current technology
2. Management innovations—in which supervisors and managers figure out how to improve operations with existing technologies
3. Process innovations—in which new technologies for procurement, assembly order processing, and distribution lead to increased efficiency

Scale-based causes of cost reductions include

1. Reduction of excess capacity—which reduces the ratio of fixed costs per unit of production
2. Scale-dependent substitutions—in which larger assembly, procurement, and distribution systems are more cost-effective per unit
3. Increased procurement power—in which increases in procurement volume lead to better deals and lower unit prices

Exhibit 5.16 outlines Alberts's (1989) view of the experience "hypothesis," although he contends that neither repetition nor growth "cause" process innovations—rather they arise through R&D investments that may or may not be linked to volume or experience. According to Alberts, experience by itself does not cause cost declines; rather it provides the opportunity for such declines. Many of the effects of experience (work specialization, for example) may become possible because the size of the operation increases, and therefore they are part of a scale effect. In fact, growth in experience usually occurs at the same

Ratio of Old Experience (n) to New Experience (q)	Learning Rate (r)					
	70%	75%	80%	85%	90%	95%
1.1	5	4	3	2	1	1
1.25	11	9	7	5	4	2
1.5	19	15	12	9	6	3
1.75	25	21	16	12	8	4
2.0	30	25	20	15	10	5
2.5	38	32	26	19	13	7
3.0	43	37	30	23	15	8
4.0	51	44	36	28	19	10
6.0	60	52	44	34	24	12
8.0	66	58	49	39	27	14
16.0	76	68	59	48	34	19

EXHIBIT 5.15
The amount of cost reduction with different levels of learning and production experience.
Source: Abell and Hammond 1979, p. 109.

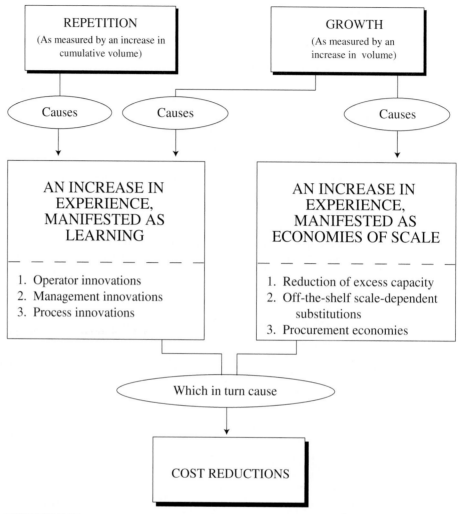

EXHIBIT 5.16
The classical view of production cost reductions: they arise from both learning and scale economics. *Source:* Alberts 1989, p. 40.

time as the size of an operation grows, although firms can use scale effects to bypass experience (as the Japanese did in the steel industry). And it is clear that process innovations will not just happen—they come from an R&D program targeted at such cost reductions.

While the experience concept is rather simple, its application in a model requires ingenuity. It is important to (1) adjust prices for inflation; (2) plot cost versus experience (not time); (3) consider cost components separately, because each may have different learning rates; (4) correct for *shared experience*, where two or more products share a common resource or activity; (5) adjust for different experience rates between competitors (firm A, a late entry, may benefit from B's experience, may be able to exploit shared experience that B cannot, may have a different proportion of value added than B, etc.); (6) begin at the right starting point choosing n and C_n in Eq. (5.15); (7) measure costs properly over a reasonably long time frame; (8) properly define the unit of analysis (a firm may have a large share of a small market yet have less experience than a competitor with a small share in a much larger market!); and (9) treat process innovation effects as separately budgeted effects.

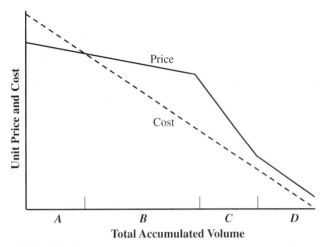

EXHIBIT 5.17
A typical price-cost relationship with costs going down faster than price during phases
A, B, and C before settling down to commodity phase D. *Source*: The Boston Consulting
Group, Inc. 1970, p. 21.

These and other practical considerations in developing and using the experience curve
are discussed by Abell and Hammond (1979), The Boston Consulting Group (1970),
Hax and Majluf (1982), Day (1986), Day and Montgomery (1983), and Alberts (1989).

The experience-curve concept is of strategic importance in business planning for many
industries. In stable industries, where profit margins remain at a constant percentage of cost,
the experience curve allows for long-range projections of cost, price, and profit.

Many situations are similar to the one illustrated in Exhibit 5.17. In phase A costs exceed
prices, as is often the case in a *start-up* situation. In phase B the market leader maintains a *price
umbrella* over higher-cost producers entering the market, trading future market share for current profit. In phase C, the *shake-out period*, one producer begins lowering prices at a faster
rate than costs are declining, perhaps because of overcapacity. In phase D *stability* occurs
when profit margins return to normal levels, paralleling industry costs again. This illustration
suggests the importance (and the risks) associated with a market-dominance strategy. While
being the market leader and operating at a low-cost position are desirable, a firm can precip-
itate a shake-out period (phase C) in a market by aggressively pursuing market share.

Aside from its use as a private sector planning tool, experience curves have been used
ex-tensively to argue for policy interventions to support accelerating the diffusion of so-
cially de-sirable technologies like alternative energy sources (see Neij, 1997).

In Chapter 10 we discuss using the experience curve to develop an optimal *monopoly*-
pricing strategy, using software called learning-curve pricing. Making informed strategic
decisions in response to experience-curve cost declines requires information about market
growth, competitive costs, and likely competitive reaction. When you can carefully model
and forecast experience-curve cost declines, you can use them in business planning.

SUMMARY

In this chapter we introduced the notion of marketing strategy as an umbrella concept within
which firms must make marketing decisions. We stressed the interconnectedness of all these
decisions, particularly functional interactions, synergies between marketing-mix elements,
and functional interactions.

To devise a marketing strategy, we must define a market appropriately and assess and forecast the demand for that market. We outlined the most common and emerging methods of forecasting sales for established products.

The structure and dynamics of markets have led marketers to develop two other key planning concepts: the product life cycle and cost dynamics. The product life cycle makes using traditional time-series and econometric forecasting methods difficult. And the dynamics of product costs—the experience-curve effect—affects market strategy and planning.

We will apply these concepts and tools in the forthcoming chapters, particularly in Chapter 6.

BOOKBINDERS BOOK CLUB CASE [1]

About 50,000 new titles, including new editions, are published in the United States each year, giv-ing rise to a $20 billion book publishing industry (in 1994). About 10 percent of the books are sold through mail order.

Book retailing in the 1970s was characterized by the growth of chain bookstore opera-tions in concert with the development of shopping malls. Traffic in bookstores in the 1980s was enhanced by the spread of discounting. In the 1990s, the superstore concept of book re-tailing was responsible for the double-digit growth of the book industry. Generally situ-ated near large shopping centers, superstores maintain large inventories of anywhere from 30,000 to 80,000 titles. Superstores are putting intense competitive pressure on book clubs, mail-order firms and retail outlets. Recently, online superstores, such as *www.amazon.com*, have emerged, carrying 1–2.5 million titles and further intensifying the pressure on book clubs and mail-order firms. In response to these pressures, book clubs are starting to look at alternative business models that will make them more responsive to their customers' preferences.

Historically, book clubs offered their readers continuity and negative option programs that were based on an extended contractual relationship between the club and its sub-scribers. In a continuity program, popular in such genres as children's books, a reader signs up for an offer of several books for a few dollars each (plus shipping and handling on each book) and agrees to receive a shipment of one or two books each month thereafter. In a neg-ative option program, subscribers get to choose which and how many additional books they will receive, but the default option is that the club's selection will be delivered to them each month. The club informs them of the monthly selection and they must mark "no" on their order forms if they do not want to receive it. Some firms are now beginning to offer books on a positive-option basis, but only to selected segments of their customer lists that they deem receptive to specific offers.

Book clubs are also beginning to use database marketing techniques to work smarter rather than expand the coverage of their mailings. According to Doubleday president Marcus Willhelm, "The database is the key to what we are doing…. We have to understand what our customers want and be more flexible. I doubt book clubs can survive if they offer the same 16 offers, the same fulfillment to everybody."[2] Doubleday uses modeling tech-niques to look at more than 80 variables, including geography and the types of books cus-tomers purchase, and selects three to five variables that are the most influential predictors.

THE BOOKBINDERS BOOK CLUB

The BBB Club was established in 1986 for the purpose of selling specialty books through direct marketing. BBBC is strictly a distributor and does not publish any of the books it sells. In anticipation of using database marketing, BBBC made a strategic decision right from the start to build and maintain a detailed database about its members containing all the relevant information about them. Readers fill out an insert and return it to BBBC which then enters the data into the database. The company currently has a database of 500,000 readers and sends out a mailing about once a month.

1. The case and the database were developed by Professors Nissan Levin and Jacob Zahavi at Tel Aviv University. We have adapted these materials for use with our software, with their permission.
2. DM News, May 23, 1994.

BBBC is exploring whether to use predictive modeling approaches to improve the efficacy of its direct mail program. For a recent mailing, the company selected 20,000 customers in Pennsylvania, New York, and Ohio from its database and included with their regular mailing a specially produced brochure for the book *The Art History of Florence*. This resulted in a 9.03 percent response rate (1806 orders) for the purchase of the book. BBBC then developed a database to calibrate a response model to identify the factors that influenced these purchases.

For this case analysis, we will use a subset of the database available to BBBC. It consists of data for 400 customers who purchased the book, and 1,200 customers who did not, thereby over-representing the response group. The dependent variable for the analysis is Choice — purchase or no purchase of *The Art History of Florence*. BBBC also selected several independent variables that it thought might explain the observed choice behavior. Below is a description of the variables used for the analysis:

Choice: Whether the customer purchased the The Art History of Florence. 1 corresponds to a purchase and 0 corresponds to a nonpurchase.

Gender: 0 = Female and 1 = Male.

Amount_purchased: Total money spent on BBBC books.

Frequency: Total number of purchases in the chosen period (used as a proxy for frequency.)

Last_purchase (recency of purchase): Months since last purchase.

First_purchase: Months since first purchase.

P_Child: Number of children's books purchased.

P_Youth: Number of youth books purchased.

P_Cook: Number of cookbooks purchased.

P_DIY: Number of do-it-yourself books purchased.

P_Art: Number of art books purchased.

EXERCISES

BBBC is evaluating three different modeling methods to isolate the factors that most influenced customers to order *The Art History of Florence*: an ordinary linear regression model, a binary logit model, and a neural network model.

1. Summarize the results of your analysis for all three models. Develop your models using the following data files, all of which contain the same data in different formats.

    ■ Linear regression: BBBC.XLS–1,600 observations for model development.
    ■ Binary logit model: BBBC.DAT–1,600 observations for model development.
    ■ Neural network model: BBBCNN.4TH–3,900 observations with 1,600 observations for model development and 2,300 observations for holdout prediction.
    ■ In addition, the file BBBCPRED.XLS contains 2,300 observations for holdout prediction using the coefficients of the linear regression and binary logit models.

2. Interpret the results of these models. In particular, highlight which factors most in-fluenced the customers' decision to buy or not to buy the book.
3. Bookbinders is considering a similar mail campaign in the Midwest where it has data for 50,000 customers. Such mailings typically promote several books. The al-located-cost of the mailing is $0.65/addressee (including postage) for the art book, and the book costs Bookbinders $15 to purchase and mail. The company allocates overhead to each book at 45 percent of cost. The selling price of the book is $31.95. Based on the model, which customers should Bookbinders target? How much more profit would you expect the company to generate using these models as compared to sending the mail offer to the entire list?
4. Based on the insights you gained from this modeling exercise, summarize the ad-vantages and limitations of each of the modeling approaches. Look at both similar and dissimilar results.
5. As part of your recommendations to the company, indicate whether it should invest in developing expertise in either (or all) of these methods to develop an in-house capability to evaluate its direct mail campaigns.
6. How would you simplify and automate your recommended method(s) for future modeling efforts at the company.

CHAPTER 6

Models for Strategic Marketing Decision Making

In Chapter 5 we described several building blocks for marketing strategy. In this chapter we discuss some important marketing-strategy problem areas in which the marketing engineering approach has been effective:

- Market entry and exit decisions—how to time market entry and exit and the issues associated with market pioneering and order of entry
- Shared-experience models—how we can learn from the experiences of successful firms
- Product portfolio models—how to manage products and businesses as an integrated group
- Models of competition—how the nature of the market and competitive response influences marketing strategy

Decisions in these areas all depend on the key strategic-marketing decision: what is the best way to allocate the firm's marketing resources in the long term? Deciding when to enter or exit a market is a question of timing: when is the best time to invest (or divest)? Shared-experience models can help us learn from the investment experience of successful organizations to benchmark and improve our own marketing investment strategy. Product portfolio models help us to establish internal consistency in our investments: when marketing investment alternatives compete for scarce resources, how should we prioritize and allocate those resources? Finally, models of competition help us analyze the likely reaction of competitors to our investment decisions and how we should address those reactions.

MARKET ENTRY AND EXIT DECISIONS

A critical issue in formulating a dynamic market strategy is timing market entry in light of market-pioneering or first-mover advantages. Lieberman and Montgomery (1980) suggest that first-mover advantages arise from three sources:

1. Technological leadership that comes from being further down the learning curve than competitors (experience-curve effect) or from success in R&D or patents.

2. Preemption of scarce assets such as limited raw materials, channels of distribution, shelf space, and scarce, specially skilled employees.
3. Switching costs and buyer risk aversion, which influence buyers to avoid switching from their current product; late entrants must invest more (provide lower prices or more value) to overcome the costs and risks buyers incur in switching.

Robinson and Fornell (1985) use the PIMS database to show that pioneers on average had higher market shares than early followers. The early followers in turn had higher market shares than late followers. Their explanation of these effects is that early entry affects four factors: product quality, breadth of product line, product price, and product cost. Urban et al. (1986), in a study of 129 consumer packaged goods, also found that entry order had a significant effect on market share, as did Parry and Bass (1990), who found differences based on industry type and end-user purchase amount.

Kalyanaram, Robinson, and Urban (1995) summarize their findings about entry timing in three generalizations:

Generalization 1: For mature consumer and industrial goods, there is a negative relationship between the order of market entry and market share.

Generalization 2: For consumer packaged goods, the new entrant's forecasted market share divided by the first entrant's market share roughly equals one divided by the square root of the order of market entry.

Generalization 3: In mature consumer and industrial goods markets, early entrant market share advantages slowly decline over time.

These generalizations and others (Lilien and Yoon 1990) provide important information about the likely outcomes of market entry decisions. For example, Bayus (1997) taking a trade-off approach, shows that fast development of low performance products is optimal when there is a short window of market opportunity, weak competitors, and high development costs. In addition to timing, the firm should consider the likely consumer reaction to the product, the likely competitive response, market evolution, and the like.

EXAMPLE

Yoon and Lilien (1985) studied the success rate of a sample of 112 new industrial products as measured by the market share of those products after one year (Exhibit 6.1). They classified the products as

Original new products (ORNPs), technological breakthroughs, often relying on technologies never before used in the industry (also called new product lines and new-to-the-world products)

Reformulated new products (RFNPs), extensions or modifications of existing products, which usually reduce costs or enlarge the range of possible uses (also called cost reductions, improvements, and additions)

The success of these new products is related to the firm's delay in launching the product after it is technically ready. For ORNPs they found that first-year market share increases with delay up to a certain point and decreases thereafter. For RFNPs they found that first-year market share steadily decreases with delay. This contrast between product types may reflect the level of market development; the market is ready for RFNPs: the longer an incremental innovation takes to get to

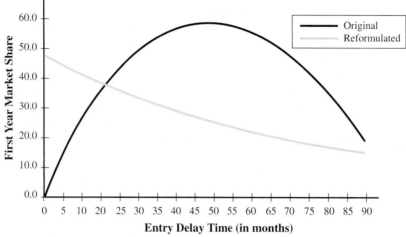

EXHIBIT 6.1
New product success for a sample of industrial products, showing that market share at the
end of the first year is highest when reformulated new products are introduced immediately,
whereas for original new products a delay helps. *Source*: Yoon and Lilien 1985, p. 142.

market, the greater its risk of failure due to changing market conditions, competitive response, or further technological advances.

EXAMPLE

In a study sponsored by the U.S. Department of Energy (DOE), Kalish and
Lilien (1986) looked at market-entry timing for a demonstration program for the
residential use of photovoltaics (solar batteries). DOE was considering funding a
proposal from a developer in the southwestern United States to incorporate photovoltaics in a 100-home development. At the time of the proposal (1980) photo-
voltaic products were not technically ready, and the results of a survey and expert
judgments suggested that a demonstration program at that time (when the risk of
failure or even fire damage to a home's roof was not insubstantial) could have a
negative impact on the rate of penetration into the marketplace. Kalish and Lilien
developed a market penetration model (a modification of the Bass diffusion model
we describe in Chapter 7) to look at the likely rate of diffusion of the product into
the market.

Their formal analysis showed that, given DOE's objective of maximizing
market penetration after 10 years, it was better for DOE to delay the demonstration program for 5 years (and get the bugs out of the technology) than to demonstrate the current state of the technology. In addition, by delaying the DOE would
save money. Partly on the basis of this analysis, the DOE did not fund the residential demonstration program.

The empirical generalizations and the examples above demonstrate that the timing of market entry should depend on the nature of the product (new versus reformulated), of the market (industrial versus consumer; mature versus immature), and of competition (number in market before you; entry order). Premature market entry can be a mistake that is as costly as excessive delay.

How can we address the timing of market entry? We describe a set of methods that rely on new product diffusion theory in the next chapter. Here we describe decision analysis or decision-tree analysis, which can also be used to address these issues.

The reactions of the market, consumers, and competitors to the entry of a new product are uncertain, and marketing managers deal with uncertainty in several ways. Some do worst-case analyses and go ahead with product launches only if the launch is still projected to pay off with poorer market response and higher costs than projected. Others run a series of spreadsheet scenarios, looking at a number of possible futures, and choose among them.

The increasing availability of various kinds of decision support software makes these kinds of decisions easier to quantify. One of the methods that is most appropriate for handling decisions under conditions of uncertainty is decision analysis. Decision analysis is appropriate for solving problems with the following characteristics:

- A choice or sequence of choices must be made among various courses of action.
- The choice or sequence of choices will ultimately lead to some consequence; but the decision maker cannot be sure in advance what the consequence will be, because it depends not only on his or her decisions but also on an unpredictable event or sequence of events.

The choice of action should depend on the likelihood that the decision maker's action will have various possible consequences, as well as the desirability of the various consequences.

The decision-analysis approach usually includes four steps:

1. *Structuring the problem*: To structure the problem one must define general objectives, specify measures of effectiveness, identify restrictions on actions, and characterize the problem chronologically. One should also identify alternative courses of action.
2. *Assigning probabilities to possible consequences*: One needs to assess the possibilities of various consequences occurring, depending on managerial actions. This assessment can be purely subjective or can include analysis of past system behavior.
3. *Assigning payoffs to consequences*: The decision maker must explicitly include his or her preferences for possible outcomes. (These preferences, or payoffs, relate to the objectives and goals we outlined in Chapter 2.)
4. *Analyzing the problem*: To analyze the problem we use a method called averaging out and folding back, which we illustrate with the following example.

EXAMPLE

This example is based on Keeney (undated notes). The QRS Company must decide whether or not to introduce a new product now. If it chooses to introduce the product, sales will either be high or low. For simplicity we assume that the firm's objective is to maximize expected profits. The firm is considering a market survey to collect information on expected sales. The market research firm contacted will report one of three results: great, good, or poor, where great means that high sales are likely. Marketing management feels that if the firm introduces the product now, its probability of high sales is 0.4. The company has had past experience with this market research firm and knows that 60 percent of high-sales products in the past had great survey results, 30 percent had good survey results, and 10 percent had poor survey results. Similarly, 10 percent of its low-sales products had great survey results, 30 percent had good survey results, and 60 percent had poor survey results. If sales are high, the firm expects net profits (excluding the cost of the survey) to be $100,000; if sales are low, it expects a net loss of $50,000 (excluding survey costs).

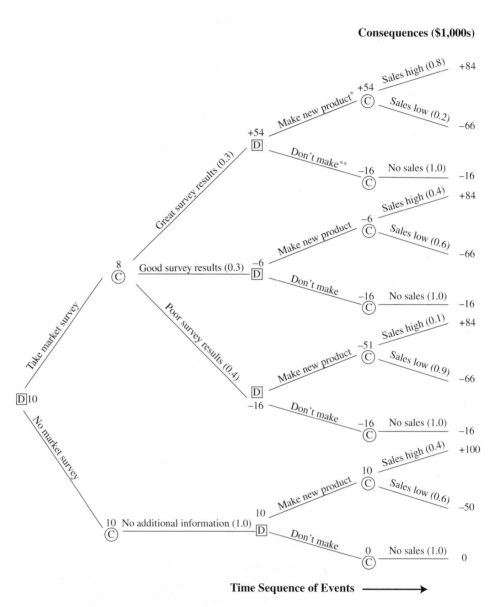

Consequences ($1,000s)

Time Sequence of Events ⟶

* Read as: Introduce new product now.
** Don't introduce new product now; delay introduction or "kill" the project.

EXHIBIT 6.2
Structure of decision tree for QRS Company, where the nodes marked D are decision nodes and those marked C are chance nodes.

This problem can be structured as a decision tree (Exhibit 6.2). The chronology of events begins on the left and flows to the right. The first thing that happens is that marketing management must decide whether or not to run a market survey. If it does run a survey, it then learns the results and decides whether or not to introduce the product. Finally, it learns sales results.

A decision tree has two types of nodes: decision nodes (marked D), meaning management has control over the course of action; and chance nodes (marked C), where the decision maker has no control.

At the end of each path of the decision tree, the consequences of the several courses of action are indicated. For instance, if the firm runs a market survey, that survey reports great results, the firm manufactures the product, and sales are high, the result is a net gain of $84,000: $100,000 less the $16,000 survey cost. All consequences are measured against the do-nothing strategy of no survey, no manufacturing, and no sales.

Beside those segments of the tree beginning at chance nodes are the conditional probabilities (the numbers in parentheses) that the event associated with that segment occurs, given that everything else up to that point in the tree *does* occur. Thus, for instance, the probability that the survey is *great*, given that the firm runs the survey, is 0.3, or 30 percent. The conditional probability that sales are high, given that survey results are great and the firm decides to manufacture, is 0.8, or 80 percent.

To summarize the given information, the firm knows from past experience that

$$p(\text{great survey} \mid \text{high sales}) = 0.6,$$
$$p(\text{good survey} \mid \text{high sales}) = 0.3,$$
$$p(\text{poor survey} \mid \text{high sales}) = 0.1,$$
$$p(\text{great survey} \mid \text{low sales}) = 0.1,$$
$$p(\text{good survey} \mid \text{low sales}) = 0.3,$$
$$p(\text{poor survey} \mid \text{low sales}) = 0.6,$$
$$p(\text{high sales}) = 0.4,$$
$$p(\text{low sales}) = 0.6. \tag{6.1}$$

To get the probability that the survey would be great, we use the theorem of total probabilities:

$$
\begin{aligned}
p(\text{great survey}) &= p(\text{great survey} \mid \text{high sales})p(\text{high sales}) \\
&\quad + p(\text{great survey} \mid \text{low sales})p(\text{low sales}) \\
&= 0.6 \times 0.4 + 0.1 \times 0.6 = 0.3. \tag{6.2}
\end{aligned}
$$

Similarly

$$p(\text{good survey}) = 0.3,$$
$$p(\text{poor survey}) = 0.4.$$

To get $p(\text{high sales} \mid \text{great survey})$, we use Bayes's theorem:

$$p(\text{high sales} \mid \text{great survey}) = \frac{p(\text{great survey} \mid \text{high sales})p(\text{high sales})}{p(\text{great survey})}$$

$$= \frac{0.6 \times 0.4}{0.3} = 0.8. \tag{6.3}$$

Similarly, we get

p(high sales | good survey) = 0.4,

p(high sales | poor survey) = 0.1,

p(low sales | great survey) = 0.2,

p(low sales | good survey) = 0.6,

p(low sales | poor survey) = 0.9.

We can now use these probabilities to average out the consequence and fold back the decision tree. The numbers beside each node represent the expected profit associated with being at that node. If we conduct a market survey, have great results, and introduce the product now, then there is an 80 percent chance of high sales, implying a net profit of $84,000, and a 20 percent chance of low sales, with a net loss of $66,000. Thus, the expected profit (averaging out) of being at that chance node is

$$(0.8)(\$84,000) - (0.2)(\$66,000) = \$54,000. \tag{6.4}$$

At the node immediately below, if we have the same great results on the survey and then choose not to manufacture, we will lose $16,000.

Now backing up (folding back) to the decision node before these chance nodes, the firm can either introduce the product with expected profit of $54,000 or not introduce the product now with an expected loss of $16,000. The best choice is to make the product; therefore the expected profit of that decision node is $54,000. In addition, if we fold back to the start, we find the best choice is not to do the survey.

Decision analysis is a powerful tool that can help managers to structure decisions of this type and others. The tree can easily be expanded to include market entry timing. For example, suppose an alternative decision at each "introduce" decision node is to delay one quarter. Suppose management judges that a competitor can enter the market with probability = 0.20 (i.e., a 20 percent chance of not being the pioneer, with an associated lower reward, even for a successful product). But if that delay allows the firm to develop a better quality product (product quality improvement over time as happened with photovoltaics in our example and with other truly new products), the likelihood of high sales may increase. Decision trees provide a convenient framework within which managers can make such judgments and trade-offs explicit and quantified, and currently available software makes constructing such decision trees simple. Through cut-and-paste operations, users can easily duplicate such trees (introduce now, wait one period, wait two periods, etc.) and obtain other important diagnostics: "What probability of success—after a good market survey, for example—would make us just indifferent between introducing and not introducing the product?" "What would the consequences be of an increase or decrease of 10 percent in the return from this project?" These diagnostics also give the user two other pieces of useful information: the expected value of sample information and the expected value of perfect information.

The expected value of sample information is the most the firm should pay for a survey. What price on the survey would make the decision maker just indifferent between conducting the survey and doing no marketing research?

EXAMPLE

From our analysis we learned that the survey information the firm could obtain was not worth $16,000. Just how much is it worth? If we label the survey cost as S and average out and fold back, we find that the value of being at the first chance node is $24,000 minus S. If S is $14,000, the firm is indifferent between taking a survey and not taking it, since the decision "no market survey" is worth an expected $10,000. Thus, $14,000 is the maximum one should pay for the survey.

The expected value of perfect information is the most the firm should pay for a "perfect" survey—one that told it reliably whether the product would succeed or fail.

EXAMPLE

The expected value of perfect information is important, because no survey can give us perfect information and thus it represents a benchmark for the most one should ever pay for sample information.

By "perfect information" we mean a forecast such that

$$p(\text{high forecast} \mid \text{high sales}) = 1,$$
$$p(\text{low forecast} \mid \text{low sales}) = 1, \tag{6.5}$$

and other outcomes have a probability of zero of occurring.

If perfect information reveals a high sales forcast, the best strategy is to introduce the product. This forecast will occur with probability 0.4:

$$p(\text{high forecast}) = p(\text{high sales}) = 0.4. \tag{6.6}$$

The net profit associated with introducing the new product is $100,000 minus R, where R is the cost of the perfect information. Similarly the probability of the forecast being low is 0.6, and in that case the best strategy is not to make the product. This strategy has a net profit associated with it of minus R.

Therefore the expected profit with perfect information is

$$(0.4)(\$100,000 - R) + (0.6)(-R) = \$40,000 - R. \tag{6.7}$$

When $R = \$30,000$ the marketing manager should be indifferent between obtaining the perfect information and not doing a market survey. Both strategies would have an expected net profit of $10,000. Thus the expected value of perfect information is $30,000.

Thus decision analysis not only helps resolve decisions under conditions of uncertainty, it helps determine how much it is worth to collect information that reduces that uncertainty. In our experience (Brown, Lilien, and Ulvila 1993) it often takes a surprisingly small reduction in market uncertainty, especially when potential payoffs are large, to justify fairly substantial market research expenditures, and decision analysis is quite useful for that justification task. Another benefit of decision analysis is that it forces managers to separate uncertainties from preferences. As a result, they are less likely to fall into the trap of believing that desirable outcomes are more likely to occur.

In the preceding discussion we assume that such information can affect management decisions. If management is already committed to a new-product-entry decision, then the best one can do using decision analysis is to provide the (expected) opportunity cost of the inappropriate decision. While we think that the wider availability of marketing engineering tools will help systematize such decisions, so far there has been only limited use of decision trees in marketing.

EXAMPLE

(From Ulvila and Brown 1982, pp. 134–135.) How will Honeywell's defense division grow? In late 1979 the manager of planning for the defense systems division of Honeywell, Inc., faced the task of planning the division's growth over the next 10 years. A major part of the work involved finding how to stay within the R&D budget and yet pursue new product opportunities to increase the division's sales and profits.

After he screened the new product opportunities according to their fit with the rest of the division, the manager needed forecasts of the products' sales, profits, and investment requirements. The products' successful development, the strength of competition, and their eventual market success were all uncertain. In addition the chances for success of some of the products were interrelated, and several products offered the chance of significant collateral business.

The approach the analysts took was to build a composite forecast for the division by combining decision-tree analyses of individual products. During the project Honeywell's planners worked closely with decision-analysis consultants and, by the time they finished, acquired the skills needed to carry out the analyses in-house. This type of analysis is now a regular part of Honeywell's project evaluation, planning, and forecasting activity.

The analysts developed a model for each product. The analysis team worked closely with each project manager and his or her staff to build the decision tree, assess probabilities and values, and discuss results and sensitivities.

The two analyses differed significantly, however, in a number of ways. First, the results of Honeywell's analysis were to be used for forecasting as well as for decision making. This use meant that the analysts would need to model additional factors and would have to make the form the outputs took suitable for forecasting.

Second, because the success of some products was related to the success of others, the analysts had to include in the analysis such factors as common investments, collateral business opportunities, and marketing interactions.

Third, Honeywell's problem presented no clear single criterion according to which management could make a decision. Honeywell considered several financial criteria such as internal rate of return, net present value, and yearly streams of profits, investments, and return on investment.

Honeywell developed a forecast based on decision-tree analyses of three main products and two collateral business opportunities. The analysts first developed decision trees for each product to determine the distributions of sales in the event that a market sufficient to support full production either did or did not emerge. Then they developed a second level of analysis to model the key interdependencies among the products; specifically, the probability of any particular product being in full production depended on which other products were also in full production.

That forecast showed that low sales were expected from the products for the first seven years. After that sales for the next six years were expected to be about $75 million per year. That amount was not certain, however. The forecast, for instance, showed a 24 percent chance of sales being below $25 million in 1989.

The supporting decision-tree analyses were useful for explaining the shape of each year's forecast. For example, because of uncertainty about which products would have sufficient markets to support full production by 1988, the forecast for sales were "lumpy." The reasons for these uncertainties are detailed in the decision-tree analyses.

This analysis helped Honeywell to assess the chances that these products would meet sales goals, the uncertainties in the assessment, and the reasons for the uncertainties. By detailing the chain of events that would produce different levels of sales, it also identified points of leverage—places where Honeywell could take action to change probabilities and improve sales.

The analysts also used the decision trees to forecast yearly profits, fund flows, assets, research and development investments, and the related financial quantities of net present value, internal rate of return, and annual return on investment. Their forecasts indicated that these products could be expected to exceed requirements on all factors and that, unless Honeywell was very risk averse, they were attractive.

Honeywell's managers compared forecasts to decide which product opportunities to pursue. These comparisons provided an additional screen since some products were clearly worse than others on *all* factors. But because the analysis did not show the relative importance of each factor—some products were projected to perform better on certain factors (for example, internal rate of return and net present value) and other products were projected to perform better on other factors (for example, return on investment)—an unambiguous ordering of the products was impossible. Honeywell's managers might have had such an ordering if their analysts had used techniques like multi-attribute utility methods or the Analytic Hierarchy Process (described later in this chapter).

Urban and Hauser (1993) provide other examples of the use of decision analysis for planning new products, and Raiffa (1968) provides a good basic treatment of decision-analysis concepts. Decision analysis can also be used to assess the responses of the market and competition to other strategic and tactical moves. If the firm is considering a price increase, it can use decision analysis to structure the likely competitive and market response, assigning values to various scenarios and the likelihood of those scenarios so that the firm can choose the best course of action. The Treeage software (included with this book) gives you an opportunity to experiment with and explore this methodology. It allows you to focus on representing and formulating the problem, and it handles all the associated computations automatically.

Because market entry disrupts the nature of a competitive marketplace, the concepts and methods of game theory (see later part of this chapter) have been used to explore the market entry timing decision. For example, Bayus, Jain, and Rao (1997) show how both the capabilities of an entering firm and those of its competitors can affect timing decisions. In another paper (2001) the authors show that firms' announcements of vaporware (announced software that may either never materialize or materialize well after the announced date of introduction) can deter competitive market entry timing decisions. And Narasimhan and Zhang (2000) show that it is often rational for a stronger firm to delay market entry, waiting for a weaker firm to enter the market first, incurring the cost of learning about and developing the early market.

SHARED-EXPERIENCE MODELS: THE PIMS APPROACH

People use a wide variety of other tools in practice to support market-strategy decisions; these approaches can be roughly classified as follows:

1. Shared-experience models (the PIMS approach)
2. Product portfolio models
   a. Standardized
   b. Customized
   c. Financial
3. Normative-resource-allocation models

All of these approaches explicitly or implicitly incorporate life-cycle analysis, experience-curve effects, market definition effects, and market structure effects. We describe shared-experience models and product portfolio models in this chapter; see Wind and Lilien (1993) for a discussion of the normative-resource-allocation models.

The PIMS (profit impact of marketing strategy) project began in 1960 at General Electric as an intrafirm analysis of the relative profitability of its businesses. It is based on the notion that the pooled experiences of diverse successful and unsuccessful businesses will provide useful insights and guidance about the determinants of business profitability. By the term *business*, we mean a strategic business unit, which is an operating unit selling a distinct set of products to an identifiable group of customers in competition with a well-defined set of competitors. By the mid-1980s the PIMS database of about 100 data items per business included about 3000 businesses from about 450 participating firms.

Perhaps the most publicized use of the PIMS data is the PAR regression model, which relates return on investment (ROI = pretax income/investment averaged over four years of data) to a set of independent variables (Buzzell and Gale 1987). Exhibit 6.3 presents the results of that analysis for the entire PIMS database. The most widely cited results of the PIMS studies are those relating to market selection and strategic characteristics associated with profitability (Exhibit 6.4).

Firms participating in the PIMS program receive PAR reports for their business, which compare its actual return on investment and return on sales (ROI and ROS) with the ROI and ROS (ROS = pretax income/sales averaged over 4 years of data) that PIMS predicts for that business (based on its market and strategic characteristics). This type of analysis, showing the deviation of the actual ROI from the PAR ROI, yields insights into how well and why the business has met its strategic potential. Another useful output from PIMS is the Limited Information Report (LIM), containing the results of an abbreviated version of the PAR ROI model. The Limited Information Model contains only 18 variables, which can be assessed using a subset of the total data required for PIMS (Exhibit 6.5).

EXAMPLE

(Drawn from Sudharshan 1995.) The Central Air Conditioner Division of Scott-Air Corp. invested $85 million to increase its capacity to produce 1 1/2- to 10-ton air conditioners. With this new capacity its break-even sales volume was $56 million, higher than the previous year's record volume of $52 million. More important, corporate management demanded at least a 22 percent return on capital. The division manager used the PIMS LIM report to guide his strategy to accomplish this objective.

CAC management used the LIM report to examine the impact of increasing sales to $100 million per year; however, when considering the whole market, that volume amounted to only about an 8.3 percent market share, a share too low to be consistent

| | — Impact on — | |
Profit Influences	ROI	ROS
Real market growth rate	0.18	0.04
Rate of price inflation	0.22	0.08
Purchase concentration	0.02**	
Unionization, %	−0.07	
Low purchase amount and		
Low importance of purchase***	6.06	1.63
High importance of purchase	5.42	2.10
High purchase amount and		
Low importance of purchase	−6.96	−2.58
High importance of purchase	−3.84	−1.11**
Exports minus imports, %	0.06**	0.05
Customized products	−2.44	−1.77
Market share	0.34	0.14
Relative quality	0.11	0.05
New products, %	−0.12	−0.05
Marketing, % of sales	−0.52	−0.32
R&D, % of sales	−0.36	−0.22
Inventory, % of sales	0.49	−2.09
Fixed capital intensity	−0.55	−2.10
Plant newness	0.07	0.05
Capacity utilization, %	0.31	0.10
Employee productivity	0.13	0.06
Vertical integration	0.26	0.18
First in first out inventory valuation	1.30*	0.62
R^2	.39	.31
F	58.3	45.1
Number of cases	2,314	2,314

Note: All coefficients, except those starred, are significant ($p < .01$).   ROI = Return on investment
    * Significance level between .01 and .05.   ROS = Return on sales
   ** Significance level between .05 and .10.
  *** Products for which the typical purchase amount is low and the importance of the purchase to
      customers is also low.

EXHIBIT 6.3
Multiple-regression equation for return on investment (ROI) and return on sales (ROS) for the entire PIMS database. *Source*: Buzzell and Gale 1987, p. 274.

with the high ROI target. That low market share was consistent with poor market position, poor distribution, and low capacity utilization, leading to the low ROI figures.

On the basis of that analysis the CAC managers decided to focus on narrow market segments: modernization and replacement. If Scott could achieve its $100 million sales target in these narrower market segments (where it had both product and strategic strengths), its projected segment market share (28 percent rather than 8.3 percent) would be consistent with a PIMS ROI of more than the 22 percent target. The LIM report in this case helped the managers to identify a strategy in which the firm's goals would at least be consistent with the performance of the businesses in the PIMS database.

This brief example illustrates the benefits and some of the risks associated with using a model like PIMS for benchmarking. On the one hand, firms can use PIMS as a diagnostic de-

Some market characteristics associated with high profitability
- A growing market
- Early life cycle
- High inflation
- Few suppliers
- Small purchase levels
- Low unionization
- High exports/low imports

Some strategic factors associated with high profitability
- High market share
- Low relative costs
- High perceived quality
- Low capital intensity
- Intermediate level of vertical integration

EXHIBIT 6.4
Some general PIMS principles relating market selection and strategic planning to profitability. *Source*: Buzzell and Gale 1987, p. 274.

	This Business (%)	Losers (%)	Winners (%)
Actual ROI	18.0	5.9	26.2
Cash flow/investment	−3.0	−1.3	4.7
Total R&D/sales	6.2	4.8	2.8
Total marketing/sales	1.2	9.1	11.4
Relative % new products	0.0	3.7	−2.6
Fixed-capital intensity	44.0	57.0	33.1

EXHIBIT 6.5
The PIMS Limited Information Report compares the focal business to winners and losers in the same market. The Limited Information Model requires only a subset of the data that the full PIMS model requires. *Source*: Cole and Swire 1980.

vice to indicate what range of outcomes (for ROI and related performance measures) are consistent with a business's market position and strategy. On the other hand, a firm is on a weak foundation if it uses the model for making specific strategy recommendations like "by defining our market more narrowly, we will increase our market share and hence our ROI." (For a direct challenge to this type of focus on market share, see Anterasian, Grahame, and Money [1996].) Because PIMS has been the most widely publicized and widely supported source of cross-sectional information about business strategy, the results emerging from the program have undergone considerable scrutiny both by academics (who question the way the data have been collected and the structure of the models) and by practitioners (who challenge the relevance of both the specific recommendations and the data—most of which were collected more than a decade ago—to current business problems). Our view is that PIMS is simply a good method of benchmarking. It provides reference points and allows managers to ask questions about business performance and the relevance of specific business strategies, but the PIMS results should not be used normatively to recommend policies by themselves. (The portfolio analysis exercise helps you to explore the PIMS models in detail.) Another good method of benchmarking is the use of the ADVISOR model (Chapter 8).

The PIMS program has provided a useful resource to explore how, historically, a number of critical issues such as the impact of cost structures, access to scarce resources, corporate culture, and the nature of the competitive environment mediate the relationship between marketing strategy and firms' performance. (See Boulding and Staelin 1993, and Jacobson 1990, for example). As noted in Chapter 2 new methods of collecting benchmarking data use the Internet and the notion of "data currency."

PRODUCT PORTFOLIO MODELS

Wind (1981) classifies the many product portfolio models as standardized models, customized models, and financial models.

Standardized product portfolio models assume that the value of market position or market share depends on the structure of competition and the stage of the product life cycle. Thus in one way or another competitive strength and rate of market growth play prominent roles in all such models.

The Boston Consulting Group (BCG) approach

The earliest and most widely cited standardized approach is the growth/share matrix developed by the Boston Consulting Group (BCG). In this approach the company classifies all of its strategic business units (SBUs) in the business portfolio matrix (also called the growth/share matrix), shown in Exhibit 6.6. There are several things to notice:

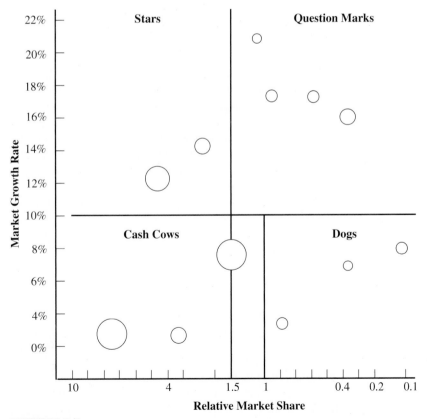

EXHIBIT 6.6
The BCG business portfolio matrix. *Source*: Lilien, Kotler, and Moorthy 1992, p. 554.

- The vertical axis, the market growth rate, shows the annualized rate at which the various markets in which each business unit is located are growing. Market growth is arbitrarily divided into high and low growth by a 10 percent growth line.
- The horizontal axis, relative market share, shows the market share for each SBU relative to the share of the industry's largest competitor. Thus a relative market share of 0.4 means that the company's SBU stands at 40 percent of the leader's share, and a relative market share of 2.0 means that the company's SBU is the leader and has twice the share of the next-strongest company in the market. Relative market share conveys more information about competitive standing than absolute market share; an absolute market share of 15 percent may or may not mean market leadership until we know the leader's share. The more SBUs with a relative market share greater than 1.5 that a company has, the more markets it leads. The relative market share is drawn on a logarithmic scale.
- The circles depict the growth/share standings of the company's various SBUs. The areas of the circles are proportional to the SBUs' dollar sales.
- Each quadrant represents a distinct type of cash flow situation, leading to the following classification of SBUs:
    1. *Stars* are high-growth, high-share SBUs. They often use cash because they need cash to finance their rapid growth. Eventually their growth will slow down, and they will turn into cash cows and become major cash generators supporting other SBUs.
    2. *Cash cows* are low-growth, high-share SBUs. They throw off a lot of cash that the company uses to meet its bills and to support other SBUs that are cash using.
    3. *Question marks* (also called *problem children* or *wildcats*) are low-share SBUs in high-growth markets. They need a lot of cash to maintain and increase their shares. Managers must think hard about whether to spend more to build these question marks into leaders; if they do not, they will have to phase the question marks down or out.
    4. *Dogs* (also called *cash traps*) are low-growth, low-share SBUs. They may generate enough cash to maintain themselves, but they do not promise to be large sources of cash.
- The higher an SBU's market share, the higher its cash-generating ability, because higher market shares are accompanied by higher levels of profitability. On the other hand, the higher the market growth rate, the higher are the SBU's requirements for cash to help it to grow and maintain its share.
- The distribution of the SBUs in the four quadrants of the business portfolio matrix suggests the company's current state of health and desirable future strategic directions. The company in Exhibit 6.6 is fortunate in having some large cash cows to finance its question marks, stars, and dogs.
- As time passes SBUs will change their positions in the business portfolio matrix. Many SBUs start out as question marks, move into the star category if they succeed, later become cash cows as market growth falls, and finally turn into dogs toward the end of their life cycles.
- Management's job is to project a future matrix showing where each SBU is likely to be, assuming no change in its strategy. By comparing the current and future matrices, management can identify the major strategic issues facing the firm. Its task in strategic planning is then to determine what role it should assign to each SBU in the interest of allocating resources efficiently. Managers usually evaluate four basic strategies:
    1. Build or improve market position and forgo short-term earnings to achieve this goal.
    2. Hold or preserve the current market position.
    3. Harvest or get a short-term increase in cash flow regardless of the long-term effect.

4. Divest, sell, or liquidate the business because the firm can use its resources better elsewhere.

The main concept behind the BCG approach is that of cash balance—that the long-run health of the corporation depends on some products generating cash (and profits) and others using that cash to grow. Unless a company has an unusually favorable cash flow, it cannot afford to sponsor too many products with large cash appetites. On the other hand, if resources are spread too thin, the company may end up with a number of marginal businesses and reduced capacity to finance promising future opportunities.

The GE/McKinsey approach

While easy to understand, the BCG approach has been criticized by some as too inflexible and simplistic to be universally applicable. Indeed the growth/share dimensions of the BCG approach can be viewed as elements (or as a special case) of the multifactor portfolio matrix pioneered by General Electric (GE): the *GE/McKinsey multifactor matrix*. In the GE/McKinsey approach businesses are displayed against two composite dimensions: *industry attractiveness* and the company's *business strength*. These dimensions in turn are composed of a series of weighted factors that make up the composite dimension. Both the factor weights and the factors themselves may vary from one application to another. For example, industry attractiveness includes measures of market size, growth rate, competitive intensity, and the like, while business strength includes such measures as market share, share growth, and product quality.

Management gives each business a rating for each factor and gives each factor a weight. These factor ratings are multiplied by the weights and summed to arrive at a position in the strength/attractiveness matrix.

The matrix has nine cells. The three cells in the upper right are those in which the company has a strong position and should be considered for investment and growth. The three cells along the diagonal are of intermediate overall attractiveness, and the company should consider a policy selectively enhancing businesses in those cells to generate earnings. Finally, the cells in the lower left corner are low in overall attractiveness, and the company should consider harvesting and divesting businesses in those cells.

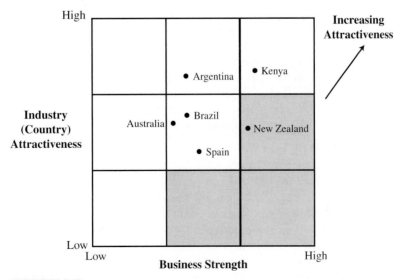

EXHIBIT 6.7
Portion of GE/McKinsey matrix for Ford tractors' multinational portfolio. *Source*: Sudharshan 1995, p. 258.

EXAMPLE

(From Sudharshan 1995.) Ford Motor Company's tractor division uses the GE/McKinsey approach to evaluate a portfolio of country markets (Exhibit 6.7). In this application, managers defined business attractiveness for tractors in a country as follows:

Business attractiveness = Market size

+ 2 × Market growth

+ 0.5 × Price control/Regulation rating

+ 0.25 × Ratification requirements

+ 0.25 × Local content and compensatory report requirements

+ 0.35 × Inflation

+ 0.35 × Trade Balance

+ 0.30 × Political factors.

Note that the factors Ford uses to address business attractiveness are quite specific to a portfolio-of-countries problem; for other applications, even for tractors, the factors might be quite different.

While more complete than the BCG approach, the GE approach shares the benefits and problems associated with all standardized portfolio approaches. Its benefit is that it is easy to implement, communicate, and understand. Its limitation is that it attempts to boil down business strategy to the interplay of a small number of somewhat arbitrary dimensions that may ignore important specific aspects of the business planning environment.

In contrast to the standardized portfolio approaches, customized approaches do not pre-specify dimensions or objectives. (The GE portfolio planning software allows you to build a customized matrix and the portfolio analysis exercise allows you to apply this tool to a product portfolio problem.)

The product-performance matrix approach (Wind and Claycamp 1976) allows managers to select dimensions. In an application at a major industrial firm, management selected four dimensions: industry sales, product sales, market share, and profitability. In allocating resources this approach follows the BCG method, but it is based on projected sales response to alternative marketing strategies.

Financial models

The analogy between the business portfolio problem and the stock portfolio problem has prompted the adaptation of financial portfolio models to this problem area. Financial portfolio analysis deals with investments in holdings of securities generally traded through financial markets. The objective is typically to create an efficient portfolio—one that maximizes return on investment for a given level of risk or that minimizes risk for a specified level of return. To apply this approach to business portfolios, managers must be able to assess the expected rate of return, the variance of that return, and the correlation between returns for any pair of businesses.

The approach is theoretically appealing. In practice, however, it has proved difficult to obtain reliable estimates of the key data inputs needed and it has seen limited application. P. Anderson (1979, 1981) and Cardozo and Wind (1980) discuss its applications further.

Analytic Hierarchy Process

The Analytic Hierarchy Process (AHP) is another approach for assessing and allocating resources in a portfolio. AHP is particularly useful when a firm can bring a logical structure to a problem but has great difficulty making quantitative assessments of the economic consequences of alternatives, a frequent problem in strategic-marketing decisions.

The AHP is an interactive, structured process that brings together the key decision makers who represent diverse functions and experiences. As a group they integrate "objective" market data with subjective management judgment. The process is based on three steps:

1. Structuring the problem as a hierarchy of levels (Exhibit 6.8). In constructing the hierarchy, the decision makers generate creative options and identify the criteria for their evaluation.
2. Evaluating the elements at each level along each of the criteria at the next higher level of the hierarchy. The decision makers use a nine-point scale to make the evaluation and base it on a series of paired comparisons.
3. Weighting the option. The model uses a weighting algorithm to determine the importance of their options in relation to multiple criteria or objectives. The algorithm is based on the idea that pairwise comparisons recover the relative weights (importance) of items or objects at any level of a hierarchy.

Given, for example, n objects, $A_1, \ldots, A_n$ and an unknown vector of corresponding weights $w = (w_1, \ldots, w_n)$, we can then form a matrix of pairwise comparisons of weights:

$$
A = \begin{array}{c} \\ A_1 \\ \vdots \\ A_n \end{array}
\begin{array}{c} A_1 \cdots A_n \\ \begin{bmatrix} \dfrac{w_1}{w_1} & \cdots & \dfrac{w_1}{w_n} \\ \vdots & \ddots & \vdots \\ \dfrac{w_n}{w_1} & \cdots & \dfrac{w_n}{w_n} \end{bmatrix} \end{array}.
\tag{6.8}
$$

We can recover the scale of weights, $w_1, \ldots, w_n$ through some simple matrix calculations such that the computed weights recover the respondents' pairwise judgments as closely as possible. (The procedure also synthesizes the weights at each level of the hierarchy to obtain overall priorities for each decision alternative.) Unlike the product portfolio model where the user directly provides the weights assigned to the criteria, the AHP model infers these weights based on a set of simple pairwise judgments.

This process produces explicit guidelines for selecting a strategy based on the decision makers' prioritization of the strategic options. The resulting strategy can be made to satisfy the corporate mission and a set of multiple objectives under alternative environmental scenarios and time horizons.

Secondary output from the AHP includes explicit weights for the objectives or criteria used for evaluating the options. The AHP provides a consistency index for a set of pairwise judgments (a good guide to the quality of those judgments) and also provides a simple way to conduct sensitivity analysis on the results. Through its computer software (Expert Choice, included with this book) the process also helps identify areas requiring the collection of additional information—those relationships on which people cannot reach consensus and for which the results can vary significantly depending on which of the conflicting views is accepted.

EXAMPLE

Ciba-Geigy, one of the top 10 pharmaceutical groups in the world, needs to determine a long-term international strategy for its dermatological unit. The dermatological unit is a part of Ciba-Geigy's Other Therapeutic Areas (OTA) Division, and it is a relatively small but profitable business. The promotional efforts for dermatological products have been irregular; the world market share has dropped correspondingly. Nevertheless, a new segment of this market is developing. The corporation can count on significant competitive advantages for a market entry because of its research and development efforts in the field. Management identified three possible strategies for the dermatological unit:

1. Milking the existing business based on its topical cortisone (TC) products and a product to be launched in the near future. It would abandon or license products in development. This option uses the minimal R&D efforts and marketing expenses necessary to maintain a presence in the marketplace.
2. Expand the existing business. It would launch TC products in development to improve performance in this segment. R&D and marketing efforts would be set accordingly.
3. Expand the existing business and create a new segment. Develop and launch nonsteroidal topical products, greatly increasing R&D and marketing expenses.

The strategy guidance committee is in charge of evaluating the strategic consistency of product groups' actions in terms of market opportunities and resource allocations. Its objective is to ensure maximization of results based on compatibility with overall strategy and objectives, organizational constraints and political aspects of the decision, market opportunities, investment and costs, competitive advantages, and risk. The committee used the AHP model to assess the alternatives identified for the dermatological unit with respect to the foregoing objectives.

The committee constructed a three-level hierarchy to help it determine the appropriate strategy to follow. Exhibit 6.8 gives two levels of criteria; for example, one criterion (level 1) is compatibility and consists of two criteria at a secondary level: consistency and support. Exhibit 6.9 shows the output of the analysis: for these input values, the third option (to expand and create a new segment) is best along all criteria except the level of risk.

A useful aspect of the Expert Choice software is its ability to conduct sensitivity analyses visually. These analyses show how changes in the relative importance of a criterion alter the relative attractiveness of each of the alternatives.

In running the AHP model, one should consider the possibility of rank reversal. Rank reversal occurs when alternative A is perferred to B before a (third) alternative C is intro-

Overall Goal
1.00

Level 1	Compatibility (.108)	Market Opportunity (.446)		Inventory & Cost (.065)	Competitive Advantage (.262)	Risk (.119)

| Level 2 | Consistency (.047) Support (.062) | Growth (.183) Geographic Concentration (.041) Volume (.041) $$$Level (.116) | | Fixed Costs (.022) Variable Costs (.035) Substitution Costs (.007) | Differentiation (.209) Current Position (.052) | Technical (.060) Marketing (.024) Distribution (.024) Conjuncture (.012) |

| Level 3 (example) | Support Creation (.047) Expansion (.027) Milking (.015) | | | | | |

Criterion	Definition
$$$ LEVEL	Expected price acceptance level
COMPETITIVE ADVANTAGE	Competitive advantage with respect to proposed solution
COMPATIBILITY	Compatibility of solution with overall group strategy
CONJUNCTURE	Sensitivity to conjuncture
CONSISTENCY	Apparent consistency with overall objectives
CURRENT POSITION	Current position on the relevant market
DIFFERENTIATION	Differentiation toward competition
DISTRIBUTION	Risk of physical distribution failure
FIXED COSTS	Fixed costs of solution (mid entry)
GEO CONCENTRATION	Geographic dilution of the relevant market
GROWTH	Growth of relevant segment
INVESTMENTS & COSTS	Investments and costs required by solution
MARKETING	Commercial risk of failure
MARKET OPPORTUNITIES	Market opportunities of solution
RISK	Uncertainty raised to solution
SUBSTITUTION COSTS	Costs of substitution (disengagement)
SUPPORT	Likeliness of affiliated support
TECHNICAL	Technical risk of failure
VARIABLE COSTS	Variable costs of solution (margin)
VOLUME	Volume of the relevant market

EXHIBIT 6.8
This decision hierarchy for the Ciba-Geigy example has two levels of criterion importance (levels 1 and 2) and their evaluation of one node for the three alternatives (level 3).

duced. The Expert Choice software provides two options to address this problem: (1) the ideal mode (which preserves ranks with the addition of alternatives) and (2) the distributive mode, which allows ranks to change. The ideal mode should be used when decision alternatives are not all distinct and you do not want the presence of copies or near-copies of alternatives to affect the outcome. The distributive mode allows weights to change consistently by assigning higher weights to alternatives that are both better than others on important criteria and differ markedly from other alternatives.

AHP has broad applicability for marketing strategy. Saaty and Vargas (1994) report its use in pricing new products, developing corporate strategy, determining the market attrac-

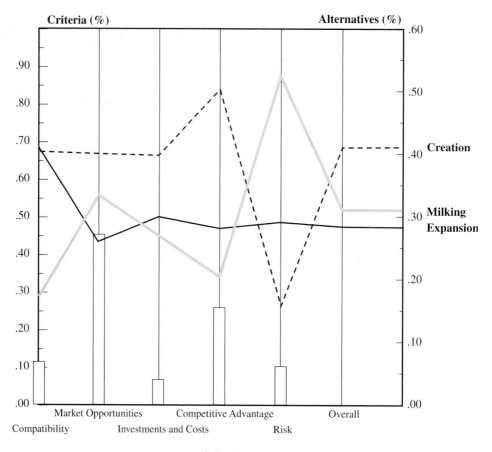

EXHIBIT 6.9
For the Ciba-Geigy example, the "creation" alternative performs well on all criteria except the level of risk.

tiveness of developing countries, and other applications, and Calantone et al. (1999) show how it can be used in the new product screening process.

COMPETITION

Substitutes exist for most products, and it is naive to assume that a firm can investigate marketing strategy without regard to competition. Dolan (1981) presents an overview of approaches to competition from microeconomics and marketing, as well as empirical evidence about types of competition from various industry studies.

In the cases of monopoly and perfect competition, microeconomic theory provides unambiguous results for optimal marketing-mix decisions. But for oligopoly, the problem of specifying competitors' behavior makes it difficult to determine what the optimal marketing mix should be. The models of oligopoly provide no single solution or strategy for a firm to follow (Singer 1968).

Considering the entire sequence of moves and countermoves by competitors is hopelessly complex. Instead, Baumol (1972) proposes one of two approaches: (1) ignore the interdependence between competitors or (2) assume each competitor is a rational economic agent and then determine a likely set of actions that will allow it to maximize its expected utility.

These two approaches relate to work on *reaction functions*, first proposed by Cournot in the nineteenth century, and to *game-theory* models. The classical reaction-function hypothesis is that each seller assumes the output (action) of rival firms to be fixed and then sets a price to maximize profits. This approach leads to unrealistic results that are apparently nonoptimal (Mansfield 1979; Scherer 1980), although Green and Krieger (1991) claim this approach closely approximates actual market behavior.

Dolan (1981) points out that many people in marketing think that game-theory models would solve many competitive issues if only some critical mathematical hurdles could be overcome. This is unlikely to be the case: game theory has "insuperable problems as a prescriptive theory of rational decisions in conflict situations [and] the prescriptive aspect of game theory ought to be written off" (Rapoport 1966, pp. 202–203). A main problem is that game-theoretic results depend critically on assumptions about the objectives, on the amount and nature of information available to the players, and on the analytical capabilities of *all* competitors, factors the decision-making firm is unlikely to know. However, the models are quite important for gaining insight into market structure and operation (Lilien, Kotler, and Moorthy 1992, especially Chapters 4–6). (For some assessments of the uses and limitations of game theory, see Aumann [1987] and Rubinstein [1991].)

Another approach to understanding competition comes from the area of industrial organizations, which explores the nature of the structural variables that influence competitive behavior. Porter (1980) attributes the type and intensity of competition to eight major factors:

1. Number and size distribution of competitors
2. Industry growth rate
3. Cost structure and storage costs
4. Extent of product differentiation
5. Divisibility of capacity additions
6. Diversity of competitors
7. Importance of the market to firms
8. Heights of exit barriers

Dolan (1981) has examined a number of industry studies to determine the extent to which these structural variables determined the mode of competition. He summarizes his results in four lessons:

1. High fixed costs promote competitive responses to share gain attempts.
2. Low storage costs reduce competitive reactions.
3. Growing primary demand reduces competitive reactions.
4. Large firms avoid price competition.

He suggests that structural dimensions of the market affect the likelihood of market response and the form of that response, but these are broad guidelines at best.

An econometric approach to modeling competition uses *reaction matrices*. We illustrate a reaction matrix with an example. Two competitors in the market compete on price (P) and advertising (A). Exhibit 6.10 shows their reaction matrix. Under the assumption that these elasticities are constant and stable over time and that a multiplicative function is a reasonable representation of the structure of interaction, the η's (elasticities) in Exhibit 6.10(a) can be estimated via the following equations.

$$\log P_1(t) = a_1 + b_1 \log P_2(t) + b_2 \log A_2(t), \tag{6.9a}$$

$$\log A_1(t) = a_2 + b_3 \log P_2(t) + b_4 \log A_2(t); \tag{6.9b}$$

Then b_1 is an estimate of η_{P1P2}, b_2 is an estimate of η_{P1A2}, and so on. A portion of the reaction matrix for the application reported in Lambin, Naert, and Bultez (1975) is reproduced in Exhibit 6.10(b). All the diagonal elements are significantly different from zero, signifying that firm 2 reacts directly to any change in the marketing mix of firm 1 (it changes price in response to a price change, for example). In addition, the lagged advertising-price elasticity is also significant, showing that indirect responses are important as well. This example shows that reaction behavior is complex, involving multiple responses and potential lags in time; therefore tracking direct responses could lead to mistaken inferences (Leeflang and Wittink, 2001).

Firm 2

	P_2	A_2
P_1	$\eta_{P_1 P_2}$	$\eta_{P_1 A_2}$
A_1	$\eta_{A_1 P_2}^{\dagger}$	$\eta_{A_1 A_2}$

Firm 1

$^{\dagger}\eta_{A_1 P_2}$ = percentage change in A_1 with a 1% change in P_2.

EXHIBIT 6.10(a)
Reaction matrix: two firms, two marketing variables.

Firm 2

	Price	Advertising (Lagged)
Price	$0.664^{\dagger}$ (0.030)	$1.898^{\dagger}$ (0.825)
Advertising	0.008 (0.005)	$0.273^{\dagger}$ (0.123)

Firm 1

† Significant at the 0.05 level.

EXHIBIT 6.10(b)
Partial reaction-function example showing that firms not only react in kind (price decline following price decline, for example) but firm 2 increases advertising when firm 1 lowers price. *Source*: Lambin, Naert, and Bultez 1975, p. 119.

Bensoussan, Bultez, and Naert (1978) have used this approach to optimize marketing-mix decisions in a competitive environment. Lambin (1976) and Hanssens, Parsons, and Schultz (2001) report additional applications of the approach for assessing competitive behavior. Hanssens (1980) extends the basic model to explicitly represent multiple competitors and to develop interrelationships among the marketing elements within a particular firm, and Carpenter and colleagues (1988) show how to address markets where competitive effects are differentially and asymmetrically distributed among competitors.

Strategy	Key Elements	Generic Strategies	Key Limitations
Organizational economics	Competition versus collusion Isolating mechanisms	Cost competition Product differentiation Strategic group competition (inter- versus intra-group)	Interaction between cost and quality Nature of "mixed" strategies Stability of groups
Sports games	Planning and coordination Importance of time Impact of rule change	Offensive Defensive Imitative Innovative	Territorial logic of the game Fixed rules Degree of control
Military	The role of signaling Direction vs. surprise Multiple time periods	Direct confrontation Flanking Guerrilla Avoidance	Focus on conflict Importance of terrain Focus on external factors and logistics
Evolutionary ecology	Scope of competition Forms of organization Interaction between firms and their markets	Generalist Specialist Niche	Nature of competition Level and unit of analysis Every species has a "niche"

EXHIBIT 6.11

An overview of competitive strategy analogies and their potential application to marketing-strategy problems. *Source*: Sudharshan 1995, p. 55.

One of the main insights and contributions of this approach is the measurement of what drives the sales that result from a firm's action in a competitive market. A firm can gain sales in a market by increasing its market share or by maintaining its share while the market grows. The market can grow as a direct result of what the firm does (increasing its advertising) or as an indirect result as competitors respond to the firm's actions: competitors respond to the firm's advertising program by increasing their advertising as well, leading to an indirect effect, an increase in total market sales. Formally this approach decomposes sales elasticity as follows:

$$\text{Sales elasticity} = \text{Shared effect} + \text{Size effect}; \tag{6.9}$$

$$\text{Share effect} = \text{Direct effect} + \text{Competitive-response effect}; \tag{6.10}$$

$$\text{Size effect} = \text{Direct effect} + \text{Competitive-response effect}. \tag{6.11}$$

This decomposition permits a more careful assessment of the firm's marketing-mix options as well as their direct and indirect effects. The Acme liquid cleanser exercise with the competitive advertising software illustrates some of the complexities of studying competitive response.

Sudharshan (1995) brings an interesting perspective to the analysis of competition by looking at four domains that have studied competition extensively: industrial organization economics (IO), sports games, military operations, and evolutionary ecology. Each domain can be characterized by the key elements in the way it handles competition, and the types of competitive strategy guidelines or insights one can glean from studying the area.

Exhibit 6.11 summarizes Sudharshan's evaluation of these approaches. For example, industrial organizational economics recognizes strategic groups and mobility barriers as key to the critical asymmetries among competing firms and identifies three ways firms can isolate themselves from competition: they can differentiate their product offerings, they can lower their costs, or they can collude. Industrial organization economics focuses largely on the mechanisms a firm can use to isolate itself from competition.

The sports game approach focuses on the relationship between prior planning and execution, on the role of time (single play, game, season), and multiple routes to success. In addition rules are most codified in sports (second most in the industrial organization perspective and the least in the other two paradigms), making changes in rules critical in the selection and modification of competitive strategies.

As we stressed in Chapter 1, the marketing engineering approach to solving marketing decision problems provides structure and insight as well as direct policy recommendations. Perhaps this value is best illustrated in the domain of analyzing competitive market strategies, where an understanding of analogous situations provides insight, but where it is risky to apply that insight directly to a marketing problem. These analogies expand our thinking and offer a set of theories and tools that we can combine and apply in developing competitive marketing strategy (Heil and Montgomery, 2001).

SUMMARY

In making marketing-strategy decisions we must allocate marketing resources over time. A key strategic decision is to time market entry and exit. We have identified some key determinants of success in that decision and a method (decision analysis) that can prove handy. Deciding when to enter the market and analyzing a firm's portfolio of products and markets are central to allocating strategic-marketing resources. Such tools as shared-experience models, product portfolio models, and the Analytic Hierarchy Process can be very helpful to those who must structure and facilitate these resource-allocation decisions.

To determine marketing strategy one must consider the competition. Our competitive-analysis toolkit is primitive, but it is far from empty. We can combine sound competitive intelligence with such approaches as market simulations, reaction-matrix analysis, and the study of analogs to better understand the benefits and consequences of our strategic allocation decisions.

ICI AMERICAS R&D PROJECT SELECTION CASE[1]

ICI America is a subsidiary of the British-based Imperial Chemical Industries, Ltd (ICI). In 1992, ICI's sales totaled $11.2 billion, making it one of the largest chemical companies in the world. The company reported a net income of $218 million for 1992 before exceptional items and discontinued operations. Its North American subsidiaries included US-based ICI Americas (primarily in polyester film, pharmaceuticals, and specialty chemicals) and Canadian Industries Ltd. (strong in explosives, pulp and paper chemicals, and environmental services). The Canadian subsidiary marketed industrial explosives (e.g., for use in mining operations) throughout North America. ICI Americas focused on the military explosives market. The post–cold-war era had reduced this subsidiary's growth opportunities. To survive within a fast growing company, it needed new products, especially for nonmilitary applications.

ICI Americas' Canadian subsidiary discovered a new but unpatentable application for one of its products (anthraquinine or AQ): use it as an agent for reducing pulp mill water pollution. AQ acts by reacting with paper and pulp waste pollutants to form solids that can be filtered out of the paper-mill waste stream. AQ was distilled from coal tar and used principally in manufacturing dyes. Coal tar is a byproduct of coke production, and coke is used exclusively to make steel. Hence ICI's current AQ capacity was directly related to the world demand for steel.

If Canadian Industries could develop the AQ product and process on a commercial scale, it could create a large global market. Reducing the pollution from pulp and paper processing was a major goal of environmental regulatory authorities worldwide. For example, the state-of-the-art Kraft process produced offensive odors and an effluent that reddened streams.

At the time, all the AQ produced in the world would have satisfied only a small portion of the unpatented and unconfirmed market for the product as a pollution-reducing agent. One of ICI's competitors, BASF, had an alternative process for synthesizing AQ; if ICI did not move rapidly, BASF might preempt ICI's potential leadership position.

ICI needed to do a quick analysis to decide whether to go ahead with its R&D expenditures or to abandon the project.

The following were the primary issues it considered in making this decision:

- Would market tests confirm that there was a significant market for the product?
- Could the company develop a new process for making this product that was technically feasible?
- Even if there were a significant market and the process were technically feasible, would the company's board sanction an investment in a new plant necessary to produce the product on a commercial scale?
- Assuming the answers to the above questions were all *yes* and the plant were built, would the venture turn out to be successful?

Assuming that each of these four issues had a *yes* or *no* answer, the management team estimated the conditional probabilities for each event (Exhibit 1).

---

1. Adapted from Hess (1993).

Event	Probability
Market tests show there is a significant market	0.6 ± 0.15
The project turns out to be technically feasible	0.15 ± 0.10
Board sanctions plant expenditures	0.8 ± 0.2
Commercial success if introduced	0.8 ± 0.2

EXHIBIT 1
Probabilities for Water Pollution Problem

Expense or Gain	Net Present Value (Million $)
Research expense	$ 1.5 ± 0.40
Marketing Research expense	$ 0.2 ± 0.05
Process development expense (presanction)	$ 3.0 ± 0.75
Commercial development expense (presanction)	$ 0.5 ± 0.25
Commercial development expense (postsanction)	$ 1.0 ± 0.25
Value of project if commercially successful	$ 25.0 ± 12.50

EXHIBIT 2
Monetary Estimates for Water Pollution Problem

The following primary economic factors affected the profitability of the venture:

■ The research expenses to identify a new production process for the product.
■ The marketing research cost to determine whether there was a significant market.
■ The process development costs, including presanction engineering.
■ The commercial development costs, both before and after the board's sanction.
■ The venture value (net present value) if successful.

Estimates of these values are given in Exhibit 2. The plus-or-minus signs show the degree of uncertainty about the values. (All dollar values are in millions of dollars.)

The decisions and actions the firm considered were to decide whether to abandon the product now or:

■ To spend on research and marketing development. If marketing research indicates an insignificant market for the product, then abandon the project.
■ If process development research indicates that the project is not technically feasible (given positive marketing research), then abandon the project.

- If the process appears technically feasible, then invest in process development. If that research indicates that the process is technically infeasible, cut expenses and quit.
- If the project is technically feasible, spend on process development and begin commercial development. If the company board then declines to sanction the money for the new plant, cut expenses and quit.
- If the board approves, spend on further commercial development. By this time the company has made all of its decisions. If the venture turns out to be a commercial success then it gains the venture value for a success (less expenses so far). Otherwise the company has lost the money spent so far, but that is all.

EXERCISES

ICI managers thought that a decision tree analysis would be appropriate for the problem they faced. Construct a decision tree to represent this problem structure. The managers are interested in the following questions:

1. What is the maximum ICI should be willing to invest in presanction process development research?
2. What decision would the model recommend under optimistic, pessimistic, and best-guess scenarios?
3. Which probability and payoff estimates have the most impact on the decision?
4. What should ICI do and why?

PRODUCT PLANNING USING THE GE/MCKINSEY APPROACH AT ADDISON WESLEY LONGMAN CASE[1]

It was July 1997 and Mark Roth, manager of business books at Addison Wesley Longman, was facing a bit of a dilemma. He was about to present his 1998 fiscal year new book budget and had three new marketing books in his portfolio. One of them, *Marketing Engineering*, was a bit different from the other two. It did not currently have a large natural market but might ultimately be a big winner, he thought, if it were promoted properly. He was about to make his plans for annual promotion, kicking his program off at the August American Marketing Association Educator's Conference in Chicago. His main question was—How should he prioritize the promotional resources for the three new books?

BACKGROUND

Addison Wesley Longman is one of the largest global educational publishers, selling books, multimedia and learning programs in all major academic disciplines to the primary, secondary, higher education, professional, and English language teaching markets throughout the world.

AWL is part of the Pearson Group. Pearson PLC, headquartered in London, is an international provider of media content and is composed of information, education and entertainment companies. Pearson reported the following fiscal year-end figures:

1996 Sales ($ mil.): $3,746.8
1-Yr. Sales Growth: 19.5%

1996 Net Inc. ($ mil.): $413.1
1-Yr. Net Inc. Growth: (7.7%)

1996 Employees: 17,383
1-Yr. Employee Growth: (10.5%)

In addition to AWL, some of Pearson's companies include: the Financial Times Newspaper, Penguin/Putnam, The Economist Group, Pearson Professional, and Pearson Television. In 1988, Addison-Wesley was acquired by Pearson PLC. The Company merged with Longman, a sister Pearson publisher, in 1995 and became Addison Wesley Longman. In 1996, AWL acquired HarperCollins Educational Publishers, consisting of HarperCollins College and Scott Foresman, and merged those operations with AWL's.

Each company that makes up AWL has historic publishing strengths and accomplishments. Many people in the United States remember learning to read with Elson Basic Readers featuring Dick, Jane and Spot. Scott Foresman, their publisher, celebrated its centennial in 1996. Longman, which published Dr. Samuel Johnson and Wordsworth, among other British literary lights, has a distinguished 273-year tradition. The former HarperCollins College, now part of the Higher Education Publishing Group, traces its roots back to 1817 when the

---

1. Note: The individuals, events and details in this case are fictional and were created purely for pedagogic purposes. The background about AWL and the three books is real, however.

brothers Harper established a publishing house in New York City. When Melbourne Wesley Cummings published MIT physics professor Francis Sears's Mechanics in 1942, Addison-Wesley was launched as an outstanding publisher of science, mathematics and computer texts.

The college division of AWL markets books to colleges and universities throughout the world. Its main promotional resources are sampling, brochures, direct mail, exhibitions (primarily at academic meetings) and direct selling to professors. The US college division salesforce includes over 200 individuals, each of whom specializes in an academic specialty (business, science, humanities) and works in a regional territory, servicing several dozen schools. AWL managers believe that their salesforce is particularly important in encouraging instructors to consider and adopt new textbooks, and they use their salesforce as a key tool in their product introduction mix.

The new marketing texts

The three new marketing texts that AWL was introducing in the summer of 1997 were:

Advertising and Sales Promotion Strategy by Gerard J. Tellis, USC, aimed primarily at MBA advertising and sales promotion courses;

Analysis for Strategic Marketing by Vithala R. Rao, Cornell University and Joel H. Steckel, New York University, aimed at capstone MBA strategic marketing courses, particularly those with analytic content; and

Marketing Engineering by Gary L. Lilien and Arvind Rangaswamy, Penn State, a book and extensive package of software to deliver marketing tools to support marketing decision making.

The *Marketing Engineering* book was a bit different from others in that it included two volumes plus a CD with 26 software packages that could be applied immediately to both classroom and prototype professional business problems. However, as the book was sufficiently different from anything else on the market, both Mark and the authors felt that the AWL selling effort could make a critical difference in the acceptance of the book, especially in the short run.

The new marketing book promotional challenge

As Mark was finalizing his proposal, he began glancing through the *Marketing Engineering* book. He noticed that the book identified several methods that could be used to approach a problem just like his.

"What a novel idea," he thought. "Why not use the ideas and tools from *Marketing Engineering* to determine what to do here?"

He determined that one *Marketing Engineering* tool might be appropriate for his problem: the GE/McKinsey approach.

Applying the GE approach

Mark found the GE approach implemented in *Marketing Engineering* in a tool called Portfolio Planning (GE). In consultation with his planning staff, Mark came up with the following factors for the components of the composite dimensions:

Industry Attractiveness:
- Market size (total volume of books to be sold in the next three years).
- Growth rate (annual growth rate of market size).
- Technological requirements[2] (high would be "traditional book," low would be when the book needed capabilities of producing multimedia, software, etc.).
- Leading edge[2] (low would include more traditional topics; high would include new and emerging topics).

Business Strength:
- Market share (book's likely share of market after two to three years).
- Share growth (annual growth rate of market share).
- Investment/cost[2] (high means low need for investment; low means high need for investment).
- Synergy (ability of book to induce sales of other AWL books or to lead to signings of new authors).

Mark then attempted to assign weights (from 1 to 5) to the factors above. He decided that the weights depended on the strategic position of the firm—whether it wanted to view itself as a traditional publisher or as a leading-edge publisher. Hence he constructed two sets of weights: "Traditional," and "Leading Edge" (Exhibit 1). He also rated each of the businesses, Tellis, Rao/Steckel, and L&R on each of the factors (Exhibit 2).

	Traditional Weights	Leading-Edge Weights
Industry Attractiveness		
Market size	5	2
Growth rate	2	5
Technological requirements	5	1
Leading edge	1	5
Business Strength		
Market share	3	2
Share growth	1	5
Investment/cost	5	1
Synergy	1	5

EXHIBIT 1
AWL's weights for new marketing texts (1-5 scale)

2. Note: Because of the way the GE approach works, "high" means better for the firm, "low" means worse. So, "high cost" gets a low rating and "low cost" gets a high rating.

	Tellis	**Rao/Steckel**	**Lilien/ Rangaswamy**
Sales Potential	20	15	12
Industry Attractiveness			
Market size	5	3	2
Growth rate	2	4	4
Technological requirements	4	5	1
Leading edge	2	3	5
Business Strength			
Market share	3	2	2
Share growth	3	4	4
Investment/cost	4	5	1
Synergy	1	3	5

EXHIBIT 2
Ratings for new AWL marketing texts.

EXERCISE

Mark was planning to allocate his new product budget equally across the books. Using the GE approach:

1. Describe the business portfolio and the options available to AWL.
2. What does the GE approach suggest about the relationship between AWL's strategic objectives and its promotional plans?
3. What should Mark do?
4. What other factors should Mark consider in setting and allocating the budget?
5. Comment on the uses and limitations of the GE model.

APPENDIX: DETAILS OF THE THREE BOOKS FROM AWL PROMOTIONAL MATERIAL

1. *Advertising and Sales Promotion Strategy*

First Edition, 475 pages, 1998, Cloth, 0-321-01411-1

Gerard J. Tellis, University of Southern California

Unique; theoretically rigorous, rich with examples, and useful for designing successful strategies.

Promotion is a rich topic that integrates perspectives from a number of disciplines including marketing, economics, psychology, anthropology, and operations research. It is also a dynamic area that is constantly changing as firms develop new media, appeals, and methods to better compete with their rivals in a rapidly changing environment. *Advertising and Promotional Strategy* is designed to communicate all of these aspects of promotion. After reading this book, prospective managers will understand the topic of promotion well enough to be able to design successful strategies.

Hallmark Features

- Tellis's writing is simple, direct, and lively. He uses short sentences and simple language even when explaining complex ideas.
- The text has a managerial orientation—more so than any other text in the field—helping prospective managers understand the topic well enough to design successful strategies.
- The book's presentation is practical, analyzing a large number of relevant examples and describing creative promotional strategies.
- Tellis draws from the most recent research in the social sciences to ensure that students are exposed to the most current knowledge in the field.
- This book explains why phenomena occur and tries to show why certain strategies succeed, while others fail.
- Using contemporary examples, the author clearly communicates points.
- Tellis explains theories, concepts and terms from first principles—his book requires no particular prerequisites in business, marketing, economics, or psychology.
- Special topics include coverage of regulation (Chapter 2), direct marketing (Chapter 16), ethics, international strategy, and brand equity.
- Your students will enjoy the text's 16-page color advertisement insert, lavish examples and numerous illustrations.

Supplements include: Instructor's Manual with Test Bank/Transparency Masters/CD-ROM Guide, a Computerized Test Bank for Windows, a Videotape with advertisement clips for classroom use, an Instructor's CD-ROM with ad stills and clips, and an Interactive CD-ROM case on Intel that allows the student to act as a marketing manager designing a promotional strategy.

This title has the following supplements:

Instructor's Resource Manual by Siva K. Balasubramanian, Southern Illinois University includes the Instructor's Manual, Test Bank, Transparency Masters, and CD-ROM Guide. 0-321-40771-7

Instructor's CD-ROM includes a gallery of print advertisements and quick-time clips of TV commercials. 0-321-01643-2

Videotape contains advertisement clips for classroom use. 0-321-40772-5

Intel Case CD-ROM for Windows by John Quelch, Harvard University Business School, is based on a Harvard Case Study on the Advertising Campaign for Intel on introducing its product into the UK market. The student acts as a marketing manager with an advertising budget, who needs to decide who to target: the novice home computer buyer, the average business person who uses a computer, or the corporate purchasing manager. With this, they then develop an advertising and promotion campaign using a series of provided advertisements, etc. 0-321-02175-4

2. *Analysis for Strategic Marketing*

First Edition, 400 pages, 1998, Paper, 0-321-00198-2

Vithala R. Rao, Cornell University
Joel H. Steckel, New York University

Provides more modern scientific marketing methods for strategic marketing courses than any other book on the market.

Analysis for Strategic Marketing is the first book in the market to tie the aspects of strategic marketing and marketing research together. In fact, this book has no direct competitors—it simply fits in a class of its own. Rao and Steckel offer you this paperback book as a versatile tool to be used as a main text or supplement in your Senior undergraduate or MBA-level advanced Marketing Research or Strategic Marketing courses.

Hallmark Features
- This text contains a mid- to high-level mix of strategy and marketing research.
- Adding analysis and research tools to traditional marketing book material, *Analysis for Strategic Marketing* is considered unique.
- Offering four cases with solutions included in the Instructor's Manual, Rao and Steckel allow and encourage flexible use of their textbook.

This title has the following supplements:

Instructor's Manual Package by Marjorie Doyen, Cornell University, includes the Instructor's Manual, Test Bank, and Data Disk. 0-321-01900-8

3. *Marketing Engineering: Computer-Assisted Marketing Analysis and Planning*

First Edition, 350 pages, 1998, Cloth, 0-321-01417-0

Gary L. Lilien, Penn State and Arvind Rangaswamy, Penn State

This book integrates concepts, analytic marketing techniques, and operational software to train the new generation of marketers, helping them to become marketing engineers.

This textbook and the related course are aimed at educating and training marketing engineers to translate concepts into context-specific operational approaches using analytical, quantitative, and computer modeling techniques. As an underlying philosophy, this book links theory to practice and practice to theory. The entire textbook package is made up of three components: the main text; a CD-ROM that includes over 25 software packages as well as customized on-line help files; and a user manual that contains software tutorials, problem sets, and cases that enable the student to apply the concepts and software, providing them with an immediate learning experience. Lilien and Rangaswamy designed this primarily as a text for a one-semester, capstone MBA course, but the material has been used successfully in executive programs and in undergraduate classes as well.

Hallmark Features

- This book is so cutting-edge—integrating concepts, analytic marketing techniques, and operational software—that it has no direct competition.
- The text material provides a detailed, but user-oriented view of the marketing engineering approach to marketing problems in the information age.
- Chapter summaries highlight key points in each chapter while problem sets and cases enable students to apply the concepts and software.
- This book is uniquely packaged as three components: Text, User Manual, and CD-ROM. The 26 software packages on the CD-ROM allow students to implement the concepts in the course and to apply those concepts immediately—each package includes a customized set of online help files. The User Manual includes problem sets and cases, as well as a tutorial for each software package with step-by-step instructions.
- The videotape, available to adopters, provides award-winning examples of how concepts and tools have been applied profitably in a number of companies, saving them millions or even billions of dollars.

Created by the authors out of Penn State University, the book's Web site can be used for problems and continuing software updates and upgrades, so that adopters can continue to upgrade the software as it evolves.

This title has the following supplements:

Videotape that provides award-winning examples of how concepts and tools have been applied profitably in a number of companies, saving them millions or even billions of dollars. 0-321-00775-1

Instructor's Manual/Solutions Manual/Transparency Masters/Instructor's CD-ROM with PP. The Instructor's CD-ROM contains a complete PowerPoint Presentation for the professor to illustrate key concepts in each chapter. 0-321-03042-7

PORTFOLIO ANALYSIS EXERCISE

*NOTE: A version of the GE model, saved as Portfol.xls, contains the data for the four SBUs in the portfolio analysis already entered and saved. Use that version of the spreadsheet to run the exercise, or develop a customized spreadsheet using the general GE model described in the tutorial. To select Portfol.xls, go to the **Model** menu, choose **GE: Portfolio Planning** and then **Portfolio Planning Exercise**.*

In late 1995, the board of directors restructured Conglomerate, Inc. into a divisional organization with each division subdivided into a number of SBUs (strategic business units). Its Food Production and Products Division (FPPD) comprised three consumer and one industrial SBU related to the food industry. This division was placed under the leadership of Henry Antworth, and Conglomerate's board asked Henry to come up with a strategic examination of the health and future for these four businesses.

1. **The Corn-Transformation Products Group** *(TRANS)* is Conglomerate's corn-processing equipment and parts business. TRANS equipment and related supplies are used internally by Conglomerate's other corn-related businesses and are also sold to a range of customers (some of whom compete with Conglomerate in other businesses). In these product markets, which have had a negligible growth rate, TRANS is seeing sales of just over $100 million in a global industry that generates about $550 million in sales annually, making TRANS either the second- or third-largest supplier in this business. Only four percent of those sales come from products TRANS introduced in the last five years. In the last few years, TRANS has been spending about seven percent of sales on marketing activities and about 1.8 percent of sales on R&D. Margins have been tight in this business recently, and investments in new tooling have led to a return on investment of minus two percent in the last year.

2. **Salted-Corn Snackfoods Group** *(SALT)* is one of Conglomerate's consumer products SBUs, producing a range of salted snacks based mainly on corn. Conglomerate has some special plants, expertise, and holdings in corn that have allowed it to maintain a market share of over 22 percent in this $450 million market. This market is growing nearly three percent a year, and SALT earns about seven percent of its sales from products introduced in the last five years. SALT has been spending about nine percent of sales on marketing activities and a bit over two percent on R&D in recent years. Its relatively low plant utilization (75 percent) and stable sales give the firm a healthy (19 percent) return on the relatively small investment this business has been requiring.

3. **Unsweetened Breakfast Cereals Group** *(UBC)* competes with Post and Kellogg, but with a more narrow range of products based primarily on the firm's expertise in corn. UBC estimates that it has about a five percent market share of the $9.8 billion market, growing at a bit over three percent per year. In recent years it has been spending about eight percent of sales on marketing activities and just under three percent of sales on R&D. New products in this business

make up about five percent of sales, and recently the ROI for this SBU has been 17 percent.

4. **The Powerdrinks Group *(POWER)*** is Conglomerate's most recently launched consumer division. The firm considers itself the market leader in this area with about 27 percent of the approximately $470 million market. (Corn and corn products are an important base for all POWER products. It has been spending over 11 percent of sales on marketing activities and over three percent of sales on R&D in this turbulent market. That market is growing at about 5.5 percent annually and POWER sees about 15 percent of its sales from new products. POWER's most recent ROI is 13 percent.

Antworth scheduled a retreat for the first week of June 1996 with his planning staff and the SBU managers. These are some of the questions that he hoped to answer at the retreat:

1. How well or poorly were these businesses performing? (Each SBU manager had to submit a capital and operating budget request by summer's end that justified the level of proposed spending in the business.)
2. Both marketing and R&D budgets were under close scrutiny. How much seemed reasonable (best?) to invest in these activities within the division and how should those expenditures be allocated across SBUs?
3. What type of strategy should Conglomerate pursue with these SBUs? (Invest? Divest? Hold? Harvest?)

Three weeks prior to the retreat, Antworth distributed these three questions to the SBU directors. He immediately got four irate phone calls: These questions could be answered only through "business feel" and "experience." Antworth had just participated in a seminar on strategic marketing analysis (i.e. marketing engineering); he suggested that the group apply some of the analytic structures from that program to answer his three questions. In a half-day session a few days before the retreat, he had each business manager provide the data needed to run two of the models from that seminar, the PIMS model and the GE/McKinsey model. He also led them through an exercise to arrive at best-guess answers to the following questions:

Q1: If your SBU's marketing budget were increased by one percent of its present value, what increase in market share would you expect to see (by what percent of the present share)?

Q2: If your SBU's R&D budget were increased by one percent of its present value, what increase in relative quality would you expect to see (by what percent of its present level)?

After some discussion, the members of the group agreed on the following answers:

	Market Share Increase	Quality Increase
TRANS	1.8%	3.1%
SALT	2.2%	2.9%
UBC	1.9%	2.7%
POWER	1.5%	2.4%

EXERCISES

1. Using the PIMS model, the GE model, or any other approach you think is appropriate, decide what advice to give Antworth. (If your approach requires additional information, be specific about what that information is and how you plan to obtain it.)

TIP: When using the PIMS model, look at the impact on ROI of the joint changes (in spending and impact on share and quality, respectively) to see what PIMS has to say about the relative effectiveness of marketing and research spending on profitability—are we under- or oversupporting these businesses, according to PIMS?

2. Comment more generally on the uses and limitations of PIMS and the GE model for analyzing these kinds of situations at Conglomerate.
3. How does this approach compare with the Analytic Hierarchy Process, another approach that Antworth's planning staff was considering?
4. Some people claim that these models can be distorted to support any preconceived strategies that managers like those at Conglomerate bring to the table. Comment on this claim.

JENNY'S GELATO CASE

Jennifer Edson was putting the finishing touches on the business plan for a new enterprise. Jenny's Gelato, a retail establishment that will serve authentic Italian gelato by the scoop or dish or for carryout. (Gelato is a rich, tasty ice cream sold in Italy.) Wholesale sales to restaurants in the Washington, D.C., Metro area were also included in the plan. The business concept had been in Jennifer's mind since she has spent a semester abroad in Florence, Italy, during her undergraduate studies and got "hooked" on gelato.

Jennifer looked over the report and everything seemed in order—it included everything from proforma financial statements to taste-test studies that she had conducted. A venture capitalist, in fact, thought the plan was so good that she had obtained a verbal commitment for $50,000 in start-up capital. Restaurant equipment, store fixtures, and gelato-making machines had been comparison priced, and she knew that these fixed costs would eat up the entire $50K. Everything was "all systems go" for a summer opening save for the selection of a specific retail site. She felt that a downtown location was best because of the preponderance of yuppies in the area. Negotiations for a specific site had come down to two alternatives, both of which involved leasing space.

She had an option on an off-street site in the fashionable area of Georgetown in Washington, D.C. Twelve-hundred square feet of retailing space was available in a vacant store whose only entrance was via an alley off M Street (a street that was constantly congested with pedestrian and auto traffic). The attractiveness of the Georgetown location was due principally to its proximity to entertainment spots and retail shopping traffic. Lots of weekday and evening trade was available, as Georgetown was a haven for tourists and college and high school students. A long-term lease could be secured for $2,500 a month but Jennifer would absorb nearly all the costs of converting the site to a 20- to 25-seat gelateria. The option on the lease had to be exercised in two weeks.

The alternative site was in an attractive, enclosed retailing and office complex on Pennsylvania Avenue only five blocks from the White House. Shops in the mini-mall included restaurants, men's and women's clothing stores, a jewelry store, a large record and tape store, and a series of international fast-food boutiques. The base for traffic was office workers within a three-block radius, and faculty, staff and students of a large urban university whose buildings were all within three to four blocks of the complex. One thousand square feet was available for $2000 per month on a one-year lease, which would be re-negotiated by the developer each year. The developer would also receive two percent of the businesses' gross revenues. Since the location was new, the developer would custom-build wall partitions and arrange other space configurations to suit the tenant.

Jennifer developed a spreadsheet to summarize market research she had conducted on the two alternative sites (see Exhibit 1). She also prepared a spreadsheet for the proforma income statement for the business (see Exhibit 2). Two of the assumptions underlying this latter spreadsheet were:

- The price per serving of gelato was $2.00.
- The cost of goods sold would be approximately 40 percent of the retail price.

Exhibit 2 also shows the results of a comparative breakeven analysis on the two alternate sites. As expected, the higher fixed costs associated with the Georgetown site resulted in a higher breakeven point. Jennifer was unsure as to how much importance to attach

Criterion	Pennsylvania Avenue (Foggy Bottom)		'M' Street (Georgetown)	
Traffic *(hourly pedestrian count)*	*afternoon (noon-5 pm)*	*evening (5-11 pm)*	*afternoon (noon-5 pm)*	*evening (5-11 pm)*
Monday	302	142	156	524
Tuesday	286	202	215	426
Wednesday	194	114	187	394
Thursday	371	176	272	404
Friday	226	224	413	735
Saturday	75	110	521	816
Sunday	62	90	795	692
Total	1516	1058	2559	3991
Average	216.6	151.1	365.6	570.1
Average (afternoon & evening)	183.9		467.9	

EXHIBIT 1
Pedestrian Traffic Count Study*
*Each site's storefront traffic counts taken during a single week in April. Traffic count is defined as pedestrians passing by.

to this analysis because she felt that breakeven examined only downside risks. The real number she was most unsure about was forecasted sales revenues for the first year of operations.

Based on her review of trade and academic sources, Jennifer developed the following mental model of factors that would influence sales of gelato at a retail site:

- Sales of gelato would likely exhibit pronounced seasonal trends similar to those of regular ice cream, frozen yogurt, and other frozen desserts.
- Sales of gelato (like those of ice cream and other frozen desserts) represent an unplanned, impulse type of buyer behavior.
- Gelato and other frozen desserts were often bought after consumers had participated in certain activities (after a movie, during a shopping trip, after participating in or watching a sporting event, after dinner at a restaurant).
- Gelato demand would be higher among trendy, upscale yuppies who had cosmopolitan interests that often included experimenting with exotic or so-called gourmet food.
- Like many convenience retail concepts, sales for a gelateria would be heavily influenced by the volume of pedestrian traffic and proximity to complementary retail businesses, restaurants, and places of entertainment.
- Competition from other ice-cream stores was an important factor—some malls, shopping areas, and other locations had reached the point of saturation or "overstoring." The uniqueness of the gelato product, however, was expected to offset the heavy competition shown in traditional ice cream sales.

These factors suggest that even though Jennifer Edson had done her homework with lots of conceptualization, financial analyses, and observational studies she still had a complex problem on her hands in making the site-selection decision. Before she actually

	Pennsylvania Avenue (Foggy Bottom)	'M' Street (Georgetown)
Revenues	$1,500,000	$1,500,000
Cost of goods sold	600,000	600,000
Gross Profit	900,000	900,000
Rent	24,000	30,000
Landlord percentage	30,000	0.00
Depreciation	5,000	5,000
Utilities	8,500	9,000
General overhead	50,000	50,000
Advertising	100,000	100,000
Site preparation	0	20,000
Licenses & permits	1,500	1,500
Total Operating Expenses	$219,000	$229,000
Net Profit		
Operating profit	$681,000	$671,000
Interest expense	9,000	9,000
Taxable profit	672,000	662,000
Income tax	248,640	244,940
After-tax Profit	$423,640	$417,060
Breakeven Analysis		
Fixed Costs		
Rent	$24,000	$30,000
Depreciation	5,000	5,000
Utilities	8,500	9,000
General overhead	50,000	50,000
Interest	9,000	9,000
Advertising	100,000	100,000
Site preparation costs	0	20,000
Total Fixed Costs	$196,500	$223,000
Variable Costs per Unit (scoop)		
Cost of goods sold	$0.80	$0.80
Landlord percentage	0.04	0.00
Total Variable Costs	$0.84	$0.80
Contribution (per scoop)	$1.16	$1.20
Breakeven ($)	$338,793	$371,667
Breakeven (scoops)	169,397	185,833

EXHIBIT 2
Proforma Income Statement and Breakeven Analysis

Criterion	Pennsylvania Avenue (Foggy Bottom)	'M' Street (Georgetown).
Building	Brand new office/retail	Old row house converted to retail space complex
Locale	Enclosed mini-mall adjacent to PA Ave	Freestanding site in alleyway off M Street
Ambiance	Business offices, university	Upscale shops, restaurants area
Traffic base	State Dept., World Bank, government employees, faculty, staff of university	Tourists, college students, retail shoppers, patrons of entertainment spots
Avg. hourly traffic	184	468
Size	1000 sq. ft.	1,200 sq. ft.
Cost	$2000 per month, developer takes 2 percent of annual gross revenue	$2,500 per month
Breakeven volume required		10 percent higher
Site development	Substantial assistance from developer/owner	Lessee assumes all costs of improvements
Competition	Two ice-cream stores within a six-block radius of site	Five ice-cream stores within a six-block radius of site

EXHIBIT 3
Comparison of Site Alternatives

developed the Expert Choice model she decided to summarize the information that she had collected about the characteristics of the two sites (see Exhibit 3). With this, Jennifer Edson began the process of developing her Expert Choice model.

EXERCISES

1. Construct an EC model similar to the one shown in Exhibit 4 to select the best retail site for the gelateria. (Make sure your criteria reflect both the quantitative and qualitative aspects of this problem.)
2. Use EC's sensitivity analysis utility to perform a what-if analysis of the alternative. Document your assumptions.
3. Provide a one-page report (excluding tables and figures) summarizing your recommendations to Ms. Edson.

Competition	Competition at site.
Condition	Condition of store
Count	Count of traffic during business hours
Drawing Power	Drawing power of location for this type of retail store
Financial	Financial considerations
Foggy Bottom	Foggy Bottom area of Washington, D.C.
Georgetown	Georgetown area of Washington, D.C.
Landlord $	Percent of sales commission to landlord
Lease $	Cost to lease
Physical	Physical characteristics of site
Siteprep	Outlay required to prepare site
Size	Size of store
Traffic	Traffic at site
Visible	Visibility

EXHIBIT 4
EC Model for Retail-Site Selection: Select the Best Retail Site

ACME LIQUID CLEANSER EXERCISE

BACKGROUND

Conglomerate Inc.'s Acme (A) liquid household cleanser operates in a highly competitive market segment with its main competitor, Baker (B). Acme brand managers are trying to determine the appropriate level of advertising while considering Baker's likely response.

While this market has many complications, for the purpose of this analysis, Conglomerate is willing to assume that Acme and Baker share the market and that advertising is the main determinant of both total market size and market share.

THE COMPETE MODEL

The company's analytic staff has put together a simple spreadsheet that incorporates its basic assumptions about the market and has called it Compete. In this spreadsheet, a period is a quarter (four periods make up a year) and you want to do a two-year analysis (eight periods or quarters).

The Compete spreadsheet incorporates several of the important effects in the competitive household cleanser market:

- The market is responsive to total advertising spending, and sales vary between a low level (with no advertising) and an upper limit (with unlimited advertising—the most the market can absorb). The market reacts to advertising almost immediately.
- Acme's market share is partly related to its share of advertising spending and partly related to the carryover effect of past spending. (A parameter in the analysis allows you to study the impact of different levels of carryover.) Because of differences in advertising copy and product quality, Acme's spending on advertising has a different level of effectiveness than Baker's.
- To the best of Conglomerate's knowledge, Acme's production costs and Baker's are roughly the same, as are their prices to the trade.

EXERCISES

This market has been in flux recently, and it appears that Baker has been matching Acme's advertising spending pattern closely, but you are not sure that that pattern will continue. By using the spreadsheet, you can analyze different reaction patterns. Acme management has asked you to come up with an advertising budget and projections of market share and profitability for the next eight quarters. Use the spreadsheet and Excel's Solver function to support those proposals.

Scenario 1: Assume that Baker matches Acme's spending over the next eight quarters. What level of advertising spending is best for Acme? ("Best" means maximizes cumulative profit here.)

Scenario 2: Suppose that Baker does not respond (stays with $1mm per period). What is Acme's best level of advertising spending?

Scenario 3: Suppose that Baker does the same analysis that you do in question 2 and, based on the solution, optimizes its advertising spending. How much will Baker spend now? And how should Acme respond to this different level of spending?

Repeat this process of Acme → Baker → Acme → Baker until the advertising policies stabilize. Compare the levels of advertising and profit with those in scenarios 1 and 2.

Scenario 4: Suppose Baker becomes more aggressive and spends 50 percent more than Acme does each period (Level of Competitive Response = 1.5). What is Acme's best advertising policy in this case?

Scenario 5: Acme is considering acquiring Baker. If it were to do so and the Federal Trade Commission [FTC] would permit it to, what should it spend to maximize joint profits? How does that spending level and profitability compare to the other cases?

Scenario 6: Acme has recently replaced its ad agency, and it expects to get ads that perform about 20 percent better from the new agency. Revisiting scenario 1, what should its level of ad spending be and what is the projected profit in this case?

After running these scenarios (and assuming Acme does not acquire Baker) what ad spending policy do you recommend? (Run any other analyses you feel appropriate here. The policy you recommend can be adjusted annually.)

CHAPTER 7

Part III: Developing Marketing Programs

New Product Decisions

In this chapter we

- Provide a conceptual framework to highlight the major decisions in developing a new product
- Describe conjoint analysis, a method useful for making product design decisions and for evaluating new product opportunities
- Describe methods for forecasting the sales of a new product both before and shortly after it is introduced into the market

INTRODUCTION

A product is anything that can be offered in the market for attention, acquisition, use, or consumption that might satisfy a want or a need. Most of the products we think of are *physical products*. But products also include *services*, such as concerts, overnight package delivery, management consulting, vacation tours, online services such as America Online, and MBA programs. Even such entities as the American Red Cross can be viewed as products in the sense that a transaction with the Red Cross makes us feel positive toward it and about ourselves.

Marketing managers view products at three levels:

Core product: The core product is the most fundamental aspect of a product: the need or want that the customer satisfies by buying the product. As Ted Levitt (1960) noted, a customer buys a three-inch hole, not a three-inch drill-bit, or as Charles Revson of Revlon put it: "In the factory, we make cosmetics; in the store, we sell hope."

Tangible product: Marketing managers must transform the core product into a tangible product, consisting of features, styling, quality level, brand name, and packaging. They make the core product into something that customers can buy. A vacation package by Club Med helps transform customers' desires for adventure, excitement, finding a mate, or getting away from it all into a tangible product that they can conveniently purchase. A Visa credit card transforms customers' desire for secure, convenient, and quick access to credit into a tangible product.

Augmented product: The augmented product includes enhancements to the tangible product in the form of additional services and features to make the product competitively attractive, such as toll-free customer information, installation guides, delivery, warranty, and after-sale services.

The product is the most important element of the marketing mix. To develop and manage successful products managers must make key decisions during the new product development process and in managing the portfolio of existing products. Here we focus primarily on new product development (NPD), which consists of several stages (Exhibit 7.1) (Urban and Hauser 1993).

In the first stage, *opportunity identification*, people generate ideas and articulate the market opportunities associated with the ideas. For example, R. J. Reynolds Tobacco Company came up with the idea of the "smokeless cigarette" to address the opportunity represented by increasing social objections to smoking. Gillette came up with the idea of spring-mounted

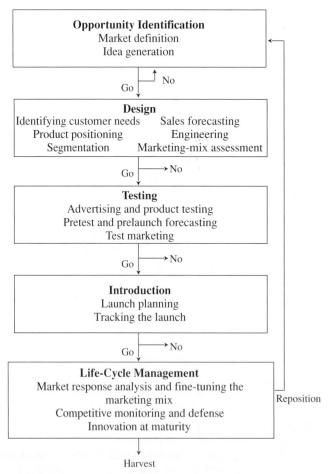

EXHIBIT 7.1

An outline showing the various stages and decisions of the new product development (NPD) process. Adapted from Urban and Hauser 1993, p. 38.

razor (Sensor) that would provide a closer and smoother shave than any other razor available in the market. If the firm decides that the new idea is attractive, it proceeds to the next stage.

In the *design* stage, the firm transforms the idea into a physical or psychological entity by giving it form, features, and meaning. For example, the smokeless cigarette was designed to heat the tobacco instead of burning it, thus reducing the "environmental" tobacco smoke in the air by 65 to 99 percent as compared with a regular cigarette. Other features included a sleek package with thin golden diagonal lines on a white background to convey the image of a "cleaner cigarette" and the brand name "Premier" to indicate a superior product.

During the design stage managers also seek a better understanding of the market segments for the product, explore alternative ways to position the product in those segments (Chapter 3), work with engineers in making cost-benefit trade-offs for various product features, develop and evaluate product prototypes, develop initial marketing plans, and generate sales forecasts for selected product designs.

In the *testing* stage, managers assess whether the product will gain market acceptance when it is introduced and whether the product will meet the firm's goals for profit and market share under a proposed marketing plan. Testing also offers diagnostic information about what changes to the product or marketing program will improve its chances of success. If the various tests (e.g., taste tests, advertising copy tests, and simulated shopping tests) indicate success, the firm introduces the product.

In the case of Premier cigarettes, test market results indicated that consumers did not value the social benefits highly enough to overcome its perceived poor taste (it leaves a charcoal-like aftertaste) and to a lesser extent its higher price and its "strangeness" (each package contained special instructions on how to light the cigarette). Most test stores reported high trial but low repeat-purchase rates. Not surprisingly, R. J. Reynolds did not introduce Premier nationally.

Introducing the product into the market calls for decisions on such issues as coordination of production and marketing plans, fine-tuning product design for manufacturability, and managing the distribution pipeline. It also calls for continuous monitoring of market performance to refine the introduction strategy (e.g., price and advertising copy).

If the firm successfully introduces the new product, it puts in place a *life-cycle management* process to maintain the growth and profitability of the product. Successful products invite competition, and the firm thus needs defensive strategies. Successful products also draw organizational resources away from other products. The firm must use portfolio management strategies across the entire product line to ensure both short-term and long-term profitability of its entire portfolio of products (Chapter 6).

At each of the five stages the firm makes a *go* or *no go* decision to move to the next stage (Exhibit 7.1). The foregoing process represents an ideal, and individual firms customize the process depending on the requirements of a specific product and the capabilities of the firm. In some cases a firm may skip a stage (e.g., testing) or iterate several times between stages before moving forward.

The costs and risks associated with new products are high. Most new products fail to achieve the objectives managers set for them, and they are withdrawn from the market. Urban and Hauser (1993, p. 61) estimate that the average costs (in 1987 dollars) were $700,000 for opportunity identification, $4.1 million for design, $2.6 million for testing, and $5.9 million for introduction. (The projects they analyzed included 60 percent industrial, 20 percent consumer durables, and 20 percent consumer nondurables.) In other categories short product cycles (e.g., a few weeks for new movies, a few months for new notebook computers) require that managers get the product right the first time rather than refining it after introduction.

Several research studies indicate that using a disciplined approach to developing new products improves the likelihood of success. For example, Hise et al. (1989) report that firms that use the full range of up-front activities associated with the stages shown in Exhibit

7.1 have a 73 percent success rate as compared with a 29 percent success rate for firms that use only a few of the up-front activities.

NEW PRODUCT DECISION MODELS

The NPD process is coming under close scrutiny as companies operating in today's competitive markets scramble to develop new products that simultaneously accomplish several objectives. New products today should be competitive in global markets, offer good value to customers, be environmentally-friendly, enhance the strategic position of the company, and enter the market at the right time. To meet these challenging objectives, companies are embracing new concepts and techniques to support changes in their NPD processes. These new approaches include such *techniques* as quality function deployment and stage-gate reviews, such *measures* as cycle time, and such *organizational mechanisms* as cross-functional teams (see, for example, Griffin 1993; Zangwill 1993). An accompanying trend has been the growth of computer models to facilitate decision making at every stage of the NPD process (Rangaswamy and Lilien 1997). We mention some of these models in the next section. In the remaining sections of this chapter we describe in detail selected models for which we provide software implementations with this book.

Models for identifying opportunities

Generating ideas: Creativity in NPD requires both divergent thinking (lateral thinking) and convergent thinking. Using such divergent thinking techniques as free association and the synectics process, people can generate a large number of ideas. They can then use convergent thinking to sort through those ideas and decide which are the most promising. Several commercial software packages are available to support the creative process, based on the premise that interaction between people and software enhances creativity.

Mindlink is a software package that implements the well-known synectics process, which combines structured problem solving with techniques for stimulating creative thinking. The user starts by stating a problem (e.g., increase battery life of notebook computers). The program encourages divergent thinking by using "wish triggers" (I wish computers could store energy the way cacti store water) and "idea triggers" (ways to realize the wishes—e.g., a battery mechanism dispersed throughout the body of the notebook computer). The software also uses a mechanism called "option triggers" to help users to evaluate ideas and to select those that are likely to be most effective in solving the problem.

Other software for generating ideas include IdeaFisher and Inspiration. IdeaFisher encourages divergent thinking for making nonobvious connections through free associations. The software combines two databases: one with 65,000 words and phrases linked by an extensive set of cross-references, and the other with a bank of about 700 questions (e.g., How would a child solve this problem?) organized in categories. When the user enters a word or phrase, the software retrieves associated words and phrases. For example, the term *new product* retrieves such associated terms as *marketing*, *imagination*, and *research experiments*, and each of these in turn triggers other connections (e.g., imaginary people and places). This process may be continued iteratively.

The Inspiration software program offers a visual environment to facilitate the creative process. Starting from a core concept, the user "spans outward" to develop links to other concepts related to the core concept using such visual aids as charts, maps, symbols, and outlines. For example, starting with the core idea of developing a notebook computer with a 10-hour battery life, the user can link this visually (with arrows) to other activities such as "check patent office for battery technology," "contact R&D in sister company," and "initiate feasibility study within the company." Each of these actions can then be visually linked to other concepts. Concepts put on a computer screen may be easily rearranged during the process.

Software packages for idea generation typically provide only minimal support for evaluating those ideas. Other decision models are available for evaluating ideas in terms of their potential value to the company and their likelihood of success if introduced.

Evaluating ideas: The Analytical Hierarchy Process (described in Chapter 6) is useful for prioritizing several new product projects based on user-provided criteria and subcriteria. The manager first establishes a hierarchical structure of criteria and subcriteria on which to evaluate the new product. Next the manager provides pairwise evaluations of the alternatives at each level on the hierarchy. The software synthesizes these evaluations across the entire hierarchy to come up with numerical scores that indicate the overall relative attractiveness of the new product ideas. AHP is particularly useful for conducting visual sensitivity analyses to explore how changes in the importance of a criterion alter the relative attractiveness of each alternative. Exhibit 7.2 shows a hierarchical model for evaluating new pharmaceutical products. Calantone, Di Benedetto, and Schmidt (1999) provide a more detailed example of the application of the AHP model for new product screening.

Another model that we can use to evaluate new product ideas is the GE Portfolio Planning model (See Chapter 6). This model is particularly useful if there are a number of ideas that need to be simultaneously screened for their strategic desirability. To simplify your ability to apply this model, we have included within the software the criteria for new product evaluation proposed by R. Cooper (1993, p. 310). Cooper studied nearly 200 new prod-

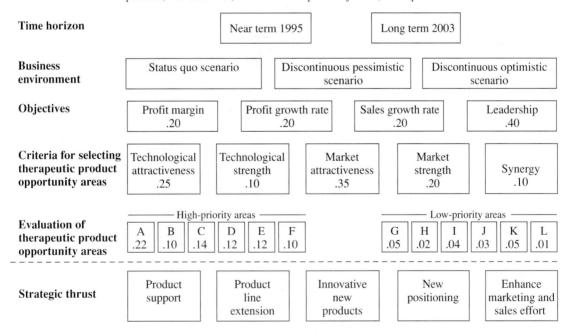

Some of the items within levels, and all numbers are disguised.
Source: Jerry Wind, The Wharton School

EXHIBIT 7.2
An example showing how a pharmaceutical firm used the Analytic Hierarchy Process (AHP) to assign numerical priorities to 12 different product opportunity areas (A through L).

uct projects using 80 variables to isolate the variables that help separate the successful products from the unsuccessful ones (R. Cooper 1986, 1992). We have marked these variables with a "C#" within the software to help you quickly identify them as Cooper-defined variables.

Finally, the *NewProd* model, also based on R. Cooper's research (1986, 1992), helps a firm to evaluate a new product idea in terms of the associated business risks and rewards and to determine the organizational resources needed to improve the product's chances of success. The current version of the model is based on 30 of the 80 variables (reduced to nine orthogonal factors) that were most instrumental in explaining the products' degrees of success.

Firms use NewProd under the guidance of a trained facilitator. Project members independently provide data on the 30 variables identified in Cooper's research and then meet to discuss differences in their inputs, repeating the process until there is general agreement about the inputs. The NewProd program compares this input profile of the new product (summarized on nine factors) with its internal database of factor scores to determine the percentile position of the new product as compared with the factor scores of products in the database. This evaluation may be customized by industry (e.g., consumer packaged goods, business markets, or electronics and communications). Several reports help the project members to determine whether the new product score on each factor is consistent with that of a successful or unsuccessful product and indicate what they should do to improve the new product's chances of success. Firms can also use this software to evaluate a number of products at different stages of development, thereby evaluating a new product in the context of the entire portfolio of new products under development. In many ways NewProd operates like PIMS, ADVISOR, and other shared-experience models (Chapters 6 and 8).

Models for product design

Many products and services can be viewed as bundles of product attributes—that is, products can be represented as combinations of levels of product attributes. For example, a Toyota Camry car could be described as SIZE = midsize, TYPE = sedan, MPG = 30 in city, ENGINE = V-6 fuel-injection, OPTIONS = sunroof, and so forth. In purchasing products, customers make trade-offs between the various attributes, for example, between a sunroof and a V-6 engine. Conjoint analysis is a formal technique for examining these trade-offs to determine an effective combination of attribute levels that will perform well in the marketplace. In particular, conjoint analysis is useful for deciding what attributes should be designed into a new product to maximize its expected performance in a market already containing competitors and for determining which market segment(s) will find a particular product configuration most appealing. In short, conjoint analysis is a formal method by which a firm can have its customers design the products that would appeal most to them. We describe conjoint analysis in detail in the next main section.

Another approach to designing new products that match customers' needs is the BUNDOPT model (Green and Kim 1991). The BUNDOPT model is particularly useful for deciding what combination of features to offer in a new product. For example, in designing a car the firm could incorporate a number of optional features such as cruise control, a roof rack, a hood air deflector, or a trailer hitch. The possible options could number 25 or more, but most customers would probably not be willing to pay for more than 5 or 10 of these. However, each customer may want different features. The manufacturer must decide which features to offer to ensure that the car will appeal to the maximum number of customers. The BUNDOPT model uses data obtained from potential customers to address this problem. It can also be used to identify which segments prefer a particular set of features, and the desirability of a particular combination of features to a target segment.

Models for new product forecasting and testing

In Chapter 5 we described several forecasting methods. Most of them require historical data. However, managers must forecast sales and success of new products before they generate any historical data. Good forecasts help firms to minimize the risk of failing in the market and maximize their use of opportunities associated with the product. For example, better forecasts might have minimized the losses on such products as Ford's Edsel, Apple's Newton Personal Digital Assistant (PDA), and General Motors' Wankel engine. Improved forecasts would also have enhanced the profits earned by such products as Mazda's Miata and Mattel's Cabbage Patch dolls, both of which were in short supply.

We can categorize new product forecasting situations based on whether the success of the product depends more on customers' first purchase (i.e., adoption) of the new product or on customers' repeat-purchase behavior. Forecasting first purchase is important for "discontinuous" innovations that *may* require customers to change their current behavior. For example, a customer who is thinking of replacing a Rolodex with an electronic personal information manager (PIM) such as a Filoflex may be reluctant to type information on a keypad instead of writing by hand. Likewise, someone adopting a microwave oven has to learn new ways to cook. These two products were made possible by enabling new technologies (inexpensive integrated chips for the PIM, and controlled microwave generation in a compact unit in the case of microwave ovens), but this need not always be the case (e.g., Chrysler used existing technologies to develop a new category of automobiles, the minivan). However, some innovations based on new technologies do not require customers to change their purchase or use behavior significantly (e.g., DirecTV satellite-based transmission of digital TV signals). Firms in business-to-business markets also need to forecast new product sales, for example, when they introduce new types of manufacturing equipment.

Forecasting repeat-purchase behavior is important for products that are purchased frequently (e.g., packaged goods such as detergents, or industrial supplies). Here the customer may already have a base of experience with which to evaluate the new product. Firms often test their new products in real or simulated markets to develop sales forecasts for them.

Most forecasting is conditional upon a specific marketing plan. Good forecasting models provide diagnostic information on how best to improve the proposed marketing plans, if necessary, by helping the firm identify those controllable variables (e.g., price, product positioning, or advertising) that are most important in driving the sales of the new product.

In the last two main sections of this chapter we describe the Bass model for forecasting first purchase and the ASSESSOR model for forecasting repeat purchase. These are well-established models for forecasting the sales of new products.

CONJOINT ANALYSIS FOR PRODUCT DESIGN

Introduction

It is helpful to view many products and services as bundles of attributes. For example, a pizza is a composite of several attributes such as type of crust and topping, and the amount of cheese. An attribute can have many options or levels (e.g., the topping can consist of pepperoni, veggie, or plain cheese). A bundle is a specific product composed of one option (or level) of each attribute selected for analysis.

Conjoint analysis uses data on customers' overall preferences for a selected number of product bundles and decomposes these overall preferences into utility values (part-worths) that the customer assigns to each level of each attribute. The set of decomposed utility values is referred to as the *part-worth function*.

In the data collection stage of conjoint analysis, the firm obtains data on respondents' preferences for a carefully selected set of product bundles. Each bundle is also called a profile. The selected bundles typically do not include those that dominate other bundles on all attributes of interest. The respondents rate or rank order the bundles to indicate their degree of preference for each bundle. In this evaluation process respondents are forced to make trade-off judgments between attributes because one product bundle may have the preferred levels of an attribute (e.g., pepperoni topping) while containing less preferred levels of other attributes (e.g., higher price). The preference data enable the firm to derive part-worth functions, which can then be used to estimate respondent preference for any product (i.e., any combination of attribute levels) *including those not directly evaluated by the respondents*. As a result managers can efficiently determine the value to respondents of many more product design options than the respondents could evaluate directly. The use of numeric part-worth functions also allows managers to develop quantitative forecasts for the sales or market shares of alternative product concepts under consideration, and to price out non-economic attributes (e.g., delivery in three weeks versus four weeks is worth $X to the respondents).

EXAMPLE

Designing a pizza: To illustrate the basic concepts of conjoint analysis, let us see how it can be used by a packaged foods firm to design a new frozen pizza. We start by assuming that pizza can be described by combinations of attributes—type of crust, type of toppings, amount and type of cheese, price, and other attributes. Suppose that the firm is considering three types of crusts (thin, thick, and pan), four types of toppings (veggie, pepperoni, sausage, and pineapple), three types of cheese (mozzarella, Romano, and mixed cheese), quantity of cheese at three levels (two, four, or six ounces), and priced at one of three levels ($7.99, $8.99, and $9.99). The pizzas are identical in all other respects, such as size, type of tomato sauce, and brand name. Even with this limited set of options there are 324 ($3 \times 4 \times 3 \times 3 \times 3$) different types of pizzas that the company can make by varying the crust, topping, type and amount of cheese, and price. Which of these will be among the most preferred by customers in a target segment?

In the typical conjoint study, marketing researchers would present potential customers in selected target segment(s) with several carefully chosen pizza alternatives. The pizzas can be described in words, shown in pictures, or better still (in this case), actually provided in samples to be taste tested. Here the respondents would evaluate as few as 16 selected pizzas out of the 324 possibilities. Because only 16 ($= 3 + 4 + 3 + 3 + 3$) discrete levels of the attributes are under study, fewer than 16 parameters need to be estimated by the model. Thus it is technically possible to estimate the part-worth that a respondent associates with each attribute level by having that respondent evaluate as few as 16 product bundles. With the information the firm obtains from this respondent's evaluation of the small number of alternatives, it can still assess how this customer will evaluate any of the 324 pizza combinations. This is possible because the basic outputs of conjoint analysis are (1) the (imputed) relative importance that each respondent attaches to each pizza *attribute* (e.g., type of topping is three times as important as amount of cheese), and (2) each respondent's part-worth for each *level of each attribute* (e.g., on a scale of 0 to 30, a customer values veggie topping at 10 points and pepperoni topping at 30 points). Exhibit 7.3 illustrates how one adds up these

Crust (15 points)	**Amount of cheese (10 points)**
Pan (0)	2 oz (0)
Thin (10)	4 oz (8)
Thick (15)	6 oz (10)

Topping (30 points)	**Price (35 points)**
Pineapple (0)	$9.99 (0)
Veggie (10)	$8.99 (20)
Sausage (25)	$7.99 (35)
Pepperoni (30)	

Types of cheese (10 points)
Romano (0)
Mixed cheese (3)
Mozzarella (10)

Ratings of three alternative pizzas for this customer based on the part-worth function

Aloha Special	**Meat-Lover's Treat**	**Veggie Delite**
Pan (0)	Thick (15)	Thin (10)
Pineapple (0)	Pepperoni (30)	Veggie (10)
Mozzarella (10)	Mixed cheese (3)	Romano (0)
4 oz (8)	6 oz (10)	2 oz (0)
$8.99 (20)	$9.99 (0)	$7.99 (35)
Utility = 38	Utility = 58	Utility = 55

Among these three pizzas, this customer most prefers the Meat-Lover's Treat.

EXHIBIT 7.3
An example of conjoint analysis showing one customer's part-worth function for frozen pizza. The numbers in parentheses are the part-worths. For this customer the topping attribute is worth 30 points (on a scale of 0 to 100), and the crust attribute is worth half as much at 15 points. Within the topping attribute, going from a pineapple topping to a veggie topping is worth 10 points and going from veggie to sausage is worth an incremental 15 points.

part-worths to compute any respondent's (or customer segment's) valuation of any possible pizza.

From the part-worths for the respondent shown in Exhibit 7.3, we can compose the ideal pizza (the pizza with the highest preference) for this respondent: a thick crust pizza with pepperoni topping, 6 oz. of mozzarella, priced at $7.99, giving a utility score of 100. This respondent's lowest-rated pizza would be a pan pizza with pineapple topping, 2 oz. of Romano cheese, priced at $9.99, giving a utility score of 0. The other 322 possible pizzas will have scores between 0 and 100. For example, the Aloha Special has a score of 38, the Veggie Delite has a score of 55, and the Meat-Lover's Treat has a score of 58. Note also that this respondent prefers pepperoni (30) to veggie (10) by 20 points (30 − 10); this respondent also prefers paying $8.99 to paying $9.99 by the same 20-point difference, implying that pepperoni topping is worth an incremental $1 to this respondent ($9.99 − $8.99) as compared with a veggie topping.

Although the firm could produce a pizza that will have a utility score of 100 for this customer, it is far from clear that doing so would be profitable. First, all the pizzas do not cost the same to produce, which means that the firm must balance customer preferences for attributes, including price, with costs to determine which pizza would generate the most profit. Second, all customers do not have preferences identical to those of the respondent shown in Exhibit 7.3. Within a target segment, customers will vary in their preferences. Although most customers in the target segment may prefer to pay the lowest price and prefer pepperoni topping, they may differ in their preferences for the type and amount of cheese and the type of crust. Thus no single pizza would be the best for everyone in the target segment. Therefore the firm might seek to develop several pizzas that are among the more preferred options for a large number of customers in a segment—a more complicated problem than simply putting together a pizza with the highest average utility score for the target segment.

As suggested by the preceding example, conjoint analysis is particularly useful for designing products that maximize measured utilities for customers in a target segment. Using the resulting information the firm can modify existing products and services and develop new products that appeal maximally to customers. Early applications of conjoint analysis were of this type. However, increasingly firms are using conjoint analysis for making strategy decisions, such as selecting market segments for which a given product delivers high utility, for planning competitive strategy, and for analyzing pricing policies (Wittink and Cattin 1989).

Conjoint analysis procedure

Conjoint analysis studies typically comprise three stages. In the first stage we design the study. In the second stage we obtain data from a sample of respondents from the target segment. In the third stage we use the data to set up simulations to explore the impact of alternative decision options (Exhibit 7.4).

Stage 1: Designing the conjoint study

Step 1.1: Select attributes relevant to the product or service category. One way to identify these attributes is by conducting a focus group study of target customers (e.g., design engineers in an industrial marketing context). Another possibility is to ask the new product development team what features and benefits it is considering. Yet another approach is to use secondary data, such as *Consumer Reports*, to identify an appropriate set of attributes. Studies that cover more than six attributes may become unwieldy, although studies have been conducted with a large number of attributes. J. Wind et al.

Stage 1—Designing the conjoint study:
    Step 1.1: Select attributes relevant to the product or service category.
    Step 1.2: Select levels for each attribute.
    Step 1.3: Develop the product bundles to be evaluated.
Stage 2—Obtaining data from a sample of respondents:
    Step 2.1 Design a data-collection procedure.
    Step 2.2 Select a computation method for obtaining part-worth functions.
Stage 3—Evaluating product design options:
    Step 3.1 Segment customers based on their part-worth functions.
    Step 3.2 Design market simulations.
    Step 3.3 Select choice rule.

EXHIBIT 7.4
Steps in designing and executing a conjoint study.

(1989) describe the design of the Courtyard by Marriott hotel using a conjoint study with 50 attributes.

Step 1.2: Select the levels of each attribute to be used in the study. We can start by asking the new product development team what specific design options it is considering. In selecting the levels of attributes, we must keep in mind several conflicting considerations:

- To improve the realism of the conjoint study, we should choose attribute levels that cover a range similar to that actually observed in existing products. We should include both the highest prevalent attribute level (e.g., highest mpg among the competing cars) and the lowest prevalent level (e.g., lowest tensile strength).
- We should include as few attributes and attribute levels as possible to simplify the respondents' evaluation task. Typically studies use between two and five levels for each attribute.
- To avoid biasing the estimated importance of any attribute, we should include roughly the same number of levels for each attribute. Otherwise, as shown by Wittink, Krishnamurthi, and Nutter (1982), some attributes may turn out to be more important simply because respondents have more levels (options) to evaluate for those attributes. We can equalize the number of levels in attributes by redefining attributes, combining two or more attributes, or breaking up an attribute into two or more attributes.

To summarize, we should use a range of attribute levels that are consistent with those observed in the marketplace and we should try to have roughly the same number of levels for each attribute, both to simplify the evaluation task for the respondents and to avoid misleading results on the importance of attributes.

Step 1.3: Develop the product bundles to be evaluated. Here we define a product as a combination of attribute levels. As in the frozen pizza example, it is unreasonable to expect a respondent to evaluate every possible combination. We must choose the product bundles (also called profiles) presented to the respondents carefully. Instead of full-factorial designs (i.e., including all possible combinations of attribute levels), we use fractional-factorial designs to reduce the number of products we ask respondents to evaluate. A common approach is to select orthogonal combinations of attribute levels to reduce the number of product bundles respondents must evaluate and, at the same time, to permit one to measure the independent contribution of each attribute to the utility function. Exhibit 7.5 presents a set of products conforming to an orthogonal design for the pizza example. We could also use nonorthogonal (or more saturated) designs to incorporate interactions between attributes. For example, if we believe that customer utility for price of a pizza depends on the type of topping, we should consider more complex designs. Green (1974) describes several such designs.

In some circumstances orthogonal designs can result in unrealistic products, such as when respondents perceive some of the attributes used in the study to be correlated—automobile horsepower (hp) and gas mileage (mpg) typically have a high negative correlation, but orthogonal designs could result in hypothetical products that combine high hp with unrealistically high levels of mpg. If a product is unrealistic in an orthogonal combination, there are several possible remedies: (1) We can combine the attributes and develop a new set of levels for the combined attribute. (For example, hp and mpg might be combined into a "performance" attribute with high performance associated with high hp and low mpg, and low performance associated with low hp and high mpg.) (2) We can replace unrealistic products by substituting other combinations (perhaps generated randomly, but not duplicating the retained combinations). While this approach com-

Product bundle #	Crust	Topping	Type of cheese	Amount of cheese	Price	Example preference score
1	Pan	Pineapple	Romano	2 oz.	$9.99	0
2	Thin	Pineapple	Mixed	6 oz.	$8.99	43
3	Thick	Pineapple	Mozzarella	4 oz.	$8.99	53
4	Thin	Pineapple	Mixed	4 oz.	$7.99	56
5	Pan	Veggie	Mixed	4 oz.	$8.99	41
6	Thin	Veggie	Romano	4 oz.	$7.99	63
7	Thick	Veggie	Mixed	6 oz.	$9.99	38
8	Thin	Veggie	Mozzarella	2 oz.	$8.99	53
9	Thick	Pepperoni	Mozzarella	6 oz.	$7.99	68
10	Thin	Pepperoni	Mixed	2 oz.	$8.99	46
11	Pan	Pepperoni	Romano	4 oz.	$8.99	80
12	Thin	Pepperoni	Mixed	4 oz.	$9.99	58
13	Pan	Sausage	Mixed	4 oz.	$8.99	61
14	Thin	Sausage	Mozzarella	4 oz.	$9.99	57
15	Thick	Sausage	Mixed	2 oz.	$7.99	83
16	Thin	Sausage	Romano	6 oz.	$8.99	70

Notes:
Preference scores could be rank orders (1 to 16), relative preference ratings (on a scale of 1 to 100), or allocation of a constant sum (e.g., 100 points) across the 16 bundles.

We can compute the relative utility of an attribute level by averaging the preference scores for the bundles in which that level occurs. For example, to compute the preference score for pan crust, compute the average of the scores of bundles 1, 5, 11, and 13, which gives a value of 45.5. Likewise, the average preference score for thick crust is 60.5, and for thin crust is 55.5. Thus, the customer gets an incremental utility of 15 points from having thick crust instead of pan crust and 5 incremental utility points from thick crust instead of thin crust. (For purposes of illustration, we made these relative utilities the same as those shown in Exhibit 7.3. As an exercise, compute the relative utilities for the other attribute levels.)

EXHIBIT 7.5
An example showing 16 product bundles that form an orthogonal design for the frozen pizza study.

promises orthogonality, it will rarely affect the estimated utility functions significantly if we replace only a few bundles (say, less than five percent). (3) We can select other orthogonal combinations (although this remedy requires special expertise).

To minimize respondent fatigue, we recommend a maximum of 25 product bundles (preferably 16 or fewer) for evaluation. When using traditional assessment procedures we should try to have about twice the number of products for evaluation as there are parameters to be estimated by the model.

The software accompanying this book uses a more flexible interactive utility assessment procedure than traditional methods, so that the number of products evaluated can be about 25 to 50 percent more than the number of parameters to be estimated. The number of independent parameters to be estimated is equal to

$$\left\{ \sum_{i=1}^{N} (n_i - 1) \right\} - 1,$$

where N is the number of attributes and n_i is the number of levels of attribute i. For each product attribute we can arbitrarily set the lowest utility value (say, equal to zero). We can also arbitrarily set the maximum total utility from any product (say, equal to 100). For the frozen pizza example the number of parameters estimated is equal to 10.

Stage 2: Obtaining data from a sample of respondents

Step 2.1: Design a data-collection procedure. Once we design the study, the next stage is to obtain evaluations of the selected product bundles from a representative sample of respondents in the target segment(s). We can present the products verbally, pictorially, or physically (using prototypes). Pictures have some advantages. They make the task more interesting and they are superior to verbal descriptions for some products (e.g., a picture of a vacation property is better than a description). Physical prototypes, while desirable, are expensive, and they are not often used in conjoint studies. Once we decide on the presentation mode, there are a number of ways to obtain data from customers:

- *Pairwise evaluations of product bundles*: One way to obtain respondent evaluations of products is to present the products two at a time and ask the respondent to allocate 100 points between the two. This task is simple, but the respondent may have to make many pairwise comparisons. For example, if there are 16 product bundles, the respondent has to evaluate 120 pairs $[(16 \times 15)/2]$, a tedious and burdensome task. (Hauser and Shugan [1980] provide further details of this approach.) Exhibit 7.6 shows a pairwise comparison for two of the alternatives from Exhibit 7.5.

- *Rank-ordering product bundles*: In this method the respondent ranks (or sorts) the products presented, with the most preferred having rank 1 and the least preferred having a rank equal to the number of products presented. If necessary, the respondent can first sort the products into piles of similarly valued products, then sort within each pile, and then finally sort the entire set. We can then use special-purpose programs such as MONANOVA (monotonic analysis of variance) or LINMAP to transform the ordinal rank-order data into a part-worth function that recovers the rank-orders as closely as possible. (Ordinary regression analysis often gives satisfactory results even with rank-ordered data.)

- *Evaluating products on a rating scale*: In this method the respondent evaluates each product on a rating scale (e.g., on a scale of 0 to 100), with larger numbers indicating greater preference. Alternatively and more difficult, the respondents can allocate a constant sum (say, 100 points) across the products presented to them. The assumption is that respondents are able to indicate how much more they prefer one product bundle to others. The advantage of this type of measurement is that we can use ordinary least squares (OLS) regression analysis with dummy variables to compute part-worth functions. Given the widespread availability of regression analysis packages, this approach is the most convenient for managers, and it is the approach used in the software accompanying this book. The last column of Exhibit 7.5 lists sample ratings for a customer in the frozen pizza study.

Step 2.2: Select a computation method for obtaining part-worth functions. Regardless of which of the foregoing methods we choose, respondents may find the evaluation task difficult if they have to evaluate many product bundles. Several approaches are available to simplify the task:

- *The hybrid conjoint model*: Here we first obtain "self-explicated" preferences, and then we combine them with a reduced set of data obtained by the traditional methods. As the name suggests the hybrid model combines two methods. In the self-explication phase (Green and Srinivasan 1990) the customer first evaluates the levels of each attribute separately on a desirability scale (say 0 to 10, with the least desirable level having a value of zero and the most desirable 10). The respondent is then asked to allocate points (say, 100) across

Product 1		Product 10
Pan pizza		Thin crust
Pineapple		Pepperoni
Romano	**OR**	Mixed cheese
2 oz. cheese		2 oz. cheese
$9.99		$8.99

Strongly
Prefer   1—2—3—4—5—6—7—8—9
Product 1

Strongly
Prefer
Product 10

EXHIBIT 7.6
Example of pairwise comparison for products 1 and 10 from Exhibit 7.5.

the attributes to reflect the relative importance of each attribute. We then obtain the initial part-worths for the attribute levels by multiplying the importance weights and the respective attribute-level desirability scores. We augment the self-explicated data with data obtained from each respondent on a smaller set of complete product bundles. Finally we compute the adjusted part-worth functions for each respondent. See Green (1984) for further details.

- *Adaptive conjoint analysis*: Another way to reduce respondent burden is adaptive conjoint analysis, which uses a computer program to obtain data from respondents interactively. The respondent first puts the attributes in rough order of importance (a simpler version of self-explication) and then refines the trade-offs between the more important attributes using pairwise comparisons. The program selects the pairs of product bundles to maximize the information content of the responses, given the respondent's previous responses. See Johnson (1987) for further details.

- *Bridging designs*: Yet another way to handle a large number of attributes is to use sophisticated designs, asking respondents to evaluate the product bundles only on a subset of attributes and on "bridging" attributes that are common across several respondents. This distributes the burden of evaluating a complete set of product bundles across several respondents. (For a discussion of these approaches, see Green and Srinivasan [1978, 1990].)

The software accompanying this book draws on ideas used in hybrid conjoint and adaptive conjoint analysis to simplify the evaluation task. The respondent first provides self-explicated preferences. The program then orders the orthogonal set of product bundles according to decreasing preference as determined from the self-explicated ratings. (The study designer can also develop customized nonorthogonal designs externally and import them into the software.) Next the customer rates each product on a scale of 0 to 100. An attractive feature of this software is that it allows respondents to view a graph of their part-worth function and fine-tune the function directly to more closely reflect their preferences. This is an interactive and iterative process, combining self-explication, ratings, and part-worth refinements.

Our software uses dummy variable regression to compute the part-worth function separately for each respondent, from the ratings the respondents provided:

$$R_{ij} = \sum_{k=1}^{K} \sum_{m=1}^{M_k} a_{ikm} x_{jkm} + \varepsilon_{ij}, \tag{7.1}$$

where

j = a particular product or concept included in the study design;

R_{ij} = the ratings provided by respondent i for product j;

a_{ikm} = part-worth associated with the mth level ($m = 1, 2, 3, \ldots, M_k$) of the kth attribute;

M_k = number of levels of attribute k;

K = number of attributes;

x_{jkm} = dummy variables that take on the value 1 if the mth level of the kth attribute is present in product j and the value 0 otherwise; and

ε_{ij} = error terms, assumed to be normal distribution with zero mean and variance equal to σ^2 for all i and j.

The a_{ikm}'s obtained from regression are rescaled so that the least preferred level of each attribute is set to zero and the maximum preferred product combination is set to 100, producing results that are more easily interpreted. Letting $\tilde{a}_{ikm}$'s denote the estimated (rescaled) part-worths, the utility u_{ij} of a product j to customer i is equal to

$$u_{ij} = \sum_{k=1}^{K} \sum_{m=1}^{M_k} \tilde{a}_{ikm} x_{jkm}. \tag{7.2}$$

Note that product j can be any product that can be designed using the attributes and levels in the study, including those that were not included in the estimation of the part-worths in Eq. (7.1).

Stage 3: Evaluating product design options

Step 3.1: Segment customers based on their part-worth functions. At this stage we can segment the market by grouping customers who have similar part-worth functions. In the frozen pizza example we might find a segment of customers who prefer thin crust pizza and another segment of customers who prefer pan pizza, with preferences on the other attributes being roughly similar for the two segments. Furthermore, we may find that these two segments differ systematically in terms of their demographic characteristics (e.g., age) and media habits (e.g., watching MTV). A simple way to identify such segments is through traditional cluster analysis (Chapter 3). There are also more sophisticated models, which we discuss in the next section.

Step 3.2: Design market simulations. A major reason for the wide use of conjoint analysis is that once part-worths ($\tilde{a}_{ikm}$'s) are estimated from a representative sample of respondents, it is easy to assess the likely success of a new product concept under various simulated market conditions. We might ask: What market share would a proposed new product be expected to achieve in a market with several specific existing competitors? To answer this question we first specify all existing products as combinations of levels of the set of attributes under study. If more than one competing product has identical attribute levels, we need to include only one representative in the simulation.

Step 3.3: Select choice rule. To complete the simulation design we must specify a choice rule to transform part-worths into the product choices that customers are most likely to make. The three most common choice rules are maximum utility, share of utility, and logit, all of which are options in the software:

- *Maximum utility rule*: Under this rule we assume that each customer chooses from the available alternatives the product that provides the highest utility value, including a new product concept under consideration. This choice rule is most appropriate for high-involvement purchases such as cars, videorecorders, equipment, and other durables that customers purchase infrequently.

We can compute the market share for a product by counting the number of customers for whom that product offers the highest utility and dividing this figure by the number of customers in the study. In computing overall market shares it may sometimes be necessary to weight each customer's probability of purchasing each alternative by the relative volume of purchases that the customer makes in the product category:

$$m_j = \frac{\sum_{i=1}^{I} w_i p_{ij}}{\sum_{j=1}^{J} \sum_{i=1}^{I} w_i p_{ij}}, \tag{7.3}$$

where

I = number of customers participating in the study;

J = the number of product alternatives available for the customer to choose from, including the new product concept;

m_j = market share of product j;

w_i = the relative volume of purchases made by customer i, with the average volume across all customers indexed to the value 1; and

p_{ij} = proportion of purchases that customer i makes of product j (or equivalently, the probability that customer i will choose product j on a single purchase occasion).

■ *Share of utility*: This rule is based on the notion that the higher the utility of a product to a customer, the greater the probability that he or she will choose that product. Thus each product gets a share of a customer's purchases in proportion to its share of the customer's preferences:

$$p_{ij} = \frac{u_{ij}}{\sum_{j} u_{ij}} \quad \text{for } j \text{ in the set of products } J, \tag{7.4}$$

where u_{ij} is the estimated utility of product j to customer i.

We then obtain the market share for product i by averaging p_{ij} across customers (weighting as in Eq. [7.3] if necessary). This choice rule is particularly relevant for low-involvement, frequently purchased products, such as consumer packaged goods.

This choice rule is widely applied in conjoint studies and often provides good estimates of market shares. However, as Luce (1959) notes, this rule requires that utilities be expressed as ratio-scaled numbers, such as those obtained from constant-sum scales where the customer allocates a fixed number of points (say, 100) among alternatives. Unfortunately, data from most conjoint studies do not satisfy this requirement.

■ *Logit choice rule*: This rule is similar to the share-of-utility rule, except that the underlying theoretical rationale is different. To apply the share-of-utility model, we assume that the utility functions are basically accurate—but an element of randomness occurs in translating utilities into choice. In applying the logit choice rule we assume that the computed utility values are mean realizations of a random process, so that the brand with the maximum utility varies randomly, say from one purchase situation to the next. The choice rule then gives the proportion of times that product j will have the maximum utility:

$$p_{ij} = \frac{e^{u_{ij}}}{\sum_{j} e^{u_{ij}}} \quad \text{for } j \text{ in the set of products } J. \tag{7.5}$$

Both the share-of-utility and the traditional logit rules share a questionable property known as IIA (independence from irrelevant alternatives). The choice probabilities from any subset of alternatives depend only on the alternatives included in the set and are independent of any alternatives not included. This property implies that if, for example, you prefer light beers to regular beers, then adding a new regular beer (an irrelevant alternative) to your choice set would nevertheless lower your probability of choosing a light beer, a counterintuitive result.

How should we select among these choice rules? The maximum utility rule (also called the first choice rule) is simple and elegant, and choices predicted by using this rule are not affected by positive linear transformations to the utility function. This rule is particularly relevant for high-ticket items and in product categories where customers are highly involved in the purchase decisions. However, this rule predicts more extreme market shares, i.e., it has a tendency to produce market shares closer to zero and one than the other choice rules. Also, it is less robust—small changes in utility values of products can drastically change their market shares. On the other hand, the market share predictions made by the share-of-preference and logit choice rules are sensitive to the scale range on which utility is measured. The market share predictions of the share-of-utility rule will change if one adds a constant value to the computed utility of each product, but they are unaltered if all utility values are multiplied by a constant. Market share predictions of the logit choice rule are not altered if one adds a constant to the utilities, but will change if one multiplies all utilities by a constant. Thus, each rule has its advantages and limitations.

One way to choose among these three rules is this: First, for each rule, compute the predicted market shares of just the existing products. Then use the choice rule that produces market shares that are closest (in the sense of least squares) to the actual market shares of these products (this assumes that we are using a representative sample of customers for the study). This approach can be formalized using yet another choice rule, called the alpha rule, proposed by Green and Krieger (1993). We describe this rule next.

■ *Alpha Rule:* This rule is a weighted combination of the maximum utility rule and the share-of-preference rule, where the weight is chosen to ensure that the market shares computed in the simulation are as close as possible to the actual market shares of the existing products. Specifically, we choose an alpha (α) in the following formula to maximally recover the observed market shares of existing products:

$$p_{ij} = \frac{u_{ij}^{\alpha}}{\sum_{j} u_{ij}^{\alpha}} \tag{7.5a}$$

To determine the best value of α, we minimize the "entropy" representing the extent of departures of computed markets shares of existing products from their actual observations:

$$Entropy = \sum_j \frac{m_j \ln(m_j)}{\hat{m}_j(\alpha)} \qquad (7.5b)$$

where j is an index to represent an existing product, m_j is the actual market share for product j, and $\hat{m}_j$ is the computed market share of product j for any given α. More details about this procedure can be found in Green and Krieger (1993). Orme and Huber (2000) have recently proposed another rule called *randomized first choice* that shows promise as an alternative to the four choice rules that we have outlined. Conceptually, it combines the ideas inherent in the logit choice rule and the alpha rule.

Other enhancements to the basic conjoint model

Measuring contribution instead of market shares: Products that deliver high market shares need not necessarily result in high profitability for the company. Our market share computations do not take into account the costs of manufacturing each product profile. A simple (and rough) way to measure incremental contribution of a product bundle (price – unit variable costs) is to first define a base product bundle and its contribution margin. Next, we can specify the incremental variable costs (positive or negative) for each attribute level, compared to the attribute level of the base product bundle. Finally, we can set the revenue index potential for the base product at 100 and measure the revenue index of every other product with respect this base level. We show this below with a numerical example:

$$\begin{array}{ccccc} \text{Unit contribution} & & \text{Market share (as per any} & & \text{Normalization} \\ \text{of base product} & \times & \text{selected choice rule)} & \times & \text{factor} & = 100 \end{array}$$

Suppose the unit contribution of the base product is \$2 and the market share as per the maximum utility rule is 25 percent, then the normalization factor is two. Now, if the incremental contribution of another product bundle is \$1 as compared to the base product, and its computed market share per the maximum utility rule is 40 percent, then its revenue index is (\$2 − \$1) × 40 × 2 = 80 We have implemented this approach in the software accompanying this book. Note that any additional fixed costs have to be added separately, outside the model. Note also that this computation ignores the price potential (i.e., what the market might be willing to pay) for all product bundles, except the base product. These simplifications suggest that the base product has to be selected carefully to make sure that interpretations of the revenue index are both meaningful and appropriate for the given context.

Segmenting customers based on their preferences: So far, we have focused on individual-level conjoint analysis and predicted market behavior by aggregating individual customer choices. That is, we implicitly grouped all customers into one segment. An important question is this: How should we conduct market simulations if the market consists of distinct groups of customers? There are several options:

1. *Post-hoc segmentation:* We could cluster-analyze the part-worth data to identify segments of customers with differing preference structures following the approaches we described in Chapter 4, and then identify the best products for each se-

lected segment. This approach works best if there is a reasonable basis to predetermine the number of segments in the market. This is the approach currently implemented in the *Marketing Engineering* software and can be applied at Step 3.1, as indicted in the previous section.

2. *Latent class segmentation:* This approach is most useful when we don't know (or cannot make a good guess about) the number of segments. Instead, we start by assuming that there are a finite number of segments (i.e., latent classes), and then let the part-worth data reveal to us the number of segments. This approach is (arguably) the most appealing on theoretical grounds. It is based on the proposition that each customer has some probability of belonging to one or more segments—for operational purposes, each customer could be assigned to the segment to which he or she has the highest probability of belonging. In spite of its theoretical elegance, this approach is not yet in wide use in conjoint analysis and has not been incorporated in our software. In Chapter 3, we describe how latent class segmentation is applied in the case of multinomial logit analysis to account for segment-level (unobserved) heterogeneity among customers.

3. *Incorporating a heterogeneity distribution:* Finally, we could assume that all customers belong to the same segment (i.e., the part-worth data comes from one population) but the customers differ from each other as specified by a heterogeneity distribution of their part-worths (e.g., a multivariate normal distribution to characterize differences in part-worths in the population). We can then estimate the parameters of the heterogeneity distribution along with the average preference structure for the entire segment. To determine the best product(s), we would sample from the estimated heterogeneity distribution to determine the preferences of any randomly selected group of respondents and then compute the market shares according to the choice rules described earlier. Jagpal (1999) explores the relative merits of each of these approaches in greater detail.

Choice-based conjoint analysis: A new approach to conjoint analysis which is becoming popular, is choice-based conjoint, originally proposed by Louviere and Woodworth (1983). Here, customers are presented with several sets of product profiles and are asked to choose the product in each set that they prefer the most. Exhibit 7.7 shows an example of a choice task with four profiles in a set. Thus, we directly measure customer choices, rather than measuring their preferences, and then converting the preferences to choices by using choice rules. The basic premise is that when we measure customer choices, the research process more closely resembles what people will actually do in the marketplace. The sets of profiles presented to customers are carefully selected according to experimental design criteria. The resulting "choice data" can then be analyzed using the multinomial logit model (Chapter 2).

Several studies comparing the relative performance of the traditional "full-profile" conjoint and choice-based conjoint seem to indicate that both models tend to predict equally well (see Elrod, Louviere, and Krishnakumar 1992). The choice-based conjoint has the advantage of offering statistical tests of attribute weights and market shares. However, it is an aggregate model that does not offer direct measures of utility functions at the individual level, making it difficult to incorporate segmentation analyses of the part-worth data. Recent developments in Hierarchical Bayes methods offer the promise of using choice-based conjoint to predict aggregate choices' while also permitting individual-level utility functions for identifying segments (see Allenby and Ginter 1995).

Contexts best suited for conjoint analysis

Conjoint analysis is one of the most widely used modeling techniques in marketing, with over 25 years of usage. Based on a survey, Wittink and Cattin (1989) determined that it is

Which Checking Account Would You Choose?

Services included with all four accounts	▪ ATM card with free unlimited use of your bank's ATM machines ▪ Unlimited free check writing with no per-check charges ▪ Unlimited free access to automated account information over telephone			
Monthly fee and minimum balance required	**Account #1** No minimum balance required. Pay a monthly fee of $10 if your account balance drops below $0.	**Account #2** Maintain a $500 minimum checking balance to avoid a $10 monthly fee.	**Account #3** Maintain a $1,500 minimum checking balance to avoid a $10 monthly fee.	**Account #4** Maintain a combined balance of at least $15,000 in your checking and savings accounts to avoid a $25 monthly fee.
Competitive interest paid on checking accounts	No	No	Yes	Yes
Use of other banks' ATM machines	$1.50 for each ATM visit	$1 for each ATM visit	$1 for each ATM visit	Free
Priority access telephone number	No	No	No	Yes
Choose the one account you prefer	❑	❑	❑	❑
		❑ None of these		

EXHIBIT 7.7
A typical choice-based conjoint task for respondents. Note that respondents can opt not to choose any of the four profiles presented. *Source*: Cohen 1997.

most commonly used for new product identification, competitive analysis, pricing, market segmentation, and product positioning. In a survey of industrial firms Anderson, Jain, and Chintagunta (1993) report that conjoint analysis is used for demand forecasting and determining price, product positioning, and new investment decisions. They also report that 85 percent of the firms classified their use of conjoint analysis as being successful for assessing how customers value products.

Conjoint analysis is a sophisticated method that has to be applied with care. The following checklist will help one to decide whether conjoint analysis is suitable in a decision context:

1. In designing the product, we must make trade-offs between various attributes and benefits offered to customers.
2. We can decompose the product or service category into basic attributes that managers can act on and that are meaningful to customers.
3. The existing products are well described as combinations of attribute levels, and new product alternatives can be synthesized from those basic attribute levels.
4. It is possible to describe the product bundles realistically, either verbally or pictorially. (Otherwise, we should consider using actual product formulations for evaluations.)

There are several limitations of the method. As indicated by Eq. (7.2), a customer's overall utility for a product is equal to the sum of the utilities of the component parts. A highly valued option on one attribute can compensate for an unattractive option on another attribute. Thus a low price can compensate for the fact that a pizza does not have pepperoni topping (Exhibit 7.3). However, in many situations customer choices are noncompensatory—for example, no matter how good a car is on other attributes, you may not want one with a stick-shift transmission. To the extent that a problem context includes non-compensatory processes, conjoint analysis can give misleading conclusions.

The validity of the study also depends on the completeness of the set of attributes. However, including too many attributes increases respondent fatigue, leading to inaccurate responses. A typical commercial application uses about 16 product bundles, which allows for about five attributes with three or four levels each.

Finally, the market-share simulation assumes that customers consider all available alternatives when choosing among them. Again, customers may idiosyncratically eliminate some alternatives from consideration (e.g., ignore all cars with stick-shift transmission). Some conjoint analysis techniques allow for this possibility (e.g., Jedidi, Kohli, and DeSarbo 1996).

FORECASTING THE SALES OF NEW PRODUCTS

Overview of the Bass model

The Bass model for forecasting first purchase has had a long history in marketing. It is most appropriate for forecasting sales of an innovation (more generally, a new product) for which no closely competing alternatives exist in the marketplace. Managers need such forecasts for new technologies or major product innovations before investing significant resources in them.

The Bass model offers a good starting point for forecasting the long-term sales pattern of new technologies and new durable products under two types of conditions: (1) the firm has recently introduced the product or technology and has observed its sales for a few time periods; or (2) the firm has not yet introduced the product or technology, but it is similar in some way to existing products or technologies whose sales history is known. The model attempts to predict how many customers will eventually adopt the new product and when they will adopt. The question of *when* is important, because answers to this question guide the firm in its deployment of resources in marketing the innovation.

EXAMPLE

While Window ME will eventually replace earlier Windows versions in home-based PCs, the timing of that replacement or substitution is critical to Microsoft and other stakeholders in the PC industry. Microsoft also continues to enhance the industrial versions of its operating system, replacing Windows NT with Windows 2000 and, eventually, with Windows XP. The expectations customers have about system developments and the speed with they adopt ME, 2000 and XP influences which systems will be adopted when, and how many of each Microsoft will sell. Microsoft needs this information to plan its production and distribution logistics, to make financial forecasts, and to inform its channel members and computer hardware and software developers (Intel, Dell, Lotus, etc.) whose decisions and operations depend on forecasts of the timing and penetration these new versions of Windows.

Exhibit 7.8 shows the "sales" trajectories for a number of innovations, including several innovative scientific articles. Some start with explosive growth, but sales fall off almost from the start. Others exhibit a "sleeper" pattern (S-shaped) where sales start out slow, then pick up momentum, and eventually decline. Surprisingly, a simple and elegant model (Bass 1969) with just three easily interpretable parameters can represent all these patterns quite well.

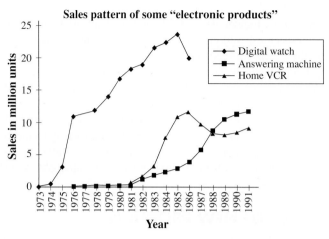

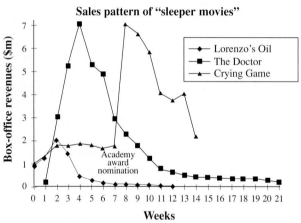

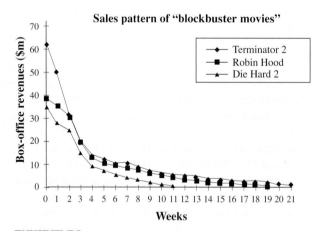

EXHIBIT 7.8
These graphs show the pattern of sales for several products in different product categories.

Citations for "sleeper" scientific articles

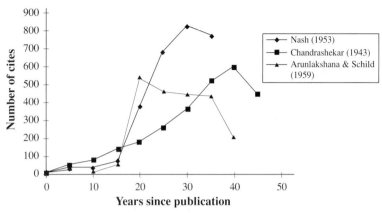

Source: Science Citation Index 1990.

Citations for "blockbuster" scientific articles

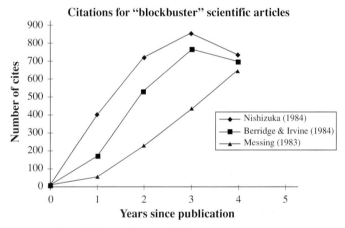

Source: Science Citation Index 1990.

EXHIBIT 7.8 (continued)

Technical description of the Bass model

Suppose that the (cumulative) probability that someone in the target segment will adopt the innovation by time t is given by a nondecreasing continuous function $F(t)$, where $F(t)$ approaches 1 (certain adoption) as t gets large. Such a function is depicted in Exhibit 7.9(a), and it suggests that an individual in the target segment will eventually adopt the innovation. The derivative of $F(t)$ is the probability density function, $f(t)$ (Exhibit 7.9b), which indicates the rate at which the probability of adoption is changing at time t. To estimate the unknown function $F(t)$ we specify the conditional likelihood $L(t)$ that a customer will adopt the innovation at exactly time t since introduction, given that the customer has not adopted before that time. Using the foregoing definition of $F(t)$ and $f(t)$, we can write $L(t)$ as (via Bayes's rule)

$$L(t) = \frac{f(t)}{1 - F(t)} \tag{7.6}$$

Bass (1969) proposed that $L(t)$ be defined to be equal to

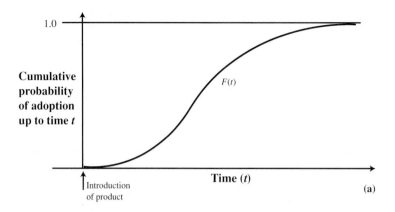

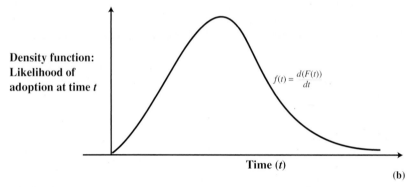

EXHIBIT 7.9
Graphical representation of the probability of a customer's adoption of a new product over time; (a) shows the probability that a customer in the target segment will adopt the product before time *t*, and (b) shows the instantaneous likelihood that a customer will adopt the product at exactly time *t*.

$$L(t) \ = \ p + \frac{q}{\overline{N}} \ N(t), \tag{7.7}$$

where

$N(t)$ = the number of customers who have already adopted the innovation by time t;

$\overline{N}$ = a parameter representing the total number of customers in the adopting target segment, all of whom will eventually adopt the product;

p = coefficient of innovation (or coefficient of external influence); and

q = coefficient of imitation (or coefficient of internal influence).

Equation (7.7) suggests that the *likelihood* that a customer in the target segment will adopt at exactly time t is the sum of two components. The first component (p) refers to a constant propensity to adopt that is independent of how many other customers have adopted the innovation before time t. The second component in Eq. (7.7) $[(q/\overline{N})N(t)]$ is proportional to the number of customers who have already adopted the innovation by time t and represents the extent of favorable interactions between the innovators and the other adopters of the product (imitators).

Equating Eqs. (7.6) and (7.7), we get

$$f(t) = \left[p + \frac{q}{\overline{N}} N(t) \right] \left[1 - F(t) \right]. \tag{7.8}$$

Noting that $N(t) = \overline{N}F(t)$ and defining the number of customers adopting at exactly time t as $n(t) (= \overline{N}f(t))$, we get (after some algebraic manipulations) the following basic equation for predicting the sales of the product at time t:

$$n(t) = p\overline{N} + (q - p)N(t) - \frac{q}{\overline{N}} [N(t)]^2. \tag{7.9}$$

If $q > p$, then imitation effects dominate the innovation effects and the plot of $n(t)$ against time (t) will have an inverted U shape. This is likely to be the case for new movies, new records, or such new technologies as cellular radios. On the other hand, if $q < p$, then innovation effects will dominate and the highest sales will occur at introduction and sales will decline in every period after that (e.g., blockbuster movies). Furthermore, the lower the value of p, the longer it takes to realize sales growth for the innovation. When both p and q are large, product sales take off rapidly and fall off quickly after reaching a maximum. By varying p and q, we can capture all the patterns shown in Exhibit 7.8 reasonably well.

Generalized Bass model: Bass, Krishnan, and Jain (1994) propose a general form of Eq. (7.8) that incorporates the effects of marketing-mix variables on the likelihood of adoption:

$$f(t) = \left[p + \frac{q}{\overline{N}} N(t) \right] \left[1 - F(t) \right] x(t), \tag{7.10}$$

where $x(t)$ is a function of the marketing-mix variables in time period t (e.g., advertising and price).

Equation (7.10) implies that by increasing marketing effort, a firm can increase the likelihood of adoption of the innovation—that is, marketing effort speeds up the rate of diffusion of the innovation in the population. In the software accompanying the book, marketing effort is measured relative to a base level indexed to 1.0. Thus if advertising at time t is double the base level, $x(t)$ will be equal to 2.0.

Estimating the Bass model parameters: There are several methods to estimate the parameters of the Bass model. These methods can be classified based on whether they rely on historical sales data or judgment for calibrating the model. Linear and nonlinear regression can be used if we have historical sales data for the new product for a few periods (years). Judgmental methods include using analogs or conducting surveys to determine customer purchase intentions.

Linear regression: We discretize the model in Eq. (7.9) by replacing continuous time t by discrete time periods, where t is the current period, $t + 1$ is the next period, and so on. We can then estimate the parameters of the following linear function (a, b, and c) using ordinary least squares regression:

$$n(t) = a + bN(t - 1) + cN^2(t - 1), \tag{7.11}$$

where

$n(t)$ = Sales in period t and $N(t)$ = cumulative sales to period t.

We can then calculate the Bass model parameters:

$$\overline{N} = \frac{-b - \sqrt{b^2 - 4ac}}{2c} \,;$$

$$p = \frac{a}{\overline{N}} \,; \text{ and}$$

$$q = p + b.$$

We need sales data for at least three periods to estimate the model. To be consistent with the model, $\overline{N} > 0$, $b \geq 0$, and $c < 0$.

Nonlinear regression: By discretizing the model in Eq. (7.8) and multiplying both sides by $\overline{N}$ we get:

$$n(t) = \left[p + \frac{q}{\overline{N}} N(t-1) \right] \left[\overline{N} - N(t-1) \right]. \tag{7.12}$$

Given at least four observations of $N(t)$ we can use nonlinear regression to select parameter values $(\overline{N}, p, q)$ to minimize the sum of squared errors. This is the approach used in the Bass model software implemented in this book, and for obtaining the parameter estimates summarized in Exhibit 7.10. An important advantage of this specification is that users need not know *when* the product was introduced into the market. They only need to know the cumulative sales of the product for the estimation periods.

Using analogous products: This approach has proved very useful in practice. First identify previous innovations that are analogous to the current product. We can then determine p and q from the sales trajectories of these previous innovations. By combining this with $\overline{N}$ estimated for the current innovation (or obtained using managerial judgment) we can forecast the sales pattern for the new product. The advantage of this approach is that instead of directly guessing the sales of a new product, managers guess the inputs to a well-established model, and the model provides a structure for incorporating these inputs in generating forecasts.

We must be careful in how we choose analogous products. Analogies based on similarities in expected market behavior work better than analogies based on product similarities. For example, in forecasting the sales path of digital cameras, it may be better to use CD-ROM drive as an analog rather than 35mm SLR camera. Thomas (1985) recommends that in selecting analogs we consider similarities along five bases: environmental context (e.g., socioeconomic and regulatory environment), market structure (e.g., barriers to entry, number and type of competitors), buyer behavior (buying situation, choice attributes), marketing-mix strategies of the firm, and characteristics of the innovation (e.g., relative advantage over existing products and product complexity). If necessary, we can consider multiple analogs and take the (weighted) average of their p and q values.

It took 27 years to sell 1 million telephones, 11 years for that many TV sets, six years for as many VCRs, five years for CDs, and two years for Hewlett-Packard's OfficeJet all-in-one printer-fax-copier-scanner. Exhibit 7.10 provides a summary of parameter estimates that have been reported for various innovations (we have included these estimates within the software to help in selecting analogs).

Product/Technology	Period of Analysis	*p*	*q*	$\overline{N}$
Agricultural				
Tractors (thousands of units)	1921-1964	.000	.134	5201.0
Hybrid corn	1927-1941	.000	.797	100.0
Artificial insemination	1943-1959	.028	.307	73.2
Bale hay	1943-1959	.013	.455	92.2
Medical Equipment				
Ultrasound imaging	1965-1978	.000	.534	85.8
Mammography	1965-1978	.000	.729	57.1
CT scanners (50-99 beds)	1980-1993	.044	.350	57.9
CT scanners (>100 beds)	1974-1993	.036	.268	95.0
Production Technology				
Oxygen steel furnace (USA)	1955-1980	.002	.435	60.5
Oxygen steel furnace (France)	1961-1980	.008	.279	88.4
Oxygen steel furnace (Japan)	1959-1975	.049	.333	81.3
Steam (vs. sail) merchant ships (UK)	1815-1965	.006	.259	86.7
Plastic milk containers (1 gallon)	1964-1987	.020	.255	100.0
Plastic milk containers (half gallon)	1964-1987	.000	.234	28.8
Stores with retail scanners (FRG, units)	1980-1993	.001	.605	16702.0
Stores with retail scanners (Denmark, units)	1986-1993	.076	.540	2061.0
Electrical Appliances				
Room air conditioner	1950-1979	.006	.185	60.5
Bed cover	1949-1979	.008	.130	72.2
Blender	1949-1979	.000	.260	54.5
Can opener	1961-1979	.050	.126	68.0
Electric coffee maker	1955-1979	.042	.103	100.0
Clothes dryer	1950-1979	.009	.143	70.1
Clothes washer	1923-1971	.016	.049	100.0
Coffee maker	1974-1979	.077	1.106	32.2
Curling iron	1974-1979	.101	.762	29.9
Dishwasher	1949-1979	.000	.213	47.7
Disposer	1950-1979	.000	.179	50.4
Fondue pot	1972-1979	.166	.440	4.6
Freezer	1949-1979	.019	.000	94.2
Frying pan	1957-1979	.142	.000	65.6
Hair dryer	1972-1979	.055	.399	51.6
Hot plates	1932-1979	.056	.000	26.3
Microwave oven	1972-1990	.002	.357	91.6
Mixer	1949-1979	.000	.134	97.7
Power leaf blower (gas or electric)	1986-1996	.013	.315	26.0
Range	1925-1979	.004	.065	63.6
Range, built-in	1957-1979	.048	.086	21.7
Refrigerator	1926-1979	.025	.126	99.7
Slow cooker	1974-1979	.000	1.152	34.4
Steam iron	1950-1979	.031	.128	100.0
Toaster	1923-1979	.038	.000	100.0
Consumer Electronics				
Cable television	1981-1994	.100	.060	68.0
Calculators	1973-1979	.143	.520	100.0
Camcorder	1986-1996	.044	.304	30.5
CD player	1986-1996	.055	.378	29.6
Cellular telephone	1986-1996	.008	.421	45.1
Cordless telephone	1984-1996	.004	.338	67.6
Electric toothbrush	1991-1996	.110	.548	14.8
Home PC (millions of units)	1982-1988	.121	.281	25.8
Radio	1922-1934	.027	.435	100.0
Telephone answering device	1984-1996	.025	.406	69.6
Television, black and white	1949-1979	.108	.231	96.9
Television, color	1965-1979	.059	.146	100.0
VCR	1981-1994	.025	.603	76.3
Average		.037	.327	
25th percentile, median, 75th percentile		.004, .025, .054	.134, .280, .435	
Average across studies, including many not listed here (Sultan et al. 1990)		0.03	0.38	

Unless indicated otherwise, the model was estimated on penetration data collected in the USA.

EXHIBIT 7.10
Parameters of the Bass model in several product categories. These parameters are based on penetration data and long data series (see Lilien, Rangaswamy, and Van den Bulte 2000, for details about how we estimated these values).

Estimating the parameters of the Generalized Bass model: Bass, Krishnan, and Jain (1994) use a modified version of nonlinear regression (described above) for estimating the parameters of the generalized Bass model.

The software accompanying this book incorporates only the effects of advertising and pricing in the generalized Bass model. We can still use any of the foregoing methods for estimating p and q of the traditional Bass model. In addition the software asks managers to provide their best guesses for the advertising and pricing coefficients.

Quarter	Sales	Cumulative sales
0	0	0
1	160	160
4	425	1,118
8	1,234	4,678
12	1,646	11,166
16	555	15,106
20	78	15,890
24	9	15,987

Example computations (from Equation 7.9)

Sales in Quarter 1 =

$$0.01 * 16,000 + (0.41 - 0.01) * 0 - (0.41 / 16,000) * (0)^2 = 160$$

Sales in Quarter 2 =

$$0.01 * 16,000 + (0.41 - 0.01) * 160 - (0.41 / 16,000) * (160)^2 = 223.35$$

Sales in Quarter 4 =

$$0.01 * 16,000 + (0.41 - 0.01) * 692.9 - (0.41 / 16,000) * (692.9)^2 = 424.8$$

EXHIBIT 7.11
Example computations showing how to use the Bass model to forecast the sales of an innovation (here, room temperature control unit). The computations are based on the estimated values of $p = 0.1$ and $q = 0.41$, and market potential $(\bar{N}) = 16,000$ units (in thousands).

Once we determine the parameter values by estimating or by using analogs, we can put these values into a spreadsheet to develop forecasts (Exhibit 7.11). The software has built-in options for sales forecasting using estimates either from the nonlinear least squares method (if there are sufficient market data for estimation) or by directly selecting p and q from analogous products.

EXAMPLE

Bass et al. (2001) describe how the Bass model helped forecast the adoption of DirecTV, a satellite-based TV broadcasting system introduced in 1994. The forecasts were made in 1992, two years before the anticipated launch of the product. We briefly describe how the company estimated the parameters of the Bass model to derive prelaunch forecasts and how it used these forecasts.

Estimating $\bar{N}$, the eventual number of adopters: The company surveyed a nationally representative sample of potential customers to determine the eventual number of adopters ($\bar{N}$) of DirecTV. The survey asked respondents about their intent to buy the product, its affordability and potential value. 32 percent of the survey participants indicated that they intended to eventually buy DirecTV.   Stated intentions typically overstate actual purchases and to account for this overstatement, the company determined deflation factors to convert intentions to actual purchases. The deflation factor was determined to be around 4 percent for purchase within the first six months after launch (i.e., only 4 percent of those who intend to buy DirecTV will actually buy it within six months after introduction) and 50 percent will buy eventually. The former figure was based on studying the actual purchases versus stated intent for several different product categories, whereas the latter figure was based on managerial judgment.

Guessing p and q: Managerial judgment provided these estimates.   Company managers felt that adoption of DirecTV would be most similar to the adoption of cable TV, which was introduced in the early 1980s.

Exhibit 7.12 shows the forecasts and the actual sales for five years after product launch. In this case, the forecasts turned out to be quite accurate. The forecasts were actually more conservative than industry estimates of 20 million subscribers six years after launch. Accurate forecasts are good, but more important for managers is the opportunity to use the forecasts for planning purposes.   Managers at DirecTV used the forecasts in the following ways:

Year	1992 Forecast Number of TV Homes Acquiring DBS (Millions)	Actual Number of TV Homes Acquiring DBS (Millions)	1992 Forecast of Percent of TV Homes with DBS (Percentage)	Actual Yearly Percent of TV Homes with DBS (Percentage)
7/01/94 – 6/30/95	0.875	1.15	0.92	1.21
7/01/95 – 6/30/96	2.269	3.076	2.37	3.21
7/01/96 – 6/30/97	4.275	5.076	4.42	5.25
7/01/97 – 6/30/98	6.775	7.358	6.95	7.55
7/01/98 – 6/30/99	9.391	9.989	9.55	10.16

EXHIBIT 7.12
A summary of the Bass model forecasts for Direct Broadcast satellite (DBS) made two years before launch and the actually realized unit sales

- To provide further justification for launching a second million-dollar satellite to expand capacity sooner than originally planned.
- To plan distribution arrangements and advertising expenditures to achieve the availability and awareness levels used in deriving the forecasts.
- To solicit funding from GM/Hughes and for developing partnerships with equipment manufactures (e.g., Sony), programming providers (e.g., Disney) and national retailers (e.g., Radio Shack).

Extensions of the basic Bass model

The Bass model makes several key assumptions. We can relax many of these assumptions by using more sophisticated models as summarized by Mahajan, Muller, and Bass (1993). However, the basic model has been widely applied. The key assumptions and possible extensions of the Bass model follow:

- *The market potential ($\bar{N}$) remains constant*: This assumption is relaxed in models in which $\bar{N}$ is a function of price declines, uncertainty about technology performance, and growth of the target segment. The software includes an option to specify the growth rate of the target segment.

- *The marketing strategies supporting the innovation do not influence the adoption process*: Considerable research has been devoted to incorporating the impact of marketing variables, particularly price, advertising, and selling effort. We described the generalized Bass model, which represents one way to relax this assumption.
- *The customer decision process is binary (adopt or not adopt)*: This assumption is relaxed in several models that incorporate multistage decision processes in which the customer goes from one phase to another over time: awareness → interest → adoption → word of mouth.
- *The value of q is fixed throughout the life cycle of the innovation*: One would, however, expect interaction effects (e.g., word of mouth) to depend on adoption time, being relatively strong during the early and late stages of a product's life cycle. This assumption is relaxed in models that incorporate a time-varying imitation parameter.
- *Imitation always has a positive impact (i.e., the model allows only for interactions between innovators and noninnovators who favor the innovation)*: Several models are available that allow for both positive and negative word of mouth. When word-of-mouth effects are likely to be positive (e.g., "sleeper" movies such as *Ghost*), it may be wise to gradually ramp up marketing expenditures, whereas when word-of-mouth effects are likely to be negative (e.g., the "mega-bomb" movie *Waterworld*), it may be better to advertise heavily initially to generate quick trials before the negative word of mouth significantly dampens sales.
- *Sales of the innovation are considered to be independent of the adoption or non-adoption of other innovations*: Many innovations depend on the adoption of related products to succeed. For example, the adoption of multimedia software depends on the adoption of more powerful PCs. Likewise such innovations as wide area networks and electronic commerce complement each other and have to be considered jointly to predict their sales. Several models are available for generating forecasts for products that are contingent on the adoption of other products.
- *There is no repeat or replacement purchase of the innovation*: There are several models that extend the Bass model to forecast purchases by both first-time buyers and by repeat buyers.
- *The effect of the Internet on diffusion:* Over the past few years, the Internet has had a growing impact on how and where people shop. This is likely to alter the parameters of the Bass model (m, p, and q), it is something to take into account when selecting parameter values using analogs.

Let us elaborate on this last point. For digital products (e.g., music, software) consumers can not only make purchases online but products can also be immediately distributed online. For such product categories, the digital medium is likely to significantly alter the diffusion proces—speeding up adoption for products that deliver good value to customers and more quickly killing off products that do not offer high value.

There are several reasons to expect speeded up online adoption of good digital products. First, the size of the available market (m) is likely to be larger because of the global reach and 24-hour, 365-days-a-year operation of many online markets. Second, and more important, the Internet alters the nature of word-of-mouth effects. Whereas offline, each innovator is perhaps is able to influence a few people, online an innovator could theoretically reach every Internet user. Thus, if word-of-mouth (w-o-m) effects are of order n offline (i.e., each person talks to n other people), the effects online could be of order n^2 (every person could theoretically reach or respond to everyone else, i.e., every one of the n persons on the Internet can reach the other (n-1) persons, leading to n(n-1) potential connections). Even if the w-o-m effect is significantly less than n^2 [say, it is of order $n^{1.1}$], it would still lead to faster spread of both positive and negative w-o-m online than offline. The low-budget movie, *The Blair Witch Project*, is thought to have succeeded through the clever use of online buzz by the movie distributor. The Web site for the film had a budget of less than $15,000, but got 75 million visits in the first week, and the movie grossed over $100 million. A third reason for the speeded up diffusion process online is that innovators would find information about new products more easily (lower search costs) and be able to try online demos, thereby speeding up their adoption of the new product. The Internet can also quickly destroy digital products that are competitively disadvantaged (e.g., Mosaic browser after Netscape was introduced).

The online medium can also alter the diffusion process of new non-digital products which are, by necessity, distributed offline. An example is the Rio, a device to play compressed music downloaded from the Internet. Within weeks after its introduction, it was selling 10,000 units per day. This occurred because of the rapid growth in web sites that offered compressed music (using MP3 format) and because of the strong and rapid word-of-mouth both online and offline.

Many people now go online to get more information about products (e.g., read a review about a new car) before purchasing it offline. Therefore, it is likely that the online medium will alter the product adoption process, even if customers choose not to actually purchase the product online. For example, according to a study by Cyber Dialogue, an Internet consulting company, 21 million people used the Internet in 1999 to get information about new vehicles. Of those, 8.4 million actually bought vehicles but only a mere 170,000 bought the vehicle directly over the Internet.

Based on the foregoing discussion, we recommend that when forecasting sales of new products that are likely to be influenced by the Internet it is first critical to determine whether the new product offers significant incremental value when compared to the value offered by existing products. If so, values of p and q based on analogs introduced in the 1990s or earlier may have to be modified upward, especially if the new product is a digital product. Over the next few years, we will get a better understanding of how exactly the Internet influences the diffusion process (Rangaswamy and Gupta 2000).

Bass Model Conclusions

The Bass model has been extensively used for understanding how successful innovations have diffused through the population. It is also being increasingly used in forecasting contexts, as in the DirecTV example (Exhibit 7.12). In applying the Bass model, especially in forecasting contexts, it is important to recognize its limitations. Most past data (from analogs) describe how successful innovations have diffused through the population, but do not account for their chances of success. Thus, such data would predict favorable forecasts for any new product, producing a forecasting success bias. To minimize such a bias, one must incorporate the probability of product failure in the model. Unfortunately, we currently know little about the sales patterns of innovations that failed. Another limitation of the Bass model is that we can estimate its parameters well from data only after making several observations of actual sales. However, by this time the firm has already made critical investment decisions. While the use of analogs can help firms make forecasts before introducing an innovation into the market, the choice of a suitable analog is critical and requires careful judgment. There is clearly a need for better ways to calibrate diffusion models before product launch, perhaps using laboratory measurement methods.

PRETEST MARKET FORECASTING

According to a Food Institute Report more than 22,000 new products were introduced in 1995 into U.S. supermarkets in the food and beverage categories alone. Over 90 percent of these were line extensions and minor modifications of existing products. Most of these products will not achieve the objectives set for them and will be withdrawn within two years of introduction. Most of the costs incurred for these new products occur after they are introduced into the market. To minimize these costs we need methods that will better forecast the sales of a new product before it is introduced into the market. We also need methods that will give firms diagnostic information so that they can identify potential problems with the product and improve its chances of success before introducing it.

Several successful pretest forecasting models have been developed and widely used in the last 20 years, primarily in the packaged goods industry. Models such as NEWS, TRACKER, SPRINTER, BASES, ASSESSOR, and LTM are available commercially. Shocker and Hall (1986) provide an overview of several of these models and summarize the similarities and differences among them. Here we describe the ASSESSOR model, which is similar to the other models in its underlying concepts and features, and the details of this model are available publicly. The following description of the model is based on Silk and Urban (1978) and Urban (1993).

Pretest market forecasting and analysis occur after the product and packaging are available (at least in trial quantities), advertising copy is ready, and the firm has formulated a preliminary plan for the marketing-mix elements such as the price, channels of distribution, and the marketing budget. Given these inputs ASSESSOR is intended to

1. Predict the new product's long-term market share and sales volume over time
2. Estimate the sources of the new product's share—that is, whether it draws its market share from competitors' brands or from other products of the same firm ("cannibalization")
3. Generate diagnostic information to improve the product, the advertising copy, and other launch materials
4. Permit rough evaluation of alternative marketing plans, including different prices, package designs, and the like

Overview of the ASSESSOR model

Exhibits 7.13 and 7.14 summarize the overall structure of the model and the measurement approach for calibrating the model. ASSESSOR consists of two models: a preference model and a trial-repeat model. If these two models provide similar forecasts, it strengthens our confidence in the forecasts. If they provide very different forecasts, an analysis of the sources of discrepancies should provide us with useful diagnostic information.

The laboratory phase of the study is conducted in a testing facility (e.g., a room in a mall or a specially equipped trailer) located in the immediate vicinity of a shopping center. The participants are about 300 individuals who have been screened to be relevant for the study and to be representative of the target segment. The participants are given about $10 each for participating.

Upon arriving at the testing facility the participants fill in a self-administered questionnaire regarding their "consideration set" (i.e., those brands that they are aware of and would consider buying in the category), the brands that they have purchased in the category in the immediate past, and their preferences for the major products (competing brands) within the consideration set. The participants then watch five or six commercials, one for each product including the new product. To avoid systematic position effects, the researchers rotate the order in which the participants see the commercials.

The participants are then sent to a simulated store, which consists of a shelf display of products in the test category along with the representative prices for all the products. They

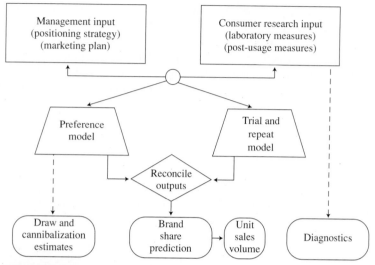

EXHIBIT 7.13

Overview of ASSESSOR modeling sequence. The model uses managerial judgment and consumer research data to make sales forecasts (brand share and sales volume) and offer diagnostics (e.g., draw and cannibalization estimates and reasons for purchase of new product). *Sources:* Silk and Urban 1978; Urban and Katz 1983.

Design	Procedure	Measurement
O_1	Respondent screening and recruitment (personal interview)	Criteria for target-group identification (e.g., product-class usage)
O_2	Premeasurement for established brands (self-administered questionnaire)	Composition of "relevant set" of established brands, attribute weights and ratings, and preferences
X_1	Exposure to advertising for established brands and new brand	
$[O_3]$	Measurement of reactions to the advertising materials (self-administered questionnaire)	Optional, e.g., likability and believability ratings of advertising materials
X_2	Simulated shopping trip and exposure to display of new and established brands	
O_4	Purchase opportunity (choice recorded by research personnel)	Brand(s) purchased
X_3	Home use, or consumption of new brand	
O_5	Post-usage measurement (telephone interview)	New-brand usage rate, satisfaction ratings, and repeat-purchase propensity; attribute ratings and preferences for "relevant set" of established brands plus the new brand

EXHIBIT 7.14

Overview of ASSESSOR data-collection procedure. *Source:* Silk and Urban 1978, p. 174, Table 1.

can use their $10 to purchase any product or combination of products in the category. (Participants may choose not to buy anything and keep their $10.) Those who do not purchase the new product receive a quantity of it free after all buying transactions are completed. This procedure parallels market behavior where some participants will try a new product on their own after seeing an ad, and others will try it if they get free samples. After allowing respondents time to use the new product at their homes, the researchers contact them by telephone for a post-usage survey. They offer participants an opportunity to repurchase the new product (to be delivered by mail) and ask them to respond to the same questions (perception and preference measurements) that they were asked in the laboratory (testing facility). The laboratory measurements provide the inputs for calibrating both the preference model and the trial-repeat model.

The preference model

The preference model transforms the measured preferences of the participants (from observations O_2 in Exhibit 7.14) into choice probabilities indicating the probability that the participants will purchase each of the products in their consideration set:

$$L_{ij} = \frac{V_{ij}^b}{\sum_{k \in C_i} V_{ik}^b}, \tag{7.13}$$

where

V_{ij} = participant i's stated preference for product j, measured on a suitable scale;

L_{ij} = an estimate of the probability that participant i will purchase product j;

C_i = the consideration set of customer i; and

b = a parameter that is estimated from the data.

$L_{ij} = 0$ for those products j that are not in the consideration set of participant i. The sum in the denominator is over all the products in participant i's consideration set. If participants differ significantly in product usage rates, L_{ij} can be weighted by usage index w_i to convert probability of purchase into market shares of the products, in a fashion similar to Eq. (7.3).

The parameter b in Eq. (7.13) is an index that indicates the rate at which preferences for products will convert to purchase probabilities for the products. If $b>1$, then high-preference brands will have disproportionately high probabilities of purchase as compared with low-preference brands. In typical applications b will be between 1.5 and 3.0. The maximum likelihood estimation procedure offers a way to estimate a value for b that maximizes the likelihood of recovering the actual product choices the participants made at *their most immediate previous purchase occasion* (as measured at O_2 in Exhibit 7.14).

To forecast the purchase probability of the new product, we measure preferences for both the new product and the existing products after the participant has used the new product for a trial period. Because the participants are aware of the new product and have had the opportunity to try it, we can assume that the new product will be in the consideration set of all the participants. We can use an equation similar to (7.13) to estimate the probability of purchase for all products, including the new product, after the participants have had an opportunity to use the new product:

$$L'_{ij} = \frac{V'^b_{ij}}{V'^b_{in} + \sum_{k \in C_i} V'^b_{ik}}, \tag{7.14}$$

where

V'_{ij} = post-use preference rating by the ith consumer for the jth product;

n = an index to denote the new product; and

L'_{in} = the probability that consumer i will choose the new product, after having used it.

In Eq. (7.14) we assume that in the laboratory setting all participants will include the new product in their consideration sets. In Eq. (7.14) b is the estimate we obtain from Eq. (7.13).

The market share obtained from (7.14) for the new product will be an optimistic forecast because not everyone in the marketplace will include the new product in their consideration sets. One way to adjust for this is to obtain estimates of the percentage of those in the target segment who will include the new product in their consideration sets and then adjust L'_{in} as follows:

$$M'_n = E_n \sum_i \frac{L'_{in}}{N},$$ (7.15)

where

E_n = proportion of participants who include the new product in their consideration set;

M'_n = the projected market share for the new product; and

N = the number of participants in the study.

To assess *draw* and *cannibalization* from other products, we first partition the participants into two hypothetical groups: those who would include the new product in the consideration set (equal to the proportion E_n) and those who would not include the new product in the consideration set (proportion equal to $1 - E_n$). (One estimate of E_n is the proportion of customers in the target segment who would eventually try the new product—a number that is estimated as part of the trial-repeat model described in the next section.) Then NE_n participants would include the new product in the consideration set, and $N(1 - E_n)$ would not. For those who do not include the new product in the consideration set, the best estimates of their choice probabilities are those provided by Eq. (7.13), which reflect product choices before trying the new product. Likewise, for those who include the new product in their consideration set, the best estimates of their choice probabilities are those provided by Eq. (7.14). Thus we obtain the best estimate of the sources of market share for the new product as follows. First we compute the market shares of the existing products j before and after the new product is introduced:

$$M_j = \sum_i \frac{L_{ij}}{N},$$ (7.16)

$$M'_j = E_n \sum_i \frac{L'_{ij}}{N} + \left(1 - E_n\right) \sum_i \frac{L_{ij}}{N},$$ (7.17)

where

M_j = the market share for product j before the new product is introduced, and $j = 1, 2, \ldots, J$, where J is the number of existing products in the competitive set (i.e., products that belong in the consideration set of at least one customer); and

M'_j = the market share for product j after the new product is introduced.

In this model M'_j will be equal to at most M_j for all existing products. Given these estimates the extent to which the new product draws from product j is given by

$$D_j = M_j - M'_j \tag{7.18}$$

Note that the sum of the draws across the existing products (i.e., $\sum_{j \in j} D_j$) is equal to the market share for the new product (M'_n). The proportion of the new product's sales that is drawn from other products sold by the firm is considered to be cannibalized; the remaining part drawn from competitors' brands is called incremental sales. A new product whose sales are primarily due to cannibalization has to be further evaluated carefully for its financial contribution to the firm, even though the ASSESSOR model may forecast that it will have high market share.

In Exhibit 7.15 we provide a numerical illustration of the computations given in Eqs. (7.13) to (7.18).

Trial-repeat model

ASSESSOR uses a standard formula to generate the long-run market share of the new product using the new product trial and repeat measures obtained from the laboratory experiment:

$$M_n = trw, \tag{7.19}$$

where

t = the cumulative proportion of the target segment that will eventually try the new product;

r = the proportion of those trying the new product who will become long-run repeat purchasers of the new product; and

w = relative usage rate, with $w = 1$ being the average usage rate in the market.

ASSESSOR estimates the trial rate (t) as follows:

$$t = \underbrace{FKD}_{\substack{\text{those} \\ \text{who try}}} + \underbrace{CU}_{\substack{\text{those} \\ \text{given} \\ \text{samples}}} - \underbrace{(FKD)(CU)}_{\substack{\text{adjustment for} \\ \text{double counting}}}, \tag{7.20}$$

where

F = the long-run probability of trial given unlimited distribution and total awareness of the new product in the target segment, the proportion of the participants who purchase the product in the simulated store (O_4 in Exhibit 7.14);

K = the long-run probability of awareness, estimated based on management judgment and the projected advertising plan;

Customer					Preference ratings				
	V_{ij} (Pre-use)				V'_{ij} (Post-use)				
	B1	**B2**	**B3**	**B4**	**B1**	**B2**	**B3**	**B4**	**New product**
1	0.1	0.0	4.9	3.7	0.1	0.0	2.6	1.7	0.2
2	1.5	0.7	3.0	0.0	1.6	0.6	0.6	0.0	3.1
3	2.5	2.9	0.0	0.0	2.3	1.4	0.0	0.0	2.3
4	3.1	3.4	0.0	0.0	3.3	3.4	0.0	0.0	0.7
5	0.0	1.3	0.0	0.0	0.0	1.2	0.0	0.0	0.0
6	4.1	0.0	0.0	0.0	4.3	0.0	0.0	0.0	2.1
7	0.4	2.1	0.0	2.9	0.4	2.1	0.0	1.6	0.1
8	0.6	0.2	0.0	0.0	0.6	0.2	0.0	0.0	5.0
9	4.8	2.4	0.0	0.0	5.0	2.2	0.0	0.0	0.3
10	0.7	0.0	4.9	0.0	0.7	0.0	3.4	0.0	0.9

Customer					Choice probabilities				
	L_{ij} (Pre-use)				L'_{ij} (Post-use)				
	B1	**B2**	**B3**	**B4**	**B1**	**B2**	**B3**	**B4**	**New product**
1	0.00	0.00	0.63	0.37	0.00	0.00	0.69	0.31	0.00
2	0.20	0.05	0.75	0.00	0.21	0.03	0.03	0.00	0.73
3	0.43	0.57	0.00	0.00	0.42	0.16	0.00	0.00	0.42
4	0.46	0.54	0.00	0.00	0.47	0.50	0.00	0.00	0.03
5	0.00	1.00	0.00	0.00	0.00	1.00	0.00	0.00	0.00
6	1.00	0.00	0.00	0.00	0.80	0.00	0.00	0.00	0.20
7	0.01	0.35	0.00	0.64	0.03	0.61	0.00	0.36	0.00
8	0.89	0.11	0.00	0.00	0.02	0.00	0.00	0.00	0.98
9	0.79	0.21	0.00	0.00	0.82	0.18	0.00	0.00	0.00
10	0.02	0.00	0.98	0.00	0.04	0.00	0.89	0.00	0.07
Unweighted market share (%)	38.0	28.3	23.6	10.1	28.1	24.8	16.1	6.7	24.3
New product's draw from each brand (unweighted %)					9.9	3.5	7.5	3.4	
New product's draw from each brand (weighted by E_n in %)					2.0	0.7	1.5	0.7	

EXHIBIT 7.15
Sample computations associated with the ASSESSOR model. There are 10 customers and four brands (B1 to B4). To convert preference ratings to choice probabilities, we used a value of 1.9 for the parameter b (Eq. 7.13). To obtain the new product's weighted draw from other brands we set E_n, the proportion of customers including the new product in their consideration set, to 0.2.

D = the long-run probability that the product will be available where the target customers shop, based on managerial judgment and expectations regarding the proportion of outlets that will eventually carry the product;

C = the probability that a customer in the target segment will receive a sample of the new product, estimated based on the introduction plan for the new product; and

U = the probability that a customer who receives a sample will use it, estimated based on past experience and managerial judgment.

The first term in Eq. (7.20), FKD, represents the proportion of customers who will be aware of the new product, have it available where they shop, and will then try it. The second term, CU, represents the proportion of customers who will obtain a trial sample. The third term, $(FKD)(CU)$, adjusts for double counting those who both purchase the new product and receive a sample. Unlike the preference model, the trial-repeat model does not provide estimates of draw and cannibalization, which are important to a firm in developing its marketing plan for the new product.

We estimate the repeat rate (r in Eq. (7.19)) from the information in the post-usage telephone survey (O_5 in Exhibit 7.14). We first formulate a brand-switching matrix that shows the proportion of customers who switch into and out of the new product at each time period:

$$t \begin{array}{c} t+1 \\ \begin{bmatrix} p_{nn} & p_{no} \\ p_{on} & p_{oo} \end{bmatrix} \end{array}, \tag{7.21}$$

where

p_{nn} = the probability that a customer who purchases the new product at time period t will also purchase it at time period $t+1$, estimated as the proportion of customers who purchased the new product in the test facility and say in the post-usage survey that they will buy the new product at the next purchase occasion;

p_{no} = $1 - p_{nn}$;

p_{on} = the probability that a customer who purchases another product at time t will purchase the new product at time $t+1$, estimated as the proportion who did not purchase the new product in the test facility but say in the post-usage survey that they will buy the new product at the next purchase occasion; and

p_{oo} = $1 - p_{on}$.

Given the switching matrix, we are interested in determining what proportion of the customers who bought the new product at some period t would buy the new product in the next period ($t+1$) if the pattern embedded in the matrix is repeated period after period indefinitely—that is, what would be the equilibrium repeat rate? The answer turns out to be given by a simple formula:

$$r = \frac{p_{on}}{1 - p_{nn} + p_{on}}. \tag{7.22}$$

The trial-repeat model summarized in Eqs. (7.19) to (7.22) provides an independent estimate of the market share for the new product, which one can compare with the estimate obtained from the preference model. When these two estimates are close, they increase managers' confidence in the forecasted market share of the new product.

The validity and value of the ASSESSOR model

Those marketing commercially available pretest market models all claim good success rates. However, ASSESSOR is one of the few models whose validation studies have been reported in academic journals (Urban and Katz 1983). The success rate of new products that go through an ASSESSOR evaluation is 66 percent, compared with a success rate of 35 percent for products that do not undergo a formal pretest model analysis. At the same time, only 3.8 percent of products that failed in ASSESSOR and were then introduced in the market succeeded. In a study of 44 new products that had undergone analysis with ASSESSOR, the average forecasted market share was 7.77 while the actual achieved market share averaged 7.16 with a standard deviation of 1.99. The correlation between the forecast and the actual market share was 0.95.

Urban and Katz (1983) also compare the average monetary gains for firms using the ASSESSOR model and for those using no market-based testing to decide whether to introduce a new product. The average incremental gain associated with the use of ASSESSOR is $11.7 million, a substantial return compared with the investment of $50,000 for the ASSESSOR model. Firms that use both ASSESSOR and a regular test market still make an incremental gain of over $300,000 by using ASSESSOR.

In summary, pretest market models have been one of the most successful areas of application of marketing engineering. These models are particularly useful for forecasting and evaluating a new product entering a well-defined category. The preference model in ASSESSOR provides diagnostic information that is useful to a firm in designing the marketing plan for introducing the new product. The preference model is likely to be accurate only in well-defined product categories where (1) customers learn about new products rapidly enough that preferences stabilize quickly and (2) the customers' usage rate for the product category would not change as a result of the new product.

We have provided a software implementation of ASSESSOR that includes both the trial-repeat and preference models, along with data for the Johnson Wax case.

SUMMARY

Firms recognize that a never-ending quest for new products is a strategic necessity to thrive. In this chapter we outlined the major stages of new product development (NPD) and the many decision models that firms can use to improve their decisions. We highlighted three models: conjoint analysis, the Bass model, and the ASSESSOR pretest market forecasting model. Firms can use these models in the early stages of developing a new product to help them make effective decisions about how much to invest in a new product.

FORTE HOTEL DESIGN EXERCISE[1]

FORTE EXECUTIVE INNES

Forte Hotels, a large European hotel chain, is developing a new hotel chain in the United States. The chain, named Forte Executive Innes, will combine the ambiance of a European hotel with American functionality and convenience. Forte decided to invest in this hotel chain partly to take advantage of the increasing numbers of business people traveling from Europe to the United States.

COMPANY BACKGROUND

Forte Hotels is the United Kingdom's largest hotel chain. Its hotel brands include Le Meridien, Forte Crest, Forte Posthouse, Forte Agip, and Forte TraveLodge. In addition, Forte Hotels includes an international group of 80 upscale hotels such as the Watergate Hotel, Washington, D.C.; Hyde Park Hotel, London; and King Edward Hotel, Toronto. Recently the company's chairman, Sir Rocco Forte, announced that he plans to sell the TraveLodge chain in the United States. In its place, Forte Hotels will develop a new chain targeted toward European and American business travelers, Forte Executive Inne.

Forte's strategy in developing the new chain is twofold. European business travelers in the United States will recognize the Forte name and associate it with comfort and service. Forte executives also expect that American business travelers will associate the new chain with "pampering" that is often lacking in the mid-priced hotel chains, while at the same time perceiving the hotel to have all the functionality of American hotel chains. Although the hotels will have a European ambiance, the facilities and services will be comparable to those available in such hotel chains as Hilton, Sheraton, and Courtyard by Marriott.

PRELIMINARY EVALUATION

A recent survey indicated that the top three reasons business travelers choose a hotel are price, location, and brand name. Forte Executive Innes would be mid-priced, around $100 per night. The company is in the process of securing several prime locations near suburban commercial centers throughout the United States. In addition, the company will leverage the Forte brand name in naming the new chain. Forte now faces the challenge of fine-tuning the specific characteristics of the hotel to ensure that it will appeal to both American and European business travelers.

A search of business databases provided some preliminary insights on the preferences of business travelers. Among men (60 percent of business travelers in the United States), price, location, and convenience are among the top reasons why a business traveler might try a new hotel. Women travelers place more emphasis on safety and cleanliness than do men. Although these considerations, combined with the overall image of the brand name, are important in generating trial, it is the hotel's unique characteristics (attributes) that encourage repeat visits. Other recent surveys have suggested a range of potential amenities that in-

---

1. This case describes a hypothetical situation. It was developed by Bruce Semisch under the guidance of Professor Arvind Rangaswamy.

Attribute [Abbreviation]	Possible Options [Abbreviation]
Room Type (All same size) [Room]	• Small suite [sm_suite] A small suite with a small bedroom area and a separate sitting area with a couch, TV, and coffee table. • Large standard room [lg_room] A room about three feet longer than a standard room with two queen-sized beds. • Room with large desk and swivel chair [rm_office] A room of the same dimensions as the large standard room with only one queen-sized bed and a well-lit work area with a large desk and swivel chair in place of the other bed.
Business Amenities [Bus_amen]	• World Wide Web (WWW) access [www access] A computer complete with software (e.g., Netscape) with access to Internet and the WWW, at a low hourly connection rate ($2 to $3 per hour). • Speakerphone in room [sp_phone] A speakerphone for group business discussions. • In-room fax machine [room_fax] A fax machine and a private fax number that expires at checkout.
Leisure Facilities [Leisure]	• Exercise room [exerc_room] A room, open 24 hours a day, equipped with Nautilus machines, free weights, stationary bikes, treadmills, stairclimbing machines, and a sauna. • Pool [pool] A standard rectangular indoor lap pool with shallow and deep ends. • Small exercise room and small pool [exerc+pool] A round pool for recreational swimming, not a lap pool, and an exercise room that lacks some features described above (e.g., no sauna and fewer machines).
Conveniences & Extras [Extras]	• Complimentary shoe shine [shoe_shine] Shoes left at the front desk or outside the room at night are shined and returned by a specified time in the morning. • Videotape library [tape_lib] A large selection of tapes will be listed in a catalog in the room and available through room service. • Complimentary fruit and cheese bowl [ft+cheese] A complimentary fruit and gourmet cheese bowl in the room. • Free newspaper [newspaper] A complimentary copy of *USA Today* outside the door.
Restaurant Delivery [Restrn_del]	• Yes [yes] From a book of menus from nearby restaurants, patrons can order food through room service, and a hotel employee will pick up and deliver the food. • No [no] No restaurant delivery service available.

EXHIBIT 1
Attributes and Options

terest at least 30 percent of business travelers. These include in-room computer facilities; on-site conference facilities; rooms with well-lit work areas with large desks and swivel chairs; and telecommunication facilities, such as speakerphones and data ports. A survey by a leading credit card company suggests that about half the European business travelers to the United States look for hotels that will look after them and let them relax. The others tended to look for hotels that would let them finish their business assignments quickly and efficiently. Given these preliminary insights, Forte realized that it needed to thoroughly understand the preferences of the hotel's target market to create a successful new hotel chain.

Conjoint Analysis (Matching hotel attributes to customer preferences)

As a first step, the company decided to explore consumer preferences for five key attributes on which Forte Executive Innes could be differentiated: room type, business amenities, leisure facilities, conveniences and extras, and restaurants and dining. Within each attribute, it defined several different options (Exhibit 1). It did not include hotel features that are common to all existing and proposed hotels among the options. Thus for comparison purposes, it considered hotel room types of roughly the same square-foot area, with data-ports and other facilities in the rooms.

Forte's challenge was to decide which combination of the attribute options in Exhibit 1 would most appeal to its target audience. The management team has authorized you to use conjoint analysis to determine this in a "scientific manner." It has recruited 300 business travelers to participate in the conjoint analysis study. For this exercise, you will use the information obtained from 40 of the respondents (Exhibit 2).

EXERCISES

1. *Design:* On the Scenario menu of the Conjoint Analysis program, choose Edit Attributes and Levels to explore the design of this conjoint study (section 1 of the tutorial). Briefly summarize the advantages and limitations of describing products as bundles of attribute options.

2. *Utility assessment:* Use the Utility Assessment command to explore your own trade-offs for the various attributes and options Forte Inne is considering (section 2 of the tutorial). First complete the prepare task (self-explicated ratings), and then complete the ratings task. Each member of a project group should do a separate utility assessment. When you are finished, insert the final set of weights for each attribute and attribute option.

   Based on your experiences in completing these tasks, summarize the advantages and limitations of conjoint analysis for obtaining preference data from customers.

3. *Analysis:* Use the Analysis menu (section 3 of the tutorial) to assess the viability of the four specific hotel concepts (Profesnl_1, Profesnl_2, Tourist, and Deluxe) that Forte is exploring for the State College area. Base this evaluation on the preferences of a sample of 40 business travelers given in the case and the rough cost estimates summarized in Exhibit 3. The preference data is already included in the hotel.cnj file. The base cost to build each hotel room (without the attributes and options listed in Exhibit 3) is expected to be about $40,000 for a 150- to 200-room hotel, regardless of the mix of room types.

   Identify the optimal product concept from among those Forte is considering. Explain how you arrived at your recommendation.

Re spond ent	Room Amen.	Bus.	Lei- sure	Ex- tras	Restrn Delivery	Sm Suite	Lg Room	Rm Office	WWW Access	Sp phone	Room Fax	Exer cise Room	Pool	Exer + Pool	Shoe Shine	Tape Lib.	Ft+ Che- ese	News paper	Del. Yes	Del. No
1	47	21	16	11	5	47	0	20	21	0	10	12	16	0	10	0	8	11	5	0
2	23	29	7	18	23	23	0	7	0	15	29	7	0	5	9	5	18	0	0	23
3	15	38	9	21	17	15	0	12	0	14	38	4	0	9	5	7	0	21	0	17
4	20	27	10	20	23	20	0	16	10	0	27	8	10	0	0	12	20	16	23	0
5	21	26	21	21	11	21	10	0	12	26	0	0	21	3	21	9	13	0	0	11
6	22	25	12	22	19	8	0	22	13	25	0	0	12	6	22	11	0	15	0	19
7	33	16	13	33	5	16	0	33	0	16	10	13	0	10	0	11	33	18	0	5
8	24	23	14	24	15	13	0	24	10	23	0	14	0	4	8	0	24	12	15	0
9	34	22	6	22	16	0	12	34	9	22	0	0	5	6	15	0	22	8	16	0
10	26	21	16	19	18	26	0	10	21	0	14	9	16	0	0	14	7	19	18	0
11	11	52	10	17	10	0	9	11	52	13	0	0	8	10	17	6	13	0	0	10
12	19	22	18	24	17	0	14	19	9	0	22	10	18	0	24	5	0	7	17	0
13	28	37	19	12	4	12	0	28	5	0	37	0	19	11	8	12	0	6	4	0
14	30	19	20	13	18	14	0	30	7	0	19	20	10	0	4	6	0	13	0	18
15	47	25	9	12	7	0	7	47	0	8	25	9	6	0	4	12	8	0	0	7
16	34	23	12	14	17	34	0	11	23	13	0	4	12	0	5	0	8	14	17	0
17	27	42	7	8	16	27	0	23	0	13	42	0	4	7	8	6	0	3	0	16
18	34	16	16	21	13	34	0	30	0	16	11	0	16	11	21	0	14	8	13	0
19	50	19	11	8	12	50	27	0	0	19	4	11	0	7	0	8	5	4	12	0
20	34	27	14	10	15	34	0	16	6	27	0	8	0	14	4	0	10	8	0	15
21	33	29	3	26	9	28	0	33	11	29	0	0	1	3	6	0	26	4	0	9
22	22	22	12	24	20	0	16	22	5	0	22	12	6	0	24	8	0	12	0	20
23	31	10	10	18	31	8	0	31	8	0	10	10	4	0	0	7	15	18	31	0
24	20	21	9	41	9	20	0	14	0	7	21	9	0	5	41	13	10	0	0	9
25	31	14	25	18	12	14	31	0	14	0	13	7	25	0	13	0	18	8	12	0
26	29	11	31	16	13	10	0	29	7	11	0	0	31	17	2	9	16	0	13	0
27	18	27	27	14	14	0	7	18	0	27	18	12	0	27	4	9	0	14	0	14
28	27	4	56	10	3	0	27	7	4	0	2	56	19	0	4	10	0	6	3	0
29	16	29	29	12	14	0	16	8	16	29	0	0	29	20	0	12	6	9	14	0
30	45	2	32	2	19	45	0	17	0	2	0	0	15	32	2	0	0	1	0	19
31	16	16	33	13	22	6	16	0	0	16	9	7	0	33	5	0	9	13	0	22
32	19	22	32	11	16	0	19	5	10	22	0	32	16	0	9	11	0	3	16	0
33	43	12	25	8	12	13	43	0	11	0	12	10	25	0	0	8	6	4	0	12
34	37	9	39	3	12	10	37	0	0	9	3	0	39	21	3	0	3	0	12	0
35	17	24	32	15	12	17	7	0	7	24	0	5	0	32	2	15	8	0	0	12
36	72	7	10	5	6	72	43	0	7	6	0	7	0	10	0	0	5	5	0	6
37	36	18	24	8	14	36	18	0	18	8	0	0	11	24	0	6	8	8	14	0
38	25	13	38	12	12	25	0	17	13	0	8	0	20	38	0	10	4	12	0	12
39	20	19	32	18	11	11	20	0	9	0	19	14	0	32	4	0	18	12	11	0
40	32	15	31	12	10	17	32	0	0	15	15	31	0	28	12	7	0	5	10	0

EXHIBIT 2
Preference Data

4. Would you recommend product concepts other than the four Forte is considering for the State College market? Explain how you arrived at your recommendation(s).
5. Summarize the major advantages and limitations of a conjoint study for new product design. What conditions favor the use of this approach in the hotel industry? (Consider such factors as types of customers and market conditions in responding to this question.)
6. After hearing about the study, a manager at Forte claimed that "A conjoint study is a major deterrent to excellence in hotel design. It's a crutch for managers with no vision and conviction. On the surface, it sounds sensible enough: find out exactly what features customers prefer before you finalize the design. But in practice, this is impossible. Customers cannot tell you what they really prefer without experiencing all the choices available to them. Even if you show them pictures or prototypes, the preferences they express are apt to veer off in the direction of mediocrity. This type of study gives you a Hyundai with a Mercedes grille, Prince tennis rackets endorsed by Ed McMahon, Big Macs with everything, and hotels with no personality! You would not produce a Mazda Miata, a Hermes tie, or the movie *Jurassic Park* with this technique." Do you agree with this statement? Why or why not?

	Incremental fixed costs per room ($) at the time of construction	Average expected incremental contribution per day per room ($)
WWW access	2,500	3.00
Speaker phone in room	200	2.00
In-room fax machine	600	2.50
Exercise room	1500	–2.00
Pool	3000	–4.00
Small exercise room & small pool	3,500	–4.50
Complimentary shoe shine	30	–0.50
Videotape library	300	–0.50
Complimentary fruit & cheese bowl	100	–5.00
Newspaper	—	–1.00
Restaurant delivery	100	–3.00
No restaurant delivery	—	—

EXHIBIT 3
Cost Data

ZENITH HIGH DEFINITION TELEVISION (HDTV) CASE[1]

On August 1, 1990, Jerry Pearlman, CEO of Zenith Electronics Corporation, met with Bruce Huber, vice president of marketing, to discuss the market potential for a new technology called high definition television (HDTV). At the end of the meeting, Mr. Pearlman asked Mr. Huber to develop, within a month, a preliminary forecast of demand for HDTV sets for a 15-year period starting in 1992. Although they both realized that any forecasts they came up with would just be best guesses, they still felt that forecasts would be useful in deciding whether and how the company should respond to this emerging technology. Many strategic decisions would depend on these forecasts, including the level and nature of the R&D and marketing research activities the company would undertake, the strategic alliances it would pursue to get a running start in the marketplace, and the extent of its participation in industrywide lobbying efforts with the Federal Communications Commission (FCC) and the U.S. Congress.

HDTV BACKGROUND

As compared to conventional TV sets, HDTV sets produce better-quality pictures with higher resolution and superior sound (CD-like). They also have wider screens. According to the Electronic Industries Association, high definition in TV can be measured by the resolution of the picture—that is, the number of horizontal and vertical lines scanned on the TV screen.

To promote the growth of HDTV several stakeholders would have to adopt a common set of standards:

- Technical specifications for the core functions and manufacture of HDTV sets;
- Production standards to enable TV and movie studios to develop content to take advantage of the superior display features of HDTV; and
- Broadcast and transmission standards regulated by the FCC to ensure high-quality transmission within the available frequency spectrum.

The Japanese government and industry adopted an HDTV standard in 1984 that had 1125 lines per frame, while the U.S. National Television Standards Committee (NTSC) standard is 525 lines per frame. In addition the U.S. NTSC standard has a 4:3 (or 16:12) aspect ratio (ratio of frame width to height), but the committee is considering a wide-screen aspect ratio of 16:9 for HDTV. Movies made after 1950 typically used wide-screen formats although not always with a 16:9 aspect ratio, while TV programs and most movies made before 1950 typically used a 16:12 aspect ratio.

The Japanese standard relied on traditional analog signals for broadcasts, but the transmission was only over satellite channels. Unless consumers had both an HDTV and a way to receive satellite signals, they would not be able to receive these programs.

In 1990, U.S. industry and government were still working together on setting standards. They had to resolve several thorny issues:

---

1. This is based on Harvard Business School case 5-591-025, written by Prof. Fareena Sultan, and is used here with the permission of the HBS Publishing Division.

Compatibility with existing TVs: The FCC wanted to ensure that whatever transmission standard the industry adopted for HDTV it would not make existing TV sets obsolete. Even with compatibility ensured, an HDTV program would leave the top and bottom of the screen empty when displayed on a standard TV set (Exhibit 1a). On the other hand, when receiving a standard-broadcast TV program, an HDTV would display a squarish picture in the middle of a wide rectangle (Exhibit 1b).

Digital versus analog standard: Several U.S. firms, including Zenith, were pushing for adoption of digital standards instead of the analog standard the Japanese had adopted. Under a digital standard, all images would be converted to the 0/1 language of computers and compressed before being transmitted by cable, satellite, or over the air. The TV receiver would convert the digital streams back into images.

Although a digital standard seemed to be better aligned with the expected convergence of computer and telecommunication technologies, industry members had several concerns. Analog signals typically degenerate gracefully under interference—that is, a small loss of signal quality results in only a small loss of picture quality. Digital signals however tend to degrade substantially with a small impairment to the signal quality. This may not be a

(a)

(b)

EXHIBIT 1
(a) HDTV broadcast as it appears on standard TV
(b) Standard NTSC broadcast as it will appear on HDTV.

major problem for cable-based transmission. Also, people have had a lot of experience with analog transmission. A digital transmission standard could require experimentation and testing over several years before adoption.

Regardless of whether the industry adopts a digital or analog transmission standard, content providers, such as TV and movie studios, would have to invest in costly equipment to produce images with higher resolution. For example, studios would either need high-definition digital cameras for shooting or equipment to convert images from a high-resolution format, such as 35mm film. A studio-quality camera would cost around $300,000 to $400,000. Production staff at TV studios would also have to adapt to the new wide-screen-aspect ratio. They would have to learn new techniques for composing scenes, editing frames, and so forth. At the same time, broadcasters (TV stations and cable TV companies) would have to invest heavily in such equipment as transmitters and towers to broadcast HDTV signals.

ZENITH HDTV EFFORTS TO DATE

In 1990, Zenith was working to develop advanced, flat-screen picture tubes that could display images in the HDTV format. The development efforts looked promising, so Zenith anticipated marketing 20-inch and wider screens by 1992. In addition Zenith and its partner, AT&T, had made significant advances in developing a "spectrum compatible" HDTV transmission system that would offer HDTV pictures in the same channel space as existing NTSC standards. (Because of the scarcity of channel bandwidth, such a system was considered to be a necessary element in the introduction of HDTV.)

THE TV MARKET

Zenith had conducted a number of studies of consumer behavior, which led to the following general conclusions:

- Consumers looked for value for their money and stayed within their budgets. Most consumers were satisfied with their existing TVs.
- Product quality was the most important criterion for evaluating brands. Consumers generally preferred large screens to small screens and considered such product features as stereo, remote control, and style to be important as well.
- Consumers tended to shy away from the lowest-priced brands because they were suspicious of poor quality.

Bruce Huber had access to several additional sources of data acquired by Zenith's marketing research department. In particular he thought the data shown in Exhibits 2 to 7 might be useful in forecasting the sales of HDTV sets.

	Size	% units	Average retail price
Small	<19"	42%	$290
Medium	20-25"	40%	$610
Large	27+"	15%	$1050

EXHIBIT 2
Breakdown of the TV set distribution in 1989 and the corresponding average prices.

	TV households	Multi-set	Color TV	Cable	VCR	Remote control
1950	10%	–	–	–	–	–
1955	67	4%	–	–	–	–
1960	87	12	–	–	–	–
1965	94	22	7%	–	–	–
1970	96	35	41	7%	–	–
1975	97	43	74	12	–	–
1980	98	50	83	20	–	–
1985	98	57	91	43	14%	29%
1989	98	63	97	53	60	72
1990	98	65	98	56	66	77

Note: Nielsen estimated U.S. TV households = 92.1 million on Jan. 1, 1990.

EXHIBIT 3
Data on the market's time pattern for adoption of past TV-related technologies. *Source: The American Enterprise* 1990, p. 97.

Year	Total units	Total $	Average $/unit	Total $ in 1989 $*	Avg. $/unit in 1989 $*
1971	11,197	$2,551,997	$228	$7,831,740	$698
1975	11,606	2,684,121	231	6,184,102	533
1980	18,143	4,798,239	264	7,220,650	398
1985	20,829	5,871,854	282	6,766,820	325
1989	24,669	6,899,762	280	6,899,761	280

*Adjusted for the Consumer Price Index

EXHIBIT 4
Summary of factory shipments of TVs in the U.S. since 1971. *Source: EIA Electronic Facts Books* (1981–1989).

Buyer type

Performance or feature	36%
Experience	34%
Price	30%

Note: Performance or feature-oriented buyers primarily consider the performance and the features of the set when making a TV purchase. Experience-oriented buyers want technology they can trust— that is, technology that is stable and has been widely used, before they adopt. Price-oriented buyers base their purchases primarily on the price of the product.

EXHIBIT 5
Summary of the results of a market segmentation study of TV buyers conducted by Zenith.

	1989	1990	1991	1992	1993	1994
Color TV forecast (Econometric model)	22.0	22.2	23.4	24.9	25.7	25.9
–Units–						
First purchase	2.1	1.8	1.6	1.6	1.5	1.5
Replacement	7.7	8.3	8.9	9.6	10.3	11.0
Additional	11.6	11.5	12.3	13.0	13.2	12.7
Institutional	0.6	0.6	0.6	0.7	0.7	0.7

EXHIBIT 6
Zenith's forecast sales of color TVs by purchase occasion (millions of units).

	1992	1993	1994	1995	1996	1997	1998	1999	2000
Industry total (millions of units)	21.4	21.9	22.4	22.9	23.5	24.1	24.7	25.2	25.9
25" and larger (millions of units)	6.0	6.1	6.2	6.4	6.8	7.2	7.5	8.0	8.5
Zenith retail price for HDTV									
26"/31"	$2500	$2000	$1700	$1500	$1400	$1350	$1300	$1300	$1300
22"/27"				1100	1000	900	900	900	
Zenith retail price with conventional tube									
26"/31"	$3000	$2500	$2100	$1900	$1700	$1550	$1550	$1550	$1500
22"/27"				1200	1100	1000	1000	1000	

EXHIBIT 7
Zenith's forecasts of U.S. sales of large screen TVs, which have price points that are likely to be similar to those of the HDTV.

FORECASTS OF HDTV SALES

A few months earlier, the Electronic Industries Association (EIA) had forecast that HDTV would penetrate 25 percent of U.S. households by the year 2000. Jerry Pearlman was not that optimistic but still predicted that HDTV would garner about 10 percent of the TV industry sales by 1999.

Some industry observers believed that both of these forecasts were optimistic because picture quality alone will not sell HDTV sets without significant levels of HDTV programming and broadcasting. They believed that the projected levels of penetration would occur only if (1) the FCC settled on a transmission standard immediately, a highly unlikely prospect, and if (2) broadcasters invested substantial amounts of money in new equipment, which is unlikely before studios produce the content for HDTV broadcasting. There are about 1,500 TV stations in the country, each of which would have to incur equipment costs of $2–3 million to upgrade to digital transmission. These observers thought that neither of these scenarios was likely to occur for several years and that by the year 2000, sales would perhaps reach "a few hundred thousand units." Until then, HDTV would be used mostly for viewing closed-circuit TV programs, such as training films (like surgery demonstrations), or for home viewing of rented or owned movies on high-end entertainment systems.

With this preliminary research behind him, Bruce Huber was ready to tackle "the HDTV forecasting problem." He had recently acquired software called GBass for forecasting new-product sales. He wondered whether this software would be of any help in this forecasting task.

EXERCISES

1. Summarize and justify alternative scenarios (that is, consistent sets of assumptions) ranging from pessimistic to optimistic with regard to market performance of HDTV.
2. Develop forecasts of HDTV penetration in the U.S. market from 1992 through 2006 for each scenario you developed in exercise 1 along with a justification and explanation for your forecasts.

JOHNSON WAX: ENHANCE CASE (A)[1]

INSTANT HAIR CONDITIONER

In April 1979, John Sherman, product development manager for S. C. Johnson & Company, was facing a decision on the future of Enhance, a new instant hair conditioner. Enhance was designed as a companion product to Agree, the company's first hair-care product. Development of Enhance had been under way for about a year and a half.

During the development process, Enhance had been tested against the leading existing products through blind comparisons and had undergone a pretest-market testing procedure called ASSESSOR. The results of these tests would play a significant role in Sherman's recommendations, because previous experience had convinced top management that such research was valuable. In fact, the company had performed a number of ASSESSOR or similar analyses in the past, and top management had on occasion seemed anxious to skip the test market and push for introduction when the ASSESSOR results were favorable.

John Sherman's task was to recommend the next steps for Enhance. While his experience and intuitive judgment would be valued, he knew the managerial climate at S. C. Johnson would require marketing research substantiation for his recommendations.

S. C. JOHNSON & COMPANY

S. C. Johnson & Company, headquartered in Racine, Wisconsin, was founded in 1886 as a manufacturer of parquet flooring. It was incorporated as S. C. Johnson & Son, Inc. and was familiarly known throughout the world as "Johnson Wax." A privately held corporation, Johnson Wax did not publicly report sales or earnings. Still, it was recognized as one of the world's leading manufacturers of products for home, auto and personal care, for commercial maintenance and industrial markets, and for outdoor recreation and leisure-time activities. Johnson Wax and its subsidiaries employed more than 13,000 people worldwide.

The buildings that served as international headquarters had been designed by Frank Lloyd Wright. They had won numerous architectural awards, and were listed in the National Register of Historic Places. U.S. manufacturing operations were conducted at the company's Waxdale, Wisconsin manufacturing plant, about eight miles west of Racine. This plant encompassed more than 1.9 million square feet of floor space and was one of the largest and most modern facilities of its kind in the world.

Johnson Wax maintained sales offices and sales and distribution centers in 20 major U.S. metropolitan areas.

Johnson Wax Associates, Inc. (JWA) was a group of nine associated companies that manufactured and marketed products for leisure-time activities and outdoor recreation. JWA products were distributed nationally and overseas to wholesalers and retailers through a system of manufacturers' representatives and factory salespeople.

1. This case was prepared by Associate Professor Darral G. Clarke as the basis for class discussion rather than to illustrate either effective or ineffective handling of an administrative situation. This revision is by Professor Robert J. Dolan. Copyright © 1982 by the President and Fellows of Harvard College. No part of this publication may be reproduced, stored in a retrieval system, or transmitted in any form or by any means—electronic, mechanical, photocopying, recording, or otherwise—without the permission of Harvard Business School. Distributed by HBS Case Services, Harvard Business School, Boston, MA 02163. Printed in U.S.A.

The first Johnson Wax overseas subsidiary was established in England in 1914. In 1979, Johnson Wax had subsidiaries in 45 countries.

The Johnson Wax consumer product line consisted of some of the best-known brands in household, automobile, and personal-care products: Brite, Future, Glo-Coat, and Klear floor waxes; Jubilee and Pledge furniture polish; Rain Barrel Fabric Softener; Shout Stain Remover; Glory Carpet Cleaner; Glade Air Freshener; J-Wax auto care products; Raid insecticide, and Off insect repellent.

The Johnson Wax Innochem Division manufactured and distributed a complete line of heavy-duty polishes, cleaners, insecticides, and disinfectants for use by commercial and institutional customers and a specialty line of chemicals.

The U.S. consumer products were distributed to supermarkets and drug, discount, and variety outlets through the company's own national salesforce. Innochem commercial products distribution was handled through a separate salesforce and through a network of more than 400 distributors nationally. Warehouse and distribution facilities were shared by the Innochem and Consumer Products Divisions.

NEW-PRODUCT DEVELOPMENT AT JOHNSON WAX

Development of these numerous product lines over the years had given Johnson Wax considerable experience in new-product evaluation and introduction. New product ideas came from laboratory research, marketing research, and customer contact. The product development process at Johnson Wax was fairly standard: ideas went through various commercial feasibility studies, performance tests against competitive products, and test markets before national introduction or rollout.

In recent years developing a new consumer product had become so expensive that Johnson Wax, like other manufacturers, had sought ways to reduce the cost. One solution was the pre-test-market test. One source[2] estimated the expected benefit from a $50,000 pretest to be in excess of $1 million. Before the Enhance pretest, Johnson Wax had performed many such pretests, most of them ASSESSORS.

THE HAIR CONDITIONING MARKET

During the 1970s, both the variety and the number of hair-care products and brands had increased drastically. Shampoos to combat dandruff were introduced; others were custom-formulated for use on dry, normal, or oily hair. During the same period, new products were introduced that would "condition" hair as well as clean it. According to one manufacturer:

> A good creme rinse conditioner can help combat many hair problems. Hair can be easily damaged when it is combed following a shampoo, since hair is weakest when wet. Washing and towel-drying hair tend to tangle it, making it susceptible to breakage during combing. A creme rinse conditioner helps prevent this type of damage because it helps prevent tangles and makes for easy wet-combing. Creme rinse and conditioners also make hair feel softer; add to its bounce,

2. Glen L. Urban and John R. Hauser, *Design and Marketing of New Products* (Englewood Cliffs, NJ: Prentice-Hall, Inc., 1980), pp. 52–59. The cost of a nine month, two-market test market was estimated at about $1MM. The expected savings of ASSESSOR, although also $1MM, are computed from a Bayesian analysis involving: (1) costs of ASSESSOR, test markets, and national introduction; (2) probabilities of success at various stages of the new-product introduction process.

shine, and body; and help prevent the buildup of static electricity that causes hair to be "flyaway."

There were two types of hair conditioners:

- *Instant conditioners*, which were usually left on the hair for one to five minutes before being rinsed off.
- *Therapeutic conditioners*, which generally remained on the hair from five to twenty minutes before rinsing.

The term "creme rinse" was still used occasionally for conditioners that stressed easier combing and manageability. Gradually the term was being replaced by "instant conditioner." Hair conditioner sales had grown dramatically during the 1970s, spurred by new-product introductions and increased use, especially among young women.

The major instant hair conditioner brands and their market shares in 1978 were Johnson's Agree (15.2 percent), Wella Balsam (4.7 percent), Clairol Condition (9.9 percent), Flex (13.4 percent), and Tame (5.4 percent).

Manufacturers' sales were as follows:

Manufacturers' Sales ($ millions)

Year	Total Conditioner	Instant Conditioner
1975	$132	$116
1976	160	141
1977	200	176
1978	230	202

Instant conditioners were sold in a variety of packages, but generally in either clear or opaque plastic bottles, often with nozzle tops. Popular sizes were 8-, 12-, and 16-ounce bottles. Retail margins generally ranged between 30 percent and 38 percent.

AGREE

In June 1977, Johnson Wax entered the hair-care market with Agree Creme Rinse and Conditioner, soon followed by Agree Shampoo. At that time, some creme rinses and conditioners included oil in their formulation. Agree's selling proposition was that the addition of this oil, especially for people with oily hair, caused the hair to look oily, greasy, and limp soon after shampooing. A technological breakthrough by Johnson Wax enabled it to produce a virtually oil-free product (Agree) which helped "stop the greasies." According to Johnson Wax promotional material:

Agree has exceptional detangling properties making the hair easier to wet-comb. It is pleasantly scented and leaves the hair feeling clean, with healthy shine, bounce, and body. Agree contains no harsh or harmful ingredients and is pH balanced to be compatible with the natural pH of hair and scalp.

Agree had fared well in product comparison tests and an ASSESSOR pretest-market test. By 1978, Agree had a 4.5 percent share of the shampoo market and 15.2 percent share of the conditioner market.

ENHANCE PRODUCT DEVELOPMENT

Agree's early success created optimism and euphoria at Johnson Wax. Gaining a foothold in the attractive conditioner market offered an opportunity to expand the conditioner product line and subsequently make greater inroads on the even larger shampoo market.

Management felt Agree was successful largely because it solved a specific hair problem for a segment of the market. They also felt that it would be desirable to offer another personal-care product line. Enhance was conceived as an instant hair conditioner targeted toward women 25–45 years old with dry hair and was formulated to appeal to that audience. Blind paired comparisons were run against Revlon's Flex.

The study, conceived by John Sherman and Neil Ford of the company's marketing research department, was summarized as follows:

> The purpose of the study was to determine the preference levels for Enhance, both overall and on specific performance attributes, versus those of Flex, the leading instant hair conditioner. A panel of 400 hair conditioner users was preselected by telephone. Each received both Enhance and Flex, blind-labeled and in identical nonidentifiable packages and, following proper rotations, used first one for three weeks, and the other for an identical period. At the end of the six-week usage period, respondents were interviewed regarding their preferences and behavior regarding the test products. A key part of the analysis was to determine preferences of women with specific hair care problems relevant to Enhance strategy and positioning.

A digest of the results appears in Exhibits 1 and 2. The conclusions drawn by Ford in an August 1978 report to Sherman were that:

> Differences between the two products are not great, but where they exist, they tend to be focused on the problems Enhance wishes to address and on the women to whom the brand will be targeted. While work should continue to improve the product, it is suitable for use in ASSESSOR in its current state and, if need be, for use in test-market introduction.

THE ASSESSOR PRETEST MARKET

Following the blind comparison tests, further work on product formulation, product positioning, packaging, and advertising copy produced an introductory marketing plan. Advertising copy presented Enhance as a solution to the dry and damaged hair problem. Enhance samples were produced in "regular" and "extra conditioning" formulas.

When the marketing plan was agreed upon and samples were available, an ASSESSOR pretest-market procedure was arranged. The primary objectives were to estimate the ongoing market share of Enhance and determine consumer reaction to the product. Two independent techniques were used to arrive at a market share prediction one year after introduction. The observed trial and repeat levels were used to make one share prediction. Another was made from estimates of brand preference calculated from the respondents' perception of and preference for the attributes of Enhance and the existing brands. Additional qualitative and quantitative information gathered during the laboratory phase, and again after use, added support for the primary conclusions of the ASSESSOR study.

ASSESSOR[3], developed in 1973 by Management Decision Systems (MDS), of Waltham, Massachusetts, was one of a number of commercial simulated test-market procedures. The first was the Yankelovich Laboratory Test Market begun in 1968. Elrick and Lavidges's COMP, National Purchase Diary's ESP, and Burke Marketing Research's BASES followed, and by 1979, nearly 1400 applications of these models had been completed.

The Enhance ASSESSOR consisted of a laboratory and a callback phase. During the *laboratory phase*, women were intercepted in shopping malls and asked if they would participate in a test market. Those who were willing and were found to be in the target segment went through a five-step procedure, as follows:

1. *An initial questionnaire* was used to determine the brands about which the respondent could provide meaningful information. This list of brands, called the respondent's "evoked set," included brands used recently or ever, and brands that would, or would not, be considered on the next purchase occasion.

2. *The preference questionnaire* was customized for each respondent to include only those brands in her evoked set. The respondent was asked to allocate 11 imaginary chips between each pair of brands in her evoked set. These allocations were used to calculate the strength of preference for each brand in each respondent's evoked set. If there were N brands, the respondent was asked to give allocations for each of the $N(N-1)/2$ pairs.

3. *Advertising recall* was measured after the respondent was shown commercials for six creme rinse/conditioning products: Tame, Agree, Flex, Condition, Wella Balsam, and Enhance.

4. *Laboratory purchasing* took place in a simulated store where the respondent was given a $2.25 certificate. If she wanted to buy more than $2.25 in merchandise, she was asked to pay the difference. Respondents who did not purchase Enhance were given a package of Enhance as a gift. Half the nonpurchasers received a 2 oz. container; the other half received an 8 oz. container. A limited number of those who did not purchase the test product were asked a few additional questions probing their impressions of Enhance and reasons for not purchasing it.

5. *Brand ratings*. Respondents were then asked to rate several of their evoked brands on how well they performed on 22 product attributes. Enhance was also rated on these attributes. These ratings, since the respondent had not used Enhance, were based on perceptions created through advertising, price, and packaging. A 7-point rating scale was used.

The *callback phase* was designed to collect information about after-use preferences, repeat purchase rate, and diagnostics concerning product performance. Only those respondents who indicated they had used Enhance were asked to complete the interview. Callback interviews were conducted four weeks after the laboratory interview.

The field research was conducted in three markets—Atlanta, Chicago, and Denver—beginning September 25, 1978, with callback interviews approximately four weeks later. A total of 387 interviews was conducted with users of creme rinse/conditioning products. Respondents included 120 users of Agree creme rinse, a disproportionate number, in order to better determine Enhance's effect on Agree.

3. More detailed descriptions of ASSESSOR may be found in the chapter and in Alvin J. Silk and Glen L. Urban, "Pre-Test-Market Evaluation of New Packaged Goods: A Model and Measurement Methodology," *Journal of Marketing Research*, Vol. XV (May 1978), pp. 171-191.

ASSESSOR RESULTS

ASSESSOR provided results in eight major areas of interest: (1) market structure, (2) advertising recall, (3) trial, (4) repeat purchase, (5) product acceptance, (6) market share prediction, (7) cannibalization, and (8) sampling response.

1. *Market Structure:* During the laboratory phase of the fieldwork, respondents were asked to rate several of their evoked brands as well as their "ideal" brand on 22 attributes. These brand ratings were used as inputs to factor analysis a data-reduction technique used for grouping similar attributes into underlying factors or dimensions (Chapter 4). From this analysis, four basic perceptual dimensions, or factors, emerged:

Factor	Relative Importance	Attributes Combined to Form the Factor
Conditioning	33%	Nourishes dry hair
		Restores moisture
		Keeps control of split ends
		Makes dry hair healthy-looking
		Conditions hair
		Helps keep hair from breaking
		Penetrates hair
Clean	27%	Leaves hair free of residue/flakes
		Leaves hair grease- and oil-free
		Leaves hair clean looking
		Rinses out easily/completely
Manageability/effects	23%	Makes hair more manageable
		Leaves hair shiny/lustrous
		Leaves hair soft and silky
		Gives hair body and fullness
Fragrance	17%	Has pleasant fragrance while using
		Leaves hair with nice fragrance

Besides identifying the possible factors underlying the instant conditioner market, factor analysis provided a graphic representation of the consumer's positioning of the brands in a "perceptual map." This was done by using pairs of factors as axes and assigning each brand a "factor score" that served as a coordinate on each axis. Using these coordinates, a brand was assigned a position on the perceptual map. MDS produced perceptual maps for a number of market segments. The maps for the total market are shown in Exhibit 3. (Maps including the fragrance factor are not presented.)

MDS's report concluded that, in terms of market structure:

The fact that all four dimensions are important to all consumer segments considered in the study suggests that being strongly positioned on only one dimension may not be sufficient to capture a significant portion of the market.

Agree and Breck Creme Rinse have achieved the "clean" position, while Clairol Condition has succeeded in differentiating itself as the "conditioning" brand. Wella Balsam, based on these maps, appears to have virtually no image, and thus might be vulnerable to a new entry. Sassoon, a relatively new brand, appears to be enjoying a very strong positive image.

2. *Advertising Recall:* Unaided advertising recall provided a measure of how well an ad broke through the clutter of competitive advertising. Total unaided recall for Enhance was 76 percent, about average for ASSESSOR-tested products, but somewhat lower than for other Johnson Wax products subjected to ASSESSOR tests. Unaided recall did not differ across hair type segments.

   Among those who recalled the Enhance ad, almost 50 percent recalled that Enhance was "for dry hair." "Conditions" and "penetrates" received somewhat lower playback. Exhibit 4 summarizes the copy-point recall results.

3. *Trial Estimation:* Store setups had been designed to reflect local conditions and simulate the anticipated competitive environment. Enhance was available in two sizes for both regular and extra conditioning formulations. Enhance had one facing for each size and formulation, and was featured in the middle of the middle shelf. In all, 24 shampoos and conditioners were represented in 60 facings. Enhance was offered in 8- and 16-ounce sizes at $1.31 and $1.94, respectively. Agree was offered in 8- and 12-ounce sizes at $1.31 and $1.67. Flex was offered only in the 16-ounce size at the same price as Agree. Enhance prices were very similar to those of Breck, Wella Balsam, and Tame.

   Trial was measured as a percentage of total laboratory purchasing. Of the 387 respondents, 307 (79 percent) made a purchase in the store. Enhance's trial rate was 23 percent. Agree had achieved an overall trial rate of 33 percent in its ASSESSOR test. For purposes of comparison, Exhibit 5 shows trial rates for other ASSESSOR-tested products, both within and outside the health and beauty aids category.

4. *Repeat Purchase Estimation:* Repeat purchase and product acceptance were determined through telephone callback interviews four weeks after the laboratory interviews. Since all respondents who had not purchased Enhance were given samples, after-use data were potentially available for all respondents. Those who had not used Enhance were not asked to complete the phone interview. Telephone callbacks were completed with 215 respondents (55 percent of all laboratory respondents). This was lower than most ASSESSOR callback completion rates. Of those people with whom callback interviews were not completed, 23 percent (42 people) indicated they had not used Enhance because it was specifically formulated for dry hair.

   During the callback interviews, respondents were again asked to compare Enhance with other brands in their evoked sets. This information was used to see whether use altered Enhance's position in the market structure (Enh. Post in Exhibit 3).

   Respondents were also given the opportunity to purchase another bottle of Enhance at the prices found in the laboratory store. Those who decided to repurchase, plus those who said without prompting that their next conditioner purchase would be Enhance, were classified as repeaters. Repeat rates were as follows:

	Enhance	Agree
Repeat among buyers in laboratory	60%	78%
Repeat among nonbuyers (who received sample)	43	63

72 percent of those repeating purchased Enhance's "Extra Conditioning Formula" and 64 percent purchased the 16-ounce size.

The repeat purchase rates of other ASSESSOR-tested products are found in Exhibit 6.

5. *Product Acceptance:* During the callback interview the respondent was asked what she liked best about Enhance. Surprisingly, manageability, not conditioning, was mentioned most frequently, even though it was not considered a main copy point. Those who made a repeat purchase were even more likely than nonrepeaters to mention manageability. Open-ended likes and dislikes for Enhance are found in Exhibit 7. Exhibit 8 presents after-use preferences and comparisons with users' favorite brands.

6. *Market Share Prediction:* A major feature that differentiated ASSESSOR from other pretest-market procedures was the use of two convergent methods to predict market share. Market share was estimated separately with a "trial and repeat" model and a "preference" model.

Trial and repeat model

The trial and repeat model used the purchase information gathered during laboratory shopping and follow-up interview repeat measurements. The formula used was

$$M = TS$$

where

M = market share,

T = the ultimate cumulative trial rate (penetration or trial),

S = the ultimate repeat purchase rate among those buyers who have ever made a trial purchase of the brand (retention).

Retention (S) was a function of the initial repeat purchase rate and the rate at which previous triers returned to Enhance after buying another product (called switchback). The relationship is explained in Chapter 7.

As mentioned above, Enhance obtained a laboratory trial of 23 percent and a repeat rate of 60 percent. Measured through a series of callback interviews, the switchback rate was 16 percent. Retention was calculated to be 28.6 percent. Since these estimates were achieved in an environment in which every respondent was aware of Enhance advertising, and Enhance was always available, corrections had to be made to adjust these laboratory measurements to actual market conditions. Market trial was estimated by

$$T = FKD + CU - \{(FKD) \times (CU)\}$$

where

F = the trial rate in the ASSESSOR test—the trial rate that would ultimately occur if all consumers were aware of the advertising;

K = the long-run probability that a consumer will become aware of Enhance;

D = the proportion of retail outlets that will ultimately carry Enhance;

C = the proportion of the target market that receives samples;

U = the proportion of those receiving samples that will use them.

Using CU to estimate the trial resulting from sampling would overstate the extent of sampling trial, since some trial would have resulted from advertising even without sampling. This "overlap" trial ($[FKD] \times [CU]$) would be double-counted, and must therefore be subtracted from the sample-induced trial rate.

The market share estimates for Enhance depended not only on data obtained from the ASSESSOR test, but also on John Sherman's estimates of what advertising awareness and distribution levels would be realized for Enhance. Sherman had decided to initially use the advertising awareness and distribution levels realized for Agree:

awareness	70%
distribution	85%

Using these values, and ignoring sampling for the moment, market share was predicted by the trial/repeat model at 3.9 percent. Sherman's computations of Enhance market share, together with those for Agree, are found in Exhibit 9.

Preference model estimates of share

The preference model market share prediction was based on the respondents' answers to the questions about product attributes and the degree to which they perceived these attributes to be present in competing brands. The preference model predicted that Enhance would attain a 27.5 percent share of those consumers in whose evoked sets it appeared. Using the penetration rate found in the laboratory phase of the ASSESSOR study (14 percent), MDS obtained a base market share estimate of 3.8 percent (see Exhibit 9).

7. *Cannibalization:* An estimate of the cannibalization of Agree's share was also computed from the ASSESSOR results by computing Enhance's share separately for Agree users. This analysis demonstrated that Enhance would draw less than proportionately from Agree, with only a share of 2.4 percent among Agree users. This indicated that Agree would lose less than half a share point to Enhance.

   More detailed analysis indicated that Enhance would draw more than proportionately from Wella Balsam, proportionately from Flex and Sassoon, and less than proportionately from Agree, L'Oreal, and Clairol Condition.

8. *Incremental Share from Sampling:* The incremental share that might be expected from sampling could be estimated, since those respondents who had not chosen Enhance had been given a sample of the product at the end of the initial ASSESSOR interview. Their use and acceptance levels were determined during the call-back interview.

   The effects of sampling were evaluated by first determining the incremental trial rate that would result from sampling. Of those using samples, a certain percentage (equal to net cumulative trial) would have tried the product anyway; the remainder were new triers due to sampling. (See formula above.) These incremental triers would now follow the normal switching process, and their long-run share potential could be estimated like that for the advertising-induced triers. These calculations, found in Exhibit 10, estimated or incremental two percent share from a 35 million sample drop. Considering the effect of sampling, market share was estimated at 5.8 percent by the preference model and 5.9 percent by the trial/repeat model.

9. *Volume Predictions:* As a final step in the evaluation of Enhance's success potential, it was necessary to convert the share estimates into dollar sales projections. Doing this required a number of additional facts and adjustments. The 1979 volume of instant hair conditioner sales was projected to be $250 million. To find the volume that would result from a given Enhance share, it would be necessary to adjust the share for price and frequency-of-use differences between Enhance and the average for the category.

A use adjustment based on expected source of volume and frequency of use, indicated that Enhance's frequency of use would be about 0.9 times the category average. The tested Enhance prices and share of sales accounted for by the two sizes resulted in a price adjustment of 1.04. Multiplying these two adjustment factors resulted in a factor of 0.94 to be used to convert unit market share to dollar share.

Volume was then predicted, according to the two models, as follows:

	Trial/Repeat Model	**Preference Model**
Manufacturer's Category Volume	$250MM	$250MM
Enhance Unit Share	3.90%	3.80%
Enhance Dollar Share (Unit Share * .94)	3.66%	3.57%
Enhance Sales	$9.15MM	$8.93MM

Additional Sales From Promotion

Promotion Unit Share	2.0	
Promotion Dollar Share	1.88	
Enhance Sales	4.7MM	4.7MM
Total Sales	$13.85MM	$13.63MM

RECOMMENDATIONS

MDS, as a result of the ASSESSOR study, was not encouraging about Enhance's prospects. It also thought sampling would not be successful for Enhance. Johnson Wax management had set a market share of 10 percent.[4]

John Sherman knew, however, that the final recommendations were his to make. He could recommend that Enhance be abandoned; reformulated; and/or retested; or that a national rollout begin. The final decision lay somewhere higher up in the organization, but his recommendations would be considered carefully.

---

4. As a privately held corporation, Johnson Wax did not report financial data publicly. Manufacturers of health and beauty aids in general held cost data close to their chests. Exhibit 11 displays some approximate information on industry cost structure. The data are included for discussion purposes only and should not be considered indicative of Enhance's actual cost structure.

Blind Use Test Results

Incidence of Problems

	All Women	25-29	30-34	35 or Older
Dry/Damage Problems	53%	55%	53%	46%
Split ends	34	42	35	29
Dryness	32	29	35	31
Brittle/breaking	12	13	17	9
Damaged hair	13	10	18	11
Dull/Limp Problems	65%	64%	68%	58%
Hard to manage	38	32	42	39
Dull/no shine	24	16	21	30
Fine/limp hair	44	45	39	46

Each respondent was screened for the presence of any of these seven hair problems. The seven problems, in turn, were subjectively grouped into those to do with "Dry/Damage" and those to do with "Dull/Limp."

Overall Preference

	(BASE)	Prefer Enhance	Prefer Flex	No Difference
ALL USERS	(320)	48%	44%	8%
By Age				
Under 35	(166)	46	47	7
35 or over	(154)	50	40	10
By Hair Type				
Oily	(94)	51	45	4
Normal	(154)	44	47	9
Dry	(72)	53*	35	12
By Hair Quality				
Dry/damaged–net	(168)	50*	40	10
Fine/limp–net	(208)	49*	43	8

*Significant at 90 percent confidence level.

EXHIBIT 1
Johnson Wax: ENHANCE (A)

Blind Use Test Results (continued)

Preference on Specific Attributes

	Prefer Enhance	Prefer Flex	No Difference
Fragrance			
In bottle	27%	32%	41%
While using	34	37	29
After dry	28	28	44
Feels Cleaner			
While using	18	17	65
When dry	26*	19	55
Next day	26	22	52
Conditioning			
Conditioning	28	24	48
Softer	31	26	43
Body	31	32	37
More manageable	32	30	38
Better shine	14	16	70
Relieves dryness	(22)	15	63
Combing			
Easy to comb	22	20	58
Tangle free	16	16	68
Use/Application			
Applies evenly	(30)	14	56
Penetrates better	(28)	18	54
Rinses out easier	22	21	57
Product			
Better color	4	6	90
Better consistency	27	29	44

BASE: 320 Users

( ) Significant at 95 percent C.L.
* Significant at 90 percent C.L.

EXHIBIT 2
Johnson Wax: ENHANCE (A)

ASSESSOR **results**

Product map

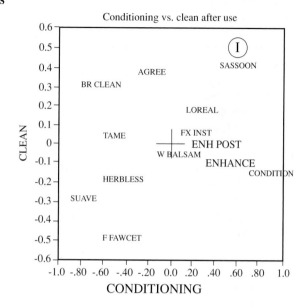

ENHANCE = Before use positioning.
ENH.POST = After-use positioning.
I = Ideal brand positioning.

ASSESSOR **results**

Product map

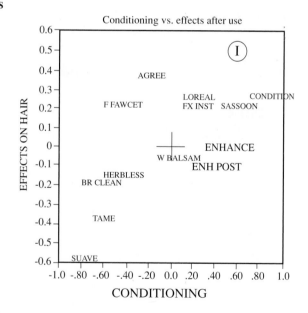

ENHANCE = Before use positioning.
ENH.POST = After-use positioning.
I = Ideal brand positioning.

EXHIBIT 3
Johnson Wax: ENHANCE (A)

ASSESSOR **Results**

Copy Point Recall

	Overall	Buyer	Nonbuyer
For Dry Hair			
Good for dry hair	46.8%	50.0%	46.1%
Nourishes hair	33.1	37.9	32.0
Prevents dry hair	5.4	1.7	6.2
Doesn't leave hair dry	0.7	0.0	0.8
Conditions	20.4%	27.6%	18.7%
Conditions hair	8.0	17.2	5.8
Good for damaged hair	5.4	5.2	5.4
Repairs hair	4.0	6.9	3.3
For brittle hair	3.3	1.7	3.7
Protects from heat damage	0.7	0.0	0.8
Mends split ends	0.7	0.0	0.8
Penetrates	19.7%	31.0%	17.0%
Penetrates hair	19.7	31.0	17.0
Doesn't just coat hair	3.3	8.6	2.1
Manageability	11.4%	17.2%	10.0%
Makes hair more manageable	7.7	12.1	6.6
Good for limp hair	3.3	3.4	3.3
Eliminates tangles	0.7	1.7	0.4
Texture of Hair	6.4%	5.2%	6.6%
Gives hair more body/bounce	4.3	1.7	5.0
Leaves hair soft	2.0	3.4	1.7
BASE:	(299)	(58)	(241)

EXHIBIT 4

Johnson Wax: ENHANCE (A)

Trial Comparison to all ASSESSOR-tested health and beauty aids products

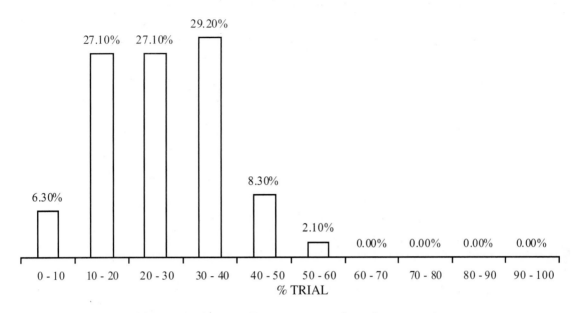

Trial comparison to all ASSESSOR-tested products.

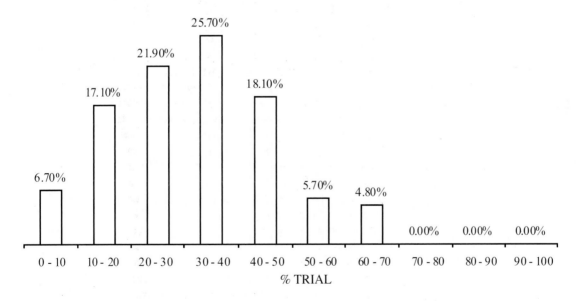

EXHIBIT 5
Johnson Wax: ENHANCE (A): Trial Comparison

Repeat Comparison to all ASSESSOR-tested health and beauty aids products

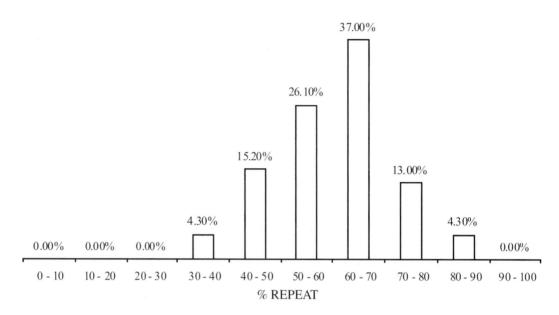

Repeat comparision to all ASSESSOR-tested products

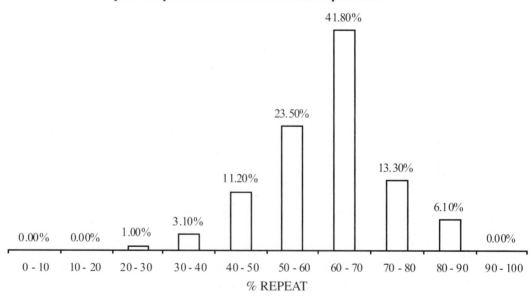

EXHIBIT 6
Johnson Wax: ENHANCE (A): Repeat-rate Comparison

ASSESSOR **Results**

Open-Ended Likes and Dislikes for Enhance (multiple mentions)

Open-Ended Likes	Overall	Repeaters	Nonrepeaters
Manageability	42%	48%	37%
Fragrance	21	14	27
Conditioning	11	12	10
Consistency	7	7	6
Application/ease of use	7	6	7
Penetrates	6	5	7
Clean	5	7	4
Base	(215)	(102)	(113)

Open-Ended Dislikes	Overall	Repeaters	Nonrepeaters
Manageability	24%	9%	38%
Fragrance	16	7	25
Conditioning	11	8	13
Consistency	1	3	0
Application/ease of use	1	1	1
Nothing Disliked	59	74	46
Base	(215)	(102)	(113)

EXHIBIT 7
Johnson Wax: ENHANCE (A)

ASSESSOR **Results**

After-Use Preferences

	*Percent Prefer Enhance**				
	1st	2nd	3rd	4th	(Base)
Dry Hair	38	32	17	7	(93)
Oily Hair	22	34	20	15	(41)
Normal	23	34	19	12	(69)
Total Sample	28	33	19	11	(215)
Total Sample (Agree)	54	26	12	2	(279)

Comparison to Regular Brand

	Among Triers		*Among Nontriers*	
	Enhance (%)	Agree (%)	Enhance (%)	Agree (%)
Much better	30	44	14	35
A little better	24	25	21	22
About the same	26	13	37	21
A little poorer	14	12	16	13
Much poorer	6	5	12	8
(Base)	(50)	(76)	(165)	(203)

*To be read, of the 93 respondents with dry hair, 38 percent rated Enhance as their favorite brand; for 32 percent it was their second choice, etc.

EXHIBIT 8
Johnson Wax: ENHANCE (A)

ASSESSOR **Results**

Market Share Prediction Trial Repeat Model

		Enhance	Agree
1.	Trial	23%	33%
2.	Awareness from advertising	.70	.70
3.	Distribution	.85	.85
4.	Net cumulative trial [(1) x (2) x (3)]	13.7%	19.6%
5.	Repeat	.60	.78
6.	Switchback	.16	.15
7.	Share of triers' choices (retention) $\dfrac{6}{[\,1+(6)-\,5]}$	28.6%	41%
8.	Base share [(4) x (7)]	3.9%	8.1

Preference Model

		Enhance	Agree
9.	Share for Enhance if everyone evokes it	27.5%	42.0%
10.	Estimated penetration [equal to (4)]	.14	.20
11.	Base share	3.8%	8.4%

EXHIBIT 9
Johnson Wax: ENHANCE (A)

ASSESSOR **Results**

Estimated Incremental Share from Sampling
for 35 Million Sample Drop with 90 Percent Delivery

Enhance vs. Agree

1. Number of samples delivered	[35M × .9]	31.5MM
2. Percent hitting target group		80%
3. Percent used*		60%
4. Number of samples used	[(1) × (2) × (3)]	15. 12MM
5. Percent using samples*	[(4) ÷ 6.0MM households]	25%
6. Overlap	[(5) × Trial Rate Advertising (line 4, Ex. 9)]	3%
7. Net incremental trial	[(5)—(6)]	22%
8. First repeat* (repeat among nonbuyers)		43%
9. Share of triers' choices (retention)		22%
10. Incremental share from sampling	[(7) × (8) × (9)]	2.0%

*Measured through ASSESSOR callbacks.

**Calculated from formula $\dfrac{SB}{1 + SB - R}$ where SB is given in line 6 of Exhibit 9 and R is line 8 of this exhibit.

EXHIBIT 10
Johnson Wax: ENHANCE (A)

Approximate Health and Beauty Aid Industry Cost Structures*
(Indexed to Suggested Retail Price)

Suggested retail price		$1.00
Expected shelf price	(large 16 oz.)	.83
	(small 8 oz.)	.73
Manufacturer's selling price		.56
Cost of goods sold		21%

*These data are not supplied by the Johnson Wax Company and are not known to be indicative of its actual costs. They are thought to reflect the average market cost structure closely enough to be helpful in the case discussion.

EXHIBIT 11
Johnson Wax: ENHANCE (A)

CHAPTER **8**

Advertising and Communications Decisions

In this chapter we will discuss the marketing engineering approach to advertising and some other communications-mix decisions. The communications mix that marketers can use includes

Advertising: Any paid form of nonpersonal presentation and promotion of ideas, goods, or services by an identified sponsor

Direct marketing: The use of mail, telephone, the Internet, and other nonpersonal contact tools to communicate with or solicit a response from specific customers and prospects

Sales promotion: Short-term incentives to encourage people to try or purchase a product or service

Public relations and publicity: Various programs designed to promote or protect a company's image or its individual products

Personal selling: Face-to-face interaction with one or more prospective purchasers for the purpose of making sales

We focus on advertising in this chapter, and we discuss the major elements of the rest of the communications mix in the next two chapters.

In this chapter, then, we deal with the following topics:

- The bewildering nature of advertising
- Advertising effects: response, media, and copy
- Advertising budgeting decisions
- Media decisions
- Advertising copy development and decisions

Software packages that are relevant for this chapter are the ADBUDG spreadsheet, developed to accompany the Blue Mountain Coffee case; ADVISOR, designed to accompany the Convection Company case; and ADCAD, a knowledge-based system for designing advertisements.

THE BEWILDERING NATURE OF ADVERTISING

One of the most important and bewildering promotional tools of modern marketing management is advertising. No one doubts that it can be effective in presenting information to, or persuading, potential buyers. Everyone agrees that it can influence customers' preferences for a product, enhance a company's image, and affect customers' purchasing behavior. Even when advertising does not directly influence sales, it may affect image and preference, which influence sales. In fact, small changes in people's preference for a product can have lasting impact, resulting in increased sales over time.

Advertising is bewildering because, among other reasons, its effects typically play out over time, may be nonlinear, and can interact with other elements in the marketing mix in creating sales. Currently no one knows what advertising really does in the marketplace. However, what advertising is supposed to do is fairly clear: advertising is supposed to increase company sales and profits. However, it rarely can create sales by itself. Whether the customer buys also depends on the product, price, packaging, personal selling, services, financing, and other aspects of the marketing process.

Even more than for other elements for the marketing mix, advertising decisions and their effectiveness are influenced by their interaction with marketing objectives, with product characteristics, and with other elements of the marketing mix. Here are some examples:

Personal selling: When personal selling is an important element in the marketing mix (in industrial markets, for example), the role of advertising is diminished. Personal selling is a far more effective (although more expensive) communication method than advertising. But because of its extra expense, it can be used most effectively when the expected level of sales to a single prospect is large (generally, sales to industrial customers, wholesalers, and retailers).

Branding: If a company produces several variations of its product under a family or company name (Kellogg's cereal, Campbell soup), it can advertise the entire line, giving attention to a special brand from time to time. When a firm carries different brand names (Procter and Gamble's Tide, Bold, and Cheer detergents, for example), the company can advertise each brand independently and make separate advertising budget, copy, and media decisions.

Pricing: The copy or message and media placement of the advertising must reinforce and be consistent with the brand's price position. A premium-priced brand should emphasize differentiating qualities, whereas a low-priced brand should stress its low price.

Distribution: The length of the distribution channel and the overall marketing strategy dictate different targets for advertising messages. To influence wholesalers or retailers a firm can use two different strategies: push versus pull. In a push strategy the firm directs its marketing efforts at salespeople or the trade, with the objective of pushing the product through the distribution channel; in a pull strategy the firm aims its marketing strategy at the ultimate consumer, with the objective of stimulating consumer demand to pull the merchandise through the distribution channels.

Batra, Myers, and Aaker (1996) define three major decisions for advertising: (1) setting objectives and budgeting (how much to spend), (2) developing copy (what message), and (3) choosing media (what media to use). Although we address these three points separately here, they are closely interrelated: advertising objectives drive copy decisions, and copy effects, which vary by response group, affect media decisions. In addition, time is an issue for all three decision areas. For budgeting, dollars must be spent over time, and firms must evaluate pulsing versus more continuous spending policies. Furthermore, advertising copy varies in its effectiveness over time, eventually wearing out, and firms must create new copy and phase it in. Finally, firms must decide what media to use in conjunction with timing and scheduling their messages.

ADVERTISING EFFECTS: RESPONSE, MEDIA, AND COPY

Advertising response phenomena

Little (1979) identifies three areas of controversy associated with advertising sales response models:

> *Shape* refers to the long-term level of sales expected at each level of advertising. Is the relationship linear? S-shaped? What are sales when advertising is zero? Is there a supersaturation point, where large amounts of advertising actually depress sales?

> *Dynamics* refers to the speed of the sales increase when advertising is increased and the rate of decay when advertising is decreased. One question is whether hysteresis exists—that is, whether advertising can move sales to a new level at which it will stay without further advertising input. Although carryover effects have been found in many empirical studies, there is little agreement about how long they last (Clarke 1976).

> *Interaction* refers to the interplay and synergy (positive and negative) between advertising and other elements in the marketing mix, such as sales promotion, personal selling, and price.

Little (1979) also reviews many empirical examples in an attempt to identify important advertising response phenomena. Exhibit 8.1 shows that advertising increases the sales rate of a packaged good: After heavy advertising, sales increased substantially. The sales rate increased within a month or so, substantially faster than many managers believe is the case.

The exhibit also shows sales leveling off during the period of heavy advertising: apparently it achieved its total effect before spending returned to its usual level.

Finally, the exhibit shows the beginning of a decay in sales following the decrease in advertising. Furthermore, sales seem to decline more slowly than they grow. Two separate phenomena are involved: the rise is related to advertising, while the decline is related to product experience, a different phenomenon, and we should expect a different rate.

Exhibit 8.2 shows sales for a line of products that have never been advertised. Supermarkets and department stores are full of house brands, price brands, and other products that have quite healthy sales even though they are not advertised. Therefore an advertising response model should admit the possibility of sales with zero advertising.

Perhaps the most interesting aspects of response to advertising are nonlinearities in the response curve. Logic suggests that a linear response curve is unreasonable: optimal advertising for a product with a linear response would be either zero or infinity, and one could increase its sales by continued increases in advertising spending. On the other hand, nonlinearity covers many alternatives, most importantly diminishing returns and an S shape. Exhibit 8.3 shows the sales of two products that display concavity, or diminishing returns to advertising "units," either dollar expenditures or an appropriate measure of exposure (Hanssens, Parsons, and Schultz 2001).

Finally, Little (1979) summarizes his observations with a list of five phenomena that a good advertising response model should admit:

1. Sales move dynamically upward in response to increases in advertising and downward in response to decreases in advertising, and frequently do so at different rates.
2. Response to advertising can be concave or S-shaped, and sales will often be positive at zero advertising.

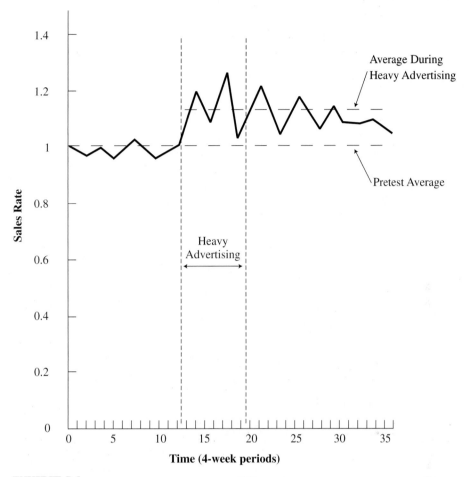

EXHIBIT 8.1
The sales rate of a packaged good rose quickly under increased advertising but declined slowly after it was removed. The vertical axis shows the ratio of sales in test areas to sales in control areas that did not receive the heavy advertising. *Source*: Little 1979, p. 637.

3. Competitive advertising affects sales, usually negatively.
4. The dollar effectiveness of advertising can change over time because of changes in media, copy, and other factors.
5. Sales of products sometimes respond to increased advertising with an increase that falls off even as advertising is held constant.

An advertising response model: Vidale and Wolfe (1957) developed a classical advertising response model to explain the rate of change of sales when advertising had both immediate and lagged effects:

$$\frac{\Delta Q}{\Delta t} = \frac{rX(V - Q)}{V} - \alpha Q, \tag{8.1}$$

where

Q = sales volume;

$\Delta Q/\Delta t$ = change in sales at time t;

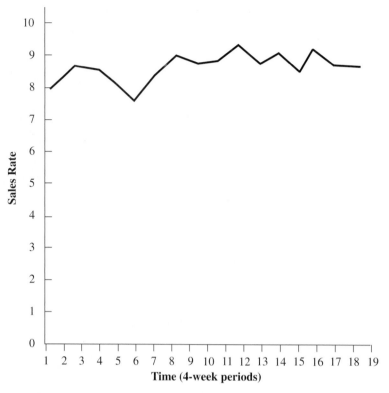

EXHIBIT 8.2
The healthy sales of a line of unadvertised food products show that advertising is not always required to sell something. *Source:* Little 1979.

X = advertising spending rate;

V = market volume;

r = sales-response constant (sales generated per dollar of advertising, X, when sales, $Q = 0$); and

α = sales-decay constant (proportion of sales lost per unit of time when advertising, $X = 0$).

The right-hand side of Eq. (8.1) means that the change in the rate of sales, $\Delta Q/\Delta t$, depends on several factors: it will be greater for higher levels of r, X, and $(V - Q)/V$ (untapped potential), and it will be lower for higher values of α and Q. Thus $\Delta Q/\Delta t$ is equal to the response rate, r, per dollar of spending times the number, X, of marketing dollars spent reduced by the percentage of unsaturated sales, $(V - Q)/V$, less sales lost through decay, αQ. The implications of this model for an advertising program of a given level of intensity that is stopped are shown in Exhibit 8.4.

Lodish et al. (1995a) provide some interesting results on how advertising works, based on split-cable TV ads. They find that in general increasing advertising does not increase sales. They also find that advertising is most likely to increase sales when it is accompanied by changes in the product (e.g., a new product), in the advertising copy, or in the media strategy and when the ads are used for product categories for which in-store merchandising effort is low. In particular, 67 percent of the tests showed no increase in sales with increased

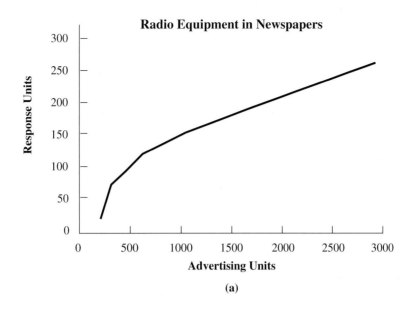

(a)

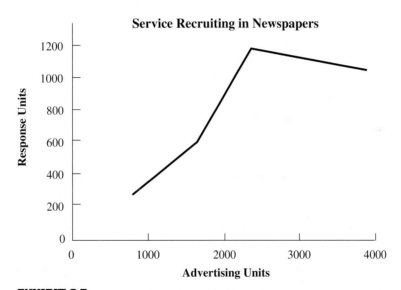

EXHIBIT 8.3
In these two examples of nonlinear response, returns diminish as advertising increases.
Source: Little 1979.

advertising for established products, and 61 percent of the tests that used existing advertising copy showed no increase in sales with increased advertising. For established products, advertising elasticity averaged 0.05; that is, a 100 percent increase in advertising would lead to a 5 percent increase in sales. Marketing researchers need to do more work of this type to determine when and how sales respond to advertising in their own product categories.

Internet and related electronic communications media are providing challenges for those attempting to draw generalizations about the effectiveness of advertising. These new media permit targeting ads on the fly and also permit new measures of direct response. (See Sherman and Deighton 2001, for example, or *www.marketswitch.com* and *www.angara.com* for examples of on-the-fly targeting.)

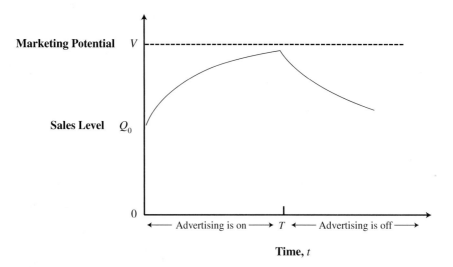

EXHIBIT 8.4
According to the Vidale-Wolfe (1957) model, during an advertising campaign of duration *T* during which spending is constant, sales increase, showing a concave response. When advertising ceases, sales decline gradually, at a different rate than they increased.

Frequency phenomena

In planning and scheduling media for advertising it is critical to understand the effect of advertising exposure over time.

The theory concerning the effects of advertisement frequency is based on laboratory research in psychology and can be traced to the work of Ebbinghaus in the late 1800s in which he showed that the forgetting rate is slowed by repeated learning of the same lessons. Zielski (1959) later applied Ebbinghaus's findings to ads for grocery products.

Appel (1971) and Grass (1968) show that response to a simple stimulus first increases, then passes through a maximum, and finally declines (Exhibit 8.5). From studies for a number of DuPont products, Grass concludes that attention increases and levels out at two exposures, while the amount of learned information increases and levels out at two or three exposures. Krugman (1972), based on his studies of brain waves and eye movements, advocates the idea that the third and subsequent exposures reinforce the effects of the second exposure.

McDonald (1971) reports on the effects of frequency, based on records 255 homemakers kept on their exposure to newspapers, magazines, and radio and TV ads for 50 product fields over a 13-week period. He found that over 9 product fields, homemakers were on average 5 percent more likely to switch to a particular brand if, between two purchases of that commodity, they saw two or more ads for that brand than if they saw zero or one ad. McDonald also found that the effect was stronger for advertising seen within four days before the second purchase.

In a study conducted for four advertisers, Ogilvy and Mather (1965) asked respondents to keep television viewing diaries; they tracked their brand preferences and related them to their number of exposures. Their study showed (1) no more than minimal effects for one exposure in an eight-week period, (2) major differences by time of day, and (3) major differences by brand. Naples (1979) reports another study within a split-cable television market in which respondents kept diaries recording their purchasing. The results indicated that at least two exposures were needed for maximum effectiveness. He also found that the brands that showed the greatest response were those with the highest share of advertising in their categories. On the basis of these studies and a review of others, Naples (1979, pp. 63–81) offers the following conclusions:

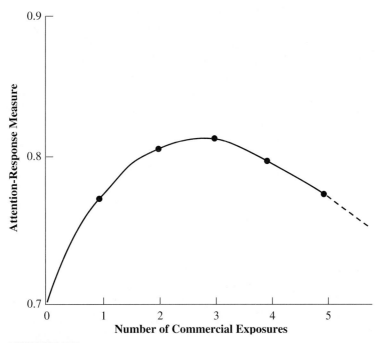

EXHIBIT 8.5
As the exposure to a TV commercial increases, people pay less attention to it. *Source*: Grass 1968.

1. Optimal frequency appears to be three or more exposures within a purchase cycle.
2. Beyond three ad exposures, effectiveness continues to increase but at a decreasing rate.
3. Advertising frequency by itself does not cause wear-out, although it can speed the decline of an effective campaign.
4. Response to advertising appears smaller for the brands with the highest market share.

Cannon (1987) lists 27 propositions (e.g., "Proposition 25: Vivid images will require low frequency since they provide unique and memorable experiences," p. 41) that summarize his feeling that frequency is an individual-, copy-, and situation-specific phenomenon and that a media schedule can at best segment the market appropriately and select media vehicles and a schedule that works best for each of those segments. (See also Cannon and Goldring 1986, and Wenzel and Speetzen 1987, and for industrial ads, Cort, Lambert, and Garret 1982.) This issue continues to be one of controversy; for example, Longman (1998) makes a case that we should question frequency as a goal of advertising programs.

Copy effects

People interested in copy or message effectiveness are most concerned with the sales effect of copy relative to media spending (advertising intensity). For example, Aaker and Carman (1982) reviewed 48 AdTel advertising experiments and reported that 30 percent showed significant results on advertising intensity while 47 percent involving ad copy showed significant results. Similarly, Fulgoni (1987) reported on more than 400 BehaviorScan tests, with 40–55 percent showing response to intensity (depending on the year) while 75 percent showed a significant response to copy. Carroll et al. (1985) reported no effect of intensity in an experiment concerning an enlistment program for the Navy but did report statistically significant results for copy tailored to the local area. Eastlack and Rao (1989), reviewing 19 advertising experiments at Campbell soup, concur, reporting that "good copy in the right media will produce sales increases without increases in budget" (p. 70). Using data on 92 British TV advertising tests, Stewart (1990) reported that 48 percent of the tests showed a significant increase in sales in response to new copy and 31 percent of the tests showed a significant sales increase for an advertising intensity test for established brands.

Given that advertising copy is so important, people have good reason to want to know what makes a good ad. Those in copy research investigate myriad phenomena from how the physical and mechanical aspects of ads relate to recognition, recall, and other measures (Hendon 1973) to the humor and seriousness of TV commercials (Wells, Leavitt, and McConnell 1971). In his review of a large number of copy-testing studies Ramond (1976) provides the following principles:

- The bigger the print ad, the more people will recognize it later (Starch 1966; Trodahl and Jones 1965; Twedt 1952; Yamanaka 1962), possibly as a function of the square root of the size increase.
- More people recognize color ads than black-and-white ads (Gardner and Cohen 1966; Twedt 1952).
- The shorter its headline, the greater the recognition of an ad (unpublished Leo Burnett bulletin).
- People recall shorter TV commercials as well as longer ones, and product class has a significant effect on recognition and recall of both TV and print ads.
- People's awareness and attitudes change with changes in the execution of TV commercials, and these changes can predict changes in brand choice (Assael and Day 1968; Axelrod 1968).
- People do not need to believe ads to remember them (Leavitt 1962; Maloney 1963).

These observations, while simplistic, have led to some contingency theories of copy and message effects—that is, what messages to use in what circumstances (Rossiter and Percy 1997). Other research in this area is promising as well. For example, Hanssens and Weitz (1980) reported that recall and readership scores for industrial ads were strongly related to such characteristics as size and position in magazines. Sewall and Sarel (1986) performed a similar analysis for radio commercials, and Goodwin and Etgar (1980) report relationships between communication effects and the type of advertising appeals. For a good treatment of what seems to drive effective TV ads, see Stewart and Furse's (1986) study of 1,000 commercials.

ADVERTISING BUDGET DECISIONS

Firms must often decide how much to spend on advertising. We will describe four of the more common methods for making this decision. Patti and Blasko (1981) and Blasko and Patti (1984) give some statistics about the use of these methods by industrial marketers (I) and consumer marketers (C), respectively. We put the percentages of each type of firm that reports using each method in parentheses following the method.

Affordable method (I = 20%, C = 33%): Many executives set the advertising budget based on what they think the company can afford. As one advertising executive explained:

> Why it's simple. First, I go upstairs to the controller and ask how much they can afford to give us this year. He says a million and a half. Later, the boss comes to me and asks how much we should spend, and I say, "Oh, about a million and a half." Then we have an advertising appropriation. (Seligman 1956, p. 123)

Setting budgets in this manner is tantamount to saying that the relationship between advertising expenditure and sales results is at best tenuous: the company should spend whatever funds it has available on advertising as a form of insurance. The basic weakness of this approach is that it leads to a fluctuating advertising budget that makes it difficult to plan for long-range market development.

Percentage-of-sales method (Anticipated: I = 16%, C = 53%; Past year's: I = 23%, C = 20%): Many companies set their advertising expenditures at a specified percentage of sales (either current or anticipated) or of the sales price. For example, a railroad company executive once said:

> We set our appropriation for each year on December 1 of the preceding year. On that date we add our passenger revenue for the next month, and then take two percent of the total for our advertising appropriation for the new year. (Frey 1955, p. 65)

Furthermore, automobile companies typically budget a fixed percentage for advertising based on the planned price of each car, and oil companies tend to set the appropriation as some fraction of a cent for each gallon of gasoline sold under their own label.

People claim a number of advantages for this method. First, advertising expenditures are likely to vary with what the company can afford. Second, it encourages managers to think in terms of the relationship between advertising cost, selling price, and profit per unit. Third, to the extent that competing firms spend approximately the same percentage of their sales on advertising, it encourages competitive stability.

In spite of these advantages the percentage-of-sales method has little to justify it. It uses circular reasoning in making sales the determinant of advertising rather than its result. And it leads executives to set the appropriation for advertising according to the availability of funds rather than according to the available opportunities. Furthermore, the method provides no logical basis for choosing a specific percentage, except what has been done in the past, what competitors are doing, or what the costs will be. Finally, it does not encourage firms to appropriate funds for advertising constructively on a product-by-product and territory-by-territory basis but instead suggests that all allocations be made at the same percentage of sales.

Competitive-parity method (I = 21%, C = 24%): Some companies set their advertising budgets specifically to match competitors' outlays—that is, to maintain competitive parity.

Two arguments are advanced for this method. One is that competitors' expenditures represent the collective wisdom of the industry. The other is that maintaining a competitive parity helps to prevent advertising wars. But neither of these arguments is valid. There are no a priori grounds for believing that the competition is using logical methods for determining outlays. Advertising reputations, resources, opportunities, and objectives are likely to differ so much among companies that their budgets are hardly guides for other firms. Furthermore, there is no evidence that appropriations based on the pursuit of competitive parity do in fact stabilize industry advertising expenditures.

Knowing what the competition is spending on advertising is undoubtedly useful information. But it is one thing to have this information and another to copy it blindly.

Objective-and-task method (I = 74%, C = 63%): In using the objective-and-task method advertisers develop their budgets by (1) defining their advertising objectives as specifically as possible, (2) determining the tasks that must be performed to achieve these objectives, and (3) estimating the costs of performing these tasks. The sum of these costs is the proposed advertising budget (Colley 1961; Wolfe, Brown, and Thompson 1962).

Firms should develop their advertising goals as specifically as possible to guide them in developing copy, in selecting media, and in measuring results. The stated goal "to create brand preference" is much weaker than "to establish 30 percent preference for brand X among Y million women in the 18 to 34 age category by next year." Colley (1961) listed 52 specific communication goals, including the following:

- Announce a special reason for buying now (price premium, etc.).
- Build familiarity and easy recognition of the package or trademark.
- Place the advertiser in a position to select preferred distributors and dealers.
- Persuade the prospect to visit a showroom and ask for a demonstration.
- Build the morale of the company's salesforce.
- Correct false impressions, misinformation, and other obstacles to sales.

This method has strong appeal and popularity among advertisers. Its major limitation is that it does not indicate how to choose the objectives and how to evaluate them and decide whether they are worth the cost of attaining them. Indeed Patti and Blasko (1981) report that 51 percent of major consumer advertisers use quantitative methods to set their budgets, although the figure for industrial advertisers is a disappointing 3 percent (Blasko and Patti 1984).

Model-based approaches: Many researchers have worked to develop decision models for setting advertising budgets. In their articles they focus on the size and allocation of the advertising budget. While the research efforts differ widely in their purpose and methodology, most are closely related to the following general approach:

Find $A_i(t)$ to

$$\max Z = \underbrace{\sum_i \sum_j \sum_t S_i\left(t \mid \{A_i(t)\}, \{C_{ij}(t)\}\right) \times m_i}_{\text{Gross Profit}} - \underbrace{\sum_i \sum_t A_i(t)}_{\text{Advertising spending}}, \qquad (8.2)$$

subject to

$$\sum_i \sum_t A_i(t) \le B \text{ (budget constraint)},$$

$$L_i \le \sum A_i(t) \le U_i \text{ (regional constraints)},$$

where

$S_i(t \mid \{A_i(t)\}, \{C_{ij}(t)\})$ = sales in area i at time t as a function of current and historical brand and competitive advertising;

$C_{ij}(t)$ = competitive advertising for competitor j in area i at time t;

$A_i(t)$ = advertising level in area i at time t;

m_i = margin per unit sales in area i;

$\{A_i(t)\}$ = entire advertising program over the planning horizon;

U_i, L_i = upper, lower regional constraints; and

B = budget constraint.

The quantitative models we discuss differ most importantly in their specifications of the form of $S_i(t)$.

As we discussed in the last section, a response model should include certain advertising phenomena. But models vary in form and incorporate these phenomena to different extents. We describe two of the simplest decision models below and a third approach (ADVISOR) based on the formal development of budgeting norms.

EXAMPLE

Rao and Miller's (1975) approach: Rao and Miller's model combines data from multiple markets over time. Their basic idea is that many national advertising campaigns provide a set of quasi-experimental conditions because exposure rates and other characteristics vary from market to market. The idea is to derive an advertising-response coefficient from each of a number of sales districts and then to combine those coefficients in a way that produces a general sales-response function.

Rao and Miller assume that advertising has an immediate effect and a lagged effect and that the lagged effect decays exponentially. Although they show how to handle price offers and other trade promotions, we concentrate here only on the aspects of the model that relate to advertising. Their individual-market model is

$$S_t = c_0 + c_1 A_t + c_1 \lambda A_{t-1} + c_1 \lambda^2 A_{t-2} + \ldots + \mu_t, \tag{8.3}$$

where

$$S_t = \text{market share at } t;$$

$$A_t = \text{advertising spending at } t;$$

$$c_0, c_1, \lambda = \text{constants } (0 < \lambda < 1); \text{ and}$$

$$\mu_t = \text{random disturbance.}$$

This equation means that an incremental expenditure of one unit of advertising in a given period will yield c_1 share points in that period, $c_1\lambda$ in the following period, $c_1\lambda^2$ in the period after that, and so on.

The distributed lag form in Eq. (8.3) can be simplified by multiplying both sides by λ,

$$\lambda S_{t-1} = \lambda c_0 + \lambda c_1 A_{t-1} + \lambda^2 c_1 A_{t-2} + \ldots + \lambda \mu_{t-1}, \tag{8.4}$$

and subtracting Eq. (8.4) from Eq. (8.3):

$$S_t = c_0(1 - \lambda) + \lambda S_{t-1} + c_1 A_t + \mu_t - \lambda \mu_{t-1}. \tag{8.5}$$

Note that the short-run effect of advertising here is

$$\frac{dS_t}{dA_t} = c_1 \text{ (short-run effect)}, \tag{8.6}$$

while the long-run effect is c_1 in the first period, then $\lambda c_1 + \lambda^2 c_1 + \ldots$ in subsequent periods, or

$$c_1 + \lambda c_1 + \lambda^2 c_1 + \cdots = \frac{c_1}{(1 - \lambda)} \text{ (long-run effect)}. \tag{8.7}$$

Now if

I =   industry sales per year in the district;

P =   the district population; and

AV   =   the average rate of advertising during the period,

then with k periods per year, by Eq. (8.6) a \$1000 increase in advertising produces a share increase of $c_1/(1 - \lambda)$. Thus the sales increase of an additional \$1000 in advertising is

$$y_i = \Delta \text{sales}_i = \frac{c_1}{(1 - \lambda)} \frac{I}{K} \quad \text{(in market } i\text{)} \tag{8.8}$$

at a per capita advertising rate of $AV_i/P = x_i$. In other words, Eq. (8.8) can be interpreted as the derivative of a general market-share response curve at the per capita spending rate AV/P.

This procedure gives a set of values (y_i, x_i) for each market i, where the $\{y_i\}$ are the derivatives of a more general response function $g(x)$, so that $y = dg/dx$. Assuming that $g(x)$ is S-shaped, Rao and Miller propose using a polynomial in x to approximate it; specifically they assume that $g(x)$ can be modeled as a cubic function in x, while $y(x)$ is a quadratic function in x:

$$y = k_1 + k_2 x - k_3 x^2 + k_4 z, \tag{8.9}$$

where

z = percent share of premium brands (an empirical adjustment factor that accounts for variability in marginal response); and

$k_1, \ldots, k_4$ = parameters to be estimated.

Given a set of $\{y_i\}$ and $\{x_i\}$ (as well as $\{z_i\}$) we can estimate the coefficients in Eq. (8.9) using standard econometric methods. We can obtain the total advertising-response function simply by integrating Eq. (8.9). After integration they obtain

$$g(x) = k_0 + k_1 x + \frac{k_2}{2} x^2 - \frac{k_3}{3} x^3 + k_4 z, \tag{8.10}$$

with k_0 unspecified. The authors assume $k_0 = 0$ (zero advertising equals zero sales), but this model can clearly accommodate a nonzero sales level at zero advertising, in line with Little's second phenomenon. Then Eq. (8.10) can be used in Eq. (8.1) to allocate an advertising budget over districts and over time.

The basic procedure is illustrated with applications to five brands. The average value of the coefficients of determination (R^2) for the within-market models, Eq. (8.5), was 0.89; and the average R^2 for the response curves, Eq. (8.9), was 0.60. Thus the fits appear adequate. Exhibit 8.6(a) graphs the relationship between marginal sales due to advertising and average expenditure levels for one of the five brands (brand B), while Exhibit 8.6(b) shows the associated advertising-response function. The authors show how this model can be used to evaluate alternative advertising policies, and they make a case for pulsing (sporadic high levels of advertising followed by lower levels) when the response is S-shaped.

Companies have applied this method widely, expanding the model to incorporate dealing and price effects as well (Rao 1978; Eastlack and Rao 1986, 1989).

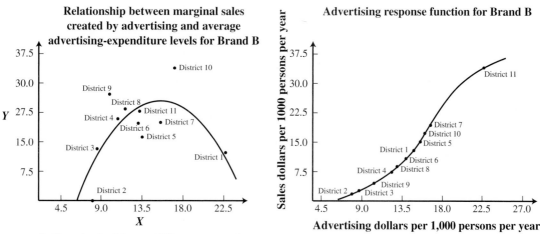

(a)   **(b)**

EXHIBIT 8.6
Rao and Miller's econometric model for advertising decisions. Graph (a) shows the inverted U-shaped relationship between advertising and the per-capita change in sales. Graph (b) shows the response function that results from integrating curve (a). *Source*: Rao and Miller 1975, p. 13.

Some products show S-shaped responses, whereas others show concave responses. Like most other econometric models this modeling approach has a variety of weaknesses. Of Little's desirable phenomena, it includes only the second, a possible S-shaped response. However, the model could be extended to include competitive effects (phenomenon 3), and copy and media effectiveness could be included as an effectiveness factor in the x's. Equation (8.4) does not readily admit differing rise and decay times. And with all econometric-based models, the data quality and its variability determine the acceptability of the model fit. In addition, while the authors report an S-shaped response, Hanssens, Parsons, and Schultz (1990) criticize their statistical methodology.

In conclusion this approach, while it has some flaws, is both simple and useful. It uses econometric methods to estimate the local conditions of a (postulated) global response curve. Furthermore, it blends well with the type of data typically collected for frequently purchased packaged goods.

The ADBUDG model: Little (1970) introduced the judgmental, decision calculus approach with his ADBUDG model. Like Rao and Miller, Little focuses on market-share response to advertising spending without explicitly considering competitive effects. Little bases the ADBUDG model on the following assumptions (Exhibit 8.7):

1. If advertising is cut to zero, brand share will decrease; but there is a floor, or minimum, to which the share will fall from its initial value by the end of one time period.
2. If advertising is increased a great deal, say, to something that could be called saturation, brand share will increase; but there is a ceiling, or maximum, on how much can be achieved by the end of one time period.

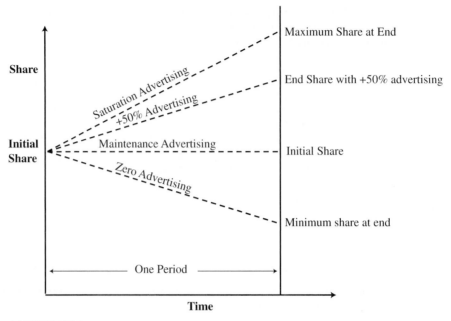

EXHIBIT 8.7
Assumptions about the one-period response for Little's ADBUDG model that can be used to develop a response function. Source: Little 1970.

3. There is some advertising rate that will maintain initial share.
4. An estimate can be made based on data analysis or managerial judgment of the effect on share by the end of one period of a 50 percent increase in advertising over the maintenance rate.

These assumptions are represented as four points on a share-response-to-advertising curve in Exhibit 8.8. This is the ADBUDG function from Chapter 2:

$$\text{share} = b + (a - b)\,\frac{\text{adv}^c}{d + \text{adv}^c}\,. \tag{8.11}$$

The constants a, b, c, and d are implicitly determined by the input data. Equation (8.11) represents a versatile but nevertheless restricted set of response relations.

The value specified for the increase in market share with a 50 percent increase in advertising is an important determinant of the advertising rate, while the values of a (maximum) and b (minimum) restrict changes to a meaningful range.

Although Exhibit 8.8 shows an S-shaped curve, Eq. (8.11) need not provide such a shape. If $c > 1$, the curve will be S-shaped; for $0 < c < 1$, it will be a concave function. The particular c will depend on the input data.

The description so far has omitted consideration of time delays. To take these into account, the model assumes

1. In the absence of advertising, share would eventually decay to some long-run minimum value (possibly zero).
2. The decay in one time period will be a constant fraction of the gap between current share and the long-run minimum; that is, decay is exponential.

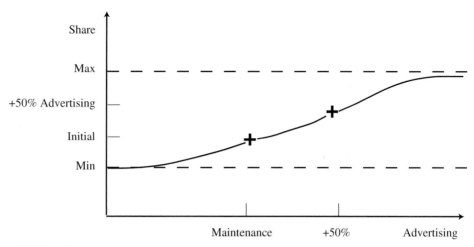

EXHIBIT 8.8
The ADBUDG model uses the data generated from the assumptions in Exhibit 8.7 to develop a smooth advertising-response function.

Let long-run min denote the long-run minimum and persistence denote the fraction of the difference between share and long-run minimum that is retained after a period of decay. Under the foregoing assumptions,

$$\text{persistence} = \frac{\text{min} - \text{long-run min}}{\text{initial share} - \text{long-run min}} ;$$

$$\text{share}_t = \text{long-run min} + \text{persistence} \times [\text{share}_{t-1} - \text{long-run min}]$$

$$+ (a - b) \frac{\text{adv}_t^c}{d + \text{adv}_t^c} . \tag{8.12}$$

This is a simple, dynamic model. It is easy to explain, and it behaves reasonably. It could be further generalized by permitting some of the constants to change with time, but that does not seem desirable at the moment.

What exactly do we mean by *advertising*? Dollars? Exposures? A product manager worries about spending rates, media, and copy. Let us construct two time-varying indices: (1) a media efficiency index, and (2) a copy effectiveness index. We will assume both have reference values of 1.0. We then hypothesize that the delivered advertising, that is, the adv_t that goes into the response function in (8.10), is given by wtd adv_t, weighted advertising:

$$\text{wtd adv}_t = \text{media efficiency}_t \times \text{media effectiveness}_t \times \text{adv dollars}_t. \tag{8.13}$$

We can determine the media efficiency and copy effectiveness indices subjectively, but better alternatives exist. Copy testing is helpful, and we can use data on media cost, exposures by market segment, and relative value of market segments to develop a media index. (We can include other effects such as product class sales effects, promotion, competition, and price in this model, but we will not deal with them here.) To summarize the model:

1. Share

$$\begin{aligned} \text{adjusted share}_t &= \text{long-run min} \\ &+ \text{persistence} \times [\text{share}_{t-1} - \text{long-run min}] \\ &+ (a - b)\,\frac{\text{wtd adv}_t^c}{d + \text{wtd adv}_t^c}. \end{aligned} \tag{8.14a}$$

2. Brand sales

$$\text{adjusted sales}_t = \text{product class sales index}_t \times \text{adjusted share}_t. \tag{8.14b}$$

3. Profits

$$\begin{aligned} \text{contribution to profit after adv}_t &= \text{contribution per sales unit}_t \\ &\times \text{brand sales}_t \\ &\times \text{adv dollars}_t. \end{aligned} \tag{8.14c}$$

The spreadsheet that accompanies the Blue Mountain Coffee case provides an implementation of the ADBUDG model that you can easily adapt to other situations.

Several of the problems with the ADBUDG model are that it does not include competition, that the one-period response limits (max and min) are independent of the market share at the beginning of the period, that advertising is independent of other marketing-mix effects, and that in the long run enough advertising can make market share exceed 100 percent. However, the model is simple and easy to understand, and it incorporates both single-period and carryover effects in an intuitively appealing manner.

As Little (1979) noted, models for budgeting advertising are seldom used. We hope that the software in this book will both demonstrate the ease with which ADBUDG can be implemented and also encourage its wider use.

Given that the effects of advertising are little understood and difficult to measure, it is not surprising that firms rely on the guidelines and informal rules of thumb outlined above as well as more formal guidelines like the ADVISOR approach.

The shared-experience approach—ADVISOR: The ADVISOR models follow the PIMS, shared experience approach (Chapter 6), but they focus more narrowly on the strategy for setting a budget for marketing industrial products. Begun in 1973 at MIT, the ADVISOR studies were sponsored by more than 80 companies that provided data on more than 300 industrial businesses.

Researchers analyzed the decision processes the sponsoring firms used in budgeting and also reviewed earlier studies. They found that models of marketing-communications spending should incorporate the effect of interaction between product and market characteristics, such as stage in the product life cycle and degree of product complexity, and should allow for a nonlinear relationship between the level of spending and those product and market characteristics.

The level of spending on advertising or marketing is dictated primarily by the sales level of the product as measured by last year's sales, and by the number of customers the marketing effort must reach. The firm then modifies that spending level to accommodate such factors as stage in the life cycle of the product, customer concentration, and technical complexity of the product.

A simple model that reflects these concepts is multiplicative:

$$\text{marketing}_t = b_0 \times \text{sales}_{t-1}^{b_1} \times \text{users}_2^{b_2} \times \text{var}_3^{b_3} \times \cdots \times \text{var}_9^{b_9}, \tag{8.15}$$

where

$b_0, \ldots, b_9$ = regression coefficients;

marketing = spending on marketing, in dollars (primarily personal selling, technical service, and marketing-communication expenditures);

sales = sales dollars (lagged one year);

users = number of individuals the marketing program must reach; and

var_i = other variables (stage in life cycle, product plans, etc.).

Exhibit 8.9 gives the main results of the ADVISOR models. Both advertising and marketing are strongly and positively related to sales (column 1). As sales increase, advertising gets less of the marketing dollar, perhaps because the number of trade journals is limited, while no such limit exists on the salesforce (row 2). As the number of users increases, firms spend more money on marketing and on advertising, but there is no obvious effect on the *A/M* ratio (column 2).

Researchers have developed other models to consider media selection, choice of distribution channels, changes in spending patterns, and use of trade shows (Lilien 1979, 1993). Furthermore, Lilien and Weinstein (1984) have replicated the results of these studies for a sample of 80 products in Europe, with remarkably consistent results. The Convection Company case provides you with a context in which to use the ADVISOR model to evaluate industrial-marketing budgeting decisions.

Thus advertising causes many different responses in the market, many of which have been reported in empirical studies (Leone 1995; Lodish et al. 1995b; Kaul and Wittink 1995). Still we need more knowledge about the dynamics of the effects and their estimation. Advances in measurement through electronic point-of-sale equipment and purchases on the Internet will improve our understanding of advertising phenomena, and this will permit us to further refine advertising models and make better advertising decisions.

MEDIA DECISIONS

Ad agencies specialize in two major decision areas: the creative decision, discussed next, and the media decision. In selecting media, the agencies try to find the best way to expose the target audience to a message the desired number of times and to schedule those exposures over the planning period.

We will elaborate on the concept of "desired number of exposures." Presumably the advertiser wants a response to its advertising from the target audience. Assume that the desired response is a certain level of product trial, which depends on, among other things, the level of brand awareness in the audience. Suppose product trial increases at a diminishing rate with the level of audience awareness (Exhibit 8.10a). Then if the advertiser wants to achieve a product trial rate of T^*, it must achieve a brand-awareness rate of A^*, and the task is to find out how many exposures E^* it needs to produce this awareness.

The effect of an advertisement on audience awareness depends on that ad's reach, frequency, and impact:

Reach (R): The number of persons or households exposed to a particular ad at least once during a specified time period. The media model assumes that if someone is exposed to a particular media vehicle carrying an ad, then that person is also "exposed" to the ad.

	Continuous Variables				Dichotomous Variables									
Dependent Variable	Sales (LSLS)	Number of Users (LUSERS)	Customer Concentration (LCONC)	Fraction of Sales Made to Order (LSPEC)	Prospect Customers/Product Attitudes Difference (DIFF)	Sales Direct to Users (LDIR-USER)	Stage in Life Cycle (LCYCLE)	Product Plans (PLANS)	Product Complexity (PROD)	Constant	R^2	F	SSE	N
Advertising (LADV)	+0.618 (9.1)	+0.104 (3.6)	−1.881 (3.1)	−1.989 (4.4)	a	a	−0.892 (3.2)	−1.503 (6.0)	a	−0.651	0.59	25.0	1.12	110
A/M [Logit (A/M)]	−0.232 (4.5)	a	a	a	+0.383 (2.0)	−0.255 (2.1)	a	a	−0.230[b] (1.2)	+0.544	0.24	7.5	0.91	100
Marketing (LMKTG)	+0.712 (12.6)	+0.082 (3.1)	−1.633 (3.1)	−0.993 (2.8)	−0.305 (1.7)	−0.194[b] (0.6)	−0.424 (2.0)	−0.809 (3.9)	+0.528 (2.5)	+0.185	0.72	28.2	0.91	110

Note: t statistics in ( ); all equations significant at $\alpha < 0.001$.   [a]Variable insignificant and logically irrelevant.   [b]Variable retained for logical consistency.

EXHIBIT 8.9

ADVISOR model coefficients for advertising (A), the advertising-to-marketing (M) ratio (logit(A/M) = log[A/(M − A)]), and marketing. LMKTG means that the equation for advertising (ADV) is linear after taking logs (Eq. 8.15). Source: Lilien 1979.

Average frequency (F): The average number of times within the specified time period that a person or household in the target segment is exposed to the message.

Impact (I): The qualitative value of an exposure through a given medium (thus a food ad would have a higher impact in *Good Housekeeping* than it would have in *Popular Mechanics*).

Exhibit 8.10(b) shows the relationship between audience awareness and reach. Audience awareness is greater the higher the exposures' reach, frequency, and impact. Furthermore, there are trade-offs among reach, frequency, and impact. For example, suppose the media planner has an advertising budget of $1 million and the cost per thousand exposures of average quality is $5. Then he can buy 200 million exposures (equal to $1,000,000 × 1,000/$5). If he seeks an average exposure frequency of 10, then he can reach 20 million people (equal to 200,000,000/10) with the $1 million budget. But if he wants to use higher-quality media, costing $10 per thousand exposures, he can reach only 10 million people, unless he is willing to decrease the frequency of exposures.

The following concepts capture the relationship among reach, frequency, and impact:

Total number of exposures (E) is the reach times the average frequency, that is, $E = R \times F$. It is also called gross rating points (GRP). If a given media schedule reaches 80 percent of the homes with an average exposure frequency of three, the media schedule is said to have a GRP of 240 (80×3). If another media schedule has a GRP of 300, it can be said to have more weight, but we cannot tell from GRP alone how this weight breaks up into reach and frequency.

Weighted number of exposures (WE) is the reach times the average frequency times the average impact, that is,

$$WE = R \times F \times I. \tag{8.16}$$

We can view the problem of planning as follows. With a given budget what is the most cost-effective combination of reach, frequency, and impact to buy?

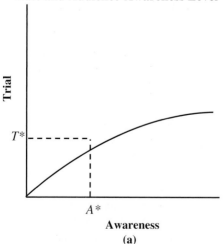

Relationship Between Product Trial Rate and Audience-Awareness Level

Trial

T*

A*

Awareness

(a)

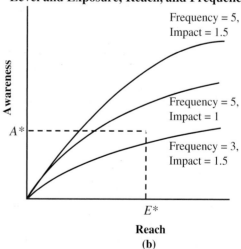

Relationship Between Audience-Awareness Level and Exposure, Reach, and Frequency

Awareness

Frequency = 5, Impact = 1.5

Frequency = 5, Impact = 1

A*

Frequency = 3, Impact = 1.5

E*

Reach

(b)

EXHIBIT 8.10

Relationship among trial, awareness, and the exposure function: Increasing the reach of an ad leads to an increase in the level of awareness (b), which in turn leads to an increase in trial for a new product (a).

In choosing a combination of media types, the media planner considers (1) the media habits of the target audience, (2) the characteristics of the product, (3) the message, and (4) the relative costs. On the basis of media impacts and costs, the planner chooses specific subgroups within each media type (PC magazines, daytime TV, daily newspapers in 20 major markets) that produce the desired response in the most cost-effective way. He or she then makes a final judgment on which specific vehicles will deliver the best combination of reach, frequency, and impact for the money.

Some agencies (and firms) use mathematical models to help them in making media plans. The media-decision problem can be stated as follows:

Given a media budget, an advertising message and copy, a set of media alternatives, and data describing the audiences and the costs of the media alternatives, decide (1) what media alternatives to use, (2) how many insertions in each and their timing, and (3) what type of advertising units (e.g., the size and color for print ads) for each of the media alternatives in such a way that you maximize the effect (measured in some way) of the media budget. The output of the media-decision process is called the media schedule, and it actually depends on your choice of an objective function. The most desirable measure of the effect of different media schedules is their impact on company profits. However, most media models do not presume a knowledge of the current or long-run sales or profit that advertisements placed in different media will generate. Instead they use various communication surrogates to measure the effectiveness of advertising when future sales would be difficult or impossible to measure. In media models the surrogate that is used most often is the number of exposures to members of the target audience—that is, the weighted number of exposures, defined in (8.16). To determine the total weighted-exposure value of a media schedule we must know two things: (1) the net cumulative audience of each media vehicle as a function of the number of exposures and (2) the level of audience duplication across all pairs of vehicles. In the case of two media alternatives we would typically use the following equation for net coverage:

$$R = r_1(X_1) + r_2(X_2) - r_{1,2}(X_{1,2}), \tag{8.17}$$

where

$$R = \text{reach of media schedule (i.e., total weighted-exposure value with replication and duplication removed);}$$

$$r_i(X_i) = \text{number of persons in audience of media } i; \text{ and}$$

$$r_{1,2}(X_{1,2}) = \text{number of persons in audience of both media vehicles.}$$

With three media alternatives, their reach would be

$$R = r_1(X_1) + r_2(X_2) + r_3(X_3) - r_{1,2}(X_{1,2}) - r_{1,3}(X_{1,3}) - r_{2,3}(X_{2,3}) + r_{1,2,3}(X_{1,2,3}). \tag{8.18}$$

In this case net coverage is found by summing the separate reaches of the three vehicles with the triplicated group and subtracting all the duplicated audiences. This equation can be generalized to the case of n media alternatives.

Obtaining data on the size of audience overlap for different sets of media vehicles requires large and expensive samples. Agostini (1961) has developed a useful estimation formula based on data from a French study of media-audience overlap, showing that total reach for magazine insertions can be estimated by

$$C = \frac{1}{K(D/A) + 1} A, \tag{8.19}$$

where

C = total reach;

K = constant, estimated as 1.125;

$$A = \sum_{j=1}^{n} r_j\left(X_j\right)$$

= total number of persons in audiences of media 1, 2, . . ., n; and

$$D = \sum_{j=1}^{n} \sum_{k=j+1}^{n} r_{jk}\left(X_{jk}\right),$$

= total of all pairwise duplicated audiences.

This relationship with parameter $K = 1.125$ has been shown to be a useful approximation for American and Canadian magazines as well (Bower 1963). See Claycamp and McClelland (1968) for an analytical interpretation of the formula. In a review of reach models, Rust (1986) recommends using the Agostini model to estimate the reach of a single vehicle and recommends Hofmans's (1966) model for two or more vehicles. Rust also provides an excellent review of models that have been developed to estimate audience overlap and exposure frequency. For some other methods for estimating both reach and frequency, see Rice (1988) Rust, Zimmer, and Leone (1986), Lancaster and Martin (1988), and Danaher (1989).

Media-scheduling models can work with a sales objective function, an effective-exposure value, or with reach and frequency separately. The most appropriate measures of sales and effective exposure are also the most difficult to use, because they are the most difficult to model and measure.

There are usually three components in models for media decisions: (1) the objective function, which assigns a value (e.g., profit or effective exposures) to an insertion schedule, (2) the solution strategy (e.g., heuristic or optimization), and (3) the constraints (e.g., the budget).

There are generally five principal components of the objective function:

1. The vehicle exposure measure—used to measure the net reach, schedule exposure, or GRPs (gross rating points)
2. The repetition effect—the relative impact of successive exposures on the same person
3. The forgetting effect—the forgetting between exposures and the nature of the decay
4. The media-option source effect—the relative impact of exposures from different sources
5. The segmentation effect—who is exposed and the fraction of the audience that represents target segments

We can classify media models by their solution approaches: optimizing models and nonoptimizing approaches. Optimizing models include several classes of mathematical-programming models, and nonoptimizing approaches include heuristic-programming, stepwise or marginal-analysis procedures, and simulation models.

In the early and mid-1960s researchers working on media models focused on linear-programming approaches. The main constraints they included were the size of the advertising budget, the minimum and maximum uses of specific media vehicles and media categories, and the desirable, minimum exposure rates to different target buyers. Choosing a best plan required them to specify an effectiveness criterion, which for media selection was usually the weighted number of exposures.

These models, and others such as MEDIAC (Little and Lodish 1966), were very sophisticated and required a lot of data, many managerial judgments, and vast computer power to generate schedules. After a decade of trial, advertising agencies developed heuristic procedures embedded in decision support systems that generate very good (if not optimal) schedules in much less time and with much less effort and cost than the more sophisticated methods (Simon and Thiel 1980). In addition, media planners could understand these methods more easily.

The increasing availability of single-source data (combining purchasing patterns with exposures to advertising, electronic media and other forms of communication) and flexible database-management software makes it likely that new models will be developed (Eskin 1985; Kamin 1988). See Rust (1986) and Leckenby and Ju (1989) for reviews of media models.

ADVERTISING COPY DEVELOPMENT AND DECISIONS

Much of the effect of an advertising exposure depends on the creative quality of the ad itself. But rating the quality of ads is extremely difficult, and much controversy surrounds copy testing. An advertisement may have very good aesthetic properties and win awards, and yet it may not do much for sales (e.g., Nissan's introductory ad for its Infiniti car that did not include a picture of the car). Another advertisement may seem crude and offensive (e.g., the classic Wisk "ring around the collar" ad), and yet it may be a major force behind sales. Such properties in advertisements as humor, believability, informativeness, simplicity, and memorability have not shown consistent relationships with sales generation. In this section we discuss three topics: testing copy and measuring its effectiveness, rating the creative quality of ads, and a new approach to designing ads.

Copy effectiveness

Copy strategy is based on advertising objectives. For a new brand, copy is oriented toward building broad awareness and inducing trial, whereas for established brands it focuses on reminding individuals to use the brand, increasing the rate of use, and distinguishing the brand from other brands. Thus in creating an ad, one must find the facts and ideas that match what a brand delivers with the objectives for the copy.

The goal of copy testing is to determine if an ad is likely to work. Two elements are involved in copy testing: measuring the dependent variable (e.g., response) and the setting for the measurement. The possible measures of response include the following:

1. Attention and impression—the ability of the ad to attract attention and be memorable
2. Communication and understanding—the ability of the ad to convey the message clearly and unambiguously to people in the target market
3. Persuasion—the ability of the ad to modify people's attitudes and beliefs about the product on certain key attributes or to change their overall purchase intentions
4. Purchase—the ability of the ad to positively affect purchasing behavior

The latter two measures, while most appropriate, are also the most difficult to measure.

Copy tests can also be classified by whether they use a laboratory setting, a simulated natural environment, or a totally natural environment (i.e., market tests). Laboratory and simulated-natural-environment methods include focus group interviews and a variety of physiological recording devices, including eye cameras (measuring eye movement), polygraphs and related devices (measuring emotional or psychological responses), and pupilometers (measuring pupil dilation, which occurs when people see something interesting).

In simulated natural environments, researchers usually bring subjects to a theater, where they measure their interest, liking, and often likelihood of purchase before and after exposing them to the advertising copy. Some procedures provide on-line measurements during exposure. Rossiter and Percy (1997) recommend procedures from McCollum Spielman (ADVANTAGE/ACT) and Research Systems Corporation (ARS).

A number of companies provide market tests. Usually they limit their campaigns to a small region and ask respondents (both those exposed to the ad and those not exposed) to answer various measures of recall and preference. Burke's AdTel and IRI's BehaviorScan can use split-cable techniques and personal interviews, along with a mail panel, to measure the effects of ads.

These methods provide some measures that may (or may not) be related to product sales. In an interesting cross-cultural comparison of advertisers' attitudes toward copy testing, Boyd and Ray (1971) found that market testing companies emphasize predictive validity, explanatory power, and reliability and do not use sales as a criterion because of measurement problems.

EXAMPLE

Developing AT&T's cost-of-visit campaign: Kuritsky et al. (1982) developed and tested a new ad copy program for AT&T Long Lines—the *cost-of-visit* campaign. Their research took five years, cost over $1 million, and comprised four "projects": (1) a segmentation study of the residential long-distance market, (2) tracking studies to test customer awareness of interstate phone rates, (3) qualitative research on customer attitudes to develop an ad concept, and (4) a large-scale, split-cable experiment that measured the effect of the advertising program in the marketplace.

In the segmentation study they established that there was a light-user group that looked (demographically) just like the heavy-user group, but it was composed of people who thought phoning was expensive: they had a price barrier. The second phase showed that most people overestimated the cost of long-distance phoning by over 50 percent. The third phase established the *cost-of-visit* theme, which included four elements:

1. *Surprise* that the cost is so low

2. *Appropriateness* of a 20-minute "visit" on the phone

3. *Maximum cost* ($3.33 or less)

4. *Taxes included* (no hidden costs)

The fourth phase of the study was the AdTel, split-cable experiment. In the AdTel system two cables distribute TV programming to households. AdTel divides a geographic area into small cells of 40 to 50 subscribers in a checkerboard pattern, each of which receives either signal A or signal B. (On a checkerboard, the red squares would get program A, the black squares program B.)

AdTel tested the cost-of-visit campaign against AT&T's very successful reach-out campaign using a panel of 16,000 households. Because there is no (necessary) delay between the time an ad is shown and when someone can make a call, and because AT&T automatically records data on calls, one can read the response to advertising in this setting much more clearly than in other field environments.

The experiment lasted for over two years and had three phases: (a) pre-assessment (5 months), (b) treatment period (15 months), and (c) post-assessment (6 months).

During the pre-assessment phase, AT&T tracked the records of all households to establish a norm for their calling behavior. In addition the company sent all respondents a questionnaire to determine whether their attitudes were the same as those in an earlier study and whether the test and control groups were demographically balanced (they were).

During the treatment period AT&T aired the two ad campaigns at a rate that gave each household about three exposures per week. The objective of the *cost-of visit* campaign was to encourage all user groups, but particularly the light-user group, to call during the 60-percent-off, deep-discount period (nights and weekends). The results of the study showed that, overall, an average household made an additional one-half long distance call during the deep-discount period while the targeted light-user group made about an additional one and a half calls. (These results were significant at the 0.01 level.) In addition there was an overall increase in revenue of about 1 percent overall, and the targeted light-user group yielded a 15 percent increase in revenue.

To make these assessments and to project them to the rational level, AT&T used the following model:

USDF = usage difference between the test group (cost-of-visit) and the control group (reach-out)

   = (Average usage during treatment for the test − average usage during pre-assessment for the test group) −

   (Average usage during treatment for the control group − average usage during pre-assessment for control group)

UNOFF = dummy variable

$$= \begin{cases} 0 \text{ for pretest weeks,} \\ 1 \text{ for test weeks,} \end{cases}$$

ε = disturbance.

The regression model:

$$\text{USDF} = \alpha + \beta \times \text{UNOFF} + \varepsilon \tag{8.20}$$

models the difference in usage/household/week as a preperiod constant (a) and a treatment constant ($a + b$). So the statistical significance of b for any segment (light users in a deep-discount period, for example) can be read from standard confidence limits resulting from linear regression analysis.

To project the results to the national level, AT&T used the following model:

$$y = \sum_{i=1}^{I} \left(n_i \sum_{j=1}^{J} z_{ij} p_{ij} \right), \tag{8.21}$$

where

y = projected usage in a given area, assuming a given level of advertising exposure;

i = index of usage segment (light, regular, etc.), $i = 1, \ldots, I$;

j = index of calling category (rate period), $j = 1, \ldots, J$;

z_{ij} = usage measure per household in cell i for calling category j;

n_i = number of households of segment type i in the area; and

p_{ij} = fraction increase or decrease in cell i, category j with "cost-of-visit" versus "reach-out."

The national or any regional projection can be made by summing over the appropriate areas.

The results of the analysis showed that AT&T was projected to earn more than $100 million more from the light-user segment without any increase in capital expenditures by introducing this new ad copy.

This study is one of the few that has demonstrated a significant impact on purchase and usage behavior based on a change in ad copy strategy. It demonstrates the effectiveness of a systematic approach for testing ad copy. We expect that as e-commerce and direct marketing become more prevalent, we will see more experiments of this type.

Estimating the creative quality of ads

Several researchers have tried to relate desirable characteristics of ads to quantifiable mechanical and message elements. Most have focused on readership or recall scores for print ads, the easiest types of ads and response variables to measure. In an interesting early study of this type, Twedt (1952) regressed readership scores of 151 advertisements in *The American Builder* against a large number of variables and found that the parameters of size of the advertisement, size of illustration, and number of colors account for over 50 percent of the variance in advertising readership. Interestingly, these mechanical variables explained advertising-readership variation better than many of the content variables that Twedt also tried out in the regression.

Diamond (1968) performed a well-known regression study of the effect of advertising-format variables on readership scores. His data were 1,070 advertisements that appeared in *Life* between February 7 and July 31, 1964. For each advertisement he had six different readership scores: "noted," "seen-associated," and "read most" for both men and women readers. In addition to these six readership scores, he measured 12 variables related to each ad: product class, past advertising expenditure, number of ads in the issue, size, number of colors, bleed/no bleed, left or right page, position in the magazine, layout, number of words, brand prominence, and headline prominence.

Diamond fitted several regression models and used the coefficients to draw conclusions about the effects of different variables on readership score. He found that the readership score was higher the larger the advertisement, the greater the number of colors, and the fewer the number of advertisements in the issue; he found that right-hand-page advertisements gained more attention than left-hand-page advertisements; and that advertisements with photographs did better than advertisements with illustrations, and both did better than nonpictorial advertisements.

In a study of the effectiveness of industrial print ads, Hanssens and Weitz (1980) related 24 ad characteristics to recall, readership, and inquiry generation for 1,160 industrial ads in *Electronic Design*. They used a model of the form

$$y_i = e^a \prod_{j=1}^{p_i} x_{ij}^{b_j} \prod_{j=p_{i+1}}^{p} \left(1 + x'_{ij}\right)^{b_j} e^{\mu_i}, \qquad (8.22)$$

where

y_i = effectiveness measure for ith ad;

x_{ij} = value of jth nonbinary characteristic of the ith ad (page number, ad size), $j = 1$, . . ., p_i;

x'_{ij} = value (0 or 1) of jth binary characteristic of ith ad (bleed, color, etc.);

e^a = scale factor; and

μ_i = error term

($\prod$ means product or "times" ($\times$)).

They segmented 15 product groups into three categories—routine purchase items, unique purchase items, and important purchase items—by factor analysis of purchasing-process similarity ratings obtained from readers of the magazine. Their results are similar to those of Twedt (1952) and Diamond (1968): they found that advertising characteristics account for more than 45 percent of the variance in the "seen" effectiveness measure, more than 30 percent of the "read-most" effectiveness measure, and between 19 and 36 percent of the variance in inquiry generation. Thus the variance explained by the "seen" measure is significantly greater than that explained by the "read-most" measure, which in turn is greater than that explained by the inquiry measure. These results are consistent across the three product categories. They are also in line with a hierarchy-of-effects model, which postulates that communication variables typically have a greater effect on lower-order responses (awareness) than on higher-order responses (behavior).

Hanssens and Weitz also found that both recall and readership were strongly related to format and layout variables (ad size, colors, bleed, use of photographs/illustrations, etc.), while the effects were weaker for inquiry generation. The effects of some factors, such as ad size, were consistently related across product groups and effectiveness measures, while others, such as the use of attention-getting methods (woman in ad, size of headline, etc.), were specific to the product category and the effectiveness measure.

As noted earlier, the only reported similar study for broadcast ads was that of Sewall and Sarel (1986). Much of the research cited here and in the previous section uses some recall measure(s) as dependent variable(s) (rather than an action measure) and neglects the effect of timing of exposures, measures of advertising believability, validity and reliability assessment, and the like. See Rossiter and Percy (1997) for a good discussion of the practical issues involved in ad testing.

Advertising design

Can we, in some sense, reverse the foregoing process: that is, use information about what copy platforms work best to develop a complete advertising design? Two approaches have been suggested in the literature on how to do this. (1) One approach is to identify common and replicable patterns "templates" that characterize creative ads that are known to be effective. Goldenberg, Mazursky, and Solomon (1999) analyzed 200 award-winning print ads and were able to categorize 89 percent of those ads into just six creativity templates. Each template (e.g., the picture analogy template) is a generalizable schema that is useful for the ideation process. In controlled experiments, the authors show that individuals (either novices or experts) trained in template-based idea generation developed ads that had higher creativity, brand attitude judgments, and recall than their untrained counterparts. However, there is no software implementation of this approach currently available. (2) Burke et al. (1990) use a different approach. They build a knowledge base containing a taxonomy of the various elements that constitute an ad (presenter, message emotion, format). They also identify a set of rules and principles to link various contexts (audience characteristics, marketing conditions, product characteristics) to ad elements that will be effective in those contexts. Finally, they embed this knowledge base in an expert system called ADCAD that facilitates user interaction with this knowledge base. Through interaction with the system, the user generates a customized checklist of ad elements that are likely to be effective in the context of interest to the user. We have included an implementation of ADCAD in the Marketing Engineering software suite. We now describe this system in more detail.

ADCAD is a rule-based expert system that allows managers to translate their qualitative perception of marketplace behavior into a basis for deciding on advertising design. Exhibit 8.11 shows an overview of the stages of the advertising-design process and the operation of the ADCAD system. The ADCAD system assumes that before purchasing a brand a consumer must (1) have a need that can be satisfied by purchasing this brand, (2) be aware that the brand can satisfy this need, (3) recognize the brand and distinguish it from its close substitutes, and (4) have no other behavioral or attitudinal obstacles to purchasing the brand. Advertising can address one or more of these issues: it can stimulate demand for the product category, create brand awareness, facilitate brand recognition, and modify beliefs about the brand that might be barriers to purchase.

ADCAD starts by asking for background information about the product, the nature of competition, the characteristics of the target audience(s), and so on, and it then develops a communication strategy for each target audience. Exhibit 8.12 lists a sample of rules for setting objectives for a specific application.

ADCAD then selects communications approaches to achieve the advertising and marketing objectives based on the characteristics of the consumers, the product, and the environment. It makes recommendations concerning the position of the ad, the characteristics of the message, the characteristics of the presenter, and the emotional tone of the ad. Exhibit 8.13 lists a sample of rules that ADCAD uses in considering each of these issues.

Where do these rules (the *knowledge base*) come from? The rules and judgments come from three sources: published theoretical results, published empirical studies, and ad agency experience. To go from these rules, or the knowledge base, to concrete recommendations the program uses what is called an *inference engine*, which logically processes the rules and facts in a way that solves the problem the user poses. Specifically, ADCAD requests information on the name and product class of the brand to be advertised and the name of the target segment. It then uses the rules in a goal-driven procedure (called backward chaining) to search for alternative communication approaches and copy strategies that best meet the conditions specified by the user. ADCAD asks the user for the minimal information it needs to evaluate the current set of alternatives that it cannot infer from the user's past responses. When it seeks only a single answer or conclusion about a variable (e.g., the life-cycle stage of the product), ADCAD stops seeking further answers to that variable as soon as it gets one answer. When it could expect multiple responses regarding a variable (e.g., benefits sought), ADCAD seeks multiple answers (or recommendations).

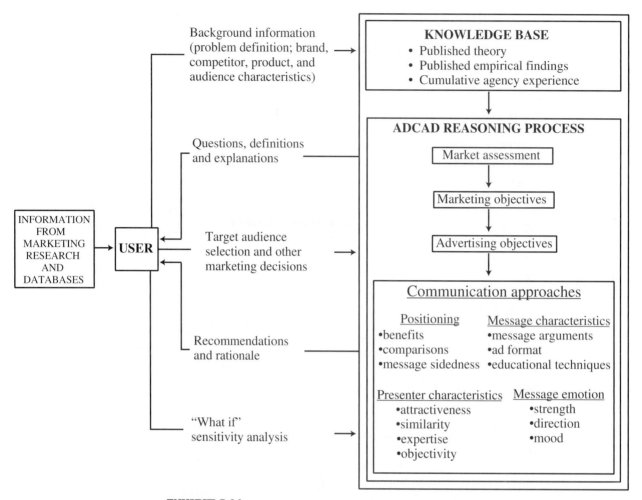

Background information
(problem definition; brand,
competitor, product, and
audience characteristics)

KNOWLEDGE BASE
- Published theory
- Published empirical findings
- Cumulative agency experience

ADCAD REASONING PROCESS

Market assessment

Marketing objectives

Advertising objectives

Questions, definitions
and explanations

INFORMATION
FROM
MARKETING
RESEARCH
AND
DATABASES

USER

Target audience
selection and other
marketing decisions

Recommendations
and rationale

"What if"
sensitivity analysis

Communication approaches

Positioning
- benefits
- comparisons
- message sidedness

Message characteristics
- message arguments
- ad format
- educational techniques

Presenter characteristics
- attractiveness
- similarity
- expertise
- objectivity

Message emotion
- strength
- direction
- mood

EXHIBIT 8.11
Overview of the major steps in advertising design and user interaction with ADCAD, showing
the interaction of the user with the environment and the role of ADCAD's knowledge base
and reasoning process in generating recommendations.

As an example, we apply ADCAD to a problem faced by the management of Suave shampoo (Albion 1984). The shampoo market is mature, competitive, and highly fragmented. Eighteen- to thirty-four-year-old women are traditionally the heaviest users of shampoo. Suave management segments this market into three groups: loyal Suave users (22 percent), consumers who have tried Suave but now use other brands (28 percent), and consumers who have never tried Suave (50 percent). The firm is targeting the third group, and the user enters this information.

Exhibits 8.14 and 8.15 show the inference process for a consultation on the Suave Shampoo case. Exhibit 8.14 shows sample input and output (ADCAD's recommendations). Exhibit 8.15 shows how the system links user inputs with rules in the knowledge base to reach conclusions.

ADCAD first asks the user questions to identify the firm's marketing objectives. When requesting information, the system provides a "What" facility in which the user can find detailed definitions regarding the terminology the system uses in questions and a "Why" facility in which the user can learn why it is using a certain piece of information in the particular decision. In the Suave example, ADCAD infers that, because shampoo is a mature

Marketing Objectives (11 rules)
- IF product life cycle stage = introduction AND innovation type = discontinuous THEN marketing objective = stimulate primary demand
- IF brand usage = none THEN marketing objective = stimulate brand trial
- IF current brand usage = some AND (brand switching = high OR product usage rate = fixed) THEN marketing objective = stimulate repeat purchase/loyalty
- IF current brand usage = some AND brand switching = low AND product usage rate = variable THEN marketing objective = increase rate of brand usage

Advertising Objectives (18 rules)
- IF marketing objective = stimulate primary demand AND product purchase motivation direction = negative THEN ad objective = convey product category information
- IF marketing objective = stimulate brand trial AND brand purchase motivation direction = positive THEN ad objective = convey brand image
- IF time of brand decision = at point of purchase AND package visibility = high AND package recognition = low THEN ad objective = increase brand recognition
- IF marketing objective = increase rate of brand usage AND new brand uses = yes THEN ad objective = convey new brand uses

EXHIBIT 8.12

Examples of the rules ADCAD employs in selecting marketing and advertising objectives, set up in the format of rule-based models.

product and most consumers use it often, it is not necessary to increase primary demand. The target audience has not used Suave, so ADCAD suggests stimulating brand trial.

Next ADCAD tries to determine appropriate advertising objectives. The user states that the motivation of the audience in purchasing a brand of shampoo is not to clean hair, but to enhance self-esteem and achieve social approval, and so ADCAD proposes that advertising should communicate a brand image, mood, or lifestyle (Rossiter and Percy 1997; Wells 1981). The case includes the information that buyers make brand decisions at the point of purchase, and so the system recommends that advertising should enhance brand recognition (Bettman 1979).

ADCAD then tries to choose a benefit to be featured in the advertisement and to determine effective communication approaches. Suave sells at a much lower price than its competitors but offers similar product features. The price attribute is important to the target audience, so ADCAD recommends positioning on value. However, the user anticipates the introduction of low-priced competing shampoos, and he or she overrides this suggestion and chooses instead to enhance the quality image of Suave. The image-oriented creative strategy dictates a one-sided message.

At the end of the consultation ADCAD presents its conclusions. Because shampoos are inexpensive, perceived brand differences are small, and health risks are minimal, ADCAD infers that the purchase decision is low involvement. ADCAD suggests that the firm use an endorsement by an attractive, recognizable, female celebrity to attract the audience's attention and communicate the quality image (Petty, Cacioppo, and Schumann 1983; Young and Rubicam 1988). The ad should be appealing, capture what the consumer feels, and use visual stimuli, imagery, and music to enhance the emotional response (Mehrabian 1982; Rossiter 1982; Young and Rubicam 1988). To make salient the audience's motivations in purchasing a brand, ADCAD proposes an emotional tone of apprehension followed by flattery (Rossiter and Percy 1997). Since the audience's evaluation of brand performance is subjective (visible benefit in use is low) and its motivation to process a message is likely to be low, ADCAD recommends making extreme claims for brand performance (Maloney 1962) and showing surrogate indicators of performance (e.g., thick suds, rich colors) (Runyon 1984). To increase brand recognition ADCAD suggests using large color photographs or extended close-ups of the brand's package (Diamond 1968; Holbrook and Lehmann 1980; Starch 1966). The user can explore how

Positioning (24 rules)
- IF objective = convey brand image or reinforce brand image AND brand purchase motivation = social approval AND brand usage visibility = high THEN possible benefit = "status" (cf. Holbrook and Lehmann 1980)
- IF an objective = convey brand information or change brand beliefs AND perceived differences between brands = small or medium AND perceived relative performance = inferior or parity AND relative performance = superior AND current brand loyalty = competitor loyal THEN message comparison = direct comparison against competition (Gorn and Weinberg 1983)
- IF ad objective = convey brand information or reinforce brand beliefs AND conflicting information = likely AND education = college or graduate AND product knowledge = high AND involvement = high THEN message sidedness = two-sided (McGuire and Papageorgis 1961)

Message Characteristics (80 rules)
- IF ad objective = increase top-of-mind awareness THEN technique = jingle, rhyme, or slogan (MacLachlan 1984)
- IF ad objective = convey brand information or reinforce brand beliefs AND market share > 18.5 AND brand switching = high AND product type = existing THEN technique = sign off (Stewart and Furse 1986)
- IF ad objective = convey brand information or change brand beliefs AND message processing motivation = low AND message processing ability = low THEN ad format = problem solution (Schwerin and Newell 1981)

Presenter Characteristics (20 rules)
- IF ad objective = convey brand information or change brand beliefs AND message processing ability = low THEN presenter expertise = high (Rhine and Severance 1970)
- IF presenter expertise = high THEN time of identification in message = early (Sternthal, Dholakia, and Leavitt 1978)
- IF ad objective = convey brand information or change brand beliefs AND involvement = high THEN presenter objectivity = high (Choo 1964)

Message Emotion (35 rules)
- IF ad objective = convey brand image or reinforce brand image or change brand image THEN emotional direction = positive (Young and Rubicam 1988)
- IF ad objective = convey brand image or reinforce brand image AND brand purchase motivation = sensory stimulation AND message processing motivation = high THEN emotional tone = elation (Rossiter and Percy 1997)
- IF ad objective = change brand beliefs AND message processing motivation = low AND purchase anxiety = low AND brand use avoids fearful consequences = yes THEN emotional tone = high fear (Ray and Wilkie 1970)

EXHIBIT 8.13
Sample rules for selecting advertising communication approaches for ADCAD. For complete references above, see Burke et al., 1990.

ADCAD reached a conclusion, and the system will report the underlying rationale for the recommendation.

The user can review and revise the input information and examine the impact of the revised information on the recommendations. In the Suave example the user considers an alternative scenario in which consumers perceive significant differences between brands. Because they are motivated by social approval and self-esteem, ADCAD infers that the psychosocial risk and involvement for the shampoo decision are now high, and it revises a number of its recommendations. The audience may be somewhat more critical of message claims, and so ADCAD suggests using strong claims with supporting information (Petty, Cacioppo, and Schumann 1983). The audience is more likely to be interested in the brand message, and so ADCAD proposes using the testimonial of an attractive presenter with whom the audience can identify (Brock 1965; Young and Rubicam 1988). ADCAD no longer recommends instilling apprehension in the ad because it assumes that the purchase motivation already exists (Rossiter and Percy 1997).

ADCAD is a marketing expert system that can help an individual who has little marketing expertise; it incorporates some of the existing knowledge in a package that is readily available and inexpensive. Its major value is its ability to consistently apply research findings and insights to decisions. ADCAD is far from a perfect system: it reasons sequentially,

INPUT: Market Assessment

Audience Characteristics:

Sex = female	Past brand usage = none
Product category usage = frequent	Product purchase interval = short
Perceived brand differences = small	Benefit "value" important = yes
Current loyalty = unfavorable brand switcher	Time of brand decision = at point of purchase
Brand purchase motivation = self-esteem, social approval	Package recognition = low

Product-Class Characteristics:

Life-cycle stage = maturity	Complexity = low
Possible to demo. "quality" = yes	Competition = heavy

Brand/Competitor Characteristics:

Brand market share = 2.0	Relative performance = parity
Brand price = $1.40	Competitor price = $3.60
Package visibility at purchase = high	Brand usage visible = low
"Quality" visibility in ad = high	"Quality" visibility in use = low
Benefit "value" unique = yes	Benefit "value" deliverable = yes
Physical/health risks = low	

OUTPUT: Marketing and Advertising Objectives

Marketing objective = stimulate brand trial	Advertising objectives = create/increase brand recognition, communicate brand image/mood/lifestyle

OUTPUT: Communication Approaches

Positioning:

Featured benefit = quality (user replaced recommend benefit = "value")	Message comparison = none
Benefit claim = extremely positive	Message sidedness = one-sided
	Number of benefits = few

Message Characteristics:

Format = demonstration of product in use, endorsement by celebrity, vignette	Technique = closeup, color illustration, long package display, music, visual stimuli/imagery, surrogate indicators of performance, capture consumer emotions

Presenter/Principal Character:

Identity = celebrity	Sex = female
Likability = high	Attractiveness = high
Identification in message = early	Recognizability = high

Message Emotion:

Strength = high	Direction = positive
Tone = apprehension/flattery	Authenticity of portrayal = high

EXHIBIT 8.14

ADCAD input and output values for a sample consultation for Suave Shampoo.

in a buildup procedure rather than holistically; it is not programmed to generate new, creative responses; it is not currently linked to outside databases, and its knowledge base is neither complete nor dynamic—it can become outdated.

On the plus side ADCAD is an emerging, marketing engineering approach to developing advertising copy, and it or its successors may provide great value in developing better ad copy.

A final decision regarding advertising copy is how many ads to create. ADCAD generally suggests a single ad platform, but most ad agencies do not (and should not) stop once they have created a single ad. The first creative idea may be the best, but typically it is not. Often clients want the agency to create and test a few alternative ideas before making a selection. The more advertising campaign themes the agency creates and pretests, the higher the probability that it will find a really first-rate one. But the more time it spends trying to create alternative themes and advertisements, the higher its costs are. Therefore there must be some optimal number of alternative advertising themes that an agency should try to create and test for the client.

If the client reimbursed the agency for the costs of creating and pretesting advertisements, then the agency might create the optimal number of advertisements for pretesting.

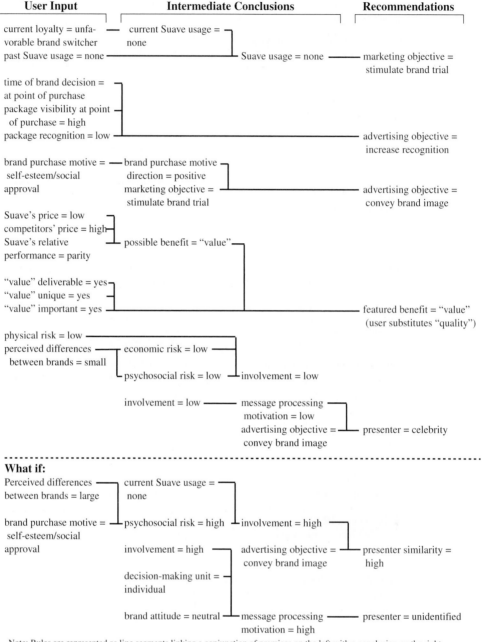

Note: Rules are represented as line segments linking a conjunction of premises on the left with a conclusion on the right.

EXHIBIT 8.15
Illustration of the ADCAD reasoning process for Suave Shampoo.

Under the normal compensation system, however, the agency's main income is a 15 percent commission on media billings. The agency has no incentive to go through the expense of creating and pretesting many alternative advertisements. Gross (1972) studied this question in an ingenious way and concluded that agencies generally create too few advertisements for pretesting. This result means that the advertiser does not typically get the best possible ad for its money but only the best (one hopes) of the few that the agency created.

To illustrate this point, Gross used some "conservative" figures for the variables in his analysis to show that the optimal expenditure for developing and testing copy should be about 15 percent of the advertising budget, more than five times the "typical" value.

Although these types of results have been challenged earlier (see Longman 1968, for example), Gross's basic result has important implications for pretesting procedures. He found that the value of pretesting depended more on the validity of the pretest (how the ad related to sale effectiveness) than on its reliability (how well the measurement is repeated in consecutive evaluations). Furthermore, he found that the higher the validity of the pretest, the greater was the justification for a large sample size to increase reliability.

Although advertisers and agencies pay lip service to Gross's idea of creating more alternatives, Jones (1986, p. 268) comments that "the system is not really concerned with generating a wide range of creative alternatives. It is really concerned with finding one alternative; the elimination of the others becomes a tool for selling this selected one."

SUMMARY

Advertising is at once one of the most potent and problematic elements of the marketing mix, and the impact of banner ads and electronic direct marketing programs exacerbate that problematic nature. Its effects are often hard to establish outside of an experimental situation. Nonetheless, managers need whatever decision support they can obtain to make informed advertising decisions.

We focused on three advertising decisions in this chapter. In budgeting advertising, the notion of the advertising-response function is central, and we explored three approaches: using judgmental information (ADBUDG and the Blue Mountain Coffee case), using historical cross-sectional and time-series data to assess likely market response (the Rao and Miller approach), and using historical norms (ADVISOR and the Convection Company case). While we have a lot to learn, these approaches make the sizing and budget allocation process more systematic.

Media-scheduling models mostly involve heuristic models (although several decades ago, optimization models were popular). The availability of expert systems and single-source data promises to revitalize interest in formal models.

Developing and deciding on advertising copy has traditionally been left to the "creative types." An expert system—ADCAD—can provide firms with support for making decisions about copy development.

BLUE MOUNTAIN COFFEE COMPANY CASE[1]

Blue Mountain's share of the coffee market had slipped badly during the past decades, although brand share has recently stabilized. The advertising manager was concerned because the increased advertising budget he had obtained the previous year had been cut back in midyear because top management was dissatisfied with the results. In addition, he thought it was vital to increase Blue Mountain's share so it would not lose distributors.

The advertising manager faced the problem of preparing and justifying an advertising budget for the coming fiscal year. He was considering using the ADBUDG model to help him.

In May 1994, Reginald Van Tassle, advertising manager for the Blue Mountain Coffee Company, tugged at his red mustache and contemplated the latest market share report. This was a dismal moment. "Blimey," he muttered, "I've got to do something to turn this darned market around before it's too late for Blue Mountain and for me. But I can't afford another mistake like last year's"

Reginald Van Tassle had been hired by James Anthoney, vice president of marketing for Blue Mountain, in the summer of 1992. Prior to that time he had worked for companies in the Netherlands and in Singapore and had gained a reputation as a sharp and effective advertising executive. Now, in the spring of 1994, he was fighting to reverse a long-term downward trend in Blue Mountain's market position.

Indeed, Lucinda Pogue (the president and a major stockholder of the Blue Mountain Company) had been dismayed to hear that Blue Mountain Coffee's share of the market was dropping back toward 5.4 percent, where it had been a year before. She had remarked rather pointedly to Reggie that if market share and profitability did not improve during the next fiscal year she might have to take "some rather drastic actions" and had murmured something about "a ticket back to Singapore."

BLUE MOUNTAIN'S MARKET POSITION

Blue Mountain Coffee was an old, established company in the coffee business, with headquarters in Squirrel Hill, Pennsylvania. Its market area included the East Coast and Southern regions of the United States and a fairly large portion of the Midwest. During its "good old days" in the 1950s, the company had enjoyed as much as 15 percent of the market in these regions. The brand had been strong and growing, and the company sponsored such popular radio and TV programs as "The Blue Mountain Comedy Hour" and "Blue Mountain Capers."

Blue Mountain began to experience some difficulties in the 1960s: TV production and time costs rose and competition stiffened as many other regional old-line companies were absorbed by giant marketers, such as General Foods and Proctor & Gamble. Furthermore, the advent of freeze-dried products and the increasing promotion and popularity of instant coffee put additional pressure on Blue Mountain, which stuck with its traditional ground vacuum-packed coffee as its only line.

---

1. This is a revised version of a case written by Professors William F. Massy, David B. Montgomery, and Charles B. Weinberg, which appeared in G. S. Day, G. J. Eskin, D. B. Montgomery, and C. B. Weinberg, *Planning: Cases in Computer and Model Assisted Marketing* Redwood City, CA: (Scientific Press 1973). The case was revised by Gary L. Lilien and Katrin Starke. The new revised software was designed by Katrin Starke and John Lin under the supervision of Professor Gary L. Lilien.

Nonetheless, Blue Mountain's troubles had only started. U.S. coffee consumption dropped steadily in the 1970s and 1980s after peaking in 1962 when 74 percent of Americans drank about three cups per day. By the end of the 1980s only about half of all Americans drank coffee and they were drinking an average of 1.7 cups per day. At the same time, the coffee market became more oligopolistic, and the "Big Three," i.e., Procter & Gamble (Folgers), Kraft General Foods (Maxwell House), and Nestle (Nescafe) together controlled over three quarters of the national market. Coffee was considered a commodity and competition was mainly on price. Under these circumstances, Blue Mountain's share slipped from 12 percent at the beginning of the 1980s to about 5 ½ percent at the end of the decade.

Since then, however, its share has been fairly stable. Management attributed this to a hard-core group of loyal buyers combined with an active (and expensive) program of consumer promotions and price-off deals to the trade. Jim Anthoney, the vice president of marketing, believed that they had halted the erosion of share just in time. A little more slippage, he said, and Blue Mountain would begin to lose distributors. This would be the beginning of the end for this venerable company.

OPERATION BREAKOUT

When Lucinda Pogue became president in 1990, her main objective was to halt the decline in market position and, if possible, to bring about a turnaround. She had succeeded in the first objective. However, she and Anthoney agreed that the strategy they were using—intensive consumer and trade promotion—would not win back much of the lost market share.

They both thought that they needed to increase consumer awareness of the Blue Mountain brand and develop more favorable attitudes about it to improve its market position. This could be done only through advertising. Since the company produced a quality product (it was noticeably richer and more aromatic than many competing coffees), they thought that a strategy of increasing advertising weight might succeed. They initiated a search for a new advertising manager, eventually hiring Reginald Van Tassle.

After a period of familiarizing himself with the Blue Mountain Company, the American coffee market, and the advertising scene, Van Tassle began developing a plan to revitalize Blue Mountain's advertising program. First, he released the company's current advertising agency and requested proposals from a number of others interested in obtaining the account. While he told them that the amount of advertising might increase somewhat, he emphasized that he was most concerned with the copy's appeal and execution. The company and the various agencies agreed that nearly all the advertising budget should go into spot television. Network sponsorship was difficult because of the regional character of Blue Mountain's markets, and no other medium could match the impact of TV for a product like coffee.

The team from Aardvark Associates, Inc., won the competition with an advertising program built around the theme "Blue Mountain Pure." Aardvark recommended a 30 percent increase in the quarterly advertising budget to give the new program a fair trial. After considerable negotiation with Lucinda Pogue and Jim Anthoney and further discussion with the agency, Van Tassle compromised on a 20 percent increase. The new campaign was to start in the autumn of 1993, which was the second quarter of the company's 1994 fiscal year (the fiscal year started July 1,1993 and would end June 30, 1994). It was dubbed "Operation Breakout."

Blue Mountain had been advertising at an average rate of $2 million per quarter for the last several years. This seemed to be enough to maintain market share at about its current level of 5.4 percent. Neither Reggie Van Tassle nor Jim Anthoney anticipated that competitors' expenditures would change much during the next few years regardless of any increase in Blue Mountain's advertising.

One basis for the 1994 plans was the expectation that the quarterly spending level of $2 million (ignoring several variations) would be enough to maintain market share at its current 5.4 percent level. Reggie felt that increasing advertising by 20 percent would increase market share to six percent.

This projected result sounded pretty good to Lucinda Pogue, especially after she had consulted the company's controller. The controller wrote her a memorandum about the advertising budget increase and its results (Exhibit 1).

August 1, 1993   CONFIDENTIAL MEMO

To: Lucinda Pogue, President
From: I. Figure, Controller
Subject: Proposed 20 percent increase in advertising

I think that Reggie's proposal to increase advertising by 20 percent (from a quarterly rate of $2.0 million to one of $2.4 million) is a good idea. He predicts that we will achieve a market share of six percent, compared to our current 5.4 percent. I can't comment about the feasibility of this assumption: that's Reggie's business, and I assume he knows what he's doing. I can tell you, however, that such a result would be highly profitable.

As you know, the wholesale price of coffee has been running about $17.20 per 12-pound case. Deducting our average retail advertising and promotional allowance of $1.60 per case and our variable costs of production and distribution of $11.10 per case leaves an average gross contribution to fixed costs and profit of $4.50 per case. Figuring a total market of about 22 million cases per quarter and a share change from 0.054 to 0.060 (a 0.006 increase), we would have the following increase in gross contribution:

$$\text{change in gross contribution} = \$4.50 \times 22 \text{ million} \times .006$$
$$= \$0.60 \text{ million}$$

By subtracting the amount of the increase in advertising expense due to the new program and then dividing by this same quantity, we get the advertising payout rate:

$$\text{Advertising Payout Rate} = \frac{\text{change in gross contribution} - \text{change in ad expense}}{\text{change in ad expense}}$$
$$= \frac{\$0.10 \text{ million}}{\$0.20 \text{ million}} = 0.50$$

That is, we can expect to make $.50 in net contribution for each extra dollar spent on advertising. You can see that as long as this quantity is greater than zero (at which point the extra gross contribution just pays for the extra advertising), increasing our advertising is a good deal.

I think Reggie has a good thing going here, and my recommendation is to go ahead. Incidentally, the extra funds we should generate in net contribution (after advertising expense is deducted) should help to relieve the cash flow bind that I mentioned last week. Perhaps we will be able to maintain the quarterly dividend after all.

EXHIBIT 1
Memo from I. Figure to L. Pogue, 1 August 1993.

Reggie had, of course, warned that the hoped-for six percent share was not a sure thing and, in any case, that it might take more than one quarter before the company saw the full effects of the new advertising program.

The new advertising campaign broke as scheduled on October 1, 1993, the first day of the second quarter of the fiscal year. Reggie was a bit disappointed with Aardvark's commercials and a little worried by the early reports from the field. The store audit report of market share for July, August, and September showed only a fractional increase in share over the 5.4 percent of the previous period. Nevertheless, Van Tassle thought that, given a little time, things would work out and the campaign would eventually reach its objective.

The October, November, and December market share report came through in mid-January. It showed Blue Mountain's share of the market to be 5.6 percent. On January 21, 1994, Reggie received a carbon copy of a memorandum to Lucinda from I. Figure (Exhibit 2).

January 20, 1994   MEMO
To: Lucinda Pogue, President
From: I. Figure, Controller
Subject: Failure of Advertising Program

I am most alarmed at our failure to achieve the market-share target projected by Reginald Van Tassle. The 0.2 point increase in market share we achieved in October-December is not sufficient to return the cost of the increased advertising. Ignoring the month of October, which obviously represents a start-up period, a 0.2 point increase in share generates only $200,000 in extra gross contribution per quarter. This must be compared to the $400,000 we have expended in extra advertising. The advertising payout rate is thus only –0.50: much less than the breakeven point.

I know Mr. Van Tassle expects shares to increase again next quarter, but he has not been able to say by how much. The new program projects an advertising expenditure increase per quarter of $400,000 over last year's winter-quarter level. I don't see how we can continue to make these expenditures without a better prospect of return on our investment.

cc: R. J. Anthoney
         R. Van Tassle

EXHIBIT 2
Memo from I. Figure to L. Pogue, 20 January 1994.

On Monday, January 24, Jim Anthoney telephoned Reggie to say that Lucinda wanted to review the new advertising program immediately. Later that week, after several rounds of discussion during which Reggie failed to convince Lucinda and Jim that the program would eventually be successful, they decided to return to fiscal 1993 advertising levels. Reggie renegotiated the TV spot contracts and by the middle of February had cut advertising back toward the $2 million per quarter rate. Aardvark Associates complained that the efficiency of their media buy suffered during February and March because of Blue Mountain's abrupt reduction in advertising expenditure. However, they were unable to say by how much. Blue Mountain also set the spring 1994 rate at the normal level of $2.0 million. Market share for the quarter beginning in January turned out to be slightly over 5.6 percent, while for the one starting in April it was about 5.5 percent.

PLANNING FOR FISCAL YEAR 1995

In mid-May of 1994, Reginald Van Tassle faced the problem of recommending an advertising budget for the four quarters of fiscal 1995. He was already very late in dealing with this assignment, since the company would have to up its media buys soon if it was to effect any substantial increase in weight during the summer quarter of 1994. Alternatively, it would have to act fast to reduce advertising expenditures below its tentatively budgeted "normal" level of $2.0 million.

During the past month, Van Tassle had spent a lot of time reviewing the difficulties of fiscal 1994. He remained convinced that a 20 percent increase in advertising should produce somewhere around a six percent market-share level. He based this partly on hunch and partly on studies performed by academic and business market researchers.

One lesson he had learned from his unfortunate experience the previous year was that presenting too optimistic a picture to top management was unwise. On the other hand, if he had made a conservative estimate he might not have obtained approval for the program. Besides, he still believed that the effect of advertising on share was greater than implied by the company's performance in the autumn of 1993. This judgment should be a part of top managers' information set when they evaluated his proposal. Alternatively, if they doubted his judgment and had good reasons to do so, he wanted to know about them. After all, Lucinda Pogue and Jim Anthoney had been in the coffee business a lot longer than he had, and they were pretty savvy.

Perhaps the problem lay in his assessment of the speed with which the new program would take hold. He had felt it would take a little time but had not tried to pin it down further. That's pretty hard, after all. He had said nothing very precise about this to management. Could he blame Mr. Figure for adopting the time horizon he did?

As a final complicating factor, Van Tassle had just received a report from Aardvark Associates about the quality of the advertising copy and the appeals used the previous autumn and winter. Contrary to expectations, these ads rated only about 0.95 on a scale that rated an "average ad" at 1.0. These tests were based on the so-called theater technique, in which the agency inserted various spots into a filmed "entertainment" program and determined their effects on the subjects' choices in a lottery designed to simulate purchasing behavior. Fortunately, the ads currently being shown rated about 1.0 on the same scale. A new series of ads scheduled for showing during the autumn, winter, and spring of 1995 appeared to be much better. The agency could not undertake theater testing until it completed production during the summer, but experts in the agency were convinced that the new ads would rate at least 1.15. Reggie was impressed with these ads, but he knew that such predictions were often optimistic. In the meantime, he had to submit a budget request for all four quarters of fiscal 1995 to management within the next week.

To help him with this problem, Reggie decided to use a marketing planning model, an adaptation of Little's (1970) ADBUDG model.

The marketing planning model

After describing his problem to Jill Stillman, director of research for Blue Mountain, Van Tassle asked Stillman to give him a list of the basic inputs the model required. After much tugging at his red mustache and several conferences with Stillman, Van Tassle arrived at a preliminary set of estimates for the basic inputs (Exhibit 3). Only the estimates relating to market share and the advertising plan itself required a lot of head scratching.

After some thought Van Tassle concluded that, if his advertising budget were reduced to zero, he would lose perhaps half his market share in the next year or about an eighth of it in the next quarter. He settled on the figure 4.7 percent as the market share at the end of the first quar-

Market share at start of period	5.4%
Maintenance advertising per period ($MM)	2.0
Market share at period end with	
Saturation advertising	6.3%
20 percent increase in advertising	5.7%
No advertising	4.7%
Market share in long run with no advertising	0.0%
Copy effectiveness	1.0
Media efficiency	1.0
Previous period market share	5.4%
Brand price ($/unit)	$17.20
Contribution ($/unit)	$4.50
Average product price ($/Unit)	$17.20
Product sales per period (MM cases)	22.0
Product sales growth rate per period	1.0%

EXHIBIT 3
ADBUDG basic input values.

ter with no advertising. Similarly, he arrived at the figures of 6.3 percent for a saturation advertising program and 5.7 percent for a 20 percent increase in advertising (figuring it would take him about three quarters of this 20 percent increase to reach a six percent share).

He then began experimenting with different values for his market share estimate and media—and copy-effectiveness estimates. He was hoping he could use the results of his analysis to explain past results and to help prepare his 1995 plan. He constructed Exhibit 4—a table of events—to help him recall the history of the program.

Recent developments: The U.S. coffee market in transition

Even though advertising budgeting was preoccupying her, Pogue kept thinking that, in light of recent trends, more could be done to help Blue Mountain's long-term position in the coffee market. What for a long time seemed to be a rather static market was now undergoing profound structural changes. In recent years, the coffee bean had begun a renaissance as consumption in the U.S. slowly climbed after more than two decades of decrease—but Blue Mountain, along with such other traditional roasters as Procter & Gamble, Philip Morris, and Nestlé, had been unable to capitalize on this trend. The growth was primarily due to specialty brews and the expansion of coffee and coffee accessory chains such as Starbucks Coffee Company of Seattle. Pogue was wary that specialty coffees, growing at about 20 percent annually, continued to grab market share at the expense of supermarket ground coffee sales. In fact, according to the latest figures, Starbucks, other regional cafes, and the gourmet whole-bean roasters had obtained nearly a quarter of the multibillion-dollar coffee market.

Pogue was wondering how best to respond to these changes and worried that Blue Mountain might already have missed the tide. It did not seem to her that the price-cutting and couponing approach of her major competitors in the ground coffee market was the answer. Pogue had been carefully following the development of Starbucks, which was holding on to its premier position in the specialty coffee business despite the increasing level of competition and imitation it encountered. Its business design differed significantly from Blue Mountain's, as Starbucks also operated a national mail order program to complement its hundreds of corporate-owned stores and its collaboration with Barnes & Noble bookstores, Nordstroms, and

ADBUDG Period	Month	Yr	Fiscal Year 94/95	AD Budget	Copy and Media	Market Share	Events
0						5.4 %	
1	July	93	1st qtr	$2.00	1.00	5.4 %	
1	Aug.	93	(FY 94)				
1	Sept.	93					
2	Oct.	93	2nd qtr	$2.40	0.95	5.6 %	Operation "Breakout"
2	Nov.	93					
2	Dec.	93					
3	Jan.	94	3rd qtr	$2.10	0.95	5.6 %	Budget cut
3	Feb.	94					
3	Mar.	94					
4	Apr.	94	4th qtr	$2.00	1.00	5.5 %	Copy effectiveness up
4	May	94				→ 5.4 %	**Now!**
4	June	94					
1	July	94			1.00		
2	Oct.	94			>1.00		

EXHIBIT 4
Blue Mountain table of events.

fine restaurants. According to a study Pogue came across, consumers of gourmet coffees were college-educated 25- to 45-year-olds who earned over $35,000 a year. They drank gourmet coffee for its prestige as well as for its taste. Gourmet coffee with price tags 80 to 100 percent higher than canned coffee was viewed as an affordable luxury. What could be a successful business model for Blue Mountain? Pogue still heard the warning of an industry analyst in her ear: "It's just like cars. Generation Xers wouldn't be caught in their fathers' Oldsmobiles, and they're not going to drink their parents' coffee brands. The traditional marketers have to come up with new appeals; the same old grind isn't going to make it."

EXERCISES

1. State precisely what you think the objectives of Blue Mountain's 1994 advertising plan should have been. Were these Van Tassle's objectives? Lucinda Pogue's? I. Figure's?
2. Evaluate the results obtained from the 1994 (FY) advertising funds. What do you think the results would have been if the 20 percent increase had been continued for the entire year?
3. What should Van Tassle propose as an advertising budget for 1995? How should he justify this budget to top management?
4. How should Van Tassle deal with the issues of seasonality and copy quality?
5. Comment on the uses and limitations of the ADBUDG model as a decision aid for this case and more generally as an advertising-budgeting decision aid.

CONVECTION CORPORATION CASE[1]

USING A COMMUNICATION PLANNING MODEL TO AID INDUSTRIAL MARKETING BUDGET DECISIONS

One of Paul Warren's major tasks following his appointment as group marketing coordinator at Convection Corporation was to develop a systematic approach to communications budgeting. The assignment was not an abstract exercise, however, since he was also to present and support his budget and media recommendations for Convection products in the annual budget review. The task was further complicated by a top management directive to cut marketing expenditures by one-third.

BACKGROUND

Convection Corporation (CC) is a Midwestern corporation founded in 1880 to produce steam boilers for use in the nearby northern Indiana steel mills. This initial product provided the experience base and opportunity to develop a more general expertise in high-temperature production process machinery and high-pressure hydraulic systems. Over the years, CC developed a diverse product line that served a wide range of industrial customers.

CC's sales reached the $2 billion level in 1997[2] despite increased competition and economic uncertainty in the utility industry, one of its major markets. During this same period, CC sought to establish a more systematic approach to marketing. Part of this process included a reorganization that created Mr. Warren's position.

In the new organization, CC marketing was directed by a senior vice president for marketing. Reporting to him were three vice presidents, each of whom supervised a number of group marketing coordinators. A number of brand managers reported to the group marketing managers. This new organization replaced the production line–oriented structure that had evolved over the years. Roles and responsibilities of the various managers were still somewhat fluid.

Mr. Warren had been given the task of recommending and justifying the marketing and communications programs for four related products managed by three product managers, Vera Stapleton, Stan Bloch, and Wayne Collins.

Vera Stapleton was the product manager for Heatcrete 4000 and Ceratam. Her background included both field sales experience and a period of time in the controller's office. Stan Bloch had been with the company for 22 years. He had done some of the development work for the Flowclean Sootblower in conjunction with several large boiler manufacturers. For the past four years he had been selling Flowclean and based on this considerable knowledge of its application, had been appointed product manager. Wayne Collins had joined the company three years earlier after completing an advanced degree in materials science. His first assignment had been research on improving the corrosion resistance of conventional steel alloys, and the first application of his work was the Corlin valve.

1. This is an updated and abridged version of a case by the same name by Gary L. Lilien and Darral G. Clarke. Copyright © 1982 by the President and Fellows of Harvard College.
2. At the time of this case, it is the end of the third quarter (both calendar and fiscal) 1997. The 1997 "actual" figures are projections from three quarters of actual data and one quarter of forecast data.

Mr. Warren and his three product managers directed the marketing efforts for four industrial equipment products. The products varied in the technical nature of the selling task, size of the sale, and age of the products.

Heatcrete 4000

Heatcrete 4000 is a castable concrete refractory material used in the construction of high-temperature furnaces, chemical reactors, and other process applications. It can be used both as a mortar for fired-brick refractories and for casting special shapes, and had been available from CC for a number of years. Similar products were offered by full-line refractory product manufacturers. Three new competitors had entered the refractory supply business during the past year, bringing the total number of competitors with over one percent market share to 28. Heatcrete 4000 sales usually occurred in conjunction with the sale of other refractory products. Ms. Stapleton estimated that there were approximately 600 Heatcrete customers that were reached through a direct sales effort (50 percent of sales) or through about 100 distributors. Heatcrete salespeople reported that they usually dealt with about three different people in a customer company involved in a given purchase decision. Industry refractory product demand in 1988 was forecast at $230 million and a growth rate of about eight percent was anticipated. Industry sales of Heatcrete-type products were forecast to be $63 million in 1988.

Ms. Stapleton was concerned about scattered sales reports of customer dissatisfaction with Heatcrete 4000 as well as its low market share. She felt that some research into possible product problems should be undertaken, and if no problems existed or if existing problems could be solved, advertising and promotion for Heatcrete 4000 could probably reach 5 percent of sales before it would start to cut into margins.

Ms. Stapleton submitted a tentative budget for Heatcrete 4000 as follows:

	1998 (plan)		**1997 (actual)**	
Heatcrete sales	$632,000		$601,000	
Market share	1%		1%	

Marketing Expenses	**Amount**	**Percent of Sales**	**Dollar Amount**	**Percent of Sales**
Personal selling	$28,000	4.4%	$20,000	3.3%
Technical service	5,300	0.8%	3,900	0.6%
Advertising	25,000	4.0%	20,000	3.3%

Ceratam

Ceratam is a ceramic material used for coating machine tool cutting inserts. Beginning in the mid-seventies, ceramics found increasing use in cutting inserts for lathes because they provided reduced friction and temperature at the tool-work interface. However, recent trends in the machine tool industry and heavy manufacturing had not been favorable and Ceratam was not yet profitable.

Making a case for coated cutting inserts required new esoteric arguments, and most end users were concerned that the coating would substantially affect their machining operations. Vera Stapleton felt that "the substantial marketing effort required to gain acceptance for the product has seriously cut into our margin. We are not sure where the market is going. We would like to hold our position and try to reduce selling costs on the one hand, but if this technology catches on we want to have a reasonable market position. We cut marketing expenses from 46.7 percent of sales in 1996 to 39.5 percent in 1997. I think we should hold marketing under 40 percent of sales to prevent further erosion of our margin."

Ceratam had about 2,000 potential customers and 40 to 50 independent distributors. About 35 percent of Ceratam orders were produced to order, which somewhat limited the role of distributors. Ms. Stapleton felt that the decision process required for an initial Ceratam purchase was complex and estimated that it required sales contact with about 11 people at each buying location. Industry sales growth was 11 percent in 1997 and industry sales for the same year were $5 million. Ceratam had three competitors with over one percent market share.

Ms. Stapleton's tentative Ceratam budget was as follows:

	1998 (plan)		1997 (actual)	
Sales	$1,200,000		$800,000	
Market share	24%		18%	
Marketing Expenses	**Amount**	**Percent of Sales**	**Dollar Amount**	**Percent of Sales**
Personal selling	$300,000	25.0%	$250,000	31.0%
Technical service	100,000	8.3%	50,000	6.3%
Advertising	75,000	6.3%	75,000	7.5%

Flowclean Sootblowers

Due to environmental pressures and increased fuel costs during the 1970s and thereafter, sootblowers were either designed into or planned to be retrofitted to virtually every large-scale fossil fuel steam boiler because they increase efficiency, reduce the need for cleaning, and reduce boiler downtime. Since sootblowers extract airborne heavy particulates from the combustion chamber, they had been adapted recently for pollution control and combustion efficiency purposes. Convection's current line of sootblowers was developed about 25 years ago and had only been slightly modified since. There were about 1,000 customers in the marketplace. Salespeople visit about five decision-makers at each location. Selling a sootblower requires working the system manufacturer as well as the buyer to understand the design parameters of the complete boiler system.

Convection was the largest of only three companies in the market. The applications are so technical that only a company with a complete understanding of boiler systems can manufacture sootblowers. Mr. Bloch explained the selling situation as follows: "When I was selling sootblowers, everybody knew me and knew that I understood the product. Sometimes I would talk to final users because the sootblowers would have to work with their existing equipment or special environmental protection procedures. In such cases it was nice to be able to show these people our ads in the key industry publications, to let them know that we were the biggest. It was always good to have some brochures that let people know that Convection was a major firm with an excellent reputation for engineering. Beyond that, it was the product specs and applications engineering that sold the product."

In 1997, Flowclean sales were $23.5 million, which represented a 50 percent market share. Forecasts for 1998 presented a muddled picture. The utilities, a major market segment, appeared to have a declining rate of expansion in generating capacity. At the same time, many facilities were converting from gas to coal. Exactly how these two oppositely directed forces would balance out for sootblower demand was uncertain.

Mr. Bloch's tentative budget for Flowclean was as follows:

	1998 (plan)			**1997 (actual)**	
Sales	$24,160,000			$23,500,000	
Market share	50%			50%	
Marketing Expenses	**Amount**	**Percent of Sales**	**Dollar Amount**	**Percent of Sales**	
Personal selling	$2,338,000	9.7%	$2,166,000	9.2%	
Technical service	314,000	1.3%	304,000	1.3%	
Advertising	248,000	1.0%	388,000	1.7%	

Corlin Valve

The Corlin valve is made from a special alloy that provides higher resistance to corrosion than was previously possible with stainless steel. The Corlin valve was felt to have a substantial potential market since it could replace existing corrosion-resistant valves that were much more expensive. Some applications involving highly corrosive substances still required existing corrosion-resistant valves. But for a wide variety of uses, the Corlin valve offered much better performance per dollar.

It hadn't been easy to convince chemical companies to switch to the Corlin valve. Mr. Collins said: "I think we need to convince customers that our product can meet their technical performance requirements. A lot of engineers just expect that any valve for corrosives must be titanium-lined. I think we should get some articles in the technical press with some specific test results for Corlin in comparison with other materials."

The market for corrosive-resistant valves was estimated at $23 million in 1996, and was growing at 15 percent. There were nearly 4,000 potential customers. Selling the Corlin valve usually required dealing with about five different people at each potential customer firm. Corlin had seven competitors with over 1 percent market share.

Mr. Collins's tentative budget was as follows:

	1998 (plan)			**1997 (actual**	
Sales	$500,000			$100,000	
Market share	1.9%			0.43%	
Marketing Expenses	**Amount**	**Percent of Sales**	**Dollar Amount**	**Percent of Sales**	
Personal selling	$225,000	45%	$130,000	130%	
Technical service	30,000	6%	20,000	20%	
Advertising	80,000	16%	55,000	55%	

ADVISOR: AN APPROACH TO MARKETING BUDGET PLANNING

Mr. Warren felt that whatever method of budgeting he developed, he would need to have at least a consensus of approval from his product managers. To achieve this consensus, he felt a meeting would be necessary to discuss various budgeting methods. During the evenings since be had been appointed to his new position, he had done considerable reading on the budgeting of industrial advertising.

He was dubious about finding a method that was better than "gut feel," but he found a description of a major cross-sectional study of industrial marketing spending behavior known as the ADVISOR Project, and thought it interesting enough to attend an ADVISOR seminar. There he learned that the ADVISOR study was based on the idea that successful industrial managers have learned how to make good communication decisions, and the project was designed to understand and generalize managers' decision experience.

ADVISOR tried to identify product and market characteristics that would affect the marketing and advertising levels for a given product. The data upon which the ADVISOR project was based were drawn from over 300 industrial products supplied by over 100 companies. Data were collected on 11 different factors found to impact budget levels, and models were constructed that computed norms called par reports for marketing and advertising spending.

When the seminar was over, Mr. Warren had no illusions that ADVISOR would solve all his budgeting problems, but he felt that the approach was sufficiently interesting to do an ADVISOR analysis on each of the four products for which he was responsible.

Summaries of the results he got are found in Exhibits 1a to 1d. (A discussion of the terms used in these exhibits is found in Exhibit 2 and an associated data form in Exhibit 3 at the end of this discussion.) When he examined the ADVISOR par reports, he felt that they made sense to him, but he wasn't sure if the product managers would feel the same way.

ADVISOR RESULTS

Product Name/ID → Ceratam

	Actual	**Norm**	**Range**
Marketing ($000)	475.0	189.0	122.8 – 289.2
Personal Selling/Tech Serv ($000)	400.0	148.8	96.7 – 227.7
Total Adv ($000)	75.0	40.2	26.1 – 61.4

EXHIBIT 1a

ADVISOR RESULTS

Product Name/ID → Heatcrete 4000

	Actual	**Norm**	**Range**
Marketing ($000)	58.3	139.3	90.6 – 213.2
Personal Selling/Tech Serv ($000)	33.3	99.4	64.6 – 152.1
Total Adv ($000)	25.0	39.9	25.9 – 61.1

EXHIBIT 1b

ADVISOR RESULTS

Product Name/ID → Sootblower

	Actual	**Norm**	**Range**
Marketing ($000)	2900.0	1335.5	868.1 – 2043.3
Personal Selling/Tech Serv ($000)	2652.0	1262.0	820.3 – 1930.9
Total Adv ($000)	248.0	73.5	47.8 – 112.4

EXHIBIT 1c

ADVISOR RESULTS

Product Name/ID → Corlin

	Actual	**Norm**	**Range**
Marketing ($000)	335.0	505.3	328.4 – 773.1
Personal Selling/Tech Serv ($000)	255.0	346.8	225.4 – 530.6
Total Adv ($000)	80.0	158.5	103.0 – 242.4

EXHIBIT 1d

Budget task force meeting

On his return to the office, Mr. Warren called his product managers together to review their budgets. He reviewed the results of his initial runs with the ADVISOR model and gave each of them a Marketing Engineering/Excel version of the program, so they could re-analyze their products, if they wished.

At this point, he asked: "Do you all feel confident of your proposed budgets? Are you sure they're right? There is one final problem I hate to bring up, but I just received a memo from John Smiley, the Comptroller, telling me to cut last year's budget by a third because of the difficult economic conditions facing the firm. His current 1998 profit projections for our products are these:

Heatcrete	$ 12,640
Ceratam	(57,200)
Flowclean	4,212,000
Corlin Valve	(197,000)

"Where do we make cuts? I don't think we'll settle this now. Will you all please meet with me again Monday morning? For that meeting I would like a justification for your present budget. Second, I need a new budget in which the total of your 1998 budgets is two-thirds of your 1997 budgets, along with a justification."

ADVISOR: A set of mathematical models that provides comparison of common industry budgeting practices among products exhibiting similar marketing characteristics.

Advertising: As used in par reports, advertising covers the following kinds of activities associated with the product:

All sales promotion	Direct mail
Trade shows	Brochures and catalogs
Space advertising	TV and radio

Customer: A purchase influencer, user or reseller. If the industry has 10 customer locations, each with 5 people involved in the purchasing decision process, it has 10 x 5 or 50 "customers." The number of customers includes distributors and any other outsiders (e.g., consultants) who might influence the decision process.

Life Cycle: We break up the product life cycle into four phases: *Introduction* refers to the period when the initial growth of the product is rather slow. This is followed by the *growth stage* in the life cycle. The growth stage can last many years; generally if the industry volume is growing by 8–10 percent or more, we consider the product to be still in the growth stage. As growth settles down and sales remain stable from year to year, the product reaches *maturity*. As the product begins being replaced by competitive technologies, it enters the *decline stage* of its life cycle.

Marketing: As used in par reports, marketing includes these activities:

All advertising
All personal selling
Technical service

Direct costs and overhead are included; sales management expenditures are not included.

Par: Par refers to the level of advertising spending that most companies agree upon. A par report compares your budgeting practices with those of other companies with products like yours.

Product or Product Market: A product market, defined by customer need, is the basis for completion of this questionnaire. Thus, if you make a unique plastic product to satisfy a need currently satisfied by steel, your competitors might include manufacturers of the competitive steel product and industry sales must be defined accordingly.

A product can be a line of products sold together or a product-market combination. Flexibility in the definition should be one that has operational meaning in your organization. The definition should rarely be so narrow that the product is considered to have no competitors, nor so broad that the questions of unit price or market share become ambiguous.

Range: Budgeting levels vary, even of similar product and marketing situations. The range gives a measure of the variability in budgeting levels in the sample. About three-fourths of the products find themselves within range. Being outside the range means you are significantly different from the norm.

Sales: Dollar value transaction of the product (by the company or industry) to external organizations. Thus internal company product transfers are not included.

EXHIBIT 2
ADVISOR Dictionary.

Product Name/Identification	Ceratam	Heatcrete	Flowclean	Corlin
1. In what stage of its life cycle would you say the total market for this type of product is?				
Introduction = 1				
Growth = 2				
Mature = 3				
Decline = 4	2	3	3	2
2. What were your company's product sales ($ millions) to your end users plus independent resellers?	1.2	0.632	24.1	0.5
3. What percent of your product's sales volume is . . .				
a. Produced to order?	35	100	100	10
b. Standard: carried inventory?	65	95	0	90
4. What percent of the industry's total dollar sales is purchased by its three largest customers?	29	40	63	15
5. How many customers (individuals influencing the purchase process in any way) were there for the industry last year?	22,230	1,650	5,224	22,480
6. If plans and objectives were developed for this product this year, indicate the main emphasis of those plans by a "1" (no more than three items should be indicated as "1").				
a. Increase share	0	1	0	1
b. Maintain share	1	0	1	0
c. Leave unprofitable market	1	0	0	0
d. Improve image	0	1	1	0
e. Retaliate against competitive action	0	0	1	0
f. More fully utilize capacity	0	0	0	1
g. Stimulate distribution channels	0	1	0	1
h. Support price	0	0	0	0
i. Decrease selling costs	1	0	0	0
j. Increase product quality	0	0	0	0

EXHIBIT 3
Convection Product Data

Product Name/Identification	Ceratam	Heatcrete	Flowclean	Corlin
7. Which one of the following categories best describes this product? 　　　Machinery and equipment 　= 1 　　　Raw material (not chemical) 　= 2 　　　Fabricated material (e.g., glass) = 3 　　　Component part 　= 4 　　　Salvage good 　= 5 　　　Chemical 　= 6 　　　Service 　= 7 　　　Partially processed material 　= 8 　　　Other 　= 9	3	3	1	1
8. Approximately what percent of your product's dollar sales volume is sold directly to users (versus through resellers/distributors)	70	51	25	80
9. How would you rate the importance of technical service in this product category? (from 1 = not very critical, to 7 = a key element in the marketing mix)	7	4	7	3
10. What percent of industry customers consider that the decision to purchase this product				
a. Is routine?	40	60	15	0
b. Needs some review?	55	35	60	10
c. Requires close analysis?	5	5	25	90
11. What is the distribution of how frequently industry customers make a decision to buy this product (as opposed to merely ordering after a purchase decision has been made)? Enter percent of customers in each category.				
a. Weekly or more frequently	0	0	0	0
b. Once/week—once/month	80	5	15	40
c. Bimonthly—twice/year	10	22.5	17.5	30
d. Yearly	10	22.5	17.5	30
e. Once/2–9 years	0	40	50	0
f. Once/10 years or less frequently	0	10	0	0
*12. What was the total amount of money ($thousands) your company spent on personal selling (including applicable overhead) for this product this year?	300	28	2338	225

EXHIBIT 3 cont'd.
Convection Product Data

Product Name/Identification	Ceratam	Heatcrete	Flowclean	Corlin
*13. What was the total amount of money ($thousands) your company spent on technical service (including applicable overhead) for this product this year?	100	5.3	315	30
*14. What was the total amount of money ($thousands) spent on advertising for this product this year?	75	25	248	80

*This information is provided for reference and comparison only; it is not used in developing the ADVISOR norms.

EXHIBIT 3 cont'd.
Convection Product Data

EXERCISES

Using the ADVISOR system, prepare an analysis that

1. (a) Identifies the products/markets, their problems, and their marketing needs.
   (b) Recommends a total level of marketing spending and its breakdown into advertising and personal selling/technical service for each product.
   (c) Justifies the recommendation.
       (Check your assumptions carefully—i.e., look at product plans in particular: re-run ADVISOR for assumptions that appear most appropriate.)
2. Viewing this set of products as a portfolio, review your analysis using the BCG Growth/Share matrix framework (Chapter 6). Is that framework useful?
3. Is it appropriate to cut one-third from the budget? Where should that cut come from? Why?

JOHNSON WAX AD COPY DESIGN EXERCISE

1. The best way to learn to use the ADCAD system is to develop the key components of a TV commercial for a familiar brand, such as Pepsi or Coke. In doing so, keep a specific target segment in mind and compare the recommendations of the system with a recent brand commercial targeted to that segment.

2. Use the ADCAD system to develop ad-copy recommendations for Enhance instant hair conditioner (Johnson Wax Enhance (A) case, Chapter 7). Use as inputs to the model the data available in the case and any other input values you think are appropriate. In your report, include the inputs you provided and the recommendations made by the system.

3. Use these recommendations to develop a one-page print advertisement for Enhance. Indicate how you used the recommendations in developing your print ad.

4. Summarize the advantages and limitations of the ADCAD system for developing ad-copy-design parameters.

5. After using the ADCAD system, a senior ad agency executive commented, "This is precisely the type of systematic approach that I would like our creatives to use. They need to develop an appreciation of the strategic rationale for an ad before they let their creative juices flow." On the other hand, after using the system, an art director commented, "Developing an ad is like making an omelette. McDonald's will consistently make us a halfway decent omelette but it takes a great chef to make one that we will remember for long. I don't think creatives will accept a mechanistic approach to ad design." Do you agree with either of these two points of view? Explain why or why not.

CHAPTER **9**

Salesforce and Channel Decisions

In this chapter we

- Highlight those salesforce decision problems that are most amenable to analytical modeling
- Describe a general resource allocation model that can be used for determining the size of the salesforce and allocating sales effort among products and markets
- Summarize the main elements of models for designing sales territories and compensation plans for the salesforce
- Describe the CALLPLAN model that helps salespeople to improve their call productivity
- List important channel decisions and describe the gravity model for selecting retail sites.

INTRODUCTION TO SALESFORCE MODELS

Sales-response models for representing the effects of sales activities

In scope and cost, selling is the most important element in the marketing mix. About 10 percent of the workforce is engaged in sales and related occupations. In addition, many company employees and other individuals perform sales functions even though their job titles do not indicate it. For example, company presidents, partners in accounting firms, management consultants, college military recruiters, and TV evangelists perform several selling functions. Many firms rely largely on the salesforce to implement their marketing strategy.

Personal selling has the following characteristics:

1. It enables the firm to target its marketing effort selectively: to high-value prospects and accounts, for example.
2. Because of the interactive nature of selling, salespeople can customize their messages: for example, they can identify and resolve specific customer problems, use visual aids or working models to demonstrate products, address specific objections, and get

feedback and information from customers that the firm can use to improve its products and customer service.

3. It involves people—recruiting, training, motivating, rewarding, and retaining employees—which makes it more complex than the other elements in the marketing mix. In particular, firms cannot change their investments in human beings as easily as they can their investments in advertising or promotions.

4. Compared with advertising, the costs per sales contact are high. Based on a survey of sales managers, Marchetti (2000) reports that the average cost of a sales call was $169 in the United States in the year 2000 (including salary, benefits, and expenses). Interestingly, *Forbes* magazine (August 28, 1995) estimated that the average cost of a single sales call was $500 in 1995, up from $71 in 1975. In contrast, a $500,000 ad insertion that reaches 20 million viewers costs just a few cents per contact.

As with other marketing investments, it is important for the firm to understand the relationship between selling effort and sales. The nature and structure of this relationship is especially difficult to determine because of the numerous functions salespeople perform:

Prospecting: Finding and cultivating new customers

Communicating: Providing information about the company's products and services to existing and potential customers

Selling: Making presentations, answering objections, closing the sale, and the like

Problem solving: Understanding customers' problems (both actual and potential) and figuring out how to solve them using the firm's products and services

Servicing: Rendering technical assistance, arranging financing, expediting delivery, and organizing after-sale service

Building relationships: Establishing long-term partnerships with customers by developing goals for the relationship, understanding customers' needs and decision-making processes, and developing shared objectives with the customer

Information gathering: Gathering information about customers and competitors (market intelligence) and recording selling activities

Analyzing and allocating: Assessing sales potential and allocating effort accordingly

Traditionally salespeople have been used primarily to generate "targeted sales volume" while marketing and company management focused on profits. However, as firms become market-driven they require their salespeople to pursue multiple objectives. In addition to tracking sales to measure their salespeople's performance, firms now use such performance measures as customer satisfaction, account relations, profit contribution, share of customers (share of product-category sales), and customer retention.

Salespeople perform a number of activities besides just selling, and their effectiveness can be measured in several ways, as just mentioned. Quantifying the link between a salesperson's input (what a salesperson does) and the outputs (what the firm observes) in the form of sales-response functions is the basis for some of the most effective implementations of salesforce modeling. These response functions may be specified at the level of the individual salesperson or at the level of the salesforce.

Our main objective in this chapter is to describe several models that can help firms improve the productivity of their field salesforce and their marketing channels. Although the salesforce models can be adapted by firms that use telemarketing or rely on external reps, we do not explore those issues specifically here. We focus on models for which we have software implementations, namely the Syntex and CALLPLAN models for allocating sales effort and the gravity model for locating retail stores. We also describe models for designing sales territories and compensating the salesforce and indicate what commercial software packages are available to address these problems.

Salesforce management decisions

Exhibit 9.1 highlights the three major categories of decisions (organization, allocation, and control) for which salesforce managers are responsible (Vandenbosch and Weinberg 1993). The four boxes and the connecting arrows offer a simple way to conceptualize decisions regarding salesforce management. The goals and objectives provide the link between the overall strategic plan for the firm and the three salesforce decision areas. The bidirectional nature of this link indicates that goals and objectives determine and are determined by each decision. Furthermore, each decision area influences and is influenced by the other decision areas. Decisions concerning the organization of the salesforce determine the internal (firm-based) context and structure for deploying the sales effort. The allocation decisions partition the total sales effort among revenue-generating entities (e.g., market segments), and control decisions are intended to motivate salespeople to adopt the firm's objectives as their own.

Salesforce organization: In organizing a salesforce the firm must decide whether to have its own direct salesforce, employ outside sales representatives, or rely on a mixture of the two. If it hires and trains its own salespeople, the firm will have greater control over which products and market segments they emphasize; outside reps, who typically handle the products of many firms, may not fully internalize the selling priorities of the firm. On the other hand, by owning the salesforce a firm increases its current and future fixed costs

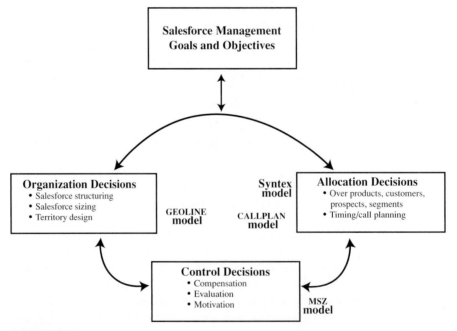

EXHIBIT 9.1
A conceptual outline of salesforce management decisions, showing the overall relationships between salesforce goals and objectives and the three major decision areas: organization, allocation, and control. In this chapter we describe the GEOLINE model for territory design, the Syntex and CALLPLAN models for allocation, and the Mantrala, Sinha, and Zoltners (MSZ) model for controlling effort deployment through compensation design.

(salary, benefits, and overhead), whereas commission-based reps give the firm more flexibility by making all costs variable.

Maintaining its own direct salesforce is likely to be a better choice for a firm when

1. Its salespeople have product-specific or firm-specific know-how that is not readily available in the marketplace.
2. Evaluating sales reps' performance is difficult because the firm cannot relate selling effort to sales with certainty (e.g., are the sales due to the superb selling skills of the salesperson or to a favorable market environment?).
3. The firm sells a product line so complex that salespeople must develop detailed knowledge of those products.
4. In conjunction with (1), the firm operates in a changing and competitive environment.
5. Effective sales performance requires skills other than selling (e.g., servicing) (Anderson 1985).

EXAMPLE

Quaker Oats used outside reps to sell its frozen food products (Aunt Jemima frozen waffles and Celeste pizza) and its own salesforce to sell its grocery items (e.g., Instant Quaker Oatmeal and Gatorade), even though both call on supermarkets. This strategy makes sense because the two require different call frequencies. The frozen food business is very competitive and the reps can get into the stores each week to maintain shelf space, whereas the firm uses periodic promotions for its grocery products, which are most effectively introduced by company-employed sales representatives. (Quaker Oats sold off its frozen foods business in 1996.)

Although research provides some guidance, which of these options the firm chooses depends on the context. The AHP model (Chapter 6), constructed using the factors mentioned above, offers one way to resolve this issue.

If the firm employs its own salespeople, how should it structure the salesforce: on a geographic, product, market, or functional basis? The answer depends partly on the overall strategy the firm pursues. Exhibit 9.2 lists some factors to consider in structuring the salesforce.

SALESFORCE SIZING AND ALLOCATION

Salesforce sizing (how many salespeople?) and allocation (how should total sales effort be allocated to different products, markets, and sales functions?) are fundamental management issues for all salesforces. Fortunately a number of well-tested models are available to support decision making in this area. However, many firms continue to employ intuitive methods even though these models have proved very effective (e.g., Lodish et al. 1988; Rangaswamy, Sinha, and Zoltners 1990).

Intuitive methods

Firms often determine the size of their salesforce by deciding "what we can afford." Typically they determine how much they can spend on the salesforce by taking a percentage of the forecasted sales for the company; they may base the actual percentage they use on historical

Approach	Influential factors
1. Geographic	Travel expenditures are high Products are mature Administrative support for sales force is low (sales force consists of "lone wolf" salespersons)
2. Customer	Customer needs or behaviors are homogeneous There are a large number of customers The firm as a whole has a market-focused organization
3. Product	Products are complex (e.g., technical content) Firm has a divisional structure organized around products The firm offers a number of products Duplication of calls (multiple salespeople calling on the same customer) is minimal
4. Functional	The buying process is complex (number of people involved, length of buying process, etc.) Effective selling requires a changing mix of skills (e.g., management consulting companies)

EXHIBIT 9.2
Factors to consider when structuring the salesforce.

norms from within the company or on the selling expense ratios for competitors. They divide the average cost of a salesperson into this figure to get the size of the salesforce:

$$\text{Number of salespeople} = \frac{\text{Selling expenses as \% of sales}}{\text{Average cost of a salesperson}}. \tag{9.1}$$

In a study of 41 packaged-goods salesforces DeVincentis and Kotcher (1995) found that the average expense for a salesforce was 3.71 percent of sales, with smaller firms (sales of less than $500 million per annum) spending between 5 and 8 percent and larger firms, about half of that. Sinha and Zoltners (2001) indicate that the average expenditure on salesforces across all industries in the U.S. is 6.8% of sales.

Another approach firms use to determine the size of the salesforce is the "breakdown method": the firm divides the sales forecast for the planning horizon by the average revenues generated by a single salesperson in that length of time:

$$\text{Number of salespeople} = \frac{\text{Forecasted sales}}{\text{Average revenues generated by a salesperson}}. \tag{9.2}$$

Once the firm has determined the total number of salespeople, it then allocates the total effort (e.g., total number of calls (visits) available) to accounts and prospects based on their actual or forecasted sales. For example, salespeople may visit accounts with high levels of sales every month and those with low levels of sales once in six months.

Intuitive methods of sizing and allocating salesforce effort are unsatisfactory for two reasons:

1. They do not account for the possibility that some accounts or prospects may respond differently from the "average" account.
2. They do not take into account that a firm cannot determine the best size for the salesforce (i.e., the total sales effort) without knowing how to allocate the total sales effort most effectively (Exhibit 9.3).

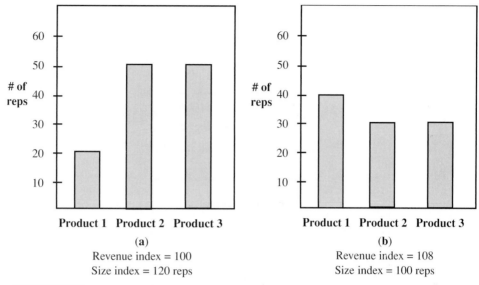

(a)
Revenue index = 100
Size index = 120 reps

(b)
Revenue index = 108
Size index = 100 reps

EXHIBIT 9.3
This exhibit illustrates the salesforce sizing dilemma—how large should the salesforce be? In case (a) (the current situation) the firm has a salesforce of 120. However, more effort is allocated to the (less responsive) products 2 and 3 at the expense of product 1. An analysis reveals that reallocation of effort toward product 1 yields anticipated sales that are higher with fewer sales representatives (case [b]). In this example the firm can realize an 8 percent increase in revenue with a 17 percent decrease in salesforce size by allocating more effort to the more responsive product (1).

Missing from Exhibit 9.3 are the "sales-response functions" that enable managers to quantify what would happen by redeploying sales efforts in different ways. We address this issue next.

Market-response methods (the Syntex model)

Market-response methods require firms to estimate response functions, which show the relationship between sales effort and sales in each *sales entity* of interest. A sales entity is anything with which we can associate potential sales for the firm—customer, prospect, market segment, geographic area, product sold by the firm, and so forth. If the firm estimates sales-response functions for each such sales entity, it can use these functions to calculate the levels of effort to allocate to each entity to maximize profits or to achieve other objectives. The sum of the sales effort across a set of nonoverlapping entities is the total sales effort the firm needs. The firm can then divide this total by the average effort of a salesperson (e.g., 750 calls per year) to estimate the number of salespeople it needs.

The Syntex model provides a general approach to the problem of sizing and allocating the salesforce effort. Lodish et al. (1988) developed the model for Syntex Laboratories, and it can be adapted for use by other multiproduct, multisegment firms that employ a field salesforce. When Lodish et al. developed the model in 1982, Syntex was selling seven prescription drugs (e.g., Naprosyn and Anaprox) that it promoted to nine physician specialties (e.g., general practice and dermatology). Syntex was considering increasing its salesforce size substantially with the expectation that this would increase the sales of its portfolio of products in the nine physician segments. Exhibit 9.4 outlines the process used in implementing the Syntex model. We describe the process

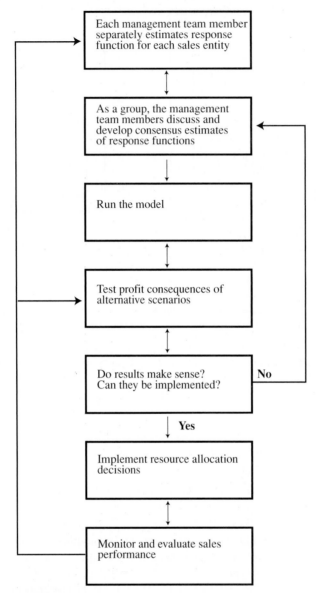

EXHIBIT 9.4
The sequence of steps for developing and implementing the Syntex salesforce resource-allocation model.

next; although we formulate the model specifically for Syntex, it is easily generalized to other firms facing similar problems.

Specification and calibration of response models: Syntex used an ADBUDG response function (Chapter 2) to model sales response for each sales entity (product or market segment). To calibrate the model senior managers from the sales, marketing, and research departments, who together had several decades of experience in selling pharmaceutical products, estimated the response functions. These managers separately answered several questions with respect to how sales of each product would respond to sales effort and how each physician segment would respond to varying levels of sales effort. The following questions illustrate the type of questions they answered:

> According to Syntex's strategic plan, if salesforce effort is maintained at the current level (indexed to 1) from 1982 to 1985, sales of product A would be the planned level (indexed to 1). What would happen to product A's year 1985 sales (compared with a base of 1 for the present levels) if during the same time period it received

1. No sales effort? X_0

2. One-half the current effort? $X_{0.5}$

3. 50 percent greater effort? $X_{1.5}$

4. A saturation level of sales effort? X_∞

After a half-day training session, each manager privately answered the questions. The four answers provided by a manager are denoted X_0, $X_{0.5}$, $X_{1.5}$, and X_∞ respectively. The answers were then summarized by a computer and the summary results provided to each manager participant.

After studying this summary the managers discussed the initial results, contemplated the differences between their own responses and the group mean, and then completed the same questionnaire again. In the Syntex study the second round led to consensus estimates for the questions. (In other situations it may take as many as three or four rounds to obtain consensus estimates; see Rangaswamy, Sinha, and Zoltners (1990).)

These consensus estimates provide inputs to calibrate the ADBUDG function. That is, the parameters a_i, b_i, c_i, and d_i in the following equation are fitted using the estimates of $r_i(X_i)$ provided by the managers at the four levels of X_i given above; the base estimate of $r_i(X_i) = 1$ when $X_i = 1$ provides another data point for the calibration:

$$r_i(X_i) = b_i + (a_i - b_i) \frac{X_i^{c_i}}{d_i + X_i^{c_i}}, \tag{9.3}$$

where

$\quad i$ = a sales entity, $i = 1, 2, 3, \ldots, I$ (# of sales entities);

$\quad X_i$ = total effort devoted to sales entity i during a planning period measured in number of calls, indexed so that current effort = 1 (for simplicity we treat this as a continuously varying quantity rather than as an integer);

$r_i(X_i)$ = indexed level of sales at entity i if the salesforce devotes X_i amount of effort to that entity;

$\quad b_i$ = minimum sales that can be expected with no sales effort allocated to sales entity i;

$\quad a_i$ = maximum sales that can be expected with an unlimited amount of sales effort allocated to sales entity i;

$\quad c_i$ = parameter that determines the shape of $r_i(X_i)$—whether it is concave or S-shaped; and

$\quad d_i$ = an index of competitive effort levels directed toward sales entity i (the larger this value, the smaller the impact of the firm's own sales effort on sales).

Syntex model description: The Syntex model allocates effort to sales entities to maximize firm profits over a planning horizon, subject to several constraints. Each run of the model requires a constraint specifying a proposed salesforce size. This constraint ensures that the model allocates effort in the best way possible for a given salesforce size. The base model follows:

Find the set of X_i's to

$$\text{maximize } Z = \sum_{i=1}^{I} r_i(X_i)S_i a_i - CF \text{ (profits)}, \tag{9.4}$$

subject to

$$\sum_{i=1}^{I} X_i e_i = F \text{ (salesforce size constraint)}, \tag{9.5}$$

where

S_i = forecasted sales for entity i according to the strategic plan;

a_i = contribution margin per incremental dollar of sales for sales entity i;

C = full costs (salary, benefits, etc.) of a single salesperson;

F = planned salesforce size (number of salespeople); and

e_i = planned deployment of sales effort to entity i according to the strategic plan.

The base model gives the optimal allocation of effort for any given salesforce size F. This model is then solved repeatedly for various levels of F, and the firm should keep adding salespersons as long as the incremental profit associated with each person is positive. At the optimal level of salesforce size, the marginal profit of an additional salesperson is 0 (Exhibit 9.5).

Constraint (9.5) can include more entity-level constraints. For example, the constraints might include minimum and maximum levels of effort allocated to any particular entity. The modified constraint set can be specified as follows:

$$\sum_{i=1}^{I} X_i e_i \leq F; \tag{9.6}$$

$$\text{LB}_i \leq X_i e_i \leq \text{UB}_i. \tag{9.7}$$

LB_i and UB_i are the lower and upper bounds on effort devoted to any particular sales entity. For example, the firm might specify that total effort devoted to Naprosyn should not exceed the equivalent of 100 salespersons (UB) and be at least 50 (LB).

Model usage: Syntex calibrated the model twice: first to allocate sales effort to products, and then to allocate effort to physician specialties. The company used these results to plan for changes in the size of the salesforce; see the Syntex Laboratories (A) case for a fuller discussion of how the company used this model. (Note that other models are available for allocating effort simultaneously to both market segments and products, such as those described by Rangaswamy, Sinha, and Zoltners [1990].)

The model can also be used to assess the overall value of the salesforce. In today's competitive environment, firms must justify every investment in terms of its opportunity

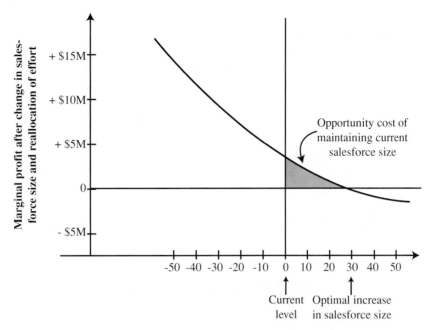

Change in salesforce size from current level

EXHIBIT 9.5
This graph shows how the results from the Syntex model can be organized to indicate (1) the opportunity cost (the shaded area) of maintaining the salesforce at the current level and (2) the required change to the current salesforce size to maximize profits.

costs. One way to meaningfully estimate opportunity cost in the context of salesforce investment is by computing the difference between profits calculated for effort levels corresponding to the selected salesforce size and the profits the firm would earn by expending zero sales effort on all sales entities (all upper bounds set to 0).

EXAMPLE

We applied the judgmental response model/Syntex approach and the corresponding marketing engineering software to C-Tek Inc. (disguised name), an industrial materials supplier that was investigating the appropriate size and allocation of one of its U.S. salesforces. The current situation was that U.S. sales were around $100 million and C-Tek employed 78 salespeople who worked out of 14 sales branches.

We ran a one-day judgmental response session with 16 senior sales reps, national sales managers, marketing managers and marketing research analysts. After a $1\frac{1}{2}$-hour introduction session, we broke the group into four subgroups, each of which built a sales response function for three to four sales branches, by essentially answering the following questions:

What would sales be in three years at this branch with:

(a) No sales force representation?
(b) One fewer sales representative?
(c) The same number of sales representatives?

(d) One more sales representative?

(e) A very large increase in the number of sales representatives?

With these and a few other model inputs (market sizes, growth rates, profit margins), we ran a number of model cases and showed that:

- Two of their (14) sales branches were significantly over-resourced whereas three others were under-resourced.
- Profits could be increased by 4 percent simply by reallocating representatives from over-resourced to under-resourced branches.
- An additional profit increase of 7percent (for a total of 11 percent) could be made by adding 25 to 30 representatives.

These results proved to be robust with respect to many sensitivity analyses we ran on profit margin, response function estimates, market growth rates, and the like. On the basis of this experience, the team decided to propose a major increase in salesforce staffing to the board at a meeting that was scheduled two weeks after the modeling work was completed. The team also decided to use the approach with another, related salesforce that was approximately twice the size of the one they had just studied. The entire process took place in $1\frac{1}{2}$ days.

Sinha and Zoltners (2001) summarize their insights from numerous implementations of sales resource allocation models. In particular, in an analysis exploring the results of 50 projects on salesforce sizing, they find that, on average, the resource allocation models were able to identify contribution improvements of 4.5 percent over the company's three-year base plan. Interestingly, only 28 percent of the incremental improvement was attributable to a size change; the rest was due to changes in resource allocation, i.e., the bulk of the gains from resource allocation models come from getting the salesforce to work smarter and not by getting it to work more. Exhibit 9.6 summarizes the results.

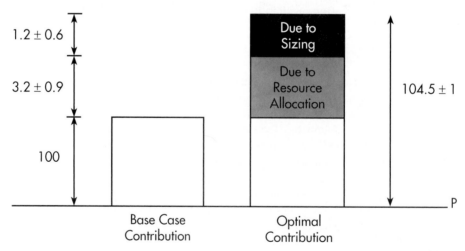

EXHIBIT 9.6
This chart shows that compared to a company's base plan, the model-based resource allocations generated an incremental contribution of about 4.5%, with 1.2% attributable to changes in the size of the salesforce and the rest to reallocation of sales effort.

EXTENDING THE SYNTEX MODEL: REALLOCATOR

The Syntex model has a number of limitations: it is static (excludes build-up/carryover effects), it includes only a single marketing mix element (sales effort), it does not explicitly consider competition, and so forth. Lilien, Kotler, and Moorthy (1992) and Leeflang et al. (2000) provide a range of mechanisms to extend this basic model structure.

We have implemented two enhancements to the Syntex model in a model we call ReAllocator (the software we used at C-Tek). First, we have relaxed the restriction that the marketing resource be sales effort. And, more importantly, we have allowed for interactions between segments or sales entities.

If the entities in ReAllocator are territories (as in C-Tek), then there is likely to be little interaction between them. However, if the entities are products, there are likely to be either complementary effects (positive synergies) or substitution effects (negative synergies). And, especially for new products where diffusion effects are important (Chapter 7), sales in some market segments are likely to influence sales in other segments via positive or negative word-of-mouth. For example, in the pharmaceutical industry, the positive or negative experience that specialists have with new drugs affects the prescribing behavior of the much-larger population of general practitioners. Recognizing that phenomenon, many pharmaceutical companies target key specialists with promotions, hoping for positive spillover effects to the more general physician population.

We have implemented this concept in ReAllocator by introducing interactive coefficients, $\{b_{ki}\}$, where

> b_{ki} = effect that an incremental dollar of spending in sales entity k has on sales in entity i relative to the direct effect of spending in entity i ($1 > b_{ki} > -1$). The restriction on b_{ki} ensures that the absolute magnitude of the complementarity or substitutability effect is less than the direct effect.

Then, the ReAllocator model is as follows (paralleling (9.4 – 9.7):

Let X_i be the (indexed) level of marketing resource (number of salespeople, $000 of ad spending, etc.). The problem is then:

Find the set of X_i's to

$$\text{Maximize } Z = \sum_{i=1}^{I} \left[r_i \left(X_i + \sum_{k \neq i} b_{ki} X_k \right) S_i a_i - d_i X_i e_i \right] \tag{9.4a}$$

where b_{ki} is defined as above

d_i is the cost per unit of X_i

and the other terms are as defined earlier. Again, constraints of the form:

$$\sum_{i=1}^{I} X_i e_i \leq F \qquad \text{(total resource constraint), and} \tag{9.6a}$$

$$LB_i \leq X_i e_i \leq UB_i \qquad \text{(sales entity constraint)} \tag{9.7a}$$

can be imposed.

As mentioned above, even with these enhancements, the ReAllocator model has several limitations. It is best suited for repetitive buying situations where the number of calls made to accounts is an important determinant of sales. In repetitive buying situations the purchase cycle is short, customers buy from an assortment of products, and the salesperson provides a much more sophisticated version of reminder advertising than one gets from other media such as TV. Here the regular contacts with customers help cement relationships and allow the salesperson to recognize potential problems in advance and deal with them. Some common examples of sales calls in repetitive buying situations are pharmaceutical reps calling on physicians, packaged goods salespeople calling on grocery stores, agricultural product reps calling on stores and farmers, and industrial parts reps calling on distributors.

SALES TERRITORY DESIGN

Firms usually structure large field salesforces geographically at some level within the organization. They assign salespeople exclusive territories in which they are responsible for sales of specified products. An important management question is how should these territories be carved out from the total market area that the firm serves.

A fundamental criterion in designing sales territories is the notion of "balance," that is, ensuring that *opportunities* or *workload* are equal across sales territories. Assigning a salesperson to a territory (a group of accounts) with low market potential, heavy competition, or too many small accounts reduces that salesperson's opportunity to perform well. Territories that do not fully utilize the time available to a salesperson or territories that demand too much work from the salesperson are suboptimal. In the former case the territory imposes a performance hurdle that is outside the control of the salesperson. This could lead to frequent turnover in personnel. In the latter case the firm suffers an opportunity loss when the salesperson does not have the time to call on profitable accounts. According to Andris Zoltners, a leading consultant, "Eighty percent of the companies in the United States have imbalanced alignments. They have too many salespeople in one territory and too few in another. This is costing companies two to seven percent in sales losses every year" (quoted by Camparelli 1994). Sinha and Zoltners (2001) find that a good territory alignment will help reduce travel times by 10 to 15 percent.

Balancing territories for potential is particularly important if the "commission" component of the salesperson's compensation package is large. On the other hand, balancing territories by workload is appropriate when salespeople are on straight salary and are not compared on the basis of the sales volume they achieve. In the latter case firms can design territories so that they require about the same number of calls per year.

Sales territories tend to become unbalanced over time because of uneven changes among geographical areas, the differential growth of the firm across sales territories, or personnel changes in salesforce, resulting in misaligned territories with highly uneven sales potential or workload. For example, Cravens (1995) describes a Fortune 500 services company that had a poorly aligned salesforce—the annual sales for 24 salespeople ranged from less than $300,000 to over $60 million! Firms should also evaluate their existing territory alignments when they reorganize or when they merge with other firms.

In addition to balance, firms use several other criteria in designing sales territories:

1. The territories should be easy to administer (e.g., conform to such geographic configurations as counties or zip codes).
2. Sales potential should be easy to estimate (e.g., if average physician prescription levels for each product are available only at the zip code level, then the standard unit of geography should be a zip code).
3. Travel time should be minimized by taking into account topography, natural geographic barriers, and the location of the territory center (home base of the salesperson).

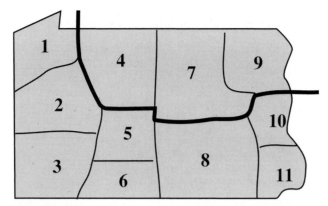

EXHIBIT 9.7
In this example, 11 SGUs have been allocated to two territories: 4, 7, and 9 to territory 1, and 1, 2, 3, 5, 6, 8, 10, and 11 to territory 2.

The GEOLINE model for territory design

The GEOLINE model was developed by Hess and Samuels (1971). It is an optimization model that simultaneously tries to accomplish three objectives: (1) to equalize workload or potential (more generally, to equalize along any activity measure of interest to salesforce management), (2) to create territories that are physically contiguous, that is, they consist of adjacent geographical units, and (3) to ensure compactness, that is, the shape of the territory minimizes travel time. The model takes the total geographic area of interest (e.g., entire United States, region, or state) and breaks it down into standard geographic units (SGUs) such as zip codes or counties. The model assigns each SGU to one or more territories (Exhibit 9.7).

Given the number of territories (I) and a starting location for the territory centers, the model assigns each SGU to a territory to minimize an objective function called the "moment of inertia." At the start each SGU is assigned to the nearest territory center. This will ensure contiguity. The objective function is the weighted sum of squared distances from a proposed territory center to all SGUs located in that territory, where the weights are determined from a measure of the magnitude of the activity for that SGU. Defining an appropriate measure is essential. An activity measure can be a general index of potential (e.g., purchasing power of consumers in an SGU) or workload (e.g., number of sales calls per year). Alternatively, an activity measure can be a specific index of potential (e.g., number of dermatologists or number of Chinese restaurants) or workload (e.g., number of sales calls to dermatologists). The number of territories can be set equal to the number of salespersons, so that each salesperson has a territory. The model also imposes two constraints: an equal activity constraint and a constraint to ensure that every SGU is assigned to at least one territory.

The model is find $\{X_{ij}\}$ to

$$\text{minimize} \sum_j \sum_i c_{ij} X_{ij} a_j \quad \text{(moment of inertia)}, \tag{9.8}$$

subject to

$$\sum_j X_{ij} a_j = \frac{1}{I} \sum_j a_j \quad \text{for } i = 1, 2, 3, \ldots, I \quad \text{(equal activity constraint)}, \tag{9.9}$$

$$\sum_i X_{ij} = 1 \qquad \text{for } j = 1, 2, 3, \ldots, J \text{ (complete assignment of SGUs)}, \quad (9.10)$$

$$X_{ij} \geq 0 \qquad \text{for } i = 1, 2, 3, \ldots, I \text{ and } j = 1, 2, 3, \ldots, J \text{ (nonnegativity)}, \quad (9.11)$$

where

X_{ij} = proportion of SGU j assigned to territory i ($i = 1, 2, 3, \ldots, I$ and $j = 1, 2, 3, \ldots, J$);

a_j = activity measure associated with SGU j; and

c_{ij} = the contribution to the moment of inertia when SGU j is assigned to territory i, calculated as the square of the distance from a proposed territory center to the location of the center of SGU j.

After the first run the model assigns territories to minimize the moment of inertia relative to the starting territory centers. However, there may be two problems with the initial solution: (1) some SGUs may be split between two or more territories, and (2) the initial territory centers may not be central to the SGUs assigned to each territory. The split-SGU problem can be addressed by reassigning split SGUs wholly to just one territory. Managers can do this judgmentally by adjusting territory centers in light of the SGUs assigned to the territories, or the model can assign each SGU automatically to the territory for which its share of activity is the largest. The model can also be programmed to automatically locate the centers at the weighted center of the territory's activity measure. These changes will disrupt the optimality of the solution, and so we must rerun the model with the new territory centers. This process must be repeated until the model output converges to a reasonably stable set of SGU assignments and territory centers.

Since Hess and Samuels (1971) developed the GEOLINE model, researchers have made several modeling enhancements in both data and computer technologies (Zoltners and Sinha 1983). A number of databases are now available from commercial sources that incorporate various geographically referenced activity measures. For example, SCAN/US sells a geodemographic database that has built-in activity measures such as buying potential and the income, age, and gender composition of each SGU. SGUs can now be defined at the level of nine-digit zip codes or even at the level of a city block. Furthermore, the database and related software packages incorporate such features as accessibility of SGUs (proximity to major highways) and nontraversibility (e.g., unbridged waterways or mountains). These data are important because GEOLINE places more weight on achieving territory compactness than on territory contiguity; that is, the moment-of-inertia criterion tends to place territory centers near the "center of gravity" of the activity measures rather than at the most accessible location.

New developments also permit managers to employ user-friendly PC software to make judgmental adjustments to results obtained from formal models such as GEOLINE. One such program is MAPS (Manpower Assignment Planning System), available from ZS Associates and widely used in the pharmaceutical and medical equipment industries. In addition to considering physical limitations (e.g., nontraversibility), it permits managers to make judgmental adjustments to the "optimal" territory alignment to account for personnel considerations, such as when a new salesperson replaces another. It is also likely that by balancing territories the firm will not necessarily be maximizing profits, i.e., there is a trade-off between profit and territory balance. Recognizing this tradeoff, Skiera and Albers (1998) developed a model called COSTA (Contribution Optimizing Sales Territory Alignment). They start by partitioning the total geography covered by the salesforce into non-overlapping regions called Sales Coverage Units (SCU), which are similar to SGUs. The model optimizes profit contribution by allocating the selling time of a salesperson (call time plus travel time) across the Sales Coverage Units, while also simultaneously assigning each SCU uniquely to a salesperson. In an application of the model to a German salesforce, the authors report that the COSTA model produces 3.8% higher predicted contribution as compared to balancing the territories according to equal sales potential.

EXAMPLE

(Adapted from Camparelli 1994.) In early 1993 Jerry Acuff, vice president and general manager of Hoescht Roussel, the pharmaceutical arm of Hoescht Celanese, realized that to stay competitive he had to take a closer look at who his customers were, where they were, and whether his 640-member salesforce was aligned properly. Market conditions were changing rapidly in the pharmaceutical industry. Traditionally salespeople sold primarily to private care physicians. However, managed care HMOs were beginning to change physicians' roles in prescribing drugs. In their new roles physicians are members of a team that may include HMO administrators, who recommend bulk purchases of certain standard drugs. Could he realign his salesforce to take advantage of the changing marketplace?

Before he implemented realignment, Acuff surveyed his customers to find out what they wanted. He conducted a five-month-long research project to gather information from customers and from cross-functional teams comprising individuals from all levels within Hoescht Roussel. According to Acuff, before the research project, "our sales force went out there with the general assumption that 65 percent of the physicians write 94 percent of the prescriptions. But when we learned that data was available that would let us know which of these 65 percent we should be focusing on and which ones we shouldn't, we decided to take action."

In reorganizing the salesforce the firm used a sales-territory-alignment model to plan the realignment around the redefined customer groups: primary care physicians' offices, managed care companies, and hospitals. Before the end of 1993 Hoescht Roussel had completed its research and modeling efforts. The model results suggested the following realignment: reduce the number of regions from nine to six and eliminate 125 sales reps. Many of these reps sold directly to physicians. In implementing these decisions the company created the position of regional operations manager. These managers would be responsible for training and deploying salespeople at the regional level (a function the home office had handled previously). Prior to the realignment, says Acuff, "the whole salesforce was deployed based on where physicians and hospitals were located. The new organization takes into account the impact of managed care." Also, within each region the company had identified high-volume and low-volume customers (the activity measure in this modeling effort was physician prescription volume). The salesforce focused on high-volume customers, and the firm devised a plan to reach lower-volume customers with direct mail and telemarketing. According to Acuff, this realignment was expected to reduce sales costs by about 14 to 15 percent, saving more than $10 million.

SALESFORCE COMPENSATION

The compensation plan for salespeople serves several objectives: (1) *compensation*, to reward individuals for their effort or performance, (2) *motivation*, to encourage salespeople to work harder and accomplish more, and (3) *direction*, to channel sales effort toward activities that are in the firm's best interests (e.g., to establish long-term relationships with customers or to emphasize new products).

Companies compensate their salespeople in a number of ways for their efforts and for their sales performance. Compensation plans may include both monetary and nonmonetary components. The monetary components can include *salary*, money in return for time worked; *commission*, money for sales revenues generated; and *bonus*, money for attaining a goal or quota. Among the possible nonmonetary components are *recognition programs* (e.g., salesperson of the month, preferred parking spots, Millionaire club), *contests* (e.g., salesperson with highest sales revenues for a month), and *noncash awards* (e.g., all-expense-paid trips, personal use of business car).

According to surveys of salesforce compensation by the Dartnell group, the most popular monetary compensation scheme is a combination plan that has a base salary component and an incentive component (commission or bonus). Even firms in the securities industry, which have traditionally relied on 100 percent commission plans, are moving toward combination plans. Approximately 70 percent of all U.S. companies use a combination plan, about 20 percent use only a straight-salary plan, and the remaining companies use all-commission plans. Smaller firms are more likely to use a commission-only plan than larger firms. Most popular is a combination of salary and bonus.

In designing a compensation plan, managers should keep several issues in mind. In most cases they are not able to fully observe the selling efforts of their field salespeople. Thus they often cannot determine how much of a salesperson's results should be attributed to effort and how much to happenstance. Further, sales are affected by many factors other than selling effort, such as the quality of the product, the reputation of the firm, and its advertising program. Therefore salespeople themselves are uncertain about the sales consequences of their efforts. Also differences between salespeople, including differences in abilities, preferences for leisure versus work, and territory potential, can account for differential results. Finally, a good compensation plan should be perceived to be equitable (i.e., perceived to offer roughly equivalent earning opportunities among the salespeople), be easy to understand, and be simple to implement.

One way for a firm to assess whether it should redesign its current incentive plan is to develop a chart, such as the one summarized in Exhibit 9.8 (Sinha and Zoltners 2001). In this example, out of a firm's 1400 salespeople, 146 were underpaid and 21 were overpaid, representing misaligned incentives for approximately 12% of the salesforce. The greater the degree of misalignment, the stronger should be the pressure for the firm to redesign its incentive scheme. Mantrala, Sinha, and Zoltners (1994) have developed and implemented a model (we call this the MSZ model) to design bonus plans in repetitive buying environments. We describe this model next.

Using conjoint analysis to design a bonus plan (the MSZ model)

The MSZ compensation model helps management to (1) set individual sales quotas that take into account differences in territory potentials and (2) design a common bonus plan that awards all salespeople the same amount of money for the same achieved percentages of their quotas. Thus, for example, all salespeople who exceed their quotas by 20 percent receive identical bonus amounts, regardless of the actual levels of the quotas assigned to the different salespeople. To design such a bonus plan, the firm first needs two types of information:

Measure(s) of sales potential in each territory: In such industries as pharmaceuticals, where MSZ implemented this model, data on territory potential are available from syn-

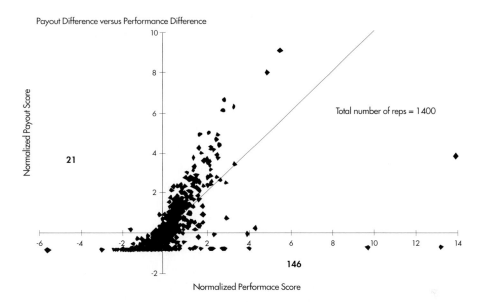

Note:
1. Sales performance is defined as the difference of actual from expection based on previous busy year's sales
2. Payouts score is defined as the number of standard deviations from the average payout.
3. Bold numbers represents number of reps in that quadrant.

EXHIBIT 9.8

This chart summarizes the relationship between a salesperson's relative incentive pay and relative performance, with each dot representing one salesperson. Performance is defined as the difference between actual sales and the expected sales derived from a regression model that incorporates the prior year's sales. Both performance and incentive pay are plotted in standard deviations above and below the mean. Salespeople in the Northwest quadrant are overpaid—their performance is substandard and they have received an above-average incentive payout. Those in the southeast quadrant are underpaid—they have above-average performance but below average incentive payout.

dicated data sources. In some other industries geodemographic databases (described in the last main section of this chapter) can be used.

Salespeople's assessments of how sales of various products are likely to respond to their individual efforts (i.e., their individual sales-response functions) and their preferences for income versus leisure: The firm can obtain this information from the salespeople by using a specially designed conjoint analysis procedure, described below. (In Chapter 7 we describe the basics of conjoint analysis.)

With this information a firm can predict how salespeople are likely to behave under various bonus plans, and it can design a good bonus plan.

The core of the MSZ model are sales-response functions, which are specified as the modified exponential described in Chapter 2:

$$r_{ij}(X_{ij}) = b_{ij} + \left(a_{ij} - b_{ij}\right)\left(1 - e^{-c_{ij}X_{ij}}\right) \tag{9.12}$$

where

X_{ij} = effort per period on product i by salesperson j; $i = 1, 2, 3, \ldots, I$ (# of products) and $j = 1, 2, 3, \ldots, J$ (# of salespeople);

$r_{ij}(X_{ij})$ = expected sales of product i per period attributable to salesperson j;

a_{ij} = maximum sales of product i that can be expected with a saturation (infinite) level of effort by salesperson j;

b_{ij} = minimum sales of product i if there is no selling effort in the territory handled by salesperson j; and

c_{ij} = parameter that determines the rate at which sales $(r_{ij}(X_{ij}))$ approach the maximum (a_{ij}) with increasing effort (X_{ij}).

In the MSZ model a_{ij} and b_{ij} are determined from external data sources, while c_{ij} is inferred from the responses that salespeople provide to the conjoint analysis task. We briefly describe the conjoint analysis task and the optimization model the firm uses to determine a good bonus plan. (For technical details of the model, see Mantrala, Sinha, and Zoltners 1994.)

Equation (9.12) can be "inverted" to determine the effort required for any desired level of sales (quota), by solving for X_{ij} as a function of sales $r_{ij}(X_{ij})$. These effort levels are then summed to determine the total effort across the products a salesperson sells, which is a function of all the c_{ij}'s associated with the products the salesperson sells. The salesperson derives "utility" from the bonus compensation, but a "disutility" from the total effort needed to get the bonus. (The larger the bonus, the higher the utility; the higher the total effort devoted to selling, the higher the disutility.) The actual trade-off between the utility value of the bonus and the disutility of work is idiosyncratic to each individual salesperson. To determine both the utility and the disutility functions and the response function coefficients (c_{ij}), the firm gives the salespeople a "conjoint ranking task," an example of which is shown in Exhibit 9.9.

We can use an ordinal regression procedure and the rank orders the salespeople provide in the conjoint task to estimate the "utility function" for each salesperson. The estimated utility function depends on the bonus amount, the territory potential, and the responsiveness parameters c_{ij} estimated from the responses to the conjoint-ranking task.

The firm then incorporates the utility functions of all the salespeople into an optimization model that selects a *common* bonus plan (i.e., the amounts it would pay for

Below are nine different bonus plans for products A and B. Also listed are possible sales objectives (quotas) for the next six-month period and the bonus that will be awarded if you achieve 100% of the sales objectives. Please rank these nine plans from "1" to "9" in terms of your preference, with "1" indicating your most preferred plan and "9" your least preferred plan.

Bonus plan	Product A sales objective	Product B sales objective	Bonus (for achieving 100% of **total** sales objectives)	Rank
1	$316,000	$45,000	$2,100	_____
2	316,000	75,000	3,200	_____
3	316,000	105,000	4,900	_____
4	526,000	45,000	4,000	_____
5	526,000	75,000	4,250	_____
6	526,000	105,000	5,100	_____
7	737,000	45,000	4,700	_____
8	737,000	75,000	5,300	_____
9	737,000	105,000	6,400	_____

EXHIBIT 9.9
A sample questionnaire for the MSZ model for estimating utility function of a salesperson (adapted from Figure A1 of Mantrala, Sinha, and Zoltners 1994). The table should be customized for each salesperson so that product sales objectives are set to lie between the minimum sales for the salesperson's territory (b_{ij}) and the maximum sales for the territory (a_{ij}).

achieving sales levels corresponding to various percentages of the quota) for all salespersons. The optimization model maximizes total firm profits generated by the entire salesforce, assuming that each salesperson will act to maximize his or her own utility and subject to an additional restriction that any new bonus plan should at least maintain the past satisfaction (utility) levels of the salespeople.

One may question whether salespeople would misrepresent their preferences in responding to the questionnaire if they knew that their responses were being used to design the bonus plan. The authors, however, report that this is rarely a problem for at least four reasons: (1) the salespeople have incomplete information about the model and therefore are unable to systematically misrepresent preferences; (2) the salespeople know that the objective of management is to set a common bonus plan rather than an individual-specific bonus plan; (3) the salespeople would find it difficult to collude to share the bonus payments; and (4) over time management has the ability to detect and penalize gaming behavior.

The MSZ model and its variants have been implemented in a number of pharmaceutical and medical products firms. In describing an early application of this model, the authors show that a new quota-bonus plan could potentially increase firm profits by 10 percent for a 12-person salesforce in an eight-month period.

We need to further develop and deploy operational models for sales compensation. In particular, existing models are weak in evaluating combination plans (salary + incentive compensation), in considering cross-product costs and sales interdependencies, and for developing compensation plans in team-selling situations.

IMPROVING THE EFFICIENCY AND EFFECTIVENESS OF SALES CALLS

In most markets customers and prospects are not all equally responsive to the efforts of the salesperson. Some customers have been buying from the firm for years and need no reselling, while some prospects need a lot of selling effort before they buy from the firm. Some customers buy large quantities of the product with each order, while others buy small quantities. Most salespeople intuitively recognize these differences. However, without formal methods they may not fully capitalize on these differences by spending more effort where likely response is high and less effort where likely response is low.

According to a survey by the Dartnell Corp. (*American Salesman*, August 1995), sales professionals make an average of 3.4 calls per day, or about 750 calls per year. In salesforces that sell packaged goods to supermarkets, salespeople ("account managers") are each responsible for two to four accounts, consisting of 40 to 120 stores, and they handle 2 to 18 products (100 to 5,000 stock keeping units [SKUs]). The average duration of a call is 60 to 90 minutes, of which the average time spent selling is 11 to 15 minutes (DeVincentis and Kotcher 1995). In industrial salesforces the percentage of time that salespeople spend in actual face-to-face selling has been around 35 percent for years (Hise and Reid 1994). Given these statistics it is not surprising that by improving the efficiency and effectiveness with which they manage sales calls, firms with large salesforces can increase their profits.

The CALLPLAN model

CALLPLAN (Lodish 1971, 1974) is an interactive call-planning system that helps salespeople to determine how many calls to make to each client and prospect (equivalently, to each category of clients and prospects) in a given time period to maximize the returns from their calls. The system determines call frequencies with respect to an *effort* period, which is the planning period used by the salesperson (e.g., one quarter). The model is based on the assumption that the expected sales to each client and prospect over a *re-*

sponse period, which is the planning period of the firm (e.g., a year), is a function of the average number of calls per effort period during that response period. The response period selected should be long enough to accommodate potential carryover effects from each effort period.

Specifying response functions: We will use a simple version of CALLPLAN to illustrate the central issues. Like the Syntex model, CALLPLAN depends on the specification of response functions. Again we use an ADBUDG response function (Chapter 2):

$$r_i(X_i) = b_i + (a_i - b_i) \frac{X_i^{c_i}}{d_i + X_i^{c_i}}, \tag{9.13}$$

where

i $= 1, 2, 3, \ldots, I$ (# of accounts or prospects);

X_i = average level of effort, measured in number of calls, expended on account i during an effort period. X_i formalizes informal statements that salespeople make in the form of "I will call on this customer twice a month";

$r_i(X_i)$ = indexed level of sales at account i if the salesperson devotes X_i amount of effort at that account;

b_i = minimum sales that can be expected with no sales effort at account i;

a_i = maximum sales that can be expected with an unlimited amount of sales effort to account i;

c_i = parameter that determines the shape of $r_i(X_i)$, whether it is concave or S-shaped; and

d_i = an index of competitive effort levels directed toward account i (the larger this value, the smaller the impact of the salesperson's effort).

The response model can be calibrated using managerial judgment as described in Chapter 2. The salesperson estimates a separate response function for each account. The salesperson can adjust the response functions based on account-specific profit-margin factors f_i if different accounts offer different levels of profitability.

Model specification: Once the response functions are specified, CALLPLAN tries to develop an effective way for the salesperson to allocate effort across the different accounts. The model assumes that the salespeople seek to maximize contribution (profits) from their selling efforts; however, they have limited time and therefore they wish to use this resource as effectively as possible. A sales territory is assumed to be divided into mutually exclusive geographic areas (e.g., zip codes). The salesperson makes trips to some or all areas in the territory in each effort period. In each trip to an area the salesperson incurs variable costs for expense items such as travel and lodging. In a trip to an area, the salesperson calls on any given account at most once.

Before we describe the formal model, we define its parameters:

n_j = number of trips per effort period to area j, where $j = 1, 2, 3, \ldots, J$. Because the salesperson calls on an account at most once during a trip, n_j is also equal to the maximum number of calls made to any account in territory j;

c_j = variable costs incurred when making a trip to area j;

t_i = time that the salesperson spends with the customer when making a call to account i (t_i may be set to be the same for all customers);

U_j = time it takes to get to area j;

e = number of effort periods in a response period (if the effort period is a month and the response period is a year, then $e = 12$);

T = total work time available to a salesperson in an effort period, which includes both selling and nonselling times;

a_i = a customer-specific profit-adjustment factor that reflects the profit contribution of sales to that customer.

The optimization model maximizes profits (Z) for a single sales territory taking into account both the costs of visiting the accounts and the expected contribution from all the accounts and prospects:

Find the set of X_i to

$$\text{maximize profits } Z = \sum_i a_i r_i(X_i) - e \sum_j n_j c_j,$$

subject to

$$\sum_i X_i t_i + \sum_j n_j U_j \leq T, \tag{9.14}$$

$$n_j = \max_i \ (X_i \text{ in geographic area } j), \tag{9.15}$$

$$\text{LB}_i \leq X_i \leq \text{UB}_i. \tag{9.16}$$

Constraint (9.14) ensures that the total time (call time plus travel time) used in an effort period does not exceed the time available to the salesperson; constraint (9.15) equates the number of trips to territory j to the maximum number of calls made to any specific account in that territory, thus ensuring that in any trip to territory j the salesperson does not call on any account more than once; constraint (9.16) allows the salesperson to incorporate judgment-based lower and upper bounds on the number of calls made to any account i in an effort period.

Model usage: We recommend that the model be run first with no upper bounds in constraint (9.16) and with a lower bound of 0 for all i. Then the model is likely to suggest that the salesperson never call on some accounts and call on some accounts too often. The salesperson may feel that such an allocation is not reasonable and can then specify minimum and maximum constraints for each account to modify these results. These judgments account for the effects of factors not explicitly included in the model. (For example, some accounts may be beta-test sites that help with testing a new product before release. However, sales effort on those accounts may not necessarily lead to increased sales.)

A salesperson should include both accounts and prospects in a calling portfolio. However, prospects typically respond weakly to sales efforts as compared with existing accounts; therefore the model will tend to exclude them from the calling plans it develops. One way to give adequate treatment to both is to run the model separately for accounts and for

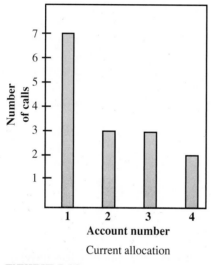

	Number of calls									
	1	2	3	4	5	6	7	8	9	10
Account 1	100	300	600	400	(300)	225	[160]	110	70	50
number 2	1400	1100	[850]	650	490	360	(250)	165	85	15
3	3600	1800	(800)	200	100	75	50	40	30	25
4	180	[170]	160	150	140	135	130	125	120	115

The numbers in each row of the matrix correspond to the response function for that account, showing incremental contribution per call at that call level.

☐ Indicates marginal contributions at current level of deployment

◯ Indicates marginal contributions at the optimal level of deployment

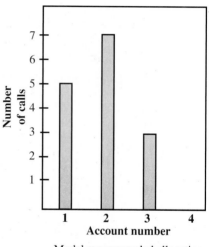

Current allocation   Model recommended allocation

EXHIBIT 9.10

Example of optimization procedure in CALLPLAN. The table at the top is a numerical representation of sales-response functions in four accounts. The bar charts at the bottom show the current and model-recommended allocation of effort to the four accounts when the salesperson makes a total of 15 calls.

prospects: Run the analysis for prospects by setting aside time equal to $T_P < T$ in constraint (9.14) to be allocated to prospects. Do the same for accounts by setting aside time equal to T_A for existing accounts such that $T_A + T_P = T$, the total time available to the salesperson. A comparison of the results with and without time set aside for prospects shows how much of the current profit the salesperson is willing to forgo to cultivate long-term prospects.

EXAMPLE

To understand the "incremental analysis" the CALLPLAN model uses to determine the optimal allocation of effort, consider a simple example with four accounts, summarized in Exhibit 9.10. Suppose that the salesperson is currently devoting 15 calls to these accounts as shown, bringing in total sales of $11,985. If the cost of a single sales call is $200, the net contribution is then $8,985.

An optimization procedure would allocate the first call to account 3, which has the highest marginal contribution ($3,600). It will also allocate the second call to this account, which has the next highest marginal contribution ($1,800). The third to the fifth calls will be allocated to account 2 with a total contribution of $3,350, the sixth call to account 3, the seventh and eighth calls to account 2 with a total contribution of $1,140, the ninth to twelfth calls to account 1 with a total contribution of $1,400, the thirteenth to account 2, the fourteenth to account 1, and the fifteenth call to account 2. This allocation procedure results in total contributions of $13,000 with a net contribution (after paying for the sales calls) of $10,000, which represents a 11.3 percent improvement over the current net contribution of these 15 calls.

Note that the model recommends making no calls on account 4. The firm should use less costly methods such as telemarketing to contact such accounts. Note also that it would not pay to make any call whose marginal contribution would be less than $200, the cost of a call. Let us explore what would happen if the salesperson were able to make more than 15 calls. Then the eighteenth call will be to account 4, with a marginal contribution of $180. Thus the maximum number of calls the salesperson makes to this set of accounts should be 17. (If the salesperson makes only 15 calls to these accounts, the opportunity loss of not making the sixteenth and seventeenth calls is equal to $25, the net contribution of making the two additional calls. The sixteenth call would be to account 1, and the seventeenth to account 3.)

Exhibit 9.11 summarizes the output from an actual application of CALLPLAN (Lodish 1971). In this example, the salesperson could increase sales by about 20 percent by fol-

	Optimal call in average three-month period	Optimal expected sales in one year	Present policy	Expected sales using present policy
Account				
Balfor	7	75	8	79
Chempro	3	14	6	22
Chemplst	10	195	3	171
Dilctx	5	15	4	8
Emerson	0	0	1	0
Ethlyn	6	64	4	52
F/C	5	37	5	37
M-I	0	0	1	2
Micro	0	0	4	2
Polyfin	1	5	3	8
Slctro	5	36	3	18
Sevema	9	59	6	38
Surf	0	0	3	2
Tri-Pt	5	72	3	36
Brdng	0	0	1	0
Marlow	0	0	1	1
Total	56	572	56	476

EXHIBIT 9.11
Optimal account call policies from an application of CALLPLAN.

lowing model recommendations to shift calls from smaller customers such as Chempro and Polyfin to larger customers such as Chemplst and Ethyln.

Firms increasingly use telemarketing and direct mailing to reach less profitable accounts. For example, W. W. Grainger distributes maintenance, repair, and operating supplies to 1.3 million customers in different market segments such as contractors, service shops, maintenance departments, hotels, and educational facilities. General Motors, its largest customer, accounts for less than 1 percent of its sales. The company has now partitioned its accounts into three groups based on their size and responsiveness. It contacts those that are not profitable enough to justify visits by salespeople through telemarketing and mailings.

A question that often arises is this: How do we know these gains from reallocating calls will actually be realized? To answer this question Fudge and Lodish (1977) conducted a study at United Airlines to assess the value of CALLPLAN. One group of salespersons used CALLPLAN to develop call frequencies for their accounts, whereas the control group used manual techniques to plan their call frequencies. However, both groups filled out the questionnaires for CALLPLAN response-function inputs. Fudge and Lodish assigned 10 pairs of "matched" salespersons randomly to each group (10 salespersons in each group) to participate in this study. At the end of the six-month study the CALLPLAN group had an 11.9 percent increase in sales from the previous year, while the control group had only a 3.8 percent increase. As a result the CALLPLAN group had an incremental sales increase of nearly $1 million over the control group. This difference between these groups was statistically significant at the 0.025 level.

Individual users should assess the value of the model in a similar fashion. A simple way to do this is to run a before-and-after study: track sales performance for six months prior to using the model and compare that with sales performance during six months when using the model. While this approach could lead to misleading results, especially if there are seasonality effects and market changes during the evaluation, it can still provide a useful assessment of the model.

Advantages and limitations of CALLPLAN: Although many salespeople believe that they should focus on high-potential prospects, they often fall back on the routine comfort of calling on friendly, established accounts. The CALLPLAN model can help them realize the consequences of such an approach on the bottom line and their commissions and nudge them to try alternative allocation strategies. Lodish (1974) notes:

> A typical first reaction from some sales managers about the procedure is "garbage in, garbage out." They are uncomfortable putting in subjective estimates of sales or odds of conversion at different call levels for each account. However, if maximizing sales or profits is the objective of the sales operation, these estimates are necessary to evaluate the profitability of utilizing the limited manpower resources. . . . After they have utilized the procedure, most managers realize this and become enthusiastic supporters of this concept. (p. 124)

In recent years several account-management software packages have become available commercially. These packages keep track of customer phone numbers and addresses, customer history, correspondence, and the like, and they also contain calendars to schedule appointments (e.g., *www.salesforce.com*). The more sophisticated packages can link to central databases to upload and download information (e.g., sales presentations or price lists). CALLPLAN complements these software packages with analytical support that helps salespeople use account information effectively.

The limitations noted under the Syntex model also apply to the CALLPLAN model. It is best suited for repetitive buying situations. In addition, in its current form the model is likely to be more useful for the "lone wolf" salesperson, but it can be adapted for team-based salesforce applications.

MARKETING CHANNEL DECISIONS

Marketing channels may be "viewed as sets of interdependent organizations involved in the process of making a product or service available for consumption or use" (Stern, El-Ansary, and Coughlan 1996). Decisions about marketing channels influence the effectiveness and the efficiency with which a firm reaches its markets. In addition, because channels require long-term commitment of corporate resources, channel decisions also affect the competitive positioning of the firm. Typically channel decisions encompass three areas:

1. *Strategy*: The firm determines the method for selling products to target markets and the types of contractual mechanisms to employ. The firm can sell directly to customers (e.g., by direct mail or the Internet) or use a variety of intermediaries (e.g., manufacturer's agents, brokers, rack jobbers, drop shippers, wholesalers, and retailers). Possible contractual mechanisms range from complete ownership of the entire marketing channel to relying only on brokers who operate entirely on commissions.
2. *Location*: The firm determines the number and locations of outlets through which it will sell its products and services. In some cases the location decision implies direct investments by the firm (e.g., Wal-Mart). In other cases, although intermediaries made the investments (e.g., McDonald's franchisees), the firm greatly influences location decisions in order to maintain system-wide control over locations.
3. *Logistics*: The firm plans and manages such activities as physical distribution and inventory to maximize the efficiency of channel operations. It tries to provide high service to customers with low transit and inventory costs.

In this section we focus on models for facilitating location decisions. In recent years firms have increasingly used such decision models because relatively inexpensive geo-demographic databases have become available. For a discussion of models concerning strategy and logistics, see Lilien, Kotler, and Moorthy (1992).

Location decisions: In selecting a location for an outlet, the firm makes two decisions: it chooses a market area, such as a city, region, or country, in which to establish an outlet, and then it chooses a specific site within that location. The former is referred to as the "macro" decision, while the latter is referred to as the "micro" decision. Many firms choose locations for retail outlets based on information about what real estate is available, deciding if the rent at that location is affordable, and then assessing the neighborhood on such criteria as profit potential and other measures of suitability. They can now use formal models in making both macro and micro location decisions because of the availability of computerized geodemographic databases. These databases overlay demographic and other types of data (e.g., psychographic) on a geocoded database containing the latitude and longitude of most households and firms in the United States. By combining these databases with quantitative computer models, such as the gravity model (Huff 1964), managers can carefully evaluate alternative retail-location options.

The gravity model

Formal models to support location decisions are intended to evaluate the combined effects of such factors as customer profiles, store image, drive times, and the locations of competing retailers on the potential value of a site. The gravity model offers managers a way to assess the impact of these and other factors in a familiar modeling framework—the discrete choice model. In its basic form the gravity model postulates that the probability that a customer or individual i will choose a store j is given by

$$p_{ij} = \frac{V_{ij}}{\sum_{n \in N} V_{in}} , \qquad (9.17)$$

where

p_{ij} = probability (proportion of times) individual(s) in geographic zone i will choose the store at the jth location;

V_{ij} = an index to indicate the attractiveness (also called value or utility) of store j to individual(s) in zone i; and

N = the set of stores that will compete with the proposed new store. (In more sophisticated versions of the model, N may be indexed by i to indicate that it may vary from zone to zone.)

Specifically, gravity models propose that value (V_{ij}) depends on several key factors. An important factor will be the size of the store (or shopping center) at location j; the larger the store, the higher the attractiveness. Larger stores typically offer greater variety and better prices. Another important factor is the distance from an individual's home to each of the competing outlets, including a proposed new outlet. The greater this distance, the less attractive a store becomes to individuals in zone i. Finally, the model permits the use of various parameters to modify the relative impact of store size and distance. We describe some examples of such parameters below. Thus shoppers in a geographical area will be "pulled" (whence the term gravity model) toward a store with higher probability if it is located closer to their homes, it is larger, and its retail image is more attractive than that of the existing competitors.

A specific form of V_{ij} in Eq. (9.17) that is used in practice is

$$p_{ij} = \frac{S_j^\alpha / D_{ij}^\beta}{\sum_{n \in N} S_j^\alpha / D_{in}^\beta} , \qquad (9.18)$$

where

p_{ij} = probability that individuals in zone i choose store at the jth location;

S_j = size of store at location j (more generally, this can be some index of store image);

D_{ij} = distance of store j from the center of zone i (more generally, this may be viewed as ease of access to the store rather than just distance);

α = a parameter to "tune" the impact of size (or image) on the decision to patronize stores; and

β = a parameter to "tune" the impact of distance (or ease of access) on the decision to patronize stores.

The example in Exhibit 9.12 shows how store choice varies as a result of changes in the parameters α and β. Note the dramatic increase in the probability of choosing store 3 when the distance component becomes more important (from 0.32 when $\alpha = 1$ and $\beta = 1$ to 0.48 when $\alpha = 1$ and $\beta = 2$).

	Store image (Index averages to 100)	Distance from geographic unit (in miles)	$\dfrac{(\text{Store image})^{\alpha}}{(\text{Distance})^{\beta}}$	Choice probability (p_{ij})
$\alpha = 1, \beta = 1$				
Store 1	100	5	20.0	0.17
Store 2	100	3	33.3	0.29
Store 3	75	2	37.5	0.32
Store 4	125	5	25.0	0.22
$\alpha = 1, \beta = 2$				
Store 1	100	5	4.0	0.10
Store 2	100	3	11.1	0.29
Store 3	75	2	18.8	0.48
Store 4	125	5	5.0	0.13
$\alpha = 2, \beta = 1$				
Store 1	100	5	2000.0	0.18
Store 2	100	3	3333.3	0.29
Store 3	75	2	2812.5	0.25
Store 4	125	5	3125.0	0.28

EXHIBIT 9.12

A numerical example illustrating the gravity model. Stores 1, 2, and 3 are existing stores, and store 4 is a proposed new store. The table shows how changes in model parameters influence store choice. The α parameter captures the impact of store image (or size) on customers' probability of selecting each store. As α increases, stores with stronger or weaker images than the average will see greater changes in the probabilities of customers' choosing them (look at changes in choice probabilities for stores 3 and 4). The β parameter captures the impact of distance (or ease of access) of a store from customers' homes on their probability of selecting each store. As β increases, the distance variable becomes more important in influencing customers' store choice (look at changes in choice probabilities for stores 1, 3, and 4).

Although gravity models have been around for many years, the recent development of commercial geodemographic databases only now makes it feasible to apply these models broadly. Without these databases it is difficult to specify exact geographic areas for analysis, and it is cumbersome to obtain distance and demographic data for a large number of geographic zones and stores. Recent data and modeling enhancements have also made it easier to use geodemographic databases in making location decisions. Managers no longer have to evaluate store attractiveness by traditional geographic units such as census tracts or zip codes. Newer databases offer finer detail, such as latitude and longitude corresponding to every geographic entity and microgrids to produce highly accurate boundaries. The user of the software is free to identify an existing or potential market area by combining grids. Also various geographic features such as streets and highways and boundaries of block groups (an area consisting of about 2,000 people) are available. In addition, company-specific data (e.g., customer records) can be overlaid on commercial databases using other databases that contain the latitude and longitude of every listed telephone in the United States. These enhancements make it possible for a company such as the Sharper Image to use its customer database of direct mail shoppers to identify potential retail store locations that are geographically close to its existing customer base.

EXAMPLE

(Adapted from Garry 1996.) Supervalue is one of the largest grocery wholesalers in the United States and is also the twelfth largest food retailer. The company serves 4,100 food stores and operates nearly 300 retail food stores. Locating its distribution facilities and its food stores in the most appropriate locations is critical to its success. Supervalue was an early adopter of geographic information systems (GIS) and gravity modeling. The company uses GIS to support a number of decisions, such as locating new stores and the mix of products to carry in a given location.

Supervalue uses GIS to evaluate potential new sites from a number of perspectives, including how a site compares with existing store sites, the kind and number of shoppers who live in the trade area, their spending potential, and the market share of competitors. In addition it uses this system to evaluate the suitability of different store formats (e.g., Cub Foods and Shop 'N Save) for a particular market area. It also uses gravity model estimates to evaluate the performance of existing stores. It uses the model to project how much business a particular store should be getting based on the number of customers who reside near the store, their access to competitors, their spending potential, and the road network. It then compares these predictions with actual store sales and associates reasons' for underperformance or superior performance with specific factors included in the model.

Steps in implementing gravity models: The software accompanying this book was developed by SCAN/US, a leading provider of geodemographic databases for marketing decision making. Although these databases have many other uses in marketing, we will focus on using them to implement a gravity model. To develop a gravity model you take the following general steps (the software tutorial has more specific instructions for implementing these steps within the SCAN/US software):

Step 1: Define the market area. Identify the geographic area that the proposed outlet is likely to serve and divide that area into its constituent zones. Ideally the zones should be relatively homogeneous in their demographic characteristics and in the availability of competitive stores and movement barriers (e.g., rivers, railway lines, high-crime neighborhoods).

Step 2: Obtain data about existing stores that might compete with the proposed store. In particular get data on the location, size, sales, and other characteristics of each competing store within the market area.

Step 3: Compute distances from each store to each zone. Commercial software packages automatically compute the distances once you specify the zones and locations of stores. (Sometimes the data from steps 2 and 3 alone are enough to indicate the potential value of a location. For example, potentially lucrative locations are likely to exist if these data indicate that sales per square foot in existing stores are much above average or that people have to travel great distances to reach existing stores.)

Step 4: Calibrate the gravity model on the existing competitors in the market area. Specifically, choose a set of parameter values for α and β that fit the existing data well. Good starting values are $\alpha = 1$ and $\beta = 1$, unless you have reason to believe that other values are more likely. For the chosen values of the parameters, compute p_{ij} from Eq. (9.18) using the size and distance information gathered in steps 2 and 3.

a. Next compute market shares for each of the existing competitors by aggregating the p_{ij}'s as follows:

$$m_j = \frac{\sum\limits_{i \in I} p_{ij} T_j}{\sum\limits_{j \in J} \sum\limits_{i \in I} p_{ij} T_j};$$

(9.19)

T_j is a measure of sales potential in zone j, I is the set of zones in the market area, and J is the number of existing stores in the market area. You can use any suitable index available in the database for measuring potential (T_j) in each zone. The actual index you select depends on the nature of the store and product category. In some cases potential may be a general index such as average annual expenditure per household or total households in a zone. In other cases it may be a product-specific index. Potential can even be indicated by *relative* measures of demographic variables, such as age or income, that are indexed to an average value of 100 (if you use indexed measures, make sure that higher index values indicate higher potential; for example, if lower age indicates higher potential, as it would for the purchase of rock music CDs, then the index should increase with decreasing age). The numerator in Eq. (9.19) is a measure of the sales potential of store j, while the denominator is a measure of the sales potential for all existing stores in the market area.

The demographic information most often included in gravity models concerns such characteristics as income, sex, age, occupation, education, family size, religion, race, and nationality. For a gravity model based on these measures of potential to be useful, these characteristics should be associated with store preferences.

b. Check that the model produces market shares m_j (or sales potential $\sum_{i \in I} p_{ij} T_j$) that are consistent with the actual market shares of sales of the existing competitors. If not, change the values of parameters α and β and repeat step 4 until the procedure settles on a realistic set of values for α and β. (There are statistical methods for choosing α and β. See, for example, Cooper and Nakanishi 1988.)

Step 5: *Evaluate the sales potential of a new store at various locations.* Introduce a new store k at a proposed location into the model and recompute the p_{ij}'s using the estimated α and β. Compute the sales potential for the new store ($= \sum_{i \in I} p_{ik} T_k$). Repeat this process to consider other locations for the new store.

Step 6: Select the location of the new store. This is where sales potential, $\sum_{i \in I} p_{ik} T_k$, is highest.

For a detailed example of implementing a gravity model in conjunction with geo-demographic databases, see Tayman and Pol (1995).

Limitations of the gravity model: Users of the gravity model should carefully scrutinize the assumptions of the model before applying it in a specific decision situation. Customers do not always try to minimize distance traveled nor do they always prefer large stores to small stores. Thus some high-fashion retailers succeed by placing a few small stores in selected locations (e.g., Hermes, the maker of fine silk scarves and ties), while others succeed by locating large stores in selected areas (e.g., Ikea furniture outlets). Despite its limitations the gravity model has turned out to be a remarkably robust method for predicting store choice, at least at the aggregate level.

The gravity model is a special case of the attraction models described in Chapter 2, which are subject to a counterintuitive phenomenon known as "independence from irrelevant alternatives." Suppose that customers are indifferent between shopping in store 1 (S1) and store 2 (S2) as long as these are the only two options, but they prefer to shop in store 3 (S3) four to one when offered a choice between S1 and S3, and they would prefer S3 four to one over S2 when offered a choice between S2 and S3. In this case, according to the model, customers would prefer S3 two-to-one over S1 and S2 when all three stores are available, whereas intuition suggests that S3 should still be preferred four to one over S1 and S2. The model forces the ratio of the attractiveness of S3 to S1 (4/1) and S3 to S2 (4/1) to remain the same, regardless of the shopping context. Thus when the customer chooses among all three stores, the probabilities (market shares) are 1/6, 1/6, and 2/3 for S1, S2, and S3, respectively. One way out of this problem is to treat highly similar alternatives as a single choice option. In the foregoing example, you could treat S1 and S2 as just one store-format option for purposes of analysis.

Another limitation of gravity models is that they ignore modes of access to a location. For example, accessibility by bus, by car, or by foot have different implications for distance measures. Where multiple modes of access are common, gravity models will perform poorly. Such situations are more likely outside the United States.

Gravity models are more difficult to interpret than multiple regression models, which are also used for making site-location decisions. The regression approach relates data from a number stores regarding store sales (dependent variable) and various independent variables such as store size, demographic characteristics associated with the store, and characteristics of competitor stores. Regression models can be used to forecast sales in new locations based on the values of the independent variables for these locations. Compared with gravity models, regression models generally do a poor job of accounting for the impact of existing competitors.

The retail world is changing. Current trends include customers making less frequent shopping trips and the growth of megastores, direct marketing, and interactive marketing over the Internet. These trends are reducing the impact of geographic constraints on shopping behavior. As these trends continue, traditional measures of market potential of a geographic area may prove inappropriate. For example, sales of PCs in North Sioux City, South Dakota (home to Gateway computers, a leading direct marketer of personal computers), would be a misleading indicator of potential for this geographical unit for the sales of a new computer game through retail outlets.

SUMMARY

In this chapter we highlighted five successful marketing engineering models for managing salesforces and marketing channels: the Syntex model for allocating sales resources, the Hess and Samuels model for aligning sales territories, the MSZ model for designing compensation plans for salespeople, the CALLPLAN model for planning sales calls, and the gravity model for locating new stores. We described how to calibrate each model and provided example applications.

The sales-management models are normative decision models (see Chapter 1) that help managers to choose a course of action from numerous available options, whereas the gravity model is a descriptive/predictive decision model, which helps managers to evaluate a few selected options very carefully. Sales-management models have resulted in incremental profits of about five percent over those the firm earned before implementing the model. Although many firms use gravity models, we did not find documented evidence in the public domain showing the incremental benefits associated with such models. However, the repeated use of the model by such companies as Supervalue is an indicator of its positive value in use.

A current trend is for companies to invest in salesforce automation and CRM (Customer Relationship Management) systems to facilitate the sales process. They are setting up "data warehouse," communications, and supporting services to provide salespeople with current information (e.g., specs for company and competitive products, authorized prices, account history, and order status) and equip salespeople and sales managers with computers so that they can access the data warehouse and upload and download information.

A good salesforce system effectively links corporate functions, customer data, managers of the field salesforce, and sales reps. The systems enable managers to monitor sales activities readily and focus on mentoring salespeople and developing strategies (not just tactics) to manage each account. The systems can include packaged software for resource allocation, lead management, account analysis, time management, and generating proposals and presentations. By linking their corporate databases to geographic information systems, firms can improve their management of channel functions and operations. As the use of information technologies in managing salesforces and marketing channels increases, we expect firms to find further applications for the models (and their variants) that we have described in this chapter.

SYNTEX LABORATORIES (A) CASE[1]

April 1982 found Robert Nelson, vice president of sales for Syntex Laboratories, considering the results of a salesforce size and allocation study. Those results presented Nelson with a dilemma. He had previously submitted a business plan increasing the number of sales representatives from 433 to 473. By now, the corporate budget cycle of which that plan was a part was well under way. The study, however, indicated that sales and contribution to profit for fiscal 1985 at the 473 level would be much less than could be obtained with an optimal salesforce size of over 700. Although Nelson was unsure how fast Syntex Labs could hire and train sales reps, the study clearly showed that a salesforce growth rate of only 40 reps per year would severely limit both present and future profitability.

The study results had been presented by Laurence Lewis, manager of promotion research, and Syntex Labs' liaison to the consultants that had done the analysis. Following Lewis's initial presentation, Nelson arranged a second presentation for Stephen Knight, senior vice president of marketing for human pharmaceuticals. They had agreed that the results were so dramatic that, if they had confidence in the results, they should attempt to interrupt the corporate planning cycle and request more sales reps.

COMPANY BACKGROUND

Syntex Corporation began in 1940 when Russell Marker, a steroid chemist, derived a cheap and abundant source of steroid hormones from the black, lumpy root of a vine growing wild in the jungles of the Mexican state of Veracruz. Syntex's first products were oral contraceptives and topical steroid preparations prescribed by gynecologists and dermatologists respectively. By 1982 Syntex Corporation had become an international life sciences company that developed, manufactured, and marketed a wide range of health and personal care products. Fiscal 1981 consolidated sales were $710.9 million with $98.6 million net income. Since 1971, Syntex had recorded a 23 percent compound annual growth rate.

SYNTEX LABORATORIES

Syntex Laboratories, the U.S. human pharmaceutical sales subsidiary, was the largest Syntex subsidiary. During fiscal 1981, Syntex Laboratories' sales increased 35 percent to $215,451,000, and grew as a percentage of total pharmaceutical sales to 46 percent, continuing a recent upward trend. Operating profit in 1981 was 27 percent of net sales. Syntex Laboratories developed, manufactured, and marketed anti-inflammatories used to treat several forms of arthritis; analgesics used to treat pain; oral contraceptives; respiratory products; and topical products prescribed by dermatologists for skin diseases. Syntex emphasized pharmaceutical research in support of these existing product lines, and in several important new therapeutic areas, including immunology, viral diseases, and cardiovascular medicine.

---

1. This case was prepared by Associate Professor Darral G. Clarke as the basis for class discussion rather than to illustrate either effective or ineffective handling of an administrative situation.

Copyright ©1983 by the President and Fellows of Harvard College. No part of this publication may be reproduced, stored in a retrieval system, or transmitted in any form or by any means—electronic, mechanical, photocopying, recording, or otherwise—without the permission of Harvard Business School. Distributed by HBS Case Services, Harvard Business School, Boston, MA 02163. Printed U.S.A.

SYNTEX LABS' PRODUCT LINE

Syntex Labs' product line consisted of seven major products. Naprosyn was by far the largest and most successful, while Norinyl and the topical steroids represented Syntex's early development as a drug manufacturer. Exhibit 1 presents retail drug purchases and market shares for Syntex products.

Naprosyn

Naprosyn[2] was the third largest selling drug in the nonsteroidal anti-inflammatory (NSAIDs) therapeutic class[3] in the country, behind Clinoril and Motrin. NSAIDs were used in the treatment of arthritis.

Major selling points for Naprosyn were its dosage flexibility (250, 375, 500 mg tablets), twice-daily regimen (less frequent than for competing products), and low incidence of side effects within a wide dosage range. The NSAI market in fiscal 1980 was $478 million. Exhibit 2 has details of NSAI market trends.

The extremely competitive arthritis drug market would soon become even more competitive as other pharmaceutical firms entered the huge and fast-growing market for alternatives to aspirin in treating arthritis. According to one expert, Naprosyn would "weather the storm (of increased competition) better than any existing agent, although its share will be lower in 1985 than today."

Anaprox

Anaprox was launched in the United States early in fiscal 1981. It was initially marketed for analgesic use and for the treatment of menstrual pain. Nearly twice as many prescriptions were written for analgesics as for anti-arthritics in the United States, making this an important, but highly competitive, market. Exhibit 2 presents details on analgesic market trends.

At the end of fiscal 1981, the U.S. Food and Drug Administration approved Anaprox for the treatment of mild to moderate, acute or chronic, musculoskeletal and soft-tissue inflammation.

Topical steroids

Lidex and Synalar were Syntex's topical steroid creams for treating skin inflammations. Fiscal 1981 sales of dermatological products, Syntex's second largest product category, were only slightly ahead of sales in 1980. U.S. patents on two of the active ingredients in Lidex and Synalar expired during 1981, but other Lidex ingredients continued to be protected under formulation patents. Syntex anticipated some continued growth from these two important products and new dermatological products were under development.

During fiscal 1980, Syntex was the only established company to increase total prescription volume in topical steroids, while two new entrants grew from smaller shares. Market shares of new prescriptions and total prescriptions are shown in Exhibit 3. Syntex had a very strong following among dermatologists—21 percent of all new topical steroid prescriptions written by dermatologists were for Syntex products. Topicort, a competitor's brand, had enjoyed 65 percent growth ($3.66 million to $6.02 million) as a result of successful selling to both dermatologists and general practitioners.

---

2. All Syntex Labs product names are registered trademarks.
3. Drugs used for similar purposes were combined for reporting purposes into groups called *therapeutic classes*.

Norinyl

Total drugstore sales for oral contraceptives (OC) in 1980 were up 23 percent over the previous year, but this dollar-volume growth was primarily the result of a price increase. Total cycle[4] sales declined by 3.5 percent. New prescriptions overall declined 1.5 percent, while new prescriptions for low-dose oral contraceptives increased by 21 percent.

Syntex's oral contraceptive, Norinyl, was available in three dosages that together totaled $37 million, or 10 percent of the market. The low-dose segment was the growth segment of the OC market; 30 percent of all new prescriptions were for low-dose products. Mid-dose products accounted for 54 percent of all new prescriptions, and high-dose products, only 16 percent.

The oral contraceptive market was extremely competitive, with seven major competitors and dozens of products. Syntex's fiscal 1981 sales increase was due primarily to larger sales to the Agency for International Development than in the previous year, price increases, and the introduction of low-dose Norinyl, which was approved by the FDA in that year. Exhibit 3 contains OC market trends.

Nasalide

Nasalide was a steroid nasal spray for the treatment of hay fever and perennial allergies. It was approved for U.S. marketing early in fiscal 1982.

THE SALES REPRESENTATIVE

The sales rep's job was to visit physicians and encourage them to prescribe Syntex drugs for their patients. This was usually done by providing the physician with samples and with information about the appropriate dosage for various medical uses. Performance of this task was complicated by the difficulty of getting appointments with busy physicians, obtaining and maintaining credibility as a reliable source of information on drug use, the number of competing sales reps vying for the physician's time, and the difficulty in measuring the results of the detailing effort.

Robert Nelson described the physician visit as follows:

> A good sales rep will have a pretty good idea of what the physician's prescribing habits are. For example, most physicians are aware of Naprosyn by now, so our sales rep would try to find out what the physician's usage level is. If the physician was not prescribing Naprosyn, the sales rep would present clinical studies comparing Naprosyn with other drugs, probably stressing Naprosyn's lower incidence of side effects and its twice-a-day regimen and then request the physician to prescribe Naprosyn for their next six rheumatism patients. The same sort of information might be used to persuade a physician to move Naprosyn up from third choice to second or first choice. Physicians already prescribing Naprosyn could be encouraged to increase the dose for severe cases from 750 to 1,000 mg per day, using recent research showing Naprosyn to be safe at those levels. New uses cleared by the FDA could also be explained, or the rep might just reinforce the physician's choice of Naprosyn and counteract competitors' claims for their drugs.

The choice of which physicians to visit, how often to visit them, and what to present was a major consideration for the individual sales rep. Though sales management might

---

4. Oral contraceptive sales were recorded by the amount of the drug used for one menstrual cycle.

set quotas and provide guidelines, on a day-to-day basis the final choice was largely the rep's. Laurence Lewis explained:

> Sales reps tend to divide the physicians in their territories into two groups: "pre-scription-productive" physicians and "easy-to-call-on" physicians. Suppose a company sets a minimum daily call average of seven. The sales rep tries to visit the most productive physicians first; they are busy physicians for the most part, so the rep may have to wait a while to see them. Later in the day the sales rep gets nervous about making the seven calls so he fills in with easy-to-call-on physicians that might not be terribly productive. His bonus, however, is based on quota and annual sales increase over the previous year, So he can't be totally unconcerned about the productivity of the physicians he visits.

Nelson felt that once the decision had been made about the number of sales reps and the sales territories had been defined and assigned, the limits of his organizational authority had about been reached. Decisions he might make about which physician specialties to visit and what drugs to feature would be subject to individual reps' interpretation and preferences. It would be necessary to educate and motivate the reps to act in accordance with the sales plan. If the reps didn't agree with the plan, strict quotas and overly directive policies would be counterproductive.

SALES MANAGEMENT AT SYNTEX LABS

Robert Nelson had been promoted to vice president of sales from director of marketing research. In his new position, he reported directly to Stephen Knight, the senior vice president of marketing for Syntex Laboratories. Reporting to Nelson through Frank Poole, the national sales manager, were 6 regional, 47 district sales managers, and 433 general sales reps. Also reporting to him separately was a group of reps that specialized in hospital sales and dermatology sales.

After some consideration, Nelson decided he had a few major decisions of a relatively strategic nature to make in managing the salesforce: the size of the sales force and its geographic allocation were of obvious importance. Call frequency, allocation of sales calls across physician specialties, and product-featuring policies were also important decisions that were relatively difficult to change once implemented.

Sales Force Size

Data available in 1980 showed that Syntex's salesforce[5] was rather small compared with those of its direct competitors:

NSAI		Oral Contraceptives		Topical Steroids	
Upjohn	930	Ortho	330	Schering	615
Merck	955	Wyeth	724	Squibb	761
McNeil	457	Searle	405	Lederle	600
Pfizer	663			Hoechst	379

---

5. This case deals only with the general salesforce and does not include the hospital salesforce. For simplicity, "salesforce" will be used to mean the general salesforce.

It was by no means obvious to Nelson, however, how much larger the Syntex sales-force needed to be. Since each competitor had a different product line that required calling on a different mix of physician specialties. it wasn't clear how the size of the Syntex salesforce should compare with the others.

Call frequency

The 433 sales reps at Syntex had been generally adequate to support a six-week call cycle (each physician was scheduled to be visited once every six weeks) with approximately 70,000 targeted physicians. Indeed. this was how the number of reps had been determined in the first place. Since many of the physicians Syntex visited were visited by other companies with four-week call cycles, Nelson had considered that possibility.

The four-week call cycle seemed attractive for at least two reasons. First, if one believed that the sales force had a positive influence on physicians' prescribing behavior, it seemed reasonable that offering less frequent positive contact than the competition had to hurt. Second. dermatologists and rheumatologists had been visited by Syntex sales reps in nearly a four-week cycle, and these were felt to be Syntex's most successful physician specialty groups.

Allocation of sales effort across products and physician specialties

The necessity to allocate salesforce effort across various physician specialties was apparent from the number of physicians in various specialties—a total of 135,229 physicians in office-based practice. Visiting all of them in a four-week call cycle would have required at least 1,200 sales reps (assuming no geographic complications). This would have been nearly three times as large as Syntex Labs' current salesforce and nearly one-third larger than that of its largest competitor.

The Syntex sales policy called for a rep to attempt to make seven sales calls per day, during which presentations would be made for two or three Syntex products. (The average was 2.7 presentations per sales call.) Which products would be featured depended on a number of factors, such as the physician's specialty, the availability of new information on Syntex product efficacy and or comparative advantages, and national sales priorities

The fact that not all physicians were likely to prescribe all of Syntex's products complicated the choice of both product presentations and physician specialties. The fact that a sales rep could make an average of seven calls and 19 presentations in a day did not necessarily mean that a recommended product-featuring schedule could be followed exactly. For example, if the rep called on four dermatologists and three obstetricians in a particular day, there would be no opportunity to make Naprosyn presentations.

Geographic allocation of sales force

When Robert Nelson became vice president of sales, geographic allocation of the sales-force seemed to be the most critical factor, so it had received immediate attention. The problem turned out to be a reasonably tractable one, however. Gathering information about the location of physicians and competitors' sales reps was a huge data-gathering task, but as Laurence Lewis explained:

> Almost everyone deploys their sales reps based on regional physician counts. We made an effort to get away from just physician counts, and looked at market potential. I know other companies have done that. In the end, it all came down to where Lilly, Pfizer, Merck, and ourselves would all have a rep in a given geo-

graphical territory. Maybe one of the big companies would have two reps in a particular territory, but regional deployment ended up being almost standard. I don't suppose any of us have any real hope of coming up with good enough data to really override that allocation, at least at the territory level. We finally built a model at the state level which is based on six factors that are weighted differentially according to management judgment. We assumed that when we got below the state level a lot of geographical things, or whatever, would have to be taken into account. We now have a comfortable deployment scheme at the state level. But we still have to know how many sales reps we should have in total and what specialties we are going to push.

SALESFORCE STRATEGY MODEL

Nelson and Knight had observed that the rapid growth of Naprosyn was changing the balance in Syntex Laboratories. According to Knight:

We had always been a specialty-oriented company. We began with a product for dermatologists, then followed that with an oral contraceptive, so we visited OB-GYNs[6] too, and for the first 15 years those were the main physicians we visited, along with a limited number of primary-care physicians.[7] So we've thought of ourselves as a small, specialty-oriented pharmaceutical company. Along came Naprosyn and suddenly we had the ninth largest selling drug in the U.S. and we were growing at over 25 percent a year. We were being forced to rethink just what kind of a company we were. It was this dynamic change in the nature of Syntex that led us to consider a more sophisticated analysis.

According to Nelson:

We knew we had some opportunities to expand the salesforce. We could see how rapidly Naprosyn was growing and that our detailing penetration with generalist doctors was very low compared to the big anti-arthritis competitors like Upjohn and Merck. They each had 900 sales reps, so we knew we were behind them. But we were trying to make major plans on the back of envelopes! We'd make notes like: If there are 60,000 generalist doctors and we've got this many people, how many calls can we make a year if each of them makes 1,360 calls a year? How are we going to divvy up those calls? We then realized we were saying that all these doctors respond to sales reps the same way, and yet we all knew that they didn't. But we could never make the differences explicit! We were assuming all products responded the same way, and we knew that wasn't right. Finally we asked ourselves if there wasn't some better way to do this.

In an effort to find a better way, Nelson created the position of manager of promotion research. The position was filled by Laurence Lewis, an analyst in the marketing research department who had earlier been a sales rep. Lewis's first task was to identify a method for determining the size of the salesforce and allocating salesforce effort across products and physician specialties. After studying the marketing research and trade literature and con-

6. OB-GYN–obstetrician and gynecologist
7. Primary-care physicians (PCP) include physicians specializing in internal medicine, general practice, and family practice.

sulting other knowledgeable people, Lewis decided to approach Leonard Lodish, a professor at the Wharton School, whose name had surfaced repeatedly during his research.

Lodish was subsequently invited to visit Syntex and make a presentation on his approach to determining salesforce size and sales effort allocation. Two aspects of his approach struck responsive chords with Knight and Nelson. Nelson stated:

> One of the attractive features of the approach was getting our sales and marketing management people together and making explicit what we believed about how each of our products responds to detailing.

Knight felt that:

> Our history had been one of increasing the salesforce size in relatively small steps. I've never been really satisfied that there was any good reason why we were expanding by 30 or 50 representatives in any one year other than that was what we were able to get approved in the budget process. Over the years I'd become impatient with the process of going to the well for more people every year with no long-term view to it. I felt that if I went to upper management with a more strategic, or longer-term viewpoint, it would be a lot easier to then sell the annual increases necessary to get up to a previously established objective in salesforce size and utilization.

Subsequently, a contract was signed with Management Decision Systems (MDS), a Boston area-based management consulting firm of which Lodish was a principal, to produce a salesforce strategy model for Syntex. Laurence Lewis was appointed liaison with MDS.

Model development process

The salesforce strategy model (SSM) was designed to help Syntex management deploy the salesforce strategically. The model would be used to calculate the amount of sales effort to direct to various Syntex products and physician specialties, and to maximize the net contribution for a given salesforce size. Repeated applications of the model with different numbers of reps could be used to make decisions on the best totals.

The technique used in the model combined management science techniques with historical data and management judgment to calculate the incremental gain in net contribution for each additional amount of sales resource (either product presentations or physician calls).

Defining the model inputs

The SSM used information from various sources. The average number of presentations per sales call, the number of sales calls per day, the contribution margin for Syntex products, and the cost per sales representative were estimated from company records and syndicated data sources. (See Exhibit 4.) The current allocation of salesforce effort was a key element in developing the model, since these data provided the background for Syntex managers to use in estimating the response of various Syntex products and physician groups to different levels of sales effort.

There were two separate, but similar, versions of the SSM model. One sought to allocate the number of *sales rep visits to physician specialties* to maximize contribution, while the other sought the optimal allocation of *sales presentations to Syntex products*. Each estimated the optimal sales force size independently of the other.

The judgmental estimates of response to sales effort were obtained during a series of special meetings held in conjunction with the annual marketing planning meetings. Leonard Lodish, Stephen Knight, Robert Nelson, Laurence Lewis, Frank Poole, and a few product managers and regional sales managers participated. According to Lewis:

> The meeting began with a short lecture on sales response and an exercise in which we were each asked to come up with an optimal sales plan for a sales rep who had six accounts and four products. Trying to do this led us to understand what the model would try to accomplish and demonstrated the impossibility of trying to plan by hand for more than 400 sales reps selling six or more products to 13 different physician specialties.

The main agenda of the meetings was to come to a group consensus on the likely response of each Syntex product and physician specialty to sales rep effort. On Monday, the first day of the annual meetings, worksheets were distributed to the participants on which they were asked to estimate the change in sales for each of seven Syntex Labs' products and nine physician specialties that would result from different levels of sales rep activity. Each manager responded to the following question for each product and specialty:

According to the strategic plan, if the current level of salesforce effort is maintained from 1982 to 1985, sales of Naprosyn (Anaprox, etc.) could be the planned level. What would happen to Naprosyn's (Anaprox, etc.) 1985 sales (compared with present levels) if during this same time period it received:

1. no sales effort?
2. one-half the current effort?
3. 50 percent greater sales effort?
4. a saturation level of sales effort?

After a summary of the participants' answers had been presented to the group and discussed, new worksheets were passed out and the process repeated. When a reasonable consensus had been obtained, the meeting was recessed.

Following this meeting, a preliminary version of the model was produced. When the group reconvened on Friday, a preliminary analysis was presented and the results were discussed. The initial analysis appeared generally reasonable to the participants and, after a final discussion and some later fine-tuning, resulted in the response estimates that appear in Exhibit 5. Commenting on the process, Knight explained:

> Of course, we knew that the responses we estimated were unlikely to be the "true responses" in some absolute knowledge sense, but we got the most knowledgeable people in the company together in what seemed to me to be a very thorough discussion and the estimates represented the best we could do at the time. We respect the model results, but we'll utilize them with cautious skepticism.

According to Poole, "We did the best we could to estimate the model. At first we were uncomfortable at having to be so specific about things we weren't too sure about. but by the end of the discussions, we were satisfied that this was the best we could do."

Model structure

The salesforce strategy model assisted a manager in determining the size of the salesforce and the allocation of sales effort across products or customers by:

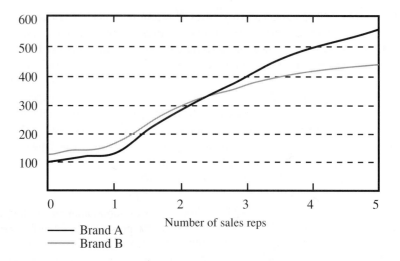

Brand A
Brand B

1. Predicting the net contribution and sales volume that would result from a particular salesforce size and allocation policy; and
2. Providing an efficient means of searching over various sales force sizes to find both the optimal sales force size and the optimal allocation policy

The basic concept of the model was quite simple: each additional sales rep should be assigned to visit the specialty which. considering the allocation of the current salesforce, would provide the highest incremental contribution. Consider the following example of a company that has

1. Two products—A and B
2. Three sales reps who sell only A, and two sales reps who sell only B
3. The response of A and B to sales effort specified below

Suppose now that the company wants to add two sales reps. The model considers the additional reps sequentially. If the first new rep is assigned to sell product A, the result will be $100 incremental contribution ($500–400). If the first new rep is assigned to sell B, only $75 incremental contribution ($375–300) will result. Thus, the first sales rep should be assigned to sell product A. The company now has 4 "A sales reps," and 2 "B sales reps." If the second new rep is assigned to sell product B, he or she could still generate $75 incremental contribution. But if assigned to sell A, only $50 could be generated.[8] So the second new sales rep should be assigned to sell B.

Exhibit 6 presents a portion of the model output allocating sales representatives to specialties. At each step in the analysis, the model indicated the number of reps already allocated, the number of new reps allocated, and to which specialty. If successive additional reps were to be allocated to the same specialty, they were accumulated in a single step.

The SSM could be used to determine the optimal number of sales reps by increasing the size of the salesforce and observing the net contribution to profit and incremental contribution per sales rep added. At each salesforce size, the salesforce was optimally deployed, and the optimal salesforce size was the one with maximum net contribution and incremental net contribution per added rep equal to zero.

8. The simplified algorithm presented here does not assure an optimal solution for S-shaped response curves. The actual SSM algorithm is the same in spirit as this example but has a refinement to assure an optimal solution for all reasonable response functions.

Syntex management had estimated response functions for both products and specialties, so running the model in both modes would provide a validity check on the approach in general. The specialty-based analysis indicated an optimum salesforce size of 768, and the product-based analysis 708 sales reps.

Results of the SSM analysis

The recommended optimal salesforce sizes computed on the basis of physician specialty and products were reasonably close together. The models differed considerably, however, in their estimation of incremental net contribution per added sales rep at levels between the current salesforce size and 600 reps. (See Exhibit 7.)

Not only did both SSM analyses indicate that the current Syntex salesforce was too small, it also showed that allocation was suboptimal. According to the specialty-based analysis, FY 1985 net contribution at the present salesforce size would be more than $7.2 million less than could be obtained with an optimal deployment policy. (See Exhibit 8.)

A direct comparison of present and optimal deployment according to the product-based analysis was somewhat more difficult, since the SSM indicated that Anaprox should either receive no sales attention or the equivalent of the next 130 sales reps. Nothing in between was optimal. This resulted in reported optimal salesforce sizes of 369 and 499 sales reps, but no report on the current size of 433. The SSM results were clear, however, that the current Syntex allocation of effort across products was even more suboptimal than it had been across specialists. Exhibit 9 shows that when 369 sales reps were optimally deployed across products, sales and net contribution would be $50.5 million and $45.7 million higher, respectively.

Finally, with both optimal salesforce size and optimal deployment, FY 1985 sales and contribution (see Exhibit 10) would be dramatically larger than with the current salesforce size and optimal deployment:

SSM Predicted FY 1985 Sales and Contribution from Optimal Deployment

According to	Sales Force Size	Sales ($MM)	Net Contribution($MM)
Specialty model			
(current)	434	$373.1	$221.1
	429	380.1	227.6
	768	447.7	251.7
Product Model			
(current)	430	$373.1	$222.2
	369	423.6	264.2
	708	485.9	279.6

Management implications

Robert Nelson had expected that the salesforce would be found to be too small and that Naprosyn probably needed more emphasis, but no one had anticipated that the optimal salesforce size would be between 700 and 800 reps. According to Laurence Lewis:

> When Len [Lodish] asked how far out he should run the thing, we were standing at 430 reps and I said. "Why don't you run it out to 550 or the maximum, whichever comes first." We knew we weren't paying enough attention to Naprosyn because our major NSAI competitors outnumbered us so far, and

that's our biggest and most important market. We also knew that Naprosyn was our most important product, but we didn't really know to what *degree* it was our most important product. We had the perception that a lot of the attention given to launching three new products had been at the expense of our smaller products, but the model showed it had come out of Naprosyn and that was exactly what we hadn't wanted to happen.

When he received the SSM analyses, Lewis decided four major conclusions could be drawn from them:

1. Until the size of the salesforce approaches 700 general representatives, profitability will not be a constraint to adding representatives.
2. From the FY 1981 base of roughly 430 representatives, Syntex Labs should grow to an optimal allocation of sales effort rather than by redeploying the current salesforce. This could be done by devoting additional sales resources largely to the primary-care audience.
3. Naprosyn was the largest product in Syntex's product line, the most sales-responsive, and highly profitable. Thus Syntex Labs should make it the driving force behind nearly all deployment and allocation decisions.
4. Syntex should consider itself a major generalist company, since optimal deployment would require the greatest portion of a large salesforce to be devoted to the generalist physician audience.

Although enthusiastic about these conclusions, Lewis added a note of caution to their acceptance:

A significant change in the marketplace that would decrease the ability of any of our products to compete would challenge the validity of the model output. Such phenomena as a product recall or a revolutionary new competitive product might act to reduce the value of this model.

Significant error in the sales response estimates of either products or specialties could lead to reduced validity of model output. The similarity between the two model outputs derived from independent response estimates hints at the low likelihood of significant error in the sales response estimates. The model would be most sensitive to significant error in the estimate of Naprosyn's sales responsiveness.

Lewis had concluded his presentations of the study results by stating that Robert Nelson and Stephen Knight were faced with two choices if they decided not to expand the salesforce to an optimal size. They could:

1. Optimize the physician sales call allocation with a smaller than optimal sales force by dramatically reducing coverage of specialists to increase calls on primary-care physicians. This option would maximize sales for the number of sales reps by leading to large gains in Naprosyn at the expense of sales losses in oral contraceptives and topical steroids.
2. Limit Naprosyn's growth to substantially less than its potential, while maintaining the present contact levels with Syntex's traditional specialist physicians and older products.

	Retail Drug Purchases (000s)			*Total RX (000s)*		
	July 80–July 81	**81–82**	**%**	**80–81**	**81–82**	**%**
Therapeutic Class						
NSAI (anti-arthritics)						
Market	$477,834	$533,980	+16%	49,759	51,466	+3%
Naprosyn	90,448	114,242	+26%	6,837	7,849	+19%
Syntex share	18.92%	21.42		13.7%	15.3%	
Analgesic (pain killers)						
Market	$315,324	$346,784	+1%	89,774	91,881	+2%
Anaprox	8,119	13,027	+60%	762	1,569	+106%
Syntex share	2.5%	3.8%		0.8%	1.7%	
Oral Contraceptives						
Market (all forms)	$359,942	$442,669	+23%	50,811	53,896	+6%
Syntex total	36,925	50,726	+37%	5,636	5,865	+4%
Syntex share	10.3%	11.42		11.1%	10.9%	
Topical Steroids (skin ointments)						
Market	$138,895	148,895	+7%	24,948	24,531	+2%
Syntex products	31,361	37,768	+20%	5,181	5,241	+1%
Syntex share	22.6%	25.4%		20.8%	21.4%	

	New RX (000s)		
	80–81	**81–82**	**%**
Therapeutic Class			
NSAI (anti-arthritics)			
Market	23,829	24,569	+3%
Naprosyn	3,323	3,656	+10%
Syntex share	13.9%	14.9%	
Analgesic (pain killers)			
Market	65,976	67,160	+2%
Anaprox	591	1,040	+76%
Syntex share	0.9%	1.5%	
Oral Contraceptives			
Market (all forms)	13,730	13,182	–0.4%
Syntex total	1,620	1,520	–7%
Syntex share	11.8%	11.5%	
Topical Steroids (skin ointments)			
Market	15,345	15,009	–2%
Syntex products	3,044	3,103	+2%
Syntex share	19.8%	20.7%	

EXHIBIT 1
Syntex Laboratories (A) Recent Sales Trends in Syntex*
*Compiled from IMS data

Nonsteroidal anti-inflammatory market trends

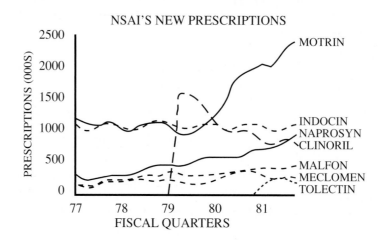

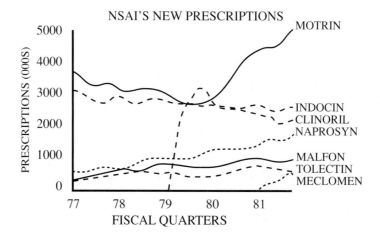

EXHIBIT 2
Syntex Laboratories (A)

Analgesic (drug store only) market trends

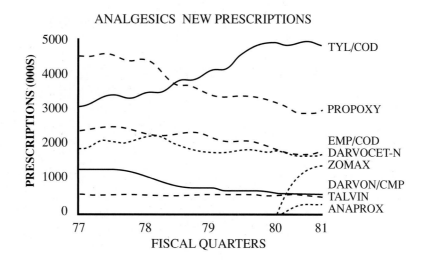

ANALGESICS NEW PRESCRIPTIONS

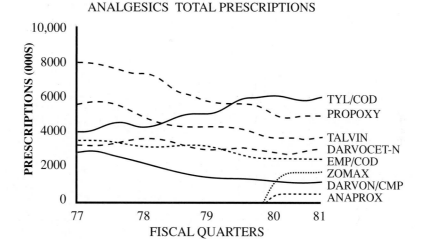

ANALGESICS TOTAL PRESCRIPTIONS

EXHIBIT 2 cont'd.
Syntex Laboratories (A)

Topical steriod market trends

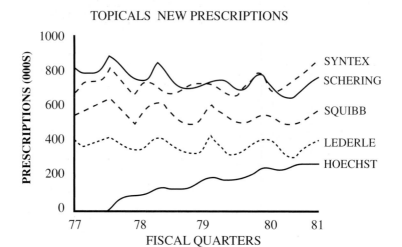

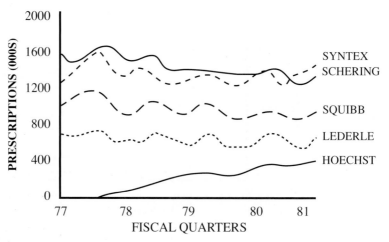

EXHIBIT 3
Syntex Laboratories (A): Topical steriod market trends

Oral contraceptive market trends

OC'S NEW PRESCRIPTIONS

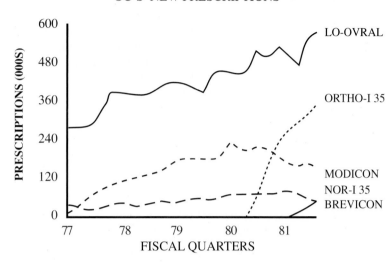

OC'S CYCLE VOLUME

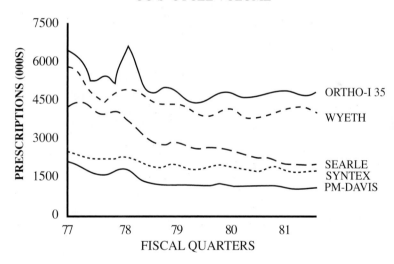

EXHIBIT 3 cont'd.
Syntex Laboratories (A): Topical steriod market trends

Normal planned 1985 calls or presentations based on FY 1981.

Products (Presentations)		Specialties (Calls)	
Naprosyn	358,000	General practice	124,000
Anaprox	527,000	Family practice	108,000
Norinyl 135	195.000	Internal medicine	98,000
Norinyl 150	89,000	Orthopedic surgeon	54,000
Lidex	101,000	Rheumatologist	13,000
Synalar	110,000	Obstetrician/	
Nasalide	210,000	gynecologist	117,000
TOTAL	1,590,000	Dermatologist	50,000
Aver/rep.	3,677	Allergist	14,000
		Ear, nose, throat	12,000
		TOTAL	590,000
		Aver/rep.	1,360

Planned 1985 sales ($000) with present policy(Syntex 1985 estimates by product, allocated to specialties on FY 1981 product by specialty distribution).

Product		Specialty	
Naprosyn	$214,400	General practice	$92,398
Anaprox	36,500	Family practice	78,083
Norinyl 135	21,200	Internal medicine	79,082
Norinyl 150	37,200	Orthopedic surgeon	19,671
Lidex	38,000	Rheumatologist	16,961
Synalar	14,600	Obstetrician/	
Nasalide	11,200	gynecologist	51,312
TOTAL	$373,100	Dermatologist	26,598
		Allergist	3,434
		Ear, nose, throat	5,561
		TOTAL	$373,100

Contribution as percent of Factory Selling Price.

Product		Specialty	
Naprosyn	70%	General practice	67.6%
Anaprox	55	Family practice	67.8
Norinyl 135	72	Internal medicine	68.1
Norinyl 150	72	Orthopedic surgeon	68.4
Lidex	62	Rheumatologist	67.5
Synalar	53	Obstetrician/	
Nasalide	52	gynecologist	66.2
		Dermatologist	55.3
		Allergist	62.5
		Ear, nose, throat	62.2

Estimated 1985 average cost per representative (excluding samples) $57,000.
Estimated 1985 fixed selling overhead (present organization) $2,800,000.

EXHIBIT 4
Syntex Corporation (A) Basic Model Inputs*
* 1985 plans have been disguised.

Product Response Functions

	No Calls	One-Half	Present	50% More	Saturation
Naprosyn	47	68	100	126	152
Anaprox	15	48	100	120	135
Norinyl 135	31	63	100	115	125
Norinyl 150	45	70	100	105	110
Lidex	56	80	100	111	120
Synalar	59	76	100	107	111
Nasalide	15	61	100	146	176

Specialty Response Functions

	No Calls	One-Half	Present	50% More	Saturation
General practice	29	62	100	120	136
Family practice	31	62	100	124	140
Internal medicine	43	69	100	111	120
Orthopedic surgeon	34	64	100	116	130
Rheumatologist	41	70	100	107	112
Obstetrician/ gynecologist	31	70	100	110	116
Dermatologist	48	75	100	107	110
Allergist	17	60	100	114	122
Ear, nose, throat	20	59	100	117	125

EXHIBIT 5
Syntex Laboratories (A)

Step No.	No. of Reps.	Chg. In Reps.	Sales (000s)	Chg In Sales (000s)	Net Profit (000s)	Chg. In Net Profit Per Rep (000s)	Alloc. To:
26	391.8	0.9	367,818	312.4	224,144	185.7	RHEU
27	392.6	0.8	368,119	300.5	224,285	176.0	ENT
28	428.7	36.1	380,052	11,933.4	230,390	169.1	ORS
29	437.0	8.3	382,766	2,713.5	231,752	164.3	GP
30	463.7	26.7	393,586	10,820.2	235,995	158.7	DERM
31	470.9	7.2	395,871	2,285.4	237,133	157.6	FP
32	477.5	6.6	397,911	2,039.6	238,149	155.0	IM
33	480.8	3.3	399,201	1,290.2	238,646	148.7	DERM
34	481.6	0.8	399,463	262.2	238,763	146.3	ENT
35	489.4	7.8	401,814	2,350.5	239,873	142.0	OBGYN
36	493.0	3.6	402,863	1,049.4	240,385	141.9	ORS
37	493.9	0.9	403,114	251.1	240,505	138.1	RHEU
38	502.2	8.3	405,412	2,297.6	241,586	130.4	GP
39	509.7	7.5	407,603	2,191.4	242,529	125.9	ALLG
40	510.6	0.9	407,874	270.8	242,645	123.9	ALLG
41	517.8	7.2	409,787	1,913.1	243,530	122.7	FP
42	524.4	6.6	411,452	1,665.1	244,291	116.1	IM
43	525.2	0.8	411,659	206.4	244,374	103.0	ENT
44	533.5	8.3	413,610	1,951.8	245,221	102.2	GP
45	534.4	0.9	413,814	203.8	245,309	101.3	RHEU

Key:
GP   general practice
FP   family practice
IM   internal medicine
ORS   orthopedic surgeon
RHEU   rheumatologist
OBGYN   obstetrician/gynecologist
DERM   dermatologist
ALLG   allergist
ENT   ear, nose, throat

EXHIBIT 6
Syntex Laboratories (A): Syntex Laboratories Sales Force Strategy Model Specialty Allocation.

Contribution to profit versus number of sales reps.

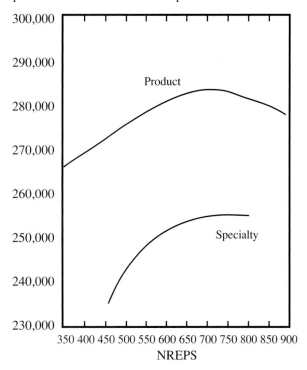

Marginal contribution versus number of sales reps.

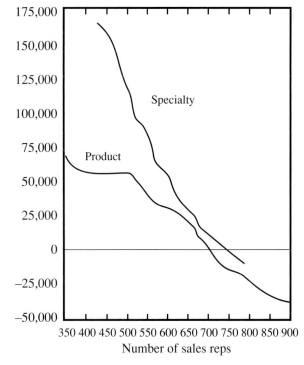

EXHIBIT 7
Syntex Laboratories (A)

Present Policy

Allocation to	Number of Reps	Sales Calls	Sales in Dollars (000s)	Gross Profit (000s)	Net Profit (000s)
GP	91.2	124,000	92,398	62,461	56,715
FP	79.4	108,000	78,083	52,940	47,938
IM	72.1	98,000	79,082	53,855	49,313
ORS	39.7	54,000	19,671	13,455	10,954
RHEU	9.6	13,000	16,961	11,449	10,844
OBGYN	86.0	117,000	51,312	33,969	28,551
DERM	36.8	50,000	26,598	14,709	12,390
ALLG	10.3	14,000	3,434	2,146	1,497
ENT	8.8	12,000	5,561	3,459	2,905
Total	433.8	590,000	373,100	242,837	221,106

SSM Recommended Policy

Allocation to	Number of Reps	Sales Calls	Sales in Dollars (000s)	Gross Profit (000s)	Net Profit (000s)
GP	116.0	157,818	103,915	70,246	63,632
FP	108.3	147,273	92,624	62,799	56,627
IM	78.6	106,909	81,586	55,560	51,079
ORS	36.1	49,091	18,622	12,737	10,680
RHEU	10.4	14,182	17,273	11,660	11,065
OBGYN	70.4	95,727	47,120	31,194	27,181
DERM	0.0	0	12,767	6,805	6,805
ALLG	0.0	0	584	365	365
ENT	8.8	12,000	5,561	3,460	2,956
Total	428.7	583,000	380,052	254,825	227,590

Key:
GP	general practice
FP	family practice
IM	internal medicine
ORS	orthopedic surgeon
RHEU	rheumatologist
OBGYN	bstetrician/gynecologist
DERM	dermatologist
ALLG	allergist
ENT	ear, nose, throat

EXHIBIT 8

Syntex Laboratories (A): Comparision of Existing Policy with Recommended Policy at Current Salesforce Levels *
(1985)

* Optimal allocations are only computed for salesforce sizes in a step (see Exhibit 6). A consequence of this is that allocations are not available for every salesforce size and thus allocated sales force sizes don't exactly match the current level.

Present Policy

Allocation to	Number of Reps	Presentations	Sales in Dollars (000s)	Gross Profits (000s)	Net Profit (000s)
N	96.8	358,000	214,400	150,080	143,981
A	142.4	527,000	36,500	20,075	11,104
N 135	52.7	195,000	21,200	15,264	11,944
N 150	24.1	89,000	37,200	26,784	25,266
L	27.3	101,000	38,000	23,560	21,840
S	29.7	110,000	14,600	7,738	5,867
N	56.8	210,000	11,200	5,824	2,246
Total	429.7	1,590,000	373,100	249,325	222,247

Recommended Policy 369 Reps

Allocation to	Number of Reps	Presentations	Sales in Dollars (000s)	Gross Profits (000s)	Net Profit (000s)
N	246.3	911,272	306,526	214,568	200,530
A	0.0	0	5,475	3,011	3,011
N 135	57.5	212,727	22,019	15,854	12,576
N 150	28.4	105,181	38,049	27,394	25,774
L	37.2	137,727	41,222	21,847	19,726
S	0.0	0	8,614	4,565	4,565
N	0.0	0	1,680	873	873
Total	369.4	1,366,909	423,585	288,115	264,257

Recommended Policy 499 Reps

Allocation to	Number of Reps	Presentations	Sales in Dollars (000s)	Gross Profits (000s)	Net Profit (000s)
N	246.3	911,273	306,527	214,569	200,530
A	129.5	479,091	33,708	18,539	11,159
N 135	57.5	212,727	22,019	15,854	12,577
N 150	28.4	105,182	38,048	27,395	25,774
L	37.2	137,727	41,222	21,848	19,726
S	0.0	0	8,614	4,565	4,565
N	0.0	0	1,680	874	874
Total	498.9	1,846,000	451,819	303,644	272,405

EXHIBIT 9

Syntex Laboratories (A): Comparision of Existing Policy with Recommended Policy at (Near) Current Levels

Optimal Sales Force Policies

Based on Specialties

Allocation to	Number of Reps	Sales Calls	Sales in Dollars (000s)	Gross Profit (000s)	Net Profit (000s)
GP	198.9	270,545	118,680	80,227	68,888
FP	173.3	235,636	104,067	70,558	60,682
IM	131.0	178.182	90,700	61,767	54,299
ORS	61.4	83,454	22,818	15,608	12,110
RHEU	16.5	22,454	18,327	12,371	11,430
OBGYN	117.3	159,545	55,389	36,667	29,980
DERM	43.4	59,091	27,551	14,685	12,208
ALLG	12.2	16,546	3,667	2,292	1,599
ENT	13.6	18,546	6,506	4,047	3,270
Total	767.6	1,044,000	447,706	298,221	251,665

Based on Products

Allocation to	Number of Reps	Sales Calls	Sales in Dollars (000s)	Gross Profit (000s)	Net Profit (000s)
NAPROSYN	263.9	976,363	309,379	216,565	201,524
ANAPROX	168.3	622,818	39,847	21,915	12,321
NORINYL 135	76.7	283,636	24,068	178,329	12,959
NORINYL 150	37.2	137,545	39,060	28,123	26,004
LIDEX	49.6	183,636	43,155	22,872	20,043
SYNALAR	29.7	110,000	14,600	7,738	6,043
NASALIDE	82.6	305.455	15,802	8,217	3,512
Total	708.0	2,619,454	485,911	322,761	279,606

Key:
GP	general practice
FP	family practice
IN	internal medicine
ORS	orthopedic surgeon
RHEU	rheumatologist
OBGYN	obstetrician/gynecologist
DERM	dermatologist
ALLG	allergist
ENT	ear, nose, throat

EXHIBIT 10
Syntex Laboratories (A)

THE JOHN FRENCH EXERCISE: SALES CALL PLANNING FOR UBC (CALLPLAN)

The Unsweetened Breakfast Cereals (UBC) division of Conglomerate, Inc. competes with Post and Kellogg but with a narrower range of products based primarily on corn. UBC estimates that it has about a five percent market share of a $9.8 billion market.

UBC has a mixed distribution system: it does mostly direct delivery to its large accounts using its own fleet of delivery trucks, but relies on distributors to deliver to small accounts. UBC account sales reps operate the trucks, restock store inventories, and interact with store managers to negotiate for shelf space, end-aisle display space, and the like. While running its own fleet is a more costly alternative than the more common industry methods, UBC has found that it achieves a higher level of sales and a higher level of retained margins (by capturing the distributor markup), which makes it a reasonable investment.

In early 1996, corporate pressures to reduce staff and to outsource noncore functions forced UBC to carefully evaluate and document the cost-effectiveness of the operation and make sure it managed the operation in the most efficient manner possible. To help it to control and justify its costs and to conform with Conglomerate's program of salesforce automation, UBC began experimenting with a software tool called CALLPLAN.

CALLPLAN relies on a salesperson's judgmental inputs about likely customer response to calling frequency to suggest optimal allocation of that salesperson's calling time.

To test the CALLPLAN system, UBC management provided its Northeastern US sales force, including its sales rep for eastern and central Pennsylvania, John French, with a prototype of the software. John covers 15 Pennsylvania counties and tries to visit his key accounts at least once a month.

John chose his four accounts in State College for a test: BiLo, Weis, Giant, and O.W. Houts. He travels through Centre County every week anyway (although he does not always stop there). In planning his visits for the next quarter, he thought as follows:

"Let's see...I can visit these accounts up to 12 times a quarter or not at all. Actually, for the large retailers, like BiLo, Weis, and Giant, I wouldn't want to visit less frequently than twice a quarter, and once a quarter would be the minimum for Houts. I'll have to check my records to see what we actually sold through these retailers last quarter and how many times I actually visited them. I also need to fill in the 'judgmental calibration' form to indicate how much more or less I think we could sell if I call more or less often. I can't possibly work more hours total than I do now, so I can spend no more time with these accounts in the next quarter (5.25 days) than I did in the last."

(Those data are saved in a version of CALLPLAN called JFrench.xls, which you should use for this analysis. Select the John French exercise under CALLPLAN in the **Model** menu of the Marketing Engineering software.)

EXERCISES

1. Set up the sales-call constraints as John has specified them and run the optimization in CALLPLAN to get a recommended calling plan. Do the results make sense? Interpret them.

2. John is thinking about putting one or more of these accounts through his distributor. (This is equivalent to removing the minimum visit restriction for each of the accounts.) How does this affect the solution in Question 1? Should he do it?

3. John is rethinking BiLo's likely response to more selling effort because its volume has grown recently. He now believes that 50 percent more effort will bring in 50 percent more sales and unlimited effort will bring in twice the current level of sales. How does this affect his calling frequency (assuming no minimum visit constraints)?

4. John's regional sales manager has suggested that he spend more time at a new Weis store that has just opened in Harrisburg. According to John's best guess, if he made two additional visits to that store each quarter, he would bring in $1,400 more in quarterly sales (with a margin similar to that of the store in State College). Should he do this if it means cutting the number of visits to his State College store-clients to four per quarter (again, assuming no minimum number of visits per quarter for any account and using the calibration from Question 3)?

5. How can CALLPLAN or a similar model be adapted to a range of products, some of which are new (whose sales will not be immediate), or to a mixture of current and prospective accounts? (Prospective accounts may or may not provide any sales at all at low levels of selling effort.) Is the model's objective the right one for these cases? What would you recommend?

J&J FAMILY VIDEO CASE[1]

Jack and Jerilyn Rodeman are longtime residents of Scottsdale, Arizona. Jack recently took early retirement from the aviation division of a leading firm in electronic instrumentation and controls after several years of successfully managing its manufacturing operations. Jeri is currently working part-time as an independent software consultant to small businesses in the Phoenix area. As Jack and Jeri planned the next phase of their life, they decided to open a small service business, such as a cybercafe, a restaurant, or a video store. After discussions with their children and friends, they decided to explore the feasibility of opening a video store close to their home.

Over 85 percent of U.S. households have a VCR and about 50 percent of American households rent a video at least once a month. A "VCR household" had an average of 47 rentals per year at an average price of $2.50 per rental. In 1996, video rentals and sales were estimated to be around $18 billion, with rentals representing about half the industry revenues, and the rest attributed to sales of used videotapes (at around $10 per tape) and other related products. Nationally, there were about 27,500 video stores, but this number had declined from a high of 31,500 in 1990. Although some industry observers believed further consolidation would lead to fewer video stores, others, like Bob Finlayson of the Video Software Dealers Association, believed that consumers will drive only a short distance (three or four miles) to rent a video, and that the number of video outlets would actually increase over the next few years. In fact, a recent trend has been the growth of video rental and sales through supermarkets ($1.9 billion in 1996), mass merchandisers such as Kmart ($200 million in 1996), and even gasoline stations.

Industry leader, Blockbuster Entertainment Group, operated 14 percent of all stores and had more than a 20 percent share of the revenues. Other large companies included Portland-based Hollywood Entertainment and Philadelphia-based West-Coast Entertainment. Blockbuster competed by offering consumers a large selection with an emphasis on recent releases, with stores carrying over 40 copies of some new releases. Blockbuster had a number of large stores that were over 6000 square feet in size, and had over 20,000 rental units under 5,000 or more titles. Smaller video stores were typically less than 2,000 square feet and carried fewer than 6,000 rental units. Video rental prices varied greatly with new releases renting for about $3.50 for two nights at Blockbuster and $3 for a single night at Hollywood Entertainment. Older movies rented for about $1.50 to $2.00 for three nights, and "family movies" rented for as little as 99 cents for two nights. Video stores often had ongoing promotions, such as half-price rentals during "happy hours" (e.g., 9 a.m. to 10 a.m.), or special pricing on selected days (e.g., Tuesdays), and senior citizens discounts.

Jack and Jeri determined that site location would be the primary factor that determined the competitive environment the new store would face and therefore its long-term viability. They hired a consultant friend, Ruby Jackson, to do preliminary research to assess the competitive environment in the catchment area within which they planned to locate their new store. Based on her experience, Ms. Jackson concluded that several factors influence what video stores consumers patronize: (1) the distance of the store from their homes, and (2) overall attractiveness of each store, which could depend on such factors as proximity to other shops, variety of videos for rent, service quality, average price, and size of

---

1. This exercise describes a hypothetical situation. It was developed by Arvind Rangaswamy and Katrin Starke using publicly available information.

the store. She identified eight existing stores with which the proposed new store would compete in the geographical area of interest and gathered preliminary information about these stores. She organized the information into the following table:

Store	Proximity to Other General Shop (1 poor to 7 good)	Estimated Number of Titles Carried	Service Quality (1 good to 7 excellent)	Estimated Average Price per Rental	Size (Square feet)	Estimated Percent Unit Market Share in Study Area (from Traffic Counts)
Discovery Video	2	2,000	6	1.95	1,200	5
Blockbuster Entertainment	6	4,000	3	2.30	4,400	25
Video Connection	2	800	6	1.70	1,000	5
Video Power	5	2,500	4	2.10	1,800	12
Hollywood Entertainment	3	3,500	5	2.20	3,000	20
Movie Arcade	7	1,500	5	1.75	1,000	10
Local Supermarket	7	300	1	2.40	200	5
Action Video	2	1,300	7	2.85	1,400	18

While Blockbuster and Hollywood offered wide variety, such stores as Action Video focused on the latest releases, adult video, and suspense and adventure titles. Video Connection and Movie Arcade focused on older movies and "seconds" of recent releases. Ruby guessed the combined annual sales of these video stores to be around $8 million per year (including sales to people outside the study area).

Jack and Jeri wanted their video store to carry only family-oriented and children's videos (PG or G ratings). They planned to carry a maximum of 1600 titles, including new releases, and they hoped to realize an average rental rate of $2.10. Jeri had access to a software program called Scan/US which she used in her work helping small businesses to develop direct marketing programs. She decided to use this software to evaluate three alternative sites where space was currently available. The table below shows the characteristics of these sites:

Location	Proximity to Other General Shops (1 poor to 7 good)	Estimated Number of Titles	Service Quality (1 good to 7 excellent)	Estimated Average Price Per Rental	Size (Square feet)
Option 1	2	1,200	6	2.10	1,200
Option 2	4	1,600	5	2.10	2,500
Option 3	3	1,200	6	2.10	1,200

EXERCISES

1. Using the tabular data, develop and justify an overall measure of store attractiveness for each existing store and for the three potential sites.

   To answer the following questions, you will need to build a gravity model using Scan/US and Microsoft Excel. Select **J&J Video and Competitors** as your location layer.

2. Insert the overall index of store attractiveness for each store into the gravity model and evaluate which of the three locations that Jack and Jeri are considering would achieve the highest market share. (To evaluate one site at a time, choose a store attractiveness index value of zero for sites not under consideration.)

3. Jeri estimated that the total annual operating costs of an established video store would be roughly $300,000 for a 1200 square-foot store and about $450,000 for a 2500 square-foot store at all three locations. She also estimated that the cost of opening a new store would be between $250,000 and $300,000, depending on its size. These initial costs cover purchasing such items as tapes, furniture and fittings, and computer equipment and software. Are any of the proposed store locations a good business proposition given this cost structure? Why or why not?

4. Jack and Jeri are also concerned about the long-term viability of video stores in view of the growth of direct TV broadcasts and the expansion of cable offerings. They wondered whether the gravity model could be modified in some way to take into account the potential threats posed by these developments. How might they accomplish that?

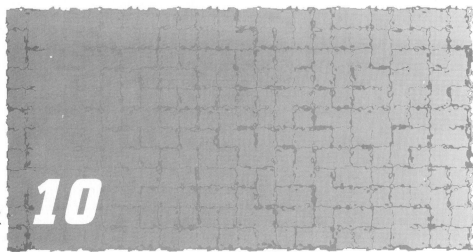

CHAPTER **10**

Price and Sales Promotion Decisions

In this chapter we cover

■ Pricing decisions—the classical economics approach
■ Pricing in practice—orientation to cost, demand, or competition
■ Interactive pricing—reference prices and price negotiations
■ Price discrimination—revenue management
■ Pricing product lines
■ Sales promotional types and effects
■ Aggregate models to analyze promotional effects
■ Analyzing individuals' responses to promotions

Price is the only marketing variable that directly affects revenue. Indeed, if one looks at a profit function as

Profit = (Unit price − Unit cost) × Quantity sold,

one sees that price is involved in all parts of the profit equation. Price affects margin (unit price less unit cost) in two ways: it is the first term (unit price) in the equation by definition, and it has an indirect effect on unit cost, which is often partly determined by the quantity sold. As price affects quantity sold (and hence unit cost indirectly), it is involved in all three components of the foregoing profit equation.

We discuss promotion along with price in this chapter since the most common promotions (deals and coupons) are in fact no more than advertised, temporary price decreases.

PRICING DECISIONS: THE CLASSICAL ECONOMICS APPROACH

From the viewpoint of the classical economist, price is the driving force that allocates goods and services in the marketplace. For the customer it is the cost of a purchase in monetary terms. For the producer or seller it helps determine the level of supply and acts to allocate economic resources on the production side.

A basic relationship in economic theory is known as the Law of Demand, which states that the quantity demanded per period (also known as the time rate of demand) is negatively related to price. This law is based on the postulate of a rational customer who has full knowledge of the available goods and their substitutes, a limited budget, and a singular drive to maximize his or her utility. For a given structure of relative prices, customers will allocate their income over goods (including savings) so as to maximize their utility. If the price relations change, they will normally substitute less expensive goods for more expensive goods; this action will increase their utility.

Central to this model is the concept of price elasticity, defined as the ratio of the percentage change in demand to a percentage change in price:

$$e_{qp} = \frac{\text{Fraction change in demand}}{\text{Fraction change in price}} = \frac{(Q_1 - Q_0) / Q_0}{(P_1 - P_0) / P_0}$$

$$= \frac{\Delta Q/Q}{\Delta P/P} = \frac{\Delta Q}{\Delta P} \frac{P}{Q}, \tag{10.1}$$

where

e_{qp} = elasticity of quantity demanded with respect to change in price;

Q_1 = quantity demanded after price change;

Q_0 = quantity demanded before price change;

P_1 = new price;

P_0 = old price;

$\Delta Q = Q_1 - Q_0$; and

$\Delta P = P_1 - P_0$.

Note that we cannot assess elasticities without specifying a model of how sales (quantity sold) respond to changes in price. In most cases price elasticities are negative. A price elasticity equal to 1.0 means that demand rises (or falls) by the same percentage that price falls (or rises). In such a case total revenue is not affected. A price elasticity greater than one means that demand rises (or falls) by more than the price falls (or rises) in percentage terms, and total revenue rises (or falls). A price elasticity less than one means that demand rises (or falls) by less than the price falls (or rises) in percentage terms, and total revenue falls (or rises).

If we know the price elasticity of demand, we can answer the question of whether the firm's price is too high or too low more precisely. If we want to maximize revenue, the price is too high if the demand elasticity at that price is less than one. Whether this rule holds true for maximizing profit depends on the behavior of costs.

Another measure of the sensitivity of demand to price is the relationship between the price of one good and the quantity demanded of another. This measure is known as the cross-price elasticity of demand, and it is computed for product X as $(\Delta Q_X/\Delta P_Y)(P_Y/Q_X)$, where Y is any other product. If the cross-price elasticity is positive, then products X and Y are substitutes. In this case (for Coke and Pepsi, say), when the price of Coke increases sales of Pepsi will increase, as customers substitute Pepsi for Coke. If the cross-price elasticity is negative, then products X and Y are complements. For example, when the price of computer equipment (hardware) goes down, the demand for related software increases.

Finally, elasticity and marginal revenue are related:

$$\text{Total revenue} = \text{TR} = PQ \quad (\text{Price} \times \text{Quantity}). \tag{10.2}$$

Therefore

$$\text{Marginal revenue} = \frac{\Delta TR}{\Delta Q} = P + Q\,\frac{\Delta P}{\Delta Q}$$

$$= P\left(1 + \frac{Q\Delta P}{P\Delta Q}\right) = P\left(1 + \frac{1}{\varepsilon_{qp}}\right). \tag{10.3}$$

This equation shows that marginal revenue varies with both price and the price elasticity of demand.

The Law of Demand does not specify the shape of the price-quantity relationship. In fact the shape varies with the particular product or product class. However, two equation forms are particularly appropriate for representing this relationship: the linear and constant-elasticity forms.

The general linear demand-price equation, where quantity goes down linearly with increases in price, is

$$Q = a - bP, \tag{10.4}$$

where a and b are constants (Exhibit 10.1). This linear relationship need not apply throughout the domain of possible prices but should be approximately true in the neighborhood of the prevailing price.

How can the price elasticity be determined in the neighborhood of a particular price, say P_1, on a linear demand curve? For the linear demand function, $\Delta Q/\Delta P = b$ and

$$\varepsilon_{qp} = \frac{\Delta Q}{\Delta P} \times \frac{P}{Q} = -b \times \frac{P}{a - bP} = -\frac{bP}{a - bP}. \tag{10.5}$$

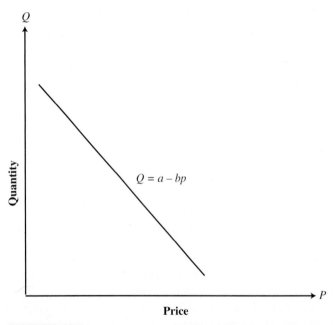

EXHIBIT 10.1
The linear demand-price function, where each $1 decrease in price leads to the same increase (*b* units) in quantity demanded.

Following from this equation:

1. The price elasticity will be minus one when $P = a/2b$.
2. The price elasticity is high (in absolute terms) at high prices, making it desirable to lower price.
3. The price elasticity is low at low prices, making it desirable to raise the price.

Another popular shape for the demand function is based on the notion of constant elasticity. This function (Exhibit 10.2) is

$$Q = aP^{-b}. \tag{10.6}$$

The exponent b is the price elasticity, which is constant for all prices. This form of demand function has been popular among modelers because it includes an explicit term for elasticity, incorporates nonlinear effects of pricing, and is easy to manipulate mathematically. (The Modeler spreadsheet allows you to investigate these simple price models.)

The classical model is based on several key assumptions that limit its applicability, including the following:

- The firm's objective in setting a price is to maximize the short-run profits to be realized from a particular product.
- The only parties to consider in setting the price are the firm's immediate customers.
- Price setting is independent of the levels set for the other variables in the marketing mix.
- The demand and cost equations can be estimated with sufficient accuracy.
- The firm has true control over price—that is, the firm is a price maker not a price taker.
- Market responses to price changes are well understood.

Each of these limitations leads to modifications of the classical model. To deal with one interesting issue—buyer reactions that vary in response to price changes—classical

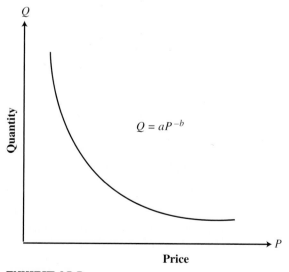

EXHIBIT 10.2
Constant-elasticity price-demand function, where each 1 percent decrease in price leads to a b percent increase in demand.

microeconomic theory usually assumes near-perfect information about market prices and a downward-sloping demand curve. However, all customers will not interpret prices in the same way. A price reduction that would normally attract more customers may not be known to all customers. Furthermore, customers may interpret changes in prices as signifying any of the following:

- The item is about to be superseded by a later model.
- The item has some faults and is not selling well.
- The firm is in financial trouble and may not stay in business to supply future parts.
- The price will come down further and it pays to wait.
- The quality has been reduced.

Conversely a price increase that would normally deter sales may carry a variety of different meanings to potential buyers:

- The item is hot and may soon be unobtainable.
- The item represents an unusually good value.
- The seller is greedy, is charging what the traffic will bear, and may charge more if the potential buyer waits.

Thus demand is affected not only by current price but by the information the price carries and expectations about future prices.

Thus in spite of its conceptual elegance and intuitive appeal, the classical model is not very useful. In practice firms tend to base their pricing decisions on one of three key factors—cost, demand, or competition—and then they rely on models that ignore the other factors.

PRICING IN PRACTICE: ORIENTATION TO COST, DEMAND, OR COMPETITION

Cost-oriented pricing

Many firms set their prices largely or even wholly on the basis of their costs. Typically they count all costs, including an allocation for overhead based on expected operating levels.

The most elementary examples of cost-oriented pricing are markup pricing and cost-plus pricing. They are similar in that price is determined by adding either a fixed amount or a fixed percentage to the unit cost.

Does the use of a rigid, customary markup over cost make logical sense in pricing products? Generally the answer is *no*. Any procedure that ignores current elasticity of demand in setting prices is not likely to lead, except by chance, to maximum profits, either in the long or in the short run. As demand elasticity changes—as it is likely to seasonally, cyclically, and over the product life cycle—the optimum markup should also change. If markup remains a rigid percentage of cost, then under ordinary conditions it would not lead to maximum profits. However, under special conditions a rigid markup at the right level may lead to optimum profit. These special conditions are (1) that average (unit) costs be fairly constant for different points on the demand curve and (2) that costs be constant over time.

Under these conditions the optimal price is

$$P* = \left(\frac{\varepsilon}{1 + \varepsilon}\right) \text{MC}, \tag{10.7}$$

where

ε = price elasticity of demand, assumed to be negative; and

MC = marginal cost.

According to this relationship the optimal price (markup over cost) goes down as price elasticity rises (in absolute value). If price = $(1 + \alpha)$MC, then α is the markup. And from Eq. (10.7), if we set $\varepsilon/(1 + \varepsilon) = (1 + \alpha)$, then $\alpha = \varepsilon/(1 + \varepsilon) - 1$. If price elasticity is low, say $(-)2.0$, as it might be in the case of branded frozen pastry, then $\alpha = 1$ and the optimal markup is high (100%). Furthermore, if the price elasticity remains fairly constant over time, then a rigid markup would be consistent with optimal pricing. Both required conditions—constant (marginal) costs and constant elasticity—characterize many retailing situations. This may explain why rigid markups are in widespread use in retailing and why they may be consistent with optimal-pricing requirements. However, for most durable consumer products and for industrial products it is less likely that the two special conditions hold.

In Chapter 5, when considering marketing strategy we described the concept of the experience curve, where costs were shown to fall with cumulative production experience. Indeed empirical studies show that the declines in costs associated with doubling cumulative production generally are in the 5 to 30 percent range (Dolan and Simon 1996). If such changes in costs can be forecast, then cost-oriented pricing becomes a dynamic phenomenon: that is, the firm can see two effects of lowering price. First, lowering price increases short-term demand. Second, these increases in short-term demand help lower costs (and raise profit margins) through the experience effect. This leads to recommendations contrary to those of the classical model: in the presence of experience-curve cost declines, one generally wants to lower price to accelerate the learning effect and to take advantage of the dynamics of cost reduction. The Price Planning for the ABCOR2000 exercise allows you to explore the impact of the learning curve on pricing decisions.

Demand-oriented pricing

Cost-oriented approaches to pricing center on the costs of producing and distributing the product. Demand-oriented approaches look at the demand for the product at various price levels: they focus on customer value. A central idea behind demand-oriented pricing is to try to charge a higher price when demand is strong and a lower price when demand is weak, even though production costs may remain the same.

Many sophisticated marketers, especially in industrial markets, practice value-based pricing after analyzing the product's value-in-use. The idea behind value-in-use analysis is that the price for a product should be related to the value that product brings to a particular customer. This approach is particularly appropriate for large-volume purchases when the salesperson has discretion in pricing. The idea is for the salesperson to imagine being in the buyer's situation and determine whether it is a good investment for the buyer to adopt the product or to replace the product currently being used with the proposed new product.

The value-in-use of a new product is defined as that price that would make a potential buyer just indifferent between continuing to use the current product and switching to the new product. This calculation is illustrated in the following example.

EXAMPLE

Suppose a chemical plant uses 200 O-rings to seal the valves on pipes that carry corrosive materials. The plant pays $5 for each O-ring and must change them during regular maintenance every two months.

A new product has twice the corrosive resisting power. We can calculate the value-in-use (VIU) of the material:

Solution 1: Annual cost of incumbent product

$$= 200 \text{ (O-rings)} \times 6 \text{ changes per year} \times \$5/\text{O-ring}$$

$$= \$6000$$

$$= 200 \text{ (O-rings)} \times 3 \text{ (changes per year)} \times \text{VIU},$$

or VIU = \$10.

Solution 2: The new material allows a longer time between shutdowns—four months vs. two months—and the cost of a shutdown is \$5,000. Then we get

$$\underbrace{\underbrace{200 \times 6 \times 5}_{\substack{\text{Equipment} \\ \text{Cost}}} + \underbrace{5000 \times 6}_{\substack{\text{Shutdown} \\ \text{Cost}}}}_{\text{Incumbent}} = \underbrace{\underbrace{200 \times 3 \times \text{VIU}}_{\substack{\text{Equipment} \\ \text{Cost}}} + \underbrace{5000 \times 3}_{\substack{\text{Shutdown} \\ \text{Cost}}}}_{\text{New}}$$

or VIU = \$35.

When doing value-based pricing, it is important to incorporate all costs, both tangible and intangible. Aside from the initial cost and operating costs suggested in the example, you must also consider the buyer's planning horizon, the cost of capital, switching costs (retraining, product reformulation, likely start-up inefficiencies), maintenance cost differences, performance differences, differences in flexibility, and the risk a buyer assumes in adopting a new product.

EXAMPLE

(From Lee 1978.) To calculate the value-in-use of a candidate material, we first calculate the cost of using the incumbent material. We call this its *use cost*. This includes not only the price of that material in cents per pound (or gallon, or square yard, etc.), but also the cost of processing, the cost of any finishing operations, the scrap cost, the inventory charges associated with stocking the material, and any other significant item of cost.

Similarly, the use cost of an incumbent *component part* includes not only its purchase price, but also the costs of assembly, adjustment, and so forth.

Finally, if we are comparing two materials or two components whose useful lives differ, and if the difference is valuable, we should take this into account by calculating use cost per year, or annual use cost. The annual use cost for an incumbent material can be calculated by

$$\text{Annual use cost}_{\text{inc.}} = (QC + C_p + C_f + \cdots)/L, \tag{10.8}$$

where

Q = quantity of incumbent material per unit of finished product;

C = purchase price of incumbent material per unit;

C_p = processing cost per unit of finished product, using the incumbent material;

C_f = finishing cost per unit of finished product, using the incumbent material; and

L = useful life of finished product, using the incumbent material.

We could use a similar equation to express the annual use cost of the candidate material. However, in this equation we insert not the price of the candidate but an unknown, V, which is the value-in-use of the candidate. We then equate the two annual use costs and solve for V.

Let us illustrate: Assume that a firm is producing an industrial fastener out of die-cast alloy, and our candidate material is a sheet metal from which it could fabricate the fastener using a combination punching-forming process. Suppose that the pertinent quantities and costs are those in Exhibit 10.3.

First we calculate the annual use cost of the incumbent material:

$$\text{Annual use cost}_{inc.} = (QC + C_{fab} + C_{fin} + XQC + YQC)/L, \qquad (10.9)$$

where

X = inventory cost, expressed as a decimal fraction; and

Y = scrap cost, expressed as a decimal fraction.

Inserting the numbers from Exhibit 10.3 and solving, we get

$$\text{Annual use cost}_{inc.} = (QC + 0.05 + 0.02 + 0.05\, QC + 0.1\, QC)/3$$

$$= 0.0281 \text{ (rounded)}.$$

Second we set up a similar equation for the annual use cost of the candidate material and simplify it, as follows:

$$\text{Annual use cost}_{cand.} = (Q'V + C'_{fab} + X'Q'V + Y'Q'V)/L'$$

$$= (Q'V + 0.10 + 0.05\, Q'V + 0.2\, Q'V)/7$$

$$= 0.00536\, V + 0.0143. \qquad (10.10)$$

Finally, we equate the two expressions for annual use costs and solve for the value-in-use of the candidate material:

$$0.00536\, V + 0.0143 = 0.0281;$$

$$V = 2.57.$$

Cost element	Die-cast	Sheet metal
Quantity in lbs per finished part	0.05	0.03
Price of material, $/lb	0.25	0.20
Fabricating cost, $/part	0.05	0.10
Finishing cost, $/part	0.02	0
Inventory cost, %**	5	5
Scrap cost, %**	10	20
Useful life of finished parts, years	3	7

** Percentages are based on value of material in finished part.

EXHIBIT 10.3
Industrial fastener cost elements for the sheet metal vs. die-cast alloy value-in-use calculations.

This tells us that if the sheet metal cost is $2.57 per pound, its annual use cost would just match that of the die-cast alloy. In other words, for this application the sheet metal is *worth* $2.57 per pound; that is, its value-in-use is $2.57 per pound. This is so much greater than its assumed price of $0.20 per pound that the fabricator would be wise to adopt the sheet metal and the seller could consider charging considerably more than $0.20 per pound.

To apply value-based pricing on a large scale, the firm normally needs to do in-depth studies at the plants of a sample of key customers to calculate a range of customer values for the product. The firm then has the strategic option of deciding whether to skim the market with the product (setting a high price—say $2.00/lb for sheet metal—and going after that part of the market that sees a high value for its product) or to penetrate the market with a price that makes its product attractive in many uses for many types of customers (charging close to $0.20/lb for sheet metal). Account planning for the ABCOR2000 exercise shows how salespeople can use this concept to customize selling strategies for different accounts.

Competition-oriented pricing

When a company bases its prices chiefly on what its competitors are charging rather than on cost or demand, its pricing policy can be described as competition-oriented. In the most common type of competition-oriented pricing, a firm tries to keep its price at the average level charged by the industry. This is called *going-rate* or *imitative pricing*.

Firms use going-rate pricing primarily for homogeneous products like oil, although the market structure itself may vary from pure competition to pure oligopoly. The firm selling a homogeneous product in a purely competitive market actually has no choice in setting its price. In an oligopoly, in which a few large firms dominate, like the plate glass industry, firms also tend to charge the same price as the competition, although for different reasons. Because there are only a few firms, each firm is aware of the others' prices and so are the buyers. The firm with the lowest price is likely to capture the most business, thereby inviting immediate decreases in price from competitors. This situation also discourages single firms from increasing prices.

On the other hand, in markets characterized by product differentiation the individual firm has more latitude in its price decision. Product differences, whether in styling, quality, or functional features, desensitize the buyer to existing price differentials. Firms make their product and marketing programs compatible within each pricing zone, and they respond to their competitors' changes in price to maintain their relative prices.

Competitive bidding is a common form of pricing in markets in which the firm competes with an unknown number of suppliers and has no way to determine their prices. Many manufacturers and service organizations that sell to the Defense Department, municipal governments, original-equipment producers, and so forth must bid against others for the work; the contract usually goes to the lowest bidder. And electronic price-discovery mechanisms like FreeMarkets (*www.freemarkets.com*) are broadening the domain for competitive bidding. Therefore the seller must carefully think through two issues regarding each bidding opportunity: (1) should the firm bid at all (the decision to bid), and (2) if so, what bid should it make (the bid-size problem)?

If a supplier makes a bid on a particular job, it must search for a price that is above its costs but below (the unknown) competitors' bids. The higher the seller sets its price above its costs, the greater will be the profit if it wins the bid but the smaller will be the probability of getting the contract. The expected profit in a potential bid is the product of the probability of getting the contract and the estimated profit on the contract:

$$E(Z_P) = f(P)(P - C),\qquad(10.11)$$

where

$E(Z_P)$ = expected profit with a bid of P;

$f(P)$ = probability of winning contract with a bid of P;

P = bid price; and

C = estimated cost of fulfilling contract.

Each possible price is associated with a certain probability of winning the contract. A company may logically choose the price that it expects to maximize the profits. Exhibit 10.4 shows four alternative bid levels and the associated probabilities and profits for a hypothetical situation. In this example the firm will be tempted to bid $10,000 because its associated expected profit is highest ($216) at this level.

However, the chief problem with this model is guessing the probabilities of winning the contract at various bidding levels. Where price is the buyer's only concern, this probability is the probability of submitting a lower bid than those of all other competitors, and the probability of submitting the lowest bid is the joint probability that the company's bid is lower than each competitor's bid. Assuming that competitors decide their bids independently, the probability of being the lowest bidder is

$$f(P) = f_1(P)f_2(P) \cdots f_j(P) \cdots f_n(P),\qquad(10.12)$$

where $f_j(P)$ is the probability that a bid of P is lower than competitor j's bid; that is, the lowest bid has to be lower than that of each of the competitors, leading to a multiplication of probabilities.

Competitors' bids are uncertain but can be based on past bidding behavior, as follows. Assume competitor j has bid on a number of past contracts and that data are available. Then for each bid competitor j's bid is related to your estimate of cost, C:

$$r_j = \frac{P_j}{C},$$

where

r_j = ratio of competitor j's bid to your company's cost;

P_j = past bid by j; and

C = your company's cost at time of bid.

Company's Bid	Company's Profit	Profitability of Getting Award with This Bid (assumed)	Expected Profit
$9,500	$ 100	0.81	$ 81
10,000	600	0.36	216
10,500	1,100	0.09	99
11,000	1,600	0.01	16

EXHIBIT 10.4
Effect of different bids on expected profit, showing that a bid of $10,000 is best.

If for a given contract your cost is C, then we might guess that the probability of competitor j's bid price being greater than ours is $h_j(r_j)$. With k competitors our likelihood of winning is $[h(r)]^k$ if all the competitors are similar, and our expected profit for a bid price of P is

$$E(Z_P) = (P - C)[h(r)]^k. \tag{10.13}$$

In the last step we knew that there would be exactly k bidders. If k is known only probabilistically, then the expected profit is calculated as

$$(P - C)q_0 + (P - C)[h(r)]q_1 + (P - C)[h(r)]^2q_2 + \cdots + (P - C)[h(r)]^Nq_N, \tag{10.14}$$

where N is the maximum number of bidders and q_k is the probability that exactly k competitors submit bids. This equation is the same as (10.13), with each profit level weighted by the probability that $0, 1, 2 \ldots$ up to N competitors actually bid.

The Competitive bidding software and the Paving I-99 exercise allows you to explore these concepts in more detail in a simulated bidding environment.

INTERACTIVE PRICING: REFERENCE PRICES AND PRICE NEGOTIATIONS

We have dealt so far with the concept of price as if it were under the direct control of a decision maker and as if it had little if any direct effect on how customers decide what products are worth. Yet in many real situations these conditions do not hold. For example, when customers cannot directly experience the quality of a product before purchasing it (cosmetics, wines, services), price can serve as an indicator of quality and price discounts may be counterproductive (reducing demand *and* margins!).

A similar and widely discussed phenomenon that undermines many of the recommendations of the classical theory is the concept of reference price; for example, a customer may believe that a four-door sedan should cost no more than $20,000. Roughly speaking, a reference price is a price that customers use to judge the actual price.

The point is that if something like a reference price exists, then the firm must take it into account in making pricing decisions. Consider the following example:

EXAMPLE

Suppose that we use the linear demand-price equation from (10.4):

$$Q = 100 - 2P. \tag{10.15}$$

If marginal production costs are (approximately) constant at $10 per unit, then we can determine profit Z from

$$Z = (P - 10) \times (100 - 2P), \tag{10.16}$$

and the profit-maximizing price P^* is $30.

With a reference price, though, (10.15) might become

$$Q = 100 - 2(P - RP), \tag{10.17}$$

where RP is the reference price. The profit-maximizing price derived from (10.16) and (10.17) is

$$P^* = \frac{120 + 2 \times RP}{4}, \tag{10.18}$$

so that if RP = 0, the optimal price from (10.18) is $30 as before; if the reference price is also $30, though, then the optimal price is $45! In general the optimal (profit-maximizing price) will go up as the reference price goes up.

As this example shows, if customers use a reference price in evaluating product offerings, the higher that reference price is, the more the firm can charge for the product and the higher the optimal price will be. Thus in the presence of reference prices it is in the best interest of the seller to consider the reference price in deciding on price and to try to influence the process by which those reference prices are set. For example, the ads for many cars compare that car to a Mercedes, showing how much the consumer can save (for supposedly comparable performance).

A key application of reference-price theory is in developing a price interactively through a bargaining process. To characterize the bargaining process, we often use a concept called *reservation price*, the upper limit on what a customer would be willing to pay for the product or service.

While many consumer markets are driven by posted prices and fixed offerings, in organizational and business markets and in consumer markets where products have high diversity and high utility, such as houses, cars, and boats, prices are generally determined in a bargaining process.

Exhibit 10.5 shows the "zone of agreement"—the zone between the seller's reservation price (or cost) s and the buyer's valuation b. If $s > b$, then there is no zone of agreement. If $s < b$, then the seller and buyer bargain to find a price p such that $s < p < b$. That price, p, then divides the "zone of agreement" $(b - s)$ into two pieces: $b - p$ (called the buyer surplus) and $p - s$ (called the seller surplus or profit).

In a simple one-time bargaining solution, where the buyer and the seller do not consider the elements found in a long-term relationship such as trust, both seek a price p that maximizes their surplus. So how will (or should) they set p?

Nash (1950) proposed an elegant solution to a more general form of this problem, under a set of reasonable assumptions such as *individual rationality* (preferring more to less); *Pareto efficiency* (there should be no solution p^* that leaves both parties better off); *symmetry*

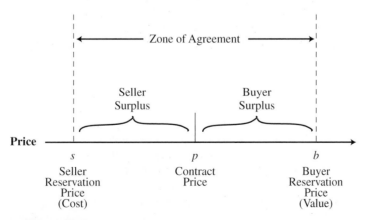

EXHIBIT 10.5
Concepts of a simple distributive bargaining situation where b, the buyer's value, is the most the buyer would pay and s, the seller's cost, is the least a seller would accept. A contract price p splits the agreement zone, providing $b - p$ to the buyer (the buyer surplus) and $p - s$ to the seller (the seller surplus or profit). (Note that if $b < s$, no zone of agreement exists.)

(or fairness) (the solution on average should leave each party as well off as the other relative to the utility of no agreement). That solution is

$$p \text{ that maximizes } U_s(p - s)U_b(b - p), \tag{10.19}$$

where $U_s(p - s)$ is the utility that the seller, with reservation price s, gets from the price p settled on (and with $U_b(b - p)$ defined similarly).

In several marketing experiments (Neslin and Greenhalgh 1983; Eliashberg et al. 1986) the Nash solution did well at predicting outcomes; however, as Neslin and Greenhalgh (1986) show, many solutions are not Nash-type. If we are to use the Nash solution in real situations, we need other price solutions that include situational contingencies and personal preferences. For example, Roth (1979) relaxes Nash's symmetry assumption to yield the weighted Nash solution

$$p \text{ that maximizes } [U_s(p - s)]^r[U_b(b - p)]^q, \tag{10.20}$$

where the values r and q are the seller's and buyer's bargaining power, respectively. Note the role that the reference price or reservation price plays in the solution. If the buyer can obtain an offer from another supplier of $b^* < b$, then the Nash solution price drops; similarly if the seller can show that circumstances (raw material costs, for example) have forced s upward, the Nash solution price rises.

Most often bargaining on price comes down to discussions about the values of b and s, so that a Nash (or Nash-like) solution will favor the party who makes the most compelling case. Situations in which information is incomplete, where the buyer does not know costs and the seller does not know buyer values, and that explicitly include outside alternatives (see Gupta and Livne 1988, and Gupta 1990, for example) have led to solutions that differ from those of Nash.

(The Value spreadsheet exercise calculates expected buyer and seller values in a two-issue selling situation and provides a tool that can facilitate such bargaining processes.)

The theoretical and empirical work on interactive price setting shows that each party should use a prenegotiation phase to determine its own reservation values and to estimate the values of the other party. Nash solutions and similar split-the-difference arrangements depend on how both parties view the reference or nonagreement points (the endpoints of the zone of agreement). Most of the negotiation process depends on calculating what those endpoints are, or should be, and then attempting to persuade the other party of one's view on those calculations.

PRICE DISCRIMINATION

Understanding price discrimination

So far we have looked at situations in which the seller seeks the best *single* price that maximizes profits. If customers are homogeneous and the firm can charge only a single price, then that is the best it can do. But if customer valuations differ, then the profit-maximizing firm can increase its profits by charging a variety of prices, that is, by *price discriminating*. We will describe some of the mechanisms for price discrimination and explain how and why they work.

Suppose there are four equal-sized segments of customers in the market for a textbook, each willing to pay a different price for it. Segment A is willing to pay up to $40, segment B up to $30, segment C up to $20, and segment D up to $10. Assume that no customer will buy more than one book and will buy only if his or her *customer surplus* (i.e., reservation price minus the price asked) is nonnegative. Suppose the firm's variable cost per book is $5, there are minimal fixed costs, and the firm wants to determine the best single price to charge. There is no point in charging a price less than $10—everyone is willing to pay at least $10, and so profits increase with a price from $5 to $10. Similarly there is no point in charging a price in between the various reservation prices. So let us begin our analysis with $10. At this price all segments will buy, and so the profits will be $4N(\$10 - 5) = \$20N$, where N is the number of customers in each segment. If the firm charged $20, then it would serve segments A, B, and C and the profits would be $3N(\$20 - 5) = \$45N$; if it charged $30, then it would serve segments A and B and the profits would be $2N(\$30 - 5) = \$50N$; and if it charged $40, then it would serve only segment A and the profits would be $N(\$40 - 5) = \$35N$. So the best single price is $30, yielding $50N$ in profits.

Now suppose that a monopolistic firm can charge four different prices to the four segments. Then it could charge $40 to segment A, $30 to segment B, $20 to segment C, and $10 to segment D. The firm's profits would be

$$N(\$40 - 5) + N(\$30 - 5) + N(\$20 - 5) + N(\$10 - 5) = \$80N.$$

Note the following features of this price-discrimination scheme:

1. The firm extracts every customer's complete surplus. (*Extraction*: "No money is left on the table.")
2. The firm serves every customer who is willing to pay at least as much as the firm's cost (in this case $5: *inclusion*).
3. The firm does not serve any customers whose willingness-to-pay is less than the firm's costs (*exclusion*).
4. Direct price discrimination is *efficient*. That is, no other pricing scheme can be found that will simultaneously improve the welfare of customers and increase the profits of the seller.

A firm trying to implement direct price discrimination in practice faces several difficulties:

1. Identifying customers' reservation prices is difficult. It is unlikely that the observable characteristics of customers will be closely correlated with their reservation prices, and you are unlikely to obtain accurate information by asking them how much they will pay (Morrison 1979).
2. Targeting a particular price to a particular segment is difficult. Most consumer goods, for example, are sold with posted prices and thus are available to everyone equally.
3. It is difficult to prevent *arbitrage*: consumers with low reservation prices may buy up a lot of the product and supply it to high-reservation-price consumers at a price lower than their reservation price.
4. Charging different prices to different segments may be illegal on various grounds, for example, sex and race discrimination, the Robinson-Patman Act governing discrimination among channel intermediaries, and so forth.
5. Customers may view price discrimination as unfair. Customers paying the high price for an item may resent the firm's giving price breaks to others unless it can position that price break positively, perhaps as charity (senior citizen discounts, student discounts). In many situations the seller may "throw in" other items in the package—free service, beneficial financing, free software, and the like—that make the price discrimination less obvious and perhaps more tolerable.

Despite these difficulties direct price discrimination schemes do exist. For example, local telephone companies discriminate between residential and business users in their prices. Senior citizen and student discounts are other forms of price discrimination. And many business products and services, whose terms and conditions of sale are customized, are priced in a discriminatory fashion. Services lend themselves particularly well to direct price discrimination. The seller (e.g., a lawyer) deals with the customer one-on-one and provides services that are difficult to resell. In all these cases the identification, targeting, arbitrage prevention, and legality requirements are satisfied.

Much price discrimination in practice is not as direct as these examples, however. In fact the need for indirectness in the price discrimination scheme is one source of the considerable variety in the pricing schemes we see today. The challenge is to identify correlations between the reservation prices of different segments (Chapter 3) and their preferences for some attributes of the product. If the firm can discover such correlations, then it can tie its different prices to the different levels of the attributes and allow customers to freely choose the level of the attribute they want to buy.

An example of this idea is the airline industry's pricing based on revenue management. Airlines offer a variety of fares with various restrictions (and some with no restriction). The higher fares are associated with no advance purchase requirements, no Saturday-stay-at-destination requirement, no cancellation penalties, and so forth. The lower fares, for example, Supersaver fares, have many of these restrictions. The effect is to create a product line differentiated on the "restrictions attribute" with different products in the product portfolio appealing to different segments. The business traveler finds the restrictions costly and opts for the higher unrestricted fares; the vacation traveler, however, finds the lower fares appealing and does not mind the restrictions.

If a market can be segmented by value and those segments can be identified (targeted), then an opportunity for price discrimination exists. The institutional differences of different markets and legal restrictions have led to a number of different methods. To implement any of these schemes, the seller must analyze customer value carefully (through choice models, conjoint analysis, value-in-use analysis, or one of the other methods we have described), segment the market, and target the various segments (Chapter 3).

To implement price discrimination, then, the firm must understand how to separate the market segments from one another and how to support the price discrimination program with advertising, distribution, and other marketing instruments. Some of the most common schemes are to rely on geographic and temporal variations in pricing, to use non-linear pricing (e.g., to base prices on customer characteristics), and to use nonprice marketing instruments. Indeed, as Patrick Kiernan notes in the *Wall Street Journal* (June 21, 2001 p. 1), "Before long the only one paying the posted price, or the 'insult price' . . . , will be a stranger to the seller with no purchase history."

Geographic price discrimination

In the days of high trade barriers, international borders facilitated price discrimination and made it particularly easy to implement. If the costs of arbitrage exceed the price differential, geographic price discrimination can be effective. The existence of so-called gray markets in many countries suggests that this is not the case. For example:

> Minolta sold cameras to its dealers in Hong Kong for a lower price than in Germany because of lower transportation costs and tariffs. The Hong Kong dealers worked on smaller margins than the German retailers who preferred high markups to high volume. Minolta's Hong Kong wholesalers noticed this price difference and shipped Minolta cameras to German dealers for less than they were paying the German distributor. The German distributor couldn't sell his stock and complained to Minolta. (Kotler 1994, p. 424)

Firms must recognize that improved information combined with lowered trade barriers, lower transportation costs, and lower costs of arbitrage is making geographic price discrimination more difficult to implement. Indeed, the absence of double and triple coupon policies among West Coast U.S. retailers (common on the East Coast) led manufacturers to issue coupons of higher face value in the West than in the East. However, coupon-clipping exchange groups have emerged on the Internet, "marketing" the higher-valued coupons back to the East Coast retail environment.

Temporal price discrimination

The idea behind temporal price discrimination is to introduce a new product at a high price initially, intending to sell it to customers whose reservation price is high, and then lower the price gradually to sell to customers with lower and lower reservation prices. For example, publishers initially introduce books in hardcover at a high price, and after about a year or so they introduce the paperback version at a lower price. One condition necessary for such skimming strategies to work is that the product be a single-purchase item. The other condition is that the customers whose reservation price is high be at least as anxious to consume the product as those whose reservation price is low. For example, the hardcover buyers who have a high reservation price for the book must want to read the book early at least as much as the paperback buyers.

Another place that temporal price discrimination plays an important role is in the service sector, in which demand for services may vary strongly over time. For example, we see

- Time of day pricing: peak-load pricing for electricity, discount prices for evening phone charges, afternoon movie rates, early-bird dinner rates, off-peak train fares, and so forth
- Time when purchased: two weeks before flight, day of flight, and the like
- Day of the week pricing: public transportation, museums, theaters, and so forth
- Seasonal pricing: air fares, hotels, vacation packages, fashion goods

In most such cases temporal arbitrage is not feasible because services cannot be stored, making price discrimination very effective (Desiraju and Shugan, 1999).

EXAMPLE

(Source: Smith, et.al. 1992.) American Airlines defines the function of yield management or revenue managment as "selling the right seats to the right customers at the right prices." American Airlines' system is divided into three major functions:

1. Overbooking—intentionally selling more reservations for a flight than there are actual seats to offset the effects of passenger cancellations and no-shows
2. Discount allocation—determining the number of discount fares to offer on a flight, limiting these fares on popular flights to preserve seats for late-booking, high-revenue passengers
3. Traffic management—controlling reservations by passenger origin and destination to provide the mix of markets (multiple-flight connecting markets versus single-flight markets) that maximizes revenue

We will describe how airlines allocate discounts. If the airline were to have only two classes of service, full fare and discount, at any point prior to departure, the system estimates p, the probability of getting a full-fare reservation if a discount fare is rejected. If

$$p \times \$\text{full fare} > \$\text{discount fare},$$

then the discount fare is rejected. In practice the airline updates p many times before the plane departs, depending on the number of remaining available seats, the time until departure, and the distribution of demand. Using a greater number of fare types (full-fare coach, moderate discount, deep discount), American extends this approach in a process called nesting. Let us assume that American has a flight with 100 seats and three classes of service, with 60 seats available for moderate discount and 30 of those 60 for deep discount. The difference in seat availability between the total number of seats and a discount-fare class is the number of seats to protect for all higher-revenue classes. Thus American protects 40 seats exclusively for full fare ($100 - 60$) and 70 seats ($100 - 30$) for full fare and moderate discount fares combined. It stops booking full-fare tickets only if the flight reaches its overbooking level.

In the following example there are seven fare classes (which American calls buckets) for a plane, and the company needs an estimate of total demand to do the calculations.

Consider a flight with the passenger and revenue results shown in Exhibit 10.6. If the airline uses no discount controls, it will accept reservations until it reaches the overbooking level. Because leisure customers typically buy the lesser-price reservations far in advance of the flight, this scenario will result in some passengers willing to pay higher prices being displaced by lower-price demand. American estimated the revenue earnings for this case as the least possible revenue that can be obtained by filling the flight to capacity. The revenue the airline would earn for a flight for which it used no discount controls is shown in Exhibit 10.7.

If it used perfect discount controls, American would realize the maximum possible revenue for each flight. In this case it would preserve the number of seats for the higher-price passengers that would exactly match the actual demand. It would turn away only the least-price passengers (and only when it had no more space available). The revenue it would earn for such a flight is shown in Exhibit 10.8.

Total revenue opportunity is defined as the difference between the perfect-controls scenario and the no-controls scenario. This difference is the amount of

Fare class	Passengers Boarded	Spilled	Total	Revenue Average	Total
Y0	12	0	12	$ 313	$ 3,756
Y1	6	0	6	258	1,548
Y2	10	0	10	224	2,240
Y3	3	0	3	183	549
Y4	30	29	59	164	4,920
Y5	16	5	21	140	2,240
Y6	32	32	64	68	2,176
Total	109	66	175		$17,429

EXHIBIT 10.6
Actual passenger and revenue information for a sample flight. The number of turned away passengers (spilled column) comes from a statistical model. In this example fare classes Y0 through Y3 are filled and no one is turned away. However, 66 passengers are turned away (spilled) and a flight with 138 seats ends up boarding only 109 passengers.

Fare class	Total demand	Passengers boarded	Revenue Average	Revenue Total
Y0	12	0	$ 313	$ 0
Y1	6	0	258	0
Y2	10	0	224	0
Y3	3	0	183	0
Y4	59	53	164	8,692
Y5	21	21	140	2,940
Y6	64	64	68	4,352
Total	175	138		$15,984

EXHIBIT 10.7
Passenger and revenue results that would have been achieved with no controls, computed by assuming demand comes from the lowest-valued fare classes first, so that high-revenue demand is turned away. This occurs because lower-fare-using passengers typically book farther in advance than higher-fare-class passengers.

Fare class	Total demand	Passengers boarded	Revenue Average	Revenue Total
Y0	12	12	$ 313	$ 3,756
Y1	6	6	258	1,548
Y2	10	10	224	2,240
Y3	3	3	183	549
Y4	59	59	164	9,676
Y5	21	21	140	2,940
Y6	64	27	68	1,836
Total	175	138		$22,545

EXHIBIT 10.8
Passenger and revenue results that would have been achieved with perfect controls computed by assuming that American knew demand exactly prior to departure, so that the airline could use ideal discount-allocation controls. Here all the passengers turned away are in fare class Y6.

revenue American could possibly obtain by controlling discount allocations. The airline can measure the amount of revenue it can attribute to controlling discount allocations by calculating the difference between the actual revenue and the no-controls revenue.

Total revenue opportunity through discount controls
= Revenue with perfect-controls − Revenue earned in the no-controls scenario
= $22,545 − $15,984
= $6,561 for the example flight.

Revenue earned through discount controls
= Actual revenue − Revenue earned in the no-controls scenario
= $17,429 − $15,984
= $1,445 for the example flight.

Thus the percentage of the discount-allocation revenue opportunity the airline earned is 1,445 divided by 6,561, or 22 percent.

The airline can measure its system-wide performance by calculating the average performance of the individual flights.

According to R. L. Crandall, president and CEO of American Airlines, at the time,

[Y]ield management is the single most important technical development in transportation management since we entered the era of airline deregulation in 1979. . . . [Yield management] creates a pricing structure which responds to demand on a flight-by-flight basis. As a result, we can more effectively match our demand to supply. . . . We estimate that yield management has generated $1.4 billion in the last three years alone [and we] expect yield management to generate at least $500 million annually for the foreseeable future. (Smith et al. 1992, pp. 30–31)

Here is another interesting example of revenue management:

EXAMPLE

[G]rants no longer are based overwhelmingly on a student's demonstrated financial need, but also on his or her "price sensitivity" to college costs, calculated from dozens of factors that all add up to one thing: how anxious the student is to attend. The more eager the student . . . the less aid he or she can expect to get. Although students and families awaiting word of college admissions this week aren't being told, these colleges are employing some of the same "yield management" techniques used to price and fill airline seats and hotel rooms.

The statistical models, which have become widespread only in the past few years, go by innocuous names like "financial aid leveraging." But they are quietly transforming the size and shape of student bodies in all sorts of ways, some of which are alarming educators. A sampling:

- The Johns Hopkins model—which the school isn't currently using but may try again in the future—suggested slashing aid to some prospects who came for on-campus interviews. The reason: Those students are statistically more likely to enroll, so need less aid to entice them. A school official now denies putting that part of the model into practice.
- At Pittsburgh's Carnegie Mellon University and other schools, eager freshmen accepted through the early-admissions program can end up with less financial aid than comparable students who apply later. "If finances are a concern, you shouldn't be applying any place early decision," says William F. Elliott, vice president for enrollment management.
- For the current school year, St. Bonaventure University in Bonaventure, N.Y., gave the poorest of its top-ranked prospects just over half the grants they needed—but gave moreaffluent prospects more than three times their need. The result: a more affluent student body, since 75% of the wealthier students decided to enroll, while only one in 11 of the neediest did so. (*Wall Street Journal*, April 1, 1996, p. 1)

The ideas of revenue management, aided by increases in computing power and customer information available through electronic transactions, are transforming pricing policies in a wide range of industries. Oberwetter (2001) discusses the impact in the entertainment industry and Cross (1997) provides numerous examples (see *www.abovetheweather.com* for a broad range of information on revenue management).

The Forte Hotel revenue-management exercise implements a simple revenue-management procedure in the hotel industry, illustrating the application of these concepts.

Nonlinear pricing or quantity discounts

Quantity discounts are a common form of price discrimination: high-volume buyers get lower prices than small-volume buyers. The correlation being exploited here is between purchase quantity and reservation price. People who avail themselves of the discounts have lower reservation prices for the later units (of a large order) than those who do not. There are various ways of implementing quantity discounts that differ in how finely they discriminate among consumers, including two-part tariffs and block tariffs (Monroe 1990):

Two-part tariff: In a two-part tariff the seller charges a fixed up-front price F and then a per-unit charge p. For example, membership clubs (like Sam's Club) charge a membership fee and offer discounted merchandise. The pricing of a durable good such as instant cameras that require specialized film or razors with specialized blades can also be thought of as two-part tariffs. Here the price of the durable good is the fixed fee, and the unit price of supplies is the per-unit charge of using the durable good.

A two-part tariff is similar to a simple linear price in that the marginal price charged and paid is constant in quantity. Everyone who buys pays the same marginal price regardless of quantity. A two-part tariff is a quantity discount scheme only because the "average price" paid—$(F/Q) + p$—decreases with the quantity Q purchased. In a linear pricing scheme, on the other hand, both marginal and average prices are constant for any quantity purchased. The presence of a fixed fee in a two-part tariff allows the seller to extract more consumer surplus than a simple linear pricing scheme.

Block tariffs: Block tariffs are the most widely used form of quantity discounts. A block tariff has at least two marginal prices; it may or may not have a fixed fee. For example,

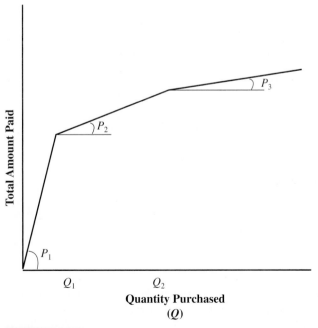

EXHIBIT 10.9
In this three-block tariff, marginal prices decrease when prices increase past points Q_1 and Q_2.

local telephone company tariffs typically have a fixed "subscription fee" as well as several price breaks built into the schedule. In Exhibit 10.9 we show a three-block pricing scheme with no fixed fee. The customer pays P_1 per unit if she purchases Q_1 or less; she pays P_1 for each of the first Q_1 units and $P_2 (< P_1)$ for each unit between Q_1 and Q_2 if she purchases between Q_1 and Q_2 units; and for purchase quantities greater than Q_2, she pays P_1 per unit for the first Q_1 units, P_2 per unit for the next $Q_2 - Q_1$ units, and P_3 per unit $(P_3 < P_2)$ for any units beyond Q_2.

The larger the number of price blocks, the finer the price discrimination possible, but also the greater the difficulty of administering and explaining the tariff to consumers. A quantity discount schedule in which each additional unit is priced differently and a simple linear schedule in which each unit is priced the same no matter how great the quantity purchased represent opposite sides of this spectrum.

Other forms of price discrimination

Promotions and coupons are another means of price discrimination. The idea is that coupon users are more price sensitive than nonusers. The manufacturer sets a price that is higher than the optimal price for the price-sensitive segment and uses coupons to promote sales to this segment. Thus the manufacturer can realize optimal prices for both the price-sensitive segment and the segment in which customers are willing to pay more.

Customer characteristics are also used for price discrimination, especially for services. The most common such characteristics are

- Age—special prices for children, senior citizens
- Income/education status—student prices for movies, subscriptions, and the like; income-linked membership fees in organizations
- Profession—government employee discounts, teacher discounts
- Membership—AAA discounts on auto rentals, employee discounts, Sam's Club

The distribution outlet can be used as a mechanism for price discrimination. For example, specialty stores charge higher prices than supermarkets.

Products themselves can be differentiated. Software companies often sell "student versions" of software packages that include all but one or two features of the $300 version (or limit spreadsheet size) for 10 percent or less of the price of the unrestricted software.

Companies also use brand differentiation as a price discrimination mechanism, particularly by selling generics at a lower (unbranded) price than their branded counterparts.

PRICING PRODUCT LINES

Most firms market more than a single product. If these products are not related, either through shared costs or through interdependent demand, then the price discrimination approaches we have outlined may be appropriate. Monroe (1990, p. 464) cites several reasons that the prescriptions arising from an analysis of single-product pricing may not be appropriate:

- Products in a line may be related to one another on the demand side, either as substitutes or as complements.
- There may be cost interdependencies such as shared production, distribution, or marketing expenditures.
- Some products may be sold as a bundle (stereo system vs. components), thereby creating complementarity.

- The price of one product in a line may influence the buyer's subjective evaluation of other products in the line.

In addition to the information on demand (i.e., price elasticities) that the firm needs for pricing a single product, it needs some knowledge of cross-price elasticities to price product lines.

Under conditions like those that lead to Eq. (10.7) (average costs are fairly constant for any level of demand and costs are constant over time), when a firm sells multiple products Reibstein and Gatignon (1984) show that the optimal price of product i in a two-product $(i + j)$ line is

$$P_i^* = \frac{\varepsilon_i}{1 + \varepsilon_i} MC_i - \frac{\varepsilon_{ij}}{1 + \varepsilon_i} \frac{Q_j}{Q_i} \left(P_j - MC_j\right). \tag{10.21}$$

What Eq. (10.21) shows is that the optimal price for a product in a demand-interdependent line is the single-product optimal price (the first term in Eq. [10.21] modified by the second term in that equation—which is a function of the product's own price and cross-price elasticity, the demand for both products, and the price and marginal production cost of the other product. If the demand-price relationship is stochastic, the function is further modified to include the effect of uncertainty in demand.

In general there will be n equations like (10.21) that the firm would have to solve simultaneously to determine optimal product-line prices for n products.

For this model and others it is often difficult to obtain key pieces of information—the self- and cross-price elasticity.

SALES PROMOTIONS: TYPES AND EFFECTS

Sales promotion comprises a wide variety of tactical promotion tools in the form of short-term incentives designed to stimulate earlier or stronger response from customers in a

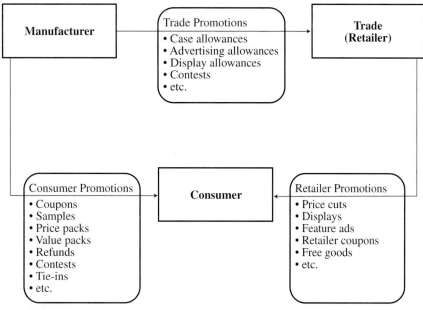

EXHIBIT 10.10
Promotion types vary widely and can be directed at either the trade (retailer) or the consumer.

target market. Most promotions can be viewed as temporary, advertised price reductions, although promotions can take many other forms. Among the more popular forms are coupons, premiums, and contests for consumer markets; buying allowances, cooperative-advertising allowances, and free goods for distributors and dealers; discounts, gifts, and extras for industrial users; and sales contests and special bonuses for members of the salesforce.

A key factor in most types of promotions is that, properly applied, they *complement* other elements of the marketing mix and therefore require a coordinated effort among retailers, wholesalers, salespersons, advertising, and (often) manufacturing and distribution. Exhibit 10.10 shows the types and the flow of promotions and suggests the importance of understanding and modeling the individual and combined effects of promotional activity at several levels.

Thus to model promotional effects we must determine (1) the objectives of the promotion, (2) the characteristics of different promotion types and their purported effects on the objectives, (3) the effectiveness of different promotions, and (4) the range of promotion decisions.

Objectives of promotions

Because sales-promotion tools are so varied in form, no single purpose can be advanced for them. For example, a free sample stimulates consumer trial, while a free management-advisory service may cement a long-term relationship with a customer. Sales-promotion techniques make three contributions:

1. *Communication:* They gain attention and usually provide information that may lead the consumer to the product.
2. *Incentive:* They incorporate some concession, inducement, or contribution designed to represent value to the receiver.
3. *Invitation:* Most include a distinct invitation to engage in the transaction now.

Exhibit 10.11 is a partial list of specific marketing objectives and the promotions that can be used to meet them.

The range of possible objectives is broad and the effects are numerous (and possibly confounding). For example, while a seller's primary purpose in a promotion may be to attract nonbrand purchasers to the brand, sellers may also want to reward brand-loyal users for their loyalty. Because both types of buyers buy during the promotion period, the seller accomplishes both purposes. Thus it is important to set objectives and measure the effect of the particular promotion, whether the objectives concern the level of retail inventory, increased retail distribution, coupon-redemption rates, or sales effects.

Characteristics of promotions

Marketing managers choose promotions for their cost-effectiveness in accomplishing their objectives. Some of the key considerations vary with promotional type.

For *sampling*, implementation can be door to door, by mail, or free with the purchase of another product. Furthermore, the size of the sample can vary. (The promotion for the introduction of Gainesburgers by General Foods, which included, in a sample pack, *half* the recommended size of a dog's meal, had less than ideal results.)

For a *manufacturer-price-off offer*, the seller must determine the total quantity of the promotion, which partly depends on the amount the retailer will accept—too small a quantity may not motivate the retailer to feature the item. The seller must carefully determine the percentage of the price off and the frequency of such offers: a too-frequent price-off offer may lead buyers to expect the discount to continue or to perceive the regular price as an increase.

Objective	Promotional Type
Increase repeat buying	In-pack coupons, continuity programs (e.g., frequent flyer, "*N* for" retail promotions)
Increase market share among brand switchers	FSI coupons, coupons targeted to users of other brands, retail promotions
Increase retailer's promotion frequency	Trade deals, combination of consumer promotions and trade deals (big-bang theory)
Enhance the product's image	Co-op image advertising with image-oriented retailers
Increase category switching	Retail promotions, FSI coupons, large rebates
Target deal-sensitive consumers	Coupons, "*N* for" retail promotions
Increase category consumption	Retailer promotions, promotions tied to events (e.g., back to school)
Increase trial among nonusers	Cross-couponing, free samples, trial packs, direct-mail coupons
Liquidate short-term inventories	Trade deals, rebates, inventory financing
Increase distribution	FSI coupons, (increase demand), trade deals (increase DPP)

"*N* for" = multiple unit promotion (e.g., 6 for 99¢)
    FSI = free standing insert in newspapers and magazines
   DPP = dealer price promotion

EXHIBIT 10.11
A range of marketing objectives and the promotions firms can use to meet those objectives.
Source: Blattberg and Neslin 1990, p. 464.

For *couponing*, the redemption rate is important (and easy to measure), and it depends on the value of the coupon (Reibstein and Traver 1982). However, as Lodish (1986) points out, most promotions are not profitable for the manufacturer and the manufacturer might more appropriately focus on the more difficult-to-measure effects of the coupons on long-term sales and profitability. As with sampling, the manufacturer has partial control of the type of household it reaches with coupons.

For premium offers included *in-* or *on-pack* (i.e., with a packaged consumer good), the selection of the premium type and the duration of the offer is important. The premium should be consistent with the quality image of the brand and if appropriate should be in place long enough so that a regular buyer can obtain a set (as with glassware).

In-store displays are effective means of moving merchandise, but display space is limited and the display must pay for itself according to the retailer's criteria for such programs.

Each promotion type has dimensions that make it unique and that affect its cost and its impact on short- and long-term brand sales.

Marketers disagree about what promotions do and how they should be viewed; however, they seem to concur that promotions (in contrast to advertising) do *not* build up long-term brand customer loyalty or increase category sales (Nijs et al. 2001).

Blattberg, Briesch, and Fox (1995, pp. G123–G125) provide some useful generalizations about promotional effects:

1. *Temporary reductions in retail price increase sales substantially*: Researchers have found that temporary retail-price promotions (promoted through supermarket flyers, for example) cause short-term sales to spike. In contrast, it is rare to see such a response for most consumer advertising on television or in other media.

2. *Brands that have higher shares of the market are less deal elastic*: That is, higher-share brands show less sales response to deals, even though they may capture a large proportion of switchers.

3. *The frequency of deals changes the consumer's reference price*: This finding is important. It explains why brands that are heavily promoted lose equity (i.e., consumers think they are less valuable). A lower consumer reference price reduces the premium the firm can charge for a brand in the marketplace.

4. *The greater the frequency of deals, the lower the height of the sales spike in response to a deal*: This result is likely to be caused by (1) consumer expectations about the frequency of deals, (2) changes in the consumer's reference price, and (3) stockpiling effects from previous deals.

5. *Cross-promotional effects are asymmetric, and promoting higher-quality brands affects weaker brands (and private label products) disproportionately*: Promoting Coke causes customers to switch from a store brand in greater numbers than promoting that store brand will cause them to switch from Coke. One possible explanation for this asymmetry in switching is differences in brand equity. An extension of this finding focuses on asymmetries in brands' perceived type. Promoting higher-tier brands generates more switching than does promoting lower-tier brands.

6. *Retailers pass through to consumers less than 100 percent of trade deals*: Because retailers are the vehicles for passing trade promotional money on to consumers, sellers should recognize that most brands receive far less than 100 percent pass-through. (*Pass-through* is the percentage of the funds a manufacturer offers to a retailer that are reflected in promotional discounts to the consumer. Greater than 100 percent pass-through means the retailer offers discounts to the end user in excess of the compensating funds received from the manufacturer.)

7. *Display and feature advertising have strong effects on item sales*: In addition, feature advertising and display interact synergistically.

8. *Advertising promotions can result in increased store traffic*: The weight of evidence is that advertised promotions of some products and categories do have an impact on store traffic. (With increased store traffic may come store switching or consumers visiting multiple stores.)

9. *Promotions affect sales in complementary and competitive categories*: Practitioners understand this effect but not its magnitude. The impact of promoting one category on the sales of a complementary or competing category is very likely a function of the type and characteristics of the categories themselves.

These general findings and those of Blattberg and Neslin (1990) lead to the following observations for modeling and evaluating promotional results:

- Brand loyalty may (or may not) be affected.
- New triers may (or may not) be attracted.
- Promotions interact with other elements of the marketing mix (advertising, in particular).
- Promotional results interact with production and distribution, affecting inventory levels rapidly and dramatically.

- Promotional frequency influences promotional effects and is linked to the average length of the product's purchase cycle (how often the consumer purchases the product).
- The type of promotion selected may have differential effects on brand loyalty and promotional attractiveness.
- Promotion size may have threshold and saturation effects, suggesting an S-shaped sales-response relationship.
- Finally, firms may experience different levels of success in implementing different promotions; a failure may be due to poor implementation, a poor promotion design, or both.

Historically, the most common technique for evaluating consumer promotions has been to compare sales or market share before, during, and after a promotion. Researchers then attribute increased sales to the impact of the sales-promotion program, all other things being equal. Exhibit 10.12 portrays results that manufacturers would like to see. In the promotion period the company's brand share rose to 10 percent. This gain in share of four percent is made up of (1) deal-prone consumers, who switched to this brand to take advantage of the deal, and (2) brand-loyal customers, who increased their purchases in response to the price incentive. Immediately after the promotion ended the brand share fell to five percent because consumers were overstocked and they were working down their inventory. After this stock adjustment brand share went up to seven percent, showing a one-percentage-point increase in the number of loyal customers. This pattern is likely to occur when the brand has good qualities that many nonbrand users did not know about.

If we assume that the effects of a promotion are short-lived, then use of this method for analyzing promotional effects seems sound. However, even with the increased availability and use of retail-scanner data, the problem of determining the effects of a promotion is quite challenging: to get accurate measures of incremental sales, we need accurate estimates of baseline

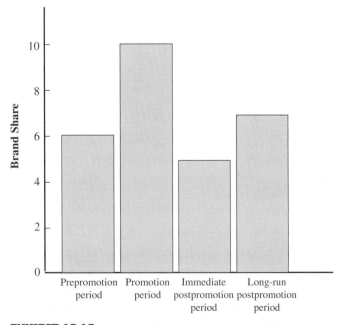

EXHIBIT 10.12
Expected effect of a consumer deal on brand share: Share increases during the promotion period, drops afterward (due to stockpiling), and returns to (perhaps) a different level in the long run.

sales—*sales for the brand that would have occurred if the promotion had not taken place.* If we use sales in a nonpromotional period (prior to the promotion) (as in Exhibit 10.12) as a base and if sales accelerate strongly, then our estimate of the baseline will be biased *downward*, and we will overstate the effect and profitability of the promotion: note that the sales rate immediately following the promotion is much lower than the long-run postpromotional sales rate.

In addition, to calculate the profitability of a trade promotion we must evaluate how much of the promotional effect is passed on to the consumer and how much is simply excess buying by the retailer to stockpile for future use. As Blattberg and Levin (1987) point out, forward buying is so extensive that it may be impossible to infer a baseline from wholesale sales data, and therefore manufacturers need good models of both consumer response to retailer promotions and retailer response to trade promotions to evaluate the profitability of trade promotions.

AGGREGATE MODELS TO ANALYZE PROMOTIONAL EFFECTS

Most of the operational models in use today, even those based on scanner data, develop some form of aggregate regression-based analysis. These response models generally focus on the level and allocation of promotional spending across different market areas.

EXAMPLE

Shapiro (1976) describes a series of studies of promotional effectiveness at H. J. Heinz company. Initial work indicated that promotional effectiveness in terms of effect on market share differed by package size within district (or market area) and differed widely across markets. The analysts captured these effects in a series of individual-market regression models, linking share of features and promotions (by size) to market-share variation in that district. They incorporated these response models into a model designed to determine the optimal level and allocation of effort, which demonstrated that Heinz could make significant improvements that would lead to the dual benefits of higher market share *and* lower cost. By implementing the model recommendations in 1973–74, Heinz reduced its promotional expenditures by 40 percent from what they had been the previous year. In addition, by concentrating its promotional efforts on the more responsive markets Heinz increased its national market share by over three share points!

The Conglomerate, Inc., promotional analysis exercise (Chapter 2) illustrates the allocation process that Shapiro employed.

As another example, consider Blattberg and Levin's (1987) model:

EXAMPLE

Blattberg and Levin developed a model to evaluate the effectiveness of trade promotions (Exhibit 10.13). They model both effects of a trade deal: (1) The trade promotion encourages the retailer to run a consumer promotion (the outcome the manufacturer desires), and (2) the promotion may also encourage the retailer to buy more during the trade period (forward buying), resulting in increased shipments during the trade period and decreased shipments afterward.

Exhibit 10.14 shows the net effect of this activity: while consumer sales (adjusted unit sales) vary very little, shipments (to retailers) show large jumps during

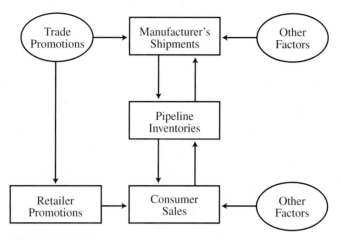

EXHIBIT 10.13
How a trade promotion influences shipments and sales: Trade promotions affect both retailer orders and the promotions that retailers run that are aimed at consumers, affecting both shipments and pipeline inventories in turn. *Source*: Blattberg and Levin 1987, p. 127.

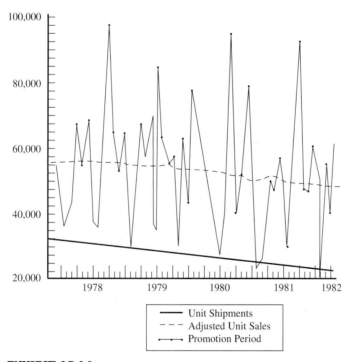

EXHIBIT 10.14
A plot of consumer sales and shipments shows major promotional peaks and troughs for shipments to the trade but less apparent effects at the consumer level. *Source*: Blattberg and Levin 1987, p. 128.

each promotional period, followed by troughs afterward. To understand the effectiveness of a trade promotion we must analyze all of the stages of the process; indeed each equation that follows represents the flow in and out of a box in Exhibit 10.13:

Manufacturer's shipment model:

$$\text{Shipments}_t = f_1(\text{Inventory}_{t-1}, \text{Trade promotions}_t, \text{Other factors}_t). \quad (10.22a)$$

Retail promotions model:

$$\text{Retail promotions}_t = f_2(\text{Trade promotions}_t, \text{Trade promotions}_{t-1}, \text{Inventories}_{t-1}). \quad (10.22b)$$

Consumer sales model:

$$\text{Consumer sales}_t = f_3(\text{Retailer promotions}_t, \text{Other factors}_t). \quad (10.22c)$$

Inventory model:

$$\text{Inventory}_t = f_4(\text{Inventory}_{t-1}, \text{Shipments}_t, \text{Consumer sales}_t). \quad (10.22d)$$

Note that Eq. (10.22d) is simply an accounting equation, as

$$\text{Inventory}_t = \text{Inventory}_{t-1} + \text{Shipments}_t - \text{Consumer sales}_t. \quad (10.22e)$$

Thus in general we will have three equations for which we must specify and estimate parameters.

Assuming that consumer sales revert to their baseline level at some time after retail promotions cease, we can assess the profitability of the promotion as the gain in gross margin associated with incremental consumer sales less the loss in gross margin associated with sales to the trade resulting from the promotion. Formally

$$\text{Promotion profitability} = I \times \text{MARGIN} - P \times \text{DISC}, \quad (10.23)$$

where

$$I = \text{incremental sales to the consumer;}$$

$$P = \text{total sales to the trade during the promotional period;}$$

$$\text{DISC} = \text{average discount per unit given to the trade during the promotional period; and}$$

$$\text{MARGIN} = \text{gross margin per unit sold.}$$

Exhibit 10.15 shows what is happening: since shipments during the trade deal are partially "stolen" from future periods and sales during that period are at a discount, these stolen shipments decrease the profitability of the promotion. In general we have

$$F = P - N - I, \quad (10.24)$$

where

$$F = \text{forward buying; and}$$

$$N = \text{"normal" (baseline) sales of the product.}$$

As F increases relative to I, the profitability of the promotion becomes lower.

Blattberg and Levin used this approach to analyze a manufacturer's trade promotions of 10 products in six markets. The data that they had were

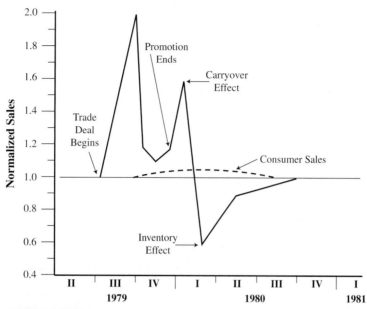

EXHIBIT 10.15

Consumer and trade sales initially climb sharply during the promotional period and then fall due to consumer stockpiling. The area under the dashed line represents the incremental sales to consumers and is (generally) much smaller than the area under the solid line during the promotional period. *Source*: Blattberg and Levin 1987, p. 137.

- Factory shipments
- Bimonthly sales data from retail audits
- Manufacturer's prices
- Trade promotions
- Advertising expenditures

The manufacturer did not have data on the promotion activity of retailers (although such data are routinely available commercially), and so the researchers dropped Eq. (10.22b) and eliminated the retailer-promotions variable from Eq. (10.22c).

The remaining models (in log-linear form) incorporated "other factors" to account for different promotional types, for the difference between retail orders and shipments, and for trends, seasonality, and the like. Blattberg and Levin estimated 60 separate cases of the shipment and consumer equations, with mean adjusted R^2's of 0.66 and 0.57, respectively. They found that

1. Trade deals significantly increase shipments.

2. Forward buying is significant, leading to significant decreases in sales after the promotional period.

3. Consumer sales increase during the promotion, but to a significantly lower degree than shipments.

Blattberg and Levin also performed the type of profitability analysis outlined above and concluded that most deals lost money.

Many regression-type models have become increasingly useful in practice because of the availability of scanner data, which reveal consumer response precisely at the retail level. The value of Blattberg and Levin's work was limited in 1987, when they did their work, because such data were not available at the time. Blattberg and Neslin (1990) describe a number of promotional models that can be used to determine the size, timing, and allocation of promotional resources.

One of the biggest challenges in analyzing the results of a promotion is to develop an appropriate baseline (i.e., an estimate of what sales would have been without a promotion). As Abraham and Lodish (1987, 1993) note in describing their PROMOTER and PROMOTION-SCAN models, this is far from a trivial task, and their models incorporate trends, seasonality, exception indices (for special factors), and promotional types in a combined multiplicative-additive model form. Neslin and Stone (1996) also discuss the difficulty of estimating a baseline, and Hanssens, Parsons, and Schultz (2001) provide an example at Glaxo Wellcome, illustrating a complete set of promotional models in practice.

ANALYZING INDIVIDUALS' RESPONSES TO PROMOTIONS

The increasing availability of scanner data linked to individual characteristics (from a scanner panel) has given a large boost to modeling individual choice behavior, including the effect of promotions. Because technical and methodological issues abound, building these models requires expertise, but many of the models share the following goal: to estimate the likelihood of an individual choosing a brand as a function of the following categories of variables (Blattberg and Neslin, 1990, p. 220):

1. Brand dummies (to represent the intrinsic value of brands)
2. Promotion occurrences
3. Last purchase effect on loyalty
4. Last purchase effect on promotion responsiveness
5. Personal and demographic characteristics

The most frequently cited (and critiqued) approach in this area is the Guadagni and Little (1983) logit model (Chapter 2):

$$P_k = \frac{e^{V_k}}{\sum_{j=1}^{J} e^{V_j}}, \quad j = 1, \cdots, J \text{ (number of brand sizes)}, \tag{10.25}$$

where

brand size is a particular size of a particular brand like "2-liter coke";

$P_k =$ the probability of buying brand-size k; and

$V_k =$ the deterministic component of utility of brand-size k at time t, where the t subscript is suppressed.

V_k is defined as

$$V_k = \sum_{l=1}^{7} \beta_l X(l, k) , \tag{10.26}$$

and where

$$X(1, k) = \text{brand-size constant} = \begin{cases} 0, & \text{not brand-size } k, \\ 1, & \text{brand-size } k; \end{cases}$$

$$X(2, k) = \text{promotion indicator} = \begin{cases} 0, & \text{not on promotion}, \\ 1, & \text{on promotion}; \end{cases}$$

$$X(3, k) = \text{regular price in dollars per ounce};$$

$$X(4, k) = \text{prior promotional purchase} = \begin{cases} 0, & \text{if the previous purchase was not} \\ & \text{brand-size } k \text{ on promotion} \\ \\ 1, & \text{if the previous purchase was} \\ & \text{brand-size } k \text{ on promotion}; \end{cases}$$

$$X(5, k) = \text{second prior promotional purchase} = \begin{cases} 0, & \text{if the second previous purchase} \\ & \text{was not brand-size } k \text{ on promotion} \\ \\ 1, & \text{if the second previous purchase} \\ & \text{was not brand-size } k \text{ on promotion} \end{cases}$$

$$X(6, k, t) = \alpha X(6, k, t-1) + (1-\alpha)\delta_1(t);$$

$$\delta_1(t) \quad = 0 \text{ if brand } k \text{ was not bought on purchase } t-1,$$

$$\quad\quad\quad = 1 \text{ if brand } k \text{ was bought on purchase } t-1;$$

$$X(7, k, t) = \gamma X(7, k, t-1) + (1-\gamma)\delta_2(t);$$

$$\delta_2(t) \quad = 0 \text{ if size } k \text{ was not bought on purchase } t-1,$$

$$\quad\quad\quad = 1 \text{ if size } k \text{ was bought on purchase } t-1;$$

$$\alpha, \gamma \quad = \text{carryover effect of previous brand (and size) purchases, respectively.}$$

Note that the model deals with the probability of an individual's buying a specific brand-size combination. This model is based on the following stylized behavioral assumption: The customer will compute his or her utility for each brand and pick the one that has the highest utility at a particular time. At any time, the utility of brand k (U_k) is the sum of the deterministic component (V_k) and a random component (ε_k). The specific form of the foregoing model measures brand loyalty in variable $X(6)$ as an exponentially decaying measure of past purchases of this brand, and it measures size loyalty similarly in $X(7)$. Variables $X(4)$ and $X(5)$ measure the effects of previous purchases on the sensitivity of the current response.

Several researchers have criticized this model for the way it handles loyalty—it assumes a homogeneous market with customers differing only in their level of loyalty, *not* in their receptivity to promotions—and for the way it deals with the effect of past purchases on customer response to current promotions. In addition, critics often think that the nature of the market and competition might better be addressed through more general models (e.g., the nested logit model in Chapter 2).

Blattberg and Neslin (1990) discuss the use of individual choice models to predict customer response to promotions and thus to guide firms' decisions about promotions. Other researchers have developed some very elaborate models to decide which brands a retailer should promote, what the level of promotion should be, what its timing should be, and the like and have obtained some very encouraging results, as the following example illustrates.

EXAMPLE

Tellis and Zufryden (1995) developed a model to help the retailer to maximize cumulative profits over a planning period. The retailer can determine which brands to discount, by how much, and when (and the model even incorporates the cost of retagging the shelves when prices change).

At the heart of this retailer model is a customer response model:

$$E(S_{ijt}) = E(Q_{ijt} \mid B, C, V) \, P_{ijt}(B \mid C, V) \, P_{it}(C \mid V), \qquad (10.27)$$

where

i = customer;

j = brand;

t = time period;

S = sales;

V = store visit;

C = category purchased;

B = brand choice;

Q = quantity purchases;

E = expectation; and

P = purchase probability.

Their model has three submodels: a purchase-incidence model, a brand-choice model, and a purchase-quantity model.

They model the customer's decision process as a (nested) logit model where the purchase incidence is a binary logit model (purchase or not) and the brand choice is a multinomial logit model. The probability that customer i will purchase in the product category during period t *given* a store visit is

$$P_{it}(C \mid V) = \frac{1}{1 + \exp\left[-\left(b_0 + b_1 \text{CatPur}_i + b_2 \text{Inv}_{it} + b_3 \text{Inc}_{it}\right)\right]}, \qquad (10.28)$$

where

CatPur_i = mean long-term probability that the customer purchases in the product category;

Inc_{it} = category attractiveness or inclusive value (log of denominator of Eq. [10.29]);

Inv_{it} = number of units of inventory the customer held at the start of period t; and

$b_0, \ldots, b_3$ = model coefficients to be estimated.

They model brand choice as a multinomial logit model (conditional on category purchase in a period) as

$$P_{ijt}(B \mid C) = \frac{\exp(\beta X_{ijt} + \gamma_j \operatorname{Disc}_{ijt})}{\sum_k \exp(\beta X_{ikt} + \gamma_k \operatorname{Disc}_{ikt})},$$ (10.29)

where

$\operatorname{Disc}_{ijt}$	= discount level available to customer i for brand j in period t;
X_{ijt}	= vector of causal variables, including brand loyalty, indicator of previous brand chosen, list price, feature indicator, and display indicator;
γ_j	= parameter for discount for brand j, to be estimated;
β	= vector of causal parameters (= $\beta_0, \beta_1, \ldots, \beta_v$, where γ is the number of casual variables); to be estimated; and
k	= index for brands in the choice set.

Finally, they model the expected quantity of brand j purchased by customer i during time period t *given* that the customer chooses brand j as

$$E(Q_{ijt} \mid B) = \exp(a_0 + a_1 \operatorname{Price}_{ijt} + a_{2j} \operatorname{Disc}_{ijt} + a_3 \operatorname{Inv}_{it} + a_4 H_{ijt}),$$ (10.30)

where

Price	= list price;
Disc	= discount for the specific brand;
Inv	= inventory of that category of household product at beginning of the period; and
H	= brand attractiveness (derived from Eq. [10.29]).
$a_0, \ldots a_4$	= model coefficients to be estimated.

H accounts for why customers buy different quantities of different brands—for example, a customer might buy a small amount of (expensive) premium coffee for guests and a larger quantity of less expensive coffee for everyday use.

Tellis and Zufryden apply the model to the saltine cracker category. Their results show that the optimal timing and level of a promotion vary with the degree of customer loyalty, with the way customers respond to changes in the marketing mix, with retail margins, and with retagging costs. Their results also suggest that retailers should give higher discounts as retail margins, customer response to discounts, and category attractiveness increase, and lower discounts as customer response to their product inventory and customer loyalty increase.

They implemented the model on a PC and optimized it in Excel, using Excel's Solver tool.

The Promotional spending analysis software and the MassMart case illustrate how this model works and how it can be used.

As the quantity and quality of data on response to promotions grow and with instant promotions (via online stores) becoming pervasive, we expect that marketers will understand promotional effects better and be able to create better models of those effects (Degeratu, Rangaswamy, and Wu 2000).

SUMMARY

While nonprice elements of the marketing mix grow in importance, price and the short-term promotional variations in price will continue to hold the central position in the marketing mix. Setting price requires knowledge of the consumer's willingness to pay for the product, the cost of producing the product, the probable reactions of competitors, and how these factors change over time. Most pricing decisions are fundamentally based on costs, on demand, or on the nature of competition, and we have described marketing engineering methods based on each of these factors. One demand-based approach to pricing relies on price discrimination and takes advantage of the different levels of need that different customers have for the product. Yield management is an effective way to implement price discrimination.

Because most firms price multiple products that interact with one another, the problem of pricing products in product lines is important. The firm must understand those interactions.

Promotions are most often short-term reductions in price. Knowledge about the effects of promotions is growing, and manufacturers and retailers are using many effective models to design and implement promotions.

With the widespread availability of scanner data and procedures to analyze the data, we are better able to understand the effect of promotions at the customer level and to use that understanding to guide firms in their promotional decisions. With these rich data sources, supplemented by measurements of consumer response to promotions in interactive Internet environments, researchers will be able to develop better operational models and make more precise empirical generalizations in the years to come.

ACCOUNT PRICING FOR THE ABCOR2000 EXERCISE

BACKGROUND

Abcor Industries, a wholly owned subsidiary of Conglomerate Inc., is one of the largest sellers of engraving-plate material and plate-making equipment in the United States. While engraving equipment is used to make brass plates for gifts and ceremonial items (plates on pictures, statuettes, and the like), its oldest and most traditional use is in engraving plates for printing business cards, high-quality stationery, invitations, and informals.

Major customers are specialty printers nationwide. Most of these printers own their own plate-making equipment and typically buy their plate stock from the manufacturer of their plate-making equipment.

In 1996, Abcor introduced new equipment using a proprietary process developed in Conglomerate's engineering polymers division—polymer plate and associated plate-making equipment. It has named the first generation of this equipment the ABCOR2000; the plate-making equipment is more costly than the metal-alloy equipment (the ABCOR1000 line), but it produces plates that are considerably less expensive than metal plates but of comparable quality. (When purchased in lots of 500 or more, metal plates range from $4.78 to $4.92 each, with prices about 10 percent higher for smaller volumes.)

With the introduction of the ABCOR2000, Abcor's support staff in sales has developed a software tool called VALUE. Initial discussions with some of Abcor's prospective customers suggest that these unsophisticated small manufacturers do not fully understand how the lower cost of materials (the plates) will compensate over time for the higher cost of the plate-making equipment. The software is designed to help the salesforce (which is given price discretion) to bid on contracts and to negotiate pricing arrangements with customers.

In introducing VALUE to the salesforce, Abcor has identified three typical prospect-accounts for a training exercise: Longform Printing of Medford, Massachusetts; Smithfields Quality Printers of Wilmington, Delaware; and Franklin Printers of Fort Lauderdale, Florida. The training exercise requires salespeople to make an initial bid (and justify it) to each of these accounts.

EXERCISES

As an Abcor salesperson, you are to prepare a bid for each of these customers as well as a justification. (You may decide that it is not in Abcor's best interest to bid on some or all of these contracts.) Salespeople at Abcor are salaried, and they are given a small bonus based on customer satisfaction measurements.

In each case, assume the following:

- Our machine costs $3,980 to produce and ship.
- The list price for our machine is $12,000. (Salespeople can generally discount up to 20 percent below list without sales management approval; larger discounts are subject to written review.)
- Metal plate prices will continue to rise three percent per year.
- The (marginal) production cost per plate (including delivery) is $0.60.
- Our machines depreciate 25 percent per year (for salvage value calculation).

- We expect to increase prices at about the same rate as metal prices

Prepare and justify bids for these three accounts:

1. Longform Printing of Medford, Massachusetts.

   - Formed in 1947 and client of ours since the mid-1950s. 15 employees.
   - Usage: 990 plates; 1994 usage: 940 plates.
   - Three-year-old ABCOR1000 (Initial price: $4,000).
   - Highly conservative firm: Looking at a 10-year time horizon and a 15 percent cost of capital.

2. Smithfields Quality Printers of Wilmington, Delaware.

   - Relatively new prospect, using competitor's equipment and material.
   - Demand is uncertain (between 250 and 500 plates per year) but appears to be growing at about 11 percent per year.
   - Old equipment worth about $3,000 on market.
   - Conservative investor: Looking at a 20 percent cost of capital. Appears to like to evaluate investments over a five-year lifetime.

3. Franklin Printers of Fort Lauderdale, Florida.

   - A small, general commercial printer that does a small amount of engraving on the side. Its business is stable.
   - Has bought 200 to 250 plates from us per year over the last four years.
   - Has an old machine of ours (an ABCOR 11), bought about 15 years ago and which is fully depreciated.
   - Evaluates investments based on a five-year payback period—i.e., it expects that (with no discounting) the sum of the simple cash flow from the investment will become positive after a maximum of five years for it to consider the investment.

The value spreadsheet

The spreadsheet contains the following relationships:

Buyer Cash Flow = Col C × (Col D − Col E) + Old Machine Salvage Machine Price in Year 1
= Col C × (Col D − Col E) in intermediate years
= Col C × (Col D − Col E) + New Machine Salvage in final year

Seller Cash Flow = Col C × (Col E − Plate Cost) + Machine Price − Machine Cost in Year 1
= Col C × (Col E − Plate Cost) in Other Years.

The discounted cash flow (DCF) columns simply discount the simple cash flow columns.

The graphing parameters allow one to plot discounted and undiscounted cash flows for a range of price possibilities.

PRICE PLANNING FOR THE ABCOR2000 EXERCISE

Abcor Industries, a wholly owned subsidiary of Conglomerate Inc., is one of the largest sellers of engraving plate material and plate-making equipment in the United States.

In 1996, Abcor introduced new equipment that uses a proprietary process developed in Conglomerate's engineering polymers division—a polymer plate and associated plate-making equipment. It has named the first generation of this equipment the ABCOR2000; it is costlier than its metal-alloy equipment (the ABCOR1000 line), but it produces plates that are much less expensive than metal plates. (For more background on Abcor and the ABCOR2000 see the Value-in-use pricing exercise: "Account pricing for the ABCOR2000.")

Abcor had developed a software tool called VALUE to support its salesforce in selling the ABCOR2000. Initial use of the VALUE model was quite successful. Salespeoples' evaluations included the following comments:

- "The VALUE software helped me close two sales in half the time."
- "I finally felt I was in control of the sales negotiation."
- "I felt comfortable making on-the-spot offers for equipment and for contracts on plates."
- "I could sell quite a few more of these machines with more aggressive pricing!"

This last comment struck Fran Collins, marketing manager for the ABCOR2000 line. Fran's background was in equipment and tool manufacture, and she felt that as Abcor gained experience producing the ABCOR2000 line it could reduce its production costs. She also felt that a coherent long-term pricing strategy would give structure to Abcor's overall marketing program.

Fran had worked with the ABCOR1000 (predecessor to the ABCOR2000), and she had noticed that costs of manufacture for that equipment seemed to drop 13 to 15 percent every time production doubled (after the first thousand machines or so). This learning-curve or experience-curve effect in manufacture was something that Abcor managers had noted in other products as well. Fran developed a simple spreadsheet model (Learner.xls) to study the learning-curve effect on short- and long-term pricing.

To address the pricing question, Fran needed to make some assumptions about the future of the product and its production costs:

- Experience-curve effect = 14 percent. (Manufacturing and related costs decrease 15 percent when production volume doubles.)
- Previous production experience = 1,000 units.
- Initial production cost = $4,000.
- Initial market price = $12,000.
- Sales forecast (at $12,000) = 3,000 units.
- Price elasticity = 15 percent (defined as percent decrease in demand with a 10 percent increase in price).
- Growth rate = 3 percent. (The underlying market demand at the current price is growing at this annual rate.)

THE PROBLEM

Fran then faced the issue of recommending a pricing policy for the ABCOR2000. To define the problem, Fran noted that although the anticipated life cycle of the ABCOR2000 is about five years, Abcor managers were split over whether to make short-term (annual) or long-term (five-year) profits their major goal. Hence Fran ran a number of analyses for comparison, seeking

- The short-term profit-maximizing price
- The single price fixed over five years that maximizes discounted five-year cumulative profit (Hint: set all cells below E47 equal to E47 and use Solver to optimize profit by changing cell E47.)
- The price policy that maximizes discounted five-year cumulative profit, with prices that can vary year by year
- The sensitivity of the above to possible changes in price elasticity (12 percent? 18 percent?) and the learning curve constant (10 percent? 20 percent?)

The baseline for comparison for the pricing program was an anticipated three percent annual price increase from the current price of $12,000.

What pricing policy do you recommend for Abcor and why?

NOTE: These are the key spreadsheet relationships in Learner.xls:

Learning curve effect:

$$C = C_0 Q^r$$

where

C = unit production cost,
C_0 = constant,
Q = cumulative production,
r = learning curve exponent (derived from the input data).

Demand/price relationship:

$$V = kP^e$$

where

V = current volume,
k = constant,
P = current price,
e = price elasticity (as a negative number).

PAVING I-99 EXERCISE:
BIDDING FOR PAVEMENT CONTRACTS BY CONGLOMERATE, INC.

Many contracts, especially those for government and institutional markets, are awarded through competitive bidding mechanisms. Although issues other than price, such as degree of qualification and past performance level, are important, the bid price is often the critical factor with the low bid winning. (Remember: When the seller—contractor here—bids, low bid wins; when the buyer bids, high price wins.)

The construction division of Conglomerate, Inc. is bidding on a series of construction contracts to pave strips of Pennsylvania Route I-99. Thirty-four such contracts are up for bid, and they are essentially designed to be approximately equivalent in cost to pave.

The actual bidding-exercise simulation is Part 2 of this exercise. In Part 1, we will attempt to convey how the likelihood of winning a bidding competition varies depending on the firm's cost to complete the contract, the number of competitors who bid, and the range of those competitive bids.

In Part 2 of the exercise, you are to simulate the effect of different bidding strategies under different competitive scenarios. As this is a public bid, the names of the firms that requested the RFQ (request for quote or bid) are public knowledge. However, all of those who requested the RFQ may not bid, so you generally know the maximum number of possible competitive bidders but not the actual number.

The best bidding strategy balances the opportunity cost of losing profitable business to a competitor (because the bid is too high) against the lost profits (or actual losses) associated with bidding too low. (The "winner's curse" is an expression that describes the theoretical and empirical finding that when costs are not known for sure but must be estimated, as here, the competitor most likely to win a contract is the one who most underestimates its costs!) Note that fluctuations in the weather, in the availability and productivity of workers, in material costs, and the like make it uncertain just what actual costs are likely to be even if you have had considerable experience in similar projects.

In this market, after you specify an upper and lower bound either for costs or for competitors' bids, the actual costs and bids are about equally likely to be found anywhere in those ranges. (They are uniformly distributed in those ranges.)

EXERCISE

Part 1: Training exercise

Use part 1 of the exercise to prepare for the competition.

1. Set up the "Bid Profit/Win Probability" so that you can see what the probability of winning the competition is when (a) your costs will be $25,000; (b) bids will be disqualified if outside the range of $25,000 to $50,000 and we are expecting one, three, or six competitors. How does the number of competitors affect your probability of winning, the best bid, and your expected profit?
2. Assume you know that there are three competitors but that the upper bid limit is $40,000 rather than $50,000. How does this affect your bid in Question 1? What if the upper limit was $50,000, but you were able to get your costs down to $20,000 in the three-competitor case. What would your optimal bid be in this case?

Part 2: The bid-competition simulation

The bid simulator allows you to study the effect on the results above when the actual number of competitors is unknown (although the maximum number is known) as well as when your own costs are known. The government is asking for bids on all 34 road segments to be submitted simultaneously (that is, not sequentially).

Your information from the state government is that four competitors (besides you) have asked for the RFQ. In addition, you have been told that the government has set a "quality floor" (lowest acceptable price) of $20,000 per strip and a maximum price of $50,000. (Bids outside these ranges will be declared nonresponsive; strips of road where there are no responsive bids will be rebid.)

Your past experience with this type of business has shown that your costs can range anywhere from $12,000 to $25,000. And you do not have the capacity to fulfill more than 10 of the contracts. (Assume that you lose $2,000 in subcontracting costs for every contract you win over your capacity.)

Conglomerate, Inc. needs guidance on the following decisions:

1. What should we bid on the contracts? Should we bid on all of them or on just a portion?
2. Our accounting firm has sent us a proposal that it claims will reduce the range of variation in our cost estimates. It is (conservatively) estimating that it can identify the causes of cost overruns and reduce the upper cost-estimate bound from $25,000 to $21,000. It is asking for $10,000 to do this work. Should we hire the firm?
3. The government is considering splitting the bidding competition into two competitions of 17 contracts each. Suppose you win three, six, or eight segments in the first round. What is your best bid for the remaining 17 segments?

FORTE HOTEL REVENUE MANAGEMENT EXERCISE

NOTE: A version of the Generalized Revenue Model called Forte Hotel Revenue Management Exercise, includes the data for this exercise.

Having recently engaged L&R Planning, Inc. to apply conjoint analysis to aid in the design of their new hotel chain, the Forte Hotels, Ltd. board, headed by Charles Long, engaged the same consultants to apply the important concept of revenue management to set prices and room allocations for these new hotels.

A unique aspect of the new Forte design was that the three types of rooms (which they were calling Premiere, Superior, and Standard) had the same physical design. The main differences were the floor level and on-floor and in-room amenities. Thus Standard rooms were on the lowest floors and included the standard-room characteristics that emerged from the conjoint analysis.

Superior rooms added bathrobes, an iron and ironing board, free use of an in-room exercycle, shoe-shine service, and twice daily room refresh (including fresh towels, if needed).

Premium rooms were all on the highest floors of the hotel and included Superior room amenities. In addition, Premium rooms offered on-floor concierge service, access to the Premiere Club rooftop lounge, which offered complimentary continental breakfast and free cocktails and hors d'oeuvres during the 5 P.M. to 7 P.M. happy hour.

These different room types tend to attract different types of customers:

Premiere room customers are typically upscale business travelers, who are not very price sensitive and want the best the hotel has to offer. They tend to use room service quite a bit, often buy personal items and family gifts in the hotel shops, and book meeting rooms and order catering at the hotel.

Superior-room customers include upscale pleasure travelers as well as business travelers with budget constraints. These customers plan somewhat farther in advance than the Premiere room customers.

Standard room customers are a mix of budget-conscious business travelers and family vacationers. The latter group, in particular, is generally on the lookout for deals and tends to plan well in advance.

As a test application, Mr. Long gave L&R the task of developing and applying a prototype of the system to their first hotel in the chain, located in Arlington, Virginia. This small hotel (consistent with Forte's plan for intimacy) has only 100 rooms and was opened in January 2000. After a year of operation, Mr. Long thought that he and his staff had a reasonable understanding of the flow of room demand during the year and how that room demand reacted to price changes. Forte's policy is to adjust prices and capacities by season, four times a year, and the first task it assigned L&R was to suggest prices (and capacities) for the three room classes for summer 2001.

The model that L&R put together required answers to a number of questions:

- What is the "price elasticity" (percent decrease in demand for each one-percent increase in price) for each room type?
- What is the expected demand level at some base price for each room type?

Because the idea was to use this model regularly, the model also asked the following questions:

- How much does this demand vary (up or down) from an annual average? (For the summer season Forte expected more pleasure travelers and fewer upscale business travelers than during the winter months, for example.)
- How does room booking come in over time? The way the model specified this was by asking, for each room type: "How many days in advance of a date of stay would 50 percent (75 percent) of the ultimate bookings be on hand?"

Thus Forte management had to supply two such estimates for each room type. Other management inputs included these:

- An estimate of incremental cost per room type: How much more the amenities and services for each room type cost the hotel as compared to the lowest-priced classes:
- An estimate of incremental revenue (multiplier): How much money above the price of the room the average customer brought into the hotel (input as a multiple of the room price).
- The maximum room price (the "rack rate" for the highest price room) and the minimal incremental price difference between room rates for adjacent price classes.

L&R's first task was to provide Mr. Long with an initial price and allocation of rooms to the three classes for summer of 2001. The tool it developed, called Generalized Revenue Model, was designed to support this decision. (A version of the model, saved as Forte Rev.xls, includes the data for this application.)

HOW THE GENERALIZED REVENUE MODEL WORKS

The spreadsheet is based on the following idea: demand for each class of service can be characterized by a total demand function of the following form:

$$D(p) = k\,p^{-e}$$

where

$$
\begin{aligned}
D &= \text{demand,} \\
p &= \text{price,} \\
e &= \text{price elasticity,} \\
k &= \text{constant,}
\end{aligned}
$$

and where k and e are determined by the user input in phase 1 of the program.

In addition, booking takes place over time. We assume that we can approximate that process with a log-normal distribution of booking arrivals. That distribution has two parameters, and in phase 2, we ask how many days in advance of the service date will 50 percent of bookings (Cell D14 for class1) and 75 percent of bookings (Cell E15 for class 1) arrive. To get the parameters of the log-normal distribution, we set $\ln(D15)$ as the mean and $\ln[(D15-E15)/3.92]$ as the standard deviation.

In cell S13, we have the booking date. According to these three inputs, if the booking date is 20 days in advance of the service date, the 50 percent days are 15 and the 75 percent days are five (i.e., D15 = 15 and E15 = 5), then we expect that log-normal (20, 2.7, 2.4) = 62 percent, or 38 percent of the ultimate demand for this date is yet to be realized. We must factor this into our original demand estimate in C38 to account for what we have observed thus far. If 20 people have booked in this class thus far, we can expect that $20/(1-62) = 53$ will be the total demand we can expect and that we can expect 33 more people to book for that date.

If demand is "lumpy," such as when a special group books a number of rooms on a given date, users of yield management systems remove that demand (and the associated booked capacity) from the system and rerun the analysis without that unusual demand spike.

We apply a greedy rule to allocate remaining unbooked space as we get closer to the booking date: any slack capacity is first allocated to the highest (most profitable) class of service up to the amount of remaining expected demand. If slack capacity remains, it is then allocated to the next highest class, etc. Thus, depending on how demand arrives, a low class of service may be fully booked 30 days in advance of the service date, but because expected demand for higher classes of service did not materialize, the yield management model may release additional space for assignment to a lower class as the booking date approaches.

EXERCISES

1. Using the Forte Hotel version of the model, suggest the number of rooms and the prices for those rooms for the June 1 through August 31, 2001, summer season.
2. How would your recommendation change if Forte management set a maximum room price of $180?
3. What if there were a 15 percent minimum increment between room classes?
4. Do the recommendations make sense? (What are the limitations and shortcomings of this analysis from Forte management's perspective?)

    The next use of the model is for daily reservations. Local management at the hotel has to decide the number of rooms of each class to book on each day. (With very rare exceptions, customers booked into a lower class who are given a "free upgrade" are happy; hence booking upward is feasible. Booking downward—giving someone who requested a Premiere room a Standard room—is not.)

    It is May 23, and the following two reservation requests have come in. Would you accept either or both of these reservations?
5. For June 7, a request from Centre for Travel, a Pennsylvania travel agency that is a steady customer, for a block of 12 Standard rooms for a Washington museum tour group: Booked to date:

Premiere:	6 rooms
Superior:	11 rooms
Standard:	59 rooms

6. For May 28, a request for 20 Standard rooms for a foreign delegation visiting the Department of Commerce:

Booked to date:	
Premiere:	9 rooms
Superior:	25 rooms
Standard:	44 rooms

    As a consultant to Mr. Long you have been asked to help him evaluate L&R's work. Comment on the appropriateness of these prototype models—specifically
7. Should they be implemented as is? (If not, what changes would you recommend?)
8. Particularly for daily reservation requests, what discretion should be given to the local hotel management in taking bookings? The reservations clerk? Why?

MASSMART INC. CASE[1]

It was Friday, February 23, 2001. Donna Sullivan, marketing manager for MassMart for the central Pennsylvania region, was in her office. She was writing a report for her boss, Jack Chen, vice president of marketing for the company. In January, Jack had asked her to do a preliminary strategic review of the company's promotion programs for its store in State College, Pennsylvania. MassMart is a leading mass merchandiser with over 80 stores in Pennsylvania, Ohio, and Maryland. The company has had a strong presence in central Pennsylvania for over 25 years. Competition has, however, increased recently with two Wal-Mart stores and one Sam's Club outlet established in State College in the last five years.

In preparing her report, Donna spent one morning at the local university library reading articles about in-store sales promotions. One article in particular (by Gerard Tellis and Fred Zufryden in *Marketing Science*) caught her eye. The authors described how to plan sales promotions in retail stores using scanner-panel data (individual-level purchase data collected by the scanner at the checkout counter). Using these data, analysts can track the purchases made by a selected sample of consumers. She knew that the State College MassMart collected this kind of data and used these data to identify trends and plan inventory.

The ideas in the article impressed her because they suggested an approach that was different from what she had been doing. She became increasingly skeptical about the current promotion strategy and excited by the prospect of developing a new promotion strategy.

BACKGROUND

MassMart established its store in downtown State College in 1975 and it was the first mass merchandiser in State College, a college town that is the home of Penn State University. The company had established relationships with several wholesalers and brokers on the East coast from whom it purchased products for sale to local residents and students. Between 1984 and 1994, as the university and the town expanded, sales at MassMart had grown over 500 percent. Its main competitors during this decade were a Sears and a J.C. Penney store located in a mall a few miles out of town. However, in the past two years, there had been increasing pressure on sales from the two Wal-Marts and the Sam's Club, also located a few miles from the town center.

Donna thought that the past increases in sales at the MassMart store in State College were in large part caused by the company's promotional policy of always passing on the trade discounts it received from wholesalers to its consumers. The logic behind this policy was simple: those discounts caused no incremental costs to MassMart but helped attract new consumers from nearby communities, some of whom would keep coming back to buy other merchandise, thereby contributing to growth in sales and profits.

When Donna met with Jack in January to review 2001's promotional activities, both thought that they needed some fresh ideas for a more intelligent strategy for promoting sales. The tougher competition had led to thinner profit margins and anything they could do to increase profitability would help them compete better.

1. This case was developed by Jianan Wu under the guidance of Professor Arvind Rangaswamy. The case describes a hypothetical situation.

SCANNER-PANEL DATA

MassMart had installed an optical scanner system in its State College store in 1988, with the primary objective of improving checkout service and the store's accounting and inventory systems. This investment paid off: The store inventory was better monitored than ever before; price changes have been easier to implement; and check out time decreased by an average of 40 percent. To keep better track of consumer needs and trends, MassMart developed its own "scanner panel," consisting of a representative sample of consumers from the shopping areas of its key stores. Panel members get a five percent discount for shopping at MassMart when they show their membership cards at checkout. Data on their purchases go into a database maintained by the company. Separately MassMart also kept records on prices, in-store promotions, special store displays, and newspaper inserts featuring specials at these stores. The complete scanner-panel database could provide all of the following data:

- The regular prices of all brands at the time of purchase
- The identification numbers of the panel members (to protect their privacy, the company did not store members' names directly in the database)
- The dates each panel member made purchases
- The product category and brands purchased
- The quantity of each item purchased
- Temporary price cuts (if any) for all the brands in a category at the time of purchase
- Whether each item purchased was part of an in-store display
- Whether each item purchased was featured in the local newspaper

(Exhibit 1 shows a sample of scanner-panel data for the liquid laundry detergent product category.)

Donna talked to Jack Chen about some of the ideas she had for using scanner data in planning promotions: "Jack, I think we should revamp our promotion program. The more I think about our current promotion strategy, the more I am convinced that we need to do something different. You know, we simply pass on trade deals directly to consumers, but we have never looked at whether this is a good strategy. These trade deals are designed by our wholesalers and the packaged-goods companies. I am not sure these discounts really serve our interests here in State College. We really have no idea what discount levels would increase our sales and profitability most."

"Donna, I guess you're right. Go on."

"We often give discounts on several brands at the same time just because we have gotten trade discounts on all of them. Our sales for all the discounted brands increase, but I wonder whether this makes sense. It might be better sometimes to combine what we get in trade deals so that we can give a larger discount on the brand Wal-Mart is promoting. Loyal consumers of the nondiscounted brands will still buy that brand."

"But Donna, won't our profits go down if we discount just the brand Wal-Mart discounts?"

"Not necessarily! According to an article I read, when two brands are on discount fewer people switch brands than when only one is discounted. If we discount both brands our opportunity costs are higher. Loyal consumers of both brands who would purchase the brand anyway without a discount are just subsidized by the discount. Of course the opportunity costs depend on the number of loyal consumers of each brand. But I think offering simultaneous discounts on two brands is likely to be less profitable than discounting just one brand."

"Donna, I think you have something. But we often get trade deals simultaneously for several brands from our wholesalers. How would we know which brand to discount and how much to discount?"

"To figure that out, I think we need to look at our promotions from the point of view of our consumers. That article I read said that the key is to understand consumer responses to price cuts, displays, and features. Response will of course vary for different brands and product categories. I think looking at our scanner-panel data may give us some insights."

"Donna, if the best discounts to offer vary by brand and category, won't we have to continuously monitor the effectiveness of our promotions and the promotions of other stores and change our discounts to suit each specific situation? If so, won't we need to use this database on an ongoing basis? All this seems so much more complicated than the simple policy we have now."

"It is! But we already have the data. The MIS department told me that it wouldn't be hard to put together a database, at least as an experiment for one or two categories. In fact, they got us some data on the liquid-detergent category last week. I also got some software from a professor in the business school so that we can build a computer model to evaluate promotion effectiveness. Let me try it out with the detergent category, and we can take it from there."

"Good idea, Donna! Let me know what you find out. I don't want to do anything new without testing it out carefully. I am also concerned about whether managers at our 79 other stores, who are not fans of all this computer stuff, will adopt your approach. What we have now is so easy for them to follow."

"I know, but easier may not be better."

THE PROMOTION MODEL

The software Donna got from her professor friend builds a choice model of consumers using the scanner-panel data and a profit model for the retailer that is based on the consumer-choice model. Together the two models incorporate three components:

Consumer-brand-choice component: This component assesses the likelihood (P) that consumers will purchase a specific brand in response to retail promotion variables, such as price discount, in-store display, and newspaper feature. The model captures consumers' loyalty to certain brands through a loyalty index that it derives from panel members' histories of past purchases of alternative brands.

Purchase-quantity component: This component of the model determines how many units of a brand a consumer will purchase once he or she decides to buy a particular brand. The quantity purchased (Q) will depend on the price cut, the consumer's current inventory of that product category, and the consumption rate of the product. The model estimates household inventory and consumption rates by examining the panel member's past purchase history.

Retailer-promotion component: The third component of the model computes retailer profits based on the brand discounted and the size of the discount. The retailer's profit function is constructed as follows:

$$Profit = \Sigma \; profit \; margin \times P \times Q$$

where P and Q together provide an estimate of the demand for a brand in a period, and the summation is over all the brands in the category. The model assumes that the retailer seeks an optimal promotion scheme to maximize profits over a planning period.

Although MassMart carries 11 brands of liquid laundry detergent, the four most popular brands are Tide, Wisk, All, and Yes, which account for more than 80 percent of the sales in the category. Donna decided to use these four brands to conduct her experiment.

With all this preliminary work behind her, Donna Sullivan pulled up this new software and began her analysis.

Customer ID	Date	Brand Purchased	Quantity	Regular Price	Discount	Display	Feature
1001	03/01/95	Tide	50 Oz	$ 3.55	$ 0.43	No	No
1001	03/29/95	Tide	64 Oz	$ 3.99	$ 0.54	Yes	Yes
1001	04/25/95	Tide	50 Oz	$ 3.55	$ 0.45	No	No
1001	05/28/95	All	50 Oz	$ 2.99	$ 0.50	Yes	No
1001	06/27/95	Tide	50 Oz	$ 3.60	$ 0.45	No	No
1001	07/22/95	Tide	50 Oz	$ 3.60	$ 0.20	No	No
1001	08/29/95	All	64 Oz	$ 3.15	$ 0.60	Yes	Yes
1001	09/24/95	Tide	50 Oz	$ 3.65	$ 0.42	No	No
1001	10/28/95	All	100 Oz	$ 4.99	$ 1.00	Yes	Yes
1001	11/25/95	Tide	50 Oz	$ 3.99	$ 0.50	No	No

EXHIBIT 1

A segment of the scanner-panel database for liquid laundry detergent shows the purchases made by a single individual over 10 periods along with the store-environment information (e.g., regular price, display) at the time of purchase.

EXERCISE

NOTE: This exercise is based on a small data set to expedite analysis. It consists of data for eight consumers over 10 periods in which they choose from four brands (providing a total of 320 data points).

1. Summarize the important factors that influence consumer brand choice within the detergent category. If a consumer chooses a particular brand, what other factors will influence the quantity that consumer will purchase?
2. Based on the sample input data, what is the best promotion strategy? Explain why you think that strategy will work. For the promotion strategy that you recommend, what will be the composition of sales? What proportion of sales comes from brand switchers, and what proportion comes from consumers stocking up (i.e., purchase acceleration)?
3. Does promoting two brands simultaneously make sense? Why or why not?
4. How do the trade deals (profit margins) affect retailers' promotion decisions (which brand and how much)? Should trade deals always be passed on to the store consumers? Why or why not?
5. Should Jack Chen adopt this approach for all MassMart stores? Why or why not?

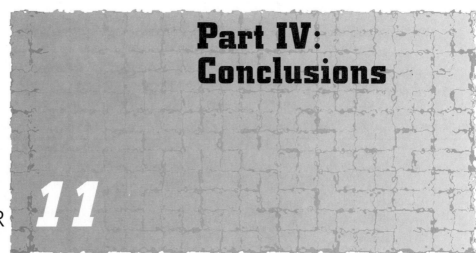

CHAPTER

Part IV: Conclusions

Marketing Engineering:
A Look Back and a Look Ahead

In this chapter we

- Summarize the main lessons that we have learned in teaching marketing engineering and that we hope you have learned from your experience with the material
- Provide tips to help you use marketing engineering successfully within an organization
- Highlight trends that we think will shape the development of marketing engineering during the next decade

MARKETING ENGINEERING: A LOOK BACK

Marketing models have become much more usable since Kotler (1971) summarized in his pioneering book what we then knew about marketing models and their value in decision making. Developments in modeling and personal computing over the past decade have given us the know-how and ability to use decision models in decision making and to do so effectively. In this book we bring together many of the new concepts, tools, and insights useful in making marketing decisions under the name *marketing engineering*. We hope you have found that marketing engineering is a practical, accessible approach, not an arcane, theoretical topic.

In developing and teaching this material we have learned several things, some of which surprised us:

Marketing engineering is marketing: We started off thinking we would be teaching marketing models and modeling in a more user-friendly way. While we did teach modeling (especially early on), we found that we were really teaching marketing in a different way. All students did not find this new way comfortable, but many now have the tools and the confidence to address marketing issues in more precise and, often, in broader terms than before. The approach and the associated tools can help you to expand your ways of thinking about marketing.

Marketing engineering is a means to an end: Marketing engineering allows marketers to take advantage of data, information, and computer models in making important marketing decisions. However, marketing engineering is not just about data, information, or analyses. It is a systematic process to help people improve decisions, and the outputs of that process are better decisions. Your experience with the decision models in this book should help you to articulate how and why you make decisions and encourage you to use these models when making those decisions.

Models require judgment: This book contains models that are relevant to both operational and strategic decisions. But models are simplified and incomplete representations of reality. Models developed to support strategic decisions (e.g., positioning) usually provide insights concerning the directions of actions but often no specific guidelines; while models developed to support operational decisions are both narrow and specific (how many sales calls should a salesperson make to a given account in the next quarter?). In using both types of models managers must temper the model results by using their own judgment. For strategic decisions managers must use judgment to translate broad guidelines into specific actions. For operational decisions managers must use their judgment to fine-tune specific recommendations to fit with the overall strategy of the firm. Decision models are very useful, but they are too simple to be trusted entirely.

Another reason for exercising judgment arises from the business context within which a model is used. Often model results suggest constructive changes to current plans, but decision makers balk at the amount of organizational disruption and resistance that would occur. As Schrage (2000, p. 25) points out, models reveal the gaps between what organizations *want* to accomplish, and what they are actually prepared to *do*. But, identifying such gaps is important for generating informed judgments about how best to implement potential actions suggested by model use.

The whole is greater than the sum of its parts: When you need to explore a major business problem you have a full marketing engineering toolkit to support you—for example, you have tools to segment a market, to select a segment to serve, to customize a product offering for that segment, to target and position that product, and to develop promotional plans and ad copy. The value of the concepts and of the associated software multiplies as the business problem broadens. The material allows you to go farther and deeper in solving marketing problems, often well beyond what individual models would permit. Ideally every tool should raise questions beyond its scope and expose unexplored areas of the total marketing system. We have found that it is usually better to build separate models and then link their insights and recommendations, rather than attempting to build a fully integrated model that simultaneously addresses all the issues. Together, the models provide a more complete and understandable set of action guidelines than any one of them can individually.

Information does not automatically result in value: We are near the end of the era when firms could gain competitive advantage merely by having market information. Today large firms have access to more market and customer information than they can use (e.g., clickstream data generated at their Web sites). To gain the most value from information, firms are trying new approaches: (1) They are using computer and communication technologies to make relevant information available in a timely manner to their entire workforce. (2) They are developing new knowledge management techniques to help employees use specialized knowledge (e.g., marketing decision models) to convert information into more effective decisions and actions throughout the organization. For example, if a firm has a superior process for developing new products, it should make sure that market information feeds that process, so that it can develop new products better tuned to customer needs and introduce them sooner than its competitors. Marketing engineering approaches that include firm-specific knowledge (e.g., a customized conjoint analysis model) can help firms to transform market information into superior products. Such uses of information are not transparent to competitors and are not likely to be replicated by them, leading to competitive advantage. Information has value only if you use it to drive decisions and actions. As Barabba and Zaltman (1991, p. 3) put it, "competitive advantage resides increasingly in how information is used rather than in who has information."

The software allows rapid prototyping: Markets are changing so quickly that decisions must reflect quick adaptation rather than careful optimization. Thus to be useful decision aids must be capable of rapid prototyping. The software accompanying the book enables you to quickly explore the potential value of a model in a particular decision context before you decide either to invest more effort in developing customized models or to use more traditional approaches. Even when a full-blown marketing engineering project is not feasible, trying out a model on a smaller, related problem can provide you with useful insights and document the potential opportunity cost of *not* doing a full-scale study.

Software empowers: In years past, we have taught many of the concepts and cases described in the book to managers, but without using the software. When managers evaluate case situations supported by the software, they often see things differently. An interesting example is the Syntex case (Chapter 9). In traditional case discussions most managers make sales resource allocation recommendations that are fairly close to those the company explored (i.e., increase salesforce size substantially and devote more resources to Naprosyn). However, managers who use the software more often make unconventional recommendations (e.g., reduce the size of the salesforce, focus all effort on a few successful products such as Naprosyn and use outside reps for selling other products). We surmise that those who use the software are more likely to determine that the potential profit associated with increasing the salesforce is not substantial, and that Syntex can get close to its current profits by reducing the size of the salesforce and reallocating the sales effort. The software enables managers to explore more options (quickly)—options that are not "anchored" only to those included in the case report.

We (Lilien et al. 2001) conducted controlled experiments to explore how MBA students use the ABB model (Chapter 3) and the Syntex model (Chapter 9). We find that the availability of models improved the quality of their resource allocation recommendations in both cases, with more resources reassigned to more profitable products and customers. However, because model users have no external criteria (e.g., market performance) to assess the quality of their recommendations, they did not perceive that they did better than people who did not have access to models. Even experts (acting as surrogates for senior management) evaluating the recommendations made by the study participants were not able to differentiate between the quality of the recommendations made by those who had access to a model and those who did not. At the same time, model availability had a significant influence on the decision process, reducing perceived decision complexity, improving discussion quality, and helping people to move farther away from anchor points (e.g., past decisions). Such process effects, in turn, had a positive effect on subjective perceptions, leading to more satisfaction with the decision, the decision process, and perceived usefulness of the model. In an experimental study using a different set of software, van Bruggen, Smidts, and Wierenga (1998) compared the relative performance of managers using a decision support system to make decisions in a simulated environment with that of managers who did not use the system. They report that managers using the system were less susceptible to anchoring current decisions to prior decisions (anchoring typically leads to poorer performance in less predictable environments). The authors also report that the superior performance was more pronounced in earlier stages of the multiperiod simulation when the managers had not yet fully grasped the important drivers of market behavior.

Empowerment has its downside: The deceptive simplicity of using the software and the presumed scientific credibility of the underlying models gives users a false sense of security. There is also a real danger in having too much data and information without having concomitant analytical capabilities to make sense of those data. In fact, the growing availability of fine-grained data, such as those from scanner panels, web logs and CRM (Customer Relationship Management) systems, encourages mechanistic applications of marketing models and a focus on finer details at the expense of exploring more difficult, strategic issues. We have also observed two interesting situations: Students with strong quantitative backgrounds are often drawn to the technical aspects of the results and sometimes miss the big picture. Students with weak analytical skills either ignore model results and go with their intuition or accept the results uncritically. For example, we saw one group inadvertently reverse the scale (changing it from low to high to high to low) on some critical data but accept the model results anyway. The best outcomes we have seen come from groups that include people with different levels of analytical abilities who pool their efforts while questioning and supporting one another. These groups use the model results as one input into a decision process that also includes common sense and educated judgment.

Marketing engineering requires lifelong learning: No book or course can communicate all the richness of marketing problems or all the opportunities and challenges associated with marketing engineering. Some of you may recall watching "slicer-dicer" demonstrations on TV: the demonstrator shows how the slicer can slice tomatoes perfectly in 15 different ways. When you try it, you get less than perfect results—learning to use the device takes time. In a similar vein, after studying marketing engineering and using the software you may underestimate the difficulties in applying this approach to new decision situations. Successful application requires a blend of modeling knowledge, common sense, sound judgment, good communication skills, patience, practice, and most important, a willingness to learn through experimentation.

Instructors should be coaches more than teachers: The pedagogic focus should be on learning by students rather than teaching by instructors. Marketing engineering cannot be taught through lectures alone. You cannot learn how to ride a bicycle by listening to a lecture, but you can learn quickly and well under the direction of a guide or coach. The same holds true for marketing engineering. The more we acted as guides, critics, and facilitators, the more students learned and the more they liked it. This is obvious in hindsight, but it was not so clear when we began. Leidner and Jarvenpaa (1995) suggest that teacher-centered methods (e.g., lectures) are efficient for imparting factual or procedural knowledge. However, learner-centered methods (e.g., hands-on cases and exercises completed with peers under the guidance of a coach) are appropriate for helping students to develop their own abilities to solve problems. Because the marketing engineering software is powerful and fairly easy to use, students can see their skills (and thinking) developing rapidly.

Marketing engineering should link academics and practitioners: In marketing, practice without theory teaches little while theory without practice means even less. Decision makers pressured to understand and operate in complex and risky markets increasingly depend on the concepts and tools of marketing engineering. For example, the executives we teach invariably try our software using some of their own data and immediately see the relevance and the benefit of the marketing engineering approach. The pressure on academics to show greater relevance for their work is increasing academic interest in marketing engineering as well. These two pressures point to an exciting marriage of convenience that should lead to improved tools for practitioners and interesting problems for academics to work on. As with all successful partnerships, both stand to gain.

USING MARKETING ENGINEERING WITHIN FIRMS

Marketing engineering succeeds because of sophisticated managers, not because of sophisticated models. Such managers recognize that decisions affect many stakeholders and that people resist change and will not embrace decision processes they do not understand or decisions not favorable to their interests. Therefore developing good decisions is only half the challenge. It is just as important to make those decisions acceptable to stakeholders within a firm, recalling that model users and decision makers may be different. Models can also help people understand and accept decisions: models improve communications among the stakeholders.

By clearly stating model assumptions and understanding the results, managers can replace positions with principles: Instead of saying "Let's do X," one might say "I believe that our objective should be A, and based on the model, X is a good way to achieve that objective." If the process of articulating model assumptions is orchestrated well, discussion will focus on the merits of those assumptions rather than on the appropriateness or validity of the model output. As we discussed in Chapter 1, models are particularly useful when they help change mental models by challenging the assumptions or beliefs underlying those mental models. A model also provides an explicit mechanism for including stakeholders in the decision process. For example, at Syntex Labs (Chapter 9) the stakeholders participated by providing inputs to the model and by helping implement model results. Managers are more likely to accept decisions resulting from a model if they know their inputs and judgments are part of the process.

The following tips and suggestions should help you to increase the likelihood of your achieving success with marketing engineering:

Be opportunistic: Select problems or issues that have a good chance of rapid and demonstrable success. A successful application of a model that favors a negative decision (e.g., do not introduce the new product) is likely to have less impact than an application of a model that favors a positive decision (e.g., introduce the new product). When managers agree that the firm needs drastic improvements in a particular area, you have an opportunity to prove the value of marketing engineering by setting more precise and defensible goals and expectations. Managers are open to new approaches in such situations, and noticeable improvements are possible. Sinha and Zoltners (2001) scrutinized hundreds of projects in which they had used marketing decision models. They argue that their models had the biggest impact in situations characterized as having moderate complexity and high measurability. They also offer the following guidelines for developing models that succeed in organizational settings: (1) build realistic models, (2) build adaptive models, (3) generate implementable solutions, (4) get it done quickly, and (5) solve the right problem.

Start simple, and keep it simple: It is best to start with problems that are understandable and familiar to the stakeholders. For example, if the firm has a large customer database and is trying to figure out how to identify and target its efforts to the most profitable accounts, choice-segmentation software might offer a quick solution. It is easy to explain: "We will target customers who, based on their previous purchase behavior, are more likely to respond favorably to our future selling efforts." The software could be programmed to tag promising accounts and update predictions regularly. Everybody wins. The salesforce is likely to increase its sales per salesperson and thus increase its commission income. Managers will be happy about the more effective use of the firm's resources. Finally, the less responsive accounts can be turned over to a newly created telemarketing salesforce, which can provide new sources of revenue.

A simple model will have served its purpose if it surprises the user with a novel insight or unearths an unexpected option. Marketing engineering should help us to use our imagination and expand our decision options, even if we are not able to use the model to make a decision.

Work backward—begin with an end in mind: Start with an understanding of the goal of the modeling effort. Is it to provide justification for a course of action? Is it to resolve an issue for which judgment seems to be inadequate? Is it to facilitate a group decision? Is it for forecasting (what will happen) or for explaining something (why did it happen)? It is also useful to undertake the marketing engineering effort with target dates for meetings and presentations in mind. This will force discipline in completing the modeling effort, and the meetings will provide a forum for discussing modeling results and facilitating follow-through.

Score inexpensive victories: Look for areas in which the costs of model development are low compared with potential benefits. For example, the salesforce-allocation model is fairly inexpensive to implement. It can be used successfully with just judgmental data. And it offers the potential of increasing current sales revenues by 5 to 10 percent by reallocating effort. As Schrage (2000, p. 57) points out, people and organizations use models when the opportunity costs of ***not*** if using them are clearly higher than the cost of use.

Develop a program, not just projects: We described marketing engineering applications at Syntex Labs and at ABB Electric that were both successful. But there was one important difference between them: the Syntex application was a project, and turnover in the original team, and in management more generally, prevented Syntex from getting the most out of this effort. The firm claimed that it could have increased its profit from the project by more than 10 percent (at no additional cost) by properly monitoring and adapting the implementation of the recommendations.

At ABB in contrast, marketing engineering has been an integral part of the organization for over two decades, affecting the allocation of sales and promotional efforts, the development of new products and advertising copy, the positioning of products, and decisions in manufacturing. Its marketing engineering program saved ABB and helped it to survive; ABB's president, Daniel Elwing, puts it this way: "It had to be a program; it could not be a project."

MARKETING ENGINEERING: A LOOK AHEAD

To improve their performance and future prospects, firms are investing heavily in information technology infrastructures linked to communication networks. The marketing function is also undergoing fundamental transformations because of these technologies: the marketing operations of direct mail firms depend on toll-free telephone systems for sales and support; salespeople keep in touch with customers and headquarters using laptop computers; large retailers cannot survive without online price-lookup systems. Firms today install computers and software everywhere, not just in their back offices. Yet many marketing managers continue to make decisions in the traditional, old-fashioned way, without using the information and decision-aiding technologies that are already available.

Some firms have recognized that one of their most important assets is relevant information whose business implications decision makers can interpret in a timely manner. To take advantage of the information available to them, firms are integrating decision-aiding technologies into the fabric of their day-to-day operations and decisions. Consider the following examples:

- *American Express* is a leading-edge user of information technologies. It developed the Authorizer's Assistant, a rule-based expert system with more than 1,000 rules, to automate the credit-approval process for purchases based on the past spending patterns of the credit card holder (this is an important function because the AmEx card does not impose a credit limit). Another model American Express is using is a complex neural network to analyze the hundreds of millions of entries in its database that include how and where its cardholders spend their money. This analysis recognizes patterns and allows the company to send cardholders special customized offers with their bills.

In another successful effort American Express uses customer records to identify stores that do not carry the card but are located in areas where there are many card members. This type of analysis, combined with a minimum sales guarantee, convinced Wal-Mart to accept the American Express card. Other information systems in the company support analyses of customer records to summarize the profile of American Express card members who use a particular establishment versus profiles of customers using competing establishments. For example, this type of analysis can be used to see if the Marriott located in downtown Philadelphia attracts more women customers than the Four Seasons Hotel located a mile away.

- *Frito-Lay*, a leading producer of snack foods, has introduced a number of successful information-technology innovations to enhance its marketing efforts. For example, its Zone Workbench System puts timely information into the hands of front-line managers. The system grew out of the company's decentralization in 1990, when it reduced the number of management levels and broadened employee responsibilities. Frito-Lay's headquarters began to manage its 10,000-person salesforce through new zone offices. The Workbench provided zone managers, each responsible for about 100 salespersons, with information they use daily in managing key accounts, overseeing the placement of promotion displays, planning sales routes, and managing expenses associated with selling. In 1991 Frito-Lay won the prestigious Computer World–Smithsonian Award for using information technology to make a positive impact on society.

- *Sensormatic* is a large electronic security firm that markets surveillance and theft-prevention equipment to businesses. It uses an information system to develop strategic plans by segments instead of treating all customers as one homogeneous group. The company has developed a large database that contains detailed customer and market information, some of which was previously unavailable to the marketing managers. This information has been the basis for improved segment-level forecasts. One of Sensormatic's executives commented that they once viewed their customers as homogeneous, but they now use information technologies to anticipate evolving customer needs and to understand the differences among customers, and they now exploit these differences to generate growth.

- *The Franklin Mint*, a worldwide direct response marketer of quality collectibles and luxury and home-decor products, has developed a system called AMOS (automatic model specification) that is a leading-edge application of database marketing. As Zahavi (1995) explains, "The most challenging part of the system was the specification problem—the process of selecting the subset of predictors that 'best' explain, in a statistical sense, the customer's choice decisions, from among a much larger set of potential predictors." For the Franklin Mint that means choosing from among more than 800 predictor variables. Its choice model incorporates past purchase history, demographic variables (often data acquired from outside vendors and appended to its database), and product attributes (theme, artist, material, etc.).

The choice model drives the Franklin Mint's entire planning and decision process, which includes such problems as

- Targeting the right audience for each promotion
- Determining how many mailings to send each customer
- Predicting the number of orders the promotion will generate
- Determining how many units of a promoted item to manufacture or procure

AMOS has resulted in increases in profitability of nearly 10 percent for the Franklin Mint over previous approaches (including a judgmental procedure and one using more standard segmentation methods like the cluster and discriminant analysis approaches we described in Chapter 3). It is now being used to support operations in Europe and Asia as well as in North America.

- *GTE Sylvania* has established a central "war room" for the staff who build rich data representations of its customers—from 16 databases and 10 external information providers. Information is maintained on 7.6 million businesses in 220 market segments, including geographic information, employee numbers, square footage of the sites, and economic growth indices for each location. They calculate the lamp-buying potential of every business from this information. This information, represented visually on wall-mounted display screens, assists GTE Sylvania as it works with its distributors to better serve product users (Source: *www.cscresearchservices.com*).

- *Travelocity*, the Web's biggest online travel site, takes strategic advantage of its Web log data to improve its promotional program. For example, in early 2000, TWA announced a special $360 round-trip fare between Los Angeles and San Juan, Puerto Rico. Typically, a traditional marketing pitch would have notified the whole Hispanic community in the L.A. area, including people with no interest in Puerto Rico. Instead, Travelocity analyzed its data warehouse, and within a few hours it had identified 30,000 customers in L.A. who had inquired about fares to Puerto Rico within the past few days. An e-mail went out to them the next morning, with an astounding 25 percent of the targeted segment either taking the TWA offer or booking another Caribbean flight (Source: *Forbes*, July 9, 2001).

We expect that during the next decade the major developments in technologies to support marketing decisions will be geared to helping managers process the information that is already available to them: to filter the relevant from the irrelevant and to draw out insights from information. Many large firms are putting together a new corporate activity called Marketing Information Systems (MKIS) to support and enhance enterprise-wide performance using marketing information. Although the concept of MKIS has existed for a number of years (see, for example, Kotler 1966), the scope and potential value of the present-day MKIS is far greater than was envisioned in those early days.

MKIS, typically located within the marketing department, is charged with harnessing marketing-related information and distributing and facilitating its use within the firm. Even as the marketing function seems to be in decline, the marketing concept itself appears to be gaining wider acceptance in firms (Doyle 1995). Marketing is becoming an enterprise-wide activity rather than the exclusive domain of a specific department. Firms see MKIS as a way to use marketing information to make everyone in the firm realize that they must be more responsive to customer needs and wants and to the competitive environment.

Historically, a major function of information systems has been to provide timely access to information. MKIS can now integrate end-user decision models with traditional information systems to enhance the firm's ability to use marketing engineering. Seven current trends favor this integration of information. Firms are

1. Investing in the infrastructure they need to develop and maintain extensive corporate databases (also called data warehouses)
2. Using On-Line Analytical Processing (OLAP) to integrate data retrieval and modeling capabilities with databases
3. Exploring the Application Service Provider (ASP) model to increase the value and flexibility of their data and models
4. Deploying intelligent systems to automate some modeling tasks

5. Developing computer simulations for decision training and for exploring multiple options
6. Installing groupware systems, such as Lotus Notes, to support group decision making
7. Enhancing user interfaces to make it easier to deploy even complex models more widely

We describe these trends next:

Data warehouses: A data warehouse is a repository of historical information that contains data collected and organized specifically to support decision making. A transaction database supports such operational tasks as looking up the *inventory level of an item*, the *price of a product* or the location of the nearest dealer. On the other hand, a data warehouse is useful for managing a business, and it can be designed to answer such questions as, "How does the response to our sales promotion in Philadelphia compare with the response in New York?" A data warehouse supports decisions in many different areas (e.g., yield management, promotions management), and it is designed to take advantage of the various transaction databases already being used by the firm. A marketing data warehouse could be structured around several databases:

- *Bank of America Corporation* maintains a data warehouse that contains 1.2 terabytes of data (each terabyte is equal to 1 trillion bytes, or roughly 250 million pages), which is a composite of 30 different databases containing 35 million records of checking, savings, and other transactions (*Business Week*, July 31, 1995; *Wall Street Journal*, November 18, 1996). One use of this database is to support the firm's phone reps who field about 100,000 calls each day from customers regarding credit balances, loan rates, and the like. They use the database to translate customer calls into business opportunities by offering other products or services tailored to the specific needs of the persons calling. For example, if a customer has more than 20 percent of his or her savings in a passbook account, a model could recognize that such a customer is likely to buy a higher-interest product. Another use of the database is to support ad hoc planning. For example, the bank found out that it was losing checking-account customers who were unhappy with the bank's fees. Using the database and some modeling efforts, the bank developed a lower-cost checking plan targeted to those customers and was able to reverse the trend.
- *Wal-Mart* has developed the world's largest commercial data warehouse consisting of more than 100 terabytes of data. This warehouse includes data on every transaction with every customer in every one of its 4200 stores for the past 65 weeks and the inventories carried in each store. Using well-structured database queries, the company can quickly determine answers to such questions as, which items are moving, what different types of customers are buying the various products, and how often it must restock shelves.

Firms can support other decision areas using different data warehouses, although they may build all the data warehouses on the same few transaction databases. To get the most value from such large databases, firms need mass-produced marketing models (Blattberg, Kim, and Ye 1994). This need is driving the development of On-Line Analytical Processing, a set of techniques to perform analyses on data retrieved from data warehouses. OLAP is described next.

On-Line Analytical Processing (OLAP): The analytical tool most widely used by corporations is the spreadsheet. The typical spreadsheet is limited to analyzing small databases, and it primarily provides a two-dimensional view of the data. Decision makers often want to cut data along several dimensions: across time (How are we doing compared with last year?), and across products and geography (Which of our products are prescribed by family practitioners in rural communities?). Database vendors such as IBM, Oracle, and Sybase offer multidimensional analytical tools for use with their database-management systems. These tools provide online decision support for managers without requiring them to learn complex database query languages. For example, Wal-Mart is using sophisticated decision support systems to help its store managers identify the top 10 to 20 products in each store on each day of the week; they then alter shelf displays and end-of-aisle displays to take advantage of the changing mix of top products by day of the week. If the Wal-Mart managers in the Wheat Ridge, Colorado, store find that it sells more diapers on a given Thursday, they will then plan special displays of diapers for the following Thursday!

Currently OLAP tools are stronger in online data retrieval than in analytic capabilities. However, as firms integrate more marketing engineering models into OLAPs, these tools will gain the ability to support complex decisions online. For example, corporations could integrate a library of models into their corporate data warehouses. Managers could then get on-line support to help them answer such questions as, "Why is thé promotion more profitable in New York than in Philadelphia?" and to help them decide whether to cut back on promotions in Philadelphia. For some decision areas the data warehouse would need to support enterprise-wide models rather than just end-user models. For example, revenue management requires the execution of complex optimization procedures on large dynamic databases. However, end-user models are still useful for many small, localized applications.

Application Service Providers (ASPs) for analytics. An exciting new development that will greatly expand OLAP capabilities is the emergence of Application Service Providers that offer online access to various types of knowledge resources (software, data, content, and models). ASPs convert knowledge resources into services (e.g., analytics, process control) accessible over the Web, instead of being packaged as products and systems. For example, *salesforce.com* is attempting to create a viable ASP model for salesforce automation by offering such online services as contact management, forecasting, e-mail communications, customizable reports, and synchronization of wireless devices. These services are made possible by dynamically linking data retrieval and analysis software to various databases. Exhibit 11.1 shows one way to implement an ASP for analytical support. With these developments, there is an emerging capability for offering marketing analytics to anyone, anytime, anywhere. Indeed, we will soon make parts of the *Marketing Engineering* suite of software available in an ASP format. Lilien and Rangaswamy (2000) discuss in more detail the value and implications of these developments for marketing modeling.

Exhibit 11.2 summarizes our beliefs about how the Internet and ASPs will influence marketing modeling in the years ahead. We classify marketing models along two dimensions: On the horizontal axis (Degree of Integration), we distinguish between standalone models (e.g., supporting a single user for a single task) on one extreme and those that are integrated with organizational processes, databases, and other aspects of the decision environment at the other extreme (e.g., single user, multiple tasks; multiple users, single task). On the vertical axis (Degree of Visibility), we distinguish between models that are embedded inside systems (i.e., a "blackbox model" that works in the background) requiring few inputs or interactions with the user, and those that are highly interactive and whose structures are visible. We discuss below four categories of models that fall at the extremes of these two dimensions and indicate how the emerging networked economy will encourage their use:

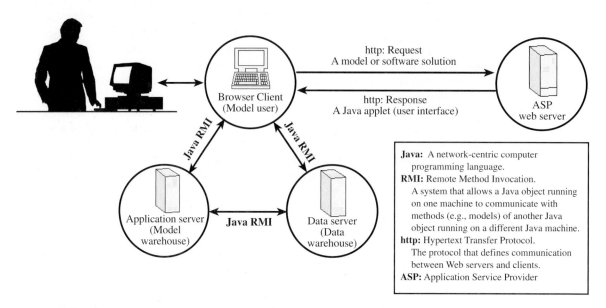

Java: A network-centric computer programming language.
RMI: Remote Method Invocation. A system that allows a Java object running on one machine to communicate with methods (e.g., models) of another Java object running on a different Java machine.
http: Hypertext Transfer Protocol. The protocol that defines communication between Web servers and clients.
ASP: Application Service Provider

EXHIBIT 11.1
The exhibit outlines one way to implement the Application Service Provider (ASP) approach for marketing engineering. Models, data, and user interfaces, which are combined together in traditional marketing models, are de-coupled in a Web environment. This enables any Internet user to have more flexibility in conducting marketing analyses and interpretations anywhere, anytime.

1. *Visible standalone models* can be put on application servers (several ASPs already do this—e.g., *www.marketswitch.com*) and accessed by client browsers. In such an environment, software renditions of marketing models can be maintained in central locations, minimizing costs of updates and distribution. Model users also benefit because they will always have access to the latest versions of the software. Visible models with user interactions can also become more valuable online. For example, applications ranging from simple computational devices, such as mortgage calculators (*www.jeacle.ie/mortgage*), to sophisticated programs, such as conjoint analysis (*www.valueharvest.com*), are available on a 24/7 basis. These applications are supported with online technical help (as well as live support), improved content (help files, tutorials, etc.), and linked to related applications that are available elsewhere on the Internet. Many traditional marketing models, such as the Bass Model, would benefit from being redesigned or re-implemented in newer software packages, for deployment over the Internet.

2. *Component objects* can be deployed more widely on the Internet because they can be structured to continuously monitor and optimize various aspects of how an organization functions. Proctor and Gamble's access to purchase data for their products at Wal-Mart allows it to deploy automated models to forecast demand, schedule production and delivery, optimize inventory holdings and even assess the effectiveness of its promotions.

3. *Integrated component objects* exploit the blurring lines between software, content, services, and applications to deliver more complete decision solutions to managers. For example, an integrated segmentation system could run not only standard clustering algorithms but could also access data from elsewhere on the Web before model execution, and then distribute customized communications to customers in different segments. Revenue management systems at the world's major airlines dy-

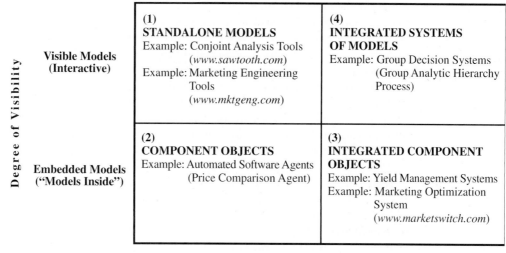

	Standalone	**Integrated**
Visible Models (Interactive)	**(1) STANDALONE MODELS** Example: Conjoint Analysis Tools (*www.sawtooth.com*) Example: Marketing Engineering Tools (*www.mktgeng.com*)	**(4) INTEGRATED SYSTEMS OF MODELS** Example: Group Decision Systems (Group Analytic Hierarchy Process)
Embedded Models ("Models Inside")	**(2) COMPONENT OBJECTS** Example: Automated Software Agents (Price Comparison Agent)	**(3) INTEGRATED COMPONENT OBJECTS** Example: Yield Management Systems Example: Marketing Optimization System (*www.marketswitch.com*)

Degree of Visibility (vertical axis label) — Degree of Integration (horizontal axis label)

EXHIBIT 11.2
Marketing models classified by degree of integration and degree of visibility that can be deployed on the World Wide Web and accessed over the Internet.

namically optimize schedules, prices and seat inventories and send messages to targeted customers about new travel opportunities that they might find attractive. Although such models may be fully automated, or used by unsophisticated users, the models themselves are likely to be quite sophisticated (akin to an autopilot for an aircraft) and require frequent updating and validation by highly skilled modelers.

4. *Integrated systems of models* put a logically linked set of models in the hands of decision makers (possibly geographically separated) who need to share their different knowledge bases for important common decisions (e.g., negotiation support, bid planning, marketing planning models). For example, Lodish et al. (1988) describe a subjectively calibrated market response model that required co-location of the decision makers. In the Internet world, such subjective data inputs can be obtained online from managers in different locations, consensus developed using models running on a server, and the resource and planning implications made available to all through a group decision support system.

The Internet could drive the prices of digital products (i.e., products, such as marketing models, that can be distributed on the Net) down to their marginal production costs which are near zero (Evans and Wurster, 2000). As a result, many Internet-based models will be available almost free, at least for limited use (or offered in exchange for viewing commercials, etc.), making them even more attractive for analysts and managerial users alike. Thus, over the next decade, we expect an explosion in the availability of customizable, scalable, and (possibly) embedded decision models on the Internet, available anytime, anywhere, for anyone.

Intelligent marketing systems: Currently most managers use marketing engineering in a reactive mode after they have identified decision problems. This limits the usefulness of marketing engineering. Herbert Simon (1977) suggested that problem solving consists of three phases: intelligence, design, and choice. In the intelligence phase the decision maker identifies problems and situations that call for decisions. In the design phase the decision maker generates many potential solutions to the problem, and in the choice phase he or she selects specific solution(s). Historically, decision models have emphasized the design and choice phases. However, information-intensive environments call for decision support systems that can also be used in the intelligence phase.

Many marketing organizations generate millions of pieces of data a day. For example, a firm might distribute 20 products to 10 accounts in each of 300 markets and employ 300 salespeople. The only way it can interpret and use the large amounts of data it accumulates is by deploying intelligent models that automate the process of interpreting the data. Several firms are experimenting with *data mining*, a process that relies on automated analysis agents to sift through the data looking for nuggets of insight.

Data mining is a catchall term for various types of analyses designed to discover relationships within a set of data. It is useful for identifying patterns in the data that indicate problems that require managers' attention and decisions. Data mining includes *correlations and associations* (e.g., people who bought Enid Blyton's *Best Stories for Five-Year-Olds* also bought J. K. Rowling's *Harry Potter and the Chamber of Secrets*), *sequences* (people who bought fresh salmon fillet also subsequently bought bananas in the same grocery shopping trip), *grouping of data through classification and clustering* (e.g., more men then women buy a particular CD), and *forecasting* (e.g., people who bought most recently are the ones likely to purchase again next week). Data mining also involves many methodologies including statistical analyses (e.g., Chapter 4), neural networks (Chapter 5), and rule-based systems (Chapter 8). We expect to see many interesting applications of data mining in marketing in the coming years.

A promising application of data mining is its potential for doing real-time customization on Web sites, dynamically adjusting the content presented to users as they interact with the Web site. For example, it is now feasible to develop systems to continuously monitor, measure, and simulate banner ad effectiveness across a network of partner sites and dynamically optimize ad deployment. If a news event at a golf tournament suddenly increases traffic at golf sites, triggering improved effectiveness of banner ads presented there, an advertiser for whom this target segment is important can then redirect more of its advertising expenditures to those sites. Such a capability will become more important as firms try to gain competitive advantage by rapid adjustment of effort deployment to reflect the continuously changing marketing response patterns characteristic of a networked economy.

Another approach to dealing with such large amounts of data is automated intelligence that links models and databases directly to customer communications. Such systems help managers automate both the modeling process and the implementation of some of the modeling results. For example, an automated segmentation and targeting system can identify attractive segments and then arrange to send segment members an e-mail message or piece of mail or arrange for a sales call.

Expert systems (also called knowledge-based systems) are a third way to automate the filtering of large amounts of data and the subsequent modeling. They are particularly useful for repetitive decision problems that have highly varying input conditions (e.g., credit authorization, automated analysis, and report writing). In such situations we can specify the structure of the problem and the range of variation in inputs reasonably well in advance, but we cannot anticipate what to do under every combination of input conditions that we might encounter. For example, Mrs. Fields Cookies, Inc., has developed an expert system to cut down on errors in signing store leases. With 800 stores, the company is trying to ensure that idiosyncratic local conditions are properly incorporated into the contract along with appropriate overall terms. "The expert system can check each lease," says Fields (Light 1992).

An important application for expert systems in marketing is in automatically generating top-line management reports based on statistical analyses of frequently collected

To: Sizzle Brand Manager
From: CoverStory
Date: 07/05/89
Subject: Sizzle Brand Summary for Twelve Weeks Ending May 21, 1989

Sizzle's share of type in total United States was 8.3 in the C&B Juice/Drink category for the twelve weeks ending 5/21/98. This is an increase of 0.2 points from a year earlier, but down .3 from last period. This reflects volume sales of 8.2 million gallons. Category volume (currently 99.9 million gallons) declined 1.3% from a year earlier.

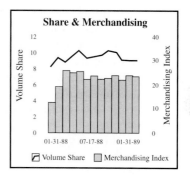

Sizzle's share of type is 8.3—up 0.2 from the same period last year.

Display activity and unsupported price cuts rose over the past year—unsupported price cuts from 38 points to 46. Featuring and price remained at about the same level as a year earlier.

Components of Sizzle Share

Among components of Sizzle, the principal gainer is:
Sizzle 64 oz: up 0.5 points from last year to 3.7

and losers:
Sizzle 48 oz: down 0.2 to 1.9
Sizzle 32 oz: down 0.1 to 0.7

Sizzle 64 oz's share of type increase is partly due to 11.3 points ride in % ACV with Display vs. year ago.

Competitor Summary

Among Sizzle's major competitors, the principal gainers are:
Shakey: up 2.5 points from last year to 32.6
Private Label: +.5 to 19.9 (but down .3 since last period)

and loser:
Generic Seltzer: –.7 to 3.5

Shakey's share of type increase is ...

EXHIBIT 11.3
The first page of a CoverStory memorandum shows how an expert system can generate a coherent management report with no human intervention. *Source*: Schmitz, Armstrong, and Little 1990, p. 38.

marketing data. Two such systems that analyze scanner data are CoverStory (Schmitz, Armstrong, and Little 1990) and INFER (Rangaswamy, Harlam, and Lodish 1991). Exhibit 11.3 shows a sample report that CoverStory generated automatically after extensive data analysis. A related system called Salespartner (Schmitz 1994) tunes its report to the needs of the sales representative for consumer packaged goods rather than to the needs of managers. Its report focuses on customer-specific programs and events that the salesperson can talk about during customer visits.

Customer service employees in many firms have diagnostic tools at their disposal to help solve customer problems. These tools—and the entire service encounter—represent other promising areas for commercial applications of expert systems. Firms can use these systems to increase their profitability by improving customer service, helping customers use products and solve problems. For example, a customer service representative at a help desk supported by expert systems can find out if a customer is a candidate for other programs, update information about the customer's new needs (product design feedback), and provide early warning about major problems. These technologies are also being deployed at some Web sites to provide product and service recommendations. Trade-off analyses are also being used for this purpose (see *www.activebuyersguide.com*).

Expert systems are most useful when we need models that (1) explain their behavior or recommendations (e.g., why they came to a specific conclusion in a report) or (2) simulate the recommendations of expert decision makers in well-specified decision areas. Many early expert systems failed because they were expensive to develop and maintain and because they operated on specialized hardware not linked to other systems within the firm. However, the new generation of "embeddable expert systems" that are linked to conventional systems have gained wider acceptance, use, and a secure role in industry (Hayes-Roth and Jacobstein 1994). In the next decade we expect to see many more embedded expert systems that support marketing managers.

Simulations: Managers use market simulations to learn marketing concepts (business simulations such as MarkStrat and InduStrat are widely used in MBA and executive programs) and to explore and understand the possible outcomes of potential decision options.

EXAMPLE

(Adapted from Whitaker 1995.) Lufthansa's consulting group developed an eight-period (each period corresponds to six months) simulation to train its managers to prepare for privatization and deregulation of the airline industry in Europe. In the simulation three airlines start out with identical resources and market positions, and they have complete freedom to decide their frequencies of flights, fares, marketing policies, and purchases of fleet after the airlines are deregulated. The simulation covers most day-to-day activities of running an airline and embodies relationships that reflect real market data. However, it ignores some complex issues, such as traffic feeding across the hub, code-sharing alliances with other carriers, and negotiations with labor unions.

Managers participating in these simulations learn by making errors, which Lufthansa hopes they will avoid on the job. For example, they may order aircraft in anticipation of demand that does not materialize. This error will teach them to use modeling approaches to more carefully consider the costs (e.g., higher debt and loan payments) and benefits (e.g., improved punctuality, lower fuel and maintenance costs) in uncertain situations before ordering new aircraft. Likewise, when competition intensifies managers might start investing large amounts of money in marketing without seeing adequate returns. This error will teach them to use modeling approaches to more carefully evaluate where, how, and why they should increase their marketing dollars before making such an investment.

In addition to their use in training, computer simulations are increasingly being used in actual decision making. For example, surgeons can first practice a complex surgical procedure on a computer-generated replica of their patient before carrying out the actual surgery. This process is called *anticipatory learning*. Marketing managers can do the same thing—make decisions in a simulated marketplace before committing to a course of action. For example, conjoint analysis reports often include a market simulator that managers can use to explore options that they were not considering when they commissioned the conjoint study. Firms use simulations (like our simplified bidding-analysis software) in competitive bidding situations for oil leases and for broadcast spectrum rights.

With simulation, marketing managers can experiment on a simulated representation of the marketplace and see the likely result of their actions. And they can do so at low cost and more rapidly than any real market experiment would allow. Organizations can also use simulations effectively to spread learning and new thinking among their employees (Senge and Lannon 1990).

The objective of marketing simulation is not necessarily to predict the future, but to help managers understand what they should do to adapt to various possible futures given their beliefs about the likelihood of the occurrence of those futures. Thus, simulation facilitates backcasting – what we should do now to either bring about a certain kind of future, or to adapt in some way if that future were to actually occur. It is immaterial whether the simulated scenarios actually occur. What matters most is that executives learn about how their company, and the industry, will react to alternate futures. Schrage (2000) offers many insights and examples of how companies are using simulations profitably.

Groupware for decision support: *Groupware* is a general term that describes a variety of computer- and communications-based systems that enhance the efficiency and effectiveness with which a group of people make decisions. Using groupware, project teams can share information (e.g., reports and presentations) as well as make and record decisions (e.g., on-line voting). Such systems can circumvent temporal, geographic, and organizational barriers in supporting collaborative work:

- *Price Waterhouse Coopers*, a leading accounting firm, has one of the world's largest installed bases of Lotus Notes to support collaborative decision making. About 40,000 of its employees (consultants) each have a Lotus Notes program with which they access corporate-wide Lotus Notes databases, as well as databases specific to individual projects. With the systems Price Waterhouse Coopers can make specialized expertise widely available within the company and quickly put together and support ad hoc teams that make decisions to take advantage of emerging opportunities.
- *Computer Language Research* (CLR) is a leading firm in the tax software business, designing and marketing hundreds of different software packages for managing audits and taxes for such customers as banks, accounting firms, and corporate tax departments. Because of changing tax laws, the firm must be able to modify and enhance existing products quickly and develop new products for new customers in other industries. CLR has used Lotus Notes to improve both the speed and quality of its new products. For example, team members make many decisions on-line without having to arrange face-to-face meetings, which helps compress product-development time. Also, project teams have improved access to expertise available within the company and improved coordination in reporting and fixing problems before the new product is shipped, both of which improve product quality.

In the future we expect firms to use the marketing engineering approach to enhance groupware, incorporating further decision-aiding components. As a step in this direction Ventana Corporation has developed a software package called GroupSystems that organizations can use to set up electronic brainstorming with a number of participants. The system can be used to create agendas (e.g., problems to be resolved), to record ideas generated simultaneously and anonymously by participants, to obtain votes on action items, to produce reports summarizing discussions, and to maintain records for future use. Participants may gather in the same room or log in from remote locations. Such systems can also be used to collect the judgmental inputs many marketing engineering models require.

Several trends promise a bright future for groupware systems. We can think of online exchanges and auction sites as groupware that facilitate and support communities involved in price discovery. As these sites grow, we expect to see many decision tools developed to support such communities with their bidding and negotiation strategies and the like. There is now a growing interest in Peer-to-Peer (P2P) networks that can support ad hoc groups. P2P networks are particularly important for groups working across organizational boundaries—e.g., a group of concerned citizens working together to analyze a pollution problem or an ad hoc group of firms that come together to jointly bid on a project. Analytical support for such groups is a promising area for groupware applications. There are also many new and interesting groupware applications that will become feasible and important as organizations deploy knowledge management systems to leverage their intellectual assets more broadly among their employees and partners.

Improving the user interface: As end-user computing increases within firms, the need for user interfaces that operate in an intuitive manner becomes critical. To be successful, decision models have to serve users who have poor computer skills. Many decision models have failed to attract users because they are incorporated in systems that are difficult to use. For example, several systems for automating the activities of the salesforce are not meeting their performance goals because they require salespeople to adapt to a nonintuitive software design. The software developers should have designed the software around familiar, existing sales processes rather than around an imagined notion of how salespeople work.

People are becoming accustomed to better designed software packages and are coming to expect ease of use from every software package they encounter. The best software hides what the novice does not need (covering the engine with a streamlined hood) and highlights those inputs and outputs that are most important to that user at that time. To ensure that increasing numbers of people use their products, software vendors must provide increasingly user-friendly packages. We have tried to make our software easy to use.

Other trends: Glazer (1991) has tried to predict what might occur in the next decade or so because of the increasing availability of information and the decreasing cost of processing that information. He expects

- shorter and less predictable product life cycles,

- a shift in power from sellers to buyers,

- more focus on product profitability and less on share,

- more (and less formal) alliances,

- more focus on cooperation and less on competition, and

- greater reliance on decision teams whose members simultaneously process shared information.

All of these changes demand rapid and coherent marketing decisions, supported by the marketing engineering approach. Shorter product life cycles mean that analysis has to be both quick and sound. Increased buyer power means that companies must better understand buyer values to succeed in the market. An emphasis on profitability means that marketers

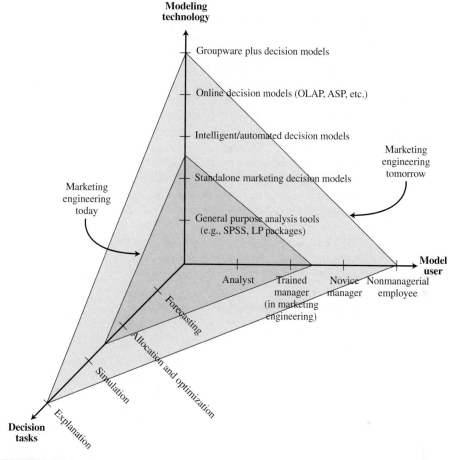

EXHIBIT 11.4
An overview of the evolution of marketing engineering to support a wider range of users and decision tasks using emerging technologies.

must focus on setting objectives. Alliances and cooperation mean that we need newer models to support these multiple decision makers. And the increase in team decisions means that groupware will increase in importance.

In Exhibit 11.4 we summarize our vision of the evolution of marketing engineering along three dimensions: (1) the type of user who uses models, (2) the type of decision tasks supported, and (3) the modeling technologies that enhance marketing engineering. Until the mid-1980s marketing engineering was carried out primarily by analysts who submitted reports to managers. Those analysts used general-purpose analysis programs running on mainframe computers (e.g., such statistical packages as SPSS and linear-programming packages) to generate forecasts and develop plans for optimally deploying organizational resources. The growth of personal computers has put managers in direct control (e.g., through spreadsheet models focused on specific decision areas), permitting richer manager-model interactions (e.g., simulations based on what-if analyses). In the future, marketing engineering will support a broadening range of users (e.g., customer service representatives) using a wider range of technologies (e.g., OLAP, intelligent systems, groupware systems) to enhance decision making by richer means (e.g., using simulation to explain market events).

While the marketing function in companies may decline in importance in the years to come, marketing can only increase in importance. Years ago Peter Drucker pointed out that marketing is too important to be left to marketers; that statement is even more true today. Marketing engineering, a bridge between conceptual marketing and disciplined, systematic marketing, is poised to take its place among the critical management tools for the successful 21st century firm.

POSTSCRIPT

Writing this book has been the most rewarding work we have undertaken. We hope that we have brought many previously abstract academic concepts and ideas to life and shown you how to apply them in business as well as in the classroom. There is nothing as rewarding as seeing good ideas used. We hope that you have found some good marketing engineering ideas and made them your own. Use them well.

We have received many suggestions from users of the first edition of this text, especially with regard to making the software more useful and user-friendly. We considered all such suggestions carefully and have implemented many of them. We conclude with a request. Please continue to send us your suggestions and share your own experiences with successful (and unsuccessful) applications of these decision models with us. This type of sharing is the surest way we know for giving life to abstract concepts. Let us hear from you at *www.mktgeng.com*!

References

Aaker, David A., and Carman, James M., 1982, "Are you overadvertising?" *Journal of Advertising Research*, Vol. 22, No. 4 (August–September), pp. 57–70.

Aaker, David A., and Day, George S., 1990, *Marketing Research*, fourth edition, John Wiley and Sons, New York, p. 574.

Abell, Derek F., and Hammond, J. S., 1979, *Strategic Marketing Planning*, Prentice Hall, Englewood Cliffs, New Jersey.

Abraham, Magid M., and Lodish, Leonard M., 1987, "PROMOTER: An automated promotion evaluation system," *Marketing Science*, Vol. 6, No. 2 (Spring), pp. 101–123.

———. 1993, "An implemented system for improving promotion productivity using store scanner data," *Marketing Science*, Vol. 12, No. 3 (Summer), pp. 248–269.

Agostini, Jean-Michel, 1961, "How to estimate unduplicated audiences," *Journal of Advertising Research*, Vol. 1, No. 3 (March), pp. 11–14.

Alberts, William W., 1989, "The experience curve doctrine reconsidered," *Journal of Marketing*, Vol. 53, No. 3 (July), pp. 36–49.

Albion, Mark S., 1984, "Suave (D)," HBS Case 9-585-020, Harvard Business School, Boston.

Allenby, Greg M., and Ginter, James L., 1995, "Using extremes to design products and segment markets, *Journal of Marketing Research*, Vol. 32, No. 4 (November), pp. 392-403.

Anderson, Erin, 1985, "Salesperson as outside agent or employee—A transaction cost analysis," *Marketing Science*, Vol. 4. No. 3 (Summer), pp. 234–254.

Anderson, James; Jain, Dipak C.; and Chintagunta, Pradeep K., 1993, "Customer value assessment in business markets: A state-of-practice study," *Journal of Business-to-Business Marketing*, Vol. 1, No. 1, pp. 3–29.

Anderson, Paul F., 1979, "The marketing management/ finance interface," in *1979 Educator Conference Proceedings*, eds. N. Beckwith, M. Houston, R. Mittelstaedt, K. B. Monroe, and S. Ward, American Marketing Association, Chicago, pp. 325–329.

———. 1981, "Marketing investment analysis," *Research in Marketing*, Vol. 4, ed. J. N. Sheth, JAI Press, Greenwich, Connecticut, pp. 1–38.

Anterasian, Cathy; Grahame, John L.; and Money, R. Bruce, 1996, "Are U.S. managers superstitious about market share?" *Sloan Management Review*, Vol. 37, No. 4, p. 67.

Appel, Valentine, 1971, "On advertising wear-out," *Journal of Advertising Research*, Vol. 11 (February), pp. 11–14.

Armstrong, J. Scott, 1985, "The ombudsman: Research on forecasting: A quarter century review, 1960–1984," *Interfaces*, Vol. 16, No. 1 (January–February), pp. 89–109.

———. 2001a, *Principles of Forecasting*, Kluwer, Boston, Massachusetts.

———. 2001b, "Selecting forecasting methods," in J. Scott Armstrong, ed., *Principles of Forecasting*, Kluwer, Boston, Massachusetts, pp. 365-386.

———. 2001c, "Combining forecasts," in J. Scott Armstrong, ed., *Principles of Forecasting*, Kluwer, Boston, Massachusetts, pp. 417-440.

Assael, Henry, and Day, George S., 1968, "Attitudes and awareness as predictors of market share," *Journal of Advertising Research*, Vol. 8, No. 4 (December), pp. 3–10.

Assael, Henry, and Roscoe, A. Marvin, Jr., 1976, "Approaches to market segmentation analysis," *Journal of Marketing*, Vol. 40, No. 4 (October), pp. 67–76.

Aumann, R., 1987, "What is game theory trying to accomplish?" In *Frontiers of Economics*, eds. K. J. Arrow and S. Honkapohja, Blackwell, Oxford, UK.

Axelrod, Joel N., 1968, "Attitude measures that predict purchase" *Journal of Advertising* Research, Vol. 8, No. 1 (March), pp. 3–17.

Barabba, Vincent P., and Zaltman, Gerald, 1991, *Hearing the Voice of the Market: Competitive Advantage Through Creative Use of Market Information*, Harvard Business School Press, Boston.

Baron, Jonathan, and Hershey, John C., 1988, "Outcome bias in decision evaluation," *Journal of Personality and Social Psychology*, Vol. 54, No. 4 (April), Washington, pp. 569–579.

Bass, Frank M., 1969, "A new product growth model for consumer durables," *Management Science*, Vol. 15, No. 4 (January), pp. 216–227.

Bass, Frank M.; Gordon, Kent; Ferguson, Teresa L.; and Githens, Mary Lou, 2001, "DIRECTV: A case history of forecasting diffusion of a new technology prior to product launch," *Interfaces, Special Issue on Marketing Engineering*, Vol. 31, No. 3, Part 2 (May-June), pp. S82–S93.

Bass, Frank M.; Krishnan, Trichy V.; and Jain, Dipak C., 1994, "Why the Bass model fits without decision variables," *Marketing Science*, Vol. 13, No. 3 (Summer), pp. 204–223.

Batra, Rajeev; Myers, John G.; and Aaker, David A., 1996, *Advertising Management,* fifth edition, Prentice Hall, Englewood Cliffs, NJ.

Baumol, William J., 1972, *Economic Theory and Operations Analysis*, Prentice Hall, Englewood Cliffs, NJ.

Bayus, Barry L., 1997, "Speed-to-market and new product performance trade-offs," *The Journal of Product Innovation Management*, Vol. 14, No. 6 (November), pp. 485–497.

Bayus, Barry L.; Jain, Sanjay; and Rao, Ambar G., 1997, "Too little, too early: Introduction timing and new product performance in the personal digital assistant," *Journal of Marketing Research*, Vol. 34, No 1 (February), pp. 50–63.

———. 2001, "Truth or consequences: An analysis of vaporware and new product announcements," *Journal of Marketing Research*; Vol. 38, No. 1 (February), pp. 3–13.

Bensoussan, Alain; Bultez, Alain; and Naert, Philippe, 1978, "Leader's dynamic marketing behavior in oligopoly," *TIMS Studies in the Management Sciences*, Vol. 9, pp. 123–145.

Berrigan, John, 1999, "From Customer Knowledge to Segments of One: Some Working Case Histories." Presentation at *16th Annual ISBM Members' Meeting*, June 16–18, State College, PA.

Bettman, James R., 1971, "The structure of consumer choice processes," *Journal of Marketing Research*, Vol. 8 (November), pp. 465–471.

———. 1979, "Memory factors in consumer choice: A review," *Journal of Marketing*, Vol. 43, No. 2 (Spring), pp. 37–53.

Blasko, Vincent J., and Patti, Charles H., 1984, "The advertising budgeting practices of industrial marketers," *Journal of Marketing*, Vol. 48, No. 4 (Fall), pp. 104–110.

Blattberg, Robert C., and Hoch, Stephen J., 1990, "Database models and managerial intuition: 50 percent model and 50 percent manager," *Management Science*, Vol. 36, No. 8 (August), pp. 887–899.

Blattberg, Robert C., and Levin, Alan, 1987, "Modelling the effectiveness and profitability of trade promotions," *Marketing Science*, Vol. 6, No. 2 (Spring), pp. 124–146.

Blattberg, Robert C., and Neslin, Scott A., 1990, *Sales Promotion: Concepts, Methods, and Strategies*, Prentice Hall, Englewood Cliffs, NJ.

Blattberg, Robert C.; Briesch, Richard; and Fox, Edward J., 1995, "How promotions work," *Marketing Science*, Vol. 14, No. 3, Part 2, pp. G122–G125.

Blattberg, Robert C.; Kim, Bong-Do; and Ye, Jianming, 1994, "Large scale data bases: The new marketing challenge," in *The Marketing Information Revolution*, eds., Robert C. Blattberg, Rashi Glazer, and John D. C. Little, Harvard Business School Press, Boston, pp. 173–203.

Boeing Commercial Airplane Group, 1988, "B727 rejuvenation," *World Jet Airplane Inventory*, The Boeing Company, Seattle, p. 7.

Boston Consulting Group, 1970, *Perspectives on Experience*, Boston.

Boulding, William, and Staelin, Richard, 1993, "A look on the cost side: Market share and the competitive environment," *Marketing Science*, Vol. 12, No. 2 (Spring), pp. 144–166.

Bower, John, 1963, "Net audiences of US and Canadian magazines: Seven tests of Agostini's formula," *Journal of Advertising Research*, Vol. 3 (March), pp. 13–21.

Box, George E.P., Jenkins, Gwilym M., and Reinsel, Gregory C. (1994), Time Series Analysis: Forecasting and Control, 3rd Edition, Prentice Hall., Englewood Cliffs, NJ.

Boyd, Harper W., Jr., and Ray, Michael L., 1971, "What big agency men in Europe think of copy testing methods," *Journal of Marketing Research*, Vol. 8, No. 2 (May), pp. 219–223.

Brock, Timothy C., 1965, "Communicator-recipient similarity and decision change," *Journal of Personality and Social Psychology*, Vol. 1, No. 10, pp. 650–654.

Brokaw, Jeanne, 1997, "Software to help fine-tune direct marketing series: 13," *American Banker*, December 19, 1995, p. 17.

Brown, Rex V.; Lilien, Gary L.; and Ulvila, Jacob W., 1993, "New methods for estimating business markets," *Journal of Business-to-Business Marketing*, Vol. 1, No. 2, pp. 33–65.

Burke, Raymond R.; Rangaswamy, Arvind; Wind, Jerry; and Eliashberg, Jehoshua, 1990, "ADCAD: A knowledge-based system for advertising design," *Marketing Science*, Vol. 9, No. 3. (Summer), pp. 212–229.

Buzzell, Robert D., 1966, "Competitive behavior and product life cycles," in *New Ideas for Successful Marketing*, eds. J. S. Wright and J. L. Goldstucker, American Marketing Association, Chicago.

Buzzell, Robert D., and Gale, Bradley T., 1987, *The PIMS Principles, Linking Strategy to Performance*, The Free Press, New York.

Calantone, Roger J. C.; di Benedetto, Anthony; and Schmidt, Jeffrey B., 1999, "Using the analytic hierarchy process in new product screening," *The Journal of Product Innovation Management*, Vol. 16, No. 1, pp. 65–76.

Camerer, Colin, 1981, "General conditions for the success of bootstrapping models," *Organizational Behavior and Human Performance*, Vol. 27, No. 3, pp. 411–422.

Camparelli, Melissa, 1994, "Reshuffling the deck: Sales territory realignment," *Sales and Marketing Management*, Vol. 146, No. 6, Part 1, pp. 83–90.

Cannon, Hugh, 1987, "A theory-based approach to optimal frequency," *Journal of Media Planning*, Vol. 2, No. 2 (Fall) pp. 33–44.

Cannon, Hugh, and Goldring, Norman, 1986, "Another look at effective frequency," *Journal of Media Planning*, Vol. 1, No. 2 (Fall), pp. 29–36.

Cardozo, Richard, and Wind, Yoram, 1980, "Portfolio analysis for strategic product market planning," Working paper, Wharton School, University of Pennsylvania, Philadelphia.

Carpenter, Gregory S.; Cooper, Lee G.; Hanssens, Dominique M.; and Midgley, David F., 1988, "Modeling asymmetric competition," *Marketing Science*, Vol. 7, No. 4 (Fall), pp. 393–412.

Carroll, J. Douglas, 1972, "Individual differences and multidimensional scaling," in *Multidimensional Scaling: Theory and Applications in the Behavioral Sciences*, Vol. 2, Applications, eds. A. K. Romney, R. N. Shepard, and S. B. Nerlove, Seminar Press, New York.

Carroll, Vincent P.; Rao, Ambar G.; Lee, H. L., Shapin, A.; and Bayus, Barry L., 1985, "The Navy enlistment marketing experiment," *Marketing Science*, Vol. 4, No. 4 (Fall), pp. 352–374.

Choffray, Jean-Marie, and Lilien, Gary L., 1978, "Assessing response to industrial marketing strategy," *Journal of Marketing*, Vol. 42, No. 2 (April), pp. 20–31.

———. 1980, Market Planning for New Industrial Products, John Wiley and Sons, New York.

Clarke, Darral G., 1976, "Econometric measurement of the duration of advertising effects on sales," *Journal of Marketing Research*, Vol. 13, No. 4, pp. 345–357.

Claycamp, Henry J., and McClelland, Charles W., 1968, "Estimating reach and the magic of K," *Journal of Advertising Research*, Vol. 8 (June), pp. 44–51.

Cocks, Douglas L., and Virts, John R., 1975, "Market diffusion and concentration in the ethical pharmaceutical industry," Internal memorandum, Eli Lilly and Company, Indianapolis, IN.

Cohen, Stephen H., 1997, "Perfect union," *Marketing Research*, Vol. 9, No. 1, pp. 12–17.

Cole, Bradley, and Swire, Donald, 1980, "The limited information report," in *Marketing Strategy*, ed., D. Sudharshan, Prentice Hall, Englewood Cliffs, NJ, p. 292.

Colley, Russell H., 1961, *Defining Advertising Goals for Measured Advertising Results*, Association of National Advertisers, New York.

Cooper, Lee G., 1983, "A review of multidimensional scaling in marketing research," *Applied Psychological Measurement*, Vol. 7, No. 4 (Fall), pp. 427–450.

———. 1993, "Market share models," in *Handbooks in Operations Research and Management Science, Vol. 5, Marketing*, eds., Jehoshua Eliashberg and Gary L. Lilien, Elsevier Science Publishers B.V., North Holland, New York, pp. 259–314.

Cooper, Lee G., and Nakanishi, Masao, 1988, *Market-Share Analysis*, Kluwer, Norwell, MA.

Cooper, Robert G., 1986, "An investigation into the new product process: Steps, deficiencies, and impact," *Journal of Product Innovation Management*, Vol. 3, No. 2 (June), pp. 71–85.

———. 1992, "The newprod system: Industry experience," *Journal of Product Innovation Management*, Vol. 9, No. 2 (June), pp. 113–127.

———. 1993, *Winning at New Products*, second edition, Addison Wesley Longman, Reading, MA, p. 310.

Cort, Stanton G.; Lambert, David R.; and Garret, Paula L., 1982, "Frequency in business-to-business advertising: A state-of-the-art review," *4th Annual Business Advertising Research Conference Proceedings*, Advertising Research Foundation, New York.

Cox, William, Jr., 1967, "Product life cycles as marketing models," *Journal of Business*, Vol. 40, No. 4 (October), pp. 375–384.

Cravens, David W., 1995, "The changing role of the sales force," *Marketing Management*, Vol. 4, No. 2 (Fall), pp. 49–57.

Cross, Robert G., 1997, *Revenue management: Hardcore tactics for market domination*, Broadway Books, New York.

Daganzo, Carlos, 1979, *Multinomial Probit*, Academic Press, New York.

Danaher, Peter, 1989, "A log linear model for predicting magazine audiences," *Journal of Marketing Research*, Vol. 26, No. 4, pp. 473–479.

Day, George S., 1981, "The product life cycle: Analysis and applications issues," *Journal of Marketing*, Vol. 45, No. 4 (Fall), pp. 60–67.

———. 1986, *Analysis for Strategic Market Decisions*, West Publishing, St. Paul, MN.

Day, George S., and Montgomery, D. B., 1983, "Diagnosing the experience curve," *Journal of Marketing*, Vol. 47, No. 2 (Spring), pp. 44–58.

Day, George S.; Shocker, Allan D.; and Srivastava, Rajendra K., 1979, "Consumer-oriented approaches to identifying product markets," *Journal of Marketing*, Vol. 43, No. 4 (Fall), pp. 8–19.

Degeratu, Alexandru M; Rangaswamy, Arvind; and Wu, Jianan, 2000, "Consumer choice behavior in on-line and traditional supermarkets: The effects of brand name, price, and other search attributes," *International Journal of Research in Marketing*; Vol. 17, No. 1 (March), pp. 55–78.

Deming, W. Edward, 1987, In Robin M. Hogarth, *Judgment and Choice*, second edition, John Wiley and Son, New York, p. 199.

Desiraju, Ramarao, and Shugan, Steven M., 1999, "Strategic service pricing and yield management," *Journal of Marketing*, Vol. 63, No. 1 (January), pp. 44–56.

DeVincentis, John R., and Kotcher, Lauri Kien, 1995, "Packaged goods sales force—Beyond efficiency," *McKinsey Quarterly*, No. 1 pp. 72–85.

Diamond, Daniel S., 1968, "A quantitative approach to magazine advertisement format selection," *Journal of Marketing Research*, Vol. 5, No. 4 (November), pp. 376–386.

Dillon, William R., and Goldstein, Matthew, 1984, *Multivariate Analysis: Methods and Applications*, John Wiley and Sons, New York, pp. 173–174

Dolan, Robert J., 1981, "Models of competition: A review of theory and empirical evidence," in *Review of Marketing*, B. Enis and K. Roering, eds., American Marketing Association, Chicago, pp. 224–234.

———. 1993, *Managing the New Product Development Process*, Addison-Wesley Publishing Company, Reading, MA.

Dolan, Robert J., and Simon, Hermann, 1996, *Power Pricing*, Free Press, New York.

Dowling, Grahame R., and Midgley, David F., 1988, "Identifying the coarse and fine structures of market segments," *Decision Sciences*, Vol. 19, No. 4 (Fall), pp. 830–847.

Dowling, Grahame; Lilien, Gary L.; Rangaswamy, Arvind; and Thomas, Robert J., 2002, *Harvesting Customer Value: Understanding and Applying Customer-Value-Based Segmentation*, ISBM Press, State College, PA.

Doyle, Peter, 1995, "Marketing in the new millennium," *European Journal of Marketing*, Vol. 29, No. 13, p. 23–41.

Eastlack, Joseph O., and Rao, Ambar G., 1986, "Modelling response to advertising and price changes for 'V-8' cocktail vegetable juice," *Marketing Science*, Vol. 5, No. 3 (Summer), pp. 245–259.

———. 1989, "Advertising experiment at the Campbell Soup Company," *Marketing Science*, Vol. 8, No. 1 (Winter), pp. 57–71.

Eliashberg, Jehoshua; LaTour, Stephen A.; Rangaswamy, Arvind; and Stern, Louis W., 1986, *Journal of Marketing Research*, Vol. 23, No. 2 (May), pp. 101–110.

Elrod, Terry; Louviere, Jordan J.; and Krishnakumar, S. Davey, 1992, "An empirical comparison of ratings-based and choice-based conjoint models," *Journal of Marketing Research*, Vol. 24 (August), pp. 368–377.

Eskin, Gerald J., 1985, "Tracking advertising and promotion performance with single source data," *Journal of Advertising Research*, Vol. 25, No. 1, pp. 31–39.

Evans, Philip, and Wurster, Thomas S., 2000, *Blown to Bits: How the New Economics of Information Transforms Strategy*, Harvard Business School Press, Boston, Massachusetts.

Forsythe, John; Gupta, Sunil; Haldar, Sudeep; Kaul, Anil; and Kettle, Keith, 1999, "A segmentation you can act on," *The McKinsey Quarterly*, No. 3, pp. 6–15.

Frey, Albert Wesley, 1955, *How Many Dollars for Advertising?* Ronald Press, New York.

Fudge, William K., and Lodish, Leonard M., 1977, "Evaluation of the effectiveness of a model based salesman's planning system by field experimentation," *Interfaces*, Vol. 8, No. 1, Part 2 (November), pp. 97–106.

Fulgoni, Gian M., 1987, "The role of advertising: Is there one?" *33rd Annual Conference Proceedings*, Advertising Research Foundation, New York, pp. 153–163.

Gardner, Yehudi A., and Cohen, Burleigh B., 1966, "ROP color and its effect on newspaper advertising," *Journal of Marketing Research*, Vol. 3, No. 4 (November), pp. 365–371.

Garry, Michael, 1996, "GIS: Finding opportunity in data," *Progressive Grocer*, Vol. 75, No. 6 (June), pp. 61–69.

Garvin, David A., 1987, "Competing on the eight dimensions of quality," *Harvard Business Review*, Vol. 65, No. 6 (November–December), pp. 101–109.

Gensch, Dennis, 2001, "A marketing-decision-support model for evaluating and selecting concepts for new products," *Interfaces*, Vol. 31, No. 3, Part 2 of 2 (May-June), pp.S166–S183.

Gensch, Dennis H.; Aversa, Nicola; and Moore, Steven P., 1990, "A choice-modeling market information system that enabled ABB Electric to expand its market share," *Interfaces*, Vol. 20, No. 1 (January–February), pp. 6–25.

Glazer, Rashi, 1991, "Marketing in an information intensive environment: Strategic implications of knowledge as an asset," *Journal of Marketing*, Vol. 55 (October), pp. 1–19.

Goldberg, Lewis R., 1970, "Man versus model of man: A rationale, plus some evidence for a method of improving on clinical inferences," *Psychological Bulletin*, Vol. 73, No. 6, pp. 422–432.

Goldenberg, Jacob; Mazursky, David; and Solomon, Sorin, 1999, "The fundamental templates of quality ads," *Marketing Science*, Vol. 18, No. 3, pp. 333–351.

Goodwin, Stephen, and Etgar, Michael, 1980, "An experimental investigation of comparative advertising: Impact of message appeal, information load and utility of product class," *Journal of Marketing Research*, Vol. 17, No. 2 (May), pp. 187–202.

Grapentine, Terry H., 1995, "Dimensions of an attribute; summated scales measure the relationship between product attributes and their perceptual dimensions," *Marketing Research*, Vol. 7, No. 3 (Summer), pp. 18–27.

Grass, Robert C., 1968, "Satiation effects of advertising," *14th Annual Conference Proceedings,* Advertising Research Foundation, New York.

Green, Paul E., 1974, "On the design of choice experiments involving multifactor alternatives," *Journal of Consumer Research*, Vol. 1, No. 2 (September), pp. 61–68.

———. 1975, "Marketing applications of MDS: Assessment and outlook," *Journal of Marketing*, Vol. 39, No. 1 (January), pp. 24–31.

————. 1984, "Hybrid conjoint analysis: An expository review," *Journal of Marketing Research*, Vol. 21, No. 2 (May), pp. 155–169.

Green, Paul E., and Kim, Jonathan S., 1991, "Beyond the quadrant chart: Designing effective benefit bundle strategies," *Journal of Advertising Research*, Vol. 31, No. 6 (December), pp. 56–63.

Green, Paul E., and Krieger, Abba M., 1991, "Modeling competitive pricing and market share: Anatomy of a decision support system," *Journal of the European Operational Research Society*, Vol. 60, No. 1 (July), pp. 31–44.

————. 1993, "Conjoint analysis with product-positioning analysis," in *Handbook of MS/OR in Marketing*, Jehoshua Eliashberg and Gary Lilien, eds., Elsevier Publishing, The Netherlands, pp. 467–515.

Green, Paul E., and Srinivasan, V., 1978, "Conjoint analysis in consumer research: Issues and outlook," *Journal of Consumer Research*, Vol. 5, No. 2 (September), pp. 103–123.

————. 1990, "Conjoint analysis in marketing: New developments with implications for research and practice," *Journal of Marketing*, Vol. 54, No. 4 (October), pp. 3–19.

Green, Paul E., and Wind, Yoram J., 1973, *Multiattribute Decisions in Marketing*, The Dryden Press, Hinsdale, IL.

Green, Paul E.; Carmone, Frank J., Jr.; and Smith, Scott M., 1989, *Multidimensional Scaling: Concepts and Application*, Allyn and Bacon, Boston.

Green, Paul E.; Krieger, Abba M.; and Wind, Yoram (Jerry), 2001, "Thirty years of conjoint analysis: Reflections and prospects," *Interfaces*, Vol. 31, No. 3, Part 2 of 2 (May-June), pp. S56–S73.

Griffin, Abbie, 1993, "Metrics for measuring product development cycle time," *Journal of Product Innovation Management*, Vol. 10, No. 2 (March), pp. 112–125.

Gross, Irwin, 1972, "The creative aspects of advertising," *Sloan Management Review*, Vol. 14 (Fall), pp. 83–109.

Guadagni, Peter M., and Little, John D. C., 1983, "A logit model of brand choice calibrated on scanner data," *Marketing Science*, Vol. 2, No. 3 (Summer), pp. 203–238.

Gupta, Sunil, 1990, "Testing the emergence and effect of the reference outcome in an integrative bargaining situation," *Marketing Letters*, Vol. 1, No. 2, pp. 103–112.

Gupta, Sunil, and Livne, Z. A., 1988, "Resolving conflict situations with a reference outcome: An axiomatic model," *Management Science*, Vol. 34, No. 11, pp. 1303–1314.

Haley, Russell L., and Case, Peter B., 1979, "Testing thirteen attitude scales for agreement and brand discrimination," *Journal of Marketing*, Vol. 43, No. 4 (Fall), pp. 20–32.

Hanssens, Dominique M., 1980, "Marketing response, competitive behavior, and time series analysis," *Journal of Marketing Research*, Vol. 17, No. 4 (November), pp. 470–485.

Hanssens, Dominique M., and Weitz, Barton A., 1980, "The effectiveness of industrial print advertisements across product categories," *Journal of Marketing Research*, Vol. 17, No. 3 (August), pp. 294–306.

Hanssens, Dominique M.; Parsons, Leonard J.; and Schultz, Randall L., 1990, *Market Response Models: Econometric and Time Series Analysis*, Kluwer Academic Publishers, Boston.

————. 2001, *Market Response Models: Econometric and Time Series Analysis,* second edition, Kluwer Academic Publishers, Boston.

Harrell, Stephen G., and Taylor, Elmer D., 1981, "Modeling the product life cycle for consumer durables," *Journal of Marketing*, Vol. 45, No. 4 (Fall), pp. 68–75.

Hauser, John R., and Shugan, Steven M., 1980, "Intensity measures of consumer preference," *Operations Research*, Vol. 28, No. 2 (March–April), pp. 278–320.

Hax, Arnoldo C., and Majluf, Nicolas S., 1982, "Competitive cost dynamics: The experience curve," *Interfaces*, Vol. 12, No. 5 (October), pp. 50–61.

Hayes-Roth, Frederick, and Jacobstein, Neil, 1994, "The state of knowledge-based systems," *Communications of the ACM*, Vol. 37, No. 3 (March), pp. 27–39.

Heil, Oliver P., and Montgomery, David B, eds., 2001, "Special Issue: Competition and Marketing, *International Journal of Research in Marketing*, Vol. 18, No. 1-2 (June), 1–3.

Hendon, Donald W., 1973, "How mechanical factors affect ad perception," *Journal of Advertising Research*, Vol. 13, No. 4, pp. 39–46.

Hess, Sidney W., 1993, "Swinging on the branch of a tree: Project selection applications," *Interfaces*, Vol. 23, No. 6 (November–December), pp. 5–12.

Hess, Sidney W., and Samuels, Stuart A., 1971, "Experiences with a sales districting model: Criteria and implementation," *Management Science*, Vol. 18, No. 4, Part II (December), pp. 41–54.

Hill, Tim; O'Connor, Marcus; and Remus, William, 1996, "Neural network models for time series forecasts," *Management Science*, Vol. 42, No. 7 (July), pp. 1082–1092.

Hise, Richard T., and Reid, Edward L., 1994, "Improving the performance of the industrial sales force in the 1990's," *Industrial Marketing Management*, Vol. 23, No. 4, pp. 273–279.

Hise, Richard T.; O'Neil, Larry; McNeal, James U.; and Parasuraman, A., 1989, "The effect of product design activities on commercial success levels of new industrial products," *Journal of Product Innovation Management*, Vol. 6, No. 1 (March), pp. 43–50.

Hoch, Stephen J., and Schkade, David A., 1996, "A psychological approach to decision support systems," *Management Science*, Vol. 42, No. 1 (January), pp. 51–64.

Hofmans, Pierre, 1966, "Measuring the cumulative net coverage of any combination of media," *Journal of Marketing Research*, Vol. 3, No. 3 (August), pp. 269–278.

Hogarth, Robin M., 1987, *Judgment and Choice*, second edition, John Wiley and Sons, New York.

Holbrook, Morris B., and Lehmann, Donald R., 1980, "Form versus content in predicting Starch scores," *Journal of Advertising Research*, Vol. 20, No. 4 (August), pp. 53–62.

Huber, Joel, 1993, *CBC Manual*, Sawtooth Software, Sequim, WA.

Huff, David L., 1964, "Defining and estimating a trading area," *Journal of Marketing*, Vol. 28, No. 3 (July), pp. 34–38.

Hunt, Morton, 1982, *The Universe Within: A New Science Explores the Human Mind*, The Harvester Press Limited, Brighton, Sussex, UK, p. 72.

Jacobson, Robert, 1990, "Unobservable effects and business performance," *Marketing Science,* Vol. 9, No. 1 (Fall), pp 74–85.

Jagpal, Sharan, 1999, *Marketing Strategy and Uncertainty*, Oxford University Press, Oxford, UK.

Javalgi, Rajshekhar G., and Dion, Paul, 1999, "A life cycle segmentation approach to marketing financial products and services," *The Service Industries Journal*, Vol. 19, No. 3 (July), pp. 74–96.

Jedidi, Kamel; Kohli, Rajeev; and DeSarbo, Wayne S., 1996, "Consideration sets in conjoint analysis," *Journal of Marketing Research*, Vol. 33, No. 3 (August), pp. 364–372.

Johnson, Richard M., 1987, "Adaptive conjoint analysis," *Sawtooth Software Conference on Perceptual Mapping, Conjoint Analysis, and Computer Interviewing*, Sawtooth Software, Ketchum, ID.

Johnson, Walter E., 1994, "Special report on forecasting consumer attitudes," *National Retail Hardware Association, Do-It-Yourself Retailing*, Vol. 167, No. 1 (July), pp. 57–66.

Jolson, Marvin A., and Rossow, Gerald L., 1971, "The Delphi process in marketing decision making," *Journal of Marketing Research*, Vol. 8, No. 4 (November), pp. 443–448.

Jones, J. Philip, 1986, *What's in a Name*, Lexington Books, Lexington, MA, p. 268.

Kalish, Shlomo, and Lilien, Gary L., 1986, "A market entry timing model for new technologies," *Management Science*, Vol. 32, No. 2 (February), pp. 194–205.

Kalyanaram, G.; Robinson, W. T.; and Urban, Glen L., 1995, "Order of market entry: Established empirical generalizations, emerging empirical generalizations, and future research," *Marketing Science*, Vol. 14, No. 3, Part 2, pp. G212–G221.

Kamin, Howard, 1988, "Why not use single source measurements now?" *Journal of Media Planning*, Vol. 3, No. 1 (Spring), pp. 27–31.

Kaul, Anil, and Wittink, Dick R., 1995, "Empirical generalizations about the impact of advertising on price sensitivity and price," *Marketing Science*, Vol. 14, No. 2, Part 2, pp. G151–G160.

Keeney, Ralph L., and Raiffa, Howard, 1976, *Decisions with Multiple Objectives: Preferences and Value Tradeoffs*, John Wiley and Sons, New York.

Kotler, Philip, 1966, "A design for the firm's marketing nerve center," *Business Horizons*, Vol. 9, No. 3 (Fall), pp. 63–74.

———. 1971, *Marketing Decision Making: A Model Building Approach*, Rinehart and Winston, New York.

———. *Marketing Management: Analysis, Planning, Implementation, and Control*, seventh edition, Prentice Hall, Englewood Cliffs, NJ.

———. 1994, *Marketing Management: Analysis, Planning, Implementation, and Control*, eighth edition, Prentice Hall, Englewood Cliffs, NJ, p. 424.

———. 1997, *Marketing Management: Analysis, Planning, Implementation, and Control*, ninth edition, Prentice Hall, Englewood Cliffs, NJ, p. 284.

Krugman, Herbert E., 1972, "Why three exposures may be enough," *Journal of Advertising Research*, Vol. 12 (December), pp. 11–14.

Kumar, V., 2000, *International Marketing Research*, Prentice Hall, Upper Saddle River, NJ.

Kuritsky, A. P.; Little, J. D. C.; Silk, A. J.; and Bassman, E. S., 1982, "The development, testing and execution of a new marketing strategy at AT&T long lines," *Interfaces*, Vol. 12, No. 6 (December), pp. 22–37.

Lambin, Jean-Jacques, 1976, *Advertising, Competition and Market Conduct in Oligopoly Over Time*, North Holland, Amsterdam.

Lambin, Jean-Jacques; Naert, Philippe; and Bultez, Alain, 1975, "Optimal marketing behavior in oligopoly," *European Economic Review*, Vol. 6, No. 2, pp. 105–128.

Lambkin, Mary V., and Day, George S., 1989, "Evolutionary processes in competitive markets: Beyond the product life cycle," *Journal of Marketing*, Vol. 53, No. 3 (July), pp. 4–20.

Lancaster, Kent M., and Martin, Thomas C., 1988, "Estimating audience duplication among consumer magazines," *Journal of Media Planning*, Vol. 3, No. 2 (Fall), pp. 22–28.

Larréché, Jean-Claude, and Montgomery, David B., 1977, "A framework for the comparison of marketing models: A Delphi study," *Journal of Marketing Research*, Vol. 14, No. 4 (November), pp. 487–498.

Leavitt, Clark, 1962, "The application of perception psychology to marketing," in *Marketing Precision and Executive Action*, ed. Charles H. Hindersman, American Marketing Association, Chicago, pp. 430–437.

Leckenby, John D., and Ju, K-H., 1989, "Advances in media decision models," in *Current Issues and Research in Advertising*, Issue 2, eds. J. Leigh and C. Martin, University of Michigan, Division of Research, Ann Arbor, MI.

Lee, Donald D., 1978, *Industrial Marketing Research*, The Chemical Marketing Research Association, Technomic Publishing Co., Westport, CT.

Lee, Timothy H., and Jung, Sung-Chang, 2000, "Forecasting credit worthiness: Logistic regression versus artificial neural nets," *Journal of Business Forecasting and Methods*, Vol. 18, No. 4 (Winter), pp. 28–30.

Leeflang, Peter S. H., and Wittink, Dick R., 2000a, "Building models for marketing decisions: Past, present and future," *International Journal of Research in Marketing*, Vol. 17, Nos. 2–3 (September), pp. 105–126.

———. 2000b, "Models for marketing decision: Postscriptum," *International Journal of Research in Marketing*, Vol. 17, Nos. 2–3 (September), pp. 237–253.

———. 2001, "Explaining competitive reaction effects," *International Journal of Research in Marketing*, Vol. 18, Nos. 1–2 (June), pp. 119–137.

Leeflang, Peter S. H.; Wittink, Dick R.; Wedel, Michel; and Naert, Philippe; 2000, *Building Models for Marketing Decisions*, Kluwer Academic Publishers, Dordrecht, The Netherlands.

Leidner, Dorothy E., and Jarvenpaa, Sirkka L., 1995, "The use of information technology to enhance management school education: A theoretical view," *MIS Quarterly*, Vol. 19, No. 3, pp. 265–291.

Leone, Robert P., 1995, "Generalizing what is known about temporal aggregation and advertising carryover," *Marketing Science*, Vol. 14, No. 2, Part 2, pp. G141–G150.

Levitt, Theodore, 1960, "Marketing myopia," *Harvard Business Review*, Vol. 38, No. 4 (July–August), pp. 45–56.

Lieberman, Marvin B., and Montgomery, David B., 1980, "First mover advantages," *Strategic Management Journal*, Vol. 9, pp. 41–48.

Light, Larry, 1992, "Software even a CFO could love," *Business Week*, November 22, p. 132.

Lilien, Gary L., 1979, "ADVISOR 2: Modeling the marketing mix decision for industrial products," *Management Science*, Vol. 25, No. 2 (February), pp. 191–204.

———. 1993, *Marketing Management; Analytic Exercises for Spreadsheets*, Boyd and Fraser Publishing Company, Danvers, MA.

Lilien, Gary L., and Kotler, Philip, 1983, *Marketing Decision Making: A Model-Building Approach*, Harper and Row, New York.

Lilien, Gary L., Kotler, Philip, and Moorthy, K. Sridhar, 1992, *Marketing Models*, Prentice Hall, Englewood Cliffs, NJ.

Lilien, Gary L., and Rangaswamy, Arvind, 2000, "Modeled to bits: Decision models for the digital, networked economy," *International Journal of Research in Marketing*, Vol. 17, Nos. 2-3 (September), pp. 227-235.

———. 2001a, "The marketing engineering imperative: Introduction to the special issue," *Interfaces*, Vol. 31, No. 3, Part 2 of 2 (May-June), pp. S1–S7.

Lilien, Gary L., and Rangaswamy, Arvind, eds., 2001b, "Special Issue: Marketing Engineering," *Interfaces*, Vol. 31, No. 3, Part 2 of 2 (May–June).

Lilien, Gary L., and Weinstein, David, 1984, "An international comparison of the determinants of industrial marketing expenditures," *Journal of Marketing*, Vol. 48 (Winter), pp. 46–53.

Lilien, Gary L., and Yoon, Eunsang, 1990, "The timing of competitive market entry: An exploratory study of new industrial products," *Management Science*, Vol. 36, No. 5 (May), pp. 568–585.

Lilien, Gary L.; Rangaswamy, Arvind; Starke, Katrin; and van Bruggen, Gerrit H., 2001, "How and why decision models influence resource allocations," ISBM Report 7-2001, The Smeal College of Business Administration, Pennsylvania State University, University Park, PA, 16802.

Lilien, Gary L.;Rangaswamy, Arvind; and Van den Bulte, Christophe, 2000, "Diffusion Models: Managerial Applications and Software," in *New-Product Diffusion Models*, eds. Vijay Mahajan, Eitan Muller and Yoram Wind, Kluwer Academic Publishers, Norwell, MA, pp. 295-336.

Lilien, Gary L.; Rangaswamy, Arvind; van Bruggen, Gerrit H.; and Wierenga, Berend, 2002, "Bridging the marketing theory-practice gap in marketing engineering," *Journal of Business Research*.

Little, John D. C., 1970, "Models and managers: The concept of a decision calculus," *Management Science*, Vol. 16, No. 8 (April), pp. B466–B485.

———. 1979, "Aggregate advertising models: The state of the art," *Operations Research*, Vol. 27, No. 4 (July–August), pp. 629–667.

Little, John D. C., and Lodish, Leonard M., 1966, "A media selection model and its optimization by dynamic programming," *Industrial Management Review*, Vol. 8 (Fall), pp. 15–23.

Lodish, Leonard M., 1971, "CALLPLAN: An interactive salesman's call planning system," *Management Science*, Vol. 18, No. 4, Part 2 (December), pp. 25–40.

———. 1974, "'Vaguely right' approach to sales force allocations," *Harvard Business Review*, Vol. 52, No. 1 (January–February), pp. 119–124.

———. 1986, *The Advertising and Promotion Challenge*, Oxford University Press, New York, p. 73.

———. 2001, "Building marketing models that make money," *Interfaces*, Vol. 31, No. 3, Part 2 of 2 (May-June), pp. S45–S55.

Lodish, Leonard M.; Curtis, Ellen; Ness, Michael; and Simpson, M. Kerry, 1988, "Sales force sizing and deployment using a decision calculus model at Syntex Laboratories," *Interfaces*, Vol. 18, No. 1 (January–February), pp. 5–20.

Lodish, Leonard M.; Abraham, Magid; Kamenson, Stuard; Livelsberger, Jeanne; Lubetkin, Beth; Richardson, Bruce; and Stevens, Mary Ellen, 1995a, "How TV advertising works: A meta analysis of 389 real world split cable TV advertising experiments," *Journal of Marketing Research*, Vol. 32 (May), pp. 125–139.

Lodish, Leonard M.; Abraham, Magid; Livelsberger, Jeanne; Lubetkin, Beth; Richardson, Bruce; and Stevens, Mary Ellen, 1995b, "A summary of fifty five in-market estimates of the long term effect of advertising," *Marketing Science*, Vol. 14, No. 2, Part 2, pp. G133–G140.

Longman, Kenneth A., 1968, "Remarks on Gross' paper," *13th Annual Conference Proceedings*, Advertising Research Foundation, New York.

———. 1998, "If not effective frequency, then what? "*Journal of Advertising Research*; Vol. 37, No. 4 (July/August). pp. 44–50.

Louviere, Jordan J., and Woodworth, George, 1983, "Design and analysis of consumer choice or allocation experiments: A method based on aggregate data," *Journal of Marketing Research*, Vol. 20 (November), pp. 350–367.

Mahajan, Vijay; Muller, Eitan; and Bass, Frank M., 1993, "New-product diffusion models," in *Handbooks in Operations Research and Management Science, Vol. 5, Marketing*, eds. Jehoshua Eliashberg and Gary L. Lilien, Elsevier Science Publishers B.V., North Holland, New York, pp. 349–408.

Malhotra, Naresh K., 1993, *Marketing Research: An Applied Orientation*, Prentice Hall, Englewood Cliffs, NJ.

Maloney, John C., 1962, "Curiosity versus disbelief in advertising," *Journal of Advertising Research*, Vol. 23 (January), pp. 51–59.

————. 1963, "Copy testing: What course is it taking?" *9th Annual Conference Proceedings,* Advertising Research Foundation, New York.

Mansfield, Edwin, 1979, *Microeconomics: Theory and Applications*, Norton, New York.

Mantrala, Murali; Sinha, Prabhakant; and Zoltners, Andris, 1994, "Structuring a multiproduct sales quota-bonus plan," *Marketing Science*, Vol. 13, No. 2 (Spring), pp. 121–144.

Marchetti, Michele, 2000, "What a sales call costs," *Sales and Marketing Management*, Vol. 152, No. 9 (September), pp. 80–82.

Martino, Joseph P., 1983, *Technological Forecasting for Decision Making*, Elsevier, New York.

McCann, John M., 1974, "Market segment response to the marketing decision variables," *Journal of Marketing Research*, Vol. 11, No. 4 (November), pp. 399–412.

McCann, John M., and Gallagher, John P., 1990, *Expert Systems for Scanner Data Environments*, Elsevier Science Publishers B.V., North Holland, New York, p. 168.

McDonald, Colin, 1971, *"What is the short term effect of advertising?"* Special Report No. 71–142 (February), Marketing Science Institute, Cambridge, MA.

Mehrabian, Albert, 1982, *General Dimensions for a General Psychological Theory*, Oelgeschlager, Gunn and Hain, Cambridge, MA.

Meulman, J.; Heiser, Wilhelm; and Carroll, J. Douglas, 1986, *PREFMAP-3 User's Guide*, Bell Laboratories, Murray Hill, NJ.

Milligan, Glenn W., and Cooper, Martha C., 1987, "Methodology review's clustering methods," *Applied Psychological Measurement*, Vol. 11, No. 4 (December), pp. 329–354.

Monroe, Kent B., 1990, *Pricing, Making Profitable Decisions*, second edition, McGraw-Hill, New York, p. 464.

Moore, William L., and Pessemier, Edgar A., 1993, *Product Planning and Management*, McGraw Hill, New York.

Morrison, Donald G., 1979, "Purchase intentions and purchase behavior," *Journal of Marketing*, Vol. 43, No. 2 (Spring), pp. 65–74.

Naples, M. J., 1979, *Effective Frequency*, Association of National Advertisers, New York.

Narasimhan, Chakravarthi and Zhang, John, 2000, "Market entry strategy under firm heterogeneity and asymmetric payoffs," *Marketing Science,* Vol. 19, No. 4 (Fall), pp 313-327.

Nash, John F., 1950, "The bargaining problem," *Econometrica*, Vol. 18 (April), pp. 155–162.

Neij, Lena, 1997, "Use of experience curves to analyze the prospects for diffusion and adoption of renewable energy technology," *Energy Policy*, Vol. 25, No. 13 (November), pp. 1099-1107.

Neslin, Scott A., and Greenhalgh, Leonard, 1983, "Nash's theory of cooperative games as a predictor of the outcomes of buyer-seller negotiations: An experiment in media purchasing," *Journal of Marketing Research*, Vol. 30 (November), pp. 368–379.

————. 1986, "The ability of Nash's theory of cooperative games to predict the outcomes of buyer-seller negotiations: A dyad-level test," *Management Science*, Vol. 32, No. 4 (April), pp. 480–498.

Neslin, Scott A., and Stone, Linda G., 1996, "Consumer inventory sensitivity and the postpromotion dip," *Marketing Letters*, Vol. 7, No. 1 (January), pp. 77–94.

Nijs, Vincent R; Dekimpe, Marnik G.; Steenkamp, Jan-Benedict E. M.; and Hanssens, Dominique H., 2001, "The category-demand effects of price promotions, *Marketing Science,* Vol. 20, No. 1 (Winter), pp. 1-22.

O'Connor, Gina Colarelli; Willemain, Thomas R.; and MacLachlan, James, 1996, "The value of competition among agencies in developing ad campaigns: Revisiting Gross's model," *Journal of Advertising*, Vol. 25, No. 1 (Spring), pp. 51–62.

Oberwetter, Robert, 2001, "Building blockbuster business," *OR/MS Today* Vol. 28, No. 3 (June), pp. 40–44.

Ogilvy and Mather Research Department 1965, "An experimental study of the relative effectiveness of three television day parts," Authors, New York.

Orme, Bryan, and Huber, Joel, 2000, "Improving the value of conjoint simulations, *Marketing Research,* Vol. 12, No. 4, pp. 12–20.

Parry, Mark E., and Bass, Frank M., 1990, "When to lead or to follow? It depends," *Marketing Letters*, Vol. 1, No. 3 (November), pp. 187–198.

Patti, Charles H., and Blasko, Vincent J., 1981, "Budgeting practices of big advertisers," *Journal of Advertising Research*, Vol. 21 (December), pp. 23–29.

Peppers, Don, and Rogers, Martha, 1993, *The One to One Future: Building Relationships One Customer at a Time*, Doubleday, New York.

Petty, Richard E.; Cacioppo, John T.; and Schumann, David, 1983, "Central and peripheral routes to persuasion: The moderating role of involvement," *Journal of Consumer Research*, Vol. 10, No. 2, pp. 135–146.

Porter, Michael E., 1980, *Competitive Strategy: Techniques for Analyzing Industries and Competitors*, Macmillan, New York.

Ragsdale, Cliff T., 2000, *Spreadsheet Modeling and Decision Analysis*, third edition, Course Technology, South-Western College Publishing, Cincinnati, OH.

Raiffa, Howard, 1968, *Decision Analysis, Introductory Lectures on Choices Under Uncertainty*, Addison-Wesley, Reading, MA.

Ramond, Charles, 1976, *Advertising Research: The State of the Art*, Association of National Advertisers, New York.

Rangaswamy, Arvind, 1993, "Marketing decision models: From linear programs to knowledge-based systems," in *Handbooks in Operations Research and Management Science, Vol. 5, Marketing*, eds. Jehoshua Eliashberg and Gary L. Lilien, Elsevier Science Publishers B.V., North Holland, New York, pp. 733–771.

Rangaswamy, Arvind, and Gupta, Sunil, 2000, "Innovation Adoption and Diffusion in the Digital Environment: Some research opportunities," in *New-Product Diffusion Models*, eds., Vijay Mahajan, Eitan Muller and Yoram Wind, Kluwer Academic Publishers, Dordrecht, The Netherlands, pp. 75–95.

Rangaswamy, Arvind, and Lilien, Gary L., 1997, "Software tools for new product development," *Journal of Marketing Research*, Vol. 34, No. 1 (February), pp. 177–184.

Rangaswamy, Arvind; Harlam, Bari A.; and Lodish, Leonard M., 1991, "INFER: An expert system for automatic analysis of scanner data," *International Journal of Research in Marketing*, Vol. 8, No. 1 (April), pp. 29–40.

Rangaswamy, Arvind; Sinha, Prabhakant; and Zoltners, Andris, 1990, "An integrated model based approach for sales force restructuring," *Marketing Science*, Vol. 9, No. 4 (Fall), pp. 279–298.

Rao, Ambar G., 1978, "Productivity of the marketing mix: Measuring the impact of advertising and consumer and trade promotions on sales," paper presented at ANA Advertising Research Workshop, New York.

Rao, Ambar G., and Miller, P. B., 1975, "Advertising/sales response functions," *Journal of Advertising Research*, Vol. 15, No. 2 (April), pp. 7–15.

Rapoport, Anatol, 1966, *Two-Person Game Theory*, University of Michigan Press, Ann Arbor, MI.

Reibstein, David J., and Gatignon, Hubert, 1984, "Optimal product line pricing: the influence of elasticities and cross elasticities," *Journal of Marketing Research*, Vol. 21, No. 3 (August), pp. 259–267.

Reibstein, David J., and Traver, Phillis A., 1982, "Factors affecting coupon redemption rates," *Journal of Marketing*, Vol. 46 (Fall), pp. 102–113.

Reis, Al, and Trout, Jack, 2001, *Positioning: The Battle for Your Mind*, McGraw Hill, New York.

Rice, Marshall D., 1988, "Estimating the reach and frequency of mixed media advertising schedules," *Journal of the Market Research Society*, Vol. 30, No. 4 (October), pp. 439–451.

Rink, David R., and Swan, John E., 1979, "Product life cycle research: A literature review," *Journal of Business Research*, Vol. 7, No. 3 (September), pp. 219–242.

Roberts, John H., and Lilien, Gary L., 1993, "Explanatory and predictive models of consumer behavior," in *Handbooks in Operations Research and Management Science, Vol. 5, Marketing*, eds., Jehoshua Eliashberg and Gary L. Lilien, Elsevier Science Publishers B.V., North Holland, New York, pp. 27–82.

Robertson, Tom S., and Barich, Howard, 1992, "A successful approach to segmenting industrial markets," *Planning Review*, Vol. 20, No. 6 (November–December), pp. 4–11, 48.

Robinson, William T., and Fornell, Claes, 1985, "The sources of market pioneer advantages in consumer goods industries," *Journal of Marketing Research*, Vol. 22, No. 3 (August), pp. 305–317.

Rossiter, John R., 1982, "Visual imagery: Applications to advertising," in *Advances in Consumer Research*, Vol. 9, ed. Andrew A. Mitchell, Association for Consumer Research, Provo, Utah, pp. 101–106.

Rossiter, John R., and Percy, Larry, 1997, *Advertising and Promotion Management*, second edition, McGraw-Hill, New York.

Roth, Alvin E., 1979, "Axiomatic models of bargaining," *Lecture Notes in Economics and Mathematical Systems*, 170, Springer-Verlag, New York.

Rubinstein, Ariel, 1991, "Comments on the interpretation of game theory," *Econometrica*, Vol. 59, No. 4 (July), pp. 909–924.

Runyon, Kenneth E., 1984, *Advertising*, second edition, Charles E. Merrill Publishing, Columbus, OH.

Russo, J. Edward, and Schoemaker, Paul J. H., 1989, *Decision Traps*, Doubleday and Company, New York.

Rust, Roland T., 1986, *Advertising Media Models: A Practical Guide*, Lexington Books, Lexington, MA.

Rust, Roland T.; Zimmer, Mary R.; and Leone, Robert P., 1986, "Estimating the duplicated audiences of media vehicles in national advertising schedules," *Journal of Advertising*, Vol. 15, No. 3, pp. 30–37.

Saaty, Thomas L., and Vargas, Luis G., 1994, *Decision Making in Economic, Political, Social and Technological Environments with the Analytical Hierarchy Process*, RWS Publications, Pittsburgh, PA.

Saunders, John, 1987, "The specification of aggregate market models," *European Journal of Marketing*, Vol. 21, No. 2, pp. 1–47.

Scherer, Frederic M., 1980, *Industrial Market Structure and Economic Performance*, second edition, Rand McNally, Skokie, IL

Schmitz, John, 1994, "Expert systems for scanner data in practice," in *The Marketing Information Revolution*, eds. Robert C. Blattberg, Rashi Glazer, and John D. C. Little, Harvard Business School Press, Boston, pp. 102–119.

Schmitz, John D.; Armstrong, Gordon D.; and Little, John D. C., 1990, "CoverStory: Automated news finding in marketing," in *DSS Transactions*, ed., Linda Bolino, TIMS College on Information Systems, Providence, RI, pp. 46–54.

Schrage, Michael, 2000, *Serious Play*, Harvard Business School Press, Boston, MA.

Science Citation Index, 1990, ISI, Philadelphia, PA.

Seligman, Daniel, 1956, "How much for advertising?" *Fortune* (December), pp. 120–126.

Senge, Peter M., and Lannon, Colleen, 1990, "Managerial microworlds; Computer simulation to facilitate decision making," *Massachusetts Institute of Technology Alumni Association Technology Review*, Vol. 93, No. 5 (July), pp. 62–68.

Sewall, Murphy A., and Sarel, Dan, 1986, "Characteristics of radio commercials and their recall effectiveness," *Journal of Marketing*, Vol. 50, No. 1 (January), pp. 52–60.

Shapiro, Arthur, 1976, "Promotional effectiveness at H. J. Heinz," *Interfaces*, Vol. 6, No. 2 (February 1976), pp. 84–86.

Sherman, Lee, and Deighton, John, 2001, "Banner advertising: Measuring effectiveness and optimizing placement," *Journal of Interactive Marketing,* Vol. 15, No. 2 (Spring), pp. 60–64.

Shocker, Allan D., and Hall, William G., 1986, "Pretest market-models: A critical evaluation," *Journal of Product Innovation*, Vol. 3, No. 2 (June), pp. 86–107.

Siemer, Richard H. 1989, "Using perceptual mapping for market-entry decisions," 3rd *Sawtooth Software Conference Proceedings*, Sawtooth Software, Sequim, WA, pp. 107–114.

Silk, Alvin J., and Urban, Glen L., 1978, "Pre-test market evaluation of new packaged goods: A model and measurement methodology," *Journal of Marketing Research*, Vol. 15, No. 2 (May), pp. 171–191.

Simon, Herbert A., 1977, *The New Science of Management Decision*, Prentice Hall, Englewood Cliffs, NJ.

Simon, Hermann, and Thiel, Michael H., 1980, "Hits and flops among German media models," *Journal of Advertising Research*, Vol. 20, No. 6, pp. 25–29.

Singer, Eugene M., 1968, *Antitrust Economics: Selected Legal Cases and Economic Models*, Prentice Hall, Englewood Cliffs, NJ.

Sinha, Prabhakant, and Zoltners, Andris A., 2001, "Sales-force decision models: Insights from 25 years of implementation," *Interfaces*, Vol. 31, No. 3, Part 2, pp. S8–S44.

Skiera, Bernd, and Albers, Sonke, 1998, "COSTA: Contribution optimizing sales territory alignment," *Marketing Science*, Vol. 17, No. 3, pp. 196–213.

Smith, Barry C.; Leimkuhler, John F.; and Darrow, Ross M., 1992, "Yield management at American Airlines," *Interfaces*, Vol. 22, No. 1 (January–February), pp. 8–31.

Starch, Daniel, 1966, *Measuring Advertising Readership and Results*, McGraw-Hill, New York.

Stern, Louis; El-Ansary, Adel; and Coughlan, Anne, 1996, *Marketing Channels*, fourth edition, Prentice Hall, Englewood Cliffs, NJ.

Stewart, David W., and Furse, David H., 1986, *Effective Television Advertising: A Study of 1000 Commercials*, Lexington Books, Lexington, MA.

Stewart, M., 1990, "Was STAT scan really an advance on AMTES?" *ADMAP*, Vol. 26 (April), pp. 32–35.

Sudharshan, Devanathan, 1995, *Marketing Strategy: Relationships, Offerings, Timing and Resource Allocation*, Prentice Hall, Englewood Cliffs, NJ.

Sultan, Fareena; Farley, John U.; and Lehmann, Donald R., 1990, "A meta-analysis of applications of diffusion models," *Journal of Marketing Research*, Vol. 27, No. 1 (February), pp. 70–77.

Tayman, Jeff, and Pol, Louis, 1995, "Retail site selection and geographic information systems," *Journal of Applied Business Research*, Vol. 11, No. 2 (Spring), pp. 46–54.

Tellis, Gerard J., and Zufryden, Fred S., 1995, "Tackling the retailer decision maze: Which brands to discount, how much, when and why?" *Marketing Science*, Vol. 14, No. 3, Part 1, pp. 271–299.

Thietart, R. A., and Vivas, R., 1984, "An empirical investigation of success strategies for businesses along the product life cycle," *Management Science*, Vol. 32, No. 6 (June), pp. 645–659.

Tholke, Jurg M.; Hulfink, Erik Jan; and Robken, Henry S. J., 2001, "Launching new product features: A multiple case examination," *The Journal of Product Innovation Management*, Vol. 18, No. 1 (January), pp. 3–14.

Thomas, Charles M., and Keebler, Jack, 1994, "Focus shifts from electric to hybrid," *Automotive News* (January 17), pp. 3, 41.

Thomas, Robert J., 1985, "Estimating market growth for new products: An analogical diffusion model approach," *Journal of Product Innovation Management*, Vol. 2, No. 1 (March), pp. 45–55.

Thorelli, Hans, and Burnett, Stephen C., 1981, "The nature of product life cycles for industrial goods businesses," *Journal of Marketing*, Vol. 45, No. 4 (Fall), pp. 97–108.

Toh, Rex S; Kahn, Habibullah; and Koh, Ai-Jin, 2001, "A travel balance approach for examining tourism area life cycles: The case of Singapore," *Journal of Travel Research*, Vol. 39, No. 4 (May), pp. 426–432.

Trodahl, Verling C., and Jones, Robert L., 1965, "Prediction of newspaper advertisement readership," *Journal of Advertising Research*, Vol. 5 (March), pp. 23–27.

Twedt, Dik W., 1952, "A multiple factor analysis of advertising readership," *Journal of Applied Psychology*, Vol. 36, No. 3 (June), pp. 207–215.

Ulvila, Jacob W., and Brown, Rex V., 1982, "Decision analysis comes of age," *Harvard Business Review*, Vol. 60 (September–October), pp. 130–141.

Urban, Glen L., 1993, "Pretest market forecasting," in *Handbooks in Operations Research and Management Science, Vol. 5, Marketing*, eds. Jehoshua Eliashberg and Gary L. Lilien, Elsevier Science Publishers B.V., North Holland, New York, pp. 315–348.

Urban, Glen L., and Hauser, John R., 1993, *Design and Marketing of New Products*, second edition, Prentice Hall, Englewood Cliffs, NJ.

Urban, Glen L., and Katz, Gerald M., 1983, "Pre-test market models: Validation and managerial implications," *Journal of Marketing Research*, Vol. 20, No. 3 (August), pp. 221–234.

Urban, Glen L., and Star, Steven H., 1991, *Advanced Marketing Strategy: Phenomena, Analysis, and Decisions*, Prentice Hall, Englewood Cliffs, NJ.

Urban, Glen L.; Carter, Theresa; Gaskin, Steve; and Mucha, Zofia, 1986, "Market share rewards to pioneering brands: An empirical analysis and strategic implications," *Management Science*, Vol. 32, No. 6, pp. 645–659.

van Bruggen, Gerrit H.; Smidts, Ale; and Wierenga, Berend, 1998, "Improving decision making by means of a marketing decision support system," *Management Science*, Vol. 44, No. 5 (May), pp. 645–658.

Vandenbosch, Mark B., and Weinberg, Charles B., 1993, "Salesforce operations," in *Handbooks in Operations Research and Management Science, Vol. 5, Marketing*, eds., Jehoshua Eliashberg and Gary Lilien, Elsevier Science Publishers B.V., North Holland, New York, pp. 653–694

Vidale, H. L., and Wolfe, H. B., 1957, "An operations research study of sales response to advertising," *Operational Research Quarterly*, Vol. 5, pp. 370–381.

Ward, J., 1963, "Hierarchical grouping to optimize an objective function," *Journal of the American Statistical Association*, Vol. 58, pp. 236–244.

Wedel, Michel, and Kamakura, Wagner A., 2000, *Market Segmentation: Conceptual and Methodological Foundations*, second edition, Kluwer Academic Press, Boston, MA.

Wells, William D., 1981, "How advertising works," working paper, Needham, Harper and Steers Advertising, Chicago.

Wells, William D.; Leavitt, Clark; and McConnell, Maureen, 1971, "A reaction profile for TV commercials," *Journal of Advertising Research*, Vol. 11, No. 2 (December), pp. 11–17.

Wenzel, Wilfred, and Speetzen, Rolf, 1987, "How much frequency is enough?" *Journal of Media Planning*, Vol. 2, No. 1, pp. 5–16.

West, Patricia M.; Brockett, Patrick L.; and Golden, Linda L., 1997, "A comparative analysis of neural networks and statistical methods for predicting consumer choice," *Marketing Science*, Vol. 16, No. 4, pp. 370–391.

Whitaker, Richard, 1995, "Make believe airline," *Airline Business*, Vol. 11, No. 4 (April), pp. 46–49.

Wierenga, Berend, and van Bruggen, Gerrit H., 1997, "Integration of marketing problem-solving modes and marketing management support systems," *Journal of Marketing*, Vol. 61, No. 3 (July): 21–37.

———. 2000, *Marketing Management Support Systems*, Kluwer Academic Press, Boston, MA.

Wind, Jerry; Green, Paul E.; Shifflet, Douglas; and Scarbrough, Marsha, 1989, "Courtyard by Marriott: Designing a hotel facility with consumer-based marketing models," *Interfaces*, Vol. 19, No. 1 (January–February), pp. 25–47.

Wind, Yoram J., 1981, "Marketing-oriented strategic planning models," in *Marketing Decision Models*, eds. R. Schultz and A. Zoltners, North Holland, New York, pp. 207–250.

Wind, Yoram J., and Claycamp, Henry, 1976, "Planning product line strategy: A matrix approach," *Journal of Marketing*, Vol. 40, No. 1 (January), pp. 2–9.

Wind, Yoram J., and Lilien, Gary L., 1993, "Interaction, strategy and synergy", in *Handbooks in Operations Research and Management Science, Vol. 5, Marketing*, eds., Jehoshua Eliashberg and Gary L. Lilien, Elsevier Science Publishers B.V., North Holland, New York, pp. 773–820.

Wind, Yoram J., and Robertson, Thomas S., 1983, "Marketing strategy: New directions for theory and research," *Journal of Marketing*, Vol. 47, No. 2 (Spring), pp. 12–25.

Winston, Wayne L. and S. Christian Albright, 2000, *Practical Management Science: Spreadsheet Modeling and Applications*, second edition, Duxbury Press, Pacific Grove, CA.

Wittink, Dick R., and Cattin, Philippe, 1989, "Commercial use of conjoint analysis: An update," *Journal of Marketing*, Vol. 53, No. 3 (July), pp. 91–106.

Wittink, Dick R.; Krishnamurthi, Lakshman; and Nutter, Julia B., 1982, "Comparing derived importance weights across attributes," *Journal of Consumer Research*, Vol. 8, No. 4 (March), pp. 471–474.

Wolfe, H. B.; Brown, Joel. R.; and Thompson, G. C., 1962, "Measuring advertising results, studies in business policy," The Conference Board, New York, No. 102, pp. 62–68.

Yamanaka, Jiro, 1962, "The prediction of ad readership scores," *Journal of Advertising Research*, Vol. 2, No. 1 (March), pp. 18–23.

Yelle, Louis E., 1979, "The learning curve: Historic review and comprehensive survey," *Decision Sciences*, Vol. 10, No. 2 (April), pp. 302–327.

Yoon, Eunsang, and Lilien, Gary L., 1985, "New industrial product performance: The impact of market characteristics and strategy," *Product Innovation Management*, Vol. 2 (September), pp. 134–144.

Young and Rubicam 1988, *Non Verbal Communication in Advertising*, eds. Sidney Hecker and David W. Stewart, Lexington Books, Lexington, MA.

Yurkiewicz, Jack, 2000, "Forecasting 2000," *OR/MS Today* Vol. 27, No. 1 (February), pp. 58–65.

Zahavi, Jacob, 1995, "Franklin Mint's famous AMOS," *OR/MS Today*, Vol. 22, No. 5 (October), pp. 18–23.

Zangwill, Willard I., 1993, *Lightning Strategies for Innovation*, Lexington Books, New York.

Zielski, Hubert A., 1959, "The remembering and forgetting of advertising," *Journal of Marketing*, Vol. 23, No. 3 (January), pp. 239–243.

Zoltners, Andris A., and Sinha, Prabhakant, 1983, "Sales territory alignment: A review and model," *Management Science*, Vol. 29, No. 11 (November), pp. 1237–1256.

Subject Index

Locators in italics indicate display material; n indicates note; quotes indicate fictional item

A priori segmentation, 66, 83–84
"ABCOR2000," 419, 449–53
Accessibility of market segment, 63
Adaptive conjoint analysis, 246
Adaptive filtering approach, 163
ADBUDG model, 7, 37, 315–18, 360–61
ADCAD model, 329–35
Advertising, 303–53
Advertising budget decisions, 303, 310–19
ADBUDG model, 7, 37, 315–18, 360–61
ADCAD model, 329–35
ADVISOR model, 51, 318–19, 347–52
    affordable method, 310–11
    budget for (See Advertising budget decisions)
    case studies and exercises, 336–53
    competitive-parity method, 311
    copy development and decisions, 303, 324–35
    copy effectiveness, 324–27
    copy effects, 309–10
    cost, vs. personal selling, 355
    creative quality estimation of, 327–28
    defined, 303
    design of, 328–35
    draft commercials exercise, 28
    effects of, 304–10
    frequency phenomena, 308–9
    media decisions in, 303, 309, 319, 321–24
    model-based methods, 311–19
    models for, 305–7, 310–35
    nature of, 303–4
    objective-and-task method, 311–12

percentage-of-sales method, 311
pricing decisions, 303
response phenomena, 304–7
shared-experience model, 318–19
ADVISOR model, 51, 318–19, 347–52
Affordable method for advertising budget decisions, 310–11
Agglomerative clustering methods, 88–89
    average linkage clustering, 89
    complete linkage clustering, 89
    single linkage clustering, 89
    Ward's method, 89, 90
Agostini's formula, 322
AHP (Analytical Hierarchy Process) model, 205–8, 237, 357
AID (automatic interaction detection), 85, 90–91, 92
Alpha rule and choice rule, 249–50
ALSCAL, 129
AMOS (automatic model specification), 468–69
Analytical Hierarchy Process (AHP) model, 205–8, 237, 357
Anticipatory learning, 477
Appendices. See also Case studies and exercises
    Excel's solver and response models, 54–57
    factor analysis and positioning, 147
    PDA features guide and segmentation, 110–12
    strategic marketing decision making model, 220–22
Application Service Provider (ASP) model, 469, 471–72
AR (autoregressive) model, 164
Arbitrage and price discrimination, 427
ARMA (autoregressive and moving average) model, 164

Artificial neural networks and forecasting, 170–73
ASP (Application Service Provider) model, 469, 471–72
ASSESSOR model, 264–71
    benefit:cost ratio, 15
    in new product testing, 4
    overview of, 264–66
    preference model, 266–68
    trial-repeat model, 268–70
    validity and value of, 271
Associations and data mining, 474
Assumptions in decision modeling, 7–8
Attraction models, 45
Attractiveness of segment, 69–72, 73
Attribute-based perceptual mapping, 128–36
    factor analysis procedure outline, 129, 131–34
    illustrative list of, 130
    in joint-space maps, 140–41
    location of products in, 136
    overview, 128
    pictorial depiction of, 132
    variance and, 134–35
Augmented product, 234
Automatic interaction detection (AID), 85, 90–91, 92
Automatic model specification (AMOS), 468–69
Autoregressive and moving average (ARMA) model, 164
Autoregressive (AR) model, 164
Available market, 159
Average linkage clustering, agglomerative method, 89

Backward chaining, 329
BASES, 287
Bases of segmentation, 63, 65, 69
Bass model, 253–61
    analogous products, 258, 260
    extensions of, 261–63

forecasting overview, 253, 254–55
generalized, 257, 260–61
linear regression, 257–58
nonlinear regression, 258, 259
parameter estimation, 257, 260–61
technical description, 255–63
Bayes's theorem, 193, 255
BCG (Boston Consulting Group) model, 201–3
"Best Offer" query model, 74
Between sum of squares (BSS), 90–91
Bidding and competition-oriented pricing, 422–24
Blattberg and Levin sales promotion model, 440–44
Block tariffs, 433–34
Bonus, as salesforce compensation, 370–73
Boston Consulting Group (BCG) model, 201–3
Box-Jenkins (ARMA) method, 164
Brand-choice model, 446–47
Brand loyalty and promotion, 445
Brand sales market share models, 44–45
Brand switching, 77
Branding, 303
Bridging designs, 246
Build-up methods in cluster analysis, 88–89
BUNDOPT model, 238
Business portfolio matrix, and BCG model, 201–3
Business strength, GE/McKinsey multifactor matrix model, 203–4

Calibration in response models, 32, 37–38, 52, 361
CALLPLAN models, 356, 373–78, 386–408
Cannibalization, 267–68
Carryover effects, 43
Case studies and exercises. See also Appendices
account pricing exercise ("ABCOR2000"), 449–50
advertising and budgeting case ("Convection Corporation"), 343–52
advertising and product turnaround case (Blue Mountain Coffee), 336–42
advertising copy design exercise (Johnson Wax), 353

bidding for pavement contract exercise ("Conglomerate, Inc."), 453–54
draft commercials exercise, 28
new product design case (Zenith HDTV), 277–82
new product design exercise (Forte Hotel), 272–76
new product development case (Johnson Wax Enhance), 277–301
positioning case (Infiniti G20), 148–54
price planning exercise ("ABCOR2000"), 451–52
promotion decision case ("MassMart Inc."), 458–61
revenue management exercise (Forte Hotel), 455–57
sales call planning and CALLPLAN case ("Conglomerate, Inc."), 386–408
sales location case ("J&J Family Video"), 411–13
salesforce size and allocation case (Syntex Laboratories), 386–408
segmentation and PDA case ("Conglomerate, Inc."), 104–9
segmentation case (ABB Electric), 113–16
strategic market analysis case [Bookbinders Book Club (BBBC)], 185–87
strategic marketing decision models and R&D project selection case (ICI America), 213–15
strategic marketing decision models compete spreadsheet exercise ("Acme" liquid), 231–32
strategic marketing decision models portfolio analysis exercise ("Conglomerate, Inc."), 223–25
strategic marketing decision models product planning exercise [Addison Wesley Longman (AWL)], 216–19
strategic marketing decision models site selection exercise (Jenny's Gelato), 226–30
Cash cow strategic business units (SBUs) in BCG model, 201, 202
Cash trap strategic business units (SBUs) in BCG model, 201, 202
Causal forecasting methods, 167–75
artificial neural networks, 170–73

input-output analysis, 168–70
regression, 167–69, 173
Certainty monetary equivalent (CME), 41
Chance nodes, decision tree, 192, 193–94
Channels for marketing, 379–84. See also Salesforce
Choice models
choice-based conjoint analysis, 251
choice-based segmentation model, 3, 97–102
customer heterogeneity in, 101–2
joint-space map, 144–45
in marketing engineering, 3
segmentation case history, 115–16
Choice rule in conjoint analysis, 247–48
Classical economic approach to pricing decisions, 415–18
Classification matrix, discriminant analysis, 94
Clumping, 84
Cluster analysis in segmentation, 84–95
association measures, 84–87
divisive method, 88, 90–91
hierarchical method, 88
interpretation of, 92–95
partitioning method, 88, 91–92
Cluster profiling, 93
Clustering and data mining, 474
CME (certainty monetary equivalent), 41
Collaboration and groupware, 477
Commerce, U. S. Department of, 161
Commission, as salesforce compensation, 370
Communication decisions. See Advertising
COMP, 287
Compensation, salesforce, 369–73
Competition
-oriented pricing, 422–24
compete spreadsheet in case study, 231–32
in cost dynamic models, 182–83
models for strategic decision making, 208–12
perceptual maps, 124–26
positioning and, 118
in response models, 44–46
segment attractiveness evaluation, 69

Competitive-parity method for advertising budget decisions, 311

Competitive strategy analogies, 211–12

Complete linkage clustering, agglomerative method, 89

Component part, use cost and pricing, 420

Computer-based models. See also Software
  basic use for, 5–6
  interactive decision models, 7
  modeling methods and programs, 129

Computer World-Smithsonian Award, 468

Conceptual models for marketing, 1–5

Conjoint analysis, 239–53
  attribute bundles, 239–42
  best uses for, 251–52
  data collection, 245–47
  design and execution of, 242–44
  enhancements to basic model, 250–51
  evaluation of design options, 247–50
  hybrid conjoint model, 245–46
  idea evaluation models, 237–38
  MSZ model, 370–73
  new product design, 3
  procedure for, 242–50

Constant elasticity, 42, 418–19

Constrained optimization problem, 13

Constraint component, optimization problems, 54–55

Consumer judgments of substitutability, 78

Contribution Optimizing Sales Territory Alignment (COSTA) model, 368–69

Contribution vs. market share in conjoint analysis, 250

Controllable variables in decision modeling, 8

Convenience-group segmentation, 66

Copy, advertising
  development and decisions, 303, 324–35
  effectiveness, 324–27
  effects, 309–10

Core product, 233

Corporate mission, defined, 155–56

Corporate strategy, 156–59

Correlation coefficient, cluster analysis, 86–87

Correlations and data mining, 474

Cost and pricing decisions, 418

Cost dynamics in strategic market analysis, 180–83

Cost-of-visit advertising campaign, 325–26

Cost-oriented approach to pricing, 418–19

COSTA (Contribution Optimizing Sales Territory Alignment) model, 368–69

Coupons, 434, 436

Criteria importance and AHP, 205–8, 237, 357

Cross-classification analysis, 96–97

Cross-elasticity of demand, 76

Cross-price elasticity, 435

Customer service, 476

Customers
  decay rate, 43
  heterogeneity in choice models, 101–2
  heterogeneity of, 62
  holdover effect, 43
  response model, 446
  retention rate, 43
  segmentation of (See Segmentation)
  surplus and price discrimination, 426
  targeting of, 70–74

Customization and data mining, 474

Data
  defined, in marketing engineering, 4–5
  segmentation instrument development, 78–83
  volume, and electronic capture of, 6

Data matrix, 79, 83, 131

Data mining, 474

Data warehouse, 469, 470–72

Database marketing, 97

Decision models
  advertising budgets (See Advertising budget decisions)
  assumptions in, 7–8
  basics, 6–13
  benefits to management, 13–19
  characteristics of, 7–8
  defined, 6–7
  descriptive, 11, 13

end-user modeling, 20–21

graphical, 8, 9–10, 11, 12

for market entry and exit, 188–97

mathematical, 8, 10–11, 12

new product decisions, 233

new product development (NPD), 236–39

normative, 11, 13

predictive, 11, 13

prescriptive, 13

strategic market analysis (See Strategic marketing decision making models)

types of, 8–13

variables, 7, 8, 15, 54

verbal, 8–9, 11, 12

Decision nodes, decision tree, 192, 193–94

Decisions
  analysis for, 191, 197
  calculus for, 38–39
  defined, in marketing engineering, 4
  matrix for, 81–83
  sequence of, consumer, 76
  for strategic marketing (See under Strategic marketing)
  tree for, 192, 193
  variable component, optimization problems, 54

Decline, product life cycle (PLC), 177

Decompositional time-series method, 165–67

Delayed-response effect, 43

Delphi forecasting method, 160–61

Demand
  -oriented pricing decisions, 419–22
  cross-elasticity of, 76
  Law of, 415–18
  market, and strategic market analysis, 159–75
  strategic market analysis, 159–75
  variables in STP process, 64–74

Dendograms, 88, 90

Department of Energy (DOE), 190

Dependent variables in decision modeling, 8

Descriptive decision model, 11, 13

Descriptors
  in discriminant analysis, 94–95
  in segmentation models, 63, 64, 69

Design stage, NPD, 234, 235

Differentiation

defined, 117–18
of products and markets in targeting, 72
Diffusion models. See Bass model
Direct marketing
  choice-based segmentation, 97–100
  defined, 303
Direction, salesforce compensation to channel, 370
Discount allocation and airline price discrimination, 429–32
Discriminant analysis in cluster profiling, 94, 129
Discriminant loadings, discriminant analysis, 95
Discrimination. See Price discrimination
Dissimilarity, measures of, in cluster analysis, 86
Distance, Euclidean, 86–87, 136
Distribution and advertising, 303
Divisive methods in cluster analysis, 88, 90–91
DOE (U.S. Department of Energy), 190
Dog strategic business units (SBUs) in BCG model, 201, 202
Double exponential smoothing approach, 163
Double moving average approach, 163
Double moving average with trend adjustments, 163
Draft commercials exercise, 28
Draw
  from other products, 267–68
  proportional draw assumption in logit model, 48–49
Dual objective segmentation, 74
Dynamic effects in response models, 42–44
Dynamics, in advertising response models, 304

Economies of scale, 180, 181
Efficiency in price discrimination, 427
Effort period, CALLPLAN, 373
EIA (Electronic Industries Associations), 281
Elasticity, price, 415–18, 419
Electronic Design, 328
Electronic Industries Associations (EIA), 281

End-user modeling, marketing engineering, 20–21
Energy, Department of (DOE), 190
Entropy, 250
Entry and exit decisions, market models, 188–97
Environmental variables in decision modeling, 8
Error sum of squares (ESS), 89, 90
ESP, 287
ESS (error sum of squares), 89, 90
Euclidean distance, 86–87, 136
Euclidean space, 119, 120
Evolutionary ecology in competitive strategy analogy, 211–12
Exclusion in price discrimination, 427
Executive opinion in forecasting, 160
Exercises. See Case studies and exercises
Exit and entry decisions, market models, 188–97
Expected value of perfect information, 195
Expected value of sample information, 194
Experience
  in cost dynamic models, 182–83
  effect on production costs, 180
  and marketing decisions, 2–3
  shared experience models, 198–201
Experience curve, 180, 183, 188
Expert systems and data mining, 474–76
Exponential response model, 36
Exponential-smoothing model, 163
Exposures to advertising, 321
External analysis in joint-space mapping method, 129, 141–44
Extraction in price discrimination, 427

Factor analysis
  attribute-based perceptual mapping, 131–34
  computer program for, 129
  in segmentation, 84, 147
  variance in, 133–35
Farthest neighbor method, agglomerative method, 89
Feedforward networks, 170–72, 171
Financial product portfolio models, 204–5
First choice, randomized, 250

First choice rule, 249
First-time prospects, industrial customer segmentation, 68
Food Institute Report, 263
Forecasting
  buying intentions in, 161
  causal methods of, 167–75
  data mining, 474
  defined, 161
  judgmental methods of, 160–61
  market and product analysis, 161–62
  market tests in, 162
  new products (See Bass model)
  pretest market, 263–71
  product life cycle, 175–80
  time-series methods, 162–67
Fractional root response models, 35–36
Freehand projection, time-series, 162
Frequency
  of exposure to advertising, 321
  phenomena of, advertising, 308–9
  of promotions and effects, 439
  of sales calls and CALLPLAN, 373–74

Game-theory models, 197, 209
GE/McKinsey multifactor matrix model, 203–4
GE Portfolio Planning model, 237
General attraction models, 45
Generalized revenue model, 456–57
GENFOLD, 129
GEOLINE model, 356, 367–69
GIS (graphic information system), 382
Goal programming in response models, 41
Going-rate pricing, 422
Gompertz response models, 36–37
Graphic information system (GIS), 382
Graphical decision models, 8, 9–10, 11, 12
Gravity model for marketing channels, 379–84
Groupware, 477–78
Growth
  company, and segment attractiveness evaluation, 69, 70
  growth/share matrix, and BCG model, 201–3
  product life cycle (PLC), 177

Hard limiters, feedforward networks, 171–72

HDTV, 277–82

Heterogeneity, customer, 62

Heterogeneity incorporation in customer segmentation, conjoint analysis, 251

Hierarchical methods in cluster analysis, 88

Hit rate, discriminant analysis, 94

Hold-out sample, discriminant analysis, 94

Homogeneity of market segment, 63, 66

Hybrid conjoint model, 245–46

Hybrid decision model, 13

Hysteresis effect, 43, 44

Idea evaluation models, NPD, 237–38

Ideal-point models, 128, 129, 139, 140

Image in perceptual maps, 126–27

Imitative pricing, 422

Implementation, defined, in marketing engineering, 4, 5

In-pack sales promotion, 436

In-store display as sales promotion, 436

Incentive pay as salesforce compensation, 370, 371

Incentive through sales promotion, 436

Inclusion in price discrimination, 427

Independent variables in decision modeling, 8

Individual rationality in Nash solution, 425

INDSCAL, 129

Industrial organization (IO) in competitive strategy analogy, 211–12

Industry attractiveness, GE/McKinsey multifactor matrix model, 203–4

Inference engine, advertising design, 329

Inflation in cost dynamic models, 182

Information in marketing engineering, 4, 463–64

Innovation and cost dynamics, 181, 182

Input-output analysis, forecasting, 168–70

Input variables in decision modeling, 8

Insights, defined, in marketing engineering, 4

Installation of marketing engineering software, 23–24

Integration, Internet marketing models, 472–73

Intelligent marketing systems, 473–74

Interaction, in advertising response models, 304

Interactive decision model, 7

Interactive pricing decisions, 424–26

Internet
  ASP (Application Service Provider) model, 469, 471–72
  Bass model and diffusion, 262–63
  marketing department interaction via, 5

Introduction, product life cycle (PLC), 177

Introduction stage, NPD, 234, 235

Intuitive methods for salesforce size and allocation, 357–59

Invitation through sales promotion, 436

IO (industrial organization) in competitive strategy analogy, 211–12

Irrelevant segmentation descriptors, 63, 64

Johns Hopkins model, revenue management, 432

Joint-space mapping method, 128–44
  from external analysis, 129, 141–44
  ideal-point, 128, 129
  as perceptual mapping technique, 128, 129
  simple, 129, 139–41
  vector models, 139–43

Judgmental forecasting methods, 160–61

Jury of executive opinion, forecasting method, 160

K-means partitioning clustering method, 91–92

Knowledge base, advertising design, 329

Knowledge-based systems and data mining, 474–76

KYST, 129

LANs (local area networks), 5

Latent class customer segmentation, conjoint analysis, 251

Law of Demand for pricing, 415–18

Learning by doing, marketing engineering, 20

Learning constant, 180–81

Learning curve, 180

Learning curve pricing, 183

Learning rate, 180–81

Life cycle, product (PLC), 175–80

Life-cycle management stage, NPD, 234, 235

Lifestyle, and positioning, 118

Likelihood-of-purchase measure, 46

LIM (Limited Information Model), 198–99, 200

Limited Information Model (LIM), 198–99, 200

Linear demand-price function, 416–17

Linear response to advertising, 304

Local area networks (LANs), 5

Local optima, 56

Location and marketing channels, 379

Logistic response model, 36

Logistics, channel decision, 379

Logit choice rule, 248–49

Logit model, 46–50, 444–47

Long-run profit as response objective, 40

Loyalty, brand, and sales promotions, 445

MA (moving average) approach, 162–63, 164

Macro channel decision, 379

Management. See also specific topics
  decision model benefits to, 13–19
  market simulations and, 476–78
  in marketing process, 1–2
  salesforce decisions, 356–57, 395–96

Manpower Assignment Planning System (MAPS), 368

Mantrala, Sinha, and Zoltners (MSZ) model, 356

Manufacturer-price-off offer as sales promotion, 436

MAPE (mean-absolute-percent error), 164–65

Mapping methods

joint-space (See Joint-space mapping method)

perceptual (See Perceptual maps)

MAPS (Manpower Assignment Planning System), 368

Margin, price impact on, 414

Market

-response methods for size and allocation of salesforce, 359–64

defined, 1–2, 75–78

demand and strategic market analysis, 159–75

entry and exit models, 188–97

response models (See Response models)

segment (See Segmentation)

simulations of, 247, 476–78

specialization in, 72

Market-share models, 3, 44–45

Marketing

-mix decisions, 208, 303–10

computer-based models in, 5–6

conceptual models for, 1–5

decisions for (See Decision models)

defined, 1

forecasting (See Forecasting)

objectives for, 156–59

reengineering of, 6

strategies (See under Strategic marketing)

Marketing Engineering (ME), 1–28. See also specific topics

computer models and, 5–6, 23–26

and conceptual marketing, 3

data in, 4

decision model basics, 6–13

decision model benefits, 13–19

defined, 2–5

draft commercials exercise, 28

end-user models, 20–21

exercise, 28

within firms, 465–67

future of, 467–80

insights in, 462–65

learning by doing, 20

pedagogical aspects of, 465

philosophy of, 19–23

purpose of, 1–2

reasons for, 5–6, 31

software for, 21–25, 464–65

software overview, 23–26

vs. mental models for marketing, 1–5

Marketing Information Systems (MKIS), 114–15, 469

Markup pricing, 418–19

Matching coefficients, 85–86

Mathematical decision models, 8, 10–11, 12

Matrices

AHP model, 205–8, 237, 357

of associations, 84–88

BCG model, 201–3

classification matrix, discriminant analysis, 94

data, 79, 83

decision, 81–83

GE/McKinsey multifactor, 203–4

product-performance matrix model, 204

reaction matrix, 209–10

Maturity, product life cycle (PLC), 177

Maximum utility in choice rule, 247–48, 249

MDPREF, 129, 131

MDS (multidimensional scaling), 128

MDSCAL, 129

ME. See Marketing engineering (ME)

Mean-absolute-percent error (MAPE), 164–65

Measures

distance, in cluster analysis, 86

NPD decision models, 236

for salesforce territory

segmentation instrument development, 78–79

similarity, in cluster analysis, 85, 86

Media decisions in advertising, 303, 309, 319, 321–24

Media models, 321–24

MEDIAC model, 324

Mental models, 2–3, 16–18

Micro channel decision, 379

Military in competitive strategy analogy, 211–12

Mission statement, 155–56

MKIS (Marketing Information Systems), 114–15, 469

Models

ADBUDG, 7, 37, 315–18, 360–61

ADCAD, 329–35

for advertising budget decisions, 311–19

ADVISOR, 51, 318–19, 347–52

AHP, 205–8, 237, 357

ALSCAL, 129

AMOS, 468–69

AR, 164

ARMA, 164

ASP, 469, 471–72

ASSESSOR (See ASSESSOR model)

attraction, 45

Bass (See Bass model)

BCG, 201–3

"Best Offer" query, 74

Blattberg and Levin sales promotion, 440–44

brand-choice, 446–47

brand sales market share, 44–45

BUNDOPT, 238

choice (See Choice models)

cost dynamic, 182–83

COSTA, 368–69

decision (See Decision models)

defined, 6

descriptive decision, 11, 13

discriminant analysis, 94, 129

end-user modeling, marketing engineering, 20–21

exponential-smoothing, 163

factor analysis (See Factor analysis)

financial product portfolio, 204–5

game-theory models, 197, 209

GE/McKinsey multifactor matrix, 203–4

GE Portfolio Planning, 237

general attraction, 45

generalized revenue, 456–57

GENFOLD, 129

GEOLINE, 356, 367–69

gravity, 379–84, 379–94

hybrid conjoint, 245–46

idea evaluation, 237–38

ideal-point, 140

INDSCAL, 129

judgement required in use of, 463

KYST, 129

LIM, 198–99, 200

logit, 46–50, 444–47

MAPS, 368

market-share, 44–45

mathematical, 8, 10–11, 12

MDPREF, 129, 131

MDSCAL, 129

media, 321–24

MEDIAC, 324

mental, 2–3, 16–18

MSZ, 370–73
multinomial logit, 46, 48
NewProd, 238
opportunity identification, 236–37
PAR regression, 198–99
perceptual maps (See Perceptual maps)
PIMS, 198–201
preference, 129, 266–68
PREFMAP3, 129, 141–45
probit, 47–48
product class sales market share, 44–45
product design, 238–39
product-performance matrix, 204
product portfolio, 201–8
projection assessment, 326–27
promotion, 440–44, 460–61
purchase-incidence, 446
purchase-quantity, 446, 447
reallocator, 365–66
response (See Response models)
retailer, 446–47
revenue, 456–57
shared experience, 50–51, 182, 318–19
SSM, 392–96
strategic marketing (See Strategic marketing decision making models)
Syntex, 356, 359–64, 392–96
trial-repeat, 268–70
vector (See Vector models)
Modified exponential response model, 36
Monopoly
marketing-mix decisions, 208
pricing strategy for, 183
Monotonicity in similarity-based perceptual mapping, 137–39
Motivation, salesforce compensation for, 369–70
Moving average (MA) approach, 162–63, 164
MSZ model, 370–73
Multicriteria decision making, 41
Multidimensional scaling (MDS), 128
Multilayered-layered feedforward network, 170–72
Multinomial logit model, 46, 48
Multivariate ARMA, 164

Naive time-series methods, 162
Nash solution, 425–26

National Bureau of Economic Research, 164
Nearest neighbor method, agglomerative method, 89
Negotiation in pricing decisions, 424–26
Neighbor method, agglomerative method, 89
Networks
computer, 5
feedforward, 170–72, 171
LANs (local area networks), 5
neural and forecasting, 170–73
P2P, 478
WANs (wide area networks), 5
Neural networks and forecasting, 170–73
New Prod model, 238
New product decisions, 233–301
Bass model, 253–61
case studies and exercises, 272–301
conjoint analysis for design of (See Conjoint analysis)
decision models for, 233
development of, stages of, 233–36
entry and exit decisions, 188–97
forecasting, 253–71
introduction of, 233–36
life-cycle management stage, 234, 235
models for, 236–39
perceptual maps for, 123–24
pretest market forecasting, 263–71
sales forecasting, 253–63
testing and ASSESSOR, 4
New product development (NPD), 234–39
decision models, 236–39
idea evaluation models, 237–38
opportunity identification models, 236–37
product design models, 238–39
stages and decisions in, 233–36
New trier effect, 43, 44
Noncash awards, as salesforce compensation, 370
Noncontrollable variables in decision modeling, 8
Nonlinear optimization problems, 54, 56
Nonlinear pricing decisions, 433–35
Nonlinear response to advertising, 304, 307
Normative decision model, 11, 13

Novices, industrial customer segmentation, 68
NPD. See New product development (NPD)
Numerical taxonomy, 84

Objective-and-task method, advertising budget decisions, 311–12
Objective component, optimization problems, 54–55
Objective function in constrained optimization problem, 13
Objective setting and advertising, 303
OLAP (On-Line Analytical Processing), 469, 470–71
Oligopoly in marketing-mix decisions, 208
On-Line Analytical Processing (OLAP), 469, 470–71
On-pack sales promotion, 436
Opportunity cost and decision model, 17, 19
Opportunity identification models and stage, NPD, 234–37
Optimization problems
CALLPLAN analysis, 376–77
components of, 54
constrained, 13, 54–56
Organization economics in competitive strategy analogy, 211–12
Organizational mechanisms, NPD decision models, 236
Original new products (ORNPs), 189
ORNPs (original new products), 189
Outcome bias, 17
Output variables in decision modeling, 8
Overbooking and airline price discrimination, 429–32

Pairwise evaluations of product bundles, conjoint analysis, 245
PAR regression model, 198–99
Parameters, defined, in response models, 32
Pareto efficiency in Nash solution, 425
Parsimony of market segment, 63
Part-worth function, 139, 239, 241
Partitioning, 84
Partitioning methods in cluster analysis, 88, 91–92
PC (personal computer) use in marketing, 5–6

PDA (Personal Digital Assistant), 104–9, 110–11

Penetrated market, 159

Percentage-of-sales method for advertising budget decisions, 311

Perceptual maps, 119–39
  attribute-based methods, 128, 129, 130–36
  defined, 77, 119
  factor analysis and, 129, 131–34
  joint-space mapping method, 128, 129, 139–44
  limitations of, 139
  positioning using, 119–22
  price in, 145
  similarity-based methods, 129, 136–39, 141
  techniques for, 128–39

Perceptual maps, applications of, 122–27
  for competition identification, 125–26
  for competitive structure, 124–25
  for image or reputation, 126–27
  for new product decisions, 123–24

Perfect information, expected value of, 195

Personal computer (PC) use in marketing, 5–6

Personal Digital Assistant (PDA), 110–11

Personal selling, 303, 354–55. See also Salesforce

Philosophy of marketing engineering, 19–23

PIMS (profit impact of marketing strategy), 51, 180, 198–201

PLC (product life cycle), 175–80

Portfolio analysis ("Conglomerate, Inc.") exercise, 223–25

Positioning, 117–54
  case studies and exercise, 148–54
  defined, 63, 117–18
  factor analysis for preprocessing segmentation data, 147
  joint-space maps, 139–45
  perceptual maps, 119–39, 145–46
  phases of, 65–66
  positioning strategy, 118–19
  price in perceptual maps, 145
  STP process, 63–74, 102–3

Post-hoc customer segmentation, conjoint analysis, 250–51

Potential market, 159

Power series response model, 35

P2P (Peer-to-Peer) networks, 478

Practice standards and marketing decisions, 2–3

Predicted purchase probability, 46, 98

Predictive decision model, 11, 13

Predictive validity of discriminant analysis, 94

Preference attribute, 140

Preference maps, 128, 129, 139. See also Joint-space mapping method

Preference models, 129, 266–68

PREFMAP3 mapping model, 129, 141–45

Preprocessing segmentation data, factor analysis for, 147

Prescriptive decision model, 13

Price
  case studies and exercises, 455–61
  in cost dynamic models, 182–83
  cross-price elasticity, 435
  customer interpretation of, 418
  elasticity of, 415–18, 419
  Law of Demand, 415–18
  negotiation and pricing decisions, 424–26
  in perceptual maps, 145
  - performance and perceptual maps, 125, 126
  as price discrimination, 434
  reference, 424–26
  and sales promotion, 435–48

Price discrimination, 426–34
  defined, 426–28
  geographic, 428–29
  nonlinear, 433–34
  other forms, 434
  quantity discounts as, 433–34
  temporal, 429–33

Price umbrella and cost dynamics, 183

Pricing decisions, 415–26
  and advertising, 303
  case studies and exercises, 449–51, 453–55
  classical economic approach to, 415–18
  competition-oriented, 422–24
  cost-oriented, 418–19
  decisions and yield management, 3
  demand-oriented, 419–22
  interactive, 424–26
  nonlinear, 433–35
  product line, 434–35
  reference and price negotiation, 424–26

Probability
  in decision analysis, 193–94
  gravity model, 380–84
  predicted purchase, 46, 98
  in preference models, 266–68
  in pricing, 423–242
  in sales promotion response models
  in trial-repeat models, 268–70

Probit model, 47–48

Problem children strategic business units (SBUs) in BCG model, 201, 202

Product attribute, and positioning, 118

Product benefit, and positioning, 118

Product class sales market share models, 44–45

Product design models, 238–39

Product life cycle (PLC), 175–80

Product lines, 72, 434–35

Product-market fit and segment attractiveness evaluation, 69, 70

Product-performance matrix model, 204

Product portfolio models, 201–8
  AHP, 205–8, 237, 357
  BCG, 201–3
  financial models, 204–5
  GE/McKinsey, 203–4, 216–19
  types of, 198

Profit, 40, 414

Projection assessment model, 326–27

Promotion models, 440–44, 460–61. See also Sales promotion

Proportional draw assumption in logit model, 48–49

Prospecting for sales, 355

Public relations, 303

Publicity, 303

Purchase-incidence model, 446

Purchase probability, 46, 98

Purchase-quantity model, 446, 447

Purpose, specific, in decision modeling, 7, 8

Qualified market, 159

Qualitative response model, 51–52

Question mark strategic business units (SBUs) in BCG model, 201, 202

Randomized first choice, 250

Rank ordering product bundles, conjoint analysis, 245

Rating scale product bundles, conjoint analysis, 245

Reach, of advertising, 319
Reaction functions, 209
Reaction matrix, 209–10
Reallocator model, 365–66
Recognition programs, as salesforce
    compensation, 370
Reference price, 424–26
Reference price theory, 425
Reformulated new product (RFNP),
    189
Regionalization, 84
Regression analysis
    in advertising studies, 326
    AR model, 164
    in forecasting, 164, 167–70, 173
    for market channeling, 384
    PAR model, 198–99
    sales promotion, 444
    for salesforce bonuses, 372
    segmentation, 96–97
Relationships in decision modeling,
    7, 8
Relevant segmentation descriptors,
    63, 64
Representation
    in decision modeling, defined, 7
    in qualitative model, 51–52
Reputational studies and perceptual
    maps, 126–27
Reservation price, 425
Resource allocation
Respondent selection, segmentation
    instrument development, 79–80
Response models, 29–60
    ADBUDG, 37, 315–18, 360–61
    advertising, 305–7
    appendix, 54–57
    calibration of, 32, 37–38, 52, 361
    CALLPLAN, 356, 373–78,
        386–408
    case studies and exercise, 58–60
    characterization of, 32
    competitive effects, 44–45
    dynamic effects, 42–44
    Excel's solver appendix, 54–57
    fractional root, 35–36
    Gompertz response models, 36–37
    at individual level, 30–53
    interactions of multiple variables,
        42
    linear, 35
    logistic response model, 36
    at market level, 29–45
    market share models, 44–45
    in marketing engineering, 30–31

modified exponential, 36
objectives and, 39–42
power series, 35
promotional analysis
    ("Conglomerate, Inc.") exercise,
    58–59, 58–60
purpose of, 29–31
qualitative, 51–52
qualitative response model, 51–52
sales-response models for sales-
    force, 354–56
Saunders' phenomena of, 33–35
selection of, 52–53
semilog response model, 36
shared experience (See Shared ex-
    perience model)
Solver tool for Excel, 25, 29, 42,
    54–57
Syntex, 356, 359–64, 392–96
types of, 31–37
Response period, CALLPLAN,
    373–74
Retailer model, 446–47
Return on investment (ROI) and PAR
    model, 198–200
Return on sales (ROS) and PAR
    model, 198, 199
Revenue management, 429–33,
    472–73
Revenue model, 456–57
RFNP (reformulated new product),
    189
Risk aversion, 41
Risk premium, 41
Robinson-Patman Act, 427
ROI (return on investment) and PAR
    model, 198–200
ROS (return on sales) and PAR
    model, 198, 199
Running marketing engineering soft-
    ware, 24–25

Salary, as salesforce compensation,
    370
Sales
    -response models for salesforce,
    354–56
    call efficiency and effectiveness,
    373–78
    choice models, 3
    elasticity in, 211
    entity of, and Syntex model, 359
    and profit cycle, 175
Sales Coverage Units (SCUs) in
    COSTA model, 368–69

Sales promotion, 435–48
    and advertising, 303
    aggregate models to analyze pro-
        motional effects, 440–44
    case studies and exercises, 458–61
    characteristics of, 436–40
    effects of, 437–38
    individual responses, analysis of,
        444–48
    objectives of, 436
    observations for modeling and
        evaluation of, 438–40
    types and effects, 435–40
Salesforce, 354–413
    CALLPLAN, 373–78
    case studies and exercises,
        386–413
    compensation of, 369–73
    - composite estimates, forecasting
        method, 160
    intuitive methods for size and allo-
        cation of, 357–59
    market-response methods for size
        and allocation of, 359–64
    marketing channel and, 379–84
    objectives of, 356–57
    personal selling characteristics,
        354–55
    productivity and Syngen, 3
    sales call efficiency and effective-
        ness, 373–78
    sales-response models for, 354–56
    salesforce management decisions,
        356–57
    size and allocation of, 357–64
    Syntex model for, 359–66
    Syntex Reallocator, 365–66
    territory design, 366–69
Salesforce strategy model (SSM),
    392–96
Sample information, expected value
    of, 194
Sampling as sales promotion, 436
Sampling frame, in segmentation in-
    strument development, 79
Saunders' response model, 33, 34, 35
SBUs (strategic business units) in
    BCG model, 201–2
Scanner-panel data, 459–61, 475
Segment descriptors, 63
Segmentation, 61–116, 84
    appendix, PDA features, 110–12
    bases of, 63, 65, 69
    behavior-based, 96–100

case studies and exercises, 104–9, 113–16
cluster analysis, 84–95
in conjoint analysis, 247, 250–51
convenience-group, 66
customer heterogeneity in choice models, 101–2
defined, 61–62, 62
factor analysis, 84, 147
market, defined, 75–78
methods, 83–95
models of (See Segmentation models)
PDA features guide appendix, 110–12
phases of, 64–65, 66–70
price discrimination, 428
research studies, 78–83
STP process, 63–74, 102–3
targeting, 61, 63–74, 102–3
targeting phase, 65, 70–74
theory and practice, 62–66
Segmentation models
choice-based, 3, 97–102
cluster analysis, 84–95
cross-classification analysis, 96–97
dual objective segmentation, 74
factor analysis, 84
a priori, 66, 83–84
regression analysis, 96–97
Self-concept, and positioning, 118
Self-selection, customer, 73–74
Semiaverage projection, time-series method, 162
Semilog response model, 36
Sequences and data mining, 474
Seriation, 84
Served market, 159
SGUs (standard geographic units) in GEOLINE model, 367–69
Shake-out period and cost dynamics, 183
Shape, in advertising response models, 304
Share-of-utility in choice rule, 248, 249
Shared experience model
for advertising budget decisions, 318–19
and cost dynamics, 182
as response model, 50–51
strategic marketing decision making models, 198–201
Short-run profit as response objective, 40

Similarity
-based methods in perceptual maps, 129, 136–39, 141
measures of, in cluster analysis, 85, 86
in use behavior, 77
Simple joint-space mapping method, 129, 139–41
Simulations, market, 476–78
Single linkage clustering, agglomerative method, 89
Size of company and segment attractiveness evaluation, 69, 70
Smoothing techniques time-series method, 162–65
Snake chart or plot, 93, 122, 123
Software
end-user interface, 478–79
hardware requirements for, 22
installation of Marketing Engineering, 23–24
for Marketing Engineering, 21–25, 464–65
modeling and programs, 129
running Marketing Engineering, 24, 26
Solver tool for Excel, 25, 29, 42, 54–57
Sophisticates, industrial customer segmentation, 68
Specific purpose, in decision modeling, defined, 7
Split-down methods in cluster analysis, 88, 90–91
Sports games in competitive strategy analogy, 211–12
Spreadsheets, computer-based, Excel, 3, 5, 11, 22–24, 26, 29, 42, 54–57, 72, 96, 165, 447
SSM (salesforce strategy model), 392–96
Stability and cost dynamics, 183
Standard geographic units (SGUs) in GEOLINE model, 367–69
Standards of practice and marketing decisions, 2–3
Star strategic business units (SBUs) in BCG model, 201, 202
Start-up period and cost dynamics, 183
Stocking effect, 43, 44
Store display as sales promotion, 436
STP (segmentation, targeting, positioning) process, 63–74, 102–3

Strategic business units (SBUs) in BCG model, 201–2
Strategic market analysis, framework and tools for, 154–87
case studies and exercises, 185–87
cost dynamics, 180–83
decision making, 154–59
limitations of, 158
market demand and, 159–75
mission statement, 155–56
product life cycle, 175–80
trend analysis, 159–75
Strategic marketing decision making models, 188–232
AHP, 205–8, 237, 357
appendix, 220–22
BCG, 201–3
case studies and exercises, 216–19, 223–32
competition, 208–12
financial models, 204–5
GE/McKinsey, 203–4, 216–19
market entry and exit decisions, 188–97
PIMS, 198–201
product portfolio models, 201–8
shared experience models, 198–201
Strategy, channel decision, 379
Structural characteristics and segment attractiveness evaluation, 69, 70
Structure correlations, discriminant analysis, 95
Stylization in decision modeling, defined, 7
Substitutability, consumer judgments of, 78
Symmetry in Nash solution, 425–26
Syngen, 3
Syntex model, 356, 359–66, 392–96
Syntex ReAllocator model, 365–66

Tangible product, 233–34
Target market, 62, 159
Targeting, 61, 63–74, 102–3
Tariffs, 433–34
Techniques, NPD decision models, 236
Technology substitution, 77
Territory design for salesforce, 366–69
Tests
advertising copy, 324–25

testing stage, new product, 234, 235

Three-layered feedforward network, 170–72

Time issues
of market entry and exit, models for, 188–97
positioning, 118
price discrimination, 429

Time-series forecasting methods, 162–67
decompositional methods of, 165–67
naive methods of, 162
smoothing techniques in, 162–65
vs. neural networks, 173

Trade-off analysis in response models, 41

Trade promotion model (Blattberg and Levin), 440–44

Traffic management and airline price discrimination, 429–32

Tree, decision, 192, 193

Trend analysis in strategic market analysis,. See Forecasting

Trial-repeat models, 268–70

Two-part tariff, 433

U. S. Census of Manufacturers, 168

U. S. Department of Commerce, 161

U. S. Department of Energy (DOE), 190

Uncertainty
decision making, 195–96
and response models, 40–41

Unfolding models, 128, 129, 139

Universe, in segmentation instrument development, 79

Unrelated diversification trap, 70

Unsupervised pattern recognition, 84

Use behavior, similarities in, 77

Use cost, 420–21

Utility in choice rule, 247–48, 252–53

Utility theory, 41

Value and information, 463–64

Value-based pricing, 419–22

Value-in-use, 419–20

Variables
in cluster analysis, 84–85, 95
in decision modeling, 7, 8, 15
descriptors as, 63, 64, 69, 94–95
interactions of multiple in response models, 42
relationships among, 8

relative impact of, 13–17, 19
in segmentation process, 66, 67, 84–85, 107–9
in STP process, 64–74
types of, 8

Variance in factor analysis, 133–35

Vector models
attribute-based in perceptual map, 134
joint-space map, 139–43
in perceptual maps, 119
PREFMAP3, 129, 141–45

Verbal decision models, 8–9, 11, 12

Visibility, Internet marketing models, 472–73

WANs (wide area networks), 5

Ward's method, agglomerative method, 89, 90

Wide area networks (WANs), 5

Wildcat strategic business units (SBUs) in BCG model, 201, 202

Word-of-mouth effects, 262

Wright Patterson Air Force Base, 180

Yield management, 3, 432

Zone of agreement, pricing, 425

Company Index

Locators in italics indicate display material; n indicates note; quotes indicate fictional material

A
ABB Electric (of Wisconsin), 3, 99–100, 113–116, 467
"Abcor Industries," 451–452
abovetheweather.com, 432
"Acme" ("Conglomerate, Inc."), 231–232
Action Video, 412
activebuyersguide.com, 476
Acura (Honda), 148
Addison Wesley Longman (AWL), 216–219
AdTel, 309, 325
Agree (Johnson Wax), 285–300
Amazon.com, 1, 6, 185
America Online (AOL), 233
American Airlines, 3, 429, 432
American Express, 467–468
American Red Cross, 233
Anaprox (Syntex Laboratories), 359, 387, 393, 395, 397, 399, 402, 403, 408
angara.com, 307
AOL (America Online), 233
Apple
  Macintosh, 22, 110
  Newton PDA, 105, 110, 239
Aqua-Fresh, 137, 138
ASEA-ABB Sweden, 113
AT&T, 106, 325–326
Aunt Jemima (Quaker Oats), 357
Avis, 72, 117
AWL (Addison Wesley Longman), 216–219

B
"Baker," 231–232
Bank of America Corporation, 470
Barnes & Noble, 341
BASF, 213

"BBBC" ("Bookbinders Club"), 185–187
Beck's, 119, 120, 121
BehaviorScan (IRI), 325
Blockbuster Entertainment Group, 411, 412
"Blue Mountain Coffee," 39, 302, 318, 335, 336–342
Boeing, 72, 177, 179
Bold (Procter and Gamble), 303
"Bookbinders Club" ("BBB Club" or "BBBC"), 185–187
Boston Consulting Group, 180, 183
Brite (Johnson Wax), 284
Budweiser, 119, 120, 121, 144, 159
Buick Reatta (GM), 123–124
Burke Market Research, 287, 309

C
"C-Tek Inc.," 363–364, 365
Cabbage Patch Dolls (Mattel), 239
CAC (Central Air Conditioner Division) (Scott-Air Corp), 198–199
Campbell, 303, 310
Camry (Toyota), 238
Canadian Industries Ltd. (ICI), 213
Casio, 105
Celeste (Quaker Oats), 357
Central Air Conditioner Division (CAC) (Scott-Air Corp), 198–199
Chase Econometrics, 160
Cheer (Procter and Gamble), 303
Chemplast, 377, 378
Chempro, 378
Chevrolet Prizm (GM), 128
Chrysler, 239
Ciba-Geigy, 206, 207, 208
Clairol Condition, 285–300
Claudia Schiffer Palm, 106
Clie (Sony), 105
Clinoril, 387
Close-up, 137, 138

CLR (Computer Language Research), 477
Club Med, 233
Coke (Coca Cola), 4, 72, 77, 353, 415
Colgate, 137, 138
CompactFlash, 110
Compaq, 105
Computer Language Research (CLR), 477
"Conglomerate, Inc."
  bidding for pavement contracts exercise, 453–454
  CALLPLAN, 409–410
  compete model, 231–232
  as example, 2
  PDA introduction, 104–109
  portfolio analysis exercise, 223–225
  price planning, 451–452
  promotional analysis exercise, 58–59, 440
  response model exercise, 40–41, 60
"ConneCtor" from "Conglomerate, Inc.," 104–105
"Convection Company," 319, 343–352
Coors Light, 119, 120, 144
Corolla (Toyota), 128
Courtyard by Marriott, 3, 243
CoverStory, 475
Cub Foods, 382
Cyber Dialogue, 263

D
Dartnell Corp., 370, 373
Data Resources, 160
Dataquest, 5
Dataquest.com, 5
Dentagard, 137, 138
Diet Coke, 77
Diet Pepsi, 77
Diet Sprite, 77

DirecTV, 239, 260–261, 263
Discount Air Express, 118
Disney, 261
Doubleday, 185
Dun and Bradstreet, 79
DuPont, 72, 308

E
East Coast Telecom, 74
The Economist Group, 216
Edsel (Ford Motor Company), 238
Egg McMuffin (McDonald's), 72
Elrick and Lavidge, 287
Elson Basic Readers, 216
Enhance (Johnson Wax), 283–301, 353
EPOC (Symbian), 110, 112
Ericsson, 110
Ethyln, 377, 378
Excel (Microsoft), 3, 5, 11, 22–24, 26, 29, 42, 54–57, 72, 96, 165, 447
Expert Choice (software), 206–207

F
Filodex PIM, 239
Financial Times Newspapers, 216
First Commerce Corporation, 173
Flex (Revlon), 285–300
Folgers (Procter and Gamble), 337
Ford Motor Company, 204, 238
"Forte Hotel," 272–276, 433, 455–457
Four Seasons Hotel, 468
The Franklin Mint, 468–469
FreeMarkets, 422
Frito-Lay, 468
Frontline Systems, 56
Future (Johnson Wax), 284

G
Gainsburgers (General Foods), 436
Gateway, 384
Gatorade (Quaker Oats), 357
GBass (software), 282
General Electric (GE), 70, 99, 113, 198, 203, 217
General Foods, 336, 436
General Motors (GM), 124, 378
    Buick Reatta, 123–124
    Chevrolet Prizm, 128
    GM/Hughes, 261
    Wankel engine, 239
Gillette, 234–235

Glade Air Freshener (Johnson Wax), 284
Glaxo Wellcome, 445
Glazer, R., 478
Glo-Coat (Johnson Wax), 284
Glory Carpet Cleaner (Johnson Wax), 284
GM. see General Motors (GM)
GM/Hughes, 261
Google, 118
W. W. Grainger, 378
GroupSystems (software), 477
GTE Sylvania, 469

H
H. J. Heinz, 440
Handspring Visor, 105, 106, 110
Handy Andy, 127
HarperCollins Educational Publishers, 216
Healthy Choice, 117
Heinekin, 119, 120
H. J. Heinz, 440
Hermes, 383
Hertz, 72
Hewlett Packard, 105
    OfficeJet, 258
Hoescht Celanese, 369
Hoescht Roussel, 369
Hollywood Entertainment, 411, 412
Home Depot, 126
Honda Acura, 148
Honeywell, 196

I
IBM, 72, 156, 471
    Workpad, 110
ICI America, 213–215
ICI (Imperial Chemical Industries, Ltd), 72, 213–215
IDC, 107
IdeaFisher (software), 236
Ikea, 383
Imperial Chemical Industries, Ltd (ICI), 72, 213–215
InduStrat, 476
INFER, 475
Infiniti G-20 (Nissan), 148–154, 324
Information Resources, Inc. (IRI), 325
Innochem Division (Johnson Wax), 284
Inspiration (software), 236
Instant Quaker Oatmeal (Quaker Oats), 357

Intel, 72, 221
Iomega, 119
IRI (Information Resources, Inc.), 325

J
J. C. Penney's, 119, 458
"J & J Family Video" case, 411–413
J-Wax (Johnson Wax), 284
jeacle.ie/mortgage, 472
Jenny's Gelato, 226–230
Johnson Wax
    ad copy exercise, 3–4
    Agree hair care, 285–300
    Enhance, 283–301, 353
    Johnson Wax Associates, Inc. (JWA), 283
    overview, 284, 353
Johnson Wax Associates, Inc. (JWA), 283
Jolt Cola, 126
Jubilee (Johnson Wax), 284
JWA (Johnson Wax Associates, Inc.), 283

K
Kellogg, 58, 303
Kentucky Fried Chicken, 117
Klear (Johnson Wax), 284
Kodak, 72
Kraft General Foods, 337

L
Lexus (Toyota), 148
Lidex (Syntex Laboratories), 387
Lilly, 390
Linux, 110
Listerine, 118
Longman, 216
L'Oreal, 281
Lotus Corporation, 72
    Notes, 72, 161, 470, 477
    1-2-3, 72
Lowe's, 126
Lufthansa, 476

M
Machino Company, 167–168
Macintosh (Apple), 22, 110
Management Decision Systems (MDS), 287, 392
Marketing Tools, 6
marketswitch.com, 307, 472
MarkStrat, 476
Marriott Corporation, 3, 468
    Courtyard by Marriott, 3, 243

"Massmart Inc.," 447, 458–461
Matsushita, 110
Mattel Cabbage Patch dolls, 239
Maxwell House (Kraft General
    Foods), 337
Mazda Miata, 239
McDonald's, 72, 156, 353, 379
    Egg McMuffin, 72
    McNuggets, 72
McGraw-Edison, 99, 113
McGraw-Hill, 161
McNuggets (McDonald's), 72
MDS (Management Decision
    Systems), 287, 392
Meisterbrau, 118, 120
Melbourne Wesley Cummings, 217
Menards, 127
Mercedes, 425
Merck, 390, 391
MGM, 72
Miata (Mazda), 239
Michelob, 119, 120, 121, 122, 144
Microsoft Corporation, 5
    Excel, 3, 5, 11, 22–24, 26, 29, 42,
        54–57, 72, 96, 165, 447
    Office, 5, 72, 105
    PowerPoint, 222
    Windows 95, 22
    Windows 98, 22
    Windows 2000, 22, 23
    Windows CE, 105, 110, 112
    Windows ME (Millenium
        Edition), 22
    Windows NT, 22
    Windows on pocket PCs, 105
    Windows Operating System, 22,
        110
    Windows XP, 22, 23
Miller, 119, 120, 144
Mindlink (software), 236
Minolta, 428–429
Mosaic, 263
Motorola, 110
Motrin, 387
Movie Arcade, 412
Mrs. Fields Cookies, Inc., 474
MS. see Microsoft Corporation
MTV, 118

N
Naprosyn (Syntex Laboratories),
    359, 387, 388, 391, 393, 395,
    397, 402, 403, 408, 464
National Purchase Diary, 287

Nescafe (Nestlé), 337
Nestlé, 337, 341
"Netlink," 104, 107
netratings. com, 5
Netscape, 263
Newton PDA (Apple), 105, 110, 239
Nielson-Netratings, 5
Nissan Infiniti, 148–154, 324
Nokia, 106, 110
Nordstroms, 341
Norinyl (Syntex Laboratories), 387,
    402, 408
Notes (Lotus Corporation), 72, 161,
    470
Nyquil, 117, 118

O
Off (Johnson Wax), 284
Office (Microsoft), 5, 72, 105
OfficeJet (Hewlett Packard), 258
Ogilvy and Mather, 308
Old Milwaukee, 119, 120
Old Milwaukee Light, 120, 121
1-2-3 (Lotus Corporation), 72
Opinion Research Corporation, 161
Oracle, 471
OS/2, 110

P
Palm Inc., 105, 110
Pilot, 105, 106
PalmOS, 104, 105, 110, 112
Pearson Group, 216
Penguin/Putnam, 216
Pepsi, 72, 77, 353, 415
Pfizer, 390
Philip Morris, 178, 341
Pledge (Johnson Wax), 284
PocketPC, 105–106
Polyfin, 378
PowerPoint (Microsoft), 222
Premier cigarettes (R. J. Reynolds
    Tobacco Company), 235
Price-Waterhouse, 477
Prizm (Chevrolet), 128
Procter and Gamble, 336, 341, 472
    Bold, Cheer and Tide, 303
    Folgers, 337
ProxiWeb, 111
Psion, 105, 110

Q
"QRS Company," 191–194
Quaker Oats, 357

R
R. J. Reynolds Tobacco Company,
    234
    Premier cigarettes, 235
Raid (Johnson Wax), 284
Rain Barrel Fabric Softener (Johnson
    Wax), 284
RAND, 161
Reatta, Buick (GM), 123–124
Revlon, 233
    Flex, 285–300
Rio MP3 player, 263
Rolodex, 239
RTE Corporation, 113

S
S. C. Johnson & Son, Inc., 283
salesforce.com, 471
Sam's Club, 433, 458
Sassoon, 289
Scan/US (software), 382, 412
Scott-Air Corp., 199–200
Scott Foresman, 216
Sears, 458
Sensor (Gillette), 235
Sensormatic, 468
Shop N' Save, 382
Shout Stain Removal (Johnson Wax),
    284
Sindlinger and Company, 161
Solver tool for Excel, 25, 29, 42,
    54–57
Sony, 261
    Clie, 105
Sprite, 77
SPSS, 479
Starbucks, 341
Stroh's, 144
Suave, 330, 332, 333, 334
Supervalue, 381–382
Sybase, 471
Symbian EPOC, 110, 112
Synalar (Syntex Laboratories), 387
Syntex Laboratories, 3, 359–369,
    386–496, 397–408, 464, 466, 467
    Anaprox, 359, 387, 393, 395, 397,
        399, 402, 403, 408
    Lidex, 387
    Naprosyn, 359, 387, 388, 391,
        393, 395, 397, 402, 403, 408,
        464
    Norinyl, 387, 402, 408
    Synalar, 387

T
Tame, 285–300
3Com/Palm Computing, 110
Tide (Procter and Gamble), 303
Topicort, 387
Toyota
    Camry, 238
    Corolla, 128
    Lexus, 148
Travelocity, 469
Treeage (software), 197

U
United Airlines, 378
Unix, 110
Upjohn, 391

V
"VALUE" (software), 449–452

valueharvest.com, 472
Ventana Corporation, 477
Video Connection, 412
Visa, 234
Visor (Handspring), 105, 106, 110
Volvo, 117, 118, 139

W
W. W. Grainger, 378
Wal-Mart, 126, 127, 379, 458, 468,
    470, 471, 472
Wankel engine (GM), 239
Wella Balsam, 285–300
West-Coast Entertainment, 411
Westin Stamford Hotel, Singapore,
    121
Westinghouse, 99, 113
Wharton Econometrics, 160

Windows Operating System. see
    under Microsoft
Workpad (IBM), 110

X
Xerox Corporation, 155–156

Y
Yankelovich Laboratory Test Market,
    287
Young and Rubicam, 331, 332

Z
Zip drive (Iomega), 119
ZS Associates, 368

Name Index

Locators in italics indicate display material; n indicates note; quotes indicate fictional name.

A

Aaker, David A., 134, 303, 309
Abell, Derek F., 181, 182, 183
Abraham, Magid M., 444
Acuff, Jerry, 369
Agostini, Jean-Michel, 322
Albers, Sonke, 368
Alberts, William W., 181
Albion, Mark S., 330
Albright, S. Christian, 56
Allenby, Greg M., 251
Anderson, James, 252
Anderson, Paul F., 205
Anterasian, Cathy, 200
Appel, Valentine, 308
Armstrong, J. Scott, 160, 174, 175, 475
Arunlakshana, O., 255
Assael, Henry, 91, 92, 310
Aumann, R., 209
Aversa, Nicola, 100
Axelrod, Joel N., 310

B

Balasubramanian, Siva K., 220n
Barabba, Vincent P., 464
Barich, Howard, 68
Baron, Jonathan, 17
Barr, S. H., 19
Bass, Frank M., 189, 253, 255n, 257, 260, 261
Batra, Rajeev, 303
Baumol, William J., 208
Bayus, Barry L., 189, 197
Bensoussan, Alain, 210
Berridge, M. J., 255
Berrigan, John, 74
Bettman, James R., 331
Blasko, Vincent J., 310, 312

Blattberg, Robert C., 437, 438, 440, 441, 442, 443, 444, 445, 470
Boulding, William, 201
Bower, John, 323
Box, George E. P., 164
Boyd, Harper W., Jr., 325
Briesch, Richard, 437
Brock, T. C., 332
Brockett, Patrick L., 173
Brown, Joel R., 312
Brown, Rex V., 195, 196
Bultez, Alain, 210
Burke, Raymond R., 329
Burnett, Leo, 310
Burnett, Stephen C., 177
Buzzell, Robert D., 177, 198, 199, 200

C

Cacioppo, John T., 331, 332
Calatone, Roger J., 208, 237
Camerer, Colin, 15
Camparelli, Melissa, 366, 369
Cannon, Hugh, 309
Cardozo, Richard, 205
Carman, James M., 309
Carmone, Frank J., Jr., 128
Carpenter, Gregory S., 210
Carroll, J. Douglas, 131, 143
Carroll, Vincent P., 310
Case, Peter B., 161
Cattin, Phillipe, 242, 251
"Chen, Jack," 459–460
Chintagunta, Pradeep K., 252
Chandrasekhar, Subrahmanyan, 255
Choffray, Jean-Marie, 81, 135, 136
Clarke, Darral G., 283n, 304, 343n, 386n
Claycamp, Henry J., 204, 323
Cocks, Douglas L., 77
Cohen, Burleigh B., 252, 310
Cole, Bradley, 200
Colley, Russel H., 312
Cooper, Lee G., 45, 128, 237, 383

Cooper, Martha C., 84
Cooper, Robert G., 238
Cort, Stanton G., 309
Coughlan, Anne, 379
Cournot, Antoine Augustin, 209
Cox, William, Jr., 177
Crandall, R. L., 432
Cravens, David W., 366
Cross, Robert G., 432

D

Daganzo, Carlos, 47
Danaher, Peter, 323
Darrow, Ross M., 429, 432
Darwin, Charles, 9
Day, George S., 76, 78, 134, 178, 179, 183, 310, 336n
Degeratu, Alexandru M., 448
Deighton, John, 307
Dekimpe, Marnik G., 437
DeSarbo, Wayne S., 253
Desiraju, Ramarao, 429
DeVincentius, John R., 358, 373
Dholakia, Ruby Roy, 332
Di Benedetto, Anthony, 237
Diamond, Daniel S., 327, 328, 331
Dillon, W. R., 89, 90
Dion, Paul, 179
Dolan, Robert J., 123, 208, 209, 283n, 419
Dowling, Grahame R., 61n, 67, 102
Doyen, Marjorie, 221
Doyle, Peter, 469
Drucker, Peter, 480

E

Eastlack, Joseph O., 310, 314
Ebbinghaus, Hermann, 308
Edson, Jennifer, 226–230
El-Ansary, Adel, 379
Eliashberg, Jehoshua, 426
Eliott, William F., 432
Elrod, Terry, 251
Elwing, Daniel, 113, 467

Eskin, Gerald J., 324, 336n
Etgar, Michael, 310
Evans, Philip, 473

F
Finlayson, Bob, 411
Ford, Neil, 286
Fornell, Claes, 189
Forsythe, John, 73
Fox, Edward J., 437
Francese, Peter, 6
"French, John," 409–410
Freud, Sigmund, 9
Frey, Albert Wesley, 311
Fudge, William K., 15, 378
Fulgoni, Gian M., 309
Furse, David H., 310, 332

G
Gale, Bradley T., 198, 199, 200
Gardner, Yehudi A., 310
Garret, Paula L., 309
Garry, Michael, 381
Gatignon, Hubert, 435
Gensch, Dennis H., 99–100, 114, 115
Ginter, James L., 251
Goldberg, Lewis R., 15
Golden, Linda L., 173
Goldenberg, Jacob, 329
Goldring, Norman, 309
Goldstein, Matthew, 89, 90
Goodwin, Stephen, 310
Gorn, Gerald J., 332
Grahame, John L., 200
Grapentine, Terry H., 122
Grass, Robert C., 308, 309
Green, Paul E., 123, 128, 131, 143,
    209, 238, 243, 245, 246, 249,
    250
Greenhalgh, Leonard, 426
Griffin, Abbie, 236
Gross, Irwin, 334–335
Guadagni, Peter M., 444
Gupta, Sunil, 263, 426

H
Haley, Russell L., 161
Hall, William G., 264
Hammond, J. S., 181
Hanssens, Dominique M., 164, 210,
    304, 310, 315, 328, 437, 444
Harlam, Bari A., 475
Harper Brothers, 217
Harrell, Stephen G., 177

Hauser, John R., 49, 131, 197, 234,
    235, 245, 284n
Hax, Arnoldo C., 183
Hayes-Roth, Frederick, 476
Heil, Oliver P., 212
Heiser, Wilhelm, 143
Hendon, Donald W., 310
Hershey, John C., 17
Hess, Sidney W., 213n, 367, 368
Hill, Tim, 173
Hise, Richard T., 25, 373
Hoch, Stephen J., 16, 53
Hofmans, Pierre, 323
Hogarth, Robin M., 17
Holbrook, Morris B., 331, 332
Huber, Bruce, 277, 279, 282
Huber, Joel, 46, 250
Huff, David L., 379
Hulfink, Erik Jan, 179
Hunt, Morton, 17

I
Irvine, R. F., 255

J
Jacobson, Robert, 201
Jacobstein, Neil, 476
Jagpal, Sharan, 102, 251
Jain, Dipak C., 252, 257, 260
Jain, Sanjay, 197
Jarvenpaa, Sirkka L., 465
Javalgi, Rajshekhar G., 179
Jedidi, Kamel, 253
Jenkins, Gwilym M., 164
Johnson, Richard M., 246
Johnson, Samuel, 216
Johnson, Walter E., 126, 127
Jolson, Marvin A., 161
Jones, J. Philip, 335
Jones, Robert L., 310
Ju, K-H., 324
Jung, Sung-Chang, 173

K
Kahn, Habibullah, 179
Kalish, Shlomo, 190
Kalyanaram, G., 189
Kamakura, Wagner A., 83, 102
Kamin, Howard, 324
Katz, Gerald M., 15, 265, 271
Kaul, Anil, 318, 319
Keebler, Jack, 161
Keeney, Ralph L., 41, 191
Kiernan, Patrick, 428
Kim, Bong-Do, 470

Kim, Jonathan S., 238
Knight, Stephen, 386, 389, 390, 391,
    393, 396
Koh, Ai-Jin, 179
Kohli, Rajeev, 253
Koppelman, Frank S., 131
Kotcher, Lauri Kien, 358, 373
Kotler, Philip, 5, 41, 56, 70, 75, 121,
    130, 167, 201, 209, 365, 379,
    462, 469
Krieger, Abba M., 209, 249, 250
Krishnakumar, S. Davey, 251
Krishnamurthi, Lakshman, 243
Krishnan, Trichy V., 257, 260
Krugman, Herbert E., 308
Kumar, V., 179
Kuritsky, A. P., 325

L
Lambert, David R., 309
Lambin, Jean-Jacques, 210
Lambkin, Mary V., 178
Lancaster, Kent M., 323
Lannon, Colleen, 477
Larréché, Jean-Claude, 161
Lavidge, R. J., 8
Leavitt, Clark, 310, 332
Leckenby, John D., 324
Lee, Donald D., 420
Lee, Timothy H., 173
Leeflang, Peter S. H., 210, 365
Lehmann, D. R., 331, 332
Leidner, D. E., 465
Leimkuhler, John F., 429, 432
Leno, Jay, 148
Leone, R. P., 319, 323
Levin, A., 440, 441, 442, 443
Levin, Nissan, 185n
Levitt, Ted, 233
Lewis, Laurence, 389, 391, 392, 393,
    395
Lieberman, Marvin B., 188
Light, Larry, 474
Lilien, Gary L., xxiii, 5, 19, 41, 50,
    57, 80, 81, 104n, 135, 136, 167,
    189, 190, 195, 198, 201, 209,
    217, 218, 221–222, 236, 259,
    319, 320, 336n, 343n, 365, 379,
    464, 471
Lin, John, 336n
Little, John D. C., 5, 18, 37, 38, 304,
    305, 306, 307, 314–315, 316,
    318, 324, 340, 444, 475
Livne, Z. A., 426

Lodish, Leonard M., 15, 306, 319, 324, 357, 359, 373, 377, 378, 392, 393, 395, 437, 444, 473, 475
Long, Charles, 455
Longman, Kenneth A., 309, 335
Louviere, Jordan J., 251
Luce, R. D., 248

M
MacKay, D. B., 146
Mahajan, Vijay, 261
Majluf, Nicolas S., 183
Malhotra, Naresh K., 138
Maloney, John C., 310, 331
Mansfield, Edwin, 209
Mantrala, Murali, 356, 370, 372
Marchetti, Michele, 355
Martin, Thomas C., 323
Martino, Joseph P., 161
Marx, Karl, 9
Massy, William F., 336n
Mazursky, David, 329
McCann, John M., 97
McClelland, Charles W., 323
McConnell, Maureen, 310
McDonald, Colin, 308
McDonnel, J. C., 19
McGuire, William G., 332
Mehrabian, Albert, 331
Messing, J. W., 255
Meulman, J., 143
Midgley, D. F., 67
Miller, P. B., 313–314, 315, 335
Milligan, Glenn W, 84
Money, R. Bruce, 200
Monroe, Kent B., 433, 434
Montgomery, David B., 161, 183, 188, 212, 336n
Moore, Steven P., 100
Moore, W. L., 119, 120, 143
Moorthy, K. Sridhar, 5, 41, 56, 201, 209, 365, 379
Morrison, Donald G., 151, 427
Muller, Eitan, 261
Myers, John G., 303

N
Naert, Phillippe, 210
Nakanishi, Masao, 383
Naples, M. J., 308
Narasimhan, Chakravarthi, 197
Nash, John F., 255, 425
Neij, Lena, 183

Nelson, Robert, 386, 388, 390–391, 393, 395, 396
Neslin, Scott A., 426, 437, 438, 444, 445
Nijs, Vincent R., 437
Nishizuka, Y., 255
Nutter, Julia B., 243

O
Oberwetter, Robert, 432
O'Connor, Marcus, 28n, 173
Orme, Bryan, 250
Owen, H., 126

P
Papageorgis, Demetrios, 332
Parry, Mark E., 189
Parsons, Leonard J., 164, 210, 304, 315, 444
Patti, Charles. H., 310, 312
Pearlman, Jerry, 277, 281
Peppers, Don, 96
Percy, Larry, 310, 328, 331, 332
Pessemier, E. A., 119, 120, 143
Petty, Richard E., 331, 332
Pol, Louis, 383
Poole, Frank, 389, 393
Porter, Michael E., 69, 209
Powell, S. G., 20, 21

Q
Quelch, John, 221

R
Ragsdale, Cliff T., 41, 56
Raiffa, Howard, 41, 197
Ramond, Charles, 310
Rangaswamy, Arvind, xxiii–xxiv, 15, 113n, 148n, 217, 218, 221–222, 236, 259, 263, 272, 357, 361, 362, 411n, 448, 458n, 471, 475
Rao, Ambar G., 197, 310, 313–315, 314, 335
Rao, Vithala R., 217, 218, 221
Rapoport, Anatol, 209
Ray, Michael L., 325, 332
Reibstein, David J., 435, 437
Reid, Edward L., 373
Reis, Al, 117, 118
Remus, William, 173
Revson, Charles, 233
Rhine, R. J., 332
Rice, Marshall D., 323
Rink, David R., 177
Roberts, John H., 50

Robertson, Thomas S., 156, 157, 158
Robertson, Tom S., 68
Robinson, William T., 189
Robken, Henry S. J., 179
"Rodeman, Jack and Jerilyn," 411–413
Rogers, Martha, 96
Roscoe, A. Marvin, Jr., 91, 92
Rossiter, John R., 310, 328, 331, 332
Rossow, Gerald L., 161
Roth, Alvin E., 426
"Roth, Mark," 216–219
Rubinstein, Ariel, 209
Runyon, Kenneth E., 331
Russo, J. Edward, 14, 15
Rust, Roland T., 323, 324

S
Saaty, Thomas L., 207
Samuels, Stuart A., 367, 368
Sarel, Dan, 310, 328
Saunders, John, 33, 34, 42, 43
Scherer, Frederic M., 209
Schild, H. O., 255
Schkade, David A., 16
Schmidt, Jeffrey B., 237
Schmitz, John D., 475
Schoemaker, Paul J. H., 14, 15
Schrage, Michael, 463, 467, 477
Schultz, Randall L., 164, 210, 304, 315, 444
Schumann, David, 331, 332
Sears, Francis, 217
Seligman, Daniel, 311
Semisch, Bruce, 272n
Senge, Peter M., 477
Severance, L. J., 332
Sewall, Murphy A., 310, 328
Shanker, Venkatesh, 159n
Shapiro, Arthur, 440
Sharda, R., 19
Sherman, John, 283, 286, 292
Sherman, Lee, 307
Shocker, Allan D., 76, 78, 264
Shugan, Steven M., 245, 429
Siemer, Richard H., 125
Silk, Alvin, 264, 265, 287n
Simon, Hermann, 324, 419, 473
Singer, Eugene M., 208
Sinha, Prabhakant, 15, 19, 53, 356, 357, 358, 361, 362, 364, 366, 368, 370, 372, 466
Skiera, Bernd, 368
Smidts, Ale, 464
Smith, Barry C., 429, 432

Smith, Scott M., 128
Solomon, Sorin, 329
Srinivasan, V., 245, 246
Srivastava, Rajendra K., 76, 78
Staelin, Richard, 201
Star, Steven H., 123–124, 145
Starch, Daniel, 310, 327, 331
Starke, Katrin, 104n, 113n, 148n,
       336n, 411n
Steckel, Joel H., 217, 218, 221
Steenkamp, Jan-Benedict E. M., 437
Steiner, G. A., 8
Stern, Louis, 379
Sternthal, Brian, 332
Stewart, David W., 310, 332
Stewart, M., 310
Stone, Linda G., 444
Sudharshan, Devanathan, 198, 203,
       204, 211–212
"Sullivan, Donna," 458–461
Swan, John E., 177
Swire, Donald, 200

T
Taylor, Elmer D., 177
Tayman, Jeff, 383
Tellis, Gerard J., 217, 218, 220,
       446–447, 458
Thiel, Michael H., 324
Thietart, R. A., 180
Tholke, Jurg M., 179
Thomas, Charles M., 161
Thomas, Robert J., 258
Thompson, G. C., 312
Thorelli, Hans, 177

Toh, Rex S., 179
Traver, Phillis A., 437
Trodahl, Verling C., 310
Trout, Jack, 117, 118
Twedt, Dik W., 310, 327, 328

U
Ulvila, Jacob W., 195, 196
Urban, Glen L., 15, 49, 123–124,
       145, 189, 197, 234, 235, 264,
       265, 271, 284n, 287n

V
Van Bruggen, Gerrit H., 5, 464
Van den Bulte, Christophe, 259
Vandenbosch, Mark B., 356
Vargas, Luis G., 207
Vidale, H. L., 305
Virts, John R., 77
Vivas, R., 180

W
Ward, J., 88, 89
Wedel, Michael, 83, 102
Weinberg, Charles B., 332, 336n, 356
Weinstein, David, 319
Weitz, Barton A., 310, 328
Wells, William D., 310
West, Patricia M., 173
Whitaker, Richard, 476
Wierenga, Berend, 5, 464
Wilkie, William L., 332
Willemain, Thomas R., 28n
Willhelm, Marcus, 185
Wilson, David T., 80

Wilson, Elizabeth J., 80
Wind, Jerry, 242
Wind, Yoram J., 63, 65, 123, 125,
       131, 143, 156, 157, 158, 198,
       201, 204, 205
Winston, Wayne L., 56
Wittink, Dick R., 210, 242, 243, 251,
       318
Wolfe, H. B., 305, 312
Woodworth, George, 251
Wordsworth, William, 216
Wright, Frank Lloyd, 283
Wu, Jianan, 448, 458n
Wurster, Thomas S., 473
Wyner, G. A., 126

Y
Yamanaka, Jiro, 310
Ye, Jianming, 470
Yelle, Louis E., 180
Yoon, Eunsang, 189, 190
Yurkiewicz, Jack, 175

Z
Zahavi, Jacob, 185n, 468
Zaltman, Gerald, 464
Zangwill, Willard I., 236
Zhang, John, 197
Zielski, Hubert A., 308
Zimmer, Mary R., 323
Zinnes, J. L., 146
Zoltners, Andris A., 15, 19, 53, 356,
       357, 358, 361, 362, 364, 366,
       368, 370, 372, 466
Zufryden, Fred S., 446–447, 458